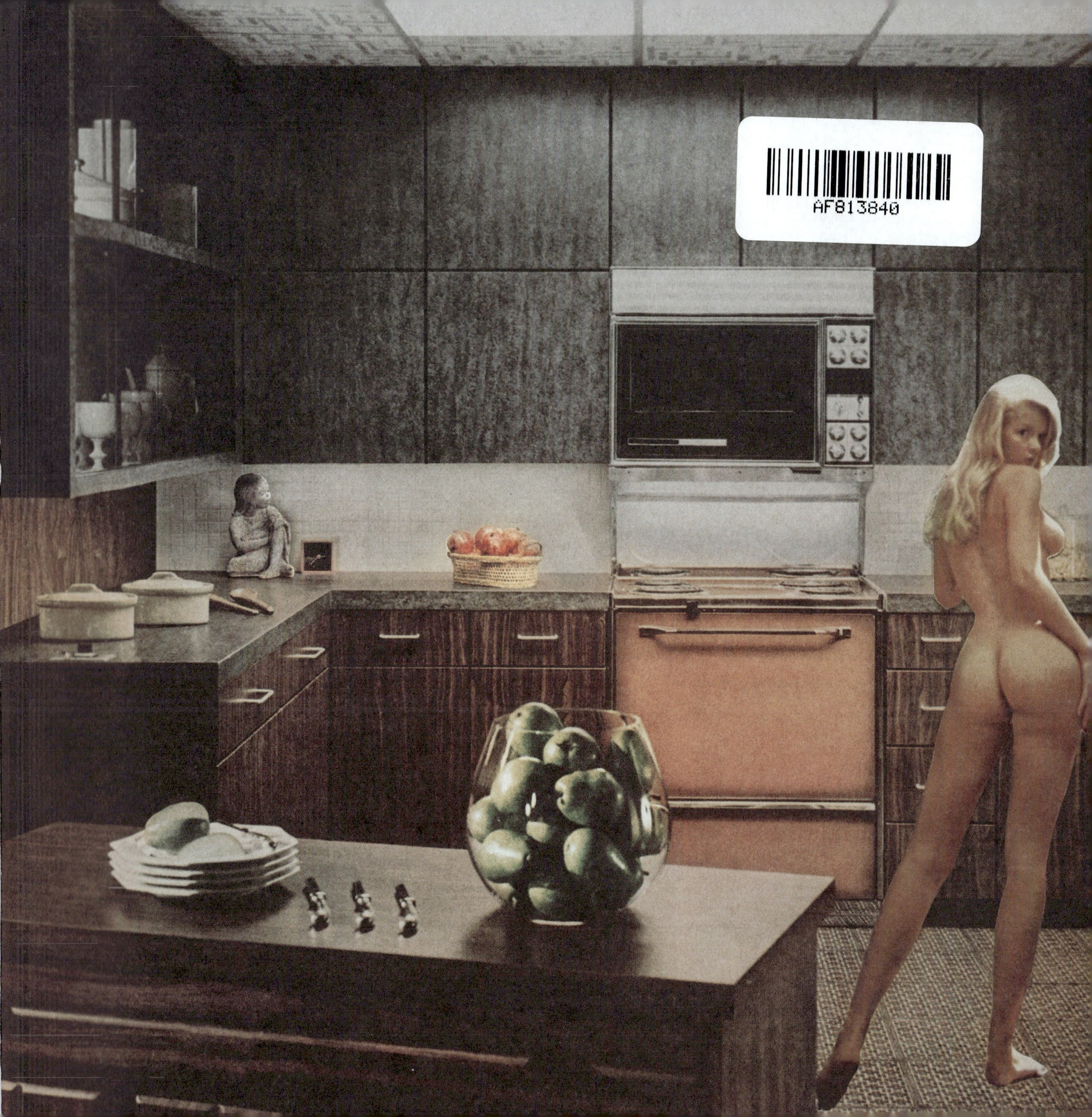

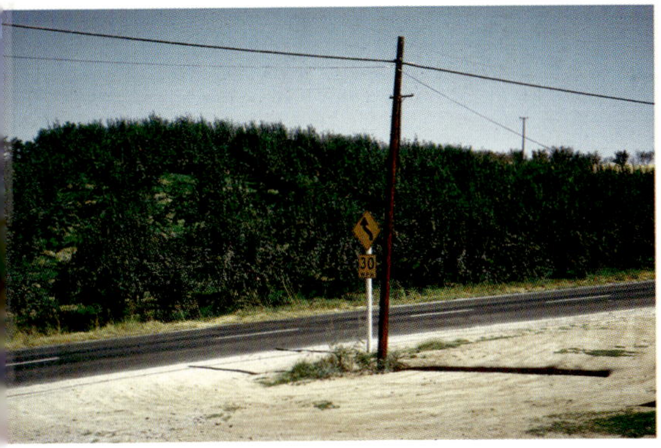
30

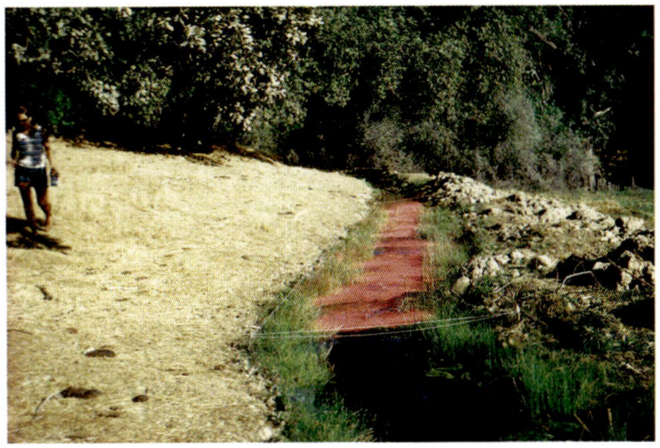

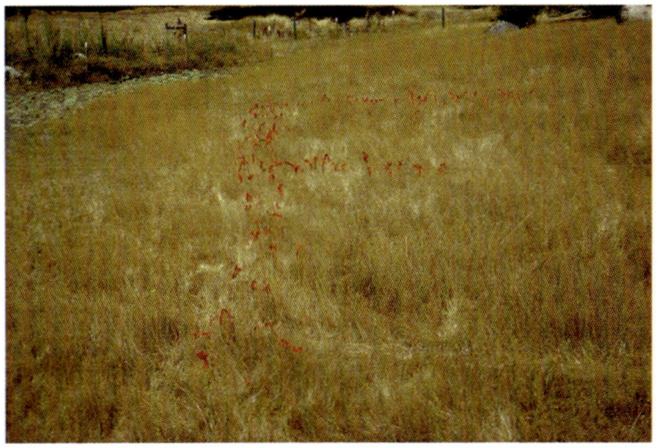

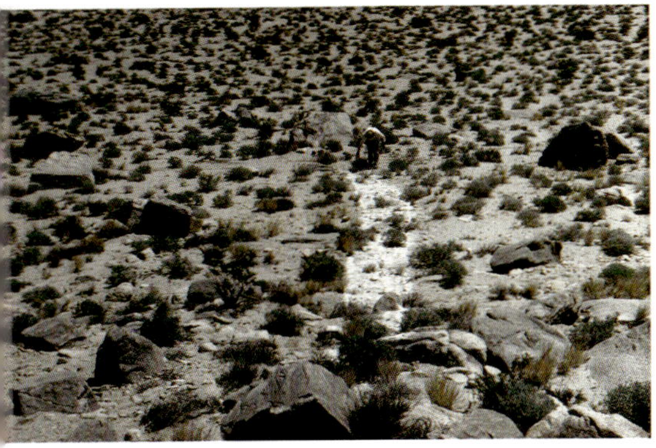

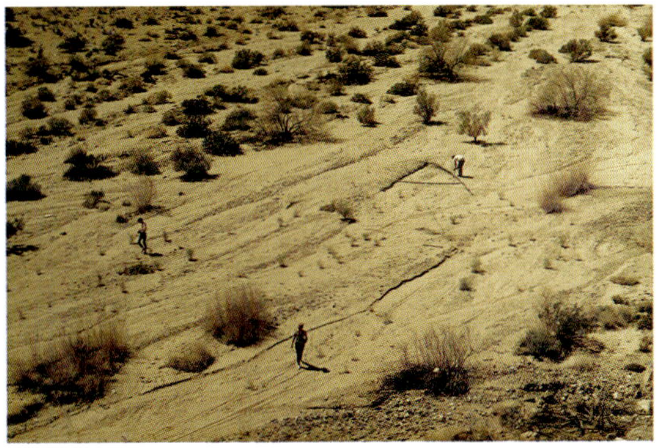

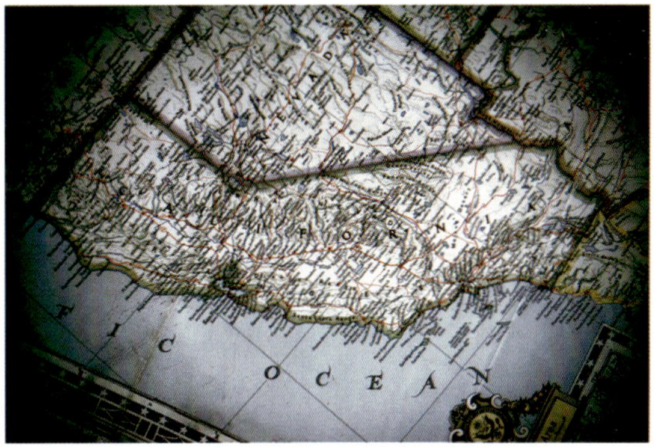
OCEAN

The publisher gratefully acknowledges the generous support of the Leo and Florence Helzel Endowment Fund in Northern California Art of the University of California Press Foundation.

State of Mind: New California Art circa 1970

Constance M. Lewallen and Karen Moss

With Additional Essays by Julia Bryan-Wilson and Anne Rorimer

PUBLISHED WITH THE ASSISTANCE OF THE GETTY FOUNDATION

UNIVERSITY OF CALIFORNIA, BERKELEY ART MUSEUM AND PACIFIC FILM ARCHIVE

ORANGE COUNTY MUSEUM OF ART

UNIVERSITY OF CALIFORNIA PRESS BERKELEY LOS ANGELES LONDON

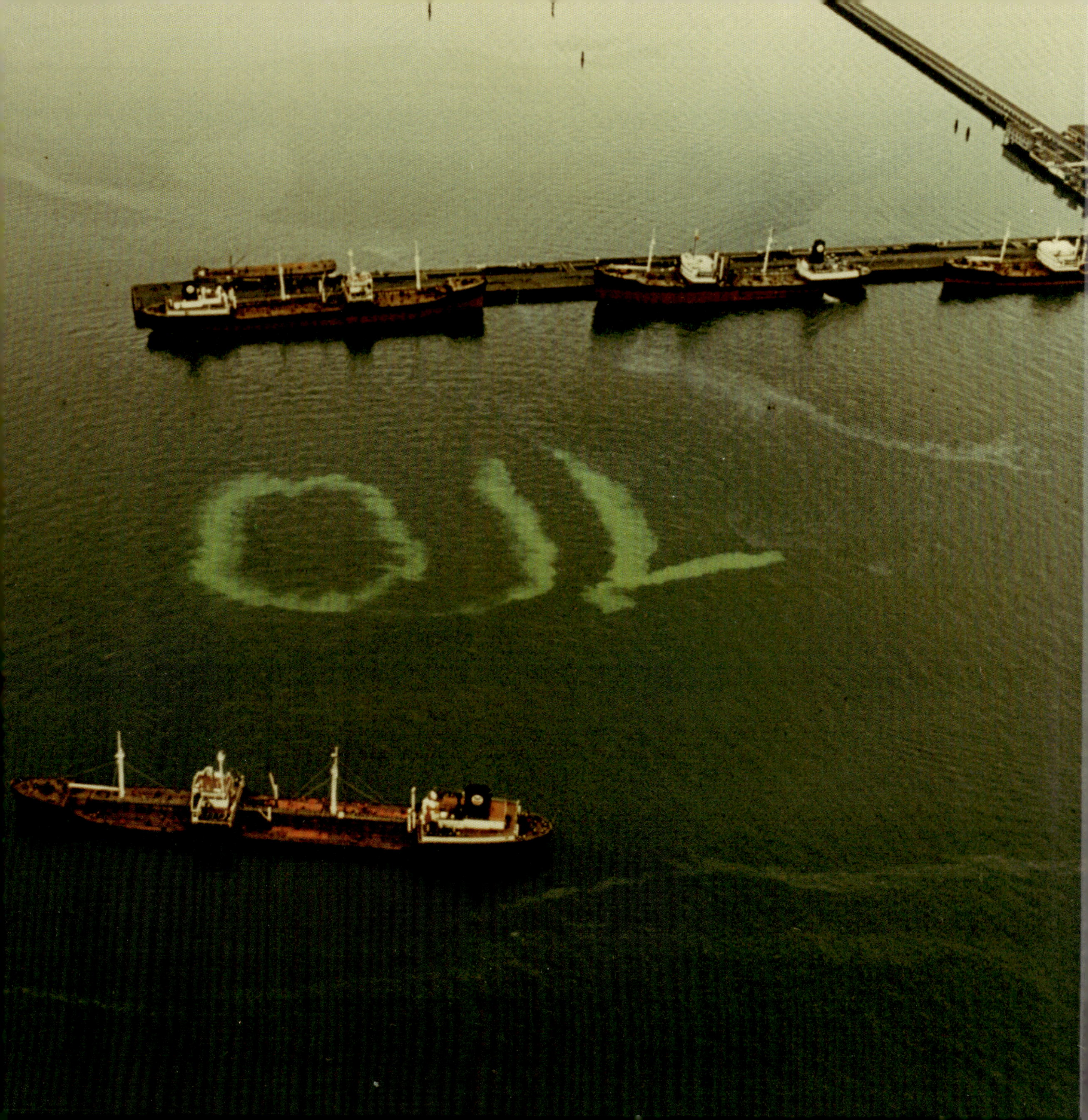
OIL

CONTENTS

LENDERS TO THE EXHIBITION

Philip Aarons and Shelley Fox Aarons, New York, NY
Adam II (the late Paul Cotton), Oakland, CA
Bas Jan Ader Estate, Santa Monica, CA
Air de Paris, Paris, France
Alexander and Bonin, New York, NY
Terry Allen, Santa Fe, NM
Marsha and Darrel Anderson, Newport Beach, CA
Gallery Paule Anglim, San Francisco, CA
Eleanor Antin, Solana Beach, CA
Artnow International, San Francisco, CA
Michael Asher, Los Angeles, CA
John Baldessari, Santa Monica, CA
Estate of Gary Beydler, Los Angeles, CA
Carolina Bilbao and Richard Massey, Miami, FL
The Box, Los Angeles, CA
Nancy Buchanan, Los Angeles, CA
Galerie Daniel Buchholz, Cologne, Germany
Chris Burden, Topanga, CA
Canyon Cinema, San Francisco, CA
Cardwell Jimmerson Contemporary Art, Culver City, CA
China Art Objects Gallery, Los Angeles, CA
Cirrus Gallery, Los Angeles, CA
Estate of Guy de Cointet, Paris, France, and New York, NY
Claire Copley and Alan Eisenberg, New York, NY
Lowell Darling, Rodeo, CA
The de Saisset Museum, Santa Clara University, Santa Clara, CA
Ronald Feldman Fine Arts, New York, NY
Morgan Fisher, Santa Monica, CA
Marita Loosen Fox, Cologne, Germany
Howard Fried, Vallejo, CA
Charles Gaines, Los Angeles, CA
Harry Gamboa Jr., Los Angeles, CA
Greene Naftali, New York, NY
Stanley and Elyse Grinstein, Los Angeles, CA
Solomon R. Guggenheim Museum, New York, NY
Doug Hall and Diane Andrews Hall, San Francisco, CA
Helen Mayer Harrison and Newton Harrison, Santa Cruz, CA
Hauser & Wirth
Mel Henderson and Susan Rannells, Nevada City, CA
Lynn Hershman, San Francisco, CA
Hudgins Family, New York, NY
Institut national de l'audiovisuel, Paris, France
Richard Jackson, Sierra Madre, CA
Stephen Kaltenbach, Davis, CA
Terri Keyser-Cooper, Reno, NV
Paul Kos, San Francisco, CA
Suzanne Lacy, Los Angeles, CA
Stephen Laub, Water Mill, NY
Margo Leavin Gallery, Los Angeles, CA
William Leavitt, Los Angeles, CA
Steven Leiber, San Francisco, CA
Fred Lonidier, La Jolla, CA
Mike Mandel, Watertown, MA
Tom Marioni, San Francisco, CA
Paul McCarthy, Altadena, CA
Tracy and Gary Mezzatesta, Burbank, CA
Mitchell-Innes & Nash Gallery, New York, NY
Linda Mary Montano, Saugerties, NY
Peter Morton, Los Angeles, CA
The Museum of Contemporary Art, Los Angeles, CA
The Museum of Modern Art, New York, NY
Nora Eccles Harrison Museum of Art, Utah State University, Logan, UT
Orange County Museum of Art, Newport Beach, CA
Patrick Painter Editions, Santa Monica, CA
Private collection, Berkeley, CA
Private collection, Long Beach, CA
Max and Jane Reid, Oakland, CA
Brenda Richardson, Baltimore, MD
Martha Rosler, Brooklyn, NY
Allen Ruppersberg, Santa Monica, CA
San Francisco Museum of Modern Art, San Francisco, CA
Darryl Sapien, San Francisco, CA
Marc Selwyn Fine Art, Los Angeles, CA
The Sender Collection, New York, NY
Bonnie Sherk, San Francisco, CA
Barbara T. Smith, Venice, CA
Estate of Larry Sultan, Greenbrae, CA
University of California, Berkeley Art Museum and Pacific Film Archive, Berkeley, CA
Susanne Vielmetter Los Angeles Projects, Culver City, CA
William Wegman, New York, NY
John Woodall, Plant City, FL
Alfred Young, Oakland, CA

<<
Frontispiece: Joe Hawley, Mel Henderson, and Alfred Young, *Oil*, September 1969. Performance event: Standard Oil docks, Richmond, CA. Nontoxic uranine marker dye on San Francisco Bay. Photo: Robert Campbell / Chamois Moon. Courtesy Mel Henderson and Susan Rannells.

DIRECTORS' FOREWORD

California was one of several global locations where Conceptual art transformed contemporary art and culture; however, the movement's contribution here was especially distinct and its influence particularly long lasting. Despite this importance, there has not been, to date, a comprehensive survey exhibition and publication exploring California Conceptualism and related practices in their seminal period, 1967 to 1974. Our two museums have been key players in the emergence, rise, and proliferation of Conceptual art, and so it is wonderfully appropriate that we have joined together to present this timely and eye-opening exhibition.

In 1970, the University of California Berkeley Art Museum and Pacific Film Archive (BAM/PFA; then known as University Art Museum) moved into a new home, a radically designed space by Mario Ciampi that was especially suited to performance and other nontraditional genres. In the late 1960s and early 1970s, the museum commissioned and hosted new works by many of the artists featured in *State of Mind,* including Paul Cotton, Terry Fox, Howard Fried, Mel Henderson, Lynn Hershman, Tom Marioni, Linda Mary Montano, and others. Over the past forty years, Conceptual art has been a core area for both museums' exhibitions and collections, and BAM/PFA now holds one of the largest archives of primary Bay Area and international Conceptual ephemera and documentation.

In the early 1960s, the Newport Harbor Art Museum, predecessor to the Orange County Museum of Art, was one of very few venues for contemporary art in Southern California. The museum organized *The Appearing/Disappearing Image/Object* (1969), an exhibition including Michael Asher, John Baldessari, and Allen Ruppersberg, among others, which was one of the earliest exhibitions of Conceptually oriented art not only in California but also nationally. In 1972, the museum presented *The San Francisco Performance*—guest curated by Marioni and featuring work by Fox, Fried, Henderson, Paul Kos, and Bonnie Sherk—and *New Art in Orange County,* with work from artists Michael Brewster, Nancy Buchanan, Chris Burden, and Barbara T. Smith, who were affiliated with the F Space, an early artist-run gallery founded by UC Irvine graduate students.

Our thanks go to the many lenders who have entrusted our institutions with their cherished, and often fragile, works of art. Lending knowledge is as valuable as lending works of art, and so we thank the numerous individuals who offered their insight in interviews and conversations with our curators and writers. Of course, behind the scenes of any exhibition is the professional museum staff; their tireless work at both of our institutions deserves our sincere gratitude. Our trustees make so much of what we do possible, and their belief in and support of this project exemplify our museums' similar commitment to groundbreaking art and scholarly excellence.

An exhibition of this scale also requires significant resources, and we are tremendously grateful to our donors: the Getty Foundation as part of the unprecedented collaborative initiative *Pacific Standard Time: Art in L.A. 1945–1980*, the National Endowment for the Arts, Dr. Rosalyn M. Laudati and Dr. James Pick, Ms. Robin Wright and Mr. Ian Reeves for the pressured air work of Michael Asher, and the continued support of BAM/PFA Trustees.

We are thrilled that Constance M. Lewallen and Karen Moss have chosen to dedicate their extraordinary curatorial and intellectual talents to documenting and interpreting the astounding legacy of California's Conceptual artists. Both scholars approach this task with decades of firsthand experience and a passion for art that stretches the boundaries of form and imagination. Finally, it is to the artists themselves that we are most grateful. They broke the rules in a spirit of hope and play—and their risks are our rewards.

Lawrence Rinder DIRECTOR, UNIVERSITY OF CALIFORNIA BERKELEY ART MUSEUM AND PACIFIC FILM ARCHIVE

Dennis Szakacs DIRECTOR, ORANGE COUNTY MUSEUM OF ART

>>
Joe Hawley, Mel Henderson, and Alfred Young, *Yellow Cabs,* November 19, 1969. Performance event: Castro and Market Streets, San Francisco. Aerial photo: Robert Campbell / Chamois Moon. Courtesy Mel Henderson and Susan Rannells.

CURATORS' ACKNOWLEDGMENTS

State of Mind: New California Art circa 1970 results from the collective efforts of many individuals and institutions. We reiterate our directors' profound thanks to our lenders and funders, especially Joan Weinstein, associate director, and Nancy Mickelberg, former senior program officer, at the Getty Foundation, as well as Andrew Perchuk, deputy director, and Rani Singh, senior research associate, at the Getty Research Institute, for their support of this exhibition and publication. Their generosity enabled us to work with a team of esteemed advisors—Michael Auping, Julia Bryan-Wilson, Renny Pritikin, David Ross, Howard Singerman, Anne Wagner, and Cécile Whiting—who counseled us wisely in the initial planning stages of our project.

Deborah Kirshman, former art editor at UC Press, was extremely helpful with her insightful advice throughout the many months of catalogue development; her replacement, Kari Dahlgren, oversaw its final stages. BAM designer Mary Kate Murphy created this beautiful book. Additional thanks go to Laura Harger, principal editor at UC Press; Laura Richard, our book editor, who guided us through the process of preparing texts; and Julia Bryan-Wilson and Anne Rorimer, who contributed thoughtful essays to this volume. Peter Cavagnaro, media relations manager at BAM, and Stacie Martinez and Johnny Sampson, curatorial associates at OCMA, were invaluable in attending to the myriad details inherent in both this publication and the exhibition.

We received strong support from our respective directors and other staff members who are too numerous to mention by name, but special thanks are due at BAM to Barney Bailey, exhibition designer; Lucinda Barnes, chief curator and director of programs and collections; Karen Bennett, associate curator for education; Ariane Bicho, communications director; Ben Blackwell, senior photographer; Lisa Calden, director of registration; Sherry Goodman, director of education and academic relations; Dave Taylor, digital media developer; Elisa Isaacson, director of foundation and corporate relations; Pamela Pack, associate registrar; and Steve Seid, video curator. We also extend particular thanks to OCMA staff Kelly Bishop, family and public programs manager; Anna Brouwer, publications manager; Albert Lopez, director of operations; Glenn Peters, deputy director; Anna Sanchez, exhibitions and collections manager; Jeanette Saunders, registrar; Kirsten Schmidt, director of marketing and communication; Lisa Silaygi, director of education and public programs; and Mary Trent, graduate research intern.

We appreciate the time taken by gallery dealers and their staffs in San Francisco, New York, and Los Angeles to answer questions and provide assistance: Caroline Alexander and Oliver Newton; Paule Anglim and Ed Gilbert; Wendy Brandow and Margo Leavin; Christine Burgin; Damon Cardwell and Tom Jimmerson; Steven Leiber; Ron Feldman and Marco Nocella; Jay Gorney and Mamie Tinker; Jack Tilton and Janine Cirincione; Mara McCarthy; Patrick Painter and Gabrielle Corchado; and Larry Miller and Sara Seagull. Additional thanks go to Sarah Aibel of the Sender Collection; Jason Burch and Emily Heick of the William Wegman studio; Mary Dean of the Ed Ruscha studio; Mark Toscano and May Haduong of the Academy Film Archive; Josh Kline and Nick Lesley at Electronic Arts Intermix; Barbara Rominski, head of the San Francisco Museum of Modern Art (SFMOMA) Research Library and Archives; Tanya Zimbardo, assistant curator of media arts, SFMOMA; Richard Armstrong, director, Susan Davidson, senior curator, collections and exhibitions, and Jodi Myers, registrar for outgoing loans at the Solomon R. Guggenheim Museum; Lindsey Kouvaris, curator of exhibitions and collections, and Jean MacDougall, collections manager, at the de Saisset Museum, Santa Clara University; Dominic Angerame of Canyon Cinema; and Brigitte Dieu of the Institut national de l'audiovisuel, France.

We are grateful for the advice and various expertise provided by Terry Allen, Terri Cohn, Kevin Concannon, Marita Loosen Fox, Mario Garcia Torres, Leta Ming, Brenda Richardson, Camille Washington, and Hans Winkler.

And last, but certainly not least, our deepest thanks go to the artists whose important work formed the basis of our endeavor and from whom we sought information time and time again.

Constance M. Lewallen
Karen Moss

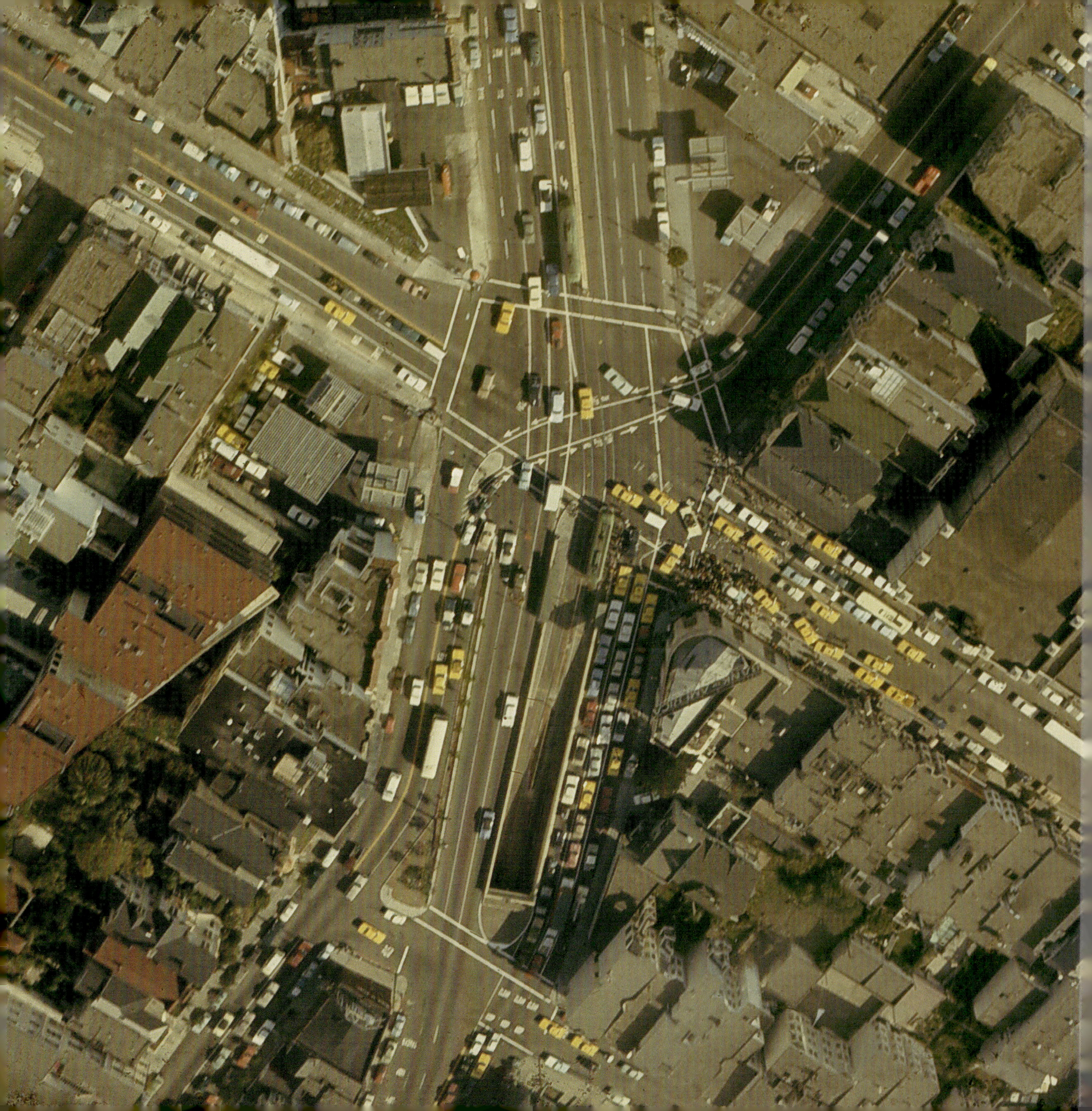

INTRODUCTION

Constance M. Lewallen and Karen Moss

Most of the artists who came to California in the late 1960s sought many of the same things that have always drawn people to the state: its beauty, climate, and relative ease of living. Moreover, by the mid-1960s, California was emerging as an incubator for social change and youth-oriented counterculture, which were strong incentives for the first generation of Conceptual artists as they looked for alternatives to established modes of art making. California also led the United States in the demand for educational reform, which was sparked by the 1964 Free Speech Movement at the University of California, Berkeley. Subsequent protests against the war in Vietnam, though nationwide, were especially strong in California due in part to the presence of the defense industry and to the state's location as the last stop en route to and back from the Pacific.[1] While social movements of the era were on a national scale, their rise was particularly strong in California precisely because of its history of discrimination and because liberation movements were tied to civil rights and antiwar efforts.[2]

The first major uprising of the decade took place in the African American neighborhood of Watts in South Central Los Angeles in 1965, and nearly four thousand people were arrested. The riots were the result of African Americans being disproportionately unemployed and drafted into the military. That same year, Cesar Chavez organized the Delano grape strike in the San Joaquin Valley. Three years later in Southern California, Chicano students' protest against racism and inequality in the public schools eventually led to the 1970 Chicano Moratorium in East Los Angeles, one of the largest off-campus antiwar demonstrations in the country. Further, 1966 saw the founding of the Black Panther Party in Oakland and the National Organization for Women (NOW) in Washington, D.C. Ignited by the 1969 Stonewall riots in New York, gay life and political activity found its nucleus in San Francisco. And a new environmental awareness was inspired by the 1962 publication *Silent Spring,* Rachel Carson's shattering look at ecological destruction, which eventually led to the first Earth Day in 1970 and the first Greenpeace action in 1971.

Some California artists—Newton Harrison and Helen Mayer Harrison, Terry Fox, Martha Rosler, Fred

Lonidier, Allan Sekula, Mel Henderson and collaborators Joe Hawley and Alfred Young, and others—made direct reference in their artwork to the tumultuous changes taking place around them. The Harrisons' concern for the degradation of the environment has defined their work from the beginning. Hawley, Henderson, and Young highlighted the dangers posed by the transport of crude oil. In both public actions and private performances, Fox expressed his despair over the deadly battles taking place in Vietnam. In scathing photomontages, Rosler responded to both the war and the exploitation of women. And, finally, Lonidier and Sekula addressed labor issues.

Young artists, whether or not actively engaged in the political and cultural movements of the time, were still caught up in the desire for change and held the fervent belief that they were forging a new, more open society. For all of these reasons and because of its relative paucity of cultural institutions, traditions, and markets vis-à-vis New York, California represented the future and freedom for experimentation of all kinds. The San Francisco Bay Area, the epicenter of the counterculture, had a particularly strong attraction. One artist told me that the Mamas and the Papas's 1967 hit song "If You Are Going to San Francisco" clinched his decision to move there.[3] Los Angeles, seductively rendered in movies and television as a place where pop culture and high art resided comfortably side by side, proved irresistible to many others. Bas Jan Ader, who lived in the city from 1963 to 1975, expressed what many of his peers felt: "I really love Los Angeles. I love the surrounding wilderness of the ocean, desert and mountains. I feel belittled by its enormous scale. I value more than anyone the solitary beauty of the freeways by night."[4] Throughout the state, numerous art schools and universities whose art departments were newly founded or expanded during the period, including the first feminist art program, were an additional attraction.[5]

This new generation of artists in California not only sought new ways to counter the increasing commercialization of art, but they also wished to inject personal, political, and social content into their work. The value of autonomous collectible objects was called into question. As artist Douglas Huebler famously put it, "The world is full of objects, more or less interesting: I do not wish to add any more."[6] If the object was not eliminated altogether, it was deemphasized in favor of the *idea* and the process that went into its making. Artists devised new, noncommercial forms of expression and communication: the photographic document, video, sound, performance, and installation—modes that pervade artistic practices today.

Conceptual artists in California who came of age in the late 1960s were not as isolated as geography might suggest. From the beginning, there were numerous interchanges between California artists and those from outside the state. These connections grew out of magazines, exhibitions, schools, and alternative spaces such as the Museum of Conceptual Art (MOCA) in San Francisco and the Los Angeles Institute of Contemporary Art (LAICA) in Los Angeles.[7] *Avalanche,* the New York–based magazine devoted to Conceptual art, covered idea-centered art activities nationally and internationally. Issues from early in its six-year run (1970–76) included interviews with California artists Chris Burden, Lowell Darling, Terry Fox, Howard Fried, Stephen Laub, Bruce Nauman, and Ed Ruscha as well as reports on the activities of Bas Jan Ader (then living in Los Angeles), Eleanor Antin, John Baldessari, Paul Cotton,

Robert Kinmont, Paul Kos, and William Wegman.[8] *Avalanche* editor Willoughby Sharp (1936–2008) was a frequent visitor to MOCA, founded in 1970 in San Francisco by Tom Marioni. That same year, in collaboration with Sharp, MOCA presented the video compilation *Body Works* at Breen's Café, where Marioni often held receptions and presented several radio and video shows. Arguably the first exhibition of body art, *Body Works* included pieces by Nauman, Wegman, Fox, Dennis Oppenheim (1938–2011), and Keith Sonnier (b. 1941). Oppenheim, a native of the Bay Area, also participated in MOCA activities, as did New York–based Vito Acconci (b. 1940), whose body-oriented performances were closely related to those by Bay Area artists Howard Fried and Terry Fox and Los Angeles–based Chris Burden. Under the auspices of MOCA, Burden performed *I Became a Secret Hippy* (1971) and *Fire Roll* (1973). In 1972, Tom Garver, director of the Newport Harbor Art Museum (now the Orange County Museum of Art), invited Marioni to curate a show. *The San Francisco Performance,* as it was called, included (in addition to Marioni) Mel Henderson, Howard Fried, Bonnie Sherk, Sam's Café, Paul Kos, and Terry Fox. George Bolling (1946–2010) and Larry Fox (b. 1943) documented the event in video and photographs. In Southern California, Baldessari invited artists from the East Coast and abroad to teach at California Institute of the Arts (CalArts) and early on established personal relationships with artists in New York and Europe.

Many artists had gallery exhibitions in Europe in the late 1960s. Michael Asher, Baldessari, Nauman, and Allen Ruppersberg were included in several landmark Conceptual exhibitions in 1969, such as *Op Losse Schroeven* (Square Pegs in Round Holes) in Amsterdam; *When Attitudes Become Form* in Bern, Switzerland; and *Konzeption-conception* in Leverkusen, West Germany (the latter two also included Stephen Kaltenbach, and the former included Richard Jackson). Fried, Jim Melchert, Baldessari, and Ruppersberg, as well as Cotton and John C. Fernie, were included in Harald Szeemann's 1972 *Documenta 5* in Kassel, West Germany. Marioni often showed and performed in Scotland and Eastern Europe during the early 1970s, and Kos was included in the 1973 *São Paulo Biennial* and in *Project 1974* in Cologne. Terry Fox, who had lived and exhibited in Europe in the late 1960s and settled in San Francisco in 1969, brought to the Bay Area information about such artists as Joseph Beuys (1921–86), whose first U.S. exhibition did not occur until 1974. However, during the succeeding decades, the group of artists identified with the beginnings of Conceptual art was narrowed, and, with a few exceptions, California Conceptual artists were less likely to be included among them.

In recent years, several important group exhibitions have explored aspects of this period in California—*Reconsidering the Object of Art: 1965–1975* and *Out of Actions: Between Performance and the Object, 1949–1979* (both at the Museum of Contemporary Art, Los Angeles, in 1995 and 1998, respectively); *Sunshine & Noir: Art in L.A., 1960–1997* (Louisiana Museum of Modern Art, Denmark, 1997); *Global Conceptualism: Points of Origin, 1950s–1980s* (Queens Museum of Art, New York, 1999); *Made in California: Art, Image, and Identity, 1900–2000* (Los Angeles County Museum of Art, 2000); *Los Angeles, 1955–1985: Birth of an Art Capital* (Centre Pompidou, Paris, 2006); and *California Video* (J. Paul Getty Museum, 2008). Earlier, *Space/Time/Sound: Conceptual Art in the San Francisco Bay Area: The 1970s* (the catalogue of a 1980 exhibition curated by Suzanne Foley at the San Francisco Museum of Modern Art) and the volume *Performance Anthology: Sourcebook for a Decade of California Performance Art* chronicled Conceptual art, especially performance activity in California in those years.[9]

This new attention to California has focused primarily on Los Angeles, and—in those few instances when the state was considered as a whole—a tendency to characterize California's Conceptual art in regional terms has persisted: an emphasis on the body, ritual, and Eastern philosophy was assigned to the north, while the importance of narrative, media, and popular culture was seen to typify the south. Such generalizations mask common threads that connected artists from San Diego to the San Francisco Bay Area during this nascent period.

To better understand why Conceptual art and the new genres that it spawned have flourished beyond all reasonable expectations, this book will consider the particular contribution of the artists who emerged in California in the late 1960s and early 1970s, a period which has yet to be thoroughly examined and critically assessed. Lewallen's essay and the organization of the exhibition itself take a thematic approach while not denying that each region maintained certain characteristics. By examining both well-known and lesser-recognized artists and artworks, the essay demonstrates the unique character and contribution of California Conceptualists across the state.

In her essay, Karen Moss discusses how the experimental ethos of the late 1960s and early 1970s demanded new sites and contexts for the production and presentation of art. She tells of the flourishing of alternative organizations, galleries, and publications, and chronicles the rise of experimental education in the art schools and universities, public interventions, and their effects on subsequent generations. Julia Bryan-Wilson considers how California artists used Conceptual and performance art at a time when gender and sexuality were being widely reconsidered in the context of feminism and gay liberation. She examines how artists played with, and also worked against, conventional images of gender and how notions of the gendered, laboring body fed into task-based performance and Conceptual practices. Finally, Anne Rorimer situates the exhibition within the broader, international context of Conceptual art's impetus to redefine traditional notions surrounding the art object with respect to its previous material and ideational manifestations. She uses linguistic, photographic, installational, time-based, and/or performative practices of East Coast and European artists such as Daniel Buren (b. 1938), Joseph Kosuth (b. 1945), and Lawrence Weiner (b. 1942) as points of comparison for the Conceptual works being produced at the same time in California.

NOTES

1 Susan Landauer, "An Overview: Countering Cultures: The California Context," in *The Art of Engagement: Visual Politics in California and Beyond*, ed. Peter Selz (Berkeley: University of California Press; San Jose, CA: San Jose Museum of Art, 2006), 6. Landauer's essay is a thorough analysis of the political and cultural conditions in California in the decades following World War II. As Landauer notes, "Between 1965 and 1968, 222,750 soldiers passed through Oakland Army Base alone."

2 Landauer, 6.

3 The song was written by John Phillips of the Mamas and the Papas and was first recorded in 1967 by Scott McKenzie to promote the Monterey Pop Festival.

4 The artist is quoted in Cathleen Chaffee, "Bas Jan Ader," in *In & Out of Amsterdam: Travels in Conceptual Art, 1960–1976,* ed. Christophe Cherix (New York: Museum of Modern Art, 2009), 54.

5 The Feminist Art Program was established in 1970 by Judy Chicago at Fresno State College (now California State University, Fresno). It subsequently relocated to the California Institute of the Arts (CalArts), where it was codirected by Chicago and Miriam Schapiro.

6 Douglas Huebler, "untitled statements" (September and December 1968), in *Arte Povera*, ed. Germano Celant (New York: Praeger, 1969), 43.

7 The acronym MOCA is not to be confused with the Museum of Contemporary Art that was founded much later in Los Angeles.

8 Paul Cotton died and was spiritually reborn as Adam II on December 24, 1969.

9 Carl E. Loeffler and Darlene Tong, eds., *Performance Anthology: Sourcebook for a Decade of California Performance Art* (San Francisco: Contemporary Arts Press, 1980).

Fig. 1.1 Fred Lonidier, *29 Arrests: Headquarters of the 11th Naval District, May 4, 1972, San Diego,* (detail), 1972. Twenty-nine black-and-white photographs and one text panel; 5½ × 8½ in. each.

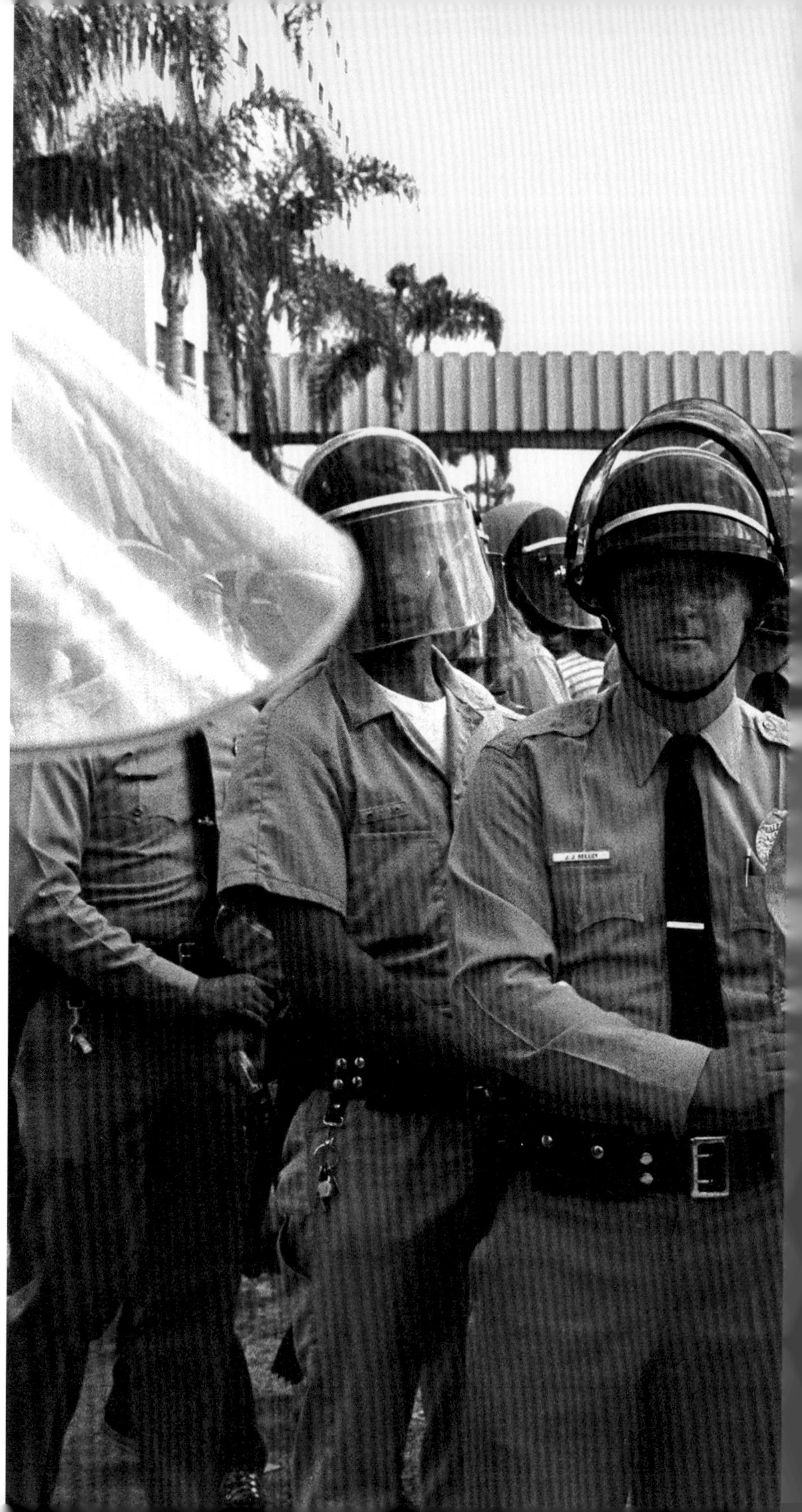

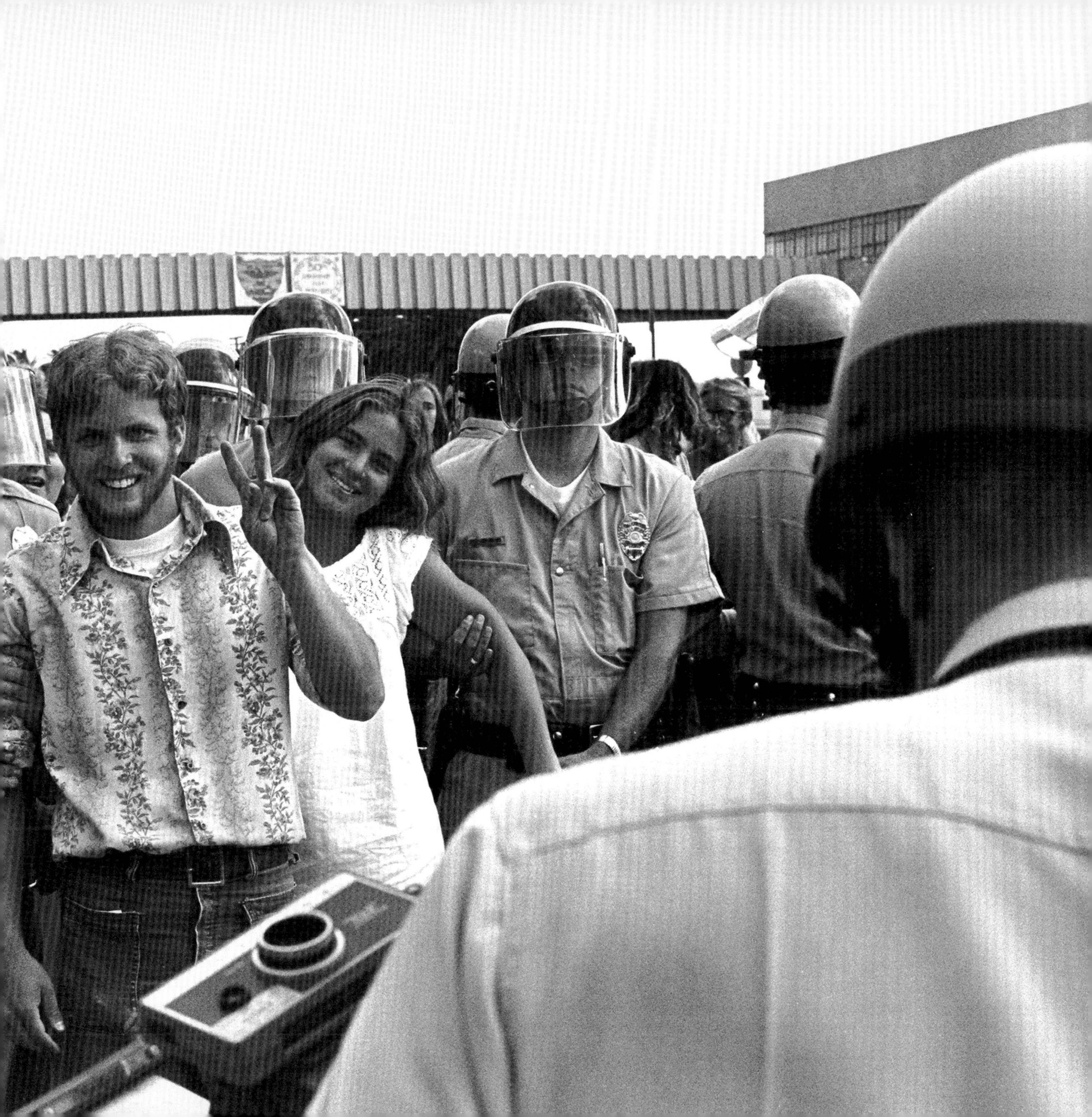

A LARGER STAGE

Constance M. Lewallen

In 1969, shortly after cremating his paintings in a ceremonial finale to his career as a painter, John Baldessari (b. 1931) transposed the letters that spell *California* as they appear on a map to their actual locations on the ground—in other words, he imposed "language on nature, and vice versa" (see frontispiece).[1] Working with his friends George and Judy Nicolaides, Baldessari traversed the state backward, first inscribing *A* at Joshua Tree National Monument with dry color, rocks, and wildflower seeds, then traveling north to end at Lake Shasta for the *C* (made with found logs), and so on. Other materials used included pigment, fabric, rocks, yarn, and a telephone pole (which, with its "fake" shadow made of black pigment, formed the *L*). Both a nod to earthworks and an absurdist literalization of the symbolic system of mapping, *California Map Project Part I: California* (1969) is one example of several works by Baldessari that adheres to one of Sol LeWitt's landmark *Sentences on Conceptual Art:* "Irrational thoughts should be followed absolutely and logically."[2] Here, Baldessari signals many of what were to become the defining features of Conceptual art: the tendency to create work outside of the studio; the emphasis on concept and process over physical objects; the absurdist idea followed to its rational conclusion; and the use of secondary material (photography and text) as documentation.

Conceptual art, defined broadly, emerged in the late 1960s more or less simultaneously among groups of young artists in the United States and elsewhere. Although most of California's first generation of Conceptual artists remain less well known than their East Coast and international peers—such as Lawrence Weiner and Sol LeWitt (New York), or Daniel Buren (France), or Art and Language (England)—they shared with them a rejection of traditional modes of art making in the context of the enormous cultural and social changes in society at large. The hyperconsumerism of the 1960s extended to the art market and offended idealistically inclined artists for whom art existed on a higher plane. Hence, they de-emphasized the creation of saleable paintings and sculpture in favor of works that privileged the concept and/or the process of art making, and documented them with some combination of maps, photographs, drawings, video, and text. Conceptual artists invented a host of new modes of artistic production and moved freely between them according to which was most appropriate to the idea.

Because many of these new genres—performance, site-specific installations, film, video, and such democratic forms as mail art and artists' books—were ill suited to or disregarded by traditional art venues, these artists colonized alternative sites, such as the city streets or non-art spaces. Even in those instances when they exhibited in galleries or museums, Conceptual artists found ways to fundamentally alter the conventional artist–viewer relationship.

With several notable exceptions, California Conceptualists relied less on systems and linguistic structures than did their New York peers. West Coast artists who used language often combined it with humor, believing that you can have serious art and humor at the same time. Californians, especially in Northern California, tended to draw their art and lives closer together, and often erased the distinction between the two. Nature played a greater role in the north—proximity to the mountains and deserts was integral to the work of artists like Paul Kos and Robert Kinmont, and others addressed environmental issues. At both ends of the state, artists were affected by widespread anti–Vietnam War and anti-establishment sentiment as well as the rise of civil rights. Conventional standards of decency were being attacked from all sides. In 1964, Southern California artist Connor Everts was arrested for work he showed at the Zora Gallery in Los Angeles (he was acquitted by the judge after the jury could not come to a decision), and Beat poet Michael McClure's play *The Beard,* featuring nudity, opened in San Francisco in 1965. Offended by the suggested sexual content of Edward Kienholz's *Back Street Dodge '38*—a truncated car with the door opened to reveal desiccated lovers in an illicit embrace—city officials threatened to close down his retrospective exhibition at the Los Angeles County Museum of Art in 1964. A last-minute compromise allowed guards to open the car door briefly at fifteen-minute intervals. In nightclubs, Lenny Bruce flouted obscenity laws with his raw language and frank observations of hypocrisy in America. But 1965 was also the year the National Endowment for the Arts was established under President Lyndon Johnson, and the next year Drs. Masters and Johnson published *Human Sexual Response,* a massive study that revealed that underneath a conventional exterior, sexual activity in America was much more varied and widespread than anyone had imagined.

The feminist and Chicano movements were especially important in Southern California, while the demand of gays and lesbians for equal rights was most strongly felt in the north. In 1968, there were massive walkouts by Chicano students in East Los Angeles, and, between 1969 and 1971, the Chicano Moratorium, a loose affiliation of Mexican American groups, combined to protest the Vietnam War not only in Los Angeles but also in Chicago, Albuquerque, Denver, San Francisco, San Diego, Oakland, and elsewhere, culminating in marches of Chicanos around the United States. The peaceful demonstrators were attacked by tear gas from helicopters, and in the ensuing melee, many were injured and four were killed in East Los Angeles.

Like the Dada artists in Europe who were sickened by the devastation of World War I, American artists saw the Vietnam War as a tragic consequence of an imperious political system from which they felt alienated. Antiwar protests raged throughout the state, although they differed in character in the north and south. In the Bay Area, the 1964 Free Speech Movement at the University of California, Berkeley, had set the stage for civil rights and antiwar protests that continued to be centered on campuses from Berkeley to San Francisco State to the University of California, Santa Cruz; in the south, the protest movement was mostly based in ethnic communities.[3] Both north and south intersected with the counterculture ethos of drug use (marijuana was to Conceptual artists what whiskey was to the Abstract Expressionists), rock music, and utopian fantasy. Following the Beat scene of the 1940s and 1950s, by the 1960s San Francisco was on the forefront of dissent, home to a flourishing underground press and radical activists like the Diggers, who gave away food and money and performed political theater in public spaces. Newly formed bands like the Grateful Dead and Big Brother and the Holding Company (Janis Joplin joined the band in 1966) established the Bay Area as the West Coast center for psychedelic rock. In short, California was ripe for artistic experimentation. Even if they were not directly engaged in protest activities, young California artists could not help but be aware that the old order was under attack; revolution was in the air; and traditional forms of art seemed remote and wholly inadequate to the concerns of the moment. The action was rarely in the studio, even less often in the museum or commercial gallery; the action was in the streets and other venues not usually associated with art.

California Conceptualists have most often been described in the following regional terms. Northern California Conceptual artists, such as Terry Fox, emphasized the body and ritual, and tended to conflate their life and art activities. In this respect, these artists had an affinity with European Conceptualists, such as Joseph Beuys (with whom Fox performed at the Kunstakademie Düsseldorf in 1971). Others, such as Tom Marioni, Linda Mary Montano, and Robert Kinmont, were influenced by Eastern philosophies. The Northern California artists worked in the full range of new genres but placed an emphasis on performance: precedence shifted from object to event, film, and video, in which time is conceived as a medium. Their Los Angeles counterparts, such as Baldessari, Robert Cumming, Lowell Darling, William Leavitt, Allen Ruppersberg, Ilene Segalove, Alexis Smith,[4] and William Wegman, drew on popular culture—print media, movies, and TV, particularly Hollywood—in terms of imagery and narrative impulse (Cumming and Leavitt were particularly fascinated by the artificiality and seductiveness of movie sets). These artists also worked in an array of nontraditional genres, although photography and video predominated. San Diego, despite its being generally conservative and home to several military bases, was the locus of highly politicized art by Martha Rosler, Allan Sekula, and others. They studied at the relatively new campus of the University of California, whose faculty—Helen Mayer Harrison and Newton Harrison, and David and Eleanor Antin as well as the German Marxist theorist Herbert Marcuse (Allan Kaprow joined the faculty in 1974)—were immersed in feminist, environmental, economic, and social issues. Rosler described their attitude as "antimodernist" in that they were against the modernist notion of art as separate from the rest of culture and society. "We were a new school, small, sitting on top of complex ties to the real world and the war. We might as well make big demands; why not do what we wanted. Either the market or the institutions were going to change or we would ignore them and make new ones."[5]

While there is some truth to these characterizations, in surveying the wide range of Conceptual practices in California, it becomes clear that artists across the state shared methodologies and themes that are as important as, and at times trump, geographic differences. I will highlight these correspondences according to the following categories: Mapping the Land; The City (the Street); Politics; Private/Public Space; Domestic Space; Art/Life; Psychological and Perceptual Space; The Body; Art about Art/the Artistic Process; and Language and Wordplay. I recognize that these categorical distinctions are fungible—a given artist might fit nicely into more than one area. For example, Paul McCarthy's oeuvre is body oriented, but in some of his first video performances, he also parodies the process of art making, and those will be discussed in the section dealing with such commentary. Despite these caveats, I believe that a thematic approach will afford a fresh look at this seminal period in California Conceptual art and demonstrate that it foreshadowed much of the work being created by young artists today.

Fig. 1.2 Ant Farm, *Truckstop Network: Phase One,* from the portfolio for *Truckstop Network* project, 1971. Drawing with collaged elements: colored pencil, felt-tipped pen, stamped ink, India ink, embossing, stickers, and photographs; 11 × 17 in.

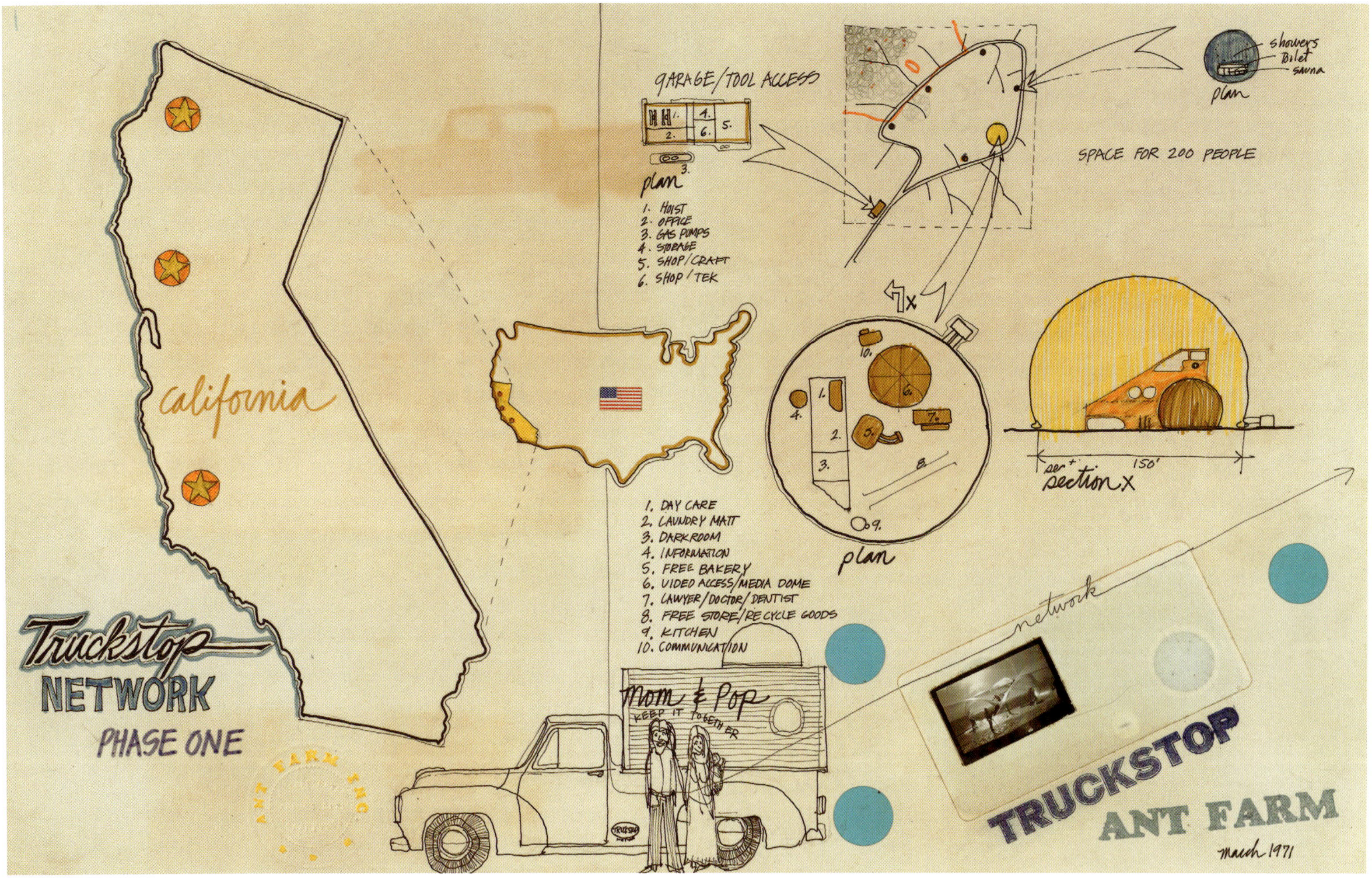

GARAGE/TOOL ACCESS
plan
1. HOIST
2. OFFICE
3. GAS PUMPS
4. STORAGE
5. SHOP/CRAFT
6. SHOP/TEK
showers
sauna
plan
SPACE FOR 200 PEOPLE
california
plan
section X
150'
1. DAY CARE
2. LAUNDRY MATT
3. DARKROOM
4. INFORMATION
5. FREE BAKERY
6. VIDEO ACCESS/MEDIA DOME
7. LAWYER/DOCTOR/DENTIST
8. FREE STORE/RECYCLE GOODS
9. KITCHEN
10. COMMUNICATION
Truckstop
NETWORK
PHASE ONE
Mom & Pop
KEEP IT TOGETHER
network
TRUCKSTOP
ANT FARM
March 1971
ANT FARM INC

MAPPING THE LAND

Baldessari was one of many California Conceptual artists who—no longer bound by the institutional and practical considerations such as scale, materials, or salability—made works outside the studio. The world became their stage. In fact, it was Baldessari who established the first post-studio program at the California Institute of the Arts (CalArts), although he credits Carl Andre with the term.[6] Post-studio practitioners argued that art based on ideas need not be created in a traditional studio space. French artist Daniel Buren summed up the attitude of many of his peers when he called the studio one of the "ossifying customs of art."[7] Art made outside of the studio tended to be ephemeral and was recorded and preserved in the form of documentation. For some artists like Douglas Huebler, the document was the work, what Seth Siegelaub calls "the primary information [the signified]."[8] For others, as in Baldessari's *California Map Project* (see frontispiece), the process—what artists did in the environment—was the work, and the documentation was simply a record, or the secondary information (the signifier). Artists' projects as disparate as those of Ant Farm, Eleanor Antin, Huebler, and Robert Kinmont used similar forms of presentation, such as an altered map, a text, a diagram, or a photograph.

Unlike Baldessari, who traveled throughout California to document his incursions in the landscape for the photographs that compose *California Map Project,* Huebler relinquished authorship and restricted his personal involvement in *Location Piece #6, Los Angeles, March 1969* (figs. 1.3–1.4) to the concept and instructions for its realization. Before he moved to Los Angeles, Huebler asked two visitors to the city to adhere small paper stickers on eight arbitrary locations in the city and to photograph the selected sites. Their intentionally unremarkable black-and-white photographs—the front tire of a car, the side of a building—accompanied by a typed explanation of the project, constitute the entirety of the work. In a 1969 interview, Huebler described his transition from painting to sculpture and, finally, to Conceptual work.[9] In the final stage of this evolution, when he moved his sculpture outside of the gallery, he realized that his work would have to be monumentally scaled to compete with the natural environment, a proposition he viewed as both arrogant and unnecessary. "The world is full of too much stuff to walk around," Huebler said, and if the purpose of an art object is to establish the relationship of the viewers to their surroundings, then there were other systematic ways of experiencing location that didn't require objects.[10]

The members of the radical architecture collective Ant Farm (Chip Lord, Curtis Schreier, Doug Michels, and Hudson Marquez) described themselves as "eco-conscious environmentalists sharing the new age technology, spreading the total awareness and demands through life (life art), i.e., playing the life game with a whole earth consciousness . . . life as art."[11] They opposed the architectural establishment and its corporate monuments, and despite the madcap character of their activities, their project—to find architectural solutions to what they saw as a nomadic future—was serious and highly influential given the widespread use of such pneumatic buildings. Ant Farm characterized their 1971 and 1972 nationwide *Truckstop Network* tours as "traveling shows of inflatable structures and environmental information circus" and documented them with clever punning and inventive graphic representation—like a U.S. map in the form of a placemat that marked their visits to colleges and universities and "pointless interests" (Paolo Soleri's Arcosanti, Earth People's Park, and Videofreex, among others) (see fig. 2.34).[12] They traveled in their customized "Media Van" and trailer, which, in addition to 35 mm cameras, audio, video, and film recording and playback equipment, included a shower, kitchen, and the inflatable structure *ICE 9,* which visitors could enter. At each stop, Ant Farm demonstrated its features: lightweight, transparent, flexible, and easily and cheaply fabricated (their 1970 *Inflatocookbook,* inspired by Stewart Brand's *Whole Earth Catalog,* provided the recipe), all befitting a society on the move.

Like Ant Farm, pioneer environmental and ecological artists Helen Mayer Harrison and Newton Harrison's passion has been to find solutions to the spoiling of the natural world, albeit their approach has been more empirical. Since they began working together in San Diego in the early 1970s, the Harrisons have created site-specific works based on research and collaboration with biologists, urban planners, and concerned specialists in other related fields. Rather than drawing attention to environmental dangers through dramatic means—like those employed by Joe Hawley, Mel Henderson, and Alfred Young, whose action *Oil* (1969; see the title page) is described later in this text—the Harrisons use straightforward, extensive mapping and documentation to tell and propose solutions to environmental "stories of place."[13] In their seminal work *The Lagoon Cycle* (1974–84; see fig. 1.5), the Harrisons describe a self-nourishing, sustainable polyculture system that mimics nature in which organisms and plants feed on one another and selective harvesting preserves the balance.[14] The Harrisons' proposition was a critique of the usual practice of harvesting everything, which may yield greater profits in the short term but is wasteful in the long term.[15]

Robert Kinmont took his measure vis-à-vis nature in *8 Natural Handstands* (1969; see fig. 1.7 and the cover image). Combining humor and death-defying skill, Kinmont executed perfect handstands in eight locations—the first at the very edge of a cliff in the Sierra Nevada mountains and then seven more at descending elevations. Vikki Kinmont recorded the series in black-and-white photographs. In *My Favorite Dirt Roads* (1969; see fig. 1.6), Kinmont, for whom nature is inseparable from his oeuvre, pointed his camera down the middle of several personally significant country roads that lead out of Bishop, California, in the eastern Sierra Nevada, where he grew up. Looking down a road, the artist says, "opens your mind in a way nothing else does."[16]

Location Piece # 6

Los Angeles, California

During late February, 1969 two persons, visiting California on other business, assisted the artist in making this piece by placing markers (1" diameter self adhering paper stickers) at eight different locations..and documenting each "marking" by photographing the site.

No structuring system was used other than that the markers were placed wherever and whenever it occured to either one of the two persons to do so.

The eight photographs of the locations, not identified otherwise, join with this statement to constitute the form of this piece.

March, 1969

Douglas Huebler

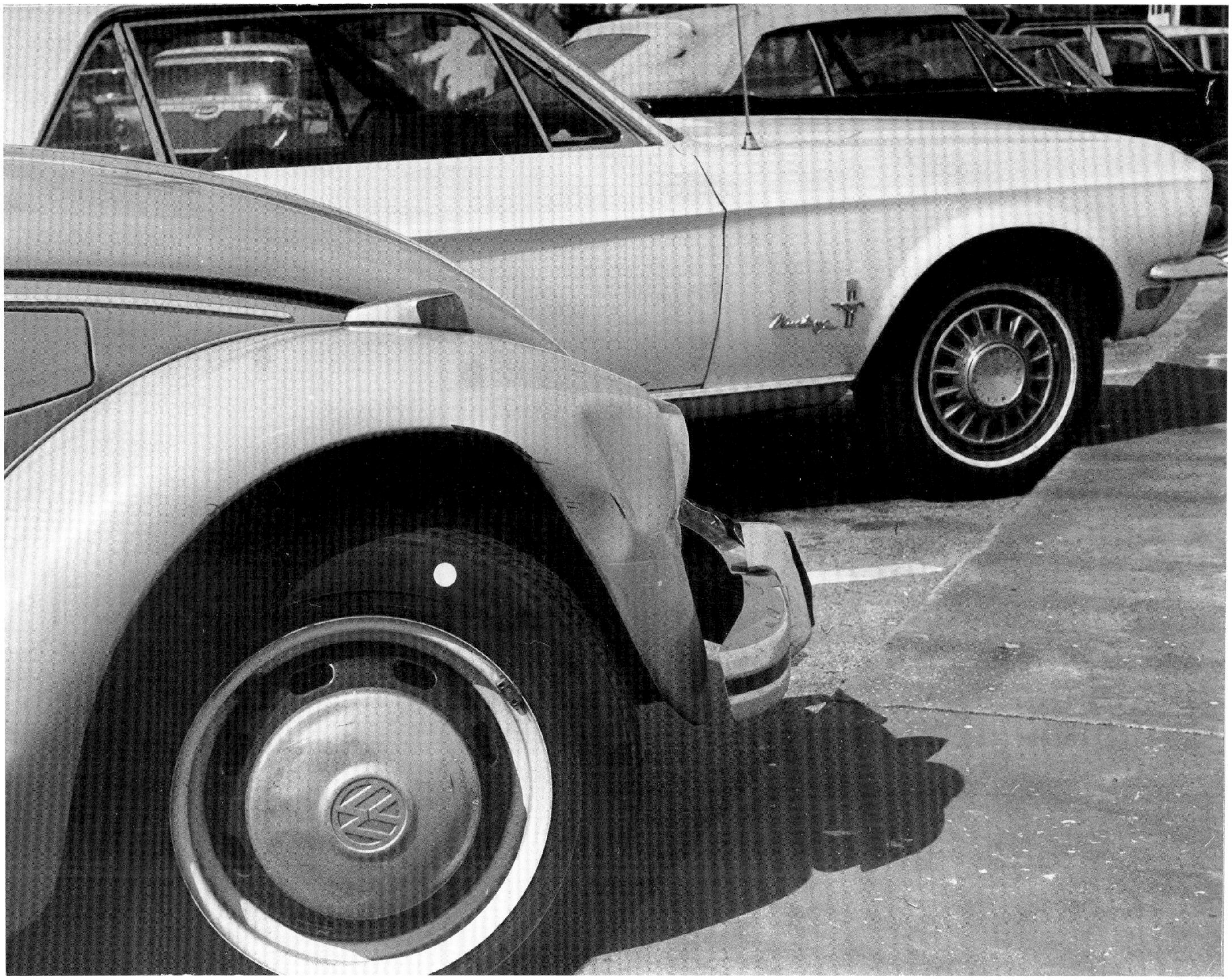

Figs. 1.3–1.4 Douglas Huebler, *Location Piece #6, Los Angeles, March 1969* (detail), March 1969. Typewritten statement and eight black-and-white photographs; statement: 11 × 8½ in.; photographs: 7 7/16 × 9 7/16 in. each.

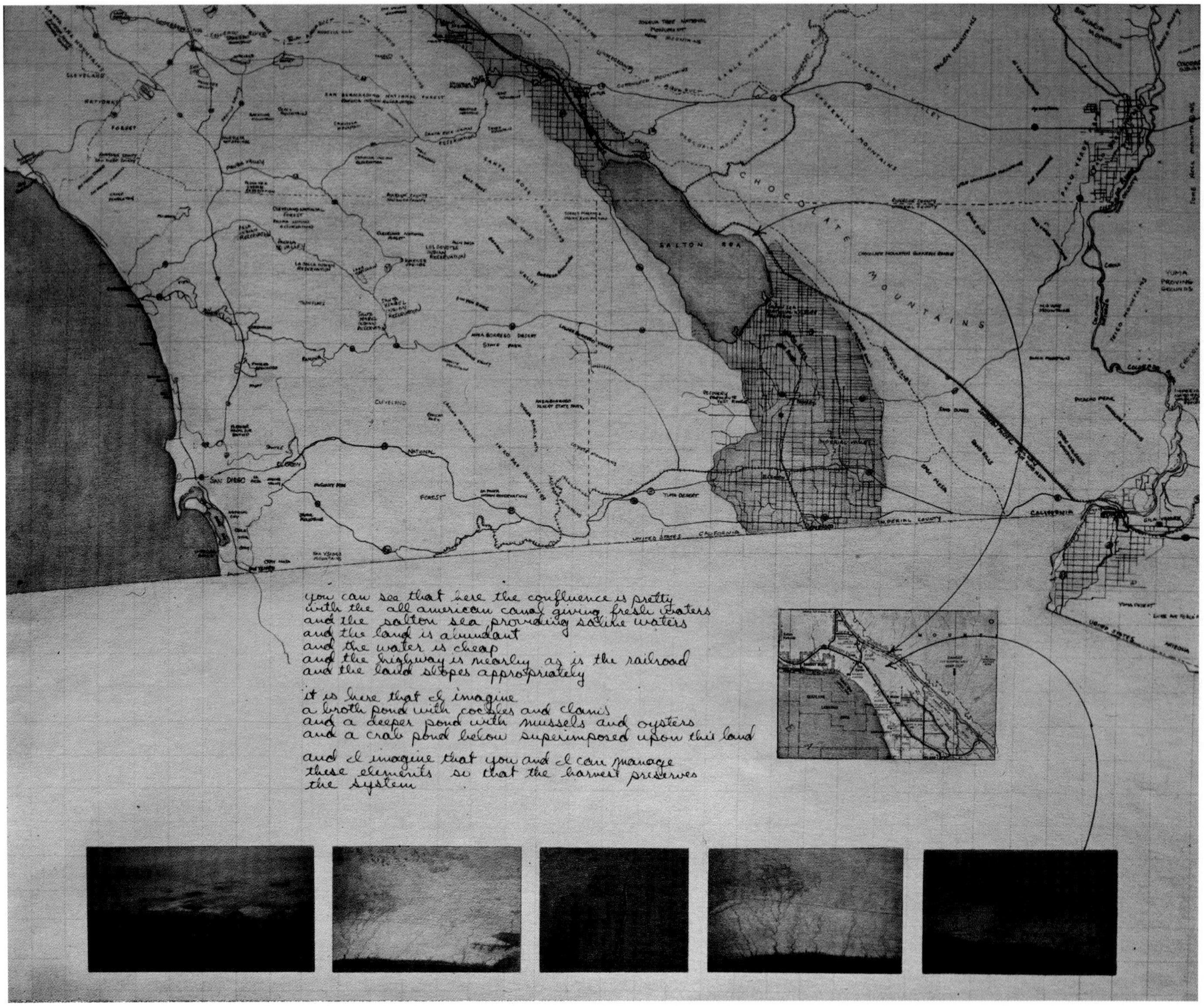

Fig. 1.5 Helen Mayer Harrison and Newton Harrison, *The Book of Lagoons, The Fourth Lagoon: On Mixing, Mapping, and Territory* (detail), 1974–84.

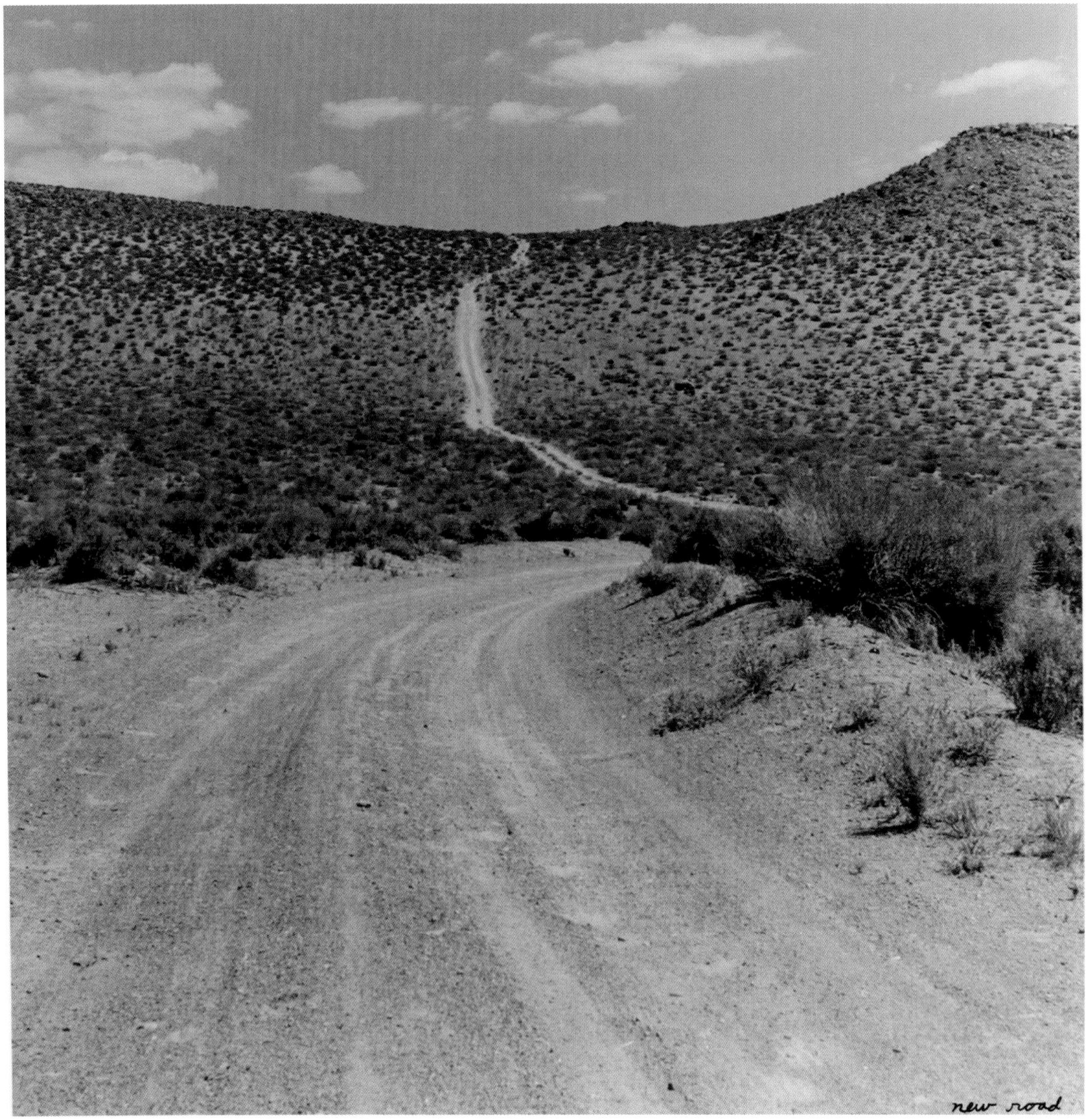

Fig. 1.6 Robert Kinmont, *My Favorite Dirt Roads* (detail), 1969/2008. Seventeen black-and-white photographs; 11 ⅛ × 10 ⅞ in. each. Photo: Jason Mandella. Courtesy of Alexander and Bonin, New York.

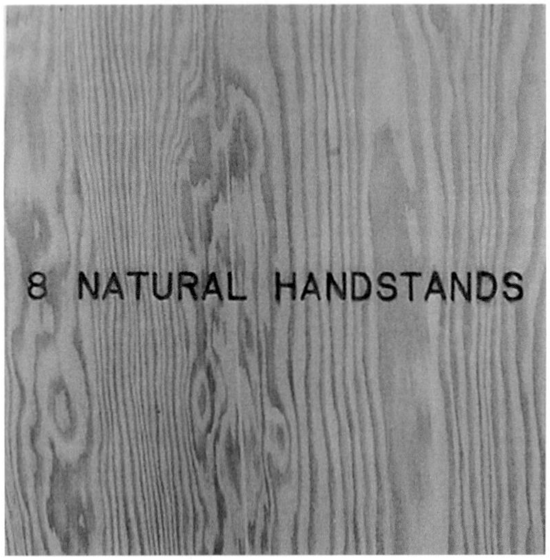
8 NATURAL HANDSTANDS

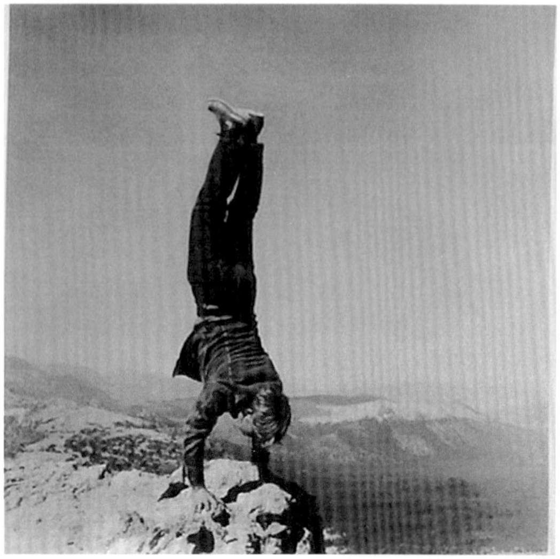

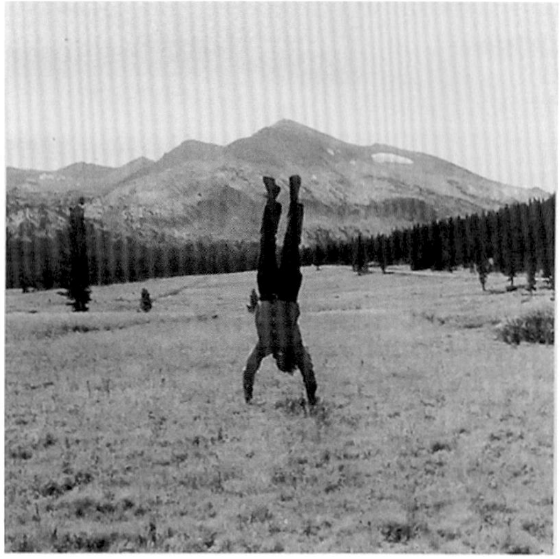

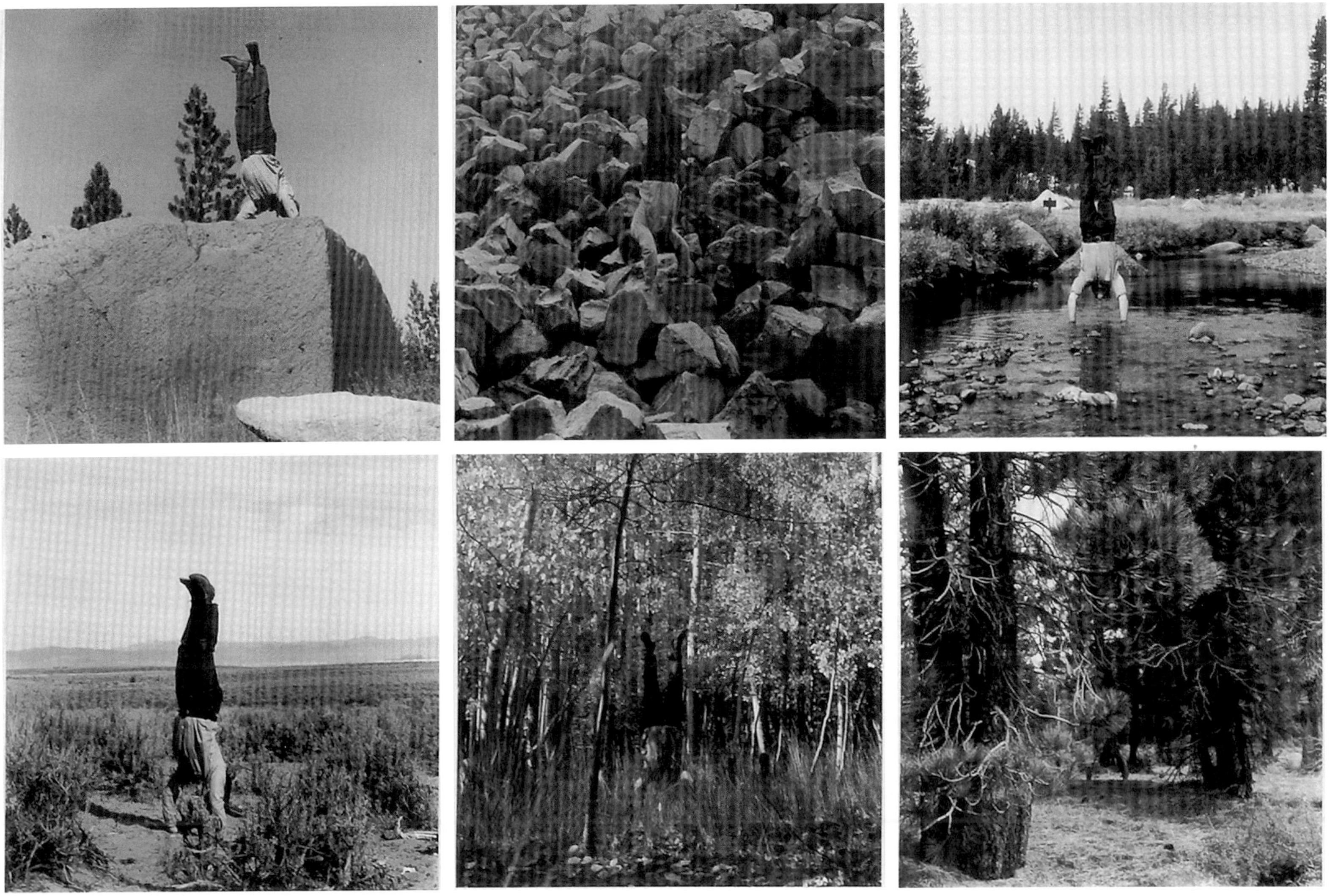

Fig. 1.7 Robert Kinmont, *8 Natural Handstands*, 1969/2009. Nine black-and-white photographs; 8 ½ × 8 ½ in. each.

Fig. 1.8 Ed Ruscha, *Every Building on the Sunset Strip,* 1966. Artist's book; 7 ¾ × 5 ⅞ in. closed; open dimensions variable.

THE CITY (THE STREET)

In the charged social climate of the time, urban space offered a new stage for artistic investigation. Ed Ruscha was a precursor to artists who elevated the mundane environment to a subject for art. His accordion-folded book *Every Building on the Sunset Strip* immortalized West Hollywood's Sunset Strip as it looked in 1966. Twenty-seven feet long when fully extended, *Sunset Strip* is the most elaborate of Ruscha's typological, pocket-sized photographic books. They capture apartments, parking lots, and swimming pools—all devoid of human presence—and other nondescript features of Los Angeles, the epitome of a late-twentieth-century, postpedestrian American city.[17] Ruscha intended these inexpensive books to be available to a wide audience but nevertheless regarded them as "the toughest part of my art."[18] Though Ruscha made the first of the series *Twentysix Gasoline Stations* in 1963, well before the advent of the Conceptual movement, his books are early examples of the type of straightforward

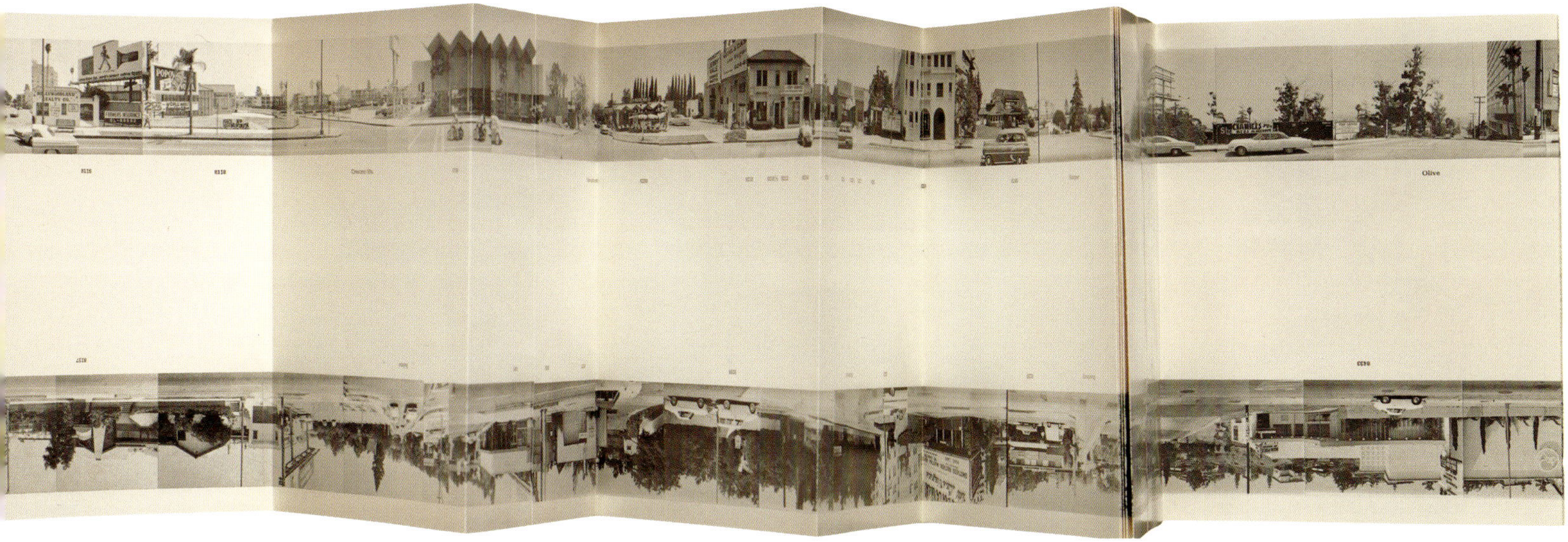

photographic document that would be almost universally used by Conceptual artists. Paul McCarthy was new to Los Angeles when he made his slide projection piece *May 1, 1971* (1971). Whereas Ruscha photographed every building he passed from a 35 mm camera mounted on the back of his pickup truck, McCarthy shot his twenty-five photographs from a stationary location—only the continuous stream of cars changes from one scene to the next. McCarthy, like Ruscha, recognized early on that the automobile, more than any building or street, defined Los Angeles.

To other young Conceptualists, the street was less a subject than a site for performance. For some, it provided the opportunity to reach a wide audience; for others, it was the backdrop for solitary actions. The street had special appeal for women and other groups who had generally been excluded from established exhibition venues even as they were entering the art world in greater numbers. Like Yayoi Kusama and Adrian Piper in New York and Valie Export in Vienna, Bonnie Sherk and Linda Mary Montano enacted several street interventions in San Francisco in the early 1970s. Sherk wanted to bring the experience of nature into the city by way of unexpected interventions. One of the first was *Portable Parks I–III* (1970; fig. 1.11), in which she and Howard Levine imported turf, palm trees, picnic tables, and live farm and zoo animals to San Francisco streets and elevated freeway ramps. (Forty years later, the collaborative art team Rebar created similar mini-parks in parking spaces in San Francisco.) Sherk's interest in animal behavior and ecological systems as microcosms and laboratories led her to found *Crossroads Community (the farm)* in 1974 (see fig. 2.31, p. 169). The farm was one of the city's first alternative art spaces and the only one devoted to urban issues. Sherk followed *Portable Parks* with the *Sitting Still* series (1970; fig. 1.12), in which she sat for approximately one hour in various city locations as a means to subtly change the environment simply by becoming an unexpected part of it. In the first performance, Sherk, dressed in an evening gown,

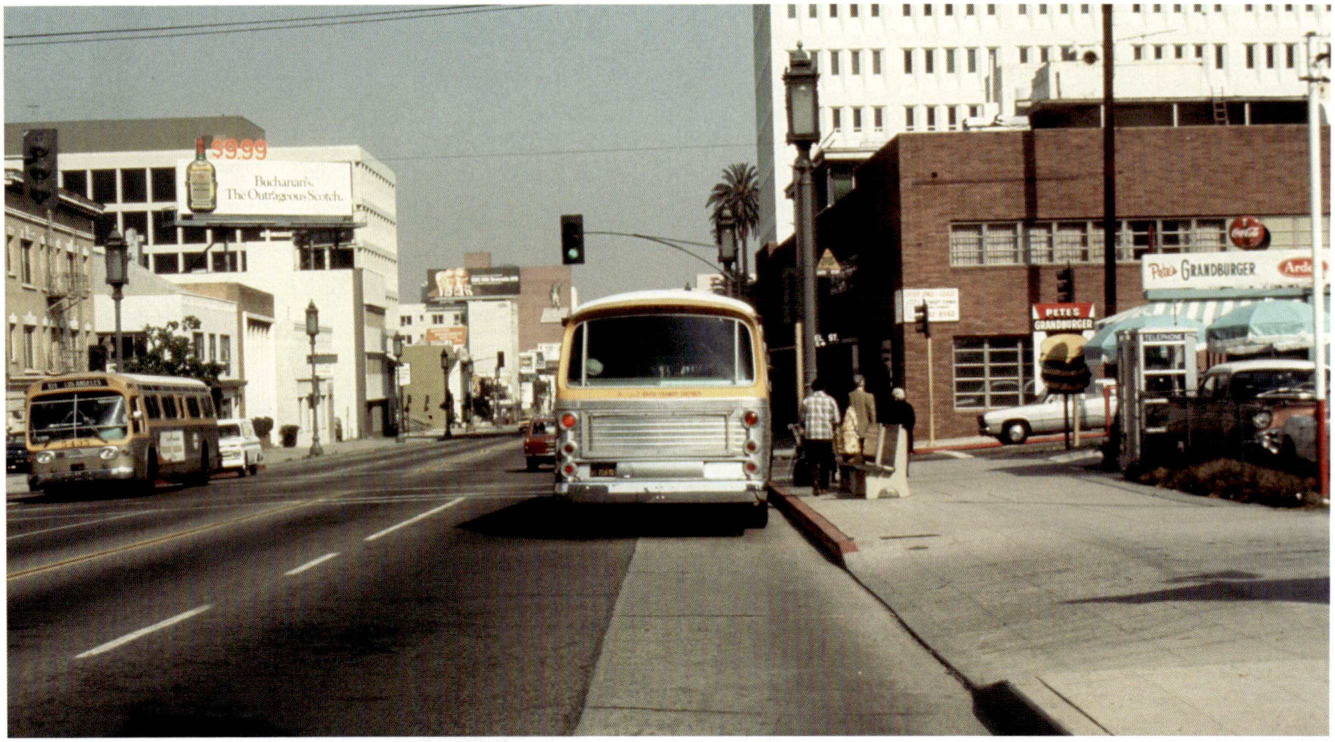
$9.99
Buchanan's,
The Outrageous Scotch.
Pete's GRANDBURGER
PETE'S
GRANDBURGER
TELEPHONE

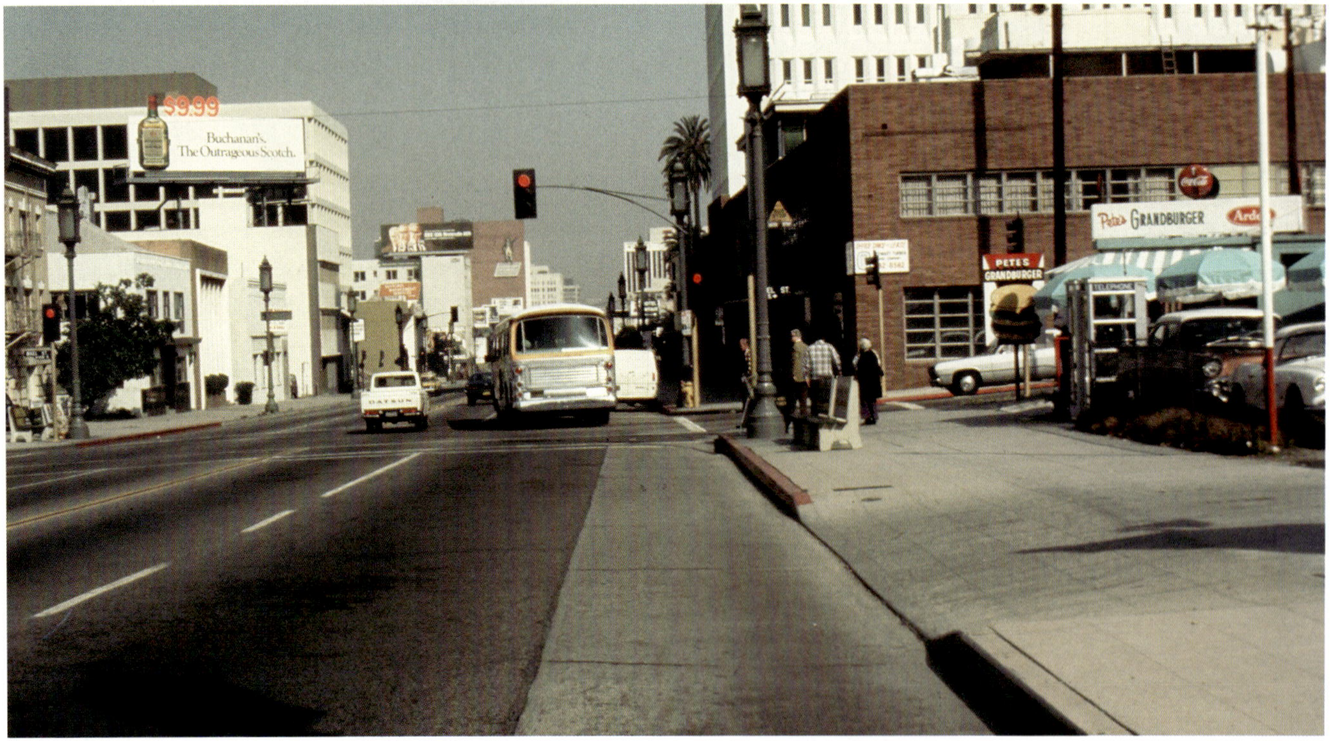
$9.99
Buchanan's,
The Outrageous Scotch.
Pete's GRANDBURGER
PETE'S
GRANDBURGER
TELEPHONE
DATSUN

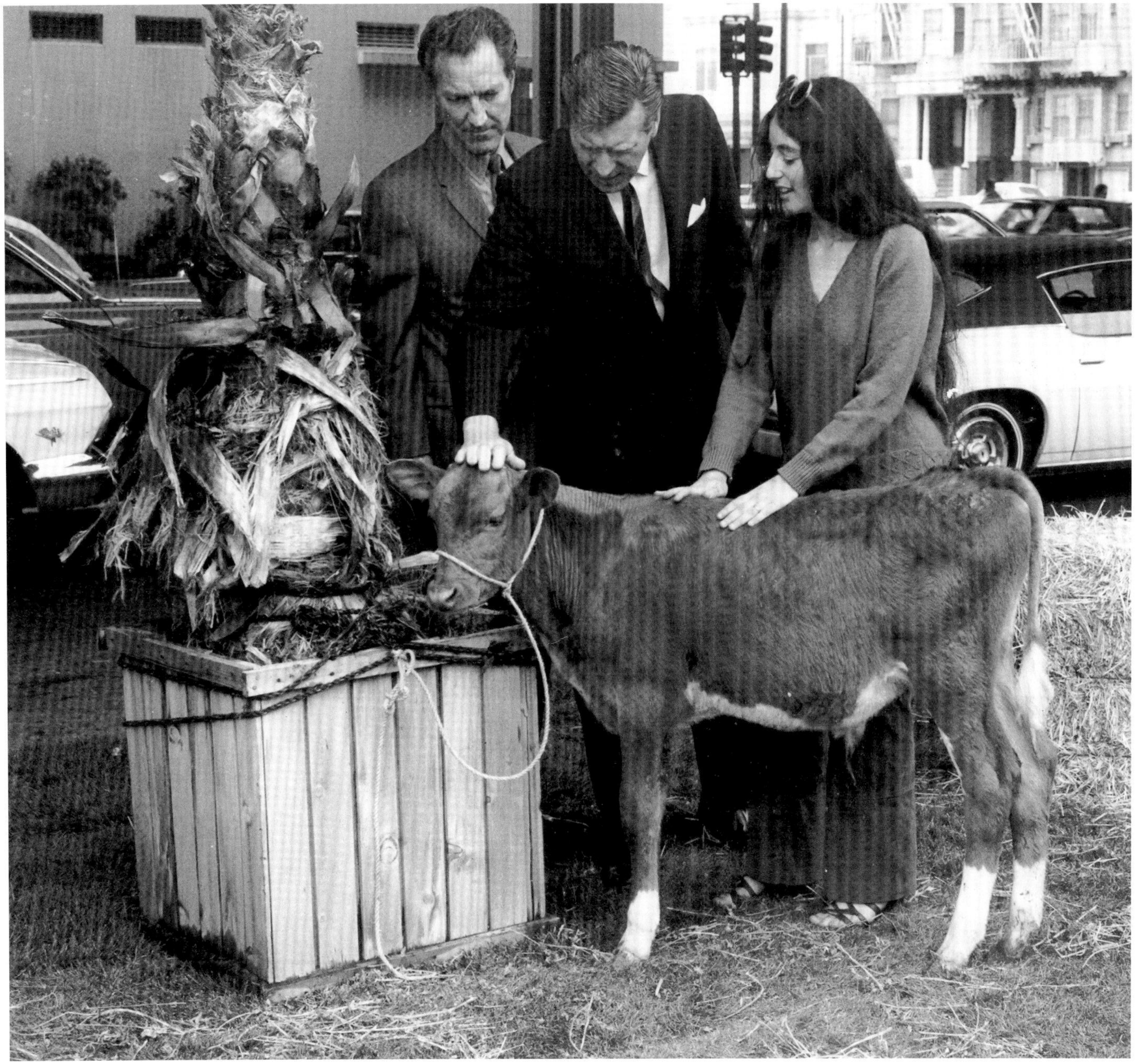

Figs. 1.9–1.10 Paul McCarthy, *May 1, 1971* (detail), 1971. Twenty-five projected slides.

Fig. 1.11 Bonnie Sherk, *Portable Park II,* 1970. Performance documentation: Sherk with CalTrans officials and cows at Mission/Van Ness off-ramp.
Courtesy of the artist, San Francisco, California.

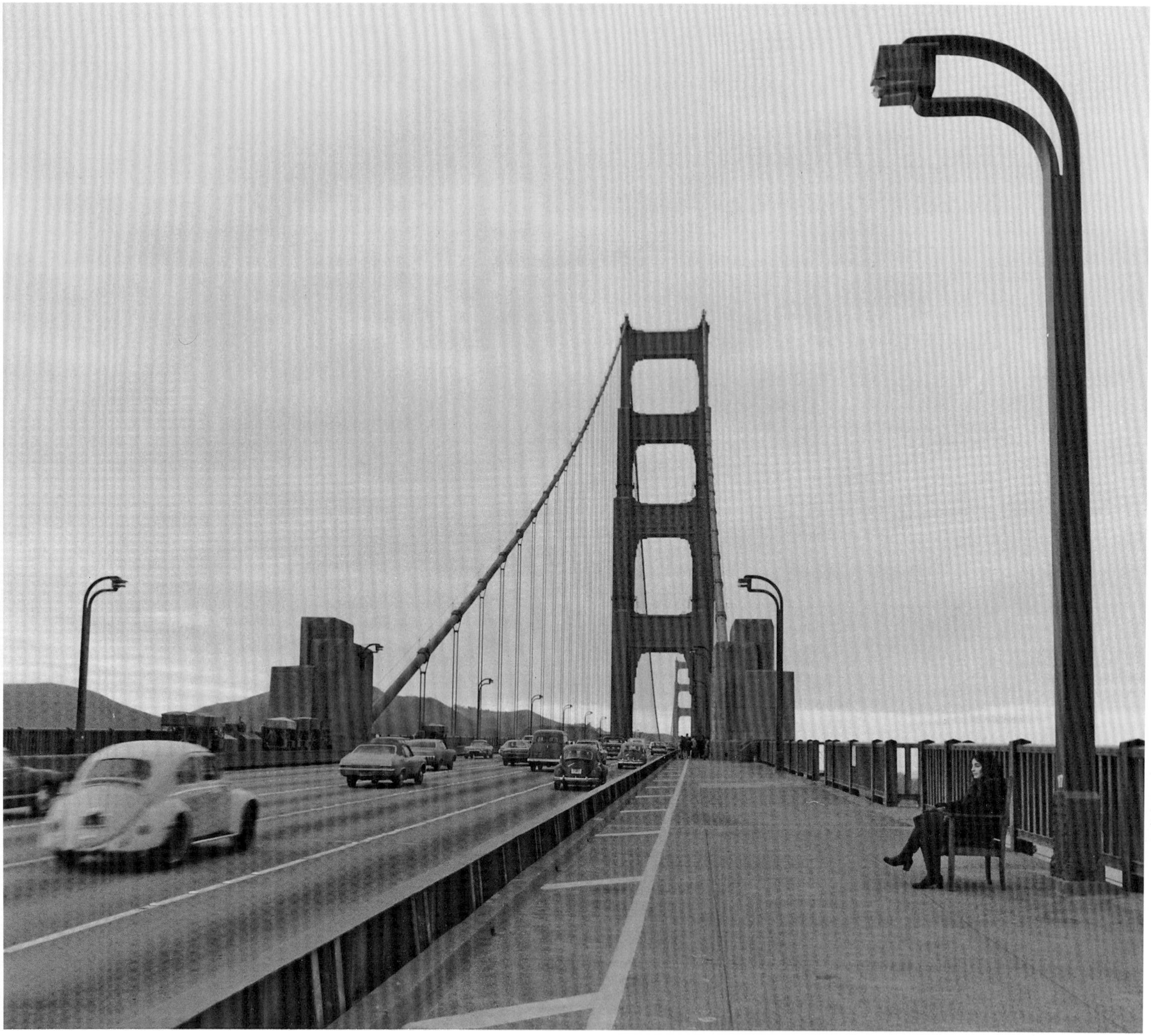

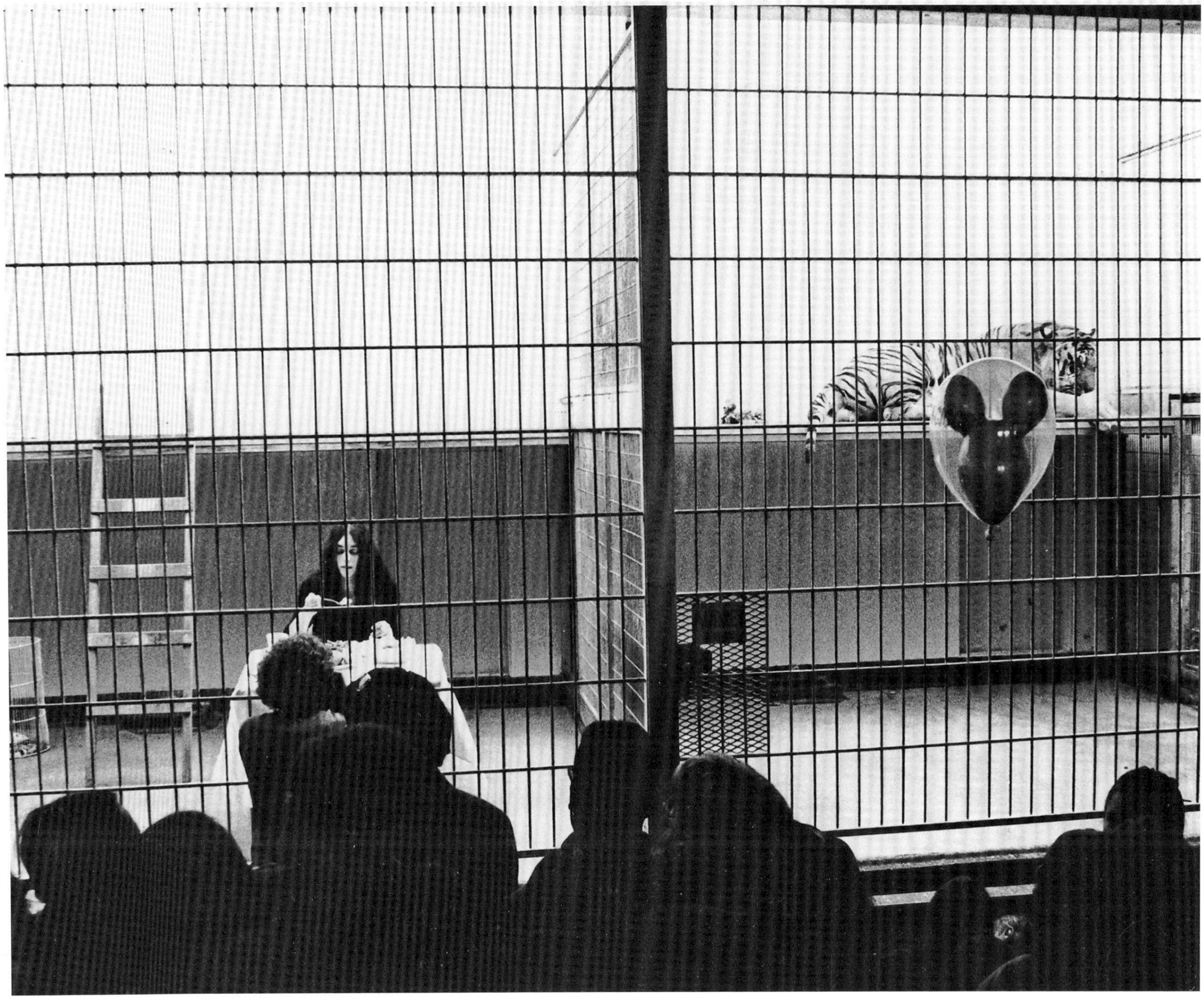

Fig. 1.12 Bonnie Sherk, *Sitting Still II,* November 1970. Performance documentation: Golden Gate Bridge, San Francisco, Photo: Courtesy SFMOMA Research Library and Archives.

Fig. 1.13 Bonnie Sherk, *Public Lunch,* 1971. Performance documentation: Lion House, San Francisco Zoo. Photo: Courtesy SFMOMA Research Library and Archives.

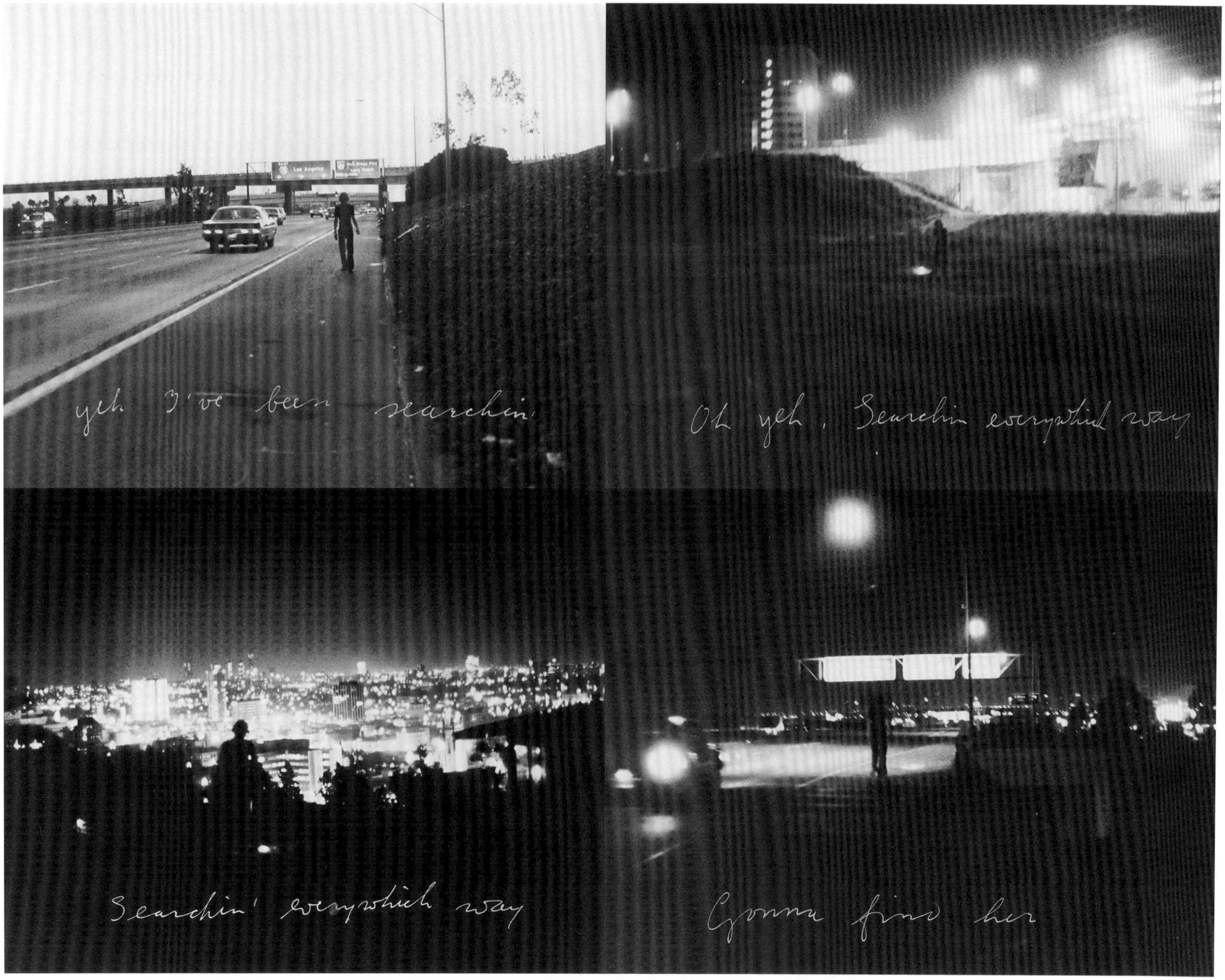

Figs. 1.15–1.18 Bas Jan Ader, *In Search of the Miraculous (One Night in Los Angeles)* (detail), 1973. Eighteen black-and-white photographs with handwritten text in white ink; 10 ¾ × 13 ½ in. each.

Fig. 1.19 Howard Fried, *Long John Servil vs. Long John Silver* (detail), 1972. Black-and-white photographs mounted on four panels; 49 ⅝ × 41 in. each. San Francisco Museum of Modern Art; purchase with the aid of funds from Rene de Rosa and the Soap Box Derby Fund. (Detail: upper Long John Servil, panel 4; lower Long John Silver, panel 1.) © Howard Fried. Photo: Courtesy of the artist.

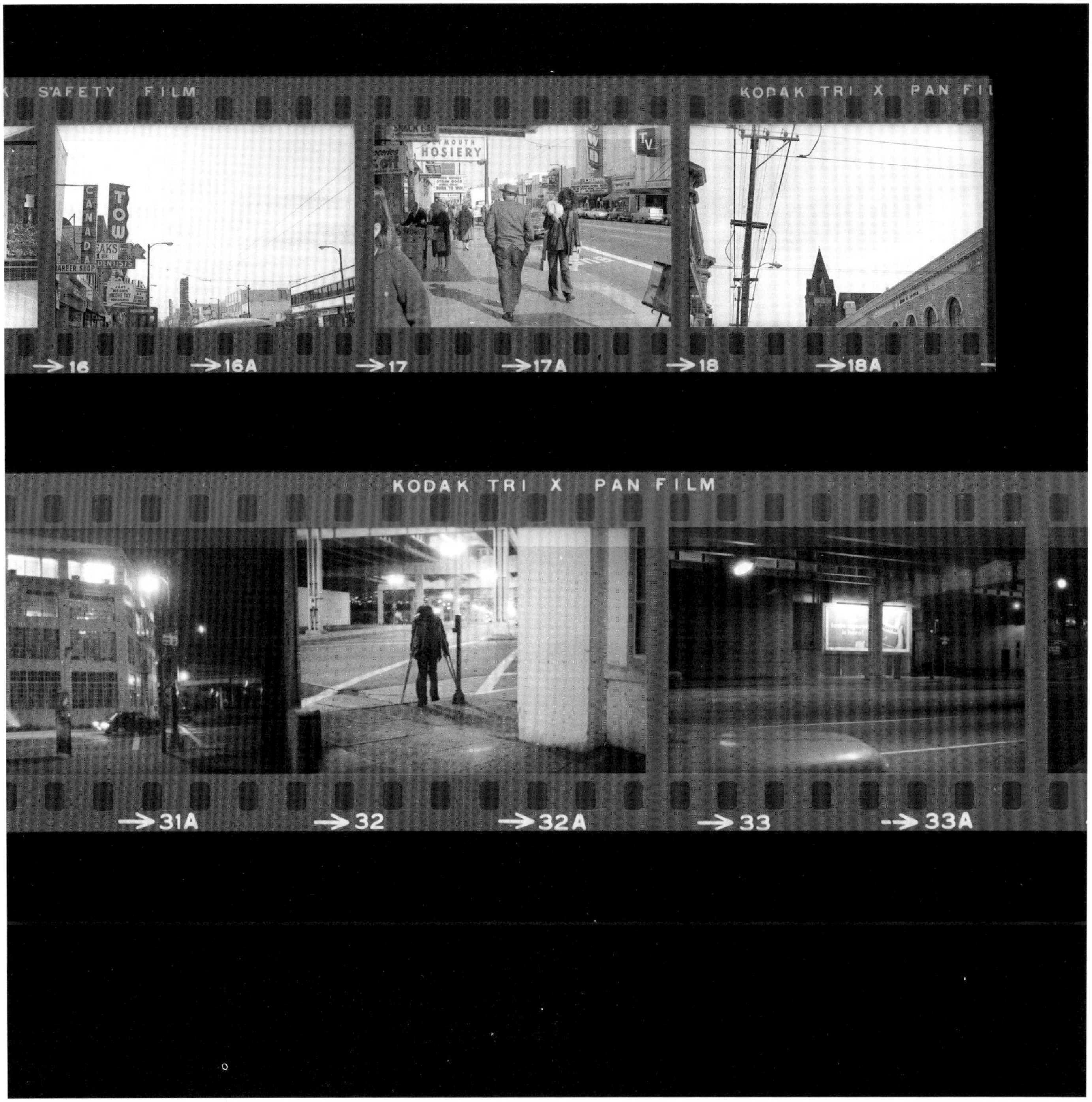
SAFETY FILM
KODAK TRI X PAN FIL
TOW
CANADA
DENTISTS
BARBER SHOP
SNACK BAR
HOSIERY
TV
→16
→16A
→17
→17A
→18
→18A
KODAK TRI X PAN FILM
→31A
→32
→32A
→33
→33A

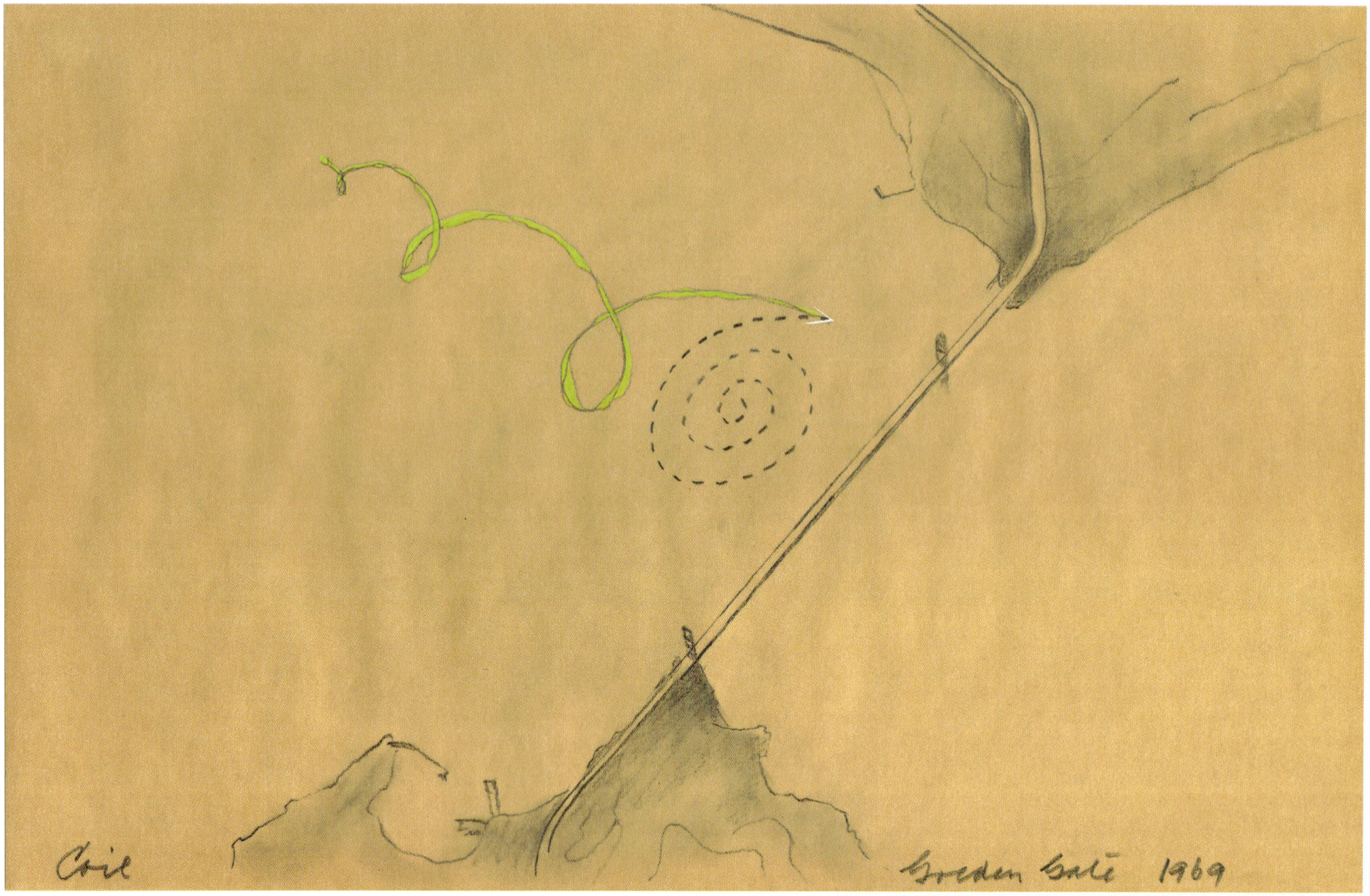

Fig. 1.20 Alfred Young, *Coil*, 1969. Ink on vellum; 16½ × 25½ in.

POLITICS

Events staged by Hawley, Henderson, and Young, as well as such actions as Paul Cotton's *The People's Prick* and Fox's *Public Theater #3: What Do Blind Men Dream* (1969; fig. 1.21), were inspired in one way or the other by the strategies of political protests that were taking place in California's streets and campuses. According to Henderson, who was deeply involved in Bay Area political activity, his events were inspired by "the energy of Berkeley and then the strike at San Francisco State," where he and his collaborators were art faculty.[22] University Art Museum, Berkeley (later University of California, Berkeley Art Museum and Pacific Film Archive) curator Brenda Richardson remembers him as a "pivotal force at San Francisco State."[23] He took part in anti–Vietnam War marches and joined with students and other faculty at San Francisco State College strikes to protest the administration's cooperation with the draft and the treatment of minority students. He drew on these experiences as well as on Allan Kaprow's Happenings, which involved large numbers of participants, in several spectacular political outdoor events. As a response to the violent repression of the riots at Attica Prison in upstate New York on September 13, 1971, in which forty-three people died, Henderson spelled out "Attica" with flashing Christmas-tree lights on the side of a hill in Southern California in March 1972 (see fig. 1.22 and Karen Moss's essay for a full description). Later, on November 10, 1973, Henderson arranged for forty-three people to walk around forty-three blocks surrounding the Hyatt Regency Hotel in San Francisco (fig. 1.24). Each participant wore a sandwich board picturing an altered American flag designed by Bruce Montgomery that had forty-three crosses in place of stars, black and white stripes representing prison bars, and "Attica" written in red letters at the bottom.[24]

Not all of the activities in which Henderson was involved were realized in the street. Henderson, again with Hawley and Young, brought attention to a massive oil spill that had taken place on January 29, 1969, along the Santa Barbara coast: the artists spelled out the word *oil* in biodegradable dye five times in San Francisco Bay off the coast of Richmond, California, home to the Standard Oil refinery. The action, which took place on September 20 of that year, was filmed and photographed by Robert Campbell from a slow, low-flying airplane, and eerily anticipated another oil catastrophe in the bay: in January 1971, two Standard Oil tankers collided near the Golden Gate Bridge in dense fog, dumping between 500,000 and 1.9 million gallons of oil into the ocean and killing upward of 20,000 birds. The three artists had been testing the idea of using dye on the bay before they successfully enacted and documented *Oil* (pp. xiii–ix). In one trial run, Young and Hawley set out with the intent that Hawley would release smoke from a plane while Young, in a speedboat containing drums of dye, would create an image on the water under the Golden Gate Bridge. Things didn't work out as planned because poor visibility prevented the airplane from arriving, but Young, seizing the opportunity, drew on the water a large, fluorescent chartreuse spiral, which the artist later titled *Coil* (fig. 1.20). Some of the actions of Hawley, Henderson, and Young were not pointedly political. *Yellow Cabs* (1969; p. xiv) was, first and foremost, a celebration of the emergent counterculture. The three artists caused a massive traffic jam when they asked one hundred people around the city to simultaneously take taxis to the busy intersection of Castro, 17th, and Market Streets. Initial annoyance and confusion dissolved, and everyone—motorists, passersby, police, and hippies high on marijuana or simply catching the spirit—seemed to be having a good time. Lighthearted as *Yellow Cabs* was, it was the artists' way of showing people that they could make their voices heard. Through the use of such highly visible staging (the entire neighborhood turned yellow), the artists drew the attention of the media, which in turn helped spread the word. This intervention anticipated by decades the recent phenomena of flash mobs, in which individuals suddenly assemble in public places after coordinating the effort via social networks.

Paul Cotton responded to current events by using the form of the political protest march. Cotton led a parade to Berkeley's contested Earth People's Park, dressed in a pink cloth penis costume that the master punster described as "an in-body-meant of the creative vision of the Student Body of the 1960s which had been 'cut off' by Governor Ronald Reagan and the National Guard."[25] Cotton claimed ownership of the park for "I-Magi-Nation" by placing a flag in the ground (as Neil Armstrong had done on the moon just three days earlier) and then burying his costume on the site. In spontaneous and scheduled performances, Cotton adopted various identities, such as the Astral-Naught Rabb-Eye and the People's Prick. He viewed his body, which he often displayed nude or with his penis exposed, as a sculptural medium in which life and death as well as all consciousness are united.

Rather than personally performing on the street, Terry Fox staged street theater events. Fox had been a painter before finding himself in the midst of the 1968 strikes in Paris, in which large numbers of students, soon joined by workers, took to the street to protest educational policies and other inequities. From that point on, Fox ceased making paintings, declaring that performing, as opposed to painting, was like "the difference between being involved in direct confrontation and reading about it."[26] His ensuing street theater actions, first in Europe and then in San Francisco, also owe a debt to French actor, poet, and playwright Antonin Artaud's pre-narrative, cathartic theater. In *Public Theater #3: What Do Blind Men Dream*, Fox arranged for two blind street musicians who sang at the same downtown San Francisco corner every evening to appear instead at the corner of Union and Buchanan Streets and mailed invitations to the event. *What Do Blind Men Dream* was in a sense a readymade—in Fox's words, "theater with no director, no actors, no plot and no script."[27]

Viewers of Fox's street theater pieces were largely fellow artists and friends, but *Defoliation* (1970; fig. 1.25), the most public of Fox's several powerful works in response to the Vietnam War, was enacted before a large unsuspecting audience. *Defoliation* took place outside of the University Art Museum's temporary quarters, in the former power plant on the University of California campus, on the night of the opening of Brenda Richardson and Susan Rannells's forward-looking exhibition *The Eighties.* Wielding a flamethrower of the type the U.S. military used to destroy vegetation in Vietnam, Fox burned an area in the bed of jasmine plants. "This was my first political work," he said. "By burning a perfect triangle right in the middle, it would look as though someone had destroyed the plants on purpose. It was also a theatrical piece. Everyone likes to watch fires . . . but at a certain point people realized what was going on. Suddenly everyone was quiet. One woman cried for twenty minutes. The next day when people came to have their lunch there, it was just a burned out plot . . . it was the same thing they were doing in Vietnam . . . burning flowers they like to sit near."[28]

Much of the politically motivated Conceptual art in Los Angeles was centered in the Chicano neighborhoods of East Los Angeles, where, beginning in 1968, students began protesting what they perceived as racism and the poor quality of their schools. The protests reached a violent end in 1970, when police shot and killed journalist Ruben Salazar during a rally by the Chicano Moratorium. In response to that event, and to the refusal of the Los Angeles County Museum of Art to exhibit work by Chicano artists, Harry Gamboa Jr.—who had been an organizer of the protests along with Willie Herrón III and Gronk—tagged the museum with spray paint. Soon Patssi Valdez joined the group, which they named Asco. More than any other artist or artist collective, Asco blended politics and art in graffiti, parades, and publications. As with Cotton and Hawley, Henderson, and Young, Asco adopted the strategies of political protest. In one parade, *Walking Mural* (1972), Asco mocked stereotypical Chicano mural style and iconography (see fig. 3.3, p. 199). They marched down Whittier Boulevard, "dressed as absurd mural characters: Patssi Valdez as the Virgin de Guadalupe-in-black; Willie Herrón as a mural consisting of multiple faces; and Gronk was a Christmas tree

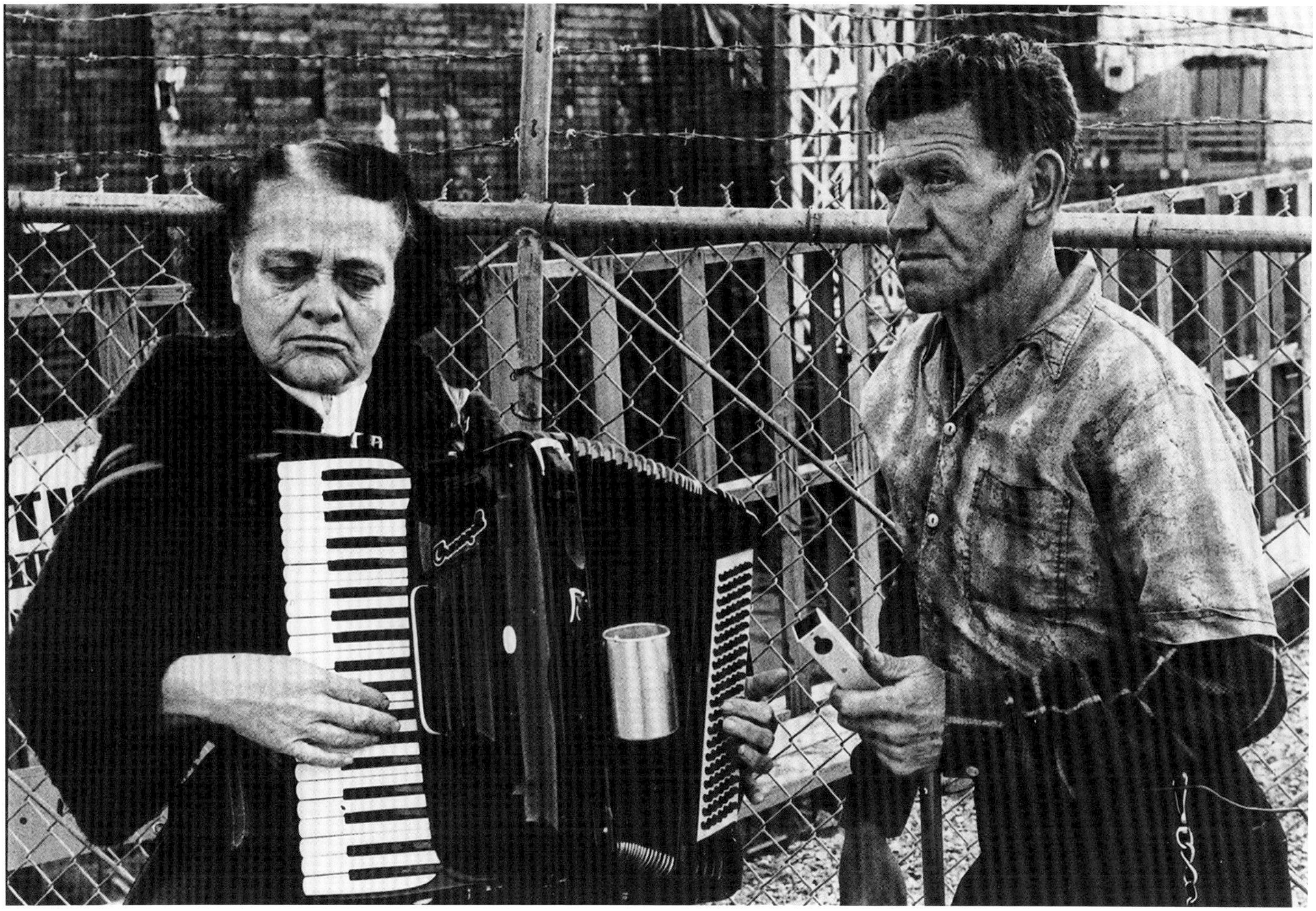

Fig. 1.21 Terry Fox, *Public Theater #3: What Do Blind Men Dream,* 1969. Performance documentation: corner of Union and Buchanan Streets, San Francisco. © The Estate of Terry Fox. Photo: Barry Klinger. Courtesy SFMOMA Research Library and Archives.

Fig. 1.22 Mel Henderson, *Attica,* March 11, 1972. From *The San Francisco Performance,* a hillside installation with Christmas tree lights, March 12–April 16, 1972, Newport Harbor Art Museum, Newport Beach, California.

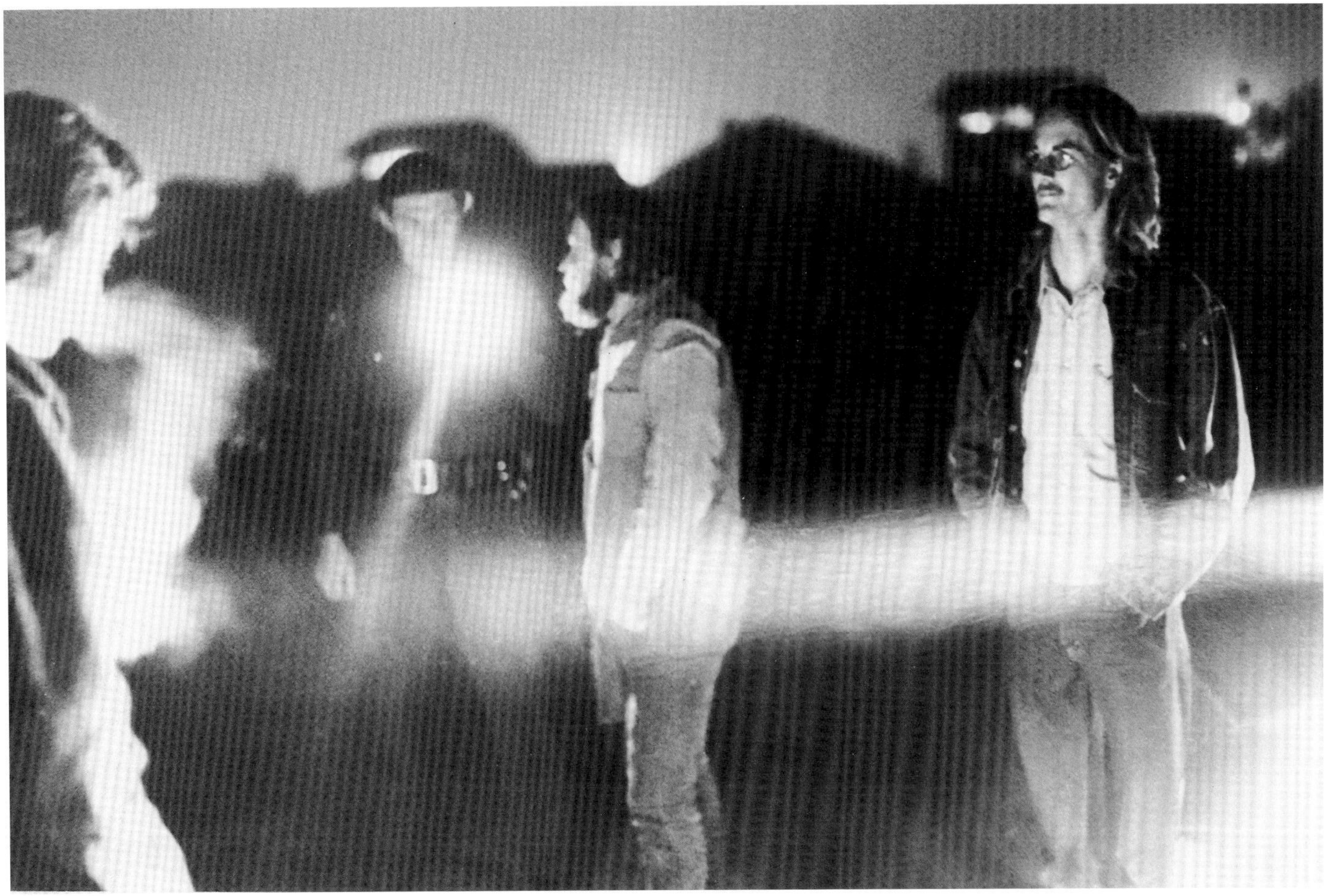

Fig. 1.23 Mel Henderson, *Untitled (Attica, The Arrest),* March 11, 1972. From *The San Francisco Performance,* March 12–April 16, 1972, Newport Harbor Art Museum, Newport Beach, California.

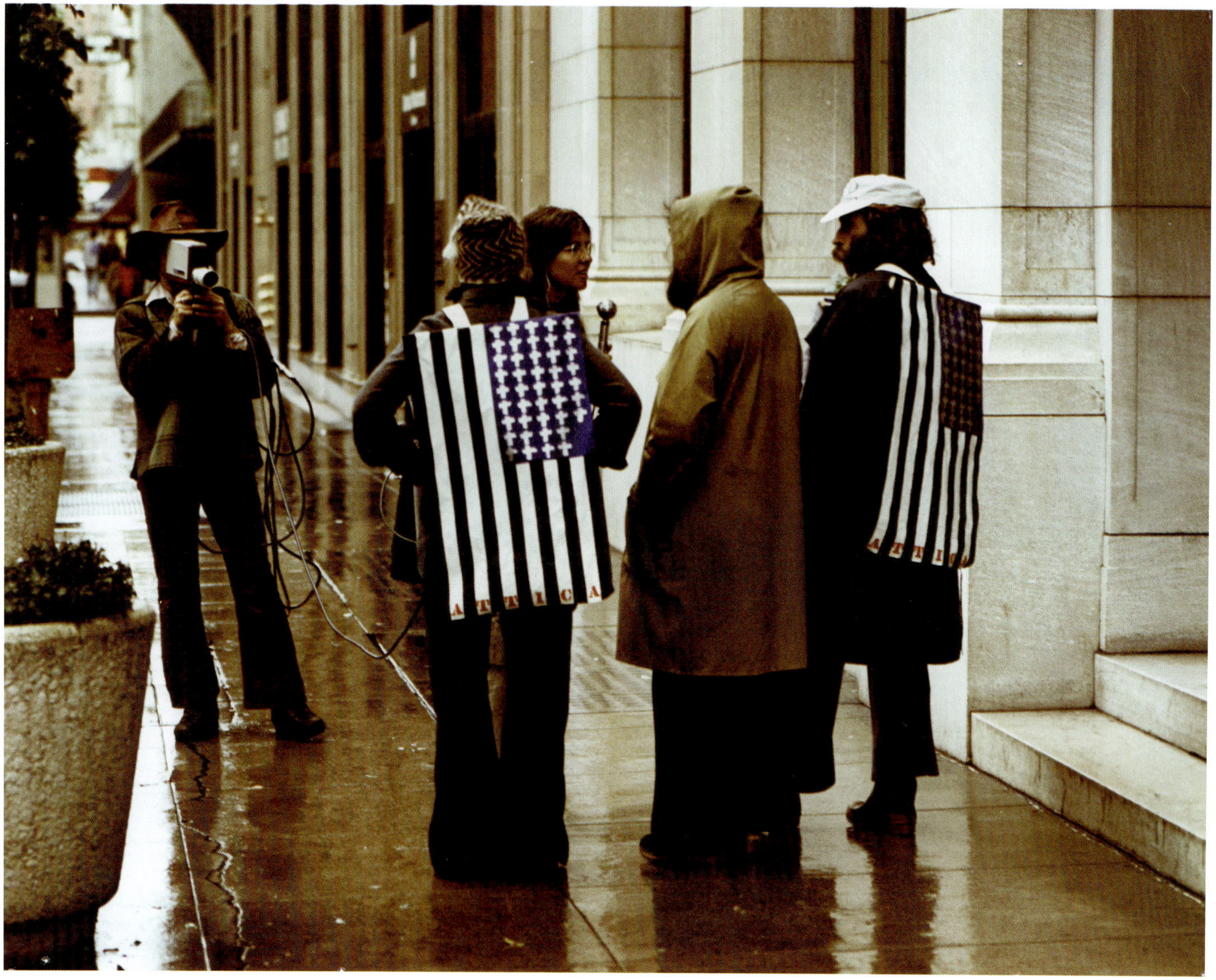

Fig. 1.24 Mel Henderson (in cooperation with Prisoners Union, San Francisco), *Attica,* 1973. Performance documentation from Artists and Educators conference, Hyatt Regency Hotel, San Francisco. Photo: Robert Campbell / Chamois Moon. Courtesy Mel Henderson and Susan Rannells.

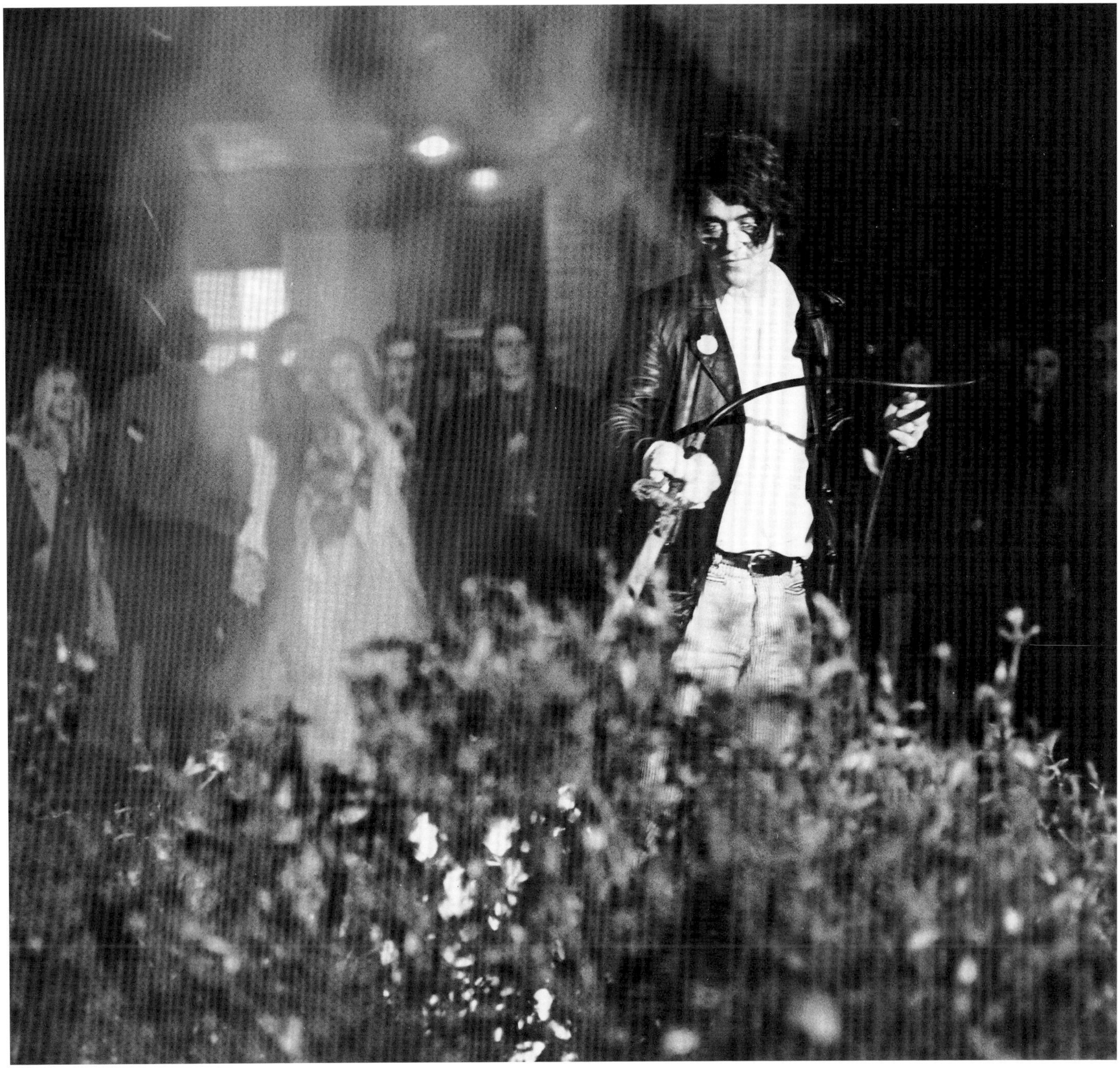

Fig. 1.25 Terry Fox, *Defoliation,* 1970. Opening-night performance, *The Eighties,* March 17, 1970, Power Plant Gallery, University Art Museum, University of California, Berkeley.

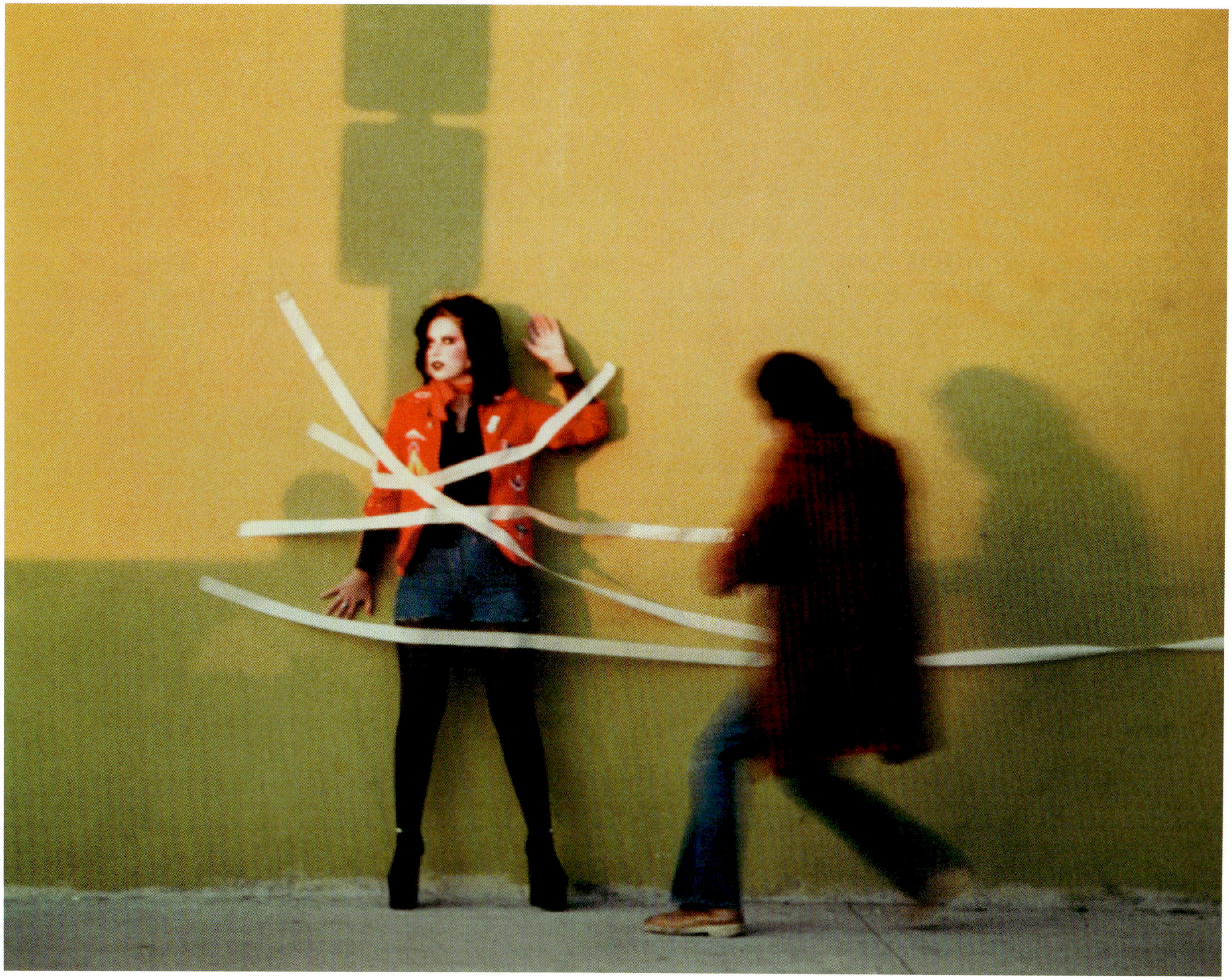

Fig. 1.26 Asco (Glugio "Gronk" Nicandro, Patssi Valdez, Willie Herrón III, Harry Gamboa Jr.), *Instant Mural,* 1974. Performance documentation (left to right: Valdez and Gronk).

Fig. 1.27 Martha Rosler, *First Lady (Pat Nixon),* 1972. Photomontage from the series *Bringing the War Home: House Beautiful,* 1967–72; 20 × 24 in.

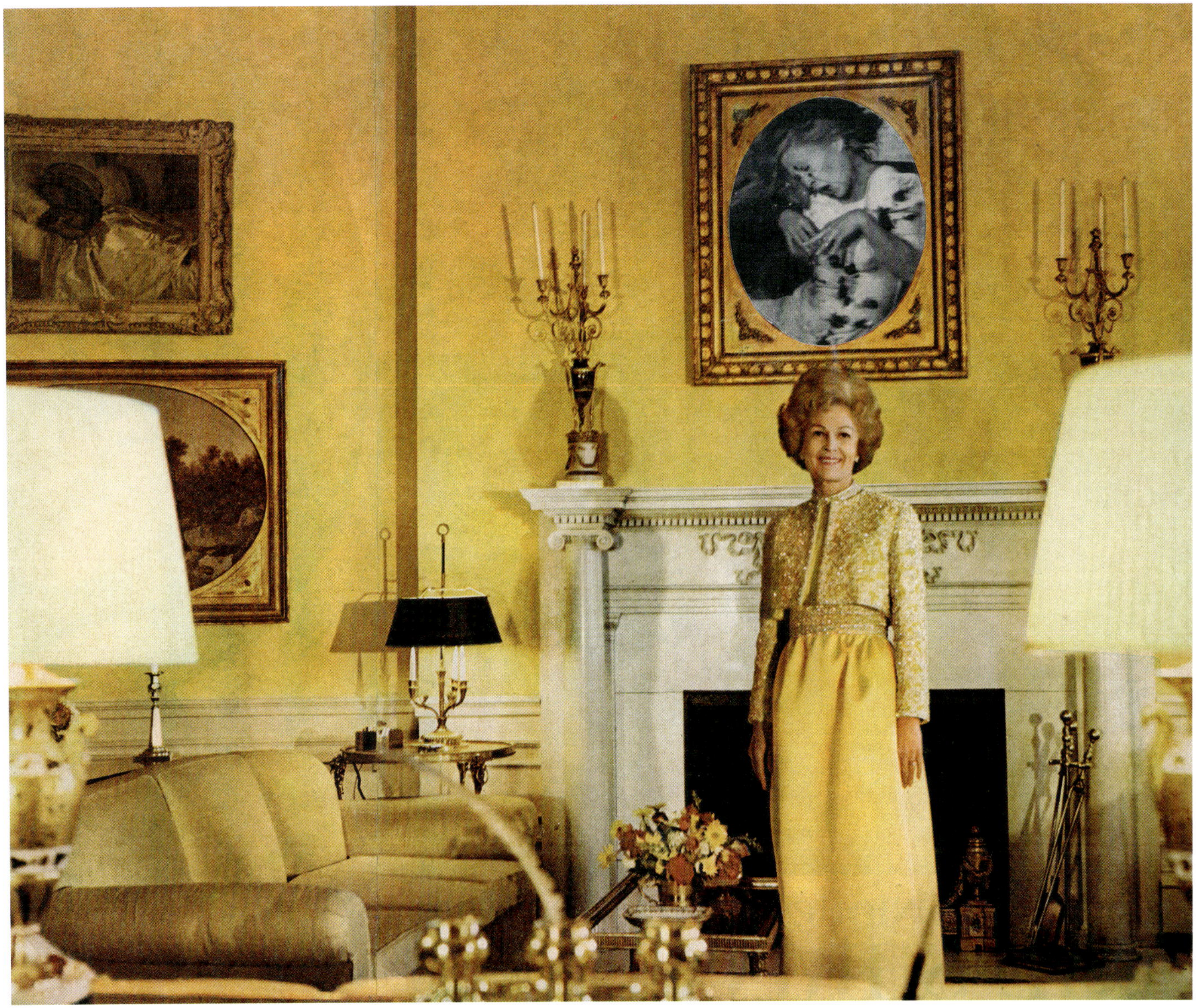

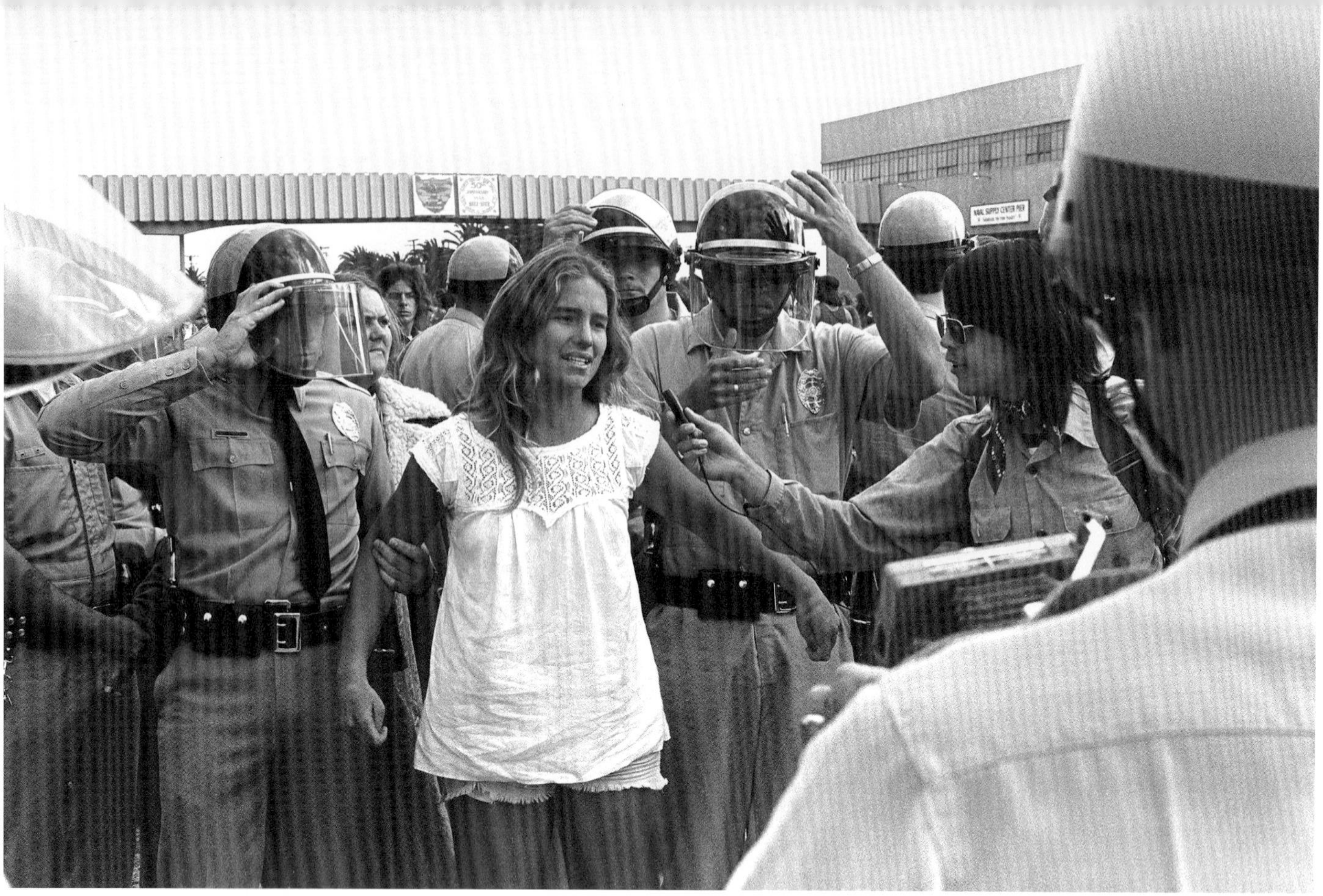

made from inverted chiffon dresses." The artists were not only critiquing the "authenticity of nationalist stereotypes" but also addressing issues of gender and sexuality that were often ignored within their community.[29] In an effort to enlist the unwitting media into their cause, they produced *No-Movies* (1973–74). These pieces consisted of a still image and text from a nonexistent film that were circulated to media outlets, which often printed them.

Further south, Fred Lonidier entered directly into a 1972 antiwar protest at the headquarters of the 11th Naval District in San Diego, where police arrested demonstrators opposed to the U.S. bombing of Cambodia. As a police officer photographed each protestor, many of them students, Lonidier stood aside and snapped his own picture. The resulting photographic series, *29 Arrests: Headquarters of the 11th Naval District, May 4, 1972, San Diego* (1972), reveals the incongruity of the police, with their helmets and protective plastic visors, and the smiling, unthreatening young arrestees (see fig. 1.28, and figs. 1.1, pp. 6–7, and 4.8, p. 232).

Rather than taking to the street, Martha Rosler trained her sights on the conflict in Vietnam in the form of photomontage. In the series *Bringing the War Home: House Beautiful* (1967–72; figs. 1.27 and 1.34),[30] she juxtaposed horrific newspaper and magazine photographs of the war with stylish home interiors from architectural and design magazines. This biting critique of American militarism and domestic complacency hasn't lost any of its sting.

Fig. 1.28 Fred Lonidier, *29 Arrests: Headquarters of the 11th Naval District, May 4, 1972, San Diego* (detail), 1972. Twenty-nine black-and-white photographs and one text panel (edition one of three); 5½ × 8½ in. each; 48 × 60 in. framed.

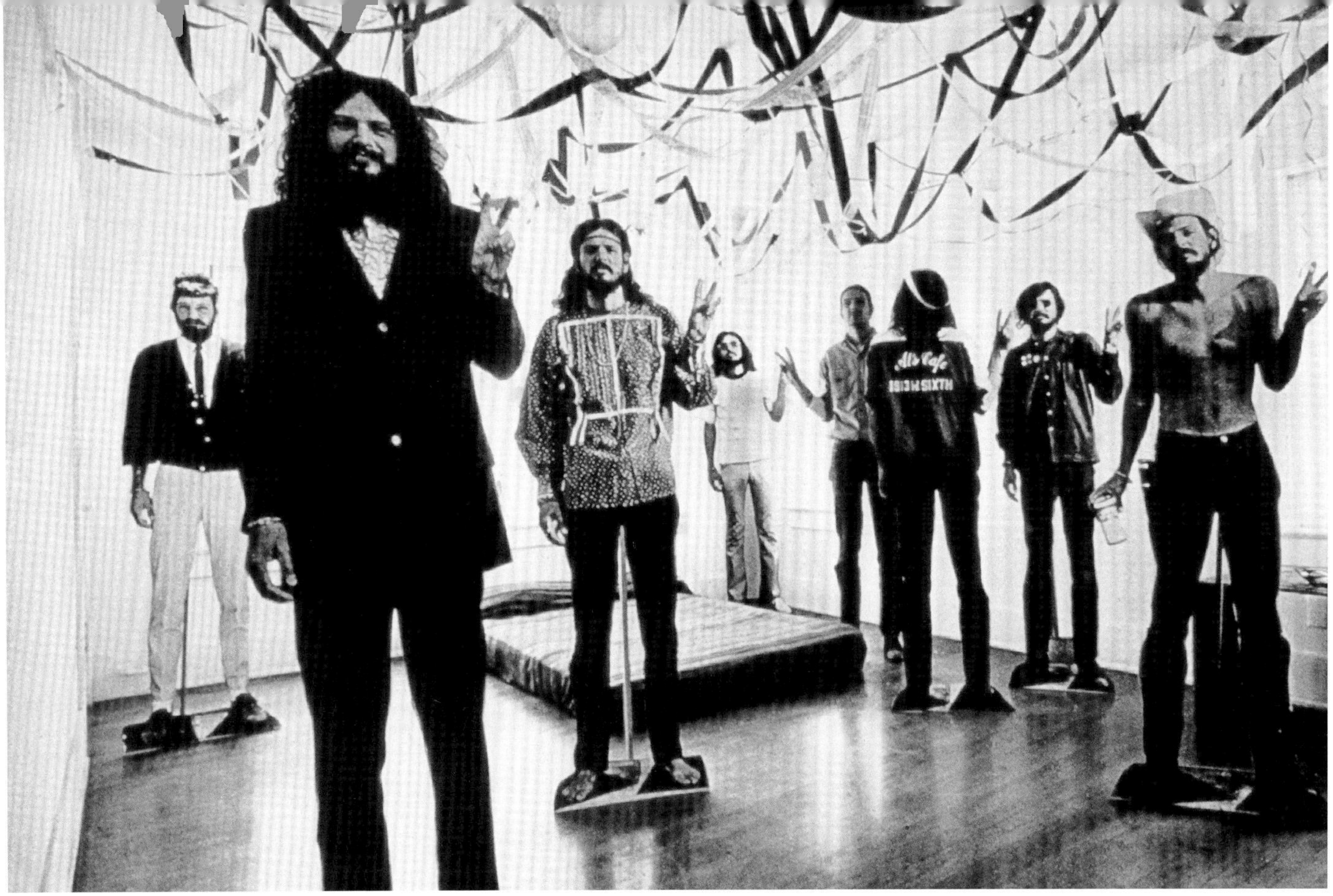

PRIVATE/PUBLIC SPACE

On weekends between May 7 and June 12, 1971, visitors could rent one of seven rooms in Allen Ruppersberg's *Al's Grand Hotel* (1971; see figs. 1.29–1.30, and 4.13–4.14, pp. 238–39). The hotel was located on Sunset Boulevard. Naming it after the 1932 MGM movie classic established its aura, and the artist designed each room—which cost the guest between fifteen and thirty dollars a night—around a theme. The Breakfast Room was outfitted with restaurant booths; the Ultra Violet Room was filled with framed notebook pages that bore the names of each of the films starring the eponymous Warhol superstar; an outsize, rough-hewn wooden cross diagonally spanned the Jesus Room; and the Al Room contained seven full-size, freestanding photographic cutouts ("standees") of the artist in various guises—the cowboy, the hippie—all of whom flashed the peace sign and bore some relationship to the artist's life. As fellow artist Allan McCollum, who experienced the hotel firsthand, wrote, "[Ruppersberg] invited his overnight guests to share a part of their own developing personal histories with the epic tale he was creating in reference to his own life. This epic was intended to include the imaginings of the other guests, the spectacle of the hotel itself, the drama of a famous, many-storied film, and the grand myth of Hollywood, all at once."[31]

A year after Ruppersberg's hotel, Lynn Hershman and Eleanor Coppola had the idea to transform two rooms in the Dante Hotel, a transient hotel in the North Beach neighborhood of San Francisco (see fig. 1.31 and the image on p.273). Their room installations opened to visitors on Halloween night, 1973. In Coppola's space, she tacked on the wall Polaroid snapshots of elements of the room. She hired a man to move in with his

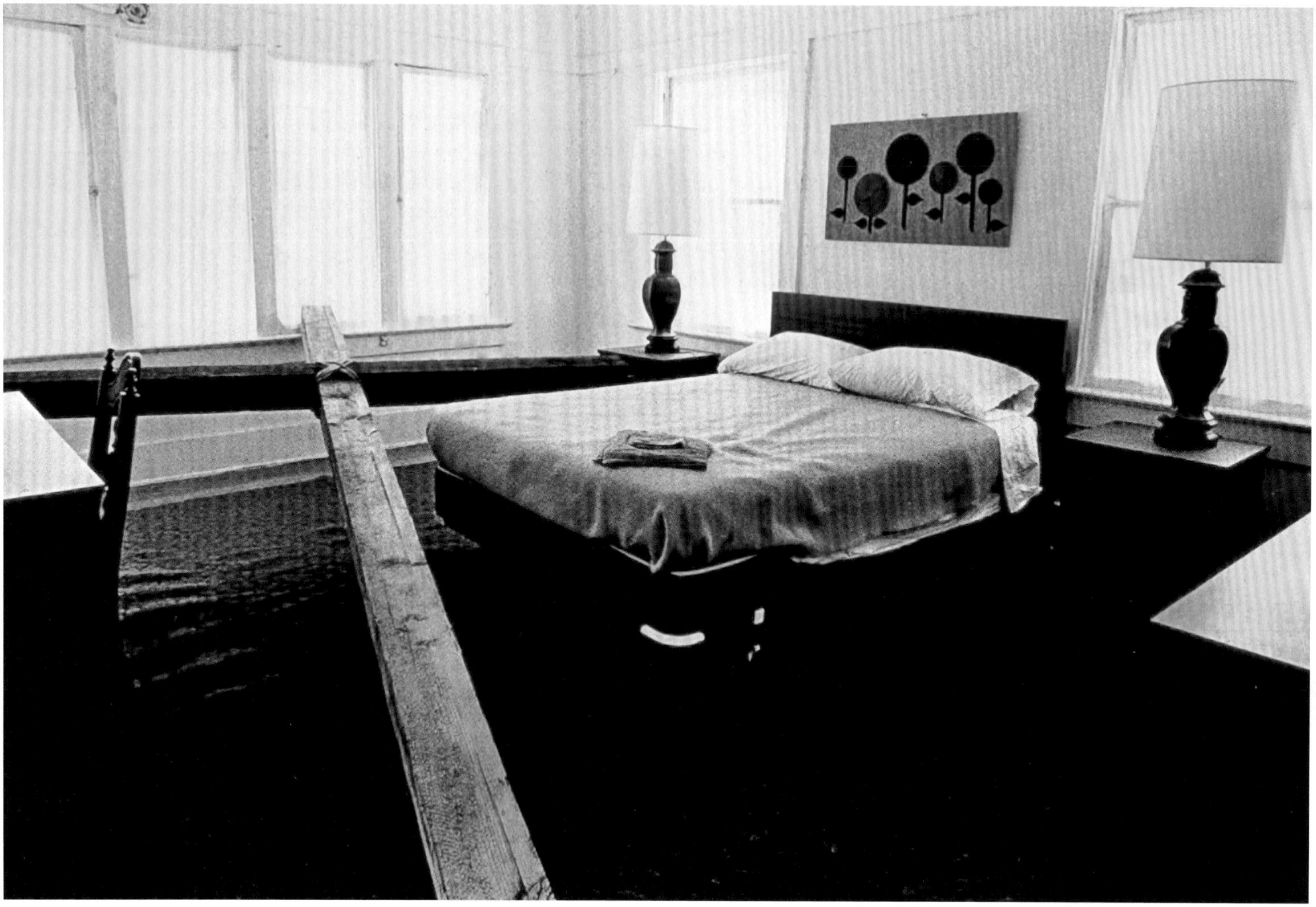

<<
Fig. 1.29 Allen Ruppersberg, The Al Room, from *Al's Grand Hotel,* 1971. Installation at 7175 Sunset Boulevard, Hollywood, California.

Fig. 1.30 Allen Ruppersberg, The Jesus Room, from *Al's Grand Hotel,* 1971. Installation at 7175 Sunset Boulevard, Hollywood, California.

Fig. 1.31 Lynn Hershman, *Dante Hotel Installation,* 1973–74. Black-and-white photograph mounted on foam core; 30 × 40 in.

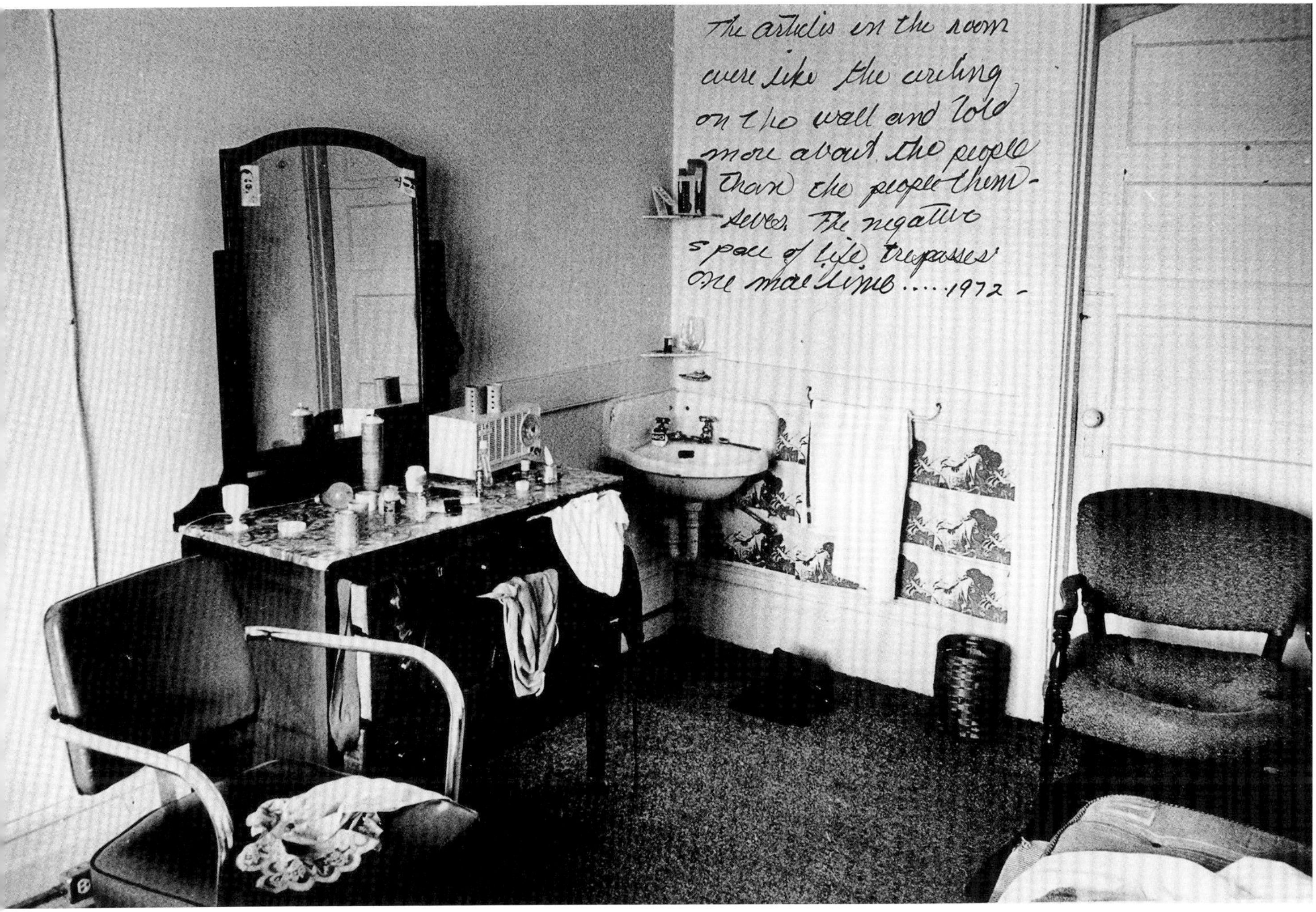
The articles in the room
were like the writing
on the wall and told
more about the people
than the people them-
selves. The negative
space of life trespasses
one more time.... 1972 -

possessions for a couple of weeks—his daily life became the stuff of the artwork.

In her room, Hershman placed two life-size wax cast figures (the heads were modeled from her own), one black and one white, under rumpled bed sheets. She surrounded them with their belongings: underwear spilling out of a bureau, cosmetics, hair rollers, cigarette butts, magazines and books, and a murky fish bowl. A radio played the local news, and lipstick-scrawled phrases covered the bureau mirror. Hershman's twenty-four-hour-a-day, nine-month-long installation ended when a visitor at 3 A.M. mistook the wax figures for corpses and called the police, who came and took all the room elements back to the station. Hershman intended for her installation to be open-ended, with no fixed last day, and was prepared to incorporate changes to the work that might occur over time.[32] The Expressionist tableaux of Edward Kienholz were an obvious influence, but, unlike him, Hershman (and Coppola) presented their environments not in a museum but in a public space. The *Dante Hotel* led directly to Hershman's extended performance *Roberta Breitmore,* in which she assumed a fictional identity over a period of several years.[33]

Despite the obvious similarities between *Al's Grand Hotel* and The *Dante Hotel,* they differed significantly. *Al's Grand Hotel* was an invention rather than intervention into an existing structure, and, more importantly, the mood and intention of each room was completely distinct. Hershman placed viewers in the role of voyeurs, whereas Ruppersberg offered them the opportunity to be part of the work; while Hershman's environment spoke of abjection, Ruppersberg's was an homage to a bygone era.

On the occasions when Conceptual artists like Tom Marioni were invited to exhibit in traditional spaces, they did so in unconventional ways. Marioni, more than any other artist, defined and encouraged the nascent Conceptual movement in the Bay Area. While still a curator at the Richmond Art Center in the East Bay, he had his own exhibition, titled *The Act of Drinking Beer with Friends Is the Highest Form of Art* (1970), at the Oakland Museum; he used the pseudonym "Allan Fish" to distinguish his work as an artist from that of a curator. The show displayed the debris (beer bottles, cigarette butts) that littered the gallery after a private party the preceding Monday, when the museum was closed. This work illustrates that for Marioni, as it was for Joseph Beuys, art is a social experience. Moreover, the act or process of art making *is* the art; what remains is the record. Marioni's program at MOCA was based on this conviction; it was primarily a site for performances, or actions, the relics of which might be displayed afterward. An even more explicit challenge by Marioni to traditional modes of exhibition occurred at the Reese Palley Gallery in San Francisco in 1972, when the artist built a room and lived in it for a week, making different kinds of action drawings each day. He named the performance *The Creation,* referring to the biblical seven-day origin of the world. Similarly, in Southern California, Chris Burden lived for periods of time in a gallery or museum. In *Bed Piece* (1972), he remained in bed in a nonprofit gallery in Venice, California, for twenty-two days. A few years later, in another endurance piece titled *White Light/White Heat,* he stayed on a platform, out of sight, for twenty-two days in the Ronald Feldman Gallery in New York. In these works, Marioni and Burden erased the distinction between the artist and the artwork; the artist—his presence and actions—was the art.[34]

Although Sam's Café (Marc and Terri Keyser and David Shire) did not live in a gallery, they made their own for a year (1969) in a former "greasy spoon" close to the UC Berkeley campus (where Terri Keyser and Shire were art students). The sign provided their collective's name; in the space, booths and fixtures were removed to create a place to launch such exhibitions as *Is America Disposable?* (fig. 1.32), a one-night display of vacuum-formed common hardware-store items. Visitors—and there were hundreds—were invited to take an artwork home. The artists took names for their mailing list, which formed the audience for future mail-art pieces. Other shows included *The Rotting Food Show* (fig. 1.33), with instruction kits for making your own rotten-food art, and *Tenney Packet* (fig. 1.35–1.36), an exhibition in an envelope—a suggestion that it was more convenient to have an art

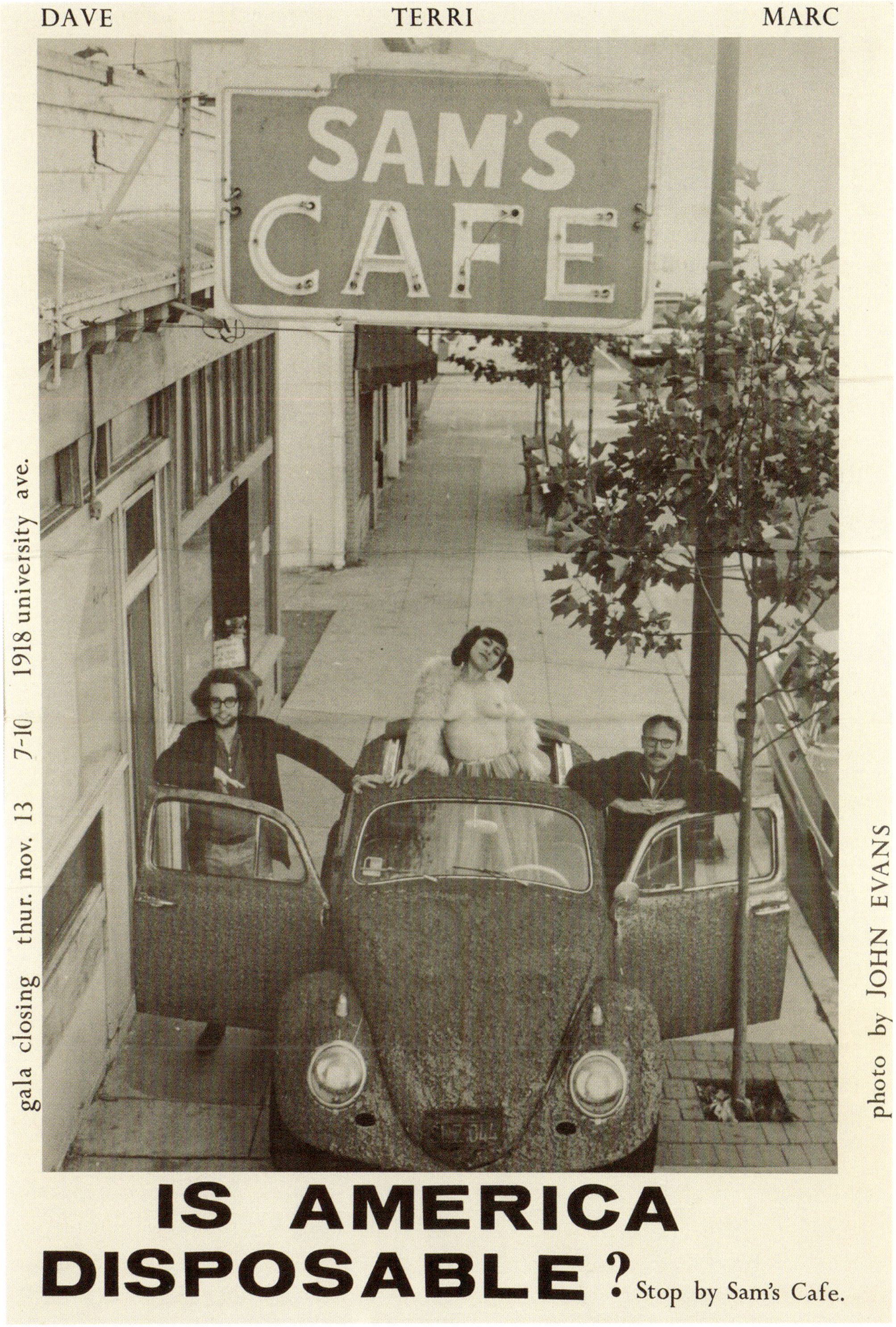

Fig. 1.32 Sam's Café (Terri Keyser, Marc Keyser, and David Shire), *Is America Disposable?,* 1970. Poster: offset lithography on paper; 30 × 20 in.

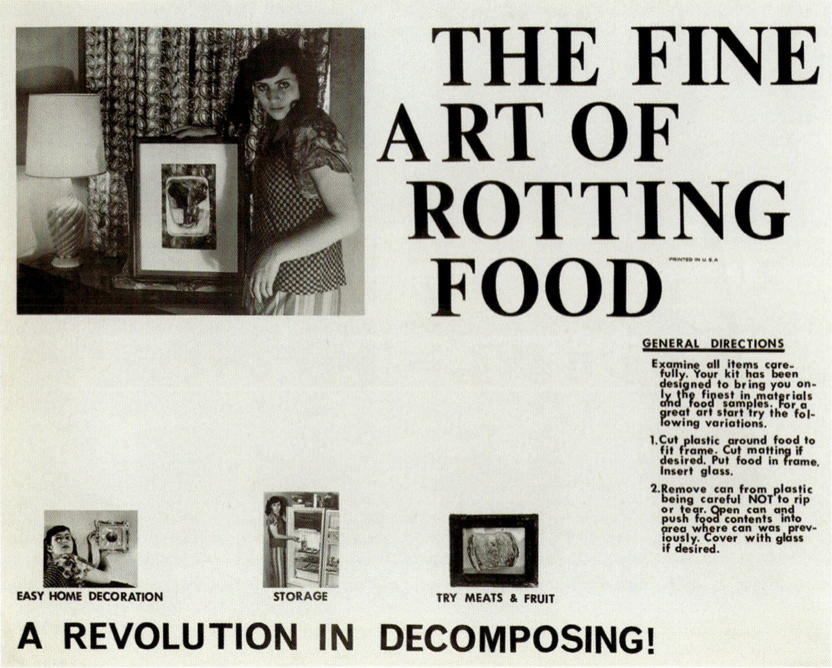

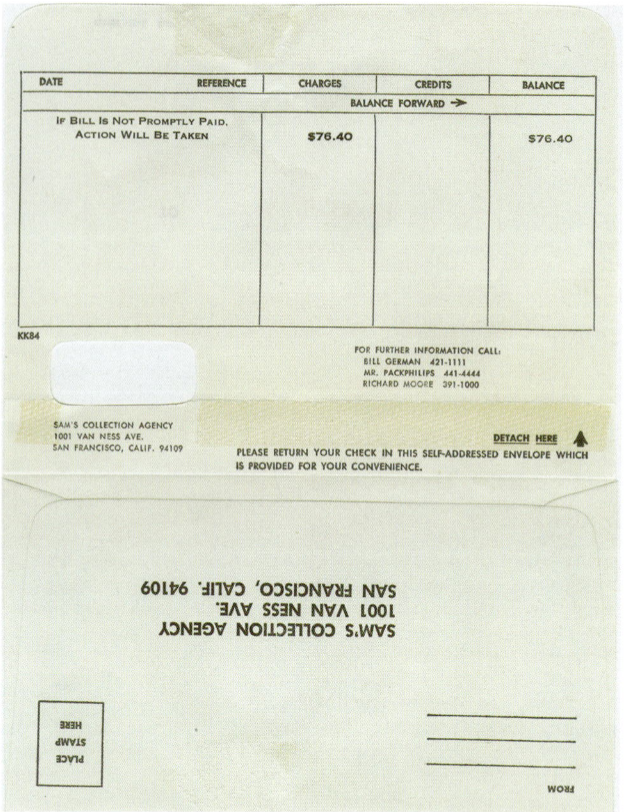

Fig. 1.33 Sam's Café (Terri Keyser, Marc Keyser, and David Shire), *The Fine Art of Rotting Food: A Revolution in Decomposing,* 1969. Poster: offset lithography on glossy paper; 17 ½ × 22 ½ in.

Fig. 1.34 Sam's Café (Terri Keyser, Marc Keyser, and David Shire), *Sam's Collection Agency Bill,* 1971. Offset lithography on paper; 8 ½ × 6 ¼ in.

>>

Figs. 1.35–1.36 Sam's Café (Terri Keyser, Marc Keyser, and David Shire), *Tenney Packet,* 1970. Offset lithography on seven cards, one sheet of paper, and envelope; cards: 5 × 7 in. each; paper: 3 ½ × 6 in.; envelope: 7 ½ × 5 ½ in.

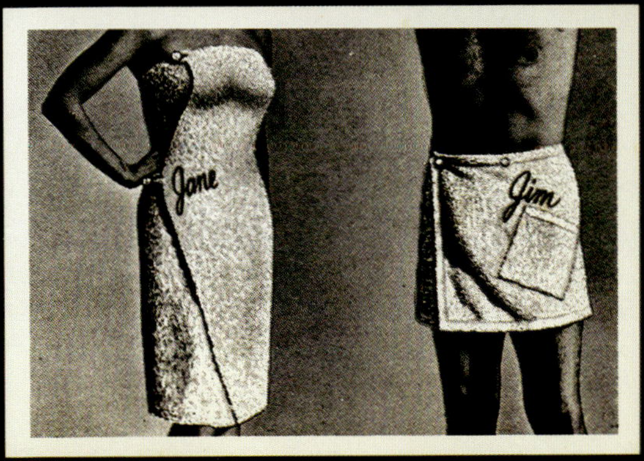
Jane
Jim

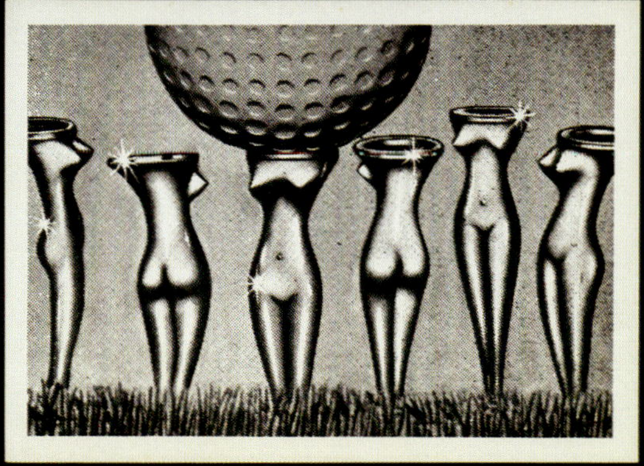

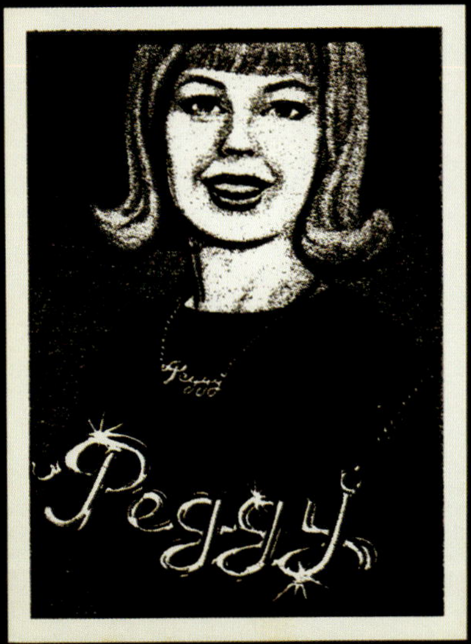
Peggy

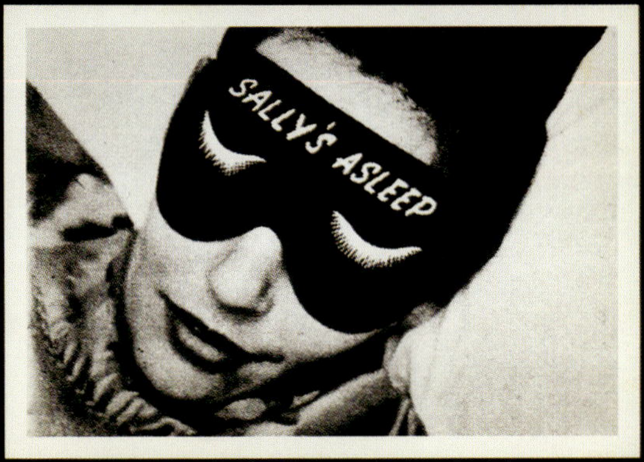
SALLY'S ASLEEP

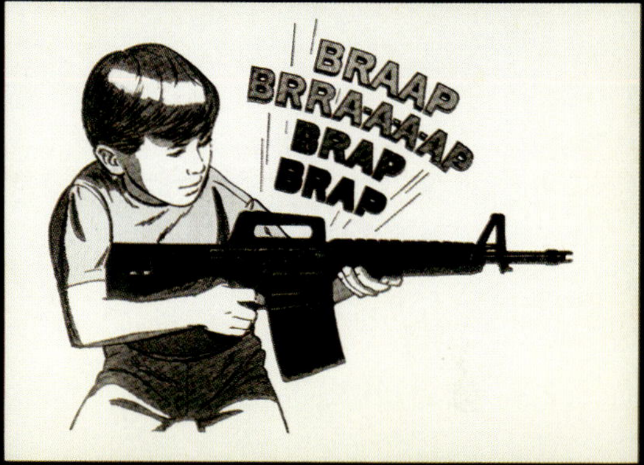
BRAAP
BRRA-A-A-AP
BRAP
BRAP

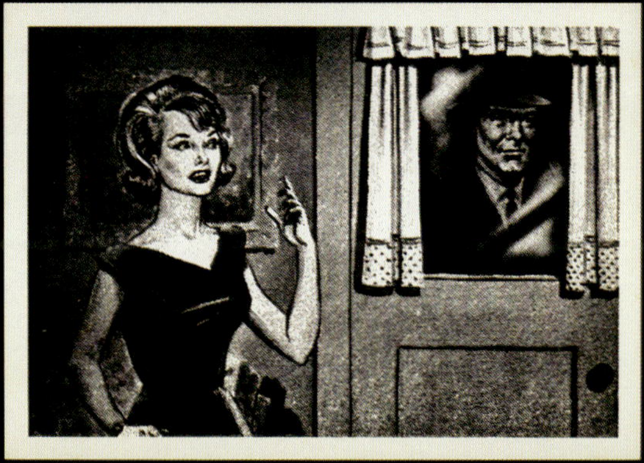

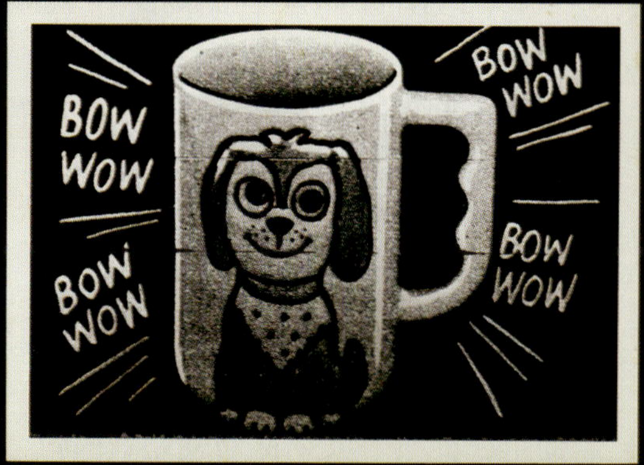
BOW WOW
BOW WOW
BOW WOW
BOW WOW

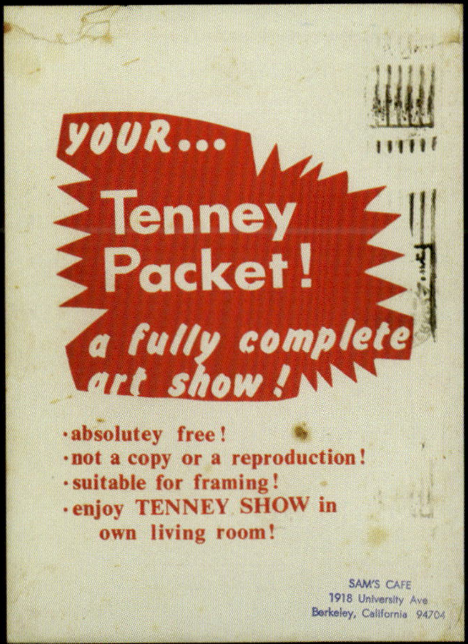
YOUR...
Tenney Packet!
a fully complete art show!
·absolutey free!
·not a copy or a reproduction!
·suitable for framing!
·enjoy TENNEY SHOW in own living room!
SAM'S CAFE
1918 University Ave
Berkeley, California 94704

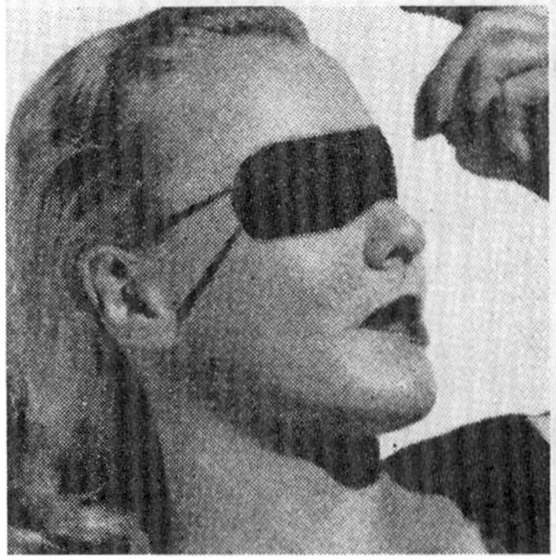

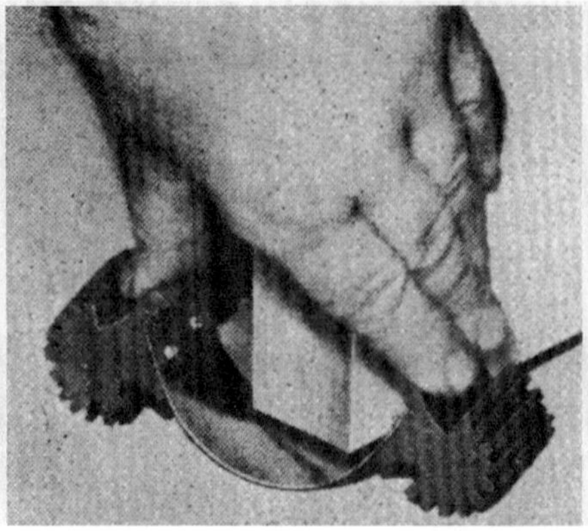

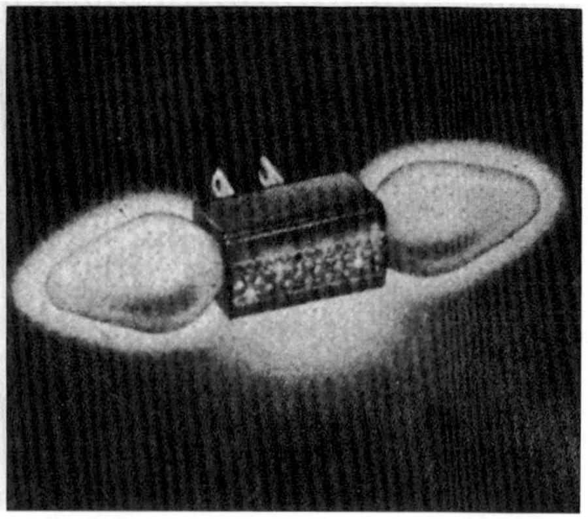

show delivered to your door. Along with advice on how to make your own photography exhibit, the packet held postcard-size advertising images taken from low-end publications that are reminiscent of the pictures in Mike Mandel and Larry Sultan's *How to Read Music in One Evening / A Clatworthy Catalog* (1974; fig. 1.37). Although Sam's Café's approach was variously humorous and repellent (they used fecal matter as well as rotten food), the group sought to bring attention to the environment and the commercialization of art.[35]

Northern California artist Stephen Kaltenbach also wanted to reach a wide audience, creating works to be experienced in unconventional sites. In 1968, he fabricated bronze *Sidewalk Plaques* (1968; figs. 1.38 and 2.45, pp. 186–187) bearing the words "art works," "earth," "air," "fire," "blood," "flesh," "skin," and "bone" in raised letters, which were intended to be embedded in pavement where they would be noticed but not necessarily perceived as art. He also inserted short texts in a year's worth of *Artforum* magazines from November 1968 through November 1969. The first simply said "Art Works"; other examples of these "micro manifestos," as the artist thought of them, included "Become a Legend," "Expose Yourself," "Tell a Lie," and "Teach Art," and one was a picture of an oddly shaped package wrapped in paper with the word "art" stamped on it several times. According to Kaltenbach, the wrapping symbolizes the art-world trappings that prevent direct communication between the artist and viewer. Like the plaques, Kaltenbach's *Artforum* "ads" were anonymous and only marginally identifiable as art. In addition, they wryly commented on the intersection of art and commerce epitomized by art magazines. Kaltenbach had already resolved to "become a legend quietly—in disguise, and through the back door." He followed through on this decision by leaving New York (where he had moved in 1967) and a promising career, spending the next three decades in relative obscurity as a professor at California State University, Sacramento. There he continued to make art, albeit at a far remove from the Conceptual works for which he was becoming known. But he carried on his Conceptual activities in private ways.[36]

The subgenre of mail art constitutes another type of alternative site, or conduit, employed by artists. For Eleanor Antin's

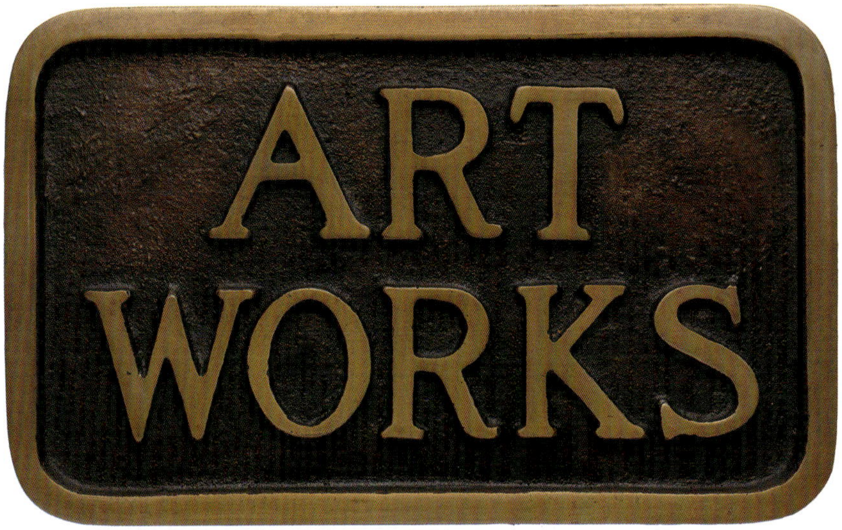

100 Boots (see fig. 2.44, p. 185), she arranged a group of one hundred black rubber boots in locations across the country, beginning on a beach in the San Diego suburb of Del Mar, where she lived, and ending in New York City. Antin documented the boots' adventures in fifty-one photographic postcards mailed at irregular intervals to one thousand people. Huebler's *Duration Piece #9, Berkeley, California—Hull, Massachusetts, January–October, 1969* (fig. 4.6, p. 228), which involved mailing a box back and forth throughout the United States, was actually realized through the U.S. Postal Service. Sam's Café subverted the postal service in the 1971 piece *Sam's Collection Agency* (fig. 1.34). The group mailed false collection notices to twenty thousand people, demanding that they each send $76.40 to the return address (which was the *San Francisco Chronicle*'s TV station). The notice listed the phone numbers of newspapers, TV stations, and the Bank of America, which were flooded with more than ten thousand angry calls. The artists made front-page news in both local newspapers. Two days later, when Sam's Café revealed themselves at a press conference—at which they handed out press kits that included vials of human excrement—they were arrested and indicted. *San Francisco Chronicle* critic Thomas Albright testified on their behalf. The case was dropped after a two-day trial. In the end, the judge shook his head and proclaimed, "Well, if the expert says it's art, it's art, but don't do it again." Sam's Café believed that by using print media, the postal service, and other ordinary means of communication, artists outside the system could reach a broad public audience. At the same time, they showed how easy it is to sabotage the U.S. Postal Service, a fact that seems particularly significant today in light of our highly sophisticated, but equally vulnerable, communication systems. Indeed, the contemporary activist artists known as Yes Men use similar tactics via the Internet to expose what they believe to be hypocrisies and false claims by the government and corporations.

Fig. 1.37 Mike Mandel and Larry Sultan, page from *How to Read Music in One Evening/ A Clatworthy Catalog*, 1974. Artists' book; 8 ⅛ × 10 ¾ in.

Fig. 1.38 Stephen Kaltenbach, *ART WORKS*, 1968/2005. Bronze; 4 ⅞ × 7 ⅞ × ⅝ in.

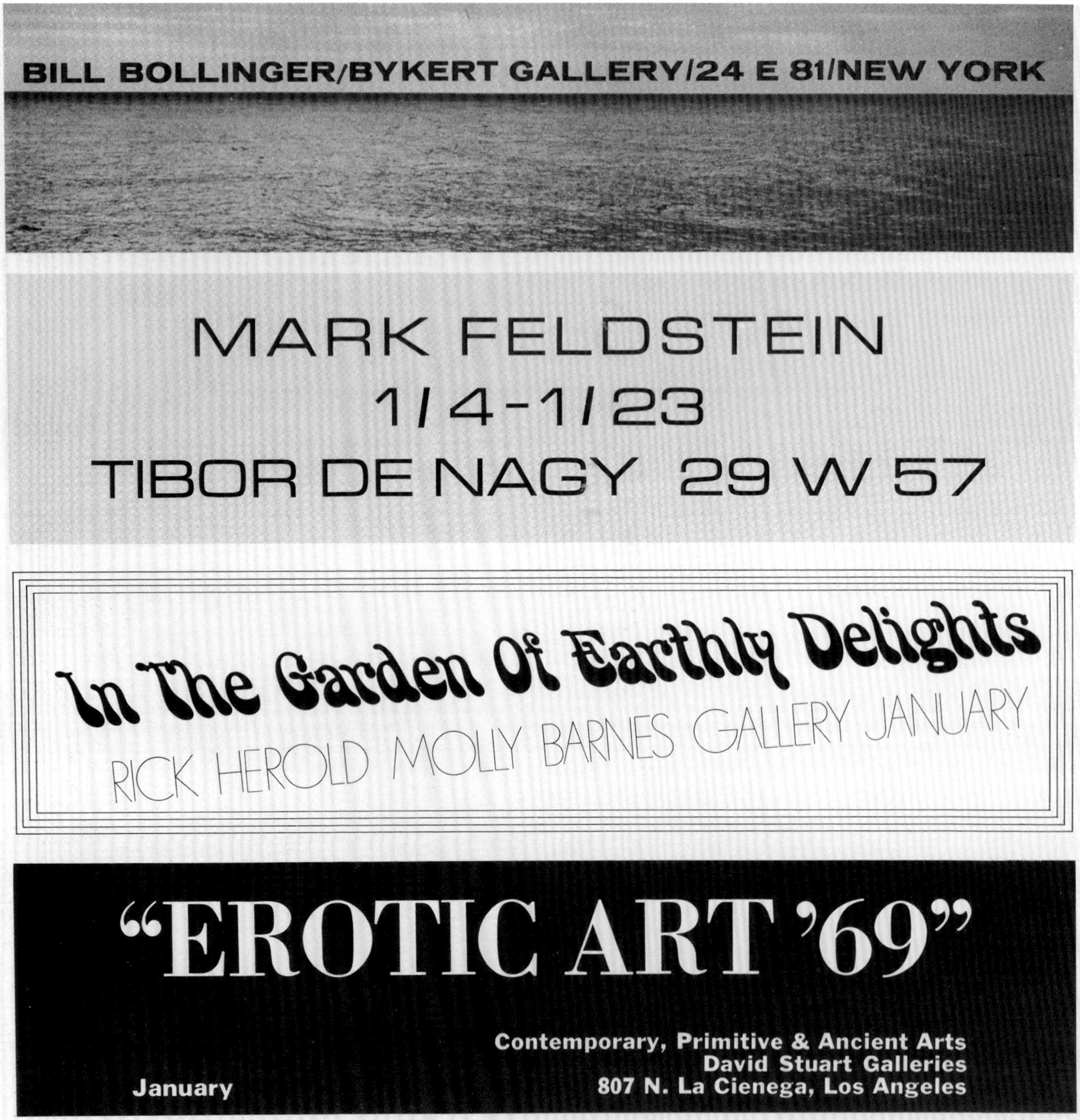

Fig. 1.39 Stephen Kaltenbach, *Artforum Ads* (detail: *Artforum,* January 1969 issue).
Photo: Benjamin Blackwell, courtesy University of California, Berkeley Art Museum and Pacific Film Archive.

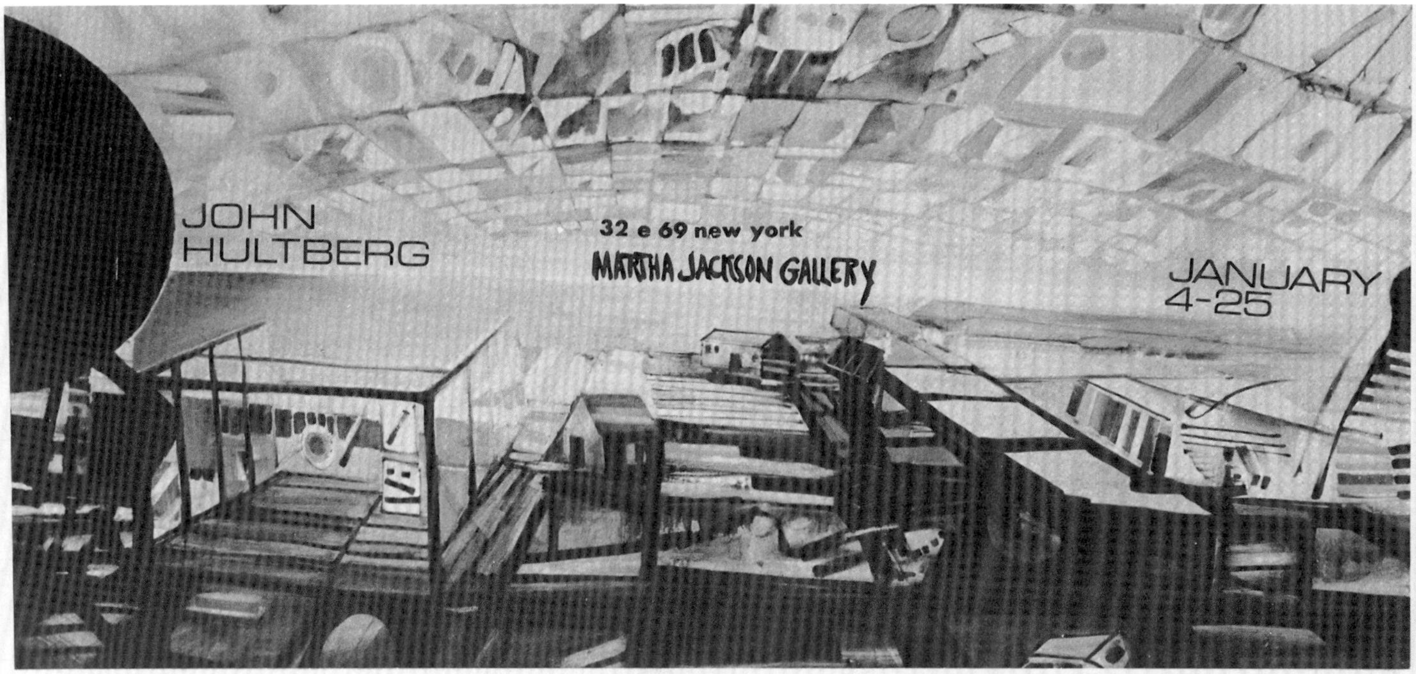
JOHN
HULTBERG
32 e 69 new york
MARTHA JACKSON GALLERY
JANUARY
4-25

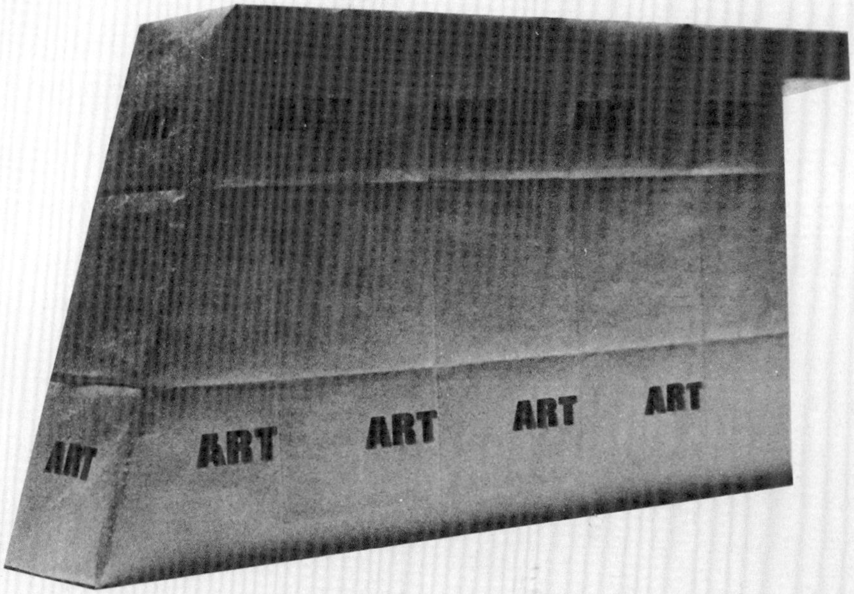
ART
ART
ART
ART
ART

Here is a delicious and very impressive dish, very French. Be sure you have an appreciative audience! I have adapted the recipe from The Art of French Cooking and Gourmet's Basic French Cookbook.

RIS DE VEAU DES GOURMETS (GOURMETS' SWEETBREADS)

Get absolutely fresh sweetbreads. Immediately soak them at least 5 hrs. in plenty of cold water, frequently changed. Drain and blanch; put in cold water, bring to boil, boil 2 mins. Plunge in cold water. Remove fat and cartilage. Spread on plate, weight heavily, and store in refrigerator a few hrs. Cook in butter 1 med. onion, sliced, and 1 large carrot, bay leaf, ½ tsp. thyme, 3 sprigs parsley (or bouquet garni) until vegetables are golden. Sprinkle with 1 tsp. flour. Add 1 cup veal or chicken stock, ½ cup dry white wine. Braise sweetbreads seasoned with salt and pepper in this stock. Reserve liquid. Place the meat in shallow casserole just large enough to fit. Cover with raw truffles sliced thick. Add reserved liquid. Cover; seal edge with flour-water paste. Bake 10 mins. in very hot oven. Serve in the dish--uncover at table.

The recipe was created by Escoffier. Enjoy it!

10

Fig. 1.40 Martha Rosler, *A Budding Gourmet* (detail), 1974. Serial postcard novel in twelve parts; first mailed January–April 1974; 3 × 5 in. each.

Fig. 1.41 Eleanor Antin, *Representational Painting*, 1971. Video: black and white; silent; 38 min.

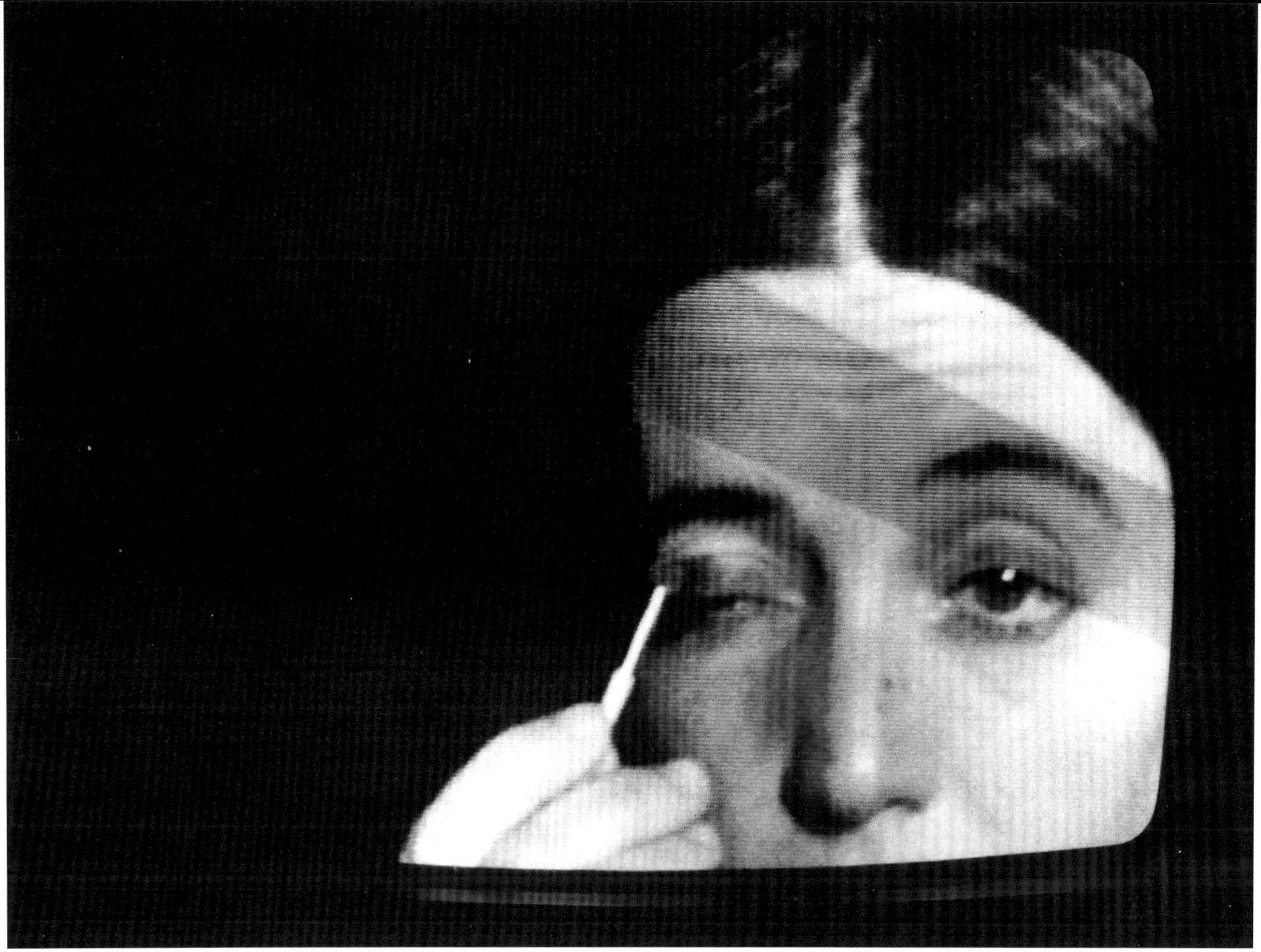

DOMESTIC SPACE

Many women who came into the art world in the early 1970s rode in on the wave of the feminist movement. Whether or not they were students in a feminist program, as were Suzanne Lacy and Susan Mogul, all were acutely aware of the need to forge an identity in an overwhelmingly male-dominated field. As Connie Butler points out in the introduction to her catalogue of the 2007 exhibition *WACK!: Art and the Feminist Revolution,* which traced the influence of feminism on art of the 1970s, feminist pioneers saw no conflict in merging their gender politics with their Conceptual practice.[37] Most embraced the new genres of performance and video not yet defined according to norms or codes. They frequently sited their performative works, which often involved role-playing, in domestic settings to call attention to the stereotyped roles assigned to women in a patriarchal culture. Martha Rosler cast herself as an aspiring gourmet cook in her serial postcard novel *A Budding Gourmet* (1974; fig. 1.40), which formed the basis of and lent its title to her first video. Here, she addresses the issues of class and private versus public space, "reflecting on the irony that whereas in the private sphere of the home the preparation of food is the duty and drudgery of the housewife, in the public realm it is a highly celebrated male domain—indicated in the videotape by a series of magisterial male chefs in their deluxe restaurants."[38]

Female chefs, on the other hand, usually found employment at the lower end of the culinary ladder, as did Bonnie Sherk, who worked, during 1973 and 1974, first as a short-order cook and then as a waitress at Andy's Donuts in San Francisco (see fig. 3.5, p. 202). She regarded her job as a performance and her work uniforms as "cultural costumes." She served on a jury for two weeks in her waitress outfit and realized that everyone else was also wearing their own cultural costumes. From that point forward, she regarded her life and her art as inseparable.[39]

As Ann-Sargent Wooster wrote, "Analysis of the representation of women remains at the heart of much video produced by women," in response to the historical representation of women as "the object of men's desire."[40] In *Representational Painting* (1971; fig. 1.41), Eleanor Antin treats the camera like a dressing-table mirror before which she transforms herself, through the careful application of makeup, from plain to, in her words, "a kind of *Vogue* hippie." The title derived from her desire to comment on traditional painting and also to address how women choose to represent themselves to the world. Antin explained, "*Representational Painting* was a feminist piece that ironically played with the idea of traditional art forms and it just started when the painting began and it ended with the final brushstroke."[41] Antin made a companion piece the next year—*Carving: A Traditional Sculpture* (fig. 1.42)—in which she documents her weight loss with 148 black-and-white photographs.

The bedroom is also the setting for Susan Mogul's humorous *Dressing Up* (1973; fig. 3.6, p. 203). In "a reverse striptease" enacted before a stationary video camera, the artist describes her shopping experiences while eating CornNuts. In her deliberately nonerotic performance, Mogul refers not only to the exploitation of the female body but also to personal history, which is similarly at the core of Ilene Segalove's *The Mom Tapes* (1974; fig. 1.43).[42] In one, "Advice

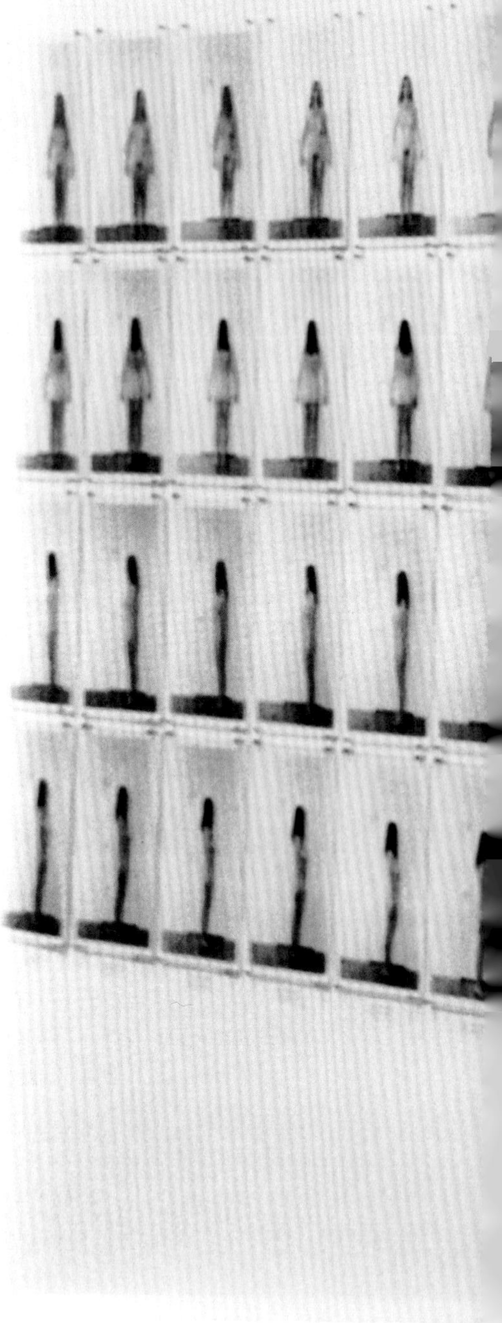

Fig. 1.42 Eleanor Antin, *Carving: A Traditional Sculpture*, 1972. 144 black-and-white photographs and text panel; photographs: 7 × 5 in. each.

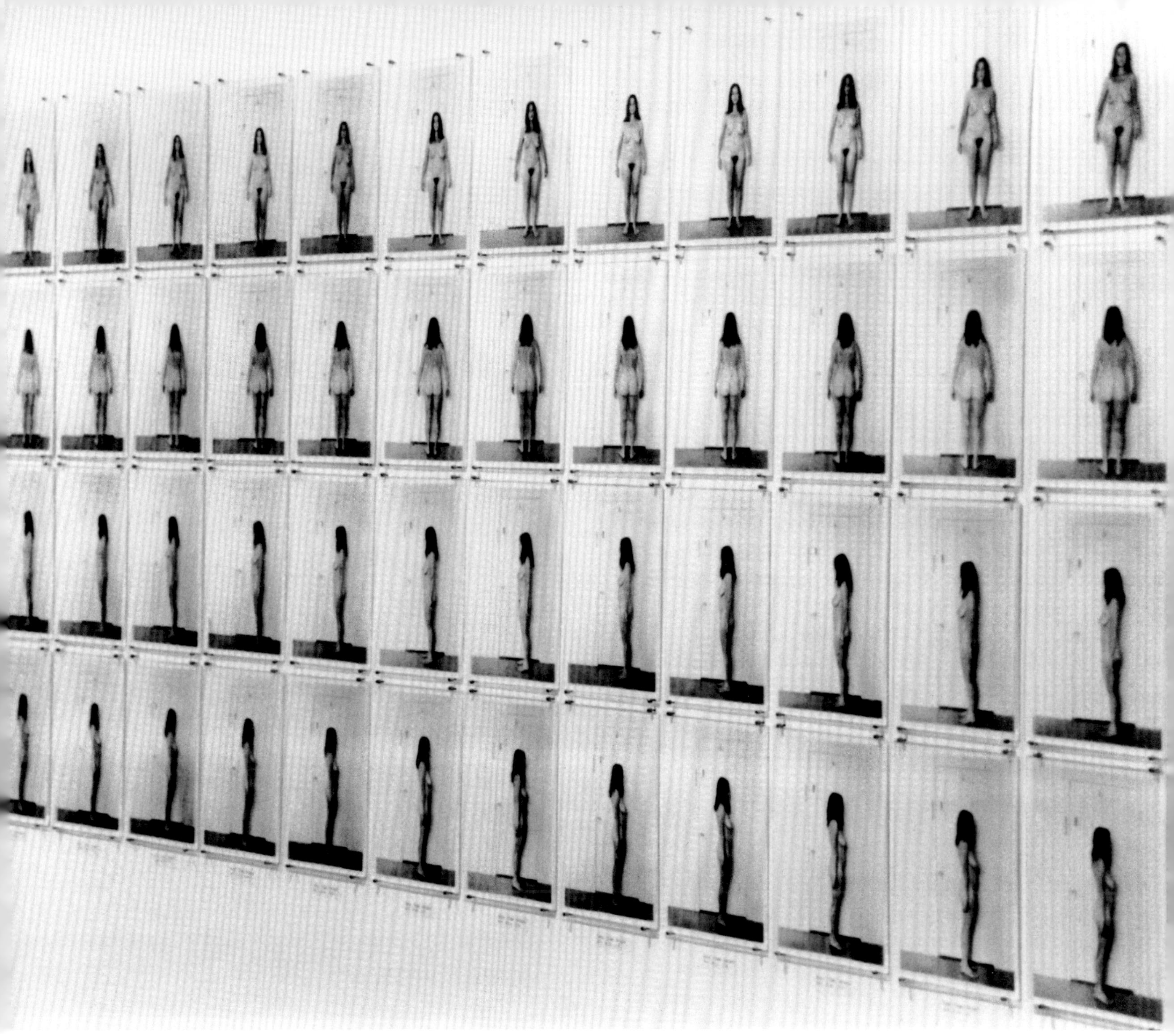

from Mom," the artist's mother offers shopping tips. Satiric but ultimately affectionate, Segalove's vignettes explore female roles in middle-class suburbia.

Perhaps no other female artist, with the possible exception of Yoko Ono in her 1965 performance *Cut Piece,* put herself more on the line to challenge received notions of female passivity and to test the limits of the artist–viewer relationship than Los Angeles–based artist Barbara T. Smith in *Feed Me,* a performance included in *All Night Sculptures* at MOCA in San Francisco.[43] On April 20–21, 1973, in a simulated boudoir, Smith allowed visitors, one by one, to enter a small space—in which she lay fully exposed— and to interact with her as they chose (fig. 1.44). On an audiocassette her voice repeated, "Feed me, feed me." By intentionally leaving herself vulnerable to any interaction, including sexual intercourse, she shifted the responsibility for behavior onto the mostly male participants. Although at the time some saw this as counter to feminist principles, for Smith it was both a method of self-transformation and "a negation of male conquest."[44] *Feed Me* anticipated Marina Abramović's *Rhythm 0* (1974), in which Abramović also assumed a passive role vis-à-vis the public, who were free to use on her any of seventy-two objects—some pleasure giving, others that would inflict pain.

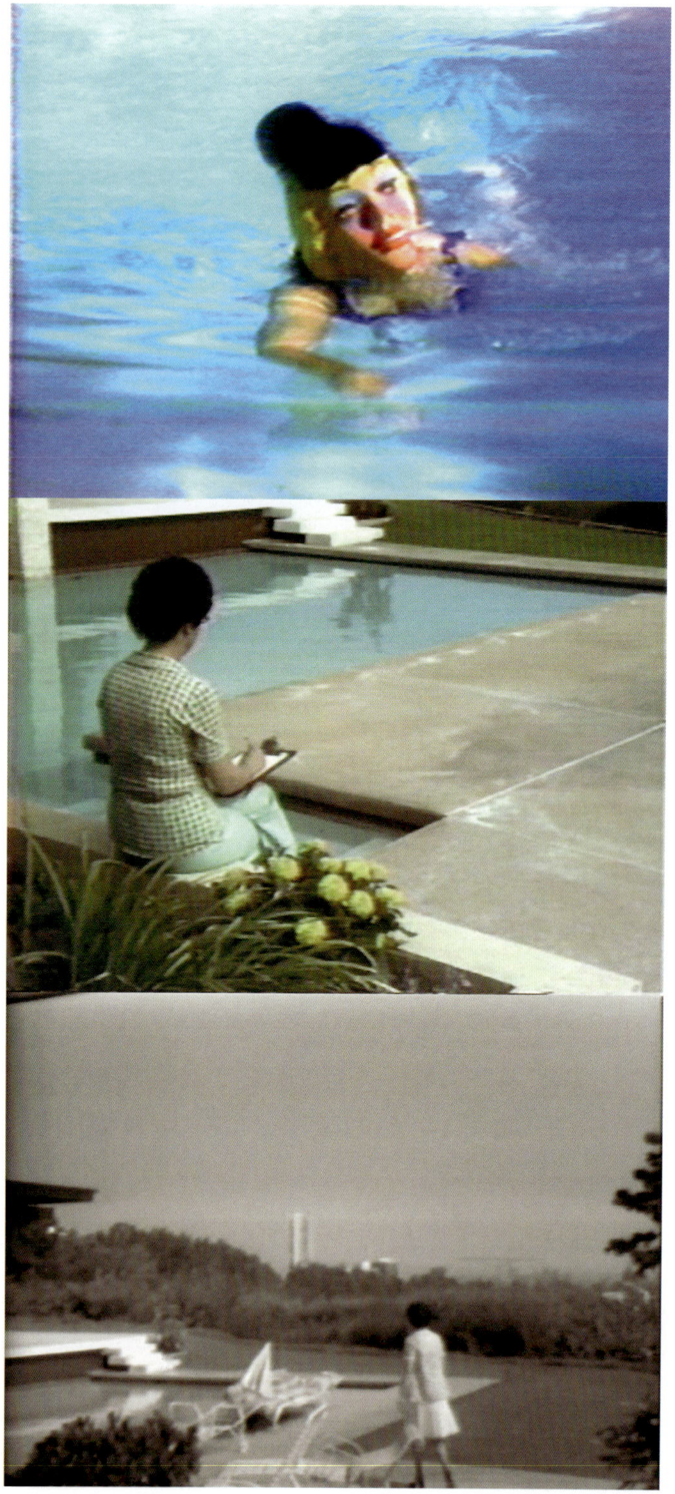

Fig. 1.43 Ilene Segalove, *The Mom Tapes,* 1974. Video: black and white and color; sound; 26:52 min.

Fig. 1.44 Barbara T. Smith, *Feed Me* (detail), 1973. Performance documentation.

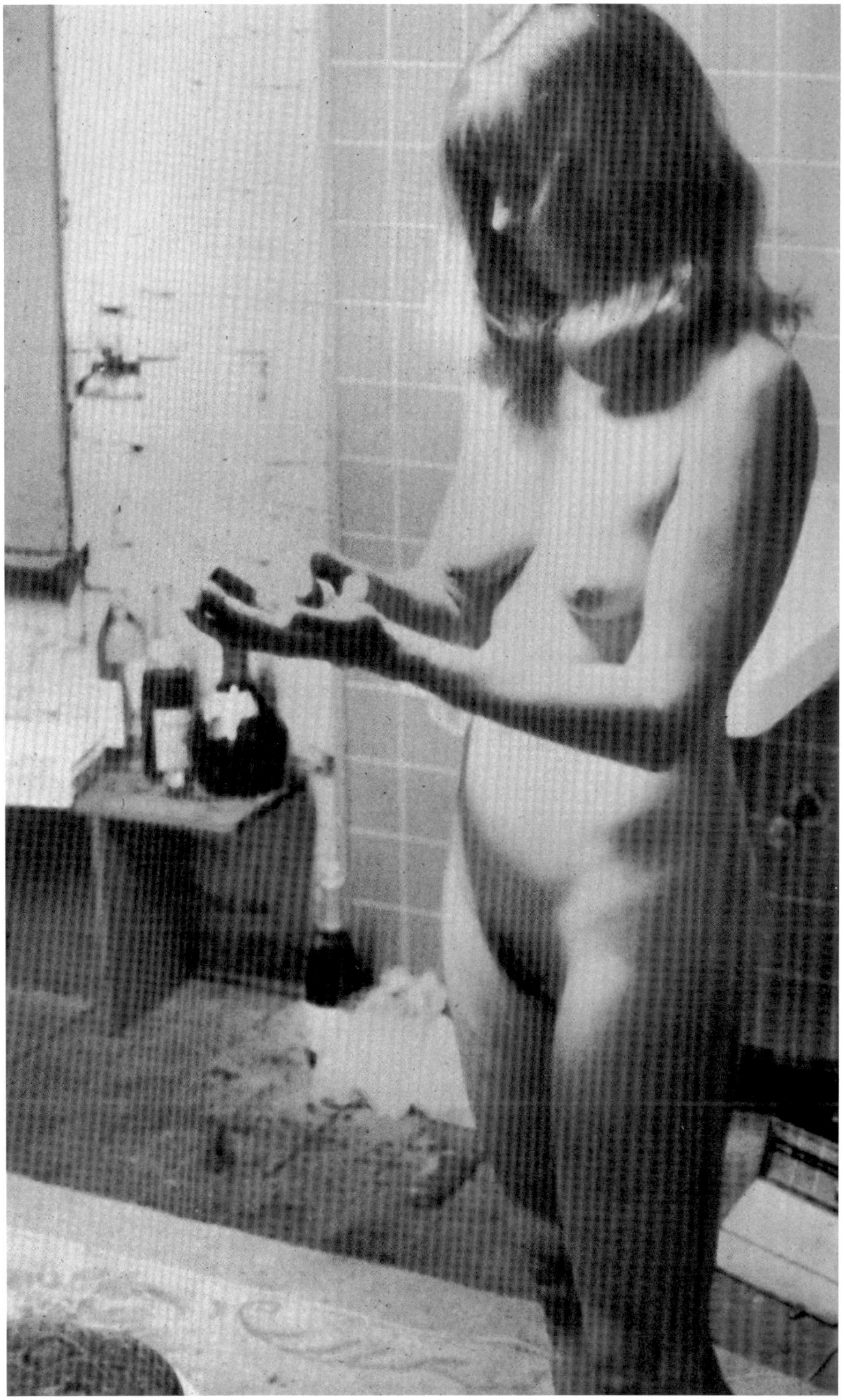

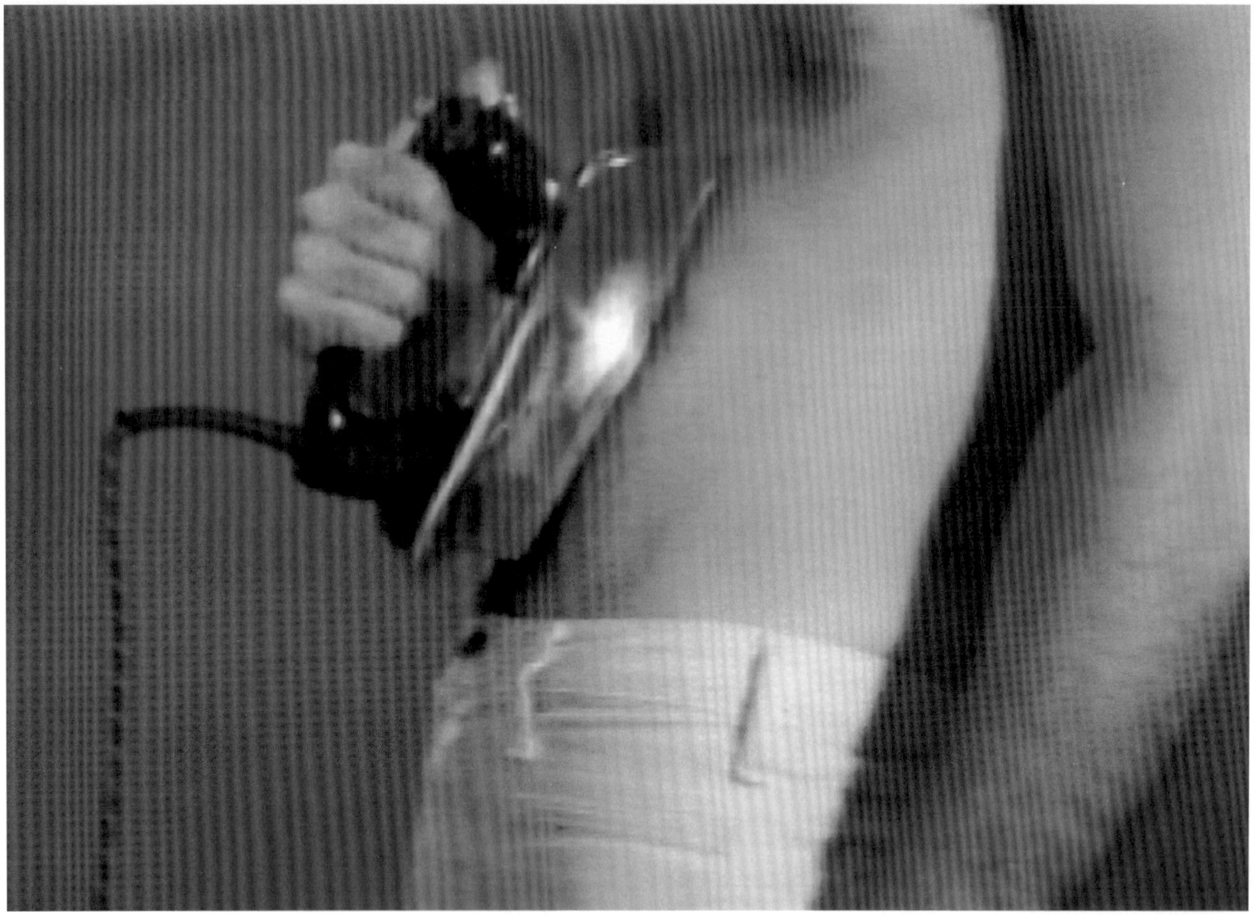

ART/LIFE

The conflation of art and daily life is associated with such Northern California artists as Kos, Fox, and Sherk, as well as Montano, who created several "living art" works in which she set aside time periods in which everything she did she considered art. Decades before Ben Kinmont, an artist associated with "relational aesthetics," offered to clean strangers' homes, Montano volunteered such services.[45] This tendency for artists to "live" their art grew out of the lack of commercial or institutional support, which had the effect of turning artists toward more personal approaches to art making. The legacy of the Beats, who focused their work on the everyday and on personal experience and who were early adherents to Zen Buddhism, was another factor. The tendency to merge art and life, which went hand in hand with role-playing, was particularly evident in the work of women both in the north and south—Segalove's *The Mom Tapes,* Mogul's *Dressing Up,* and Smith's *Feed Me* are all examples, as are Montano's many "living art" performances, such as *Lying: Dead Chicken, Live Angel (Chicken Bed)* (1972), in which for three hours a day for three days she laid on a "chicken bed" at the University Art Museum, Berkeley (see fig. 2.8, p. 133). Of this piece, she said, "I was curious about female imagery and tried making art that looked as if it were made by a woman but felt that feather-covered female, donut-shaped sculptures didn't satisfy me. Wings did. I provided some sound this time and yet was still talked to/with and even kissed on the lips by a self-designated prince."[46]

Male artists, too, assumed alter egos: Ruppersberg played the role of chef in *Al's Café* (1969) and hotel clerk in *Al's Grand Hotel;* Fried occupied the dual personae of Long John Servil and Long John Silver; and Stephen Laub merged his identity with those of others in his slide-projection performances (fig. 1.74). Paul Cotton, as noted previously, also devised a series of alter egos in his works. As the Astral-Naught Rabb-Eye, he performed spontaneously for three hours at the opening of the University Art Museum, Berkeley's new building on November 8, 1970, and again at *Documenta 5* in 1972 (fig. 1.27).

William Wegman, too, adopted multiple roles. He kept a video camera at the ready in his Los Angeles studio so that he could spontaneously enact short comedic scenes using his own body, simple props, and/or his dog. In these deceptively casual skits, Wegman switches genders or assumes various personae, often a hapless salesman peddling a useless gadget. Puns, objects found around the studio, and, of course, his dog, Man Ray, comprise his repertory. Wegman's approach to video has been compared to that of Bruce Nauman, whom Wegman knew and admired. Both artists had gone to the University of Wisconsin in Madison and arrived in Los Angeles around 1970. Joan Simon noted that they "shared a love of music, a philosophical bent, an affinity for word games, and a sense of moral intensity of the work done by artists and teachers at Madison."[47] However, Wegman's humorous and absurd vignettes, which have become classics of early video performance, owe as much to the radio comics Bob and Ray and "dumb TV" as to Nauman or other artists.[48] At the same time that he made his first videos, Wegman also made black-and-white photographs presented as single images, diptychs, or triptychs that function as mininarratives. In the diptych *Light Off/Light On* (1970; fig. 1.46), the only difference between the two photographs is the position of the light switch. This subtle alteration contrasts with the more obvious, but equally engaging, *A Basic Guide to Lettering* (1972; figs. 147–148), in which the world is literally upended from the first to the second image.

Fig. 1.45 William Wegman, *Selection of Unreleased Videos,* 1971–72. Video: black and white; sound; 17:47 min.

>>

Fig. 1.46 William Wegman, *Light Off / Light On,* 1970. Two black-and-white photographs; 11 × 11 in. each; 13 × 22¼ in. framed together.

>>

Figs. 1.47–1.48 William Wegman, *A Basic Guide to Lettering,* 1972. Two black-and-white photographs; 11 × 14 in. each.

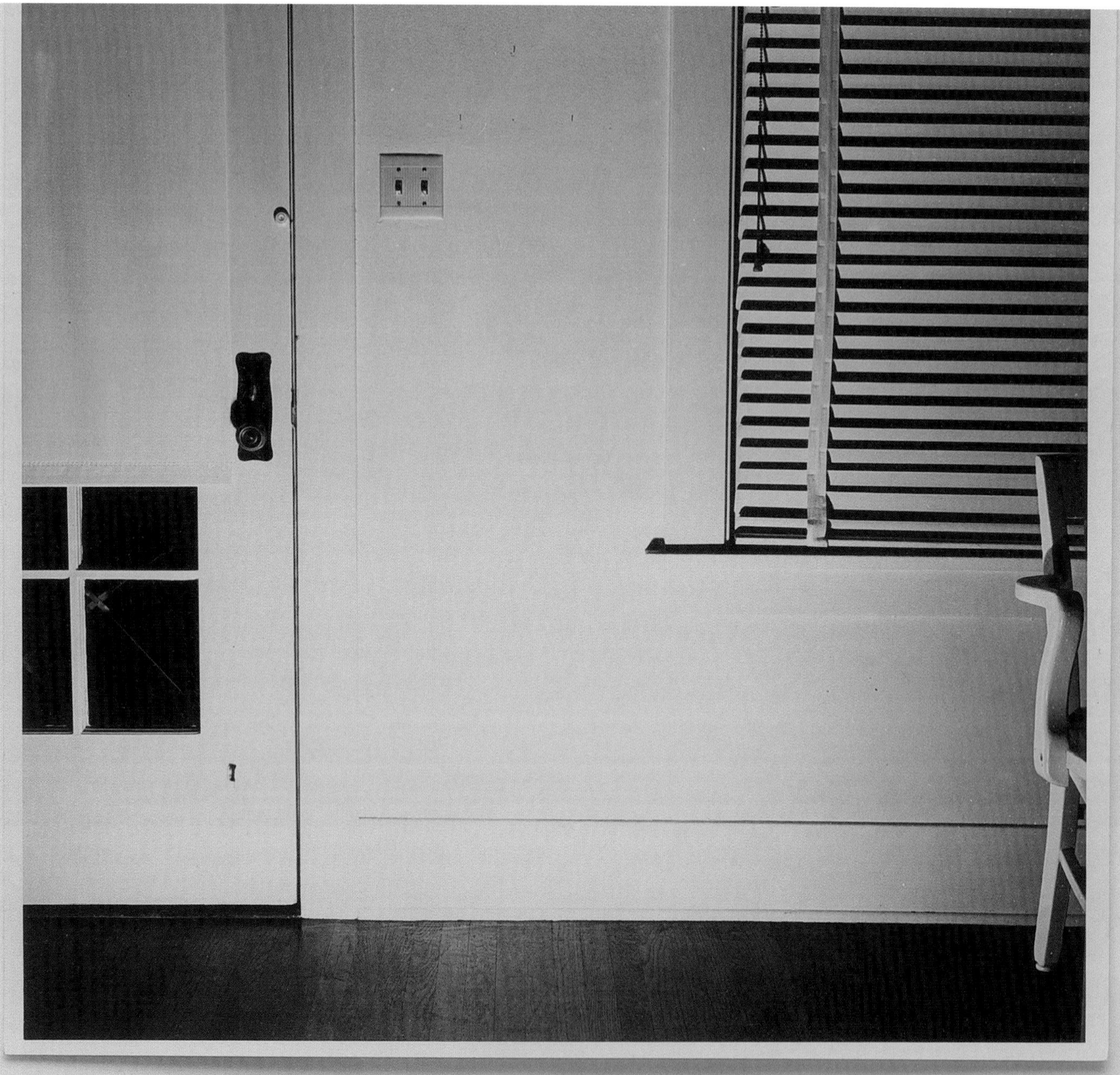

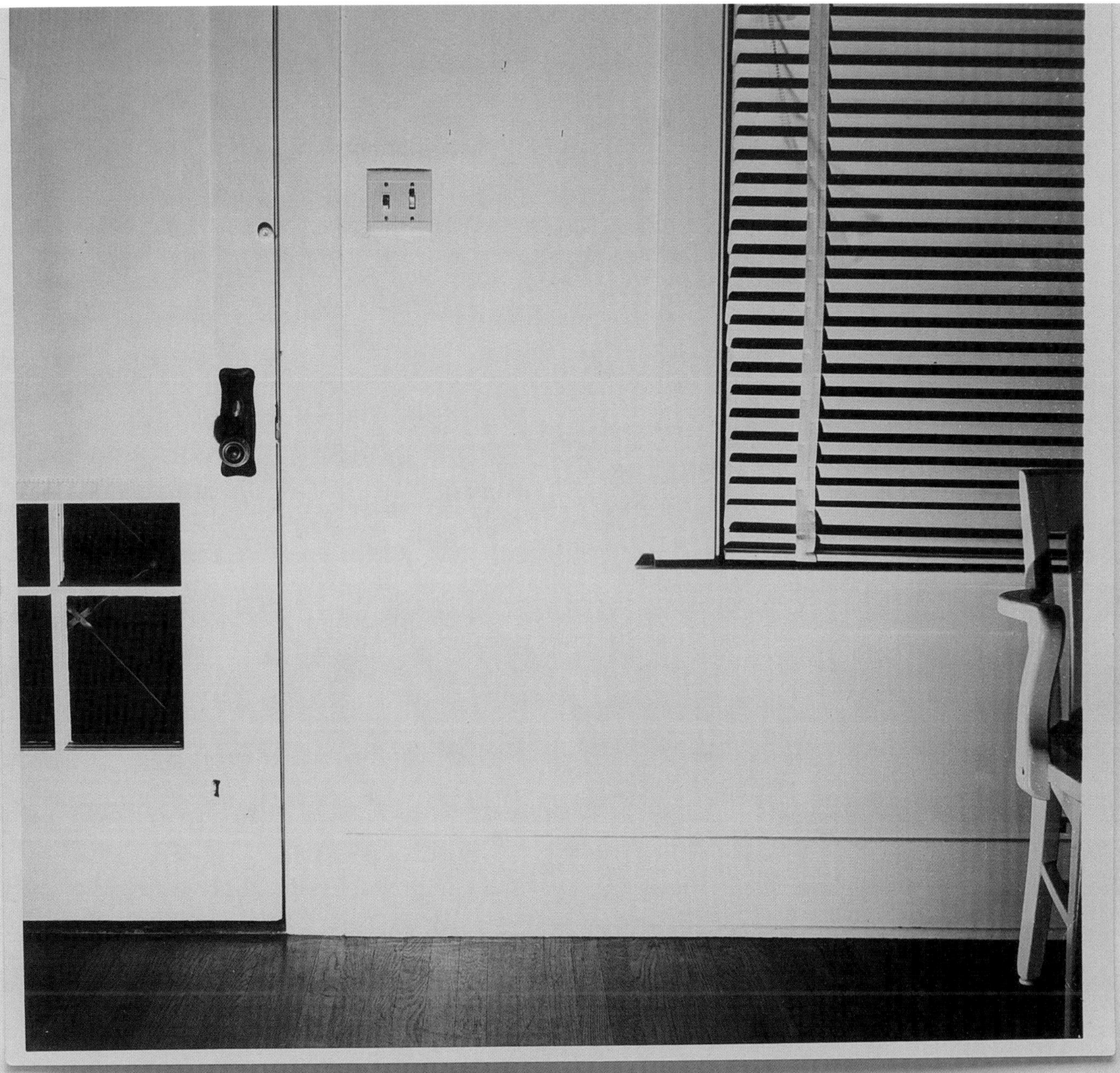

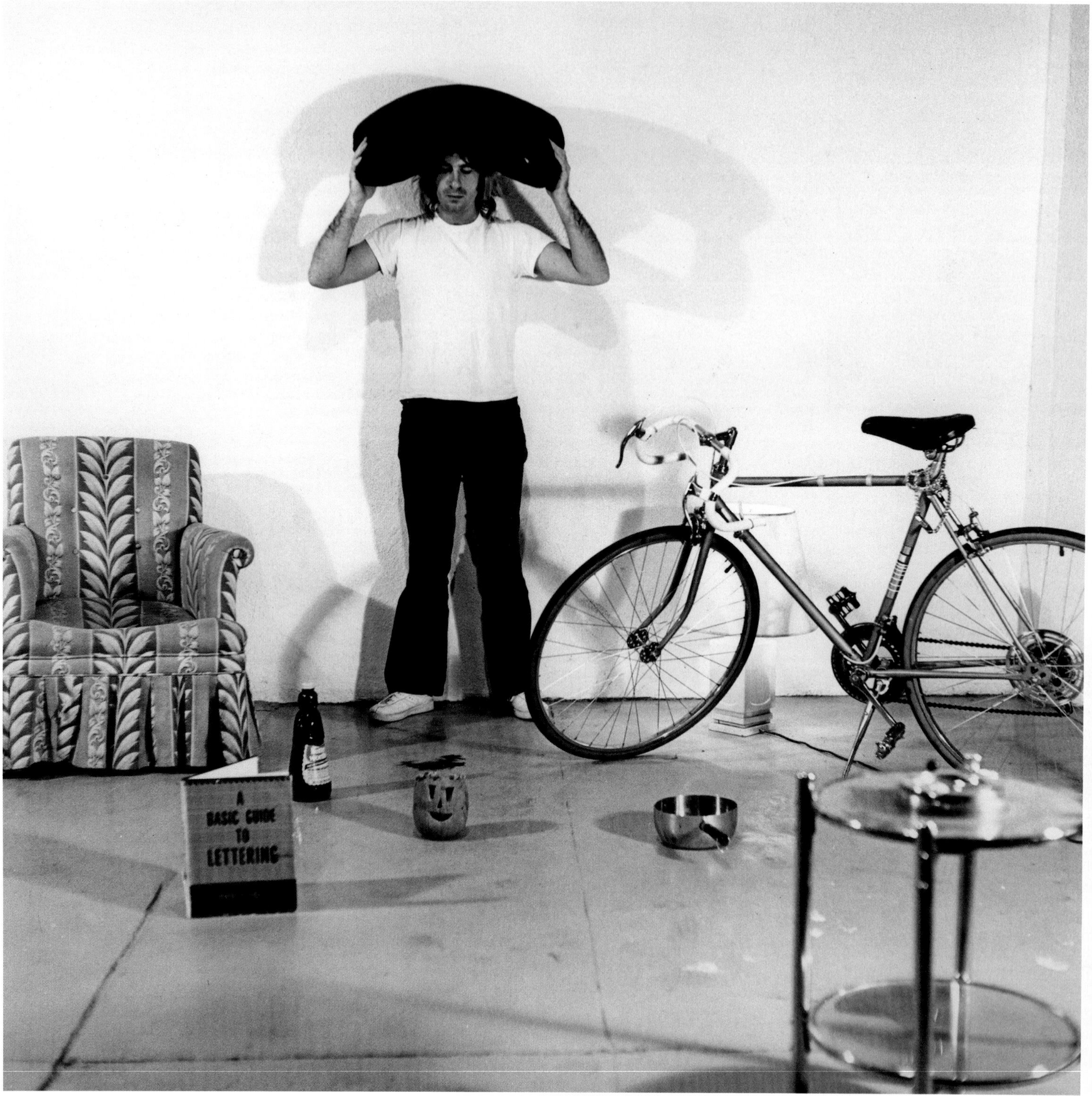
A
BASIC GUIDE
TO
LETTERING

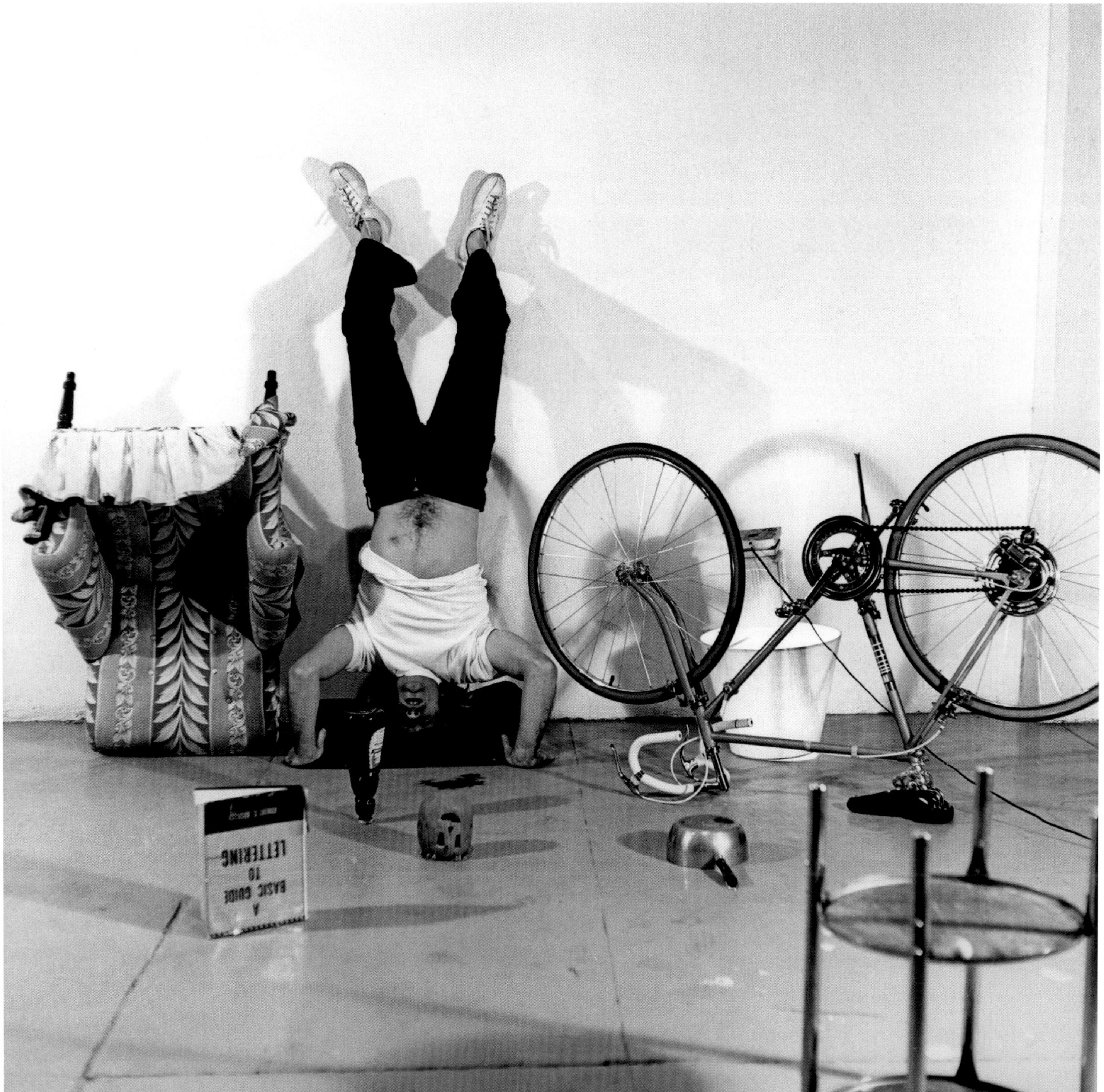
A BASIC GUIDE TO LETTERING

PSYCHOLOGICAL AND PERCEPTUAL SPACE

Artists such as Michael Asher, John Knight, Stephen Kaltenbach, and Bruce Nauman made works that altered viewers' perceptions. Asher, Kaltenbach, and Nauman created architectural installations—a hybrid form that is neither painting nor sculpture and that encompasses an entire space to interrupt ordinary experience in order to stimulate new ways of seeing. Already in 1966, Asher was making heat-molded Plexiglas wall-mounted works in which he investigated the properties of painting and sculpture and their relationship to the wall[49] (see fig. 1.49). Soon after, Asher's pieces became even more site and situationally specific so that they could not, unlike this particular sculpture, be re-created in another location. He also commenced a series of pressured-air works that were designed to take the viewer by surprise. In his words, he was "dealing with air as an elementary material of unlimited presence and availability, as opposed to visually determined elements," intervening "to structure this material given in the exhibition container itself, and to reintegrate it into the exhibition area."[50] While many Conceptual artists aspired to what Lucy Lippard described as the dematerialization of the art object, few adhered to it as purely as did Asher. Considered a founder of "institutional critique," he has consistently created installations that subtly alter the physical or other aspects of a given structure. His goal is to make viewers aware that not only does the architecture of a given exhibition space affect our understanding of it, so too do all the ways in which institutions present, publicize, and interpret works. In 1969, Asher attached nine modular walls, regularly used to divide the space according to the needs of a given exhibition, to create a partition that extended the length of the Diego Rivera Gallery at the San Francisco Art Institute (fig. 2.26, p. 163). The modular units—which Asher called "structural ambiguities" since they "constitute a static structure" but are actually moveable—were taped and painted to look like a continuous or permanent part of the architecture. The partition divided the gallery into a large, light and airy area with no exit and a darker hallway-like space. Visitors had to walk around this long wall to access the open area. What interested the artist was the way in which seemingly static forms can be arranged to redefine a space.[51] In other such interventions, Asher revealed facts not readily known or perceived. For example, in 1974 he removed the wall that divided the exhibition space from the office and storage area of the Claire Copley Gallery in Los Angeles to expose the commercial side of the gallery's function.

Knight, who like Asher often intervenes in a given place or situation with minimal materiality, created a site-specific work for a short-lived nonprofit space in Cambridge, Massachusetts, that he had never visited. *I Assumed* (fig. 4.20, pp. 248–249) is a series of fifty index cards on which Knight describes architectural features of the imagined space in statements such as, "Three of the walls to be constructed of mortar and brick." At the site, readers of the cards could compare Knight's assumptions with the actual features of the gallery. In this way, the artist characteristically, if at a distance, took the site "into full account in the construction of the work."[52]

Kaltenbach and Nauman were among the first artists to create participatory or, in the case of Kaltenbach, faux-participatory architectural installations that, like Asher's air column, elicit a psychological response. In 1967, Kaltenbach designed a series of rooms that subvert viewers' expectations by preventing access. In *Raised Floor* (fig. 1.50), one approaches the doorway only to discover that the floor inside the room has been raised about five feet above the floor outside of it, both barring entrance and causing a sense of dislocation. Viewers actually can enter Nauman's deliberately oppressive *Yellow Room (Triangular)* (1973; fig. 1.51), but both the shape of the room and the intense yellow light emitted by fluorescent fixtures disturb one's mental equilibrium.

Another example of an artist creating a discomfiting situation for the viewer is Chris Burden's never-before-shown *Being Photographed: Looking Out, Looking In* (1971; figs. 1.52–56). The piece involved 140 participants who, over several days, scaled a rickety ladder to reach a platform hanging by a chain from the ceiling, twelve to fourteen feet above the floor. After climbing onto the precarious perch and lying on their backs, viewers

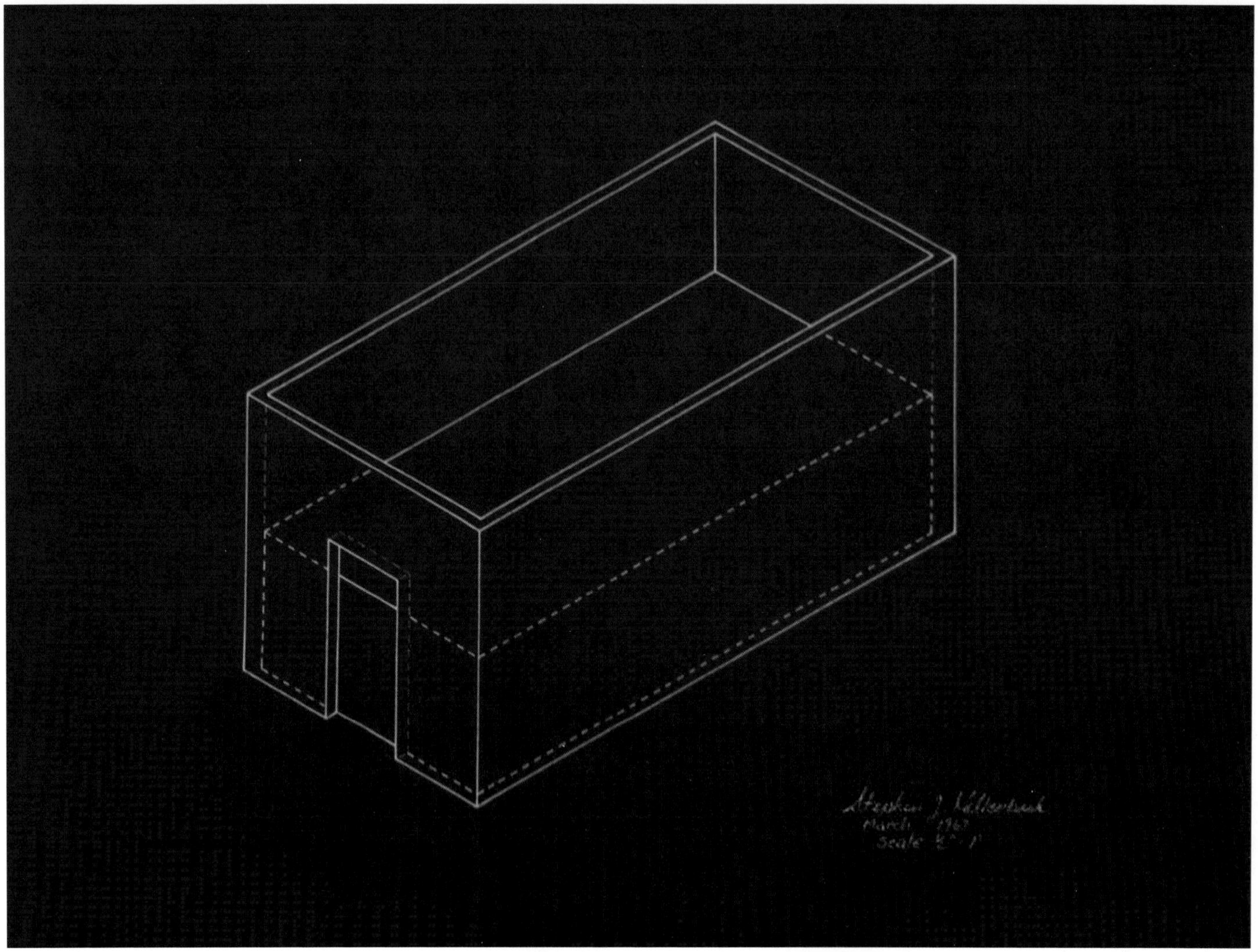

<<

Fig. 1.49 Michael Asher, no title, 1966. Heat-molded Plexiglas; 34 × 40 in.

Fig. 1.50 Stephen Kaltenbach, *Raised Floor,* 1967. Blueprint for room construction; 17 × 21 in. (approx.). Photo: courtesy of the artist and another year in LA, Los Angeles.

Fig. 1.51 Bruce Nauman, *Yellow Room (Triangular),* 1973. Painted wallboard, plywood, and fluorescent light fixtures with yellow lamps; dimensions variable; Solomon R. Guggenheim Museum, New York; Panza Collection. © 2010 Bruce Nauman / Artists Rights Society (ARS), New York.

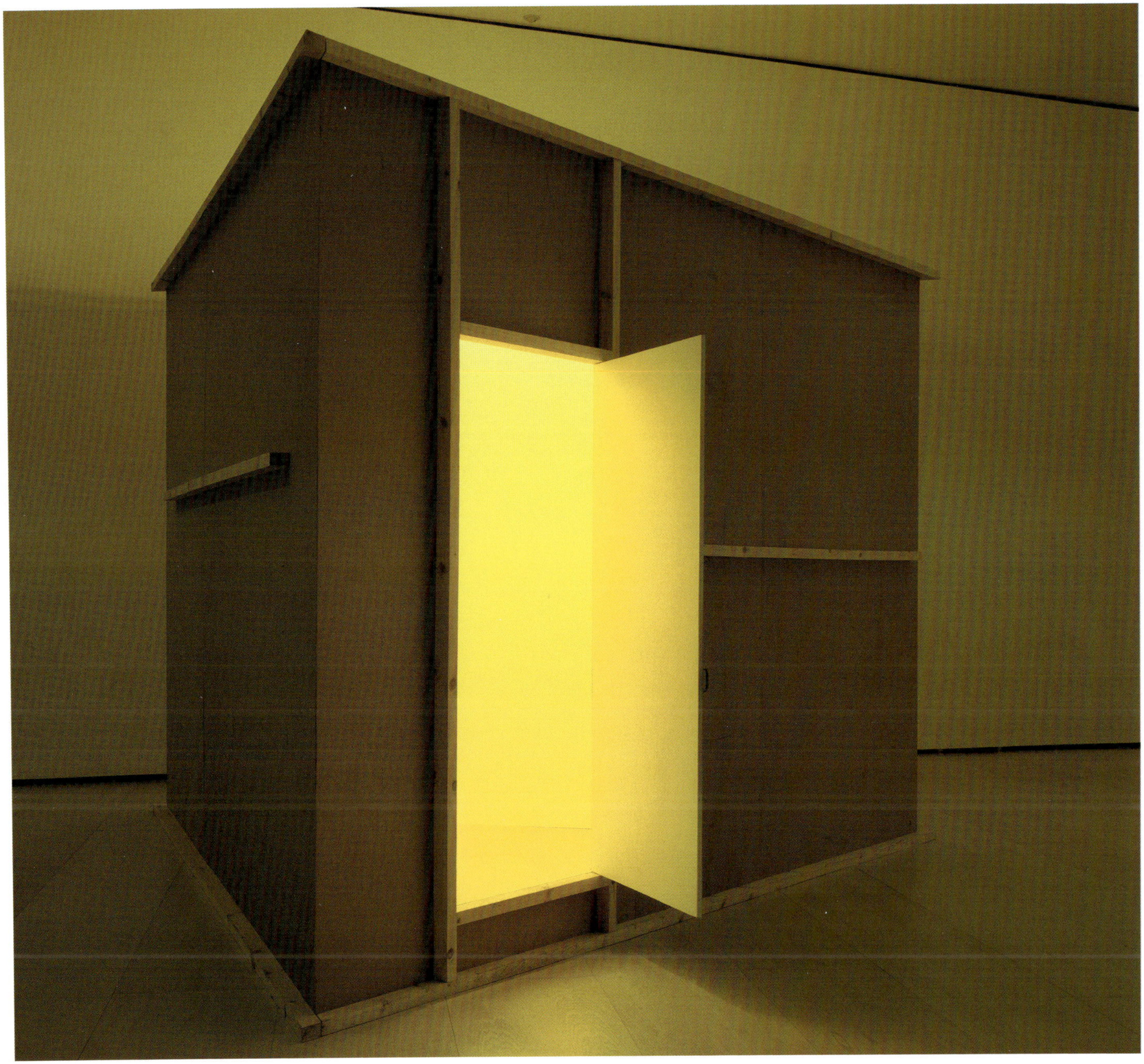

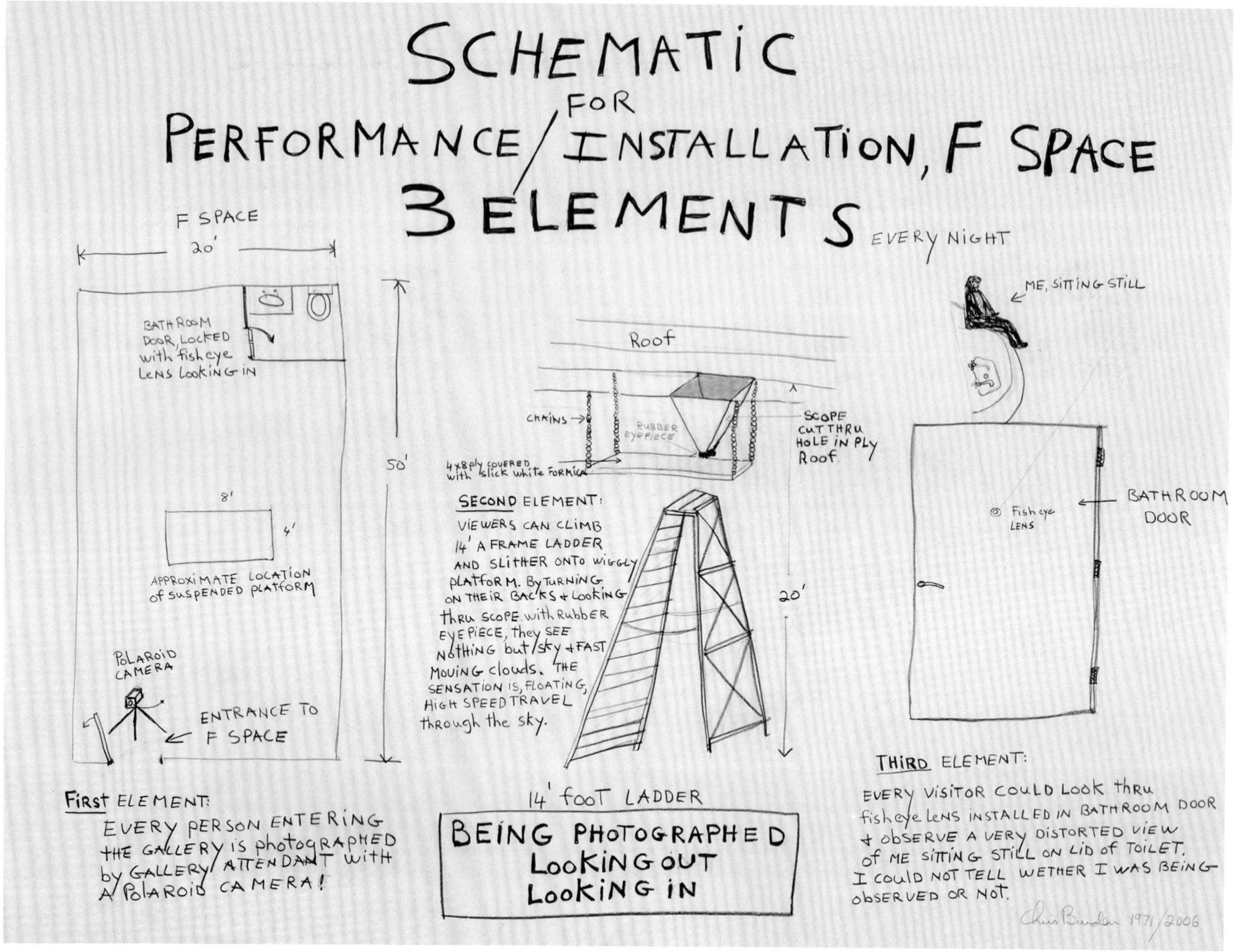

Fig. 1.52 Chris Burden, *Being Photographed: Looking Out, Looking In,* 1971. Schematic drawing for performance: ink and color on paper; 25 × 33 in.

Figs. 1.53–1.56 Chris Burden, *Being Photographed: Looking Out, Looking In,* 1971. 140 Polaroid photographs and one drawing; photographs: 25 × 133 in. overall; drawing: 25 × 33 in.

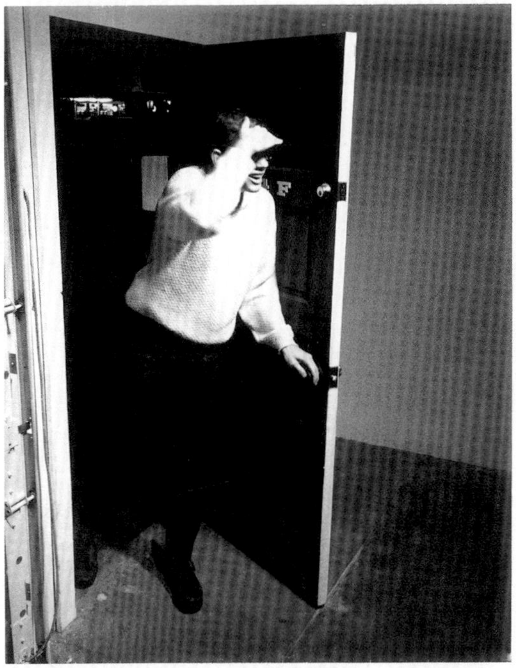

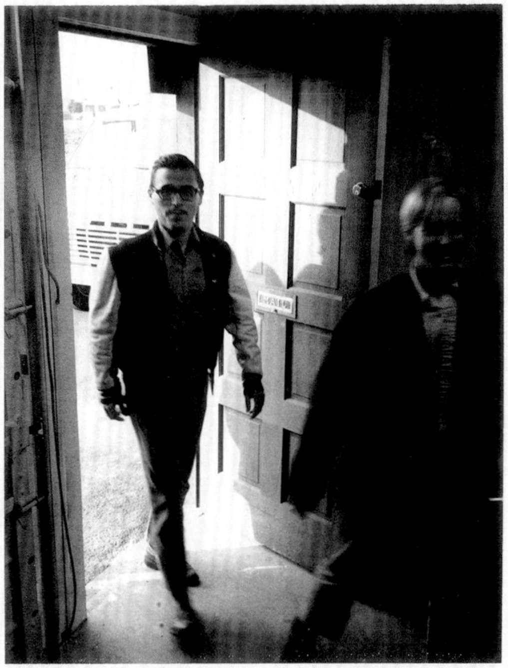

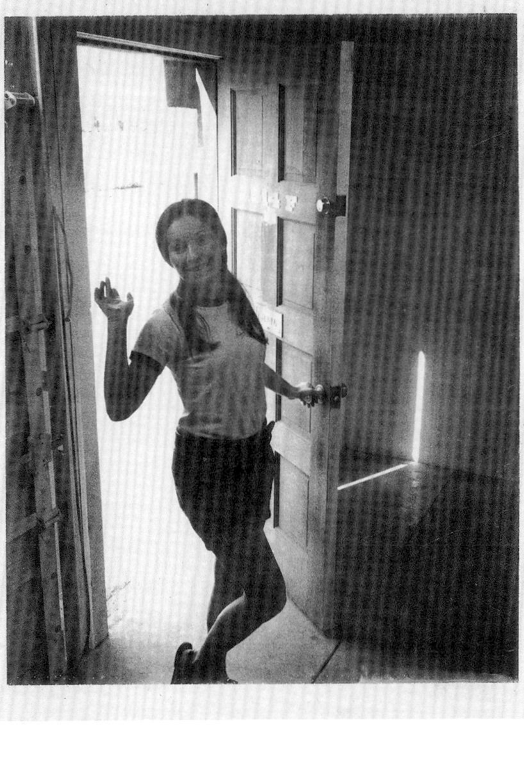

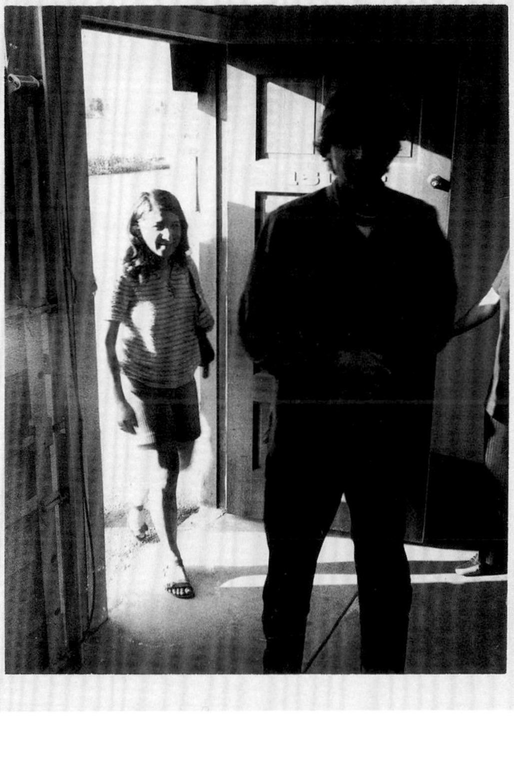

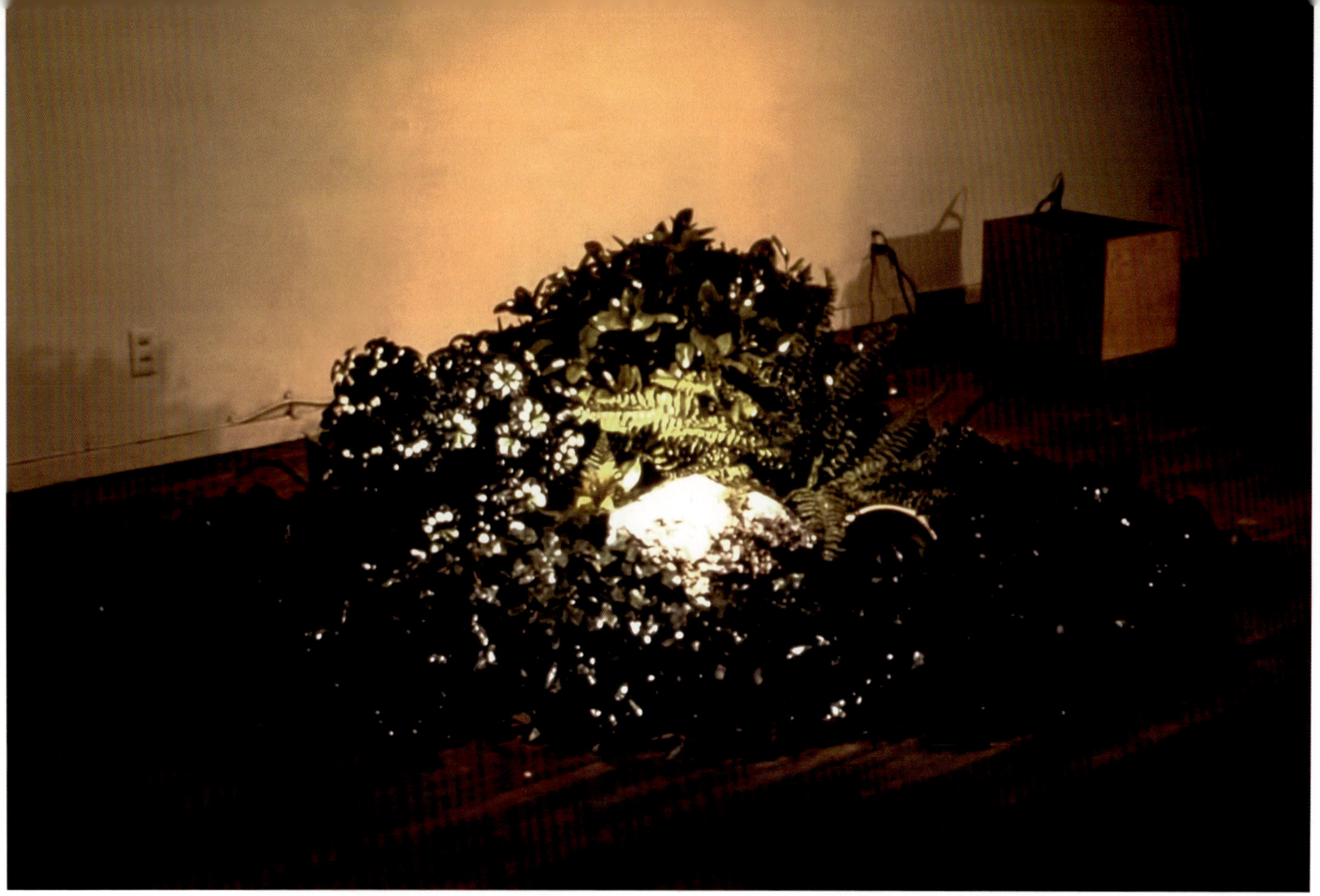

could look at the sky through a scope. According to people who experienced the work, "the psychological response created by the ascent onto this viewing platform was very powerful, creating a sense of both disorientation and freedom."[53] There was a final element to the piece. Viewers were instructed to look into a fish-eye lens in a door in the corner of the space, where they saw Burden sitting on a toilet. "Having played on participants' emotions through the situation created by the platform, he in turn allowed them to feel that they were able to 'invade' his physical and psychological space."[54]

Although some Conceptual artists created three-dimensional multimedia works that have roots in Postminimalism (e.g., Richard Serra's prop pieces or Keith Sonnier's neon assemblages), such Postminimal works, though unconventional, were still identifiable as sculpture. Other Conceptual artists went one step further. Their works often not only incorporated elements of sculpture and painting, but also they were specific to the sites they inhabited, such as Michael Asher's space alterations, and were frequently participatory, as in Nauman's *Yellow Room (Triangular)*. Some pieces, such as Kos's *Sound of Ice Melting* (fig. 1.77), included natural elements, like ice, that changed over time. William Leavitt's *Garden Sound* (1970; fig. 1.57) at first might recall one of Robert Smithson's Nonsites (figs. 4.2–4.3, pp. 222–23), in which the artist brought natural elements, such as rocks, into the gallery or museum. But Leavitt's garden is deliberate artifice, a precursor to his better-known narrative tableaux, such as *California Patio* (1972), that draw upon popular culture, specifically B movies and soap operas of the 1960s. A more apt comparison would be to Belgian artist Marcel Broodthaers's *Wintergarten,* an evocative interior ensemble of potted palms and garden furniture first shown in 1974 in Brussels. Thomas Lawson describes Leavitt's installations as "distilled narratives" pared down to "what is essential to indicate the situation," and, according to another writer, "each piece is in itself a fiction based on certain romantic attitudes to real places, social strata, styles, and taste."[55] Barbara Smith's *Field Piece* (1968–72) is, like Leavitt's, an artificial garden in which tall, colored, fiberglass resin "blades" simulate vegetation. This work is an early example of a participatory installation in which, by walking among the plastic tubes on the platform, viewers activate the various colored lights controlled by a computer (see fig. 2.1, pp. 118–19).

Unlike the artists who dealt with perceptual phenomena, Howard Fried centered his work on his own psychology, the only artist with the inner circle of Marioni's MOCA to do so. Fried's early works such as *Long John Servil vs. Long John Silver* and *Inside the Harlequin: Approach-Avoidance III and II* (1971; figs. 1.58–1.59) were objectifications of psychological states, specifically the phenomenon of approach-avoidance wherein simultaneous attraction and repulsion create a condition of stasis. *Inside the Harlequin* (in art and literature, the harlequin historically represents the artist) consists of two silent Super-8 film loops approximately eight minutes long, one slightly longer than the other, projected side by side, resulting in ever-changing juxtapositions of actions enacted by Fried and two other performers. While two men operate in opposite sides of the studio marked by different colors (shades of gray) on the walls and floors, Fried moves freely from one to the other, "acting cooperatively or antagonistically with the others."[56] One segment shows two men in mountain-climbing gear scaling a wall, while a third stands grounded on the floor. Another records Fried wrestling one of the participants as they scatter studio tools and materials; in yet another, a tower of stacked tables is cut in two with a chainsaw. Fried edited these situations into short segments that appear and reappear throughout. In his iconic first video, *Fuck You Purdue* (1971), as in *Long John Servil vs. Long John Silver,* Fried assumes two characters who interact on a set that has been divided into two roomlike spaces. The idea came from a story told by Fried's brother, who was in the Marine Corps. Two drill instructors, Purdue and Ward, each ordered their recruit to deliver the message "fuck you" to the other instructor, resulting in the recruit being punished for the insult. Fried moved from one room to the other, screaming the epithets, starting in the morning while still in bed and continuing throughout the day. The hostility and aggression of *Fuck You Purdue* recalls Nauman's equally off-putting sound work *Get Out of My Mind, Get Out of This Room* (1968), as well as several of Vito Acconci's early videos, such as *Claim* (1971), in which the artist sits blindfolded in a basement, swinging a crowbar and ordering those who venture near to leave. In fact, in their works of this time, Fried and Acconci share an interest in setting up psychologically tense and challenging scenarios.

Bay Area artists Darryl Sapien and John Woodall enacted highly theatrical, ritualistic performances that reflect knowledge of Fried's work—as well as that of Joseph Beuys—but were less psychological and more symbolic. Sapien's *War Games* (1973; figs. 1.60–1.61), performed with his partner Michael A. Hinton, symbolized conflict and cooperation as described in ethnologist Konrad Lorenz's 1966 book *On Aggression.*[57] Staged before an audience in the exposed basement of a demolished building in downtown San Francisco, two artist combatants, one painted red, the other black, fought each other in a series of ritualistic actions (according to Lorenz, such ritualized conflict can avoid intertribal warfare). The conclusion of a concurrent chess game ended the conflict. Similarly driven by rules and restrictions, Woodall's *Marking the Dilemma* (1973; fig. 1.62) was about staking out his territory—a circle drawn on the gallery floor—while impeded by self-imposed restraints. The artist nailed the heel of one shoe to the floor and wore a three-inch elevator shoe on the other foot as well as eyeglasses that blurred his vision.[58] While he stood at the center of the circle, Woodall outlined his shadow with chalk attached to the end of a stick as he moved around the circle. The result of the thirty-six overlapping cast shadow outlines at ten-degree intervals looked "something like a mandala."[59]

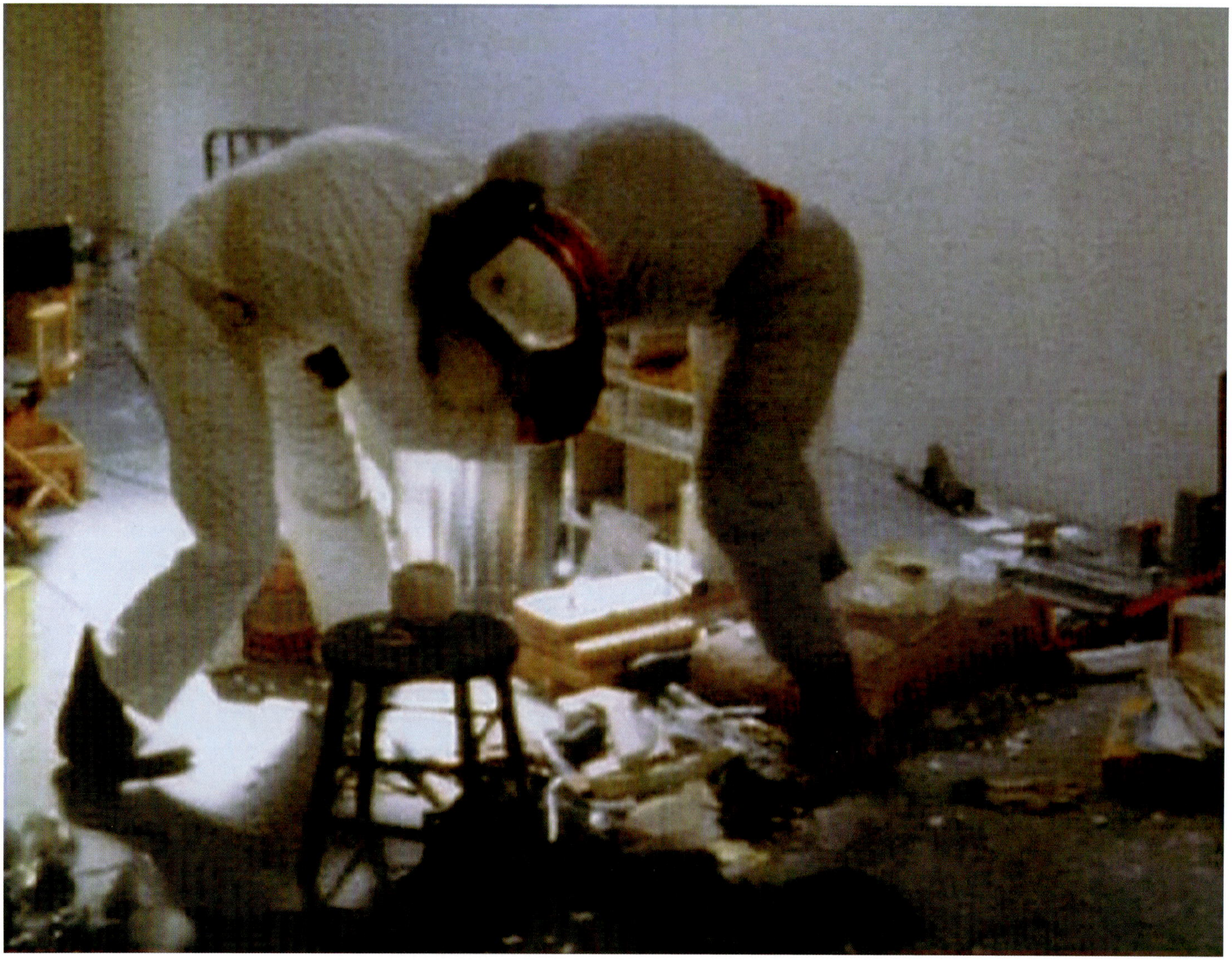

<<

Fig. 1.57 William Leavitt, *Garden Sound,* 1970. Artificial plants, plywood box, water, circulating pump, microphone, amplifier, and speaker; 84 × 144 × 144 in.

Figs. 1.58–1.59 Howard Fried, *Inside the Harlequin: Approach-Avoidance III and II* (details of wrestling and crossover sequences), 1971. Two unsynchronized Super-8 film loops transferred to video with two unsynchronized audio loops and projected images; 455 × 120 in.; 75 5⁄8 × 120 × 126 in. overall.

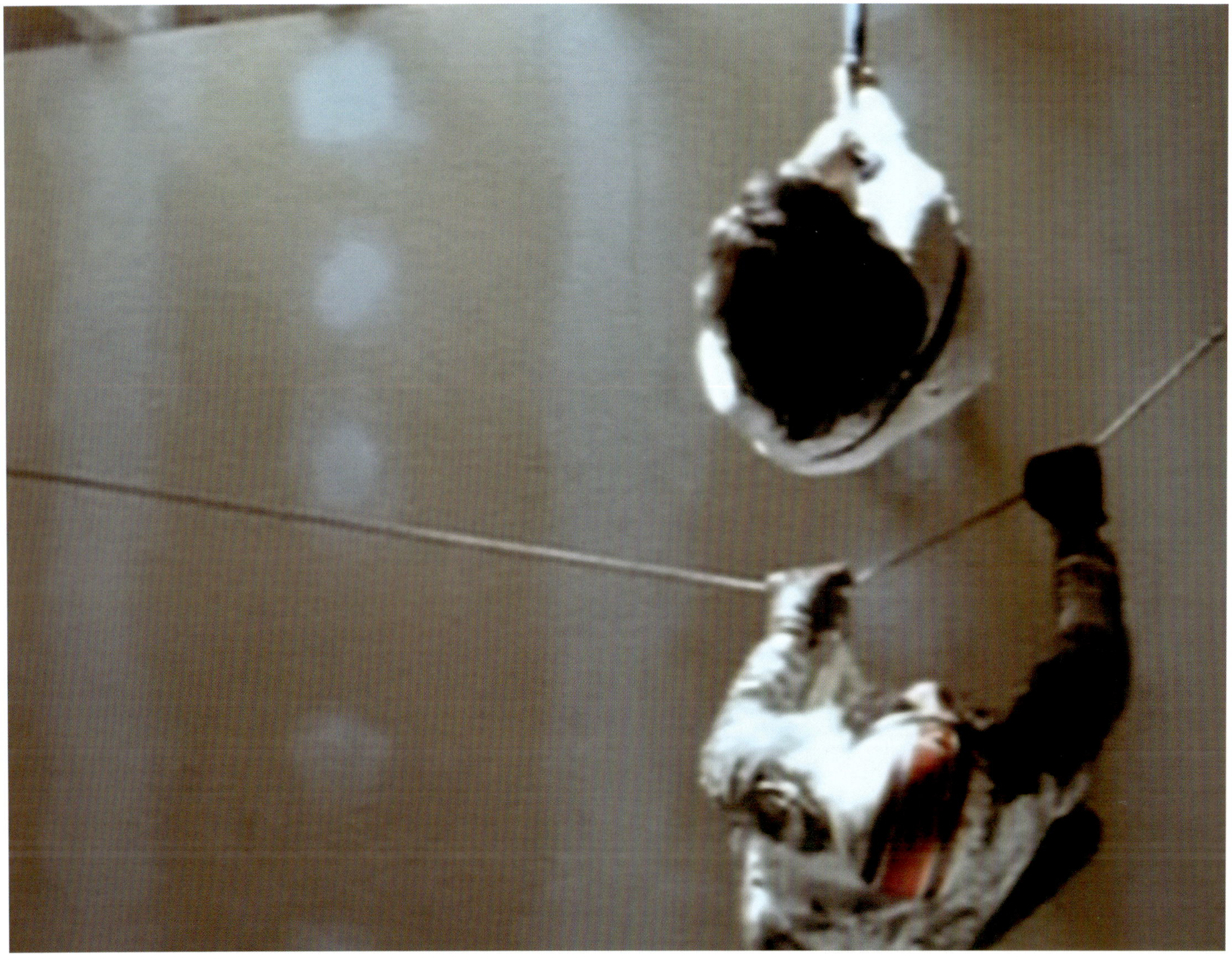

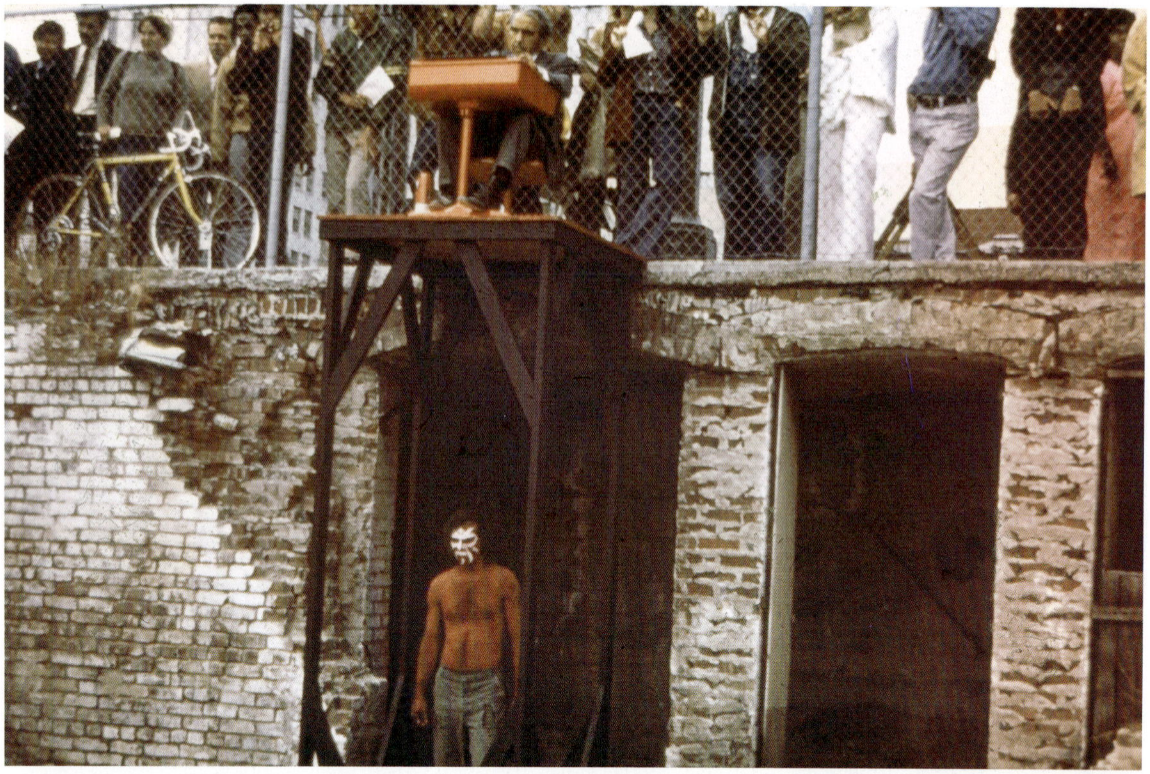

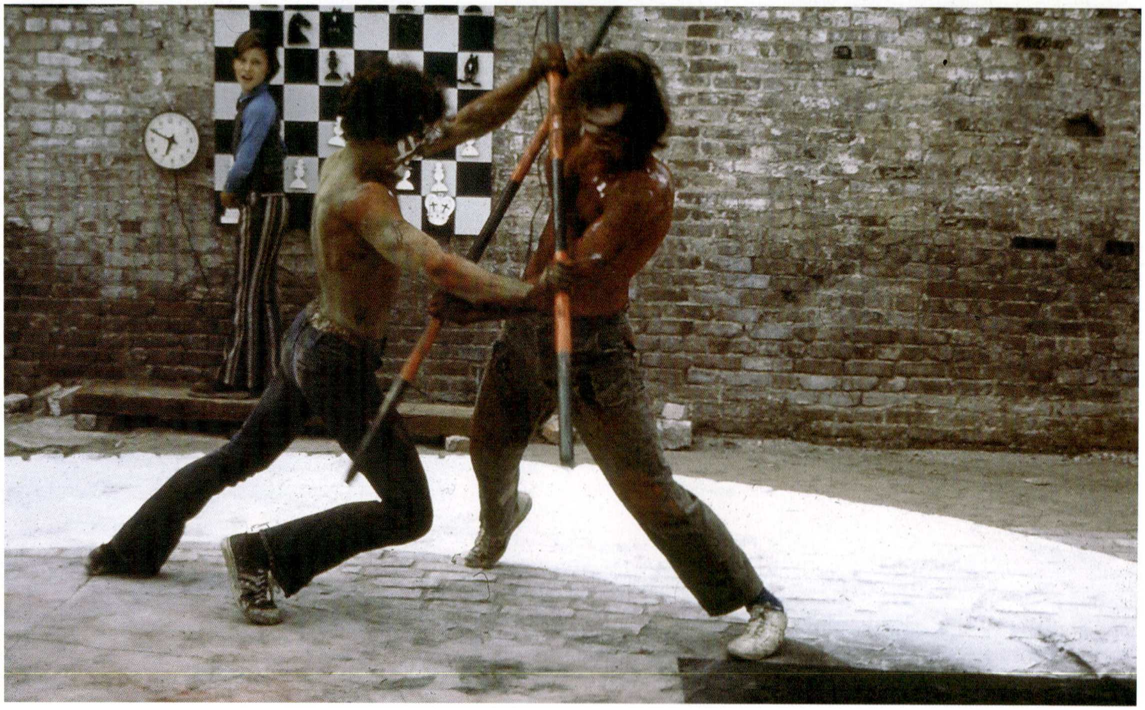

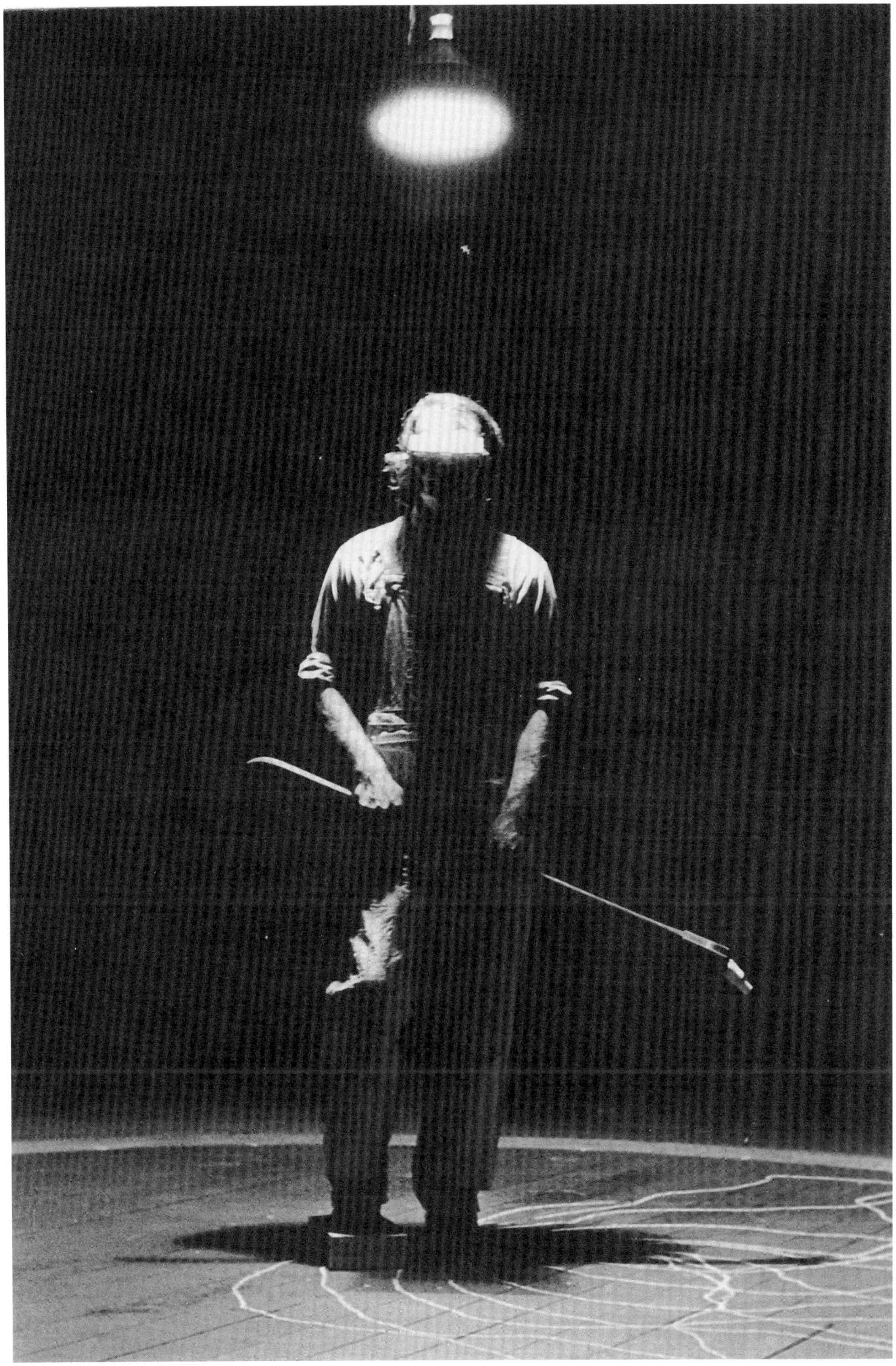

Figs. 1.60–1.61 Darryl Sapien with Michael A. Hinton, *War Games*, 1973. Performance documentation: Third and Howard Streets, San Francisco, in the ruins of a demolished building.

Fig. 1.62 John Woodall, *Marking the Dilemma,* 1973. Performance documentation from *All Night Sculptures,* Museum of Conceptual Art (MOCA), San Francisco.

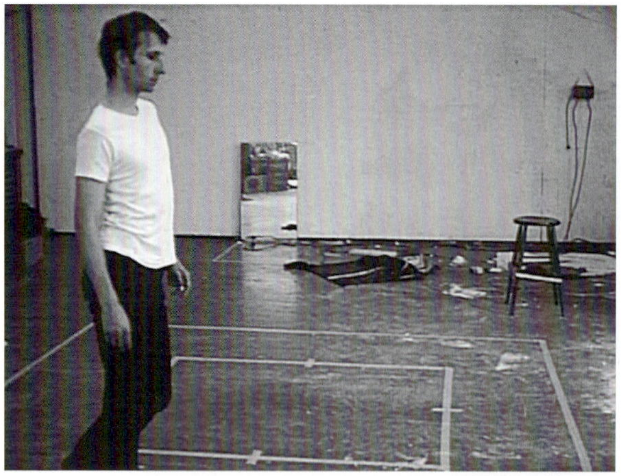

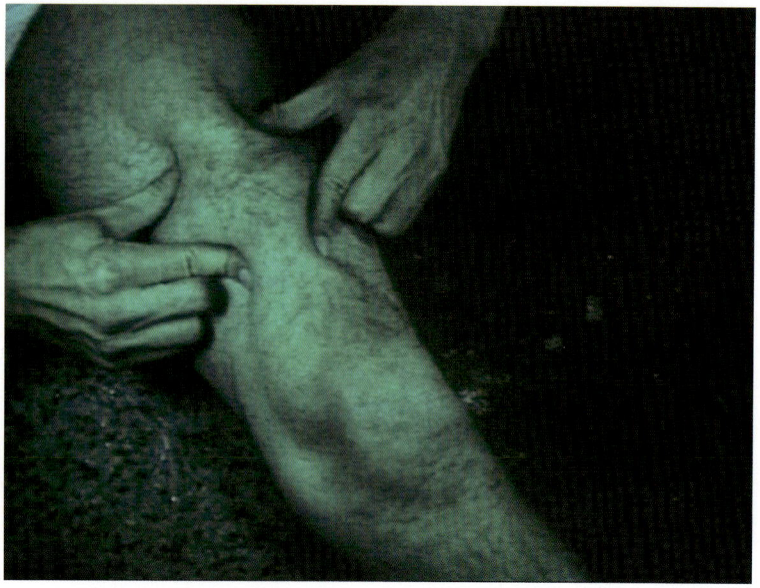

THE BODY

The use of the body as a material is one of the defining characteristics of California Conceptual art, and as has often been asserted, it is not particular to the Bay Area. Throughout the state, artists used the body as both subject and object of their artwork for a variety of reasons: to circumvent the art market; to test the body's limits; to explore its sculptural potential; to act as a means of self-understanding and transformation. Women used their bodies to investigate cultural stereotypes. In Southern California, as we have seen in Antin's *Representational Painting* and in *Carving: A Traditional Sculpture*, Mogul's *Dressing Up,* and Smith's *Feed Me,* "women artists working within the political feminist movement incorporated their bodies in performances, actions, and sculptural works in order to call attention to how the body is 'culturally marked' with differences such as gender" (see figs. 1.41–1.44, pp. 55–59, as well as fig. 3.6, p. 203).[60] Nancy Buchanan—who exhibited at the F Space group in Santa Ana along with Burden, Smith, and others—symbolically switched genders with a male performer by exchanging body hair (see fig. 2.25, p. 161). Men, too, used their bodies as material. Nauman, one of the first artists to do so, explained, "If you can manipulate clay and end up with art, you can imagine yourself in [art] as well. It has to do with using the body as a tool, an object to manipulate."[61] Nauman was still living in the Bay Area when he made his landmark films in which he engages his own body as an instrument. Most, like *Dance or Exercise around the Perimeter of a Square* and *Walking in an Exaggerated Manner around the Perimeter of a Square* (fig. 1.63) (both 1967–68), involved exercises in balance and were influenced by Bay Area avant-garde dance and minimal music pioneered by Anna Halprin, La Monte Young, and others. "I thought of them as dance problems without being a dancer," Nauman said.[62] In other works he manipulated his body. *Thighing* (1967; fig. 1.64), a 16 mm film, shows a closeup of the artist's thigh as he pinches and kneads it. He pulls at his cheeks, stretches his mouth, and in other ways contorts his face in *Studies for Holograms* (1970; fig. 1.65), a series of screen prints based on infrared photographs taken in 1968.

Paul McCarthy admired Nauman—in fact, it was because Nauman was teaching at the San Francisco Art Institute that McCarthy moved from his native Salt Lake City, Utah, to attend

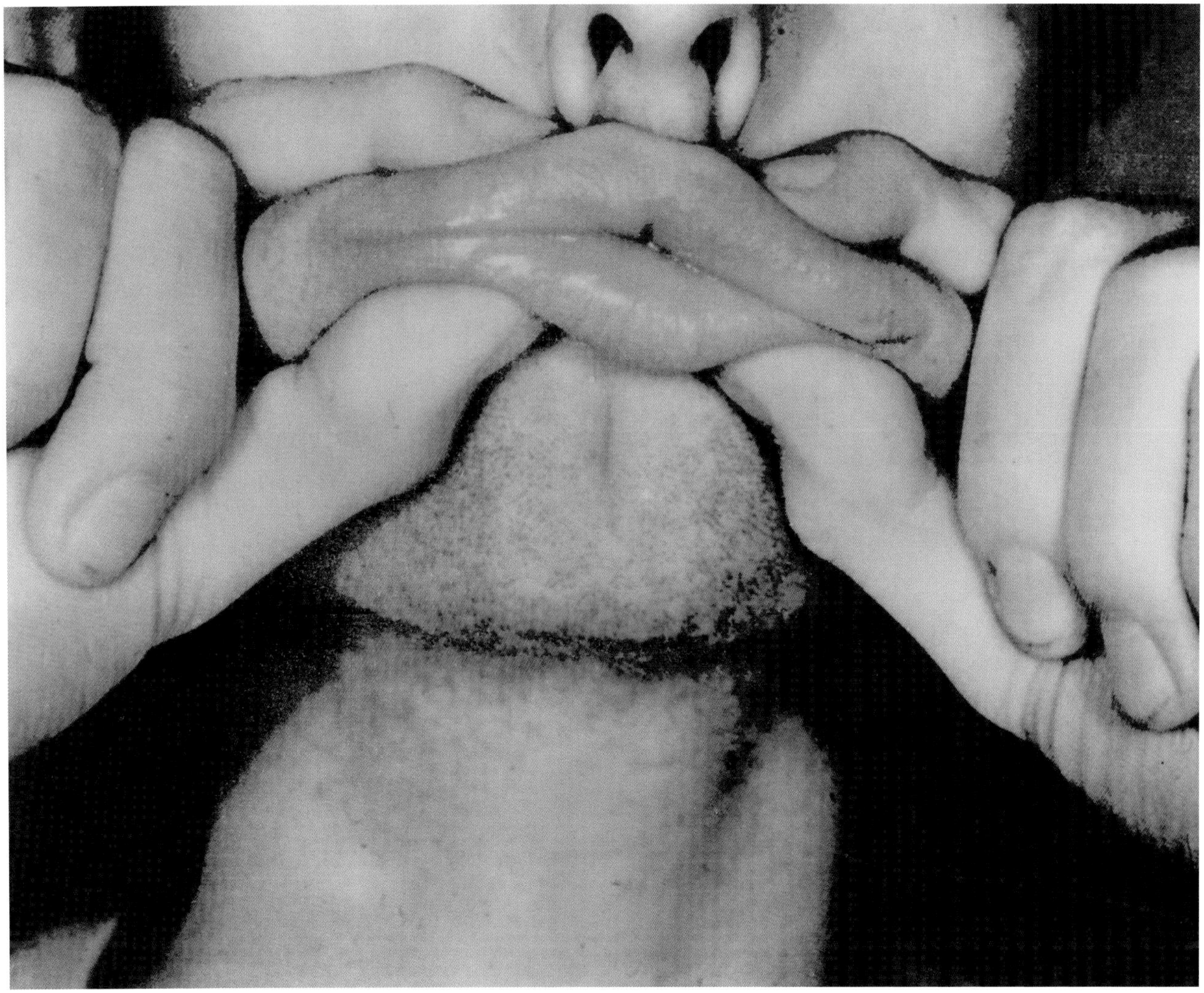

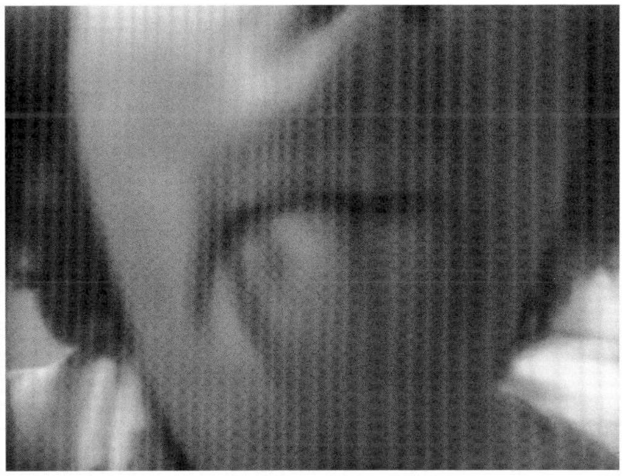

Fig. 1.63 Bruce Nauman, *Walking in an Exaggerated Manner around the Perimeter of a Square,* 1967–68. 16 mm film transferred to video; black and white; silent; 10 min.

Fig. 1.64 Bruce Nauman, *Thighing,* 1967. 16 mm film transferred to video; color; sound; 4:36 min.

Fig. 1.65 Bruce Nauman, *Studies for Holograms (Pinched Lips; Pulled Lower Lip; Pulled Neck; Pulled Cheeks; and Squeezed Lips),* (detail), 1970, Five screen prints; 25 ¾ × 25 ¾ in. each.

Fig. 1.66 Terry Fox, *Tonguings,* 1970. Video: black and white; sound; 21 min.

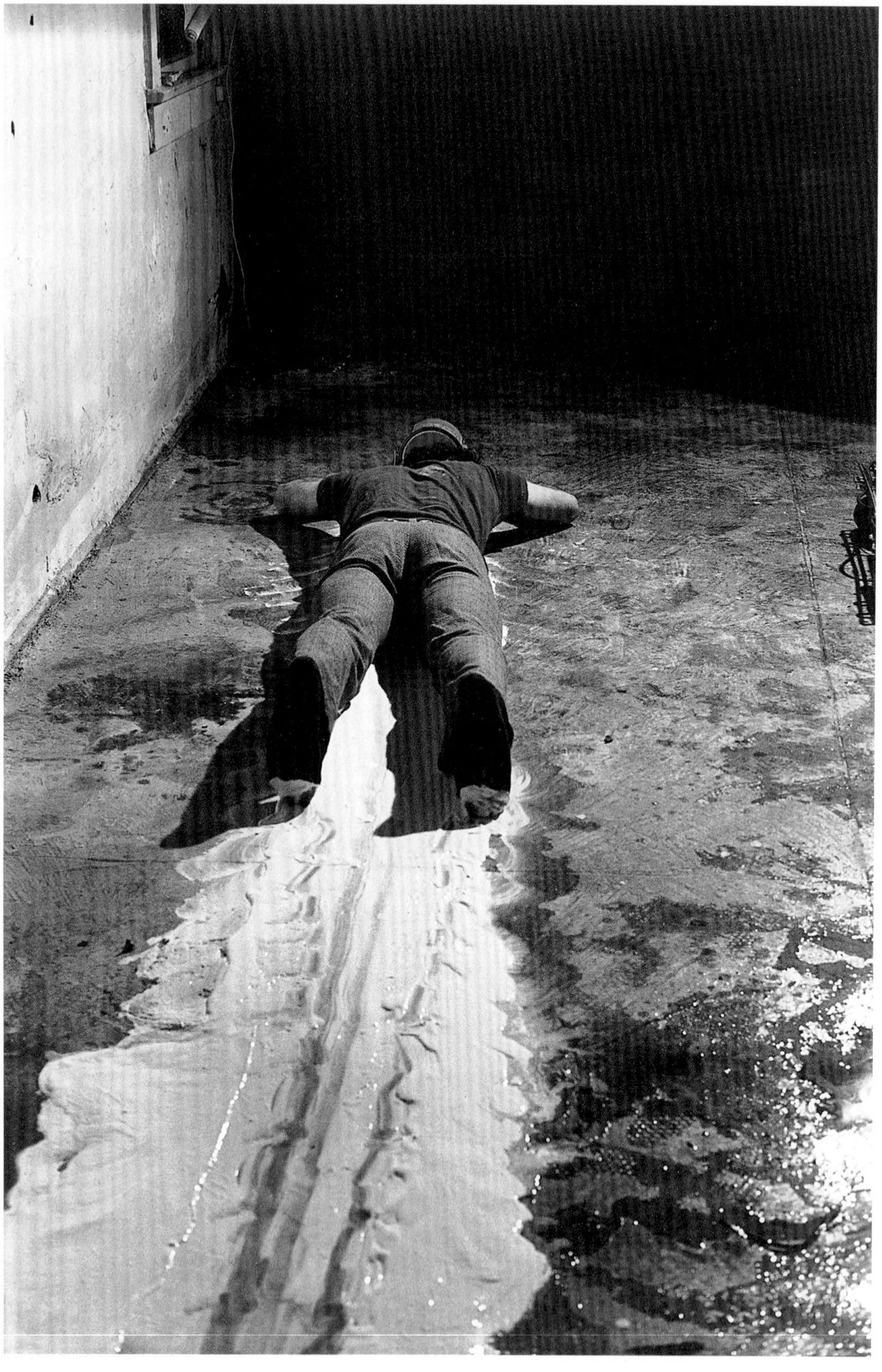

Fig. 1.67 Paul McCarthy, *Face Painting Floor, White Line,* 1972, from *Black and White Tapes,* 1970–75. Video: black and white; sound; 32:50 min.

Fig. 1.68 Terry Fox, *Pisces,* February 2 or 3, 1971. Performance documentation: *Fish, Fox, Kos,* Museum of Conceptual Art, San Francisco, and de Saisset Art Gallery and Museum, Santa Clara University. © The Estate of Terry Fox. Photo: Joel Glassman, courtesy SFMOMA Research Library and Archives.

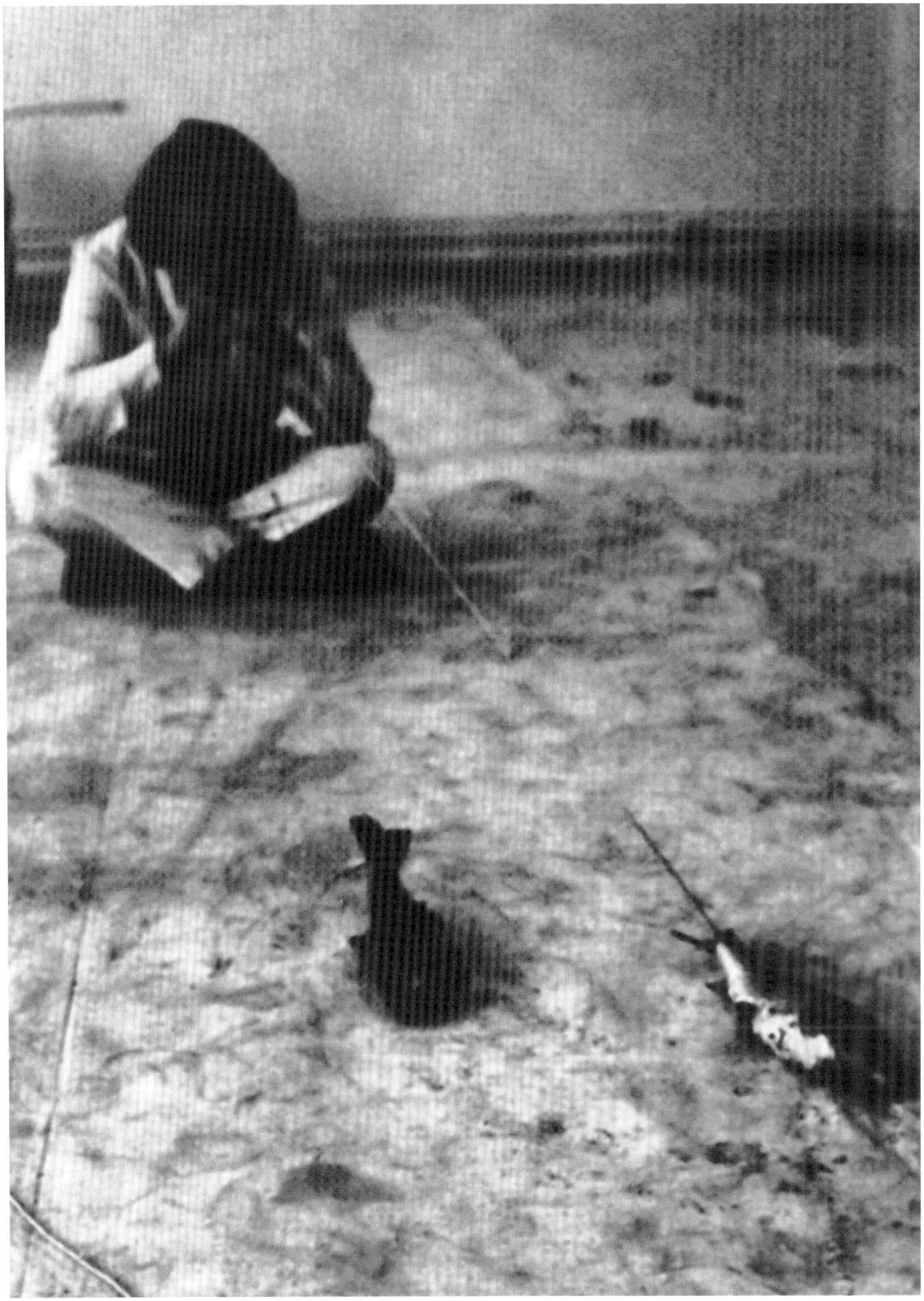

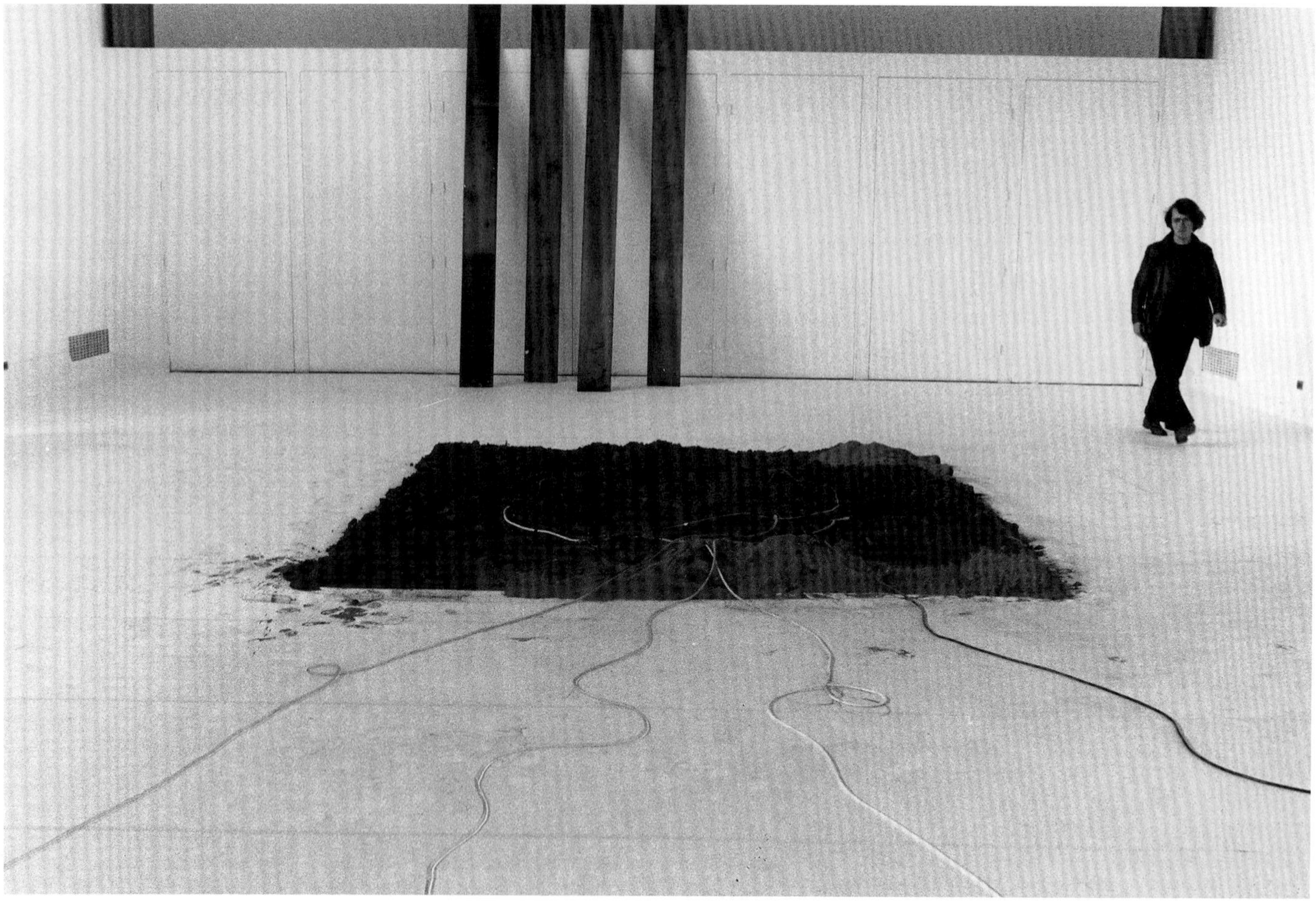

the school (although by the time McCarthy arrived, Nauman was no longer teaching).[63] McCarthy completed his graduate studies at the University of Southern California and stayed in the area, developing a highly theatrical oeuvre based on his body. In his seminal transgressive, expressionistic, and sexualized *Black and White Tapes* (1970–75; fig. 1.67), he bends, slams, and gyrates his naked torso and spits at the camera lens. His darkly humorous work has been described as Rabelaisian, but, at base, McCarthy offers a critique of consumer society. As one writer put it, he gives us "the dark side of the American Dream."[64] In addition to Nauman, McCarthy cites influences as varied as Allan Kaprow's book *Assemblages, Environments & Happenings,* which he acquired in 1966, and, through Kaprow, the Japanese Gutai group.[65] His extreme body performances also bear a strong relationship to the highly theatrical, even violent performances of the Viennese Actionists (Günter Brus, Otto Mühl, Hermann Nitsch, and Rudolf Schwarzkogler), who worked together between 1969 and 1971.[66]

In addition to the Viennese group, Californians had an affinity with Europeans, such as Beuys and Yves Klein. Terry Fox learned of Beuys in Europe in the late 1960s and even performed with him in 1971 at the Kunstakademie Düsseldorf, where Beuys was a highly influential teacher (he did not

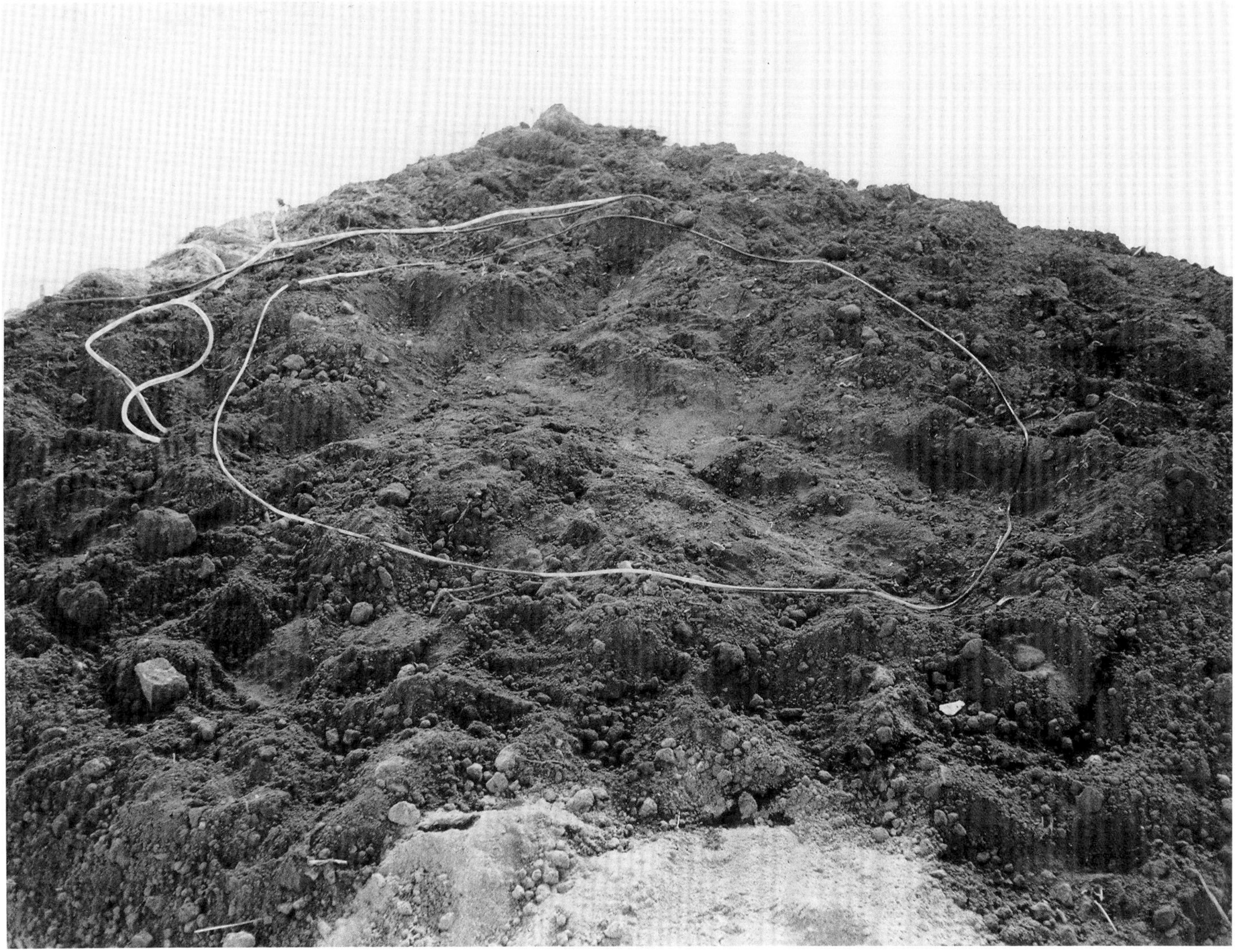

Fig. 1.69 Terry Fox, *Levitation* (installation view), 1970. Performance documentation: Richmond Art Center, September 17–21, 1970. © The Estate of Terry Fox. Photo: Larry Fox, courtesy SFMOMA Research Library and Archives.

Fig. 1.70 Terry Fox, *Levitation,* 1970. Performance documentation: imprint of Fox's body on dirt in Richmond Art Center, September 17–21, 1970. © The Estate of Terry Fox. Photo: Larry Fox, courtesy SFMOMA Research Library and Archives.

become well known in the United States until his first show in 1974 at the Rene Bloch Gallery, New York). Beuys's ritualistic actions and repeated use of certain symbolic materials, such as felt and fat, influenced Fox's own performances. While this ritualism was also important to Woodall, Marioni and Ruppersberg shared the German artist's belief in art as a social activity, as evidenced in Ruppersberg's *Al's Café* and *Al's Grand Hotel* and in Marioni's weekly free-beer get-togethers (see figs. 1.29–1.30, pp. 43–44). Marioni cites French Protoconceptualist Yves Klein's (1928–62) notorious leap from a window (*Le Saut dans le Vide,* 1958), captured in a black-and-white photograph (by photographers Harry Skunk and John Kender, whom Klein had hired to document the act), as "a symbol for the whole performance art movement." Marioni noted, "It didn't have anything to do with telling a story.[67] It was about the artist as material. The artist's body actually was the art object."[68] Paul McCarthy also cites Klein's leap, with which he was familiar as early as 1966, along with Klein's *Anthropométries,* as an influence.[69]

Like McCarthy, Fox knew of Nauman's work—he had seen Nauman's films in an exhibition at the Reese Palley Gallery in San Francisco in 1969—but did not have firsthand contact with the artist. After Fox's *Public Theater* works and *Defoliation,* he retreated into a period of private experimentation with his own body as a vehicle for art. Several such performances, like *Pisces* (1971), were both metaphors for his own precarious health (he suffered from Hodgkin's disease) and empathetic responses to the suffering caused by the war in Vietnam, and those works are described more fully in Karen Moss's essay (see fig. 1.68; see also figs. 1.21, p. 35, 1.25, p. 39, and 2.10, p. 135). Fox also made private body-related works that were documented in photographs or video.

The passage of time is the subject of *Clutch* (1971), a fifty-minute videotaped performance. In this rarely seen piece, Fox, lying on his stomach with arms extended, follows a shaft of light as it moves across the floor, then out of reach, and, finally, off screen. In other private body works, he pushed his body into

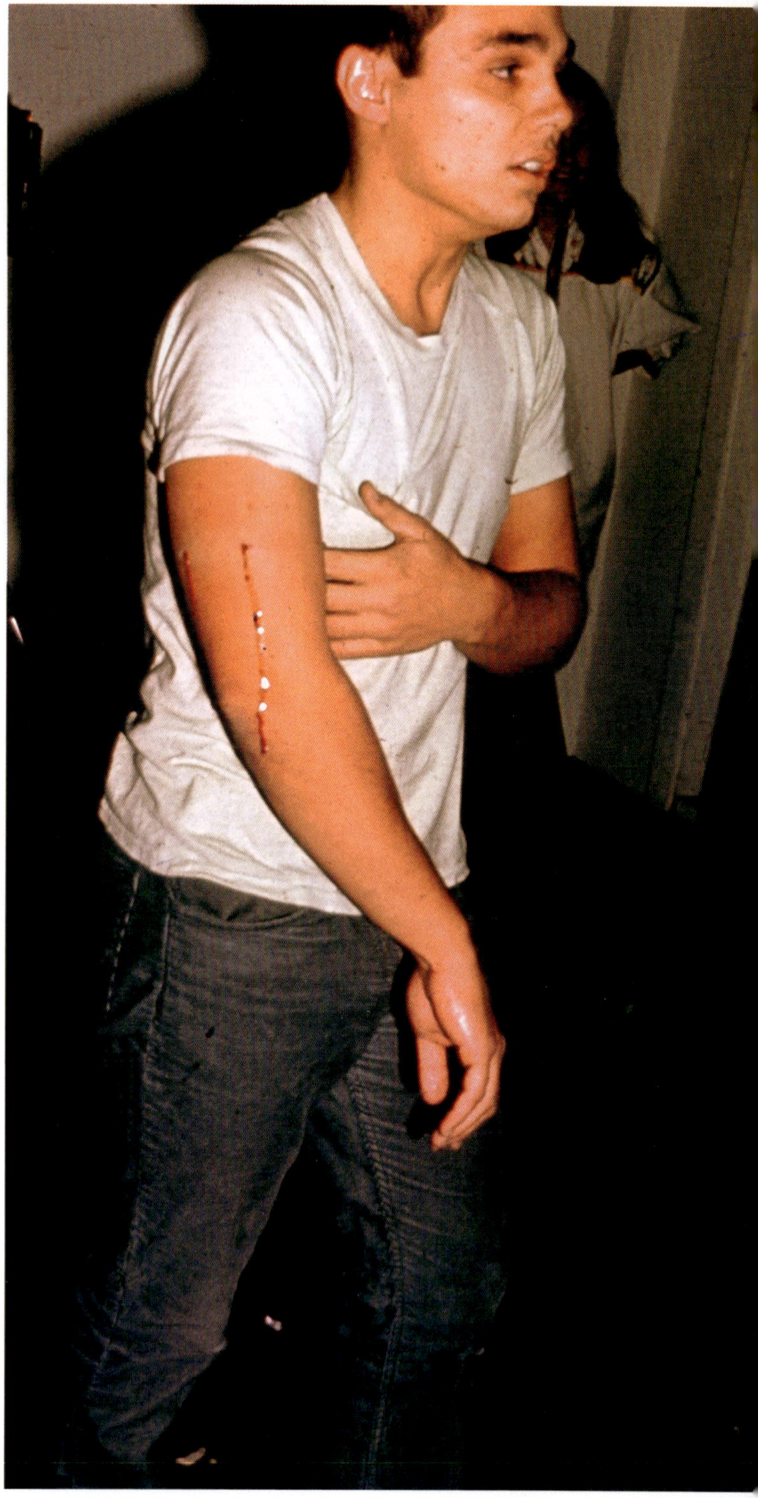

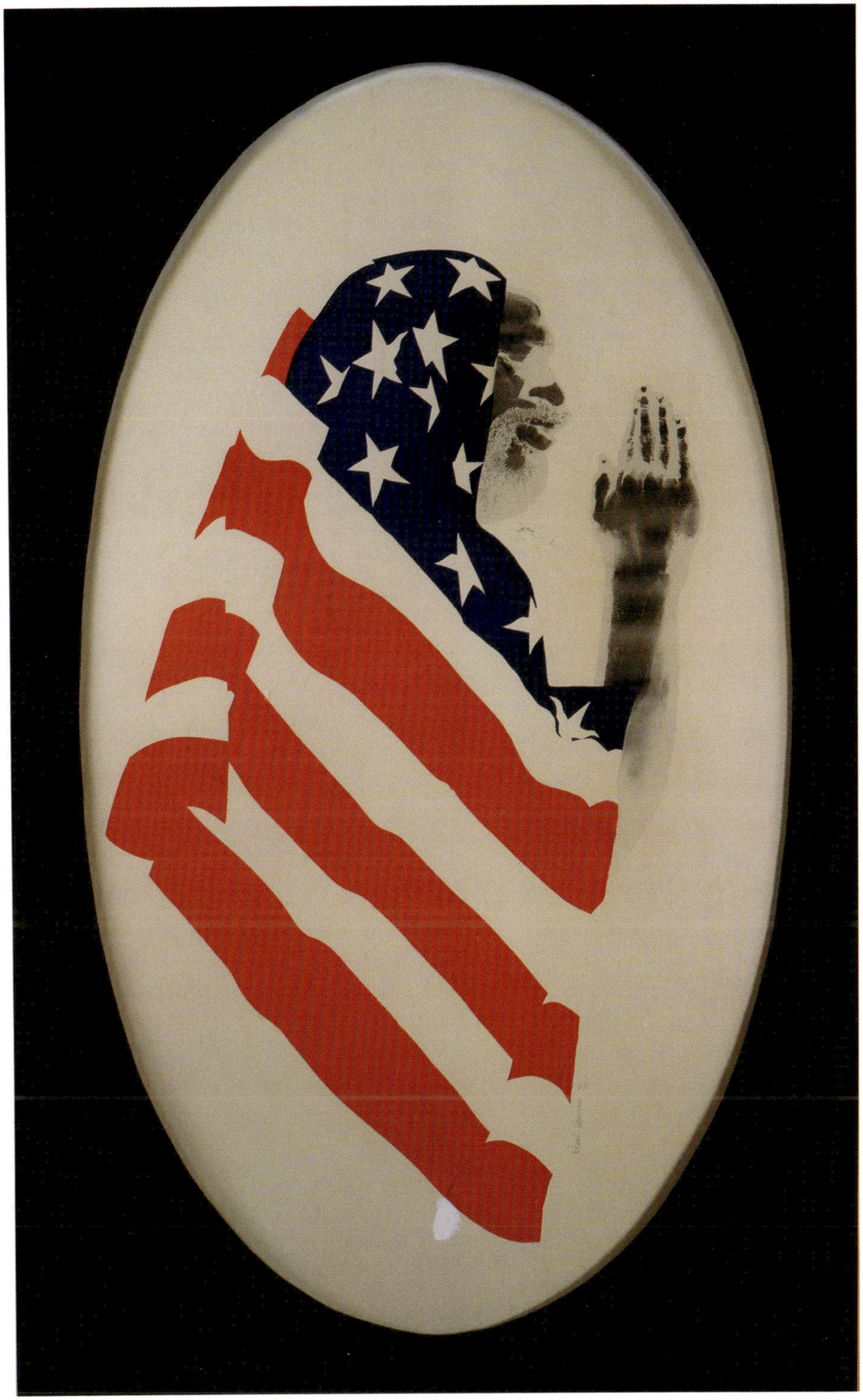

Fig. 1.71 Chris Burden, *Shoot,* November 19, 1971. Performance at F Space, Santa Ana, California.

Fig. 1.72 David Hammons, *Pray for America,* 1974. Body print, silkscreen; 60 ½ × 30 in.

>>

Fig. 1.73 Bas Jan Ader, *Fall I, Los Angeles,* 1970. 16mm film transferred to video; black and white; silent; 34 sec.

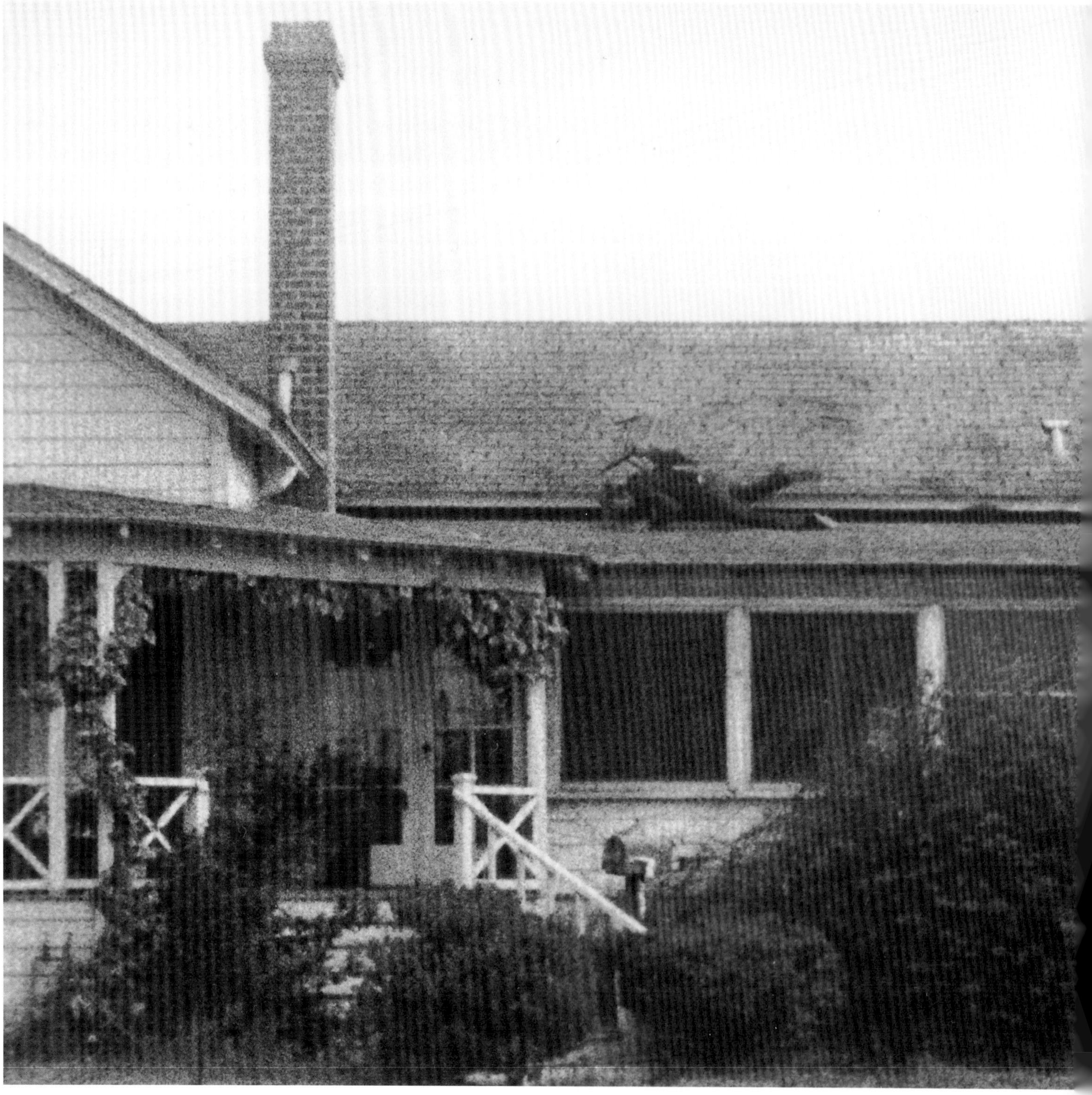

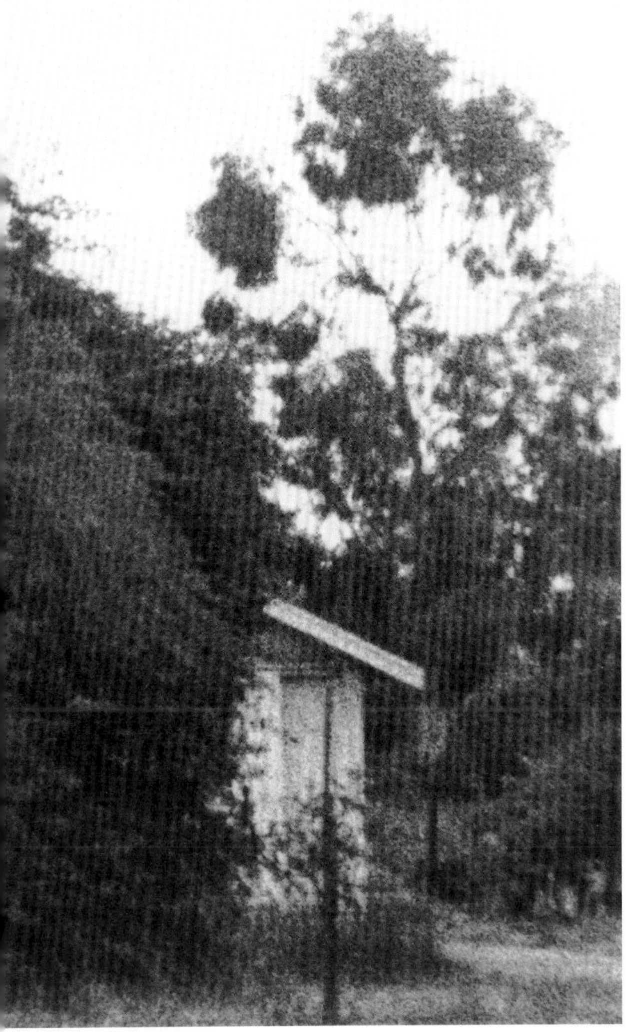

a corner of a room, blew smoke out of his mouth, and opened his hand as slowly as possible as explorations of the interactions of matter and energy. In 1970, Fox produced *Tonguings* for *Body Works,* a video exhibition organized in coordination with *Avalanche* editor Willoughby Sharp and the first body art show in the United States. In the video, Fox extends, rotates, and curls his tongue and lips for twenty-one minutes. Such corporeal manipulations have a close affinity with those of Vito Acconci, who was a frequent visitor to MOCA, as well as to those of Burden and Nauman, whose video *Thighing* Fox may have seen at this 1969 exhibition at Reese Palley Gallery, San Francisco, which also included Acconci.

Levitation (1970; figs. 1.69–70), a private performance/installation, was the most intense of Fox's body works. It took place at the Richmond Art Center, where Marioni was director. Lying on his back for six hours within a ring of blood on a mound of dirt he collected from under a freeway, Fox attached with string from his hands and feet vials of water, blood, milk, and urine, symbolically expelling spirit from flesh. "I was trying to think about leaving the ground," he wrote, "until I realized I should be thinking about entering the air. For me that changed everything, made it work."[70] When viewers entered the space after the action, they saw only the imprint of the artist's body on the earth, the vials, and a typewritten explanation of what had occurred. For Fox, who had undergone numerous hospitalizations and treatments, the effort to leave his body had particular significance: there was never any distance between his life experiences and his art.

Southern California artist Chris Burden had an affinity with Marioni's circle, especially Fox, who were exploring the body through performance. Burden flirted with danger, even death, to experience what most wish to avoid in a series of iconic performances he began while still a graduate student at the University of California, Irvine. In his most infamous, *Shoot* (fig. 1.71), a friend shot him in the arm with a .22 rifle on November 19, 1971, at F Space in Orange County. A month before, on October 3 at MOCA in San Francisco, Burden had performed a clandestine body work, *I Became a Secret Hippy* (1971; fig. 3.7, p. 204). Burden had himself photographed in a black suit, white shirt, and shaved head, in the style of an FBI agent, concealing the metal star which had been hammered into his chest earlier. Two years later, he performed *Fire Roll* also at MOCA, using his body to extinguish a fire on the floor. What distinguished Burden's body performances from those of his peers was the way in which he implicated the audience, either as complicit observers of his risky actions or by actually putting them in peril as in *Being Photographed: Looking Out, Looking In* (see figs. 1.52–1.56, pp. 70–71).

Like Burden, Dutch-born artist Bas Jan Ader, who lived in Los Angeles in the early 1970s, sought self-transformation through performance. He studied both art and philosophy and was particularly drawn to Georg Hegel, whose book *The Phenomenology of Mind* he took with him on his failed attempt to cross the Atlantic Ocean in a small boat. Hegel, in brief, writes of "the development from soul to mind and discovery of the absolute and true knowledge with the aim of becoming at one with it."[71] However, potentially harmful as they were, Ader's short, filmed performances display a certain romantic, even slapstick, whimsy—more Buster Keaton than Evel Knievel. Several works involve falling. In *Fall I, Los Angeles* (1970; fig. 1.73), filmed by William Leavitt, Ader attempts, unsuccessfully, to sit on a chair balanced on the peaked roof of his house. In *Fall II, Amsterdam,* made the same year, he rides his bike into a canal. Each film, only seconds long, ends abruptly at the end of the fall. Ader's interest was not in body art per se, but in submitting himself to natural forces, such as gravity. In the recent monograph of Ader's work, Erik Beenker posits several associations the artist might have had with fall—from the biblical to the personal (his father was killed by a firing squad of German soldiers during World War II).[72]

Stephen Laub, who had been a student of Jim Melchert at UC Berkeley, used his body in a unique series of performances that involved aligning himself with a life-size, projected photographic image from his family's album (fig. 1.74). Laub literally steps into the shoes—male and female—of relatives and friends, many of whom he never knew because his family fled Berlin at the beginning of World War II with not much more than their photo albums. Where Laub used his body in a project about "personal identity and social history," Wegman, whose early videos were made in Los Angeles during the short time he lived there, used his to more humorous effect.[73] In many of his early video performances, he positions his lips and moves his stomach to assume various comical roles.

Not all body art took the form of performance. During the time he lived in Los Angeles (1963–74), David Hammons made a series of body prints, which, although they had a performative aspect as part of their creation, were essentially works on paper that bore the imprint of the artist's grease-covered body. Hammons often printed multiple impressions on a single sheet, moving his body as he came into contact with a board or paper, or sometimes adding pigment or collage elements. In execution, but not in purpose, these body prints relate to Yves Klein's *Anthropométries,* although, unlike Klein, Hammons usually used his own body to assume various identities: a rabbi in one, the Black Panther Bobby Seale tied to a chair (as he was during the trial of the Chicago Eight) in another. Several prints include depictions of a spade in its multiple meanings, a defiant reference to the derogatory term for African Americans.[74] Often the figure is cloaked in the American flag, as in *Pray for America* (1974; fig. 1.72), a bitter reminder of the broken promise of racial equality in this country. As Holland Cotter wrote, these prints contain "a distinctive mix of popular graphics, black vernacular art, performance art and the emotional weight of Goya's prints. Humor, particularly in satirical riffs on ethnic stereotyping, prevents clear-cut reading. Yet the simple fact that the imprinted bodies are black bodies, and self-portraits, makes the racial politics volatile and profound."[75]

Fig. 1.74 Stephen Laub, *Relations (My father and a friend from school),* 1970–73. Performance documentation.

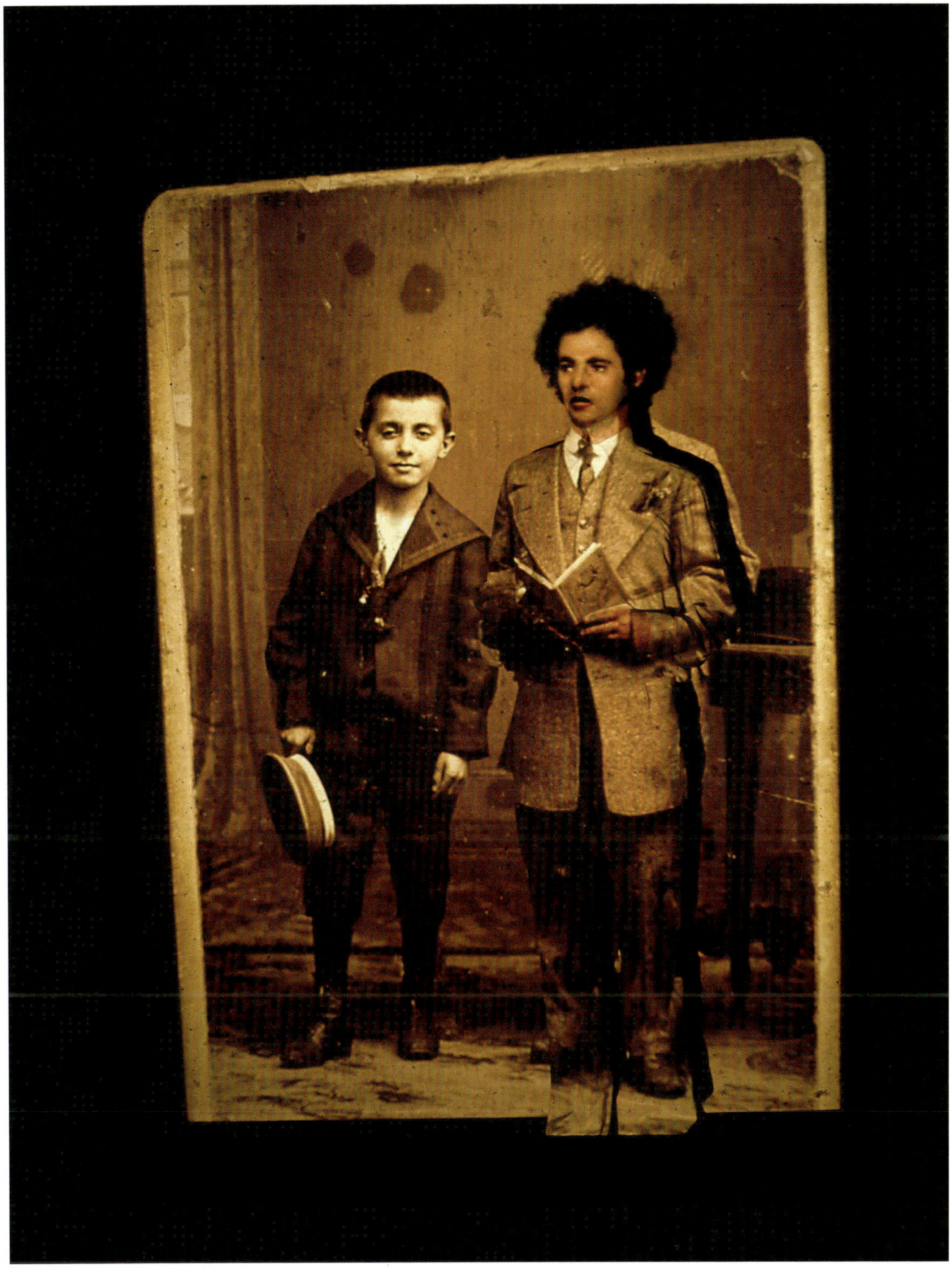

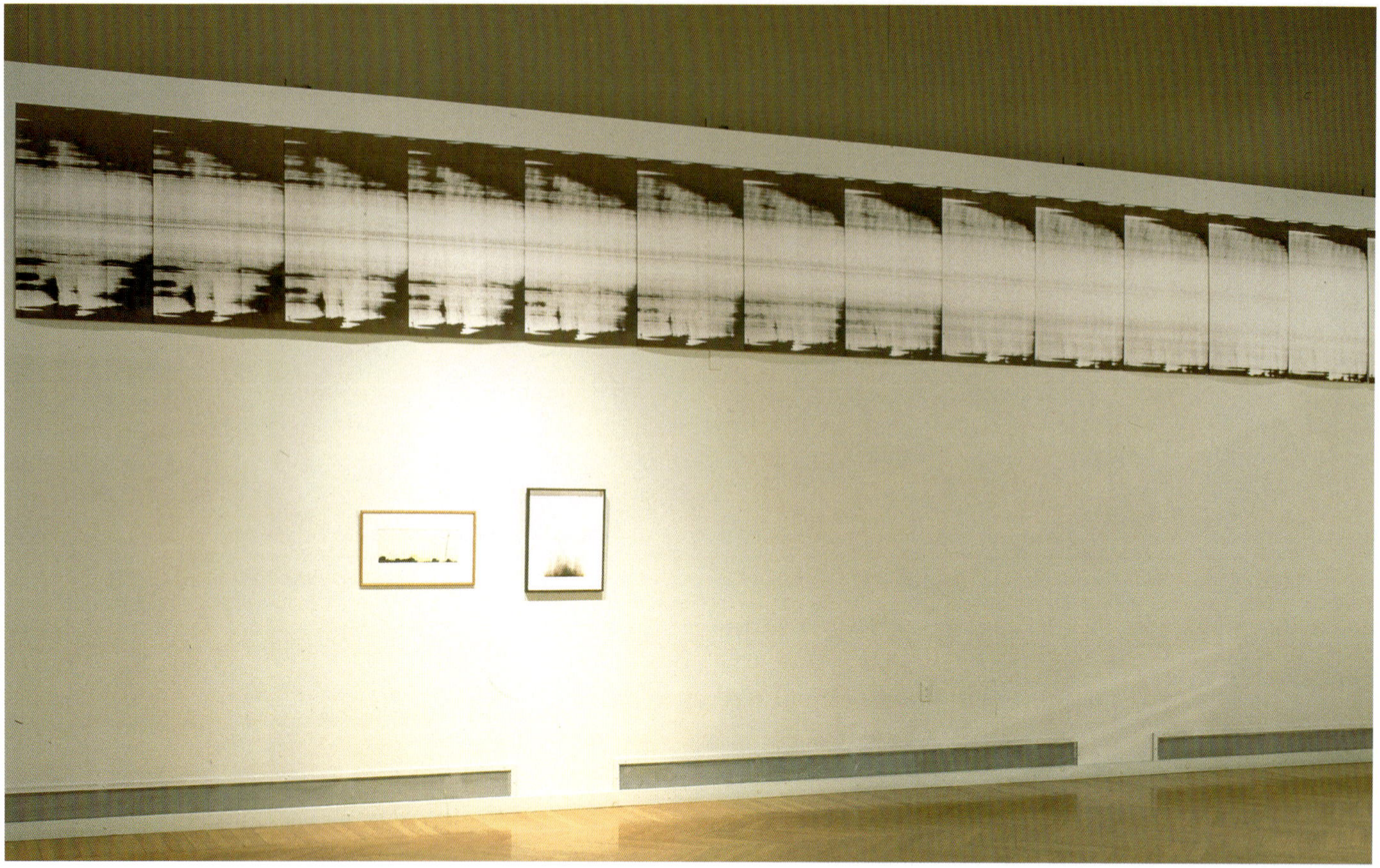

ART ABOUT ART / THE ARTISTIC PROCESS

One of the touchstones of Conceptual art, at least at its beginning stage, is that the process of art making is the art, and so the resulting object is simply a record of that activity. Marioni makes this point in *Process Print* (1969; fig. 1.75). The work consists of approximately thirty-four sheets of paper that the artist ran through a commercial offset lithography press with brown ink. Since the metal plate was devoid of an image, the gradual buildup of brown ink made a continuous filmstrip-like image. The first sheet was solid brown; the last, white. The artist sees this as "an installation work that has the visual effect of a landscape."[76]

The kinetic properties of natural materials like fire and ice were the subject of much of the early 1970s works of San

Fig. 1.75 Tom Marioni, *Process Print*, 1969. Approximately thirty-four offset lithographs; 24 × 30 in. each.

Fig. 1.76 Terry Fox, *Untitled*, 1970–71. Wood matchstick and glue on fiberboard (four sheets); 14 × 11 in. each; 22 × 61⅛ in. overall.

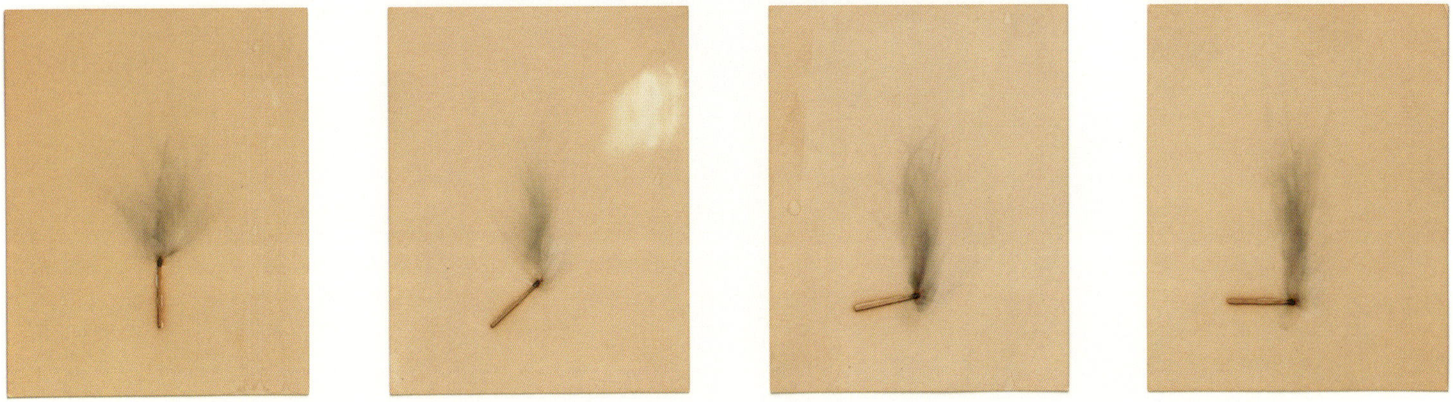

Francisco artist Paul Kos. These pieces included a series of process sculptures involving the flow of melting ice as well as installations such as *Sand Piece* (1971), in which Kos poured a ton of sand on the top floor of a gallery and let it filter through a small hole over a period of days (like an hourglass) to form a craterlike mound on the floor below. In *Sound of Ice Melting* (1970), eight live boom microphones connected to an amplifier were set up to record the sound of two large blocks of ice melting. Although the piece is silent, Kos worked with Richard Beggs, a professional sound engineer, to establish credibility. An absurdist proposition that can be understood in Buddhist terms, Kos's installation premiered in *Sound Sculpture As* at the Museum of Conceptual Art (MOCA) in San Francisco, one of the first sound exhibitions anywhere. Kos shared with Arte Povera artists—working at the same time in Italy—an interest in process-oriented sculptural works made up of unconventional, often organic, materials. He observed that many of his peers in Northern California, including Terry Fox, "liked to use objects and materials for their indigenous characteristics . . . the use of ice as a temporary object or gravity and sand falling." This more personal and local approach was in contrast to that of artists on the East Coast, "who, more aware of what was timely, directed their works toward the art world."[77] In a never-before-seen four-part work on paper from 1970–71, Fox ignited four wooden matches and placed each of them on a sheet of paper (fig. 1.76). In this way, the smoky residue fixed the ephemerality of fire. Kos also made a series of videos during his annual summer trip to his native Wyoming, including a mesmerizing Super-8 film from 1971 in which he evokes the cowboy as he attempts to rope Boar's Tusk, a volcanic plug, which in reality stood miles away (fig. 1.78). Growing up in a landscape of desert plains, buttes, mountains, and lakes, Kos developed a close relationship with nature and is one of the artists who best exemplifies the synchronicity of art and life.

The process of painting is the subject of Jim Melchert's slide transparency sequence, *Changing Walls* (1971; figs. 1.79–1.82). Eighty-one slides, projected life-size, portray artist Howard Fried painting a wall red from floor to ceiling. In the end, the surface turns out not to be a wall at all, but a sheet of paper, which the artist peels away before the sequence repeats. On one level, the piece is about creation and destruction—"this is what artists do," Melchert observed in a recent interview.[78] It also reads as a comment on the performative aspect of Abstract Expressionist painting, although Melchert deliberately chose an artist who was not a painter so that he wouldn't get too involved in the medium. However, the process is of paramount importance here, and, by extension, applies to art making in general.

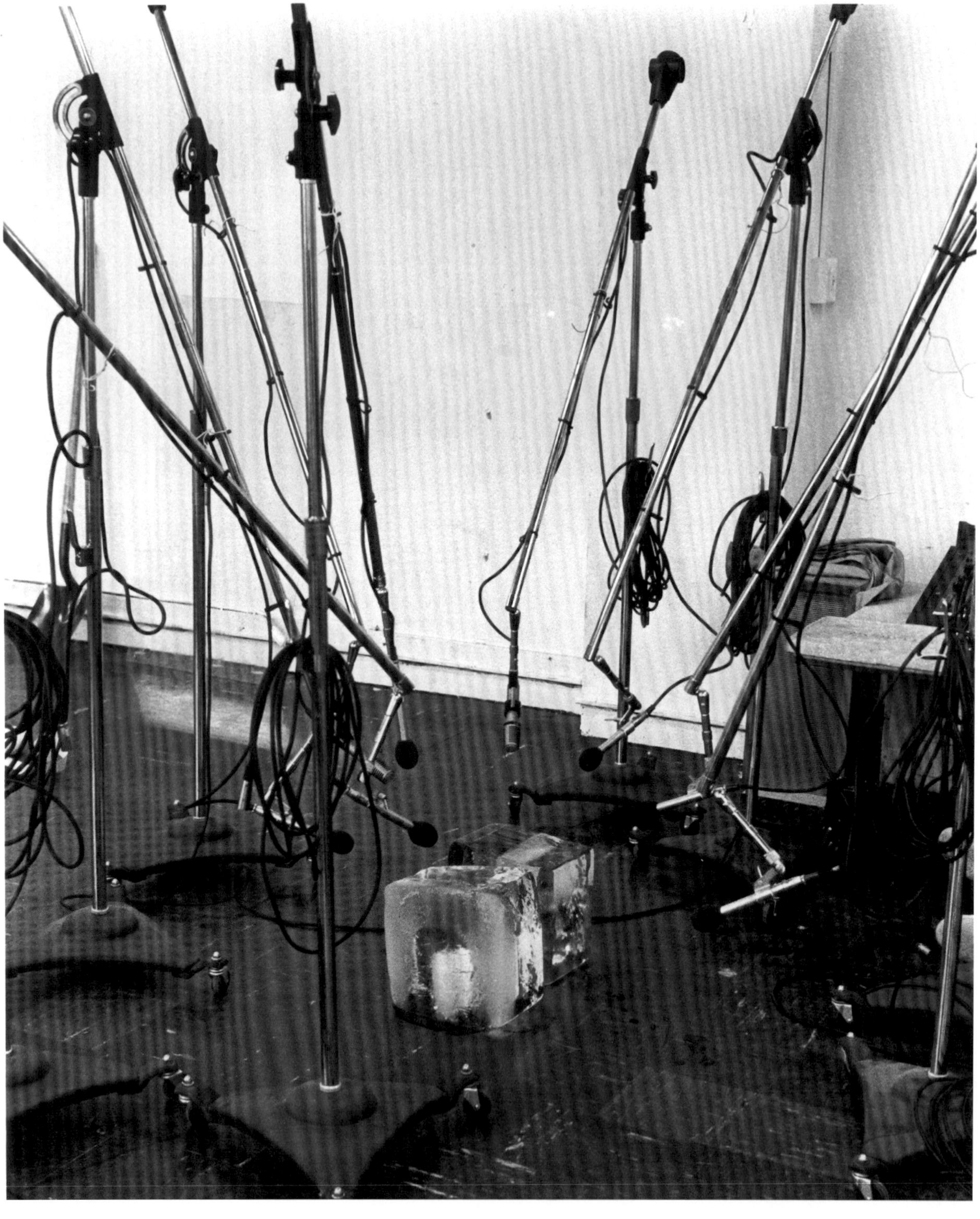

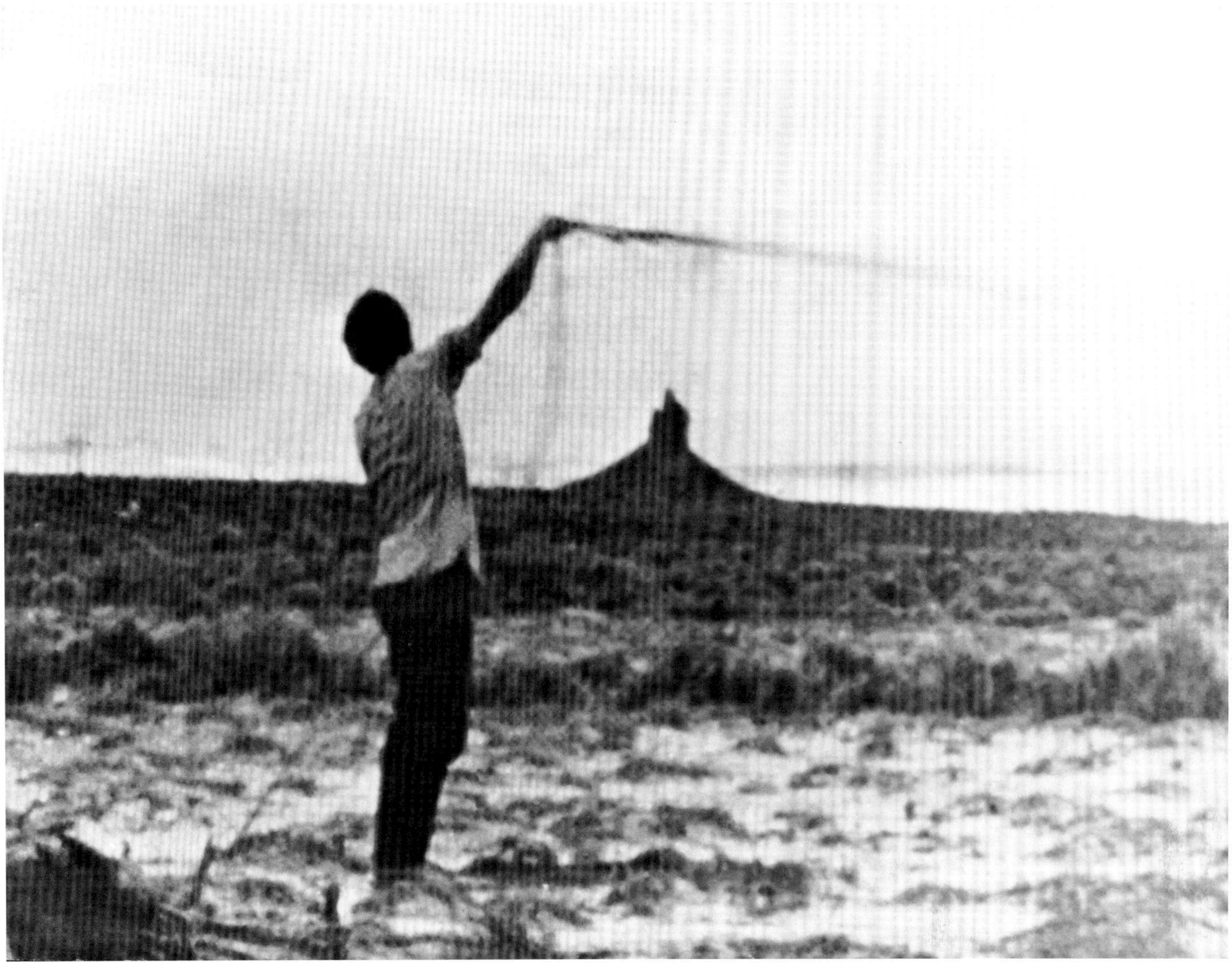

Fig. 1.77 Paul Kos, *Sound of Ice Melting,* 1970. Installation view from *Sound Sculpture As,* April 30, 1970, Museum of Conceptual Art (MOCA), San Francisco; installation with two 25-lb. blocks of ice, eight boom microphone stands, mixer, amplifier, two large speakers, and cables; 78 × 240 × 180 in.

Fig. 1.78 Paul Kos, *Roping Boar's Tusk,* 1971. Super-8 film transferred to video; one-min. loop.

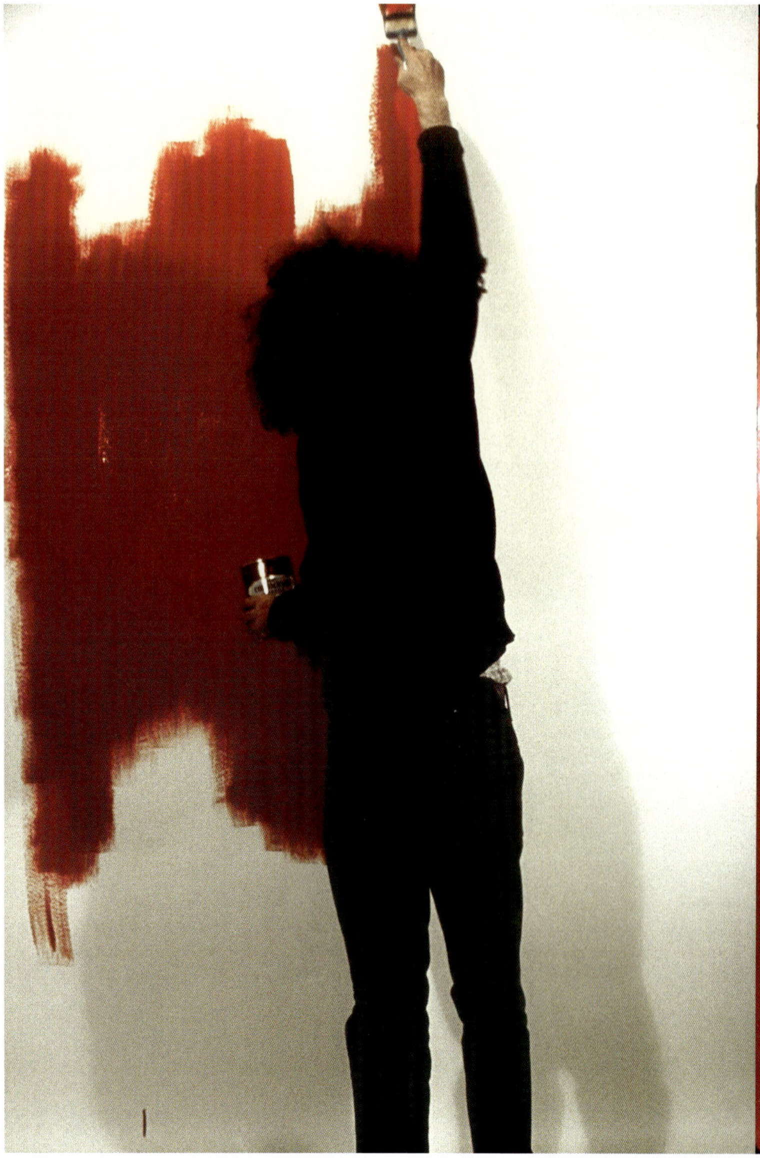
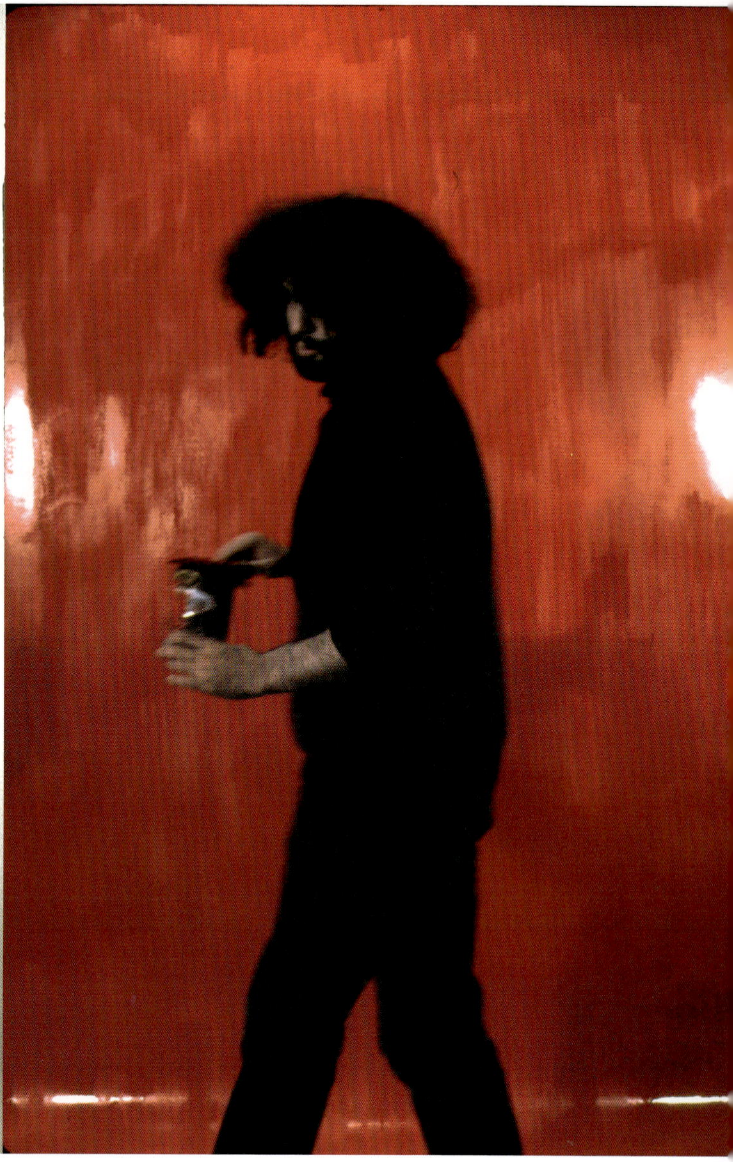

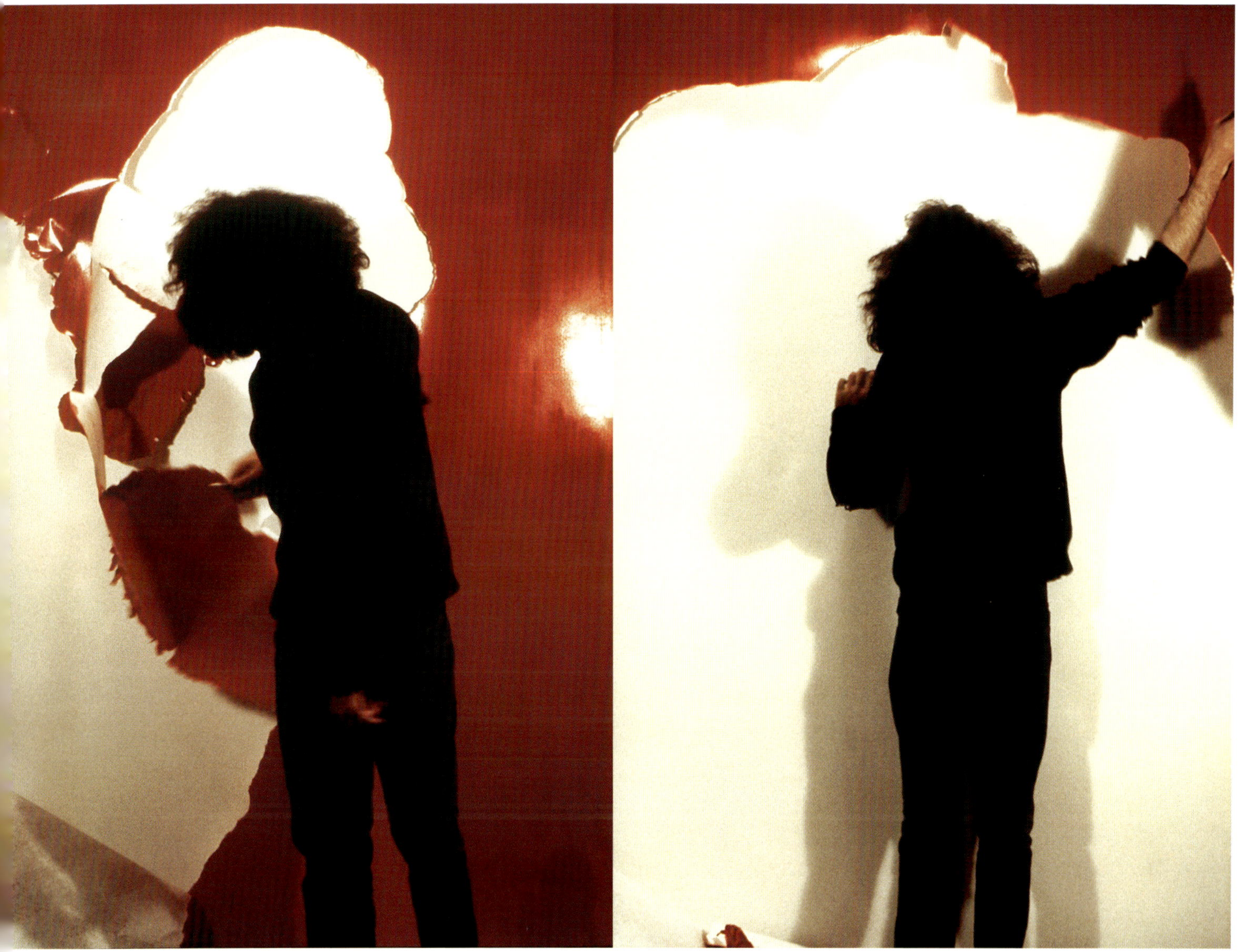

Figs. 1.79–1.82 Jim Melchert, *Changing Walls* (detail; participant: Howard Fried), 1971. Eighty-one 35mm slides and timed projection; 5:24 min.; 84 × 56 in.

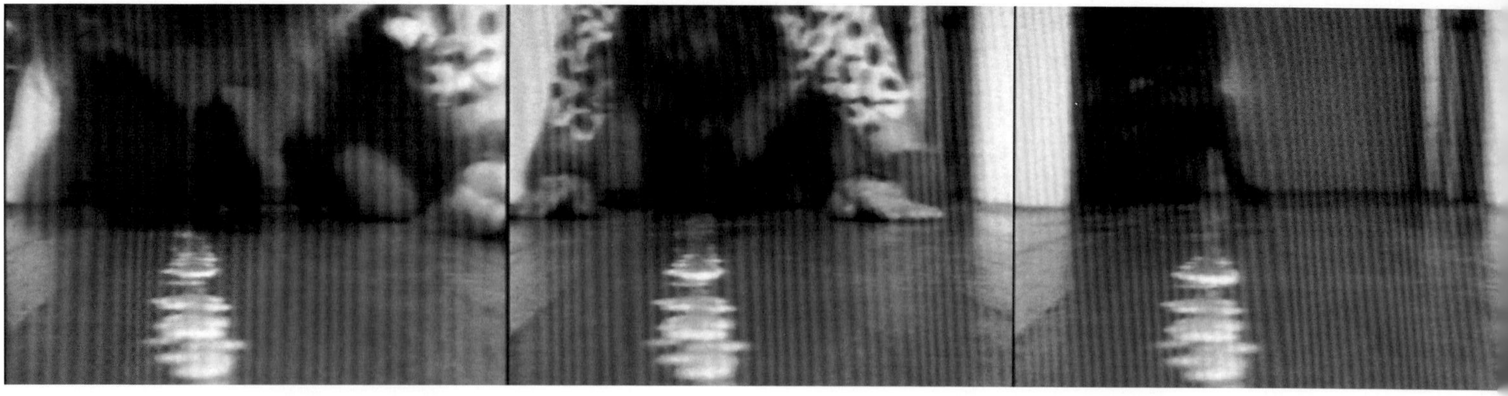

Painting is also the subject of several of McCarthy's *Black and White Tapes* (1970–75) (see fig. 1.67, p. 80). In one video, a nod to Nam June Paik's *Zen for Head* (1962), itself an interpretation of La Monte Young's *Composition 1960 #10* (for Robert Morris), McCarthy creates a white paint trail on his studio floor by pushing a can of paint with his head and torso. Here, the artist replaces the brush; the maker and the process are one. In other videos, he parodies the Abstract Expressionist gesture by flinging a paint-soaked blanket against the walls of his studio and by painting a windshield with his penis. Wegman references both McCarthy and Paik in *Milk/Floor* (1970; fig. 1.83), one of his early video skits. On hands and knees, Wegman slithers backward across the floor, spitting milk in a continuous line until he disappears around a corner. A moment later, his indomitable Weimaraner Man Ray retraces this trajectory in reverse and laps up the milk. In another work about the act of painting, a 1971 photograph titled simply *Artist* (fig. 1.84), Wegman, as the hapless painter, is shown sitting on the floor and holding a wide brush, which has presumably just created the swath of dark paint around his lips (so that they resemble the exaggerated mouth of a clown) and similarly marked a small sheet of paper on the wall. Which came first is not clear—is the artist the artwork or the creator?

Just as some Conceptual artists created works about the act of painting, Los Angeles–based filmmakers Gary Beydler and Morgan Fisher made Structuralist films that take as their subject the process of filmmaking. Beydler created an idiosyncratic portrayal of place with a painstaking and highly personal approach to cinema in two breathtaking Structuralist films, *Pasadena Freeway Stills* (1974; fig. 1.85) and *Venice Pier* (1976; figs. 1.86–1.88). In the former, he filmed as he rode through four tunnels on the oldest freeway in the state. He then made 1,400 paper prints from the 16 mm film stock negative frames. Next, he explained, "I mounted a piece of glass in my garage, with a square of tape marked out on it. I sat down behind the glass with a white T-shirt on and started shooting the stills. My wife Sarah shot the first part, and as the shots got shorter and shorter, I shot myself using a bulb hooked up to the camera that I operated with my foot." About the work, film historian Mark Toscano says, "Possibly the most lucid, vivid, and awesome demonstration of the building up of still images to create moving ones, *Pasadena Freeway Stills* simply, gracefully and powerfully shows us the process by which we are fooled by the movies." He continues, "The film is a beautiful articulation of our emotional entanglement with moving images, while simultaneously creating a form in which the illusion of cinema is brought into incredible relief as the film we're watching gradually catches up to the film Gary is holding up to the

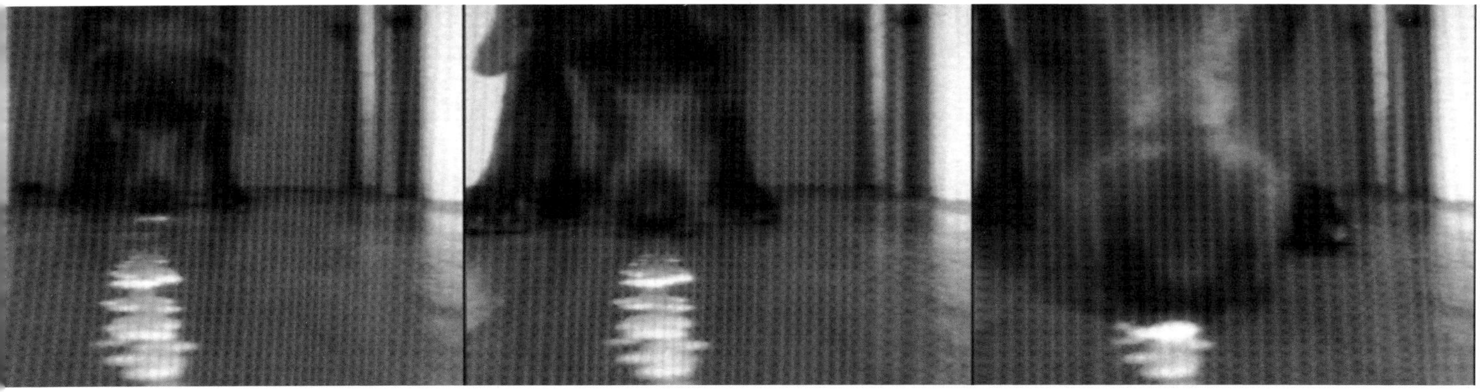

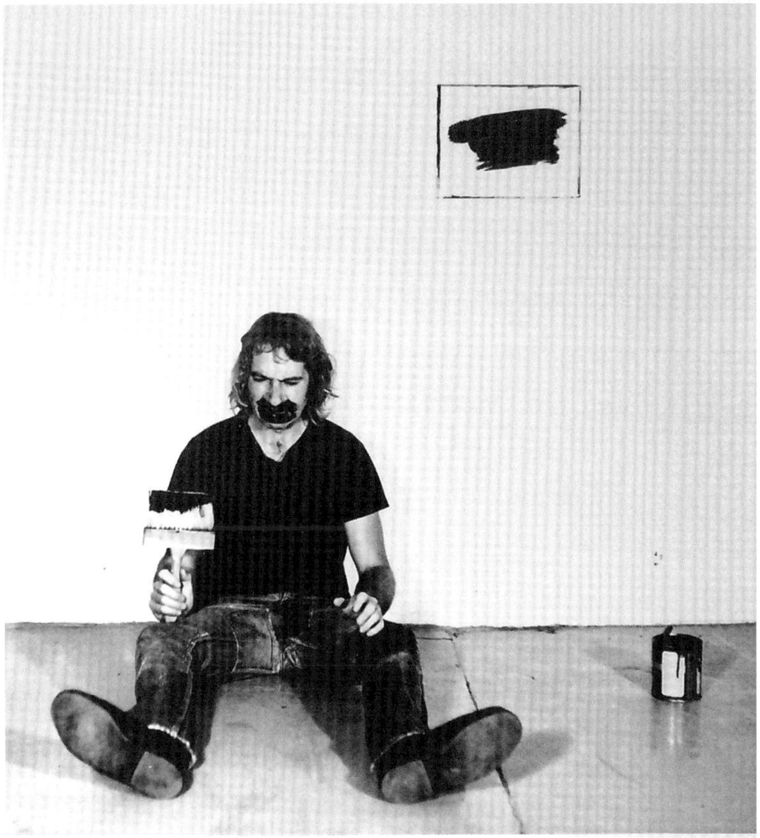

Fig. 1.83 William Wegman, *Milk/Floor,* 1970, from *Selected Works from 1970–78.* Video: black and white and color; 19:11 min.

Fig. 1.84 William Wegman, *Artist,* 1971. Black-and-white photograph; 14 × 11 in.

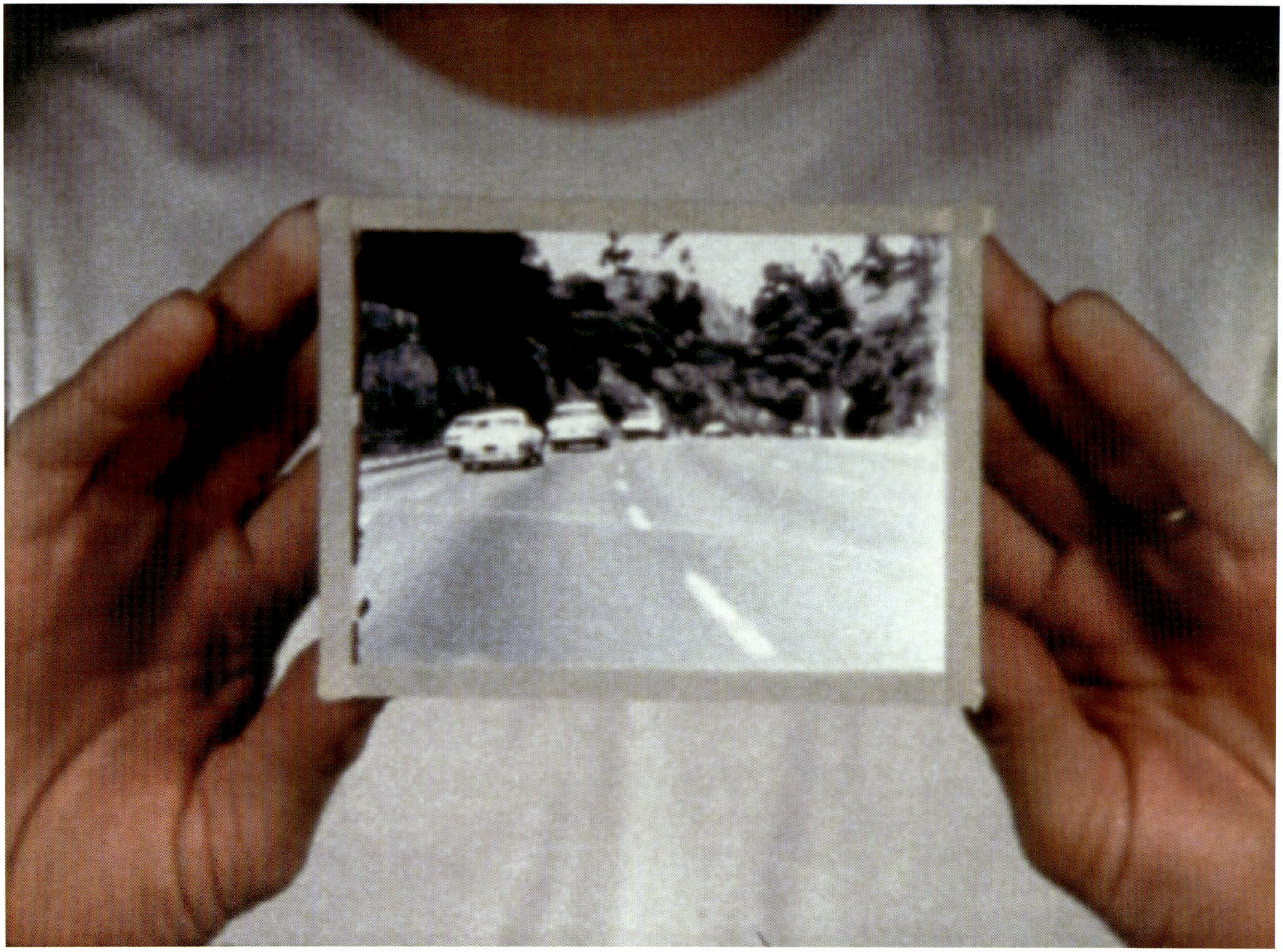

Fig. 1.85 Gary Beydler, *Pasadena Freeway Stills,* 1974. 16 mm film; color; silent; 6 min.

camera with his hands, one frame at a time."[79]

Venice Pier is a simpler, though no less affecting, construct. Over the span of a year, Beydler filmed at ten-foot intervals from the pier as it extends into the ocean and then spliced the segments together in a spatial, rather than temporal, order. The resulting film takes viewers down the pier through various seasons and hours—from a bright afternoon when crowds of people walk, bike, and buy food at the snack bar, to gloomy winter mornings when the pier is devoid of human activity—and ends with a dazzling time-lapse view of the sun setting over the ocean.

Fisher's film *Picture and Sound Rushes* (1973) seemingly embraces the commercial film industry by using some of its terms, but it also contradicts that embrace (see fig. 4.12, p. 236). And the disruptions that the film's construction produces—the disappearance of picture, of sound, and of both—subvert the smooth perfection of the films that the industry makes.

Other artists up and down the state critiqued art institutions, art criticism, or the whole enterprise of making art, often using humor as a strategy. Sometimes this took the form of sight gags (van Elk, Wegman); other times, it was wordplay and puns (Nauman, Kos, Cotton), which had roots in the previous generation of Bay Area "Funk" artists like William T. Wiley and Robert Arneson. It might be deadpan (Ruscha), slapstick (McCarthy), satiric (Mogul, Segalove), absurd (Kos, Wegman), or based on incongruous juxtapositions (Cumming, Wegman). East Coast Conceptualists disdained humor, taking it for lack of gravitas, but, to the contrary, wit can mask deadly serious content. No one has used it to greater effect than Baldessari, whose humor derives from the slightly askew way he views the world and the spirit of play with which he approaches it. Baldessari makes free use of puns, absurdist juxtapositions, and game playing to stimulate new ways of looking not only at art but also at the world. In several works, including the 1973 artist books *Throwing Three Balls in the Air to Get a Straight Line (Best of Thirty-six Attempts;* fig. 2.41, pp. 180–81) and *Throwing a Ball Once to Get Three Melodies and Fifteen Chords,* he tries—against the odds—to create an arbitrary order (to his mind, all systems of ordering are arbitrary). In *Voluble Luminist Painting for Max Kozloff* (1966–68; fig. 1.89), one of his text paintings executed by a sign painter, he pokes fun at art critical discourse by appropriating out of context phrases such as "illusionist space," "lyricism/diffidence," and, more enigmatically, "subterranean pictorial life" from an *Artforum* article written by Max Kozloff. In his video *I Am Making Art* (1971; figs. 1.90–1.92), in which he shifts body positions, repeating at each pose the phrase "I am making art," he pokes irreverent fun at the Duchampian claim adopted by Conceptual artists that art is defined by the artist. He might also have been thinking of Nauman's oft-repeated assertion that whatever an artist does in the studio is art. To the complaint heard by many viewers in regard to early, unedited videotapes, in his own 1971 video, Baldessari covers a blackboard with the phrase *I Will Not Make Any More Boring Art,* subverting the message by doing exactly the opposite.

Humor and subterfuge were strategies for the collective T. R. Uthco. Doug Hall, one of the three members, remembers that they "were looking for other ways of operating that weren't in the tradition, that were completely out of the mainstream." Hall and Jody Procter had been roommates at Harvard, where Hall had begun to experiment with performance, and Diane Andrews Hall, the third member of the group, had graduated from Tulane University with a major in painting and minor in theater. The three moved to San Francisco because "we were fleeing the pretentiousness of the East Coast."[80] They were attracted to the music, the Black Panthers, the counterculture. Hall remembers being elated at hearing Angela Davis speak at the San Francisco Art Institute. The three artists lived and worked communally and began by exploring performance ideas through photography, as in *8 Gestures* (1972; figs. 1.93–1.94). Andrews Hall directed Hall and Procter in a series of gestures that were disconnected from any context and suggestive of, but not tied to, a specific

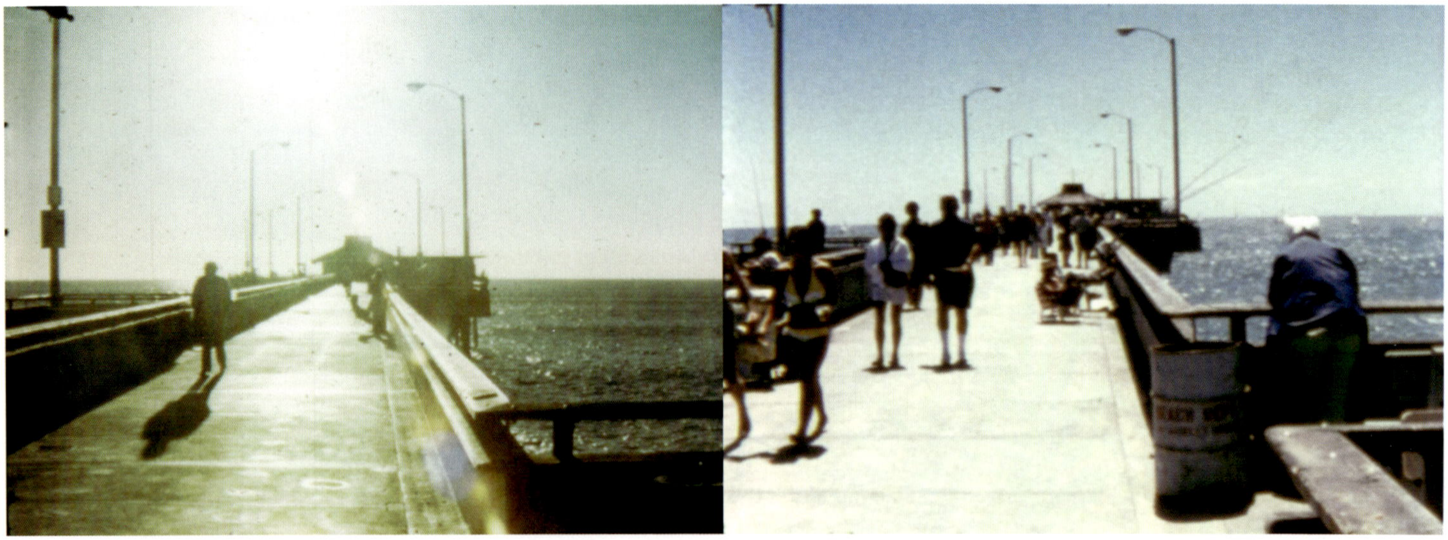

narrative. These photographs were not performance documents like Montano's photographs of her *Chicken Dances,* for example, but documents of studio events, like Wegman's *Artist* or Nauman's *Self-Portrait as a Fountain* (1966–67).

Although Conceptual photography was primarily identified with artists in Los Angeles, such as Baldessari, Cumming, Ruscha, and Wegman, the Bay Area also had practitioners, such as the team of Larry Sultan and Mike Mandel. In nearly all cases, the subject of Conceptual photography, as practiced by Californians, is the importance of context in how a photograph is understood. Sultan and Mandel's 1974 book *How To Read Music in One Evening* is a precursor to *Evidence* (1977), their groundbreaking book of appropriated and recontextualized photographs (see fig. 1.37, p. 50). The earlier volume depicts groupings of "how to" illustrations taken from comic books and low-end popular magazines. With texts excised and juxtapositions altered, images of such oddities as electric neck warmers and mechanical nose-hair trimmers suggest bizarre narratives and are a wry comment on how images acquire meaning.

Like T. R. Uthco, Robert Cumming, who moved to Southern California from Wisconsin in 1970 around the same time as his friend Bill Wegman, made photographs in his studio, but his works highlight the mutability of photographic meaning, or what he calls "perceptual glitches."[81] Influenced by movie stills he found in Hollywood and specifically the camera's ability to create the illusion of reality from slipshod constructions of ordinary materials, he devised a miniature studio "back lot" on which he built various sets. He describes the resulting "constructed" or "fabricated" photographs, an innovative approach for the time, as "a mixture of perceptual experiment, meditation on reality, while some just tinkered with logic."[82] The inspiration for *Ansel Adams Raisin Bread* (1973; fig. 1.95) was an anecdote about Ansel Adams, who, the story goes, while shooting an ad for raisin bread noticed that the raisins didn't look right. To make them appear more realistic, he inserted fresh raisins into white bread. Cumming found Adams's willingness to fake reality amusing in light of Adams's devotion to "straight" photography. In his diptych, Cumming

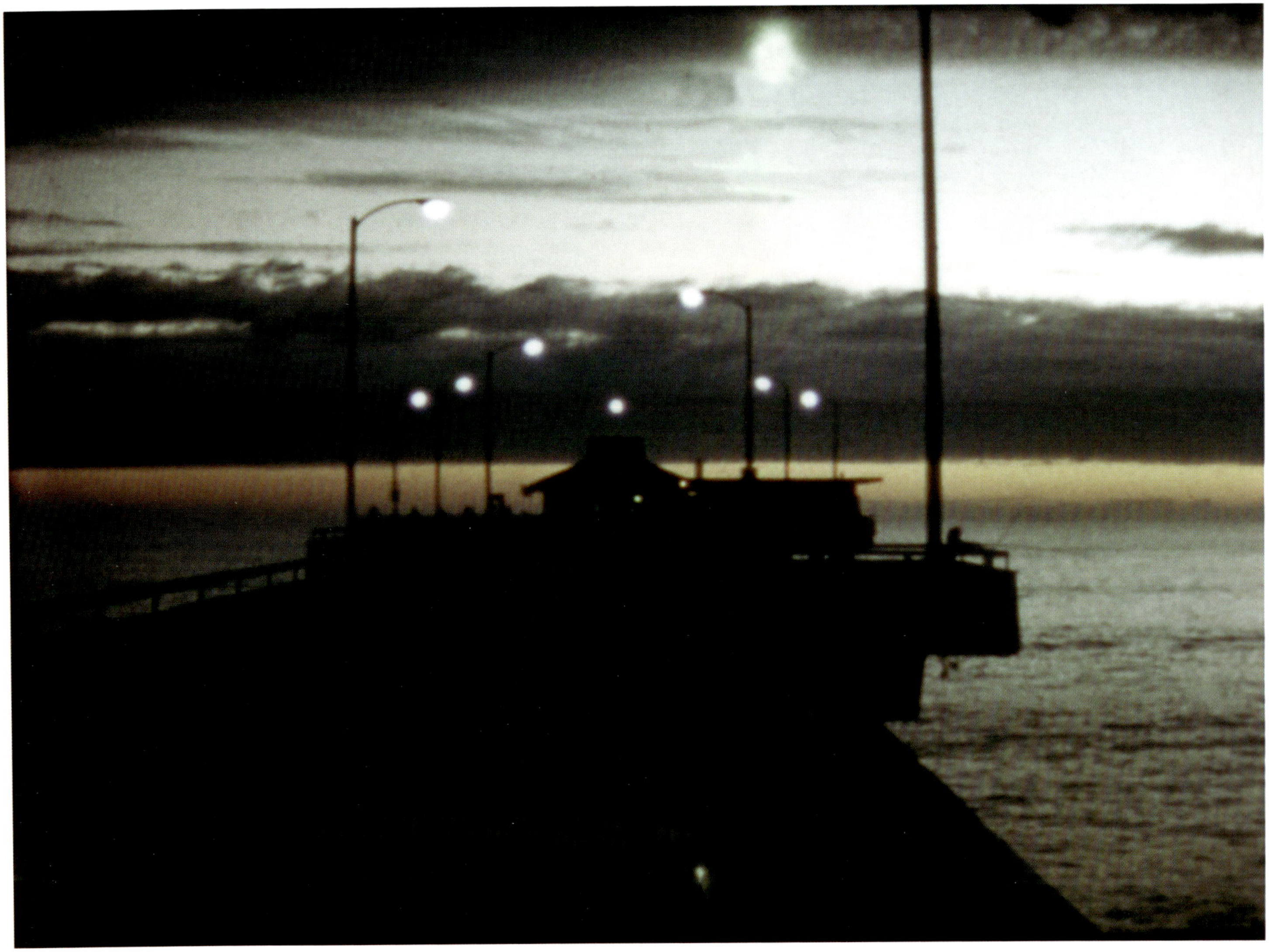

Figs. 1.86–1.88 Gary Beydler, *Venice Pier,* 1976. 16 mm film; color; sound; 16 min.

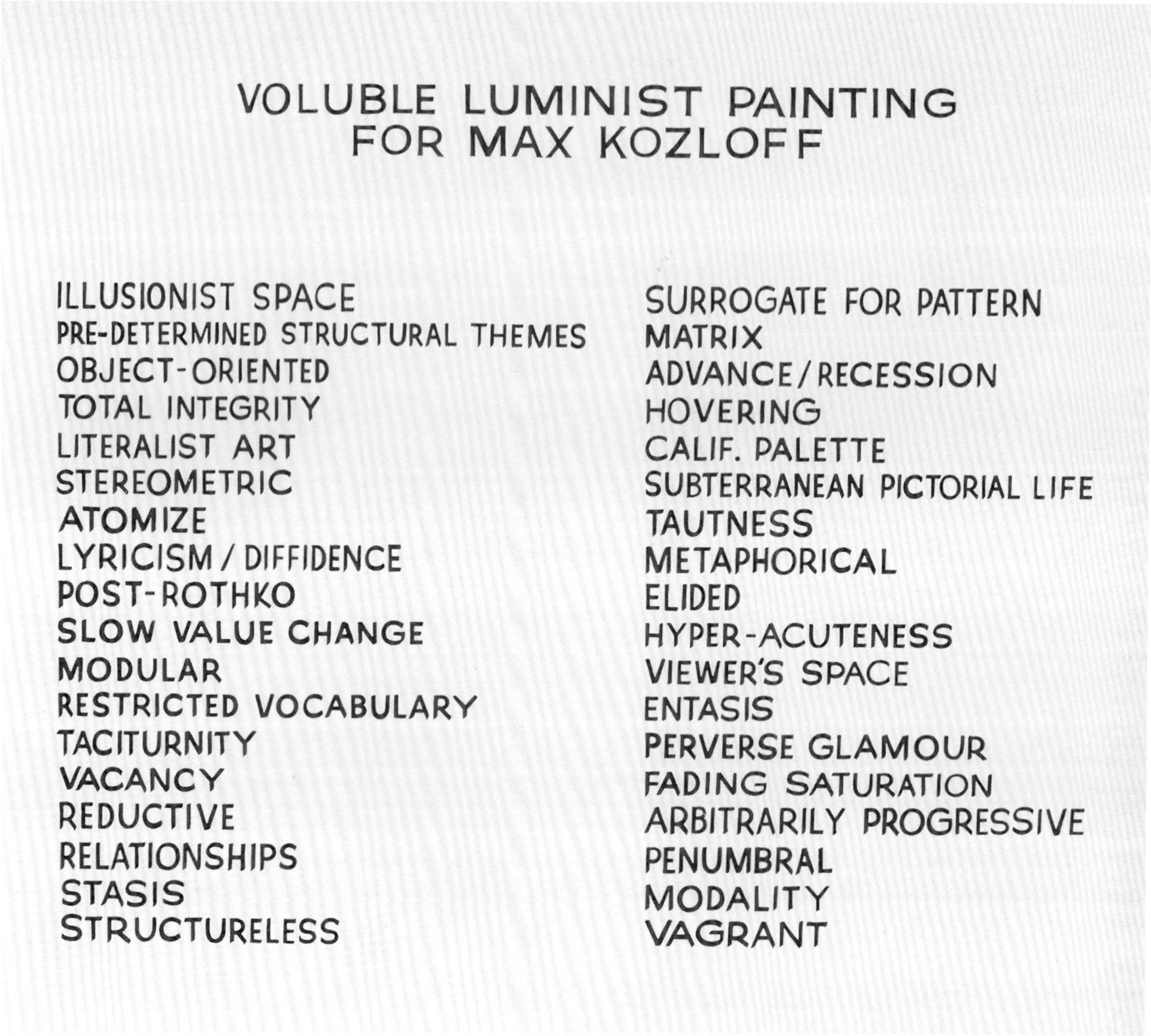
VOLUBLE LUMINIST PAINTING
FOR MAX KOZLOFF
ILLUSIONIST SPACE
PRE-DETERMINED STRUCTURAL THEMES
OBJECT-ORIENTED
TOTAL INTEGRITY
LITERALIST ART
STEREOMETRIC
ATOMIZE
LYRICISM / DIFFIDENCE
POST-ROTHKO
SLOW VALUE CHANGE
MODULAR
RESTRICTED VOCABULARY
TACITURNITY
VACANCY
REDUCTIVE
RELATIONSHIPS
STASIS
STRUCTURELESS
SURROGATE FOR PATTERN
MATRIX
ADVANCE/RECESSION
HOVERING
CALIF. PALETTE
SUBTERRANEAN PICTORIAL LIFE
TAUTNESS
METAPHORICAL
ELIDED
HYPER-ACUTENESS
VIEWER'S SPACE
ENTASIS
PERVERSE GLAMOUR
FADING SATURATION
ARBITRARILY PROGRESSIVE
PENUMBRAL
MODALITY
VAGRANT

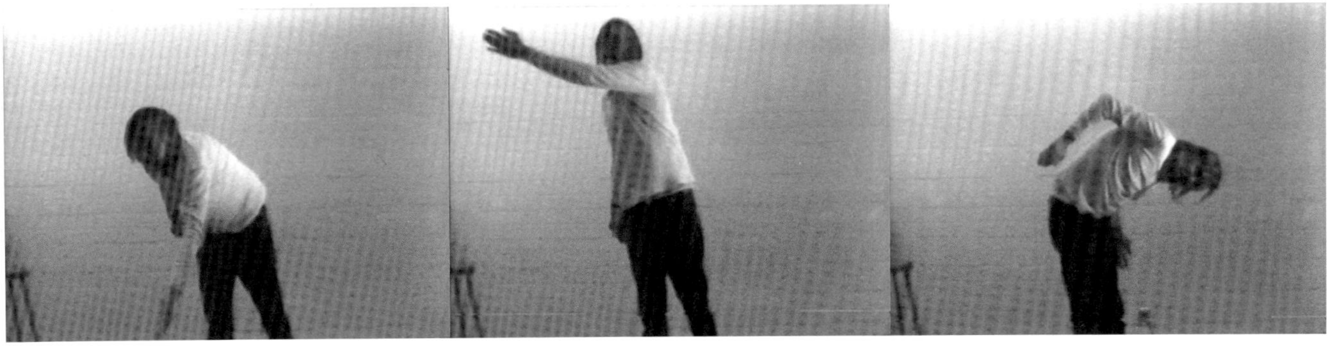

shows real raisin bread in one photo and the altered version in the other. He constructed a table to hold the bread and other objects, which "isn't horizontal but angled up while the edges are slanted back to look like perspective . . . [and] much smaller by more than half its functional counterpart. I was experimenting in those days with how cockeyed you could make an object; in reality you could see the 'prop' as highly abnormal while in a photo, things could look quite proper."[83] The clues to the artifice become apparent in the details: the raisin box is doctored to fit the scene, and what looks like a brick surface is actually contact paper. Cumming shares with Wegman a low-tech and comedic approach that belies a more serious intent—the questioning of photographic veracity and a sly commentary on art making in general.

Art education proliferated in the 1960s. Universities launched or expanded art, as distinct from art history, departments, and art schools swelled their ranks. Having an MA or MFA became de rigueur for artists, many of whom would earn their livings teaching art. (Another source of income was the Individual Artist Fellowship then offered by the National Endowment for the Arts.) It is not surprising, then, that the increased professionalization of art education was a ripe target for critique. In this atmosphere, Lowell Darling established the mail order *Fat City School of Finds Art* out of his Hollywood apartment. Anyone could request a master's degree, and Darling obliged (fig. 1.96). He often traveled to the Bay Area to conduct graduation ceremonies, handing out both masters' and "Doctors of Dada" degrees to one and all.[84] Pedagogy was also the subject of Jim Melchert's performance *Following Instructions* (1971) at the University Art Museum, Berkeley. He and a fellow performer, Dick Burgess, faced the audience and, though unable to see one another, responded to such instructions as "touch all walls" or "take an absurd position" while their actions were relayed on a video monitor.[85] Each performer interpreted the commands differently, exemplifying the subjectivity of interpretation, something Melchert, as a professor, knew only too well.

Fig. 1.89 John Baldessari, *Voluble Luminist Painting for Max Kozloff,* 1966–68. Acrylic on canvas; 59 × 59 in.

Figs. 1.90–1.92 John Baldessari, *I Am Making Art,* 1971. Video: black and white; sound; 18:40 min.

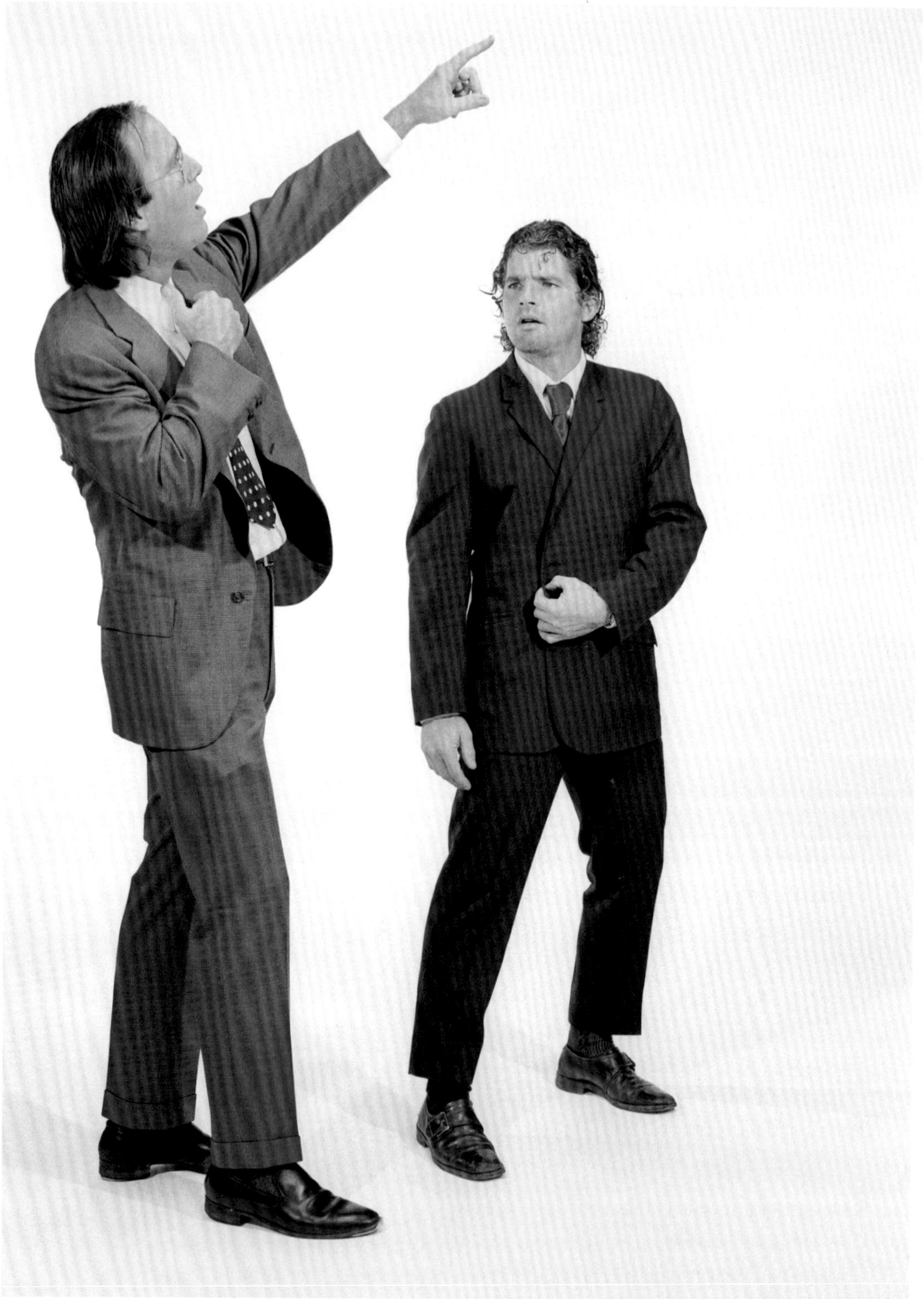

Figs. 1.93–1.94 T. R. Uthco (Doug Hall, Jody Procter, and Diane Andrews Hall), *Gestures 5* and *7*, from *8 Gestures*, 1972. Eight black-and-white photographs; 16 × 12 in. each (largest); 14 × 11 in. each (smallest).

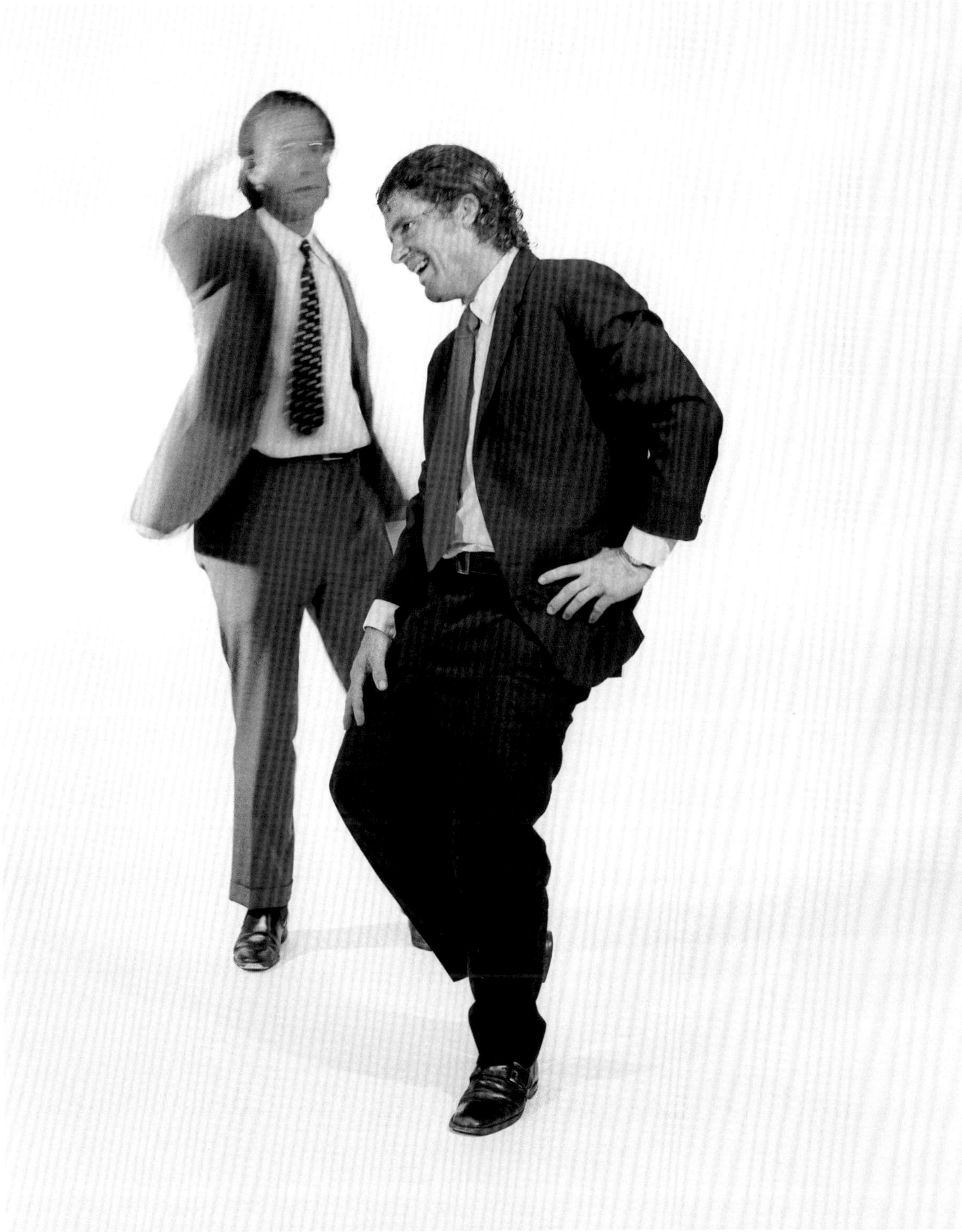

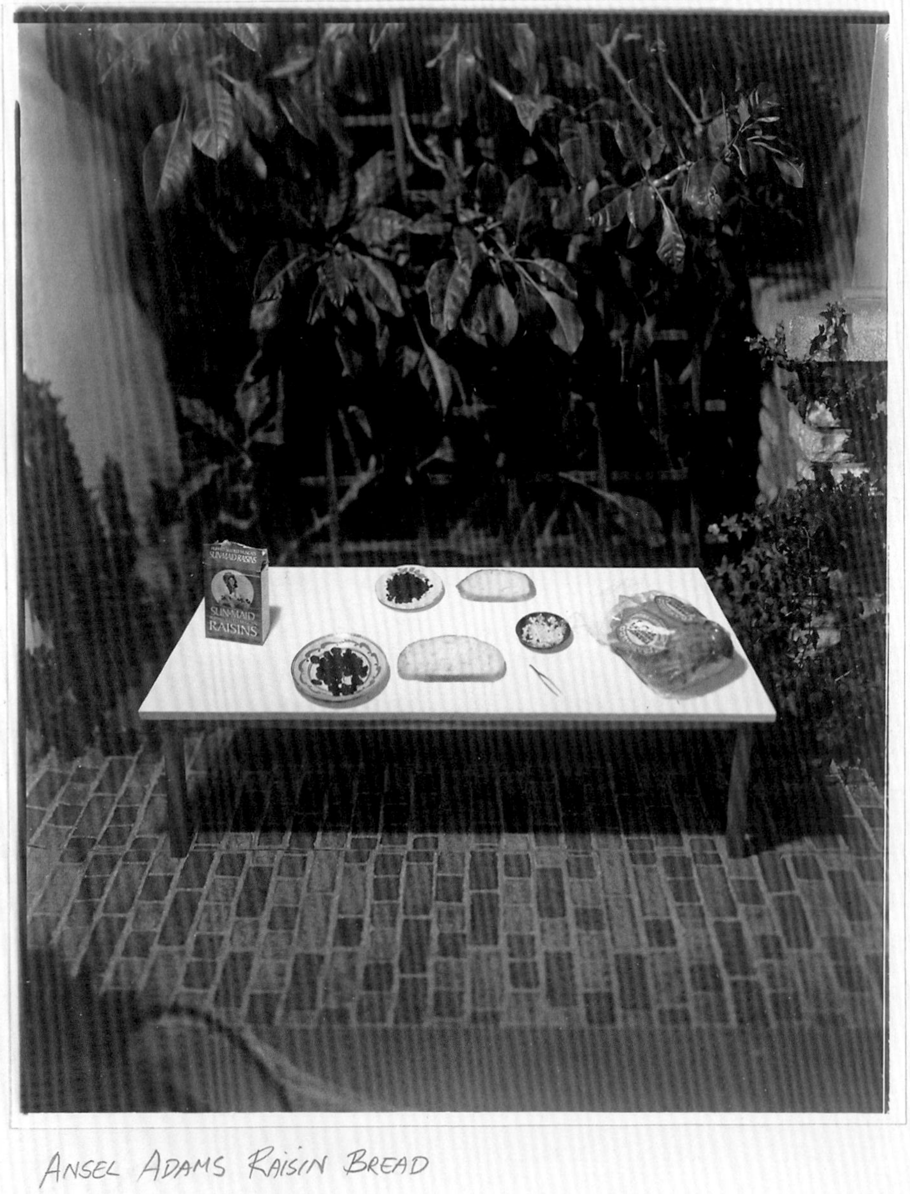

Fig. 1.95 Robert Cumming, *Ansel Adams Raisin Bread,* 1973. Two black-and-white photographs; $9\frac{15}{16} \times 17\frac{3}{8}$ in.

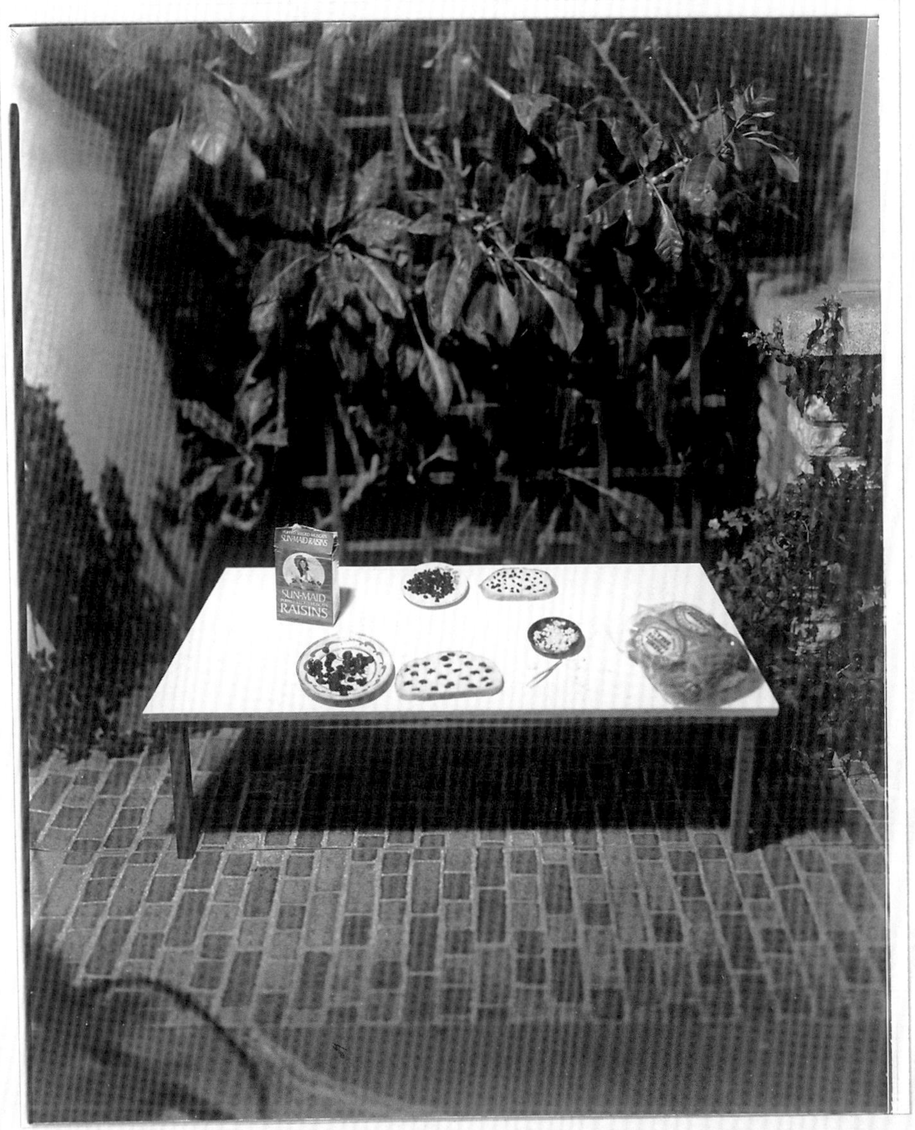

Cummings 1973

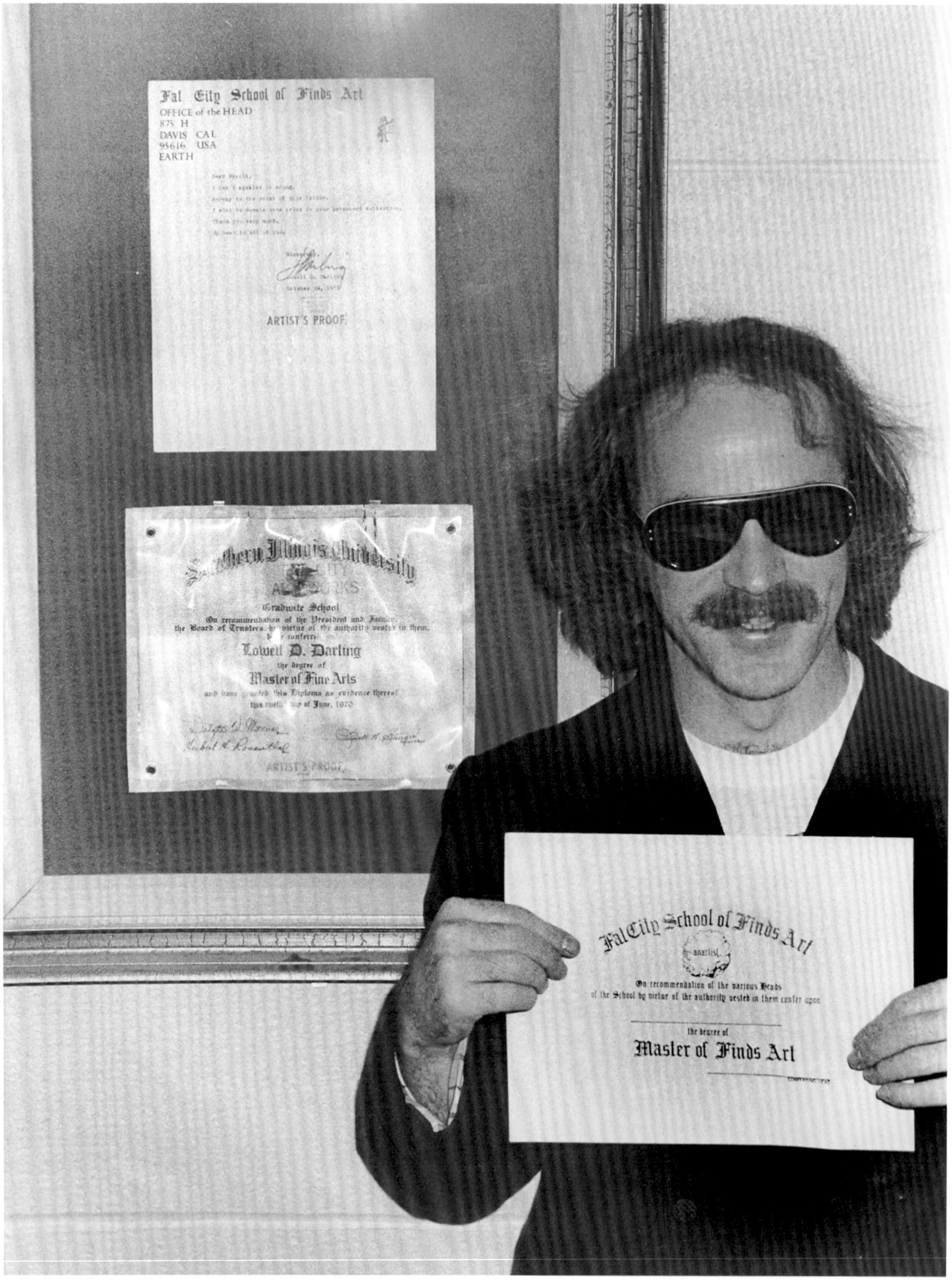
Fat City School of Finds Art
OFFICE of the HEAD
875 H
DAVIS CAL
95616 USA
EARTH
ARTIST'S PROOF
Graduate School
Lowell D. Darling
the degree of
Master of Fine Arts
ARTIST'S PROOF
FatCity School of Finds Art
On recommendation of the various Heads
of the School by virtue of the authority vested in them confer upon
the degree of
Master of Finds Art

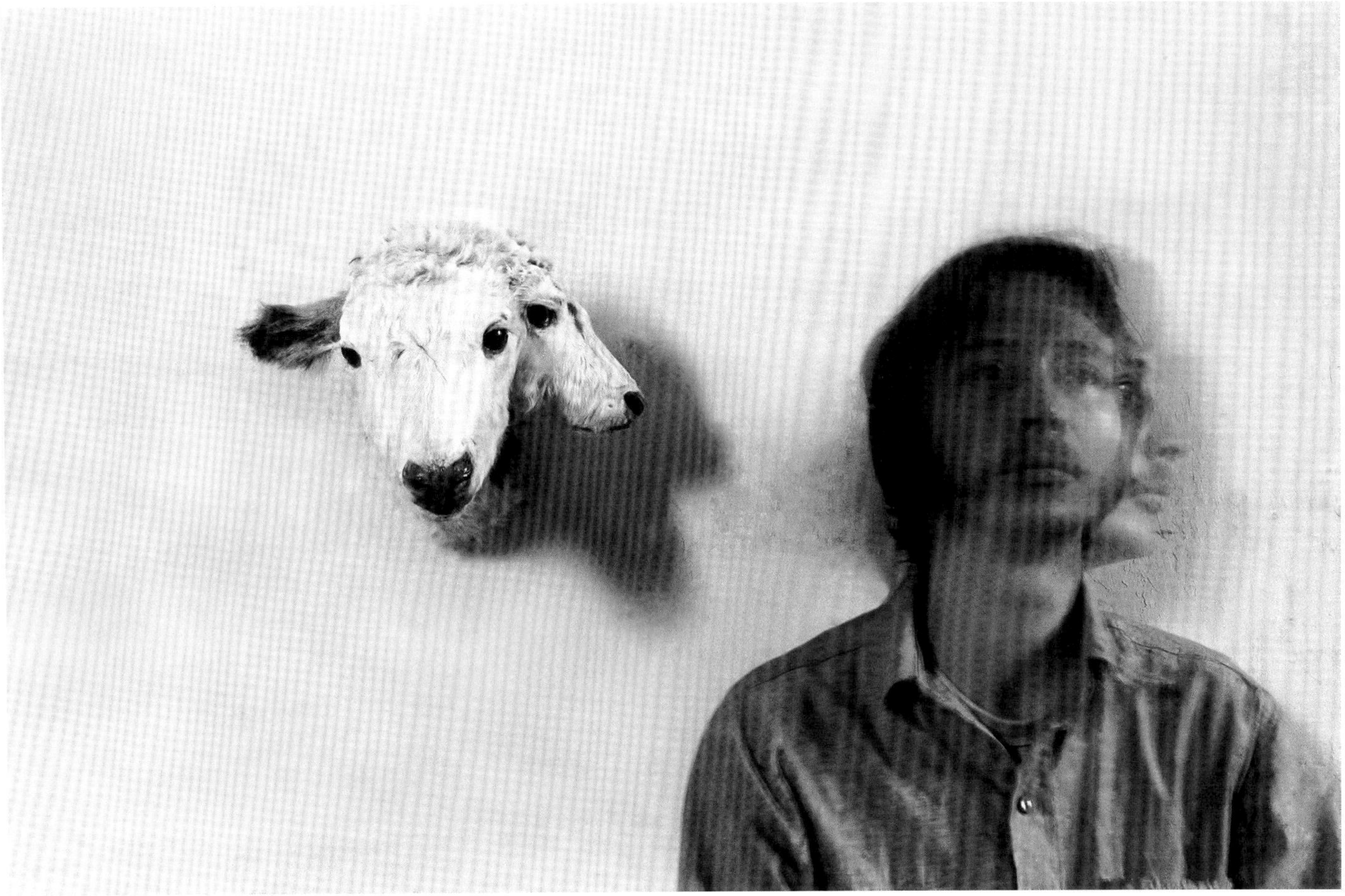

Fig. 1.96 Lowell Darling with *Fat City School of Finds Art* diploma at his alma mater, Southern Illinois University, 1972.

Fig. 1.97 Paul Kos, *A Trophy/Atrophy,* 1971. Video: black and white; sound; 3:08 min.

LANGUAGE AND WORDPLAY

Humor aside, Baldessari is one of the few West Coast artists whose art is informed by linguistic systems and in that sense is related to such rigorous East Coast Conceptualists as Joseph Kosuth.[86] Even in his most banal and comical films—singing Sol LeWitt's foundational *Sentences on Conceptual Art* to such incongruous tunes as "The Star Spangled Banner" in a 1972 video, for example—Baldessari's intent is to probe the relationship between art and language and, like Duchamp before him, to question the very definition of art.[87] Language play, however, was practiced by many—Paul Kos conflates the words "a trophy" and "atrophy" in his eponymous 1971 video (fig. 1.97). In this short piece, Kos attempts to imitate, by moving his head from right to left, a freak two-headed taxidermied calf mounted on the wall beside him. As he speeds up the film, his head blurs into a double image. Concurrently, he exposes the mutability of language as he repeats the words "a trophy" until they shift meaning. Nauman, a frequent punster, also played with the title of his book *Clea Rsky* (1967–68). But no one dabbled with language more elaborately than did Paul Cotton, who, for example, refers to himself as "eye" in describing his appointment with Los Angeles County Museum of Art's then curator Maurice Tuchman on July 28, 1969 (fig. 1.98). Cotton, who presented himself as a living sculpture (his nude body painted white), wrote at the reception desk that the purpose of his visit was "Monk-Key Business" and asked Tuchman to sign his "Docu-Mentation of a Meating" that stated that a living being was more important than any man-made object.[88] French-born Guy de Cointet (1934–83), who lived in Los Angeles from the late 1960s until his untimely death, was interested in troubling the graphic and semantic aspects of language, as in his coded text *A Page from My Intimate Journal (Part 1)* (1974; fig. 1.99). Of all the West Coast artists whose works are centered on language, Charles Gaines is the closest to East Coast and European counterparts, in particular to the work of German artist Hanne Darboven. His 1973–74 *Regression* series consists of hand-drawn gridded pages based on numeric systems (fig. 2.40, p. 179).

Language is also the subject of Robert Cumming's photograph *"A" Structure: Dana Atchley, Ken Friedman, Douglas Huebler, William T. Wiley* (1973; fig. 1.100). For this piece, Cumming built a rickety structure in his backyard and placed on it various enlarged versions of the lowercase letter *a* as written by the four artists in the title. It is one of many of the artist's "penmanship" works, which feature three-dimensional letters as abstract shapes. As with others in his backyard series, Cumming shot the scene at night using floodlights "with an under-scale house façade behind as backdrop."[89] This particular photograph was inspired by an exhibition of Jim Melchert's works that centered on the lowercase *a*. Melchert's show was inspired in turn by Raymond Queneau's 1947 book *Exercises in Style,* in which the author relates the same story in ninety-nine different styles. As Melchert told me in a recent e-mail, "I loved it. In a way my show was a single work that consisted of thirty-some variations, most but not all ceramic. Mine were things like an /a/ made three pounds lighter, 7/8 of an /a/, 'a' flat, etc. In time Cumming sent me a paper on which he'd copied four *a*'s chosen from letters he had happened to receive. He probably used an enlarger to make them so big."[90]

Fig. 1.98 Adam II (the late Paul Cotton), *Docu-Mentation of a Meating,* July 28, 1969, 3:00 P.M.; Lost Angeles County Museum of Art; Creators' proof of the Word Made Flesh meating with Maurice Tuchman who signed a valuation and contract assessing "the essential value of this living human being as greater than any Man-made artifact designated 'art'"; Historical Memo-Random of the Big-inning of the Creators' Dionysian Space Project to Land the First Man on the Earth. Camera: Peter Zecher, courtesy of Trans-Parent Teacher's Ink.

>>
Fig. 1.99 Guy de Cointet, *A Page from My Intimate Journal (Part 1),* 1974. Screenprint; 30 × 22 in.

>>>
Fig. 1.100 Robert Cumming, *"A" Structure: Dana Atchley, Ken Friedman, Douglas Huebler, William T. Wiley,* 1973. Black-and-white photograph; 10 × 8 in.

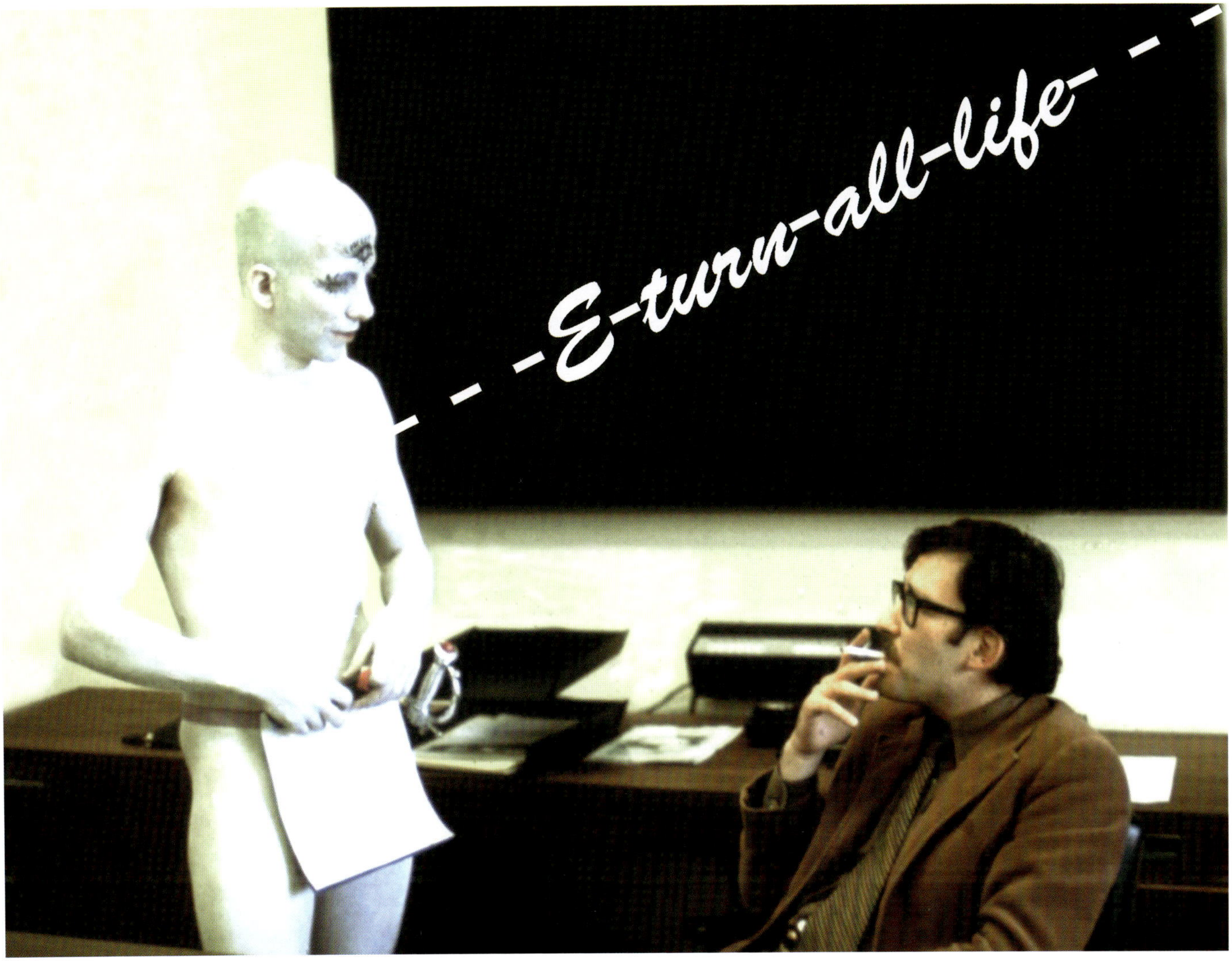
E-turn-all-life

A page from my intimate journal (Part I)

FHETOM...AGUX JY
ZAWR, SPLONV DEHTQ
UNIKMBA HESUR OCE
IR.UE DHAN WENUD,
AVSROLEM?

CEGINABFOW, EEPHN
ISRA TITUMELLOR X
EJYNWHOS L DUPSEG
VAZAC EQOMMEHL.EQ
OMMEHL! FHETO...BU
R KIIX 67 DAGZOR
SEVU AWUNNEF PEYN
IW, RODH L NCAIFEV
SHUZRYVNAW SOEDU
LTN IXW, GEJUSL TI
CAEDAN IBOLER, PHA

Printers Proof

Guy de Cointet 74

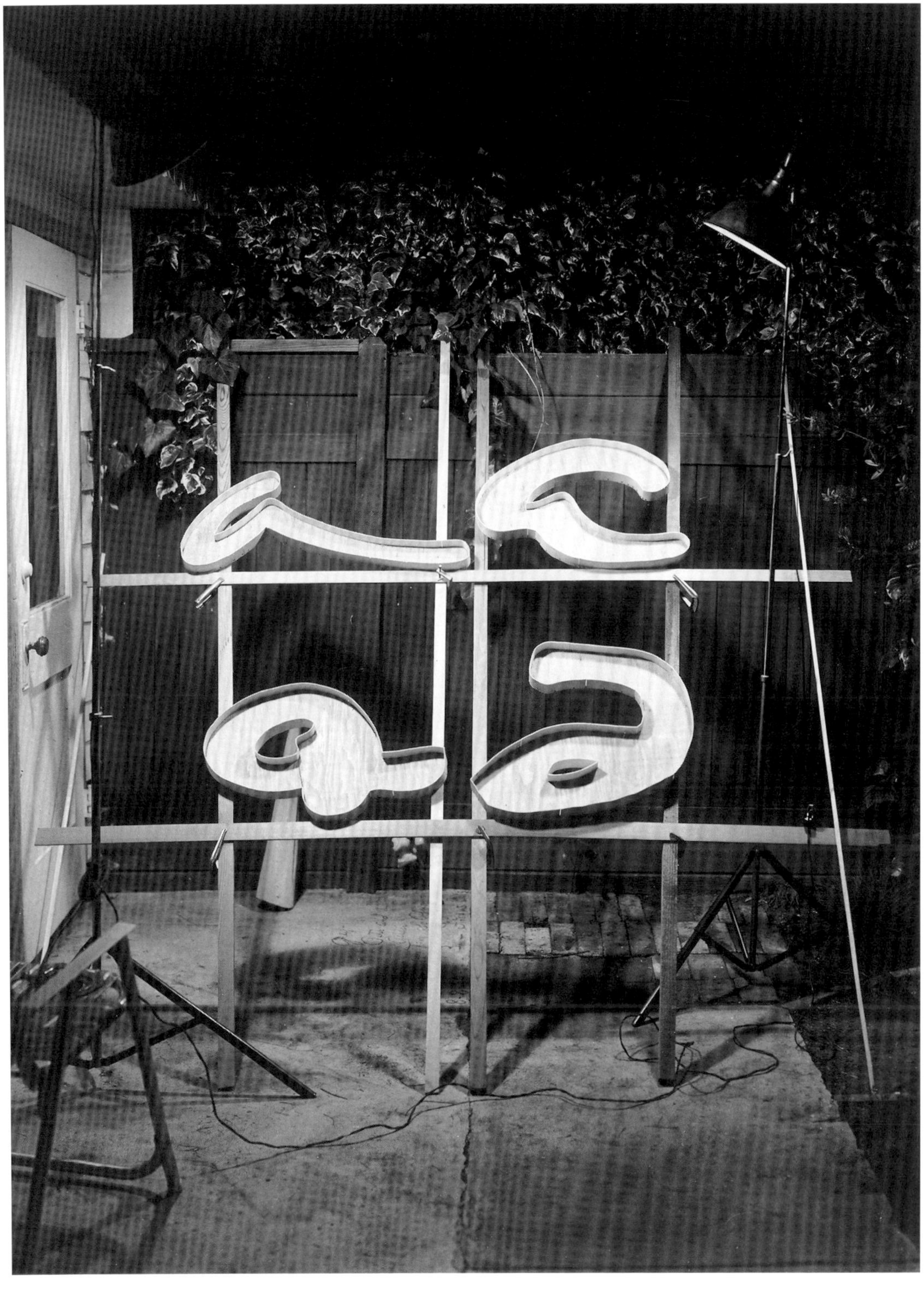

CONCLUSION

Despite these examples, in general, language and information systems did not play as central a role on the West Coast as they did on the East Coast. Instead, Californians tended to privilege the experiential over the epistemological, creating artworks that emphasized the body and performance. Although there were male practitioners of body art on the East Coast, the use of the body, whether in performance or as a material, was mostly a hallmark of the West Coast and has been one of the most enduring forms of Conceptual practice throughout many countries and cultures ever since. Similarly, the focus on nature—its processes, inspirational potential, and concern for its preservation—was also particularly strong on the West Coast.[91]

The confluence of art and life resonated with artists from all parts of the state but was especially prevalent in Northern California. It was brought to its apogee by David Ireland, who emerged a bit later than the dates covered by *State of Mind,* but whose work, especially his house-as-art at 500 Capp Street in San Francisco's Mission District, is a prime example. Many Southern California artists drew upon popular culture as manifested in print media, movies, and TV for images and narrative content. Again, though not the exclusive domain of California, these tendencies were especially strong in Southern California. In the Bay Area, the romantic, anticommercial concept of the artist promulgated by Clyfford Still, who taught at the San Francisco Art Institute from 1946 to 1950, remained powerful long after he had left the city. The Bay Area has always been characterized by a healthy strain of independence, and in general artists there tended to private and casual actions and installations. As Paul Kos explained to me recently, "If you lived in New York, you were more aware of what was timely in terms of the art world. If you lived outside, your timeliness was based on your immediate environs, your dedication to your enterprise even if it was less sophisticated. Obviously the West Coast was not part of the theoretical drive that made New York."[92] Allen Ruppersberg, who moved from

Ohio to Los Angeles in 1962, said, "There was no art history to play with, unlike New York which is all about history—in Los Angeles you started from scratch."[93] Instead of looking at other art, he said that he, Ruscha, and Leavitt were looking at colors in the environment. Although he has split his time between the coasts in subsequent years, Ruppersberg insists that California allowed him "to put more of an emotional and psychological spin on things" than would have been possible in New York, where formal concerns were more central.[94]

Of course, there have been many direct descendents of the artists in *State of Mind* who studied at CalArts, the San Francisco Art Institute, or other schools where several of the artists discussed in this essay held teaching positions. Some students stayed in California to form the next generation of Conceptual artists. Many left the area but built on the innovations of these pioneers. Baldessari's use of appropriated imagery spawned an entire movement that was the subject of the 2009 exhibition *Pictures Generation, 1974–1984* at the Metropolitan Museum of Art of New York. Furthermore, many of the artists from the 1990s who are cited as part of the international relational aesthetics movement invoked the interactive works of this earlier period, especially those of Ruppersberg and Marioni. Asher's influence, both as an artist and longtime professor at CalArts, helped define institutional critique, and Ruscha is the acknowledged progenitor of the artists' book. Nauman, who started his multifaceted career in the north of the state in the mid-1960s and moved southward to Pasadena where he worked throughout the 1970s, is arguably the most influential artist working today for his early body-based performances for film and video, his interactive installations, and his manipulations of language. Although many of the radical innovations of the late sixties and early seventies were more or less abandoned in the eighties (when studio art again flourished in a greatly expanding market), by the mid-1990s a backlash against consumerism gave rise to a new generation of artists who looked back eagerly to this first generation of Conceptualists and adapted their innovations to a globalized art world.

But what distinguishes California artists from this period is their enthusiasm for experimentation. In fact, it was the exciting prospect of being part of momentous social change that drew so many young artists from other parts of the country and abroad to California for their education. California's relative distance from the business of art and established institutions and traditions gave them the freedom to experiment, which in turn resulted in a greater variety of forms and approaches than was found among the same generation elsewhere. While many artists in this exhibition do not think of themselves as "California artists"—Baldessari is a case in point—those who moved to California from elsewhere (unlike Baldessari) made a conscious choice. In Nauman's case, it was an interest in Bay Area figurative painters (he was making paintings as an undergraduate) as well as a suggestion from one of his art teachers at the University of Wisconsin that he look into the new department at UC Davis that inspired his move; for Marioni, it was the aura of San Francisco Beat culture; for Kos, the Bay Area's proximity to nature; for Ruppersberg, Los Angeles's promise of self-invention.[95] The most enduring legacy of early California Conceptualism has been its breadth, which impressed upon succeeding generations a broader understanding of what art could be. Virtually all of the hallmarks of contemporary art practice—collectivity, emphasis on the ephemeral, body-oriented performance, participation, art as life, political commentary, and art as social interaction—were pioneered in California during Conceptualism's formative era, an era in which the very definition of art, the role of the artist, and that of its academic and institutional structures were challenged. This was the core of the Conceptual revolution.

NOTES

1 R. H. Fuchs, *John Baldessari* (Essen, Germany: Van Abbemuseum Eindhoven and Museum Folkwang), 12.

2 Lucy Lippard, *Six Years: The Dematerialization of the Art Object from 1966 to 1972* (New York: Praeger, 1973), 75. Baldessari affectionately lampoons these sentences in the video *Baldessari Sings LeWitt* (1972).

3 For an in-depth analysis of the antiwar movement in California, see Marcia A. Eymann and Charles Wollenberg, eds., *What's Going On: California and the Vietnam Era* (Oakland, Berkeley, and Los Angeles: Oakland Museum of California and University of California Press, 2004).

4 At age seventeen, the artist changed her name from Patti Anne to Alexis, after the actress, beginning her appropriation of Hollywood imagery that she would continue throughout her career.

5 Martha Rosler, conversation with author, March 21, 2009.

6 Oral history interview with John Baldessari conducted by Christopher Knight on April 4–5, 1992, Archives of American Art, Smithsonian Institution, Washington, D.C. It is believed that the term was coined by Lawrence Alloway in reference to Robert Smithson (Ann Temkin, *Gabriel Orozco* [New York: Museum of Modern Art, 2009], 11).

7 Buren quoted in Temkin, 11.

8 John Miller, "Double or Nothing: John Miller on the Art of Douglas Huebler," *Artforum* 44, no. 8 (April 2006): 117.

9 Huebler's *Bradford 2–66* was included in the landmark *Primary Structures* exhibition at the Jewish Museum, New York, in 1966.

10 Alexander Alberro and Patricia Norvell, eds., *Recording Conceptual Art: Early Interviews with Barry, Huebler, Kaltenbach, LeWitt, Morris, Oppenheim, Siegelaub, Smithson, and Weiner by Patricia Norvell* (Berkeley: University of California Press, 2001), 137.

11 Ant Farm promotional material, Ant Farm Archive, 2005.14.253.10, University of California, Berkeley Art Museum and Pacific Film Archive.

12 Quotes from "Ant Farm Timeline," in *Ant Farm (1968–1978)*, ed. Constance M. Lewallen and Steve Seid (Berkeley: University of California Press and University of California, Berkeley Art Museum and Pacific Film Archive, 2005).

13 Barbara C. Matilsky, *Fragile Ecologies: Contemporary Artists' Interpretations and Solutions* (New York: Rizzoli, 1992), 67.

14 *The Lagoon Cycle* was published in a handmade, limited-edition book, *The Book of Lagoons.*

15 Newton Harrison, e-mail message to author, June 18, 2010.

16 Kinmont in Julie Ault, "In Step with the Desert: The Morphology of Robert Kinmont," in *Robert Kinmont* (New York: Alexander and Bonin, 2009), u.p.

17 In Ken D. Allen's insightful article on Ruscha's early books and early painting, Allen notes that the kind of built environment depicted in Ruscha's books corresponds to Henri Lefebre's spatial theory "as a symptom of larger cultural and economic shifts in the late twentieth century." See Ken D. Allen, "Ed Ruscha, Pop Art, and Spectatorship in 1960s Los Angleles," *Art Bulletin* 92, no. 3 (September 2010): 243.

18 Allen, 242.

19 One cannot help but think of Marina Abromović's later sitting performances, which culminated in her marathon *The Artist Is Present* (2010) at the Museum of Modern Art, New York, where she sat still all day for seventy-two days.

20 Interview with Andrea Juno in Andrea Juno and V. Vale, *ReSearch Publications,* no. 15, 1001 (N6494P4R5): 54; "Annie Sprinkle's Post-Porn Modernist," in *Angry Women,* ed. Andrea Juno and V. Vale, 50–65 (New York: Juno, 1999).

21 Fried, letter to author, April 1, 1994.

22 Moira Roth, "Toward a History of Performance: Part One," *Arts Magazine* (February 28, 1978): 100.

23 Brenda Richardson, e-mail message to author, March 21, 2010.

24 For his contribution to *The San Francisco Performance* exhibition at the Newport Harbor Art Museum (now the Orange County Museum of Art), Henderson spelled out the word "Attica" in flashing Christmas lights on the side of a hill in Irvine, California. The California Highway Patrol ordered him to remove the piece, which was on private property. Paul Kos, who helped him install it, spent the night in jail for trespassing.

25 From Cotton's artist statement in *The Artist's Body,* ed. Tracey Warr and Amelia Jones (London: Phaidon, 1980), 79.

26 "Terry Fox: 'I wanted to have my mood affect their looks.'{hrs}" Interview by Willoughby Sharp, *Avalanche* (Winter 1971): 70–81.

27 Terry Fox, unpublished interview with author, December 3, 1991.

28 Terry Fox in Constance M. Lewallen, *Terry Fox: Articulations* (Philadelphia: Moore College of Art and Design, 1992), 15–16.

29 Chan A. Noriega, "From Beats to Borders: An Alternative History of Chicano Art in California," in *Reading California: Art, Image, and Identity, 1900–2000,* ed. Stephanie Barron, Sheri Bernstein, and Ilene Susan Fort (Los Angeles: Los Angeles County Museum of Art and University of California Press, 2001), 364.

30 The "war" image was not taken from a newspaper but rather depicts the bullet-ridden Faye Dunaway in the 1967 Arthur Penn film *Bonnie and Clyde.*

31 Allan McCollum, "What One Loves about Life," in *Allen Ruppersberg: Books Inc.* (Limoges, France: FRAC Limousin; New York: DAP, 1999), 11.

32 Lynn Hershman, e-mail message to author, April 5, 2010.

33 For a description of *Roberta Breitmore*, see Meredith Tromble, ed., *The Art and Films of Lynn Hershman Leeson* (Berkeley: University of California Press, 2005).

34 Over the years, there have been several other instances of artists living in the gallery. For example, in Marina Abromović's *The House with an Ocean View* (2002), she lived in full view of the audience for twelve days in the Sean Kelly Gallery, New York.

35 Terri Keyser-Cooper, e-mail message to author, June 8, 2010.

36 Sarah Lehrer-Graiwer, "Altered Ego," *Artforum* (September 2010): 137–38.

37 Connie Butler, "Introduction," in *WACK!: Art and the Feminist Revolution,* ed. Lisa Gabrielle Mark (Los Angeles: Museum of Contemporary Art; Cambridge, MA: MIT Press, 2007), 22.

38 Alexander Alberro, "The Dialectics of Everyday Life," in *Martha Rosler: Positions in the Life World,* ed. Catherine de Zegher (Birmingham: Ikon Gallery; Vienna: Generali Foundation; Cambridge, MA: MIT Press, 1999), 74.

39 Suzanne Foley and Constance M. Lewallen, eds., *Space/Time/Sound: Conceptual Art in the San Francisco Bay Area; The 1970s* (San Francisco: San Francisco Museum of Modern Art, 1980), 83.

40 Ann-Sargent Wooster, "The Way We Were," in *The First Generation: Women and Video, 1970–75* (New York: Independent Curators Incorporated, 1993), 34.

41 Antin in *California Video: Artists and Histories,* ed. Glenn Phillips (Los Angeles: Getty Research Institute and the J. Paul Getty Museum, 2008), 24.

42 Phillips, 178–79.

43 In this work, Ono sat passively on a stage while members of the public sheared off her clothing.

44 Jennie Klein, "The Body's Odyssey," in *The 21st Century Odyssey Part II: The Performances of Barbara T. Smith,* ed. Jennie Klein and Rebecca McGrew (Pomona, CA: Pomona College Museum of Art, 2005), 10.

45 Nicolas Bourriaud, *Relational Aesthetics* (Nice, France: Les Presse du Reel, 1998).

46 Linda Mary Montano in *Angry Women,* ed. Andrea Juno and V. Vale (New York: Juno, 1999), 55.

47 Joan Simon, *William Wegman: Funney/Strange* (New Haven, CT: Yale University Press; Andover, MA: Addison Gallery of American Art, Phillips Academy, 2006), 89.

48 David Ross, "Interview with Wegman," in *Theories and Documents of Contemporary Art: A Sourcebook of Artists' Writings,* ed. Kristine Stiles and Peter Selz (Berkeley and London: University of California Press, 1996), 450.

49 Ann Goldstein, *A Minimal Future?: Art as Object 1958–1968* (Los Angeles: Museum of Contemporary Art; Cambridge, MA: MIT Press, 2004), 160.

50 Asher quoted in Benjamin Buchloh, ed., *Michael Asher: Writings 1973–1983 on Works 1969–1979* (Halifax: Press of the Nova Scotia College of Art and Design; Los Angeles: Museum of Contemporary Art, 1983), 8.

51 The exhibition, *18′6″ × 6′9″ × 11′ 2½″ × 47′ 11 3/16″ × 29′ 8½″ × 31′ 9 3/16″*, organized by Eugenia Butler, took place from April 11 to May 3, 1969. Other artists included were Robert Barry, Iain Baxter, Eugenia Butler, James Lee Byers, Douglas Huebler, Stephen Kaltenbach, Edward Kienholz, Joseph Kosuth, Barry LeVa, Dennis Oppenheim, Rudnick, Robert Watts, and Lawrence Weiner. Asher is quoted in Buchloh, 2.

52 Anne Rorimer, *New Art in the 60s and 70s: Redefining Reality* (London: Thames and Hudson, 2001), 265.

53 Fred Hoffman, *Chris Burden* (Newcastle upon Tyne, UK: Gagosian Gallery, Locus + Publishing Ltd.), 17.

54 Hoffman, 17.

55 Thomas Lawson, "Every Picture Tells a Story, Don't It?" in *Mining for Gold: Selected Writings (1979–1996),* ed. Lionel Bovier and Fabrice Stroun (Zurich: JRP/Ringier, 2004), 29. Helene Winer quoted in Erik Bluhm, "Minimalism's Rubble: On William Leavitt's and Bas Jan Ader's *Landslide* (1969–1970)," *ArtUS* 10 (October-November 2005): 16.

56 Tanya Zimbardo, "Howard Fried: Inside the Harlequin," in *San Francisco Museum of Modern Art: Looking Forward,* ed. Janet Bishop, Corey Keller, and Sarah Roberts (San Francisco: San Francisco Museum of Modern Art, 2010), 231.

57 Sapien was a student of Fried at the San Francisco Art Institute and Woodall a classmate for one year.

58 For more complete descriptions of these and other Bay Area performances, see Foley and Lewallen.

59 Woodall, letter to author, May 2010.

60 Janet Kraynak, "Performance," in *Work Ethic,* ed. Helen Molesworth (Baltimore: Baltimore Museum of Art; University Park: Pennsylvania State University Press, 2003), 122.

61 Coosje van Bruggen, *Bruce Nauman* (New York: Rizzoli, 1988), 109.

62 Willoughby Sharp, "Nauman interview," *Arts Magazine* (March 1970), reprinted as "Two Interviews: Interview I," in *Art + Performance,* ed. Robert C. Morgan (Baltimore: Johns Hopkins University Press, 2002), 253.

63 Paul McCarthy, conversation with author, July 10, 2009.

64 Magnus Petersens, "Paul McCarthy's 40 Years of Hard Work—An Attempt at a Summary," in *Paul McCarthy: Head Shop/Shop Head, Works 1966–2006,* ed. Paul McCarthy (Göttingen: Steidl and Moderna Museet, 2006), 9.

65 Petersens, 9.

66 McCarthy, conversation with author, July 10, 2009.

67 Douglas Fogle, *The Last Picture Show: Artists Using Photography, 1960–1982* (Minneapolis, MN: Walker Art Center, 2003), 9.

68 Marioni in "California Body Art and Its International Roots," in *The Art Embodied, Musées de Marseilles, France,* reprinted in *Writings on Art: Tom Marioni 1969–1999* (San Francisco: Crown Point Press, 1999), 72.

69 McCarthy, conversation with author, July 10, 2009.

70 Lewallen, *Terry Fox: Articulations,* 11–12.

71 Erin Beenker, "The Man Who Wanted to Look beyond the Horizon," in *Bas Jan Ader: Please Don't Leave Me,* ed. Erik Beenker (Rotterdam: Museum Boijmans Van Beuningen, 2006), 16.

72 Beenker, 16.

73 Stephen Laub, e-mail message to author, September 15, 2009.

74 He said once in an interview that he was curious about why the term "spade" was used to describe African Americans, rather than, say, "club." From "An Interview with David Hammons," Brown University, www.brown.edu/Departments/MCM/people/cokes/Hammons.html (accessed February 20, 2011).

75 Holland Cotter, "Reading Fragments from an Incendiary Time," *New York Times,* November 14, 2006, E1.

76 Tom Marioni, e-mail message to author, March 10, 2010.

77 Paul Kos, e-mail message to author, May 5, 2010.

78 Melchert in an unpublished interview by Peter Samis and Tanya Zambardo for the San Francisco Museum of Modern Art, September 2010.

79 Mark Toscano, unpublished interview with the artist, August 5, 2008, included in an e-mail message to author, March 10, 2010.

80 Doug Hall, interview with author, May 6, 2010.

81 Artist quoted in Charles Hagen, "Robert Cumming's Subject Object," *Artforum* 21, no. 10 (Summer 1983): 26.

82 Robert Cumming, *The Sketch Boards for Fabricated Photos 1973–1979* (Boston: Howard Yezerski Gallery, 2001), 2.

83 Robert Cumming, e-mail message to author, April 10, 2010.

84 Thomas Albright, *Art in the San Francisco Bay Area, 1945–1980* (Berkeley: University of California Press, 1985), 204.

85 Jim Melchert, *Points of View, Slide Projection Pieces* (San Francisco: San Francisco Museum of Art, 1975), 7.

86 Los Angeles–based Charles Gaines, who created gridded drawings based on numerical systems, was perhaps most closely aligned with a New York sensibility.

87 LeWitt's *Sentences on Conceptual Art* was first published in the journal *Art-Language* in May 1969.

88 Paul Cotton, e-mail message to author, July 26, 2010.

89 Robert Cumming, e-mail message to author, April 24, 2010.

90 Jim Melchert, e-mail message to author, March 2010.

91 Paradoxically, three of the major earth artists—Walter De Maria, Michael Heizer, and Dennis Oppenheim—were born and educated in the Bay Area, although they all left the state in the late 1960s.

92 Kos, e-mail message to author, May 5, 2010.

93 Allen Ruppersberg, e-mail message to author, May 12, 2010

94 Ruppersberg in an interview with Frédéric Paul, Books, Inc., FRAC, France, published on the occasion of the *Allen Ruppersberg's Exhibition,* FRAC, Limousin, 2000, and reprinted in *You and Me or the Art of Give and Take: Allen Ruppersberg,* ed. Constance M. Lewallen (Zurich: JRP Ringier and Santa Monica Museum of Art, 2009).

95 Constance M. Lewallen, *A Rose Has No Teeth: Bruce Nauman in the 1960s* (Berkeley: University of California Press and UC Berkeley Art Museum and Pacific Film Archive, 2007), 8.

Fig. 2.1 Barbara T. Smith, *Field Piece* (installation view), 1968–72. Black-and-white photograph; 48 × 72 in.

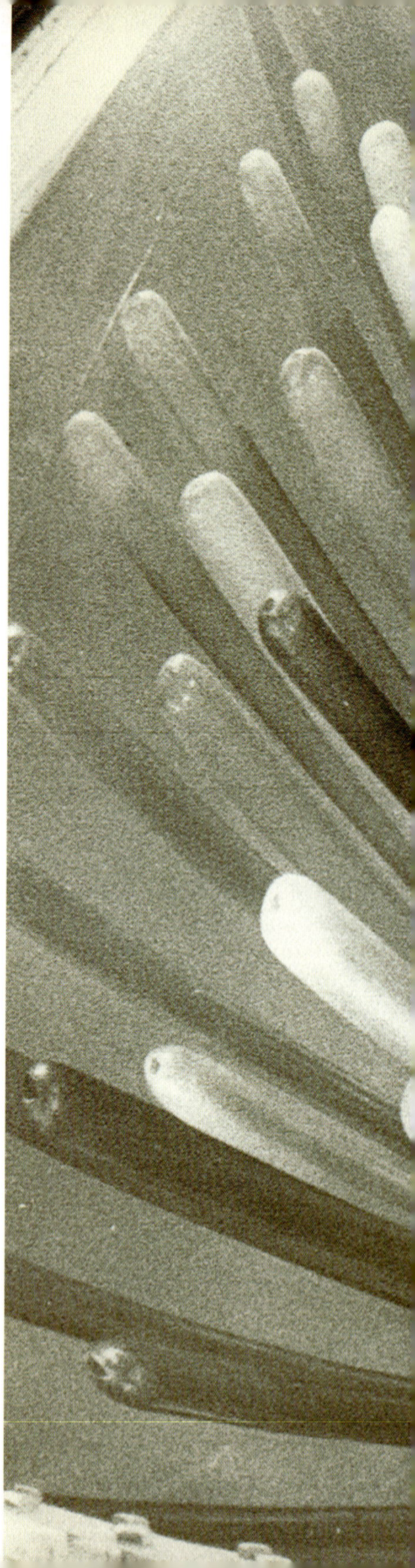

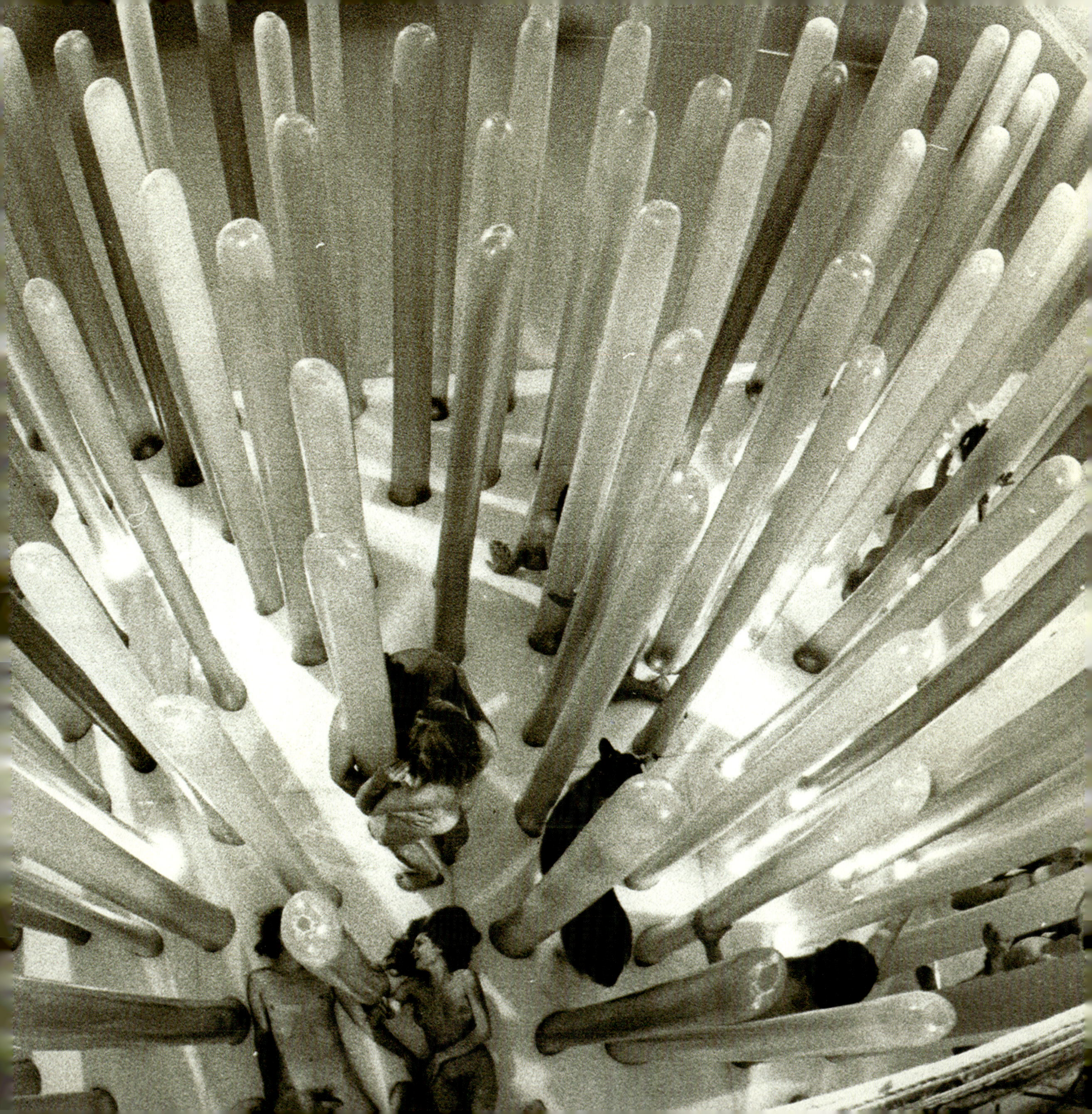

BEYOND THE WHITE CELL

EXPERIMENTATION/EDUCATION/INTERVENTION IN CALIFORNIA CIRCA 1970

Karen Moss

For more than four decades, critics, historians and, most importantly, artists have attempted to define and locate Conceptual art of the 1960s. As noted in this book's introduction, often these histories have privileged New York and Europe; however, today this continuing discourse now includes Conceptual and Postconceptual practices from locations across the globe, including California. While in our current globalized era the particularities of locality or geography may seem elusive (or even irrelevant), this was not the case in the 1960s: interrogating place and placement—particularly the specific sites of cultural production and presentation—became an integral strategy of Conceptual art.

In his introduction to *Conceptual Art: A Critical Anthology*, Alexander Alberro delineates four different trajectories, stating: "The fourth trajectory that leads to conceptual art is one that problematizes placement. Here, the subject of the work becomes both a reflection on the conventions that will frame it or situate it and a self-questioning of how it will be communicated or displayed."[1]

By the mid-1960s, artistic production radically shifted the notions of both space and site. The analysis of the art object and subjective viewing in Minimalism extended the idea of space and elicited a more differentiated concept of the subject. Subsequently, Conceptualism redefined the idea of an art object and the notion of representation. As artists took greater control of their production, they selected specific sites in public and private spaces, resulting in an *internal* interrogation of institutions and an *external* exploration of the environment. Increasingly, audience reception, participation, and performativity became integral to the artwork, eradicating the boundaries between art and life, artist and spectator, producer and production.

Conceptualism focused not only on the primacy of artists' ideas, but also, more specifically, on how both language and systems produce larger cultural meaning. As a result, many artists elected to address the public directly through different types of physical, spatial, or linguistic interventions. Some occupied or transformed existing physical structures within institutional contexts, interrogated spaces in the urban environment, or made site-specific installations or performances in the public sphere. Others interjected their work into existing journals or newspapers, while some created their own alternative publications to disseminate their ideas. Artists also pirated television airwaves and radio broadcasts and, increasingly, with the advent of video, produced their own, more radical forms of media.

This experimental ethos of Conceptualism, new genres, and post-studio practices demanded new sites of presentation and production. No longer satisfied with the museum's role as mausoleum for static art, some artists performed live events or produced interactive installations to "de-institutionalize" the institution. Others rejected the commodified gallery system and founded nonprofit artist-run galleries or alternative spaces. Within the academy, teaching artists tested experimental ideas and utopian idealism in art schools and university art departments, often in new programs supported by experimental education initiatives or through the formation of new institutions. Still other artists ventured into unusual or eccentric locations to express ideas about the larger cultural and sociopolitical discourses of the time. Finally, some worked within the alternative and underground press, created their own books and publications, or made correspondence and mail art as they sought out alternate distribution systems for their work.

Who are some of the key predecessors for these new practices, and what was the cultural milieu directly preceding this generation? How did cultural institutions receive these new practices, and in what ways did artists attempt to transform existing institutions or establish their own alternatives? How did art schools and experimental art programs in universities become primary venues for these practices, and how did experimental education infiltrate the academy? What were the systems of public address developed by artists within urban contexts, mass media, and alternative press or publications? And finally, what was the legacy of California art circa 1970 on later generations?

To better understand this period, one must go back a decade earlier to the artistic and cultural milieu of San Francisco and Los Angeles in the late 1950s and early 1960s. From Beat-inspired assemblage to experimental dance and music, there is an emphasis on everyday, quotidian action. A preference for intermedial practices and a new concern with viewer interactivity and audience participation foreshadowed Conceptualism and new genres.

INTERMEDIA AND EARLY PERFORMANCE ART IN THE BAY AREA AND LOS ANGELES

Bohemia by the Bay

Leaving school with more questions than answers, rejecting established dogmas, highly impressionable to anything that seemed new and untried, we did our post-graduate work in the streets, the bars and the coffeehouses. . . . It was a loose scene that was made up of several disparate circles—poets, artists, filmmakers, jazz musicians . . . it was small, always in flux.

Thomas Albright, "Overview: A Kind of Beatness," *San Francisco Chronicle*, February 17, 1975

As San Francisco art critic Thomas Albright observed, the bohemian Beat scene in the Bay Area of the mid-1950s revolved around the street: artists and poets created dynamic, multidisciplinary collaborations in storefront cafés and other urban locales. Artist-run bars and galleries presented live poetry readings, performance events, and spontaneous Happenings, some iconic and others virtually unknown.

Perhaps the most famous of the artist-run spaces was the King Ubu Gallery, founded in 1952 by poet Robert Duncan, artist Jess Collins (Jess), and painter Harry Jacobus. Adopting its name from Alfred Jarry's Protosurrealist play of 1898, this former automobile-repair shop became an important alternative venue for art and poetry. Closed then reopened in 1954 as the Six Gallery, this space is where Allen Ginsberg read "Howl" in October 1955, often cited as the first public event of the Beat generation and the beginning of the San Francisco poetry renaissance.[2] The Place in North Beach, run by Black Mountain College alums Knute Stiles and Leo Krikorian, became the site for "Dada" festivals and a series of weekly open-mike events—"Blabbermouth nights"—often with light shows produced by Wally Hedrick. Several other North Beach haunts—the Co-Existence Bagel Shop, Coffee House Gallery, Triangle Gallery (still extant), and Dilexi Gallery—exhibited art and held regular readings.

Most of these events occurred spontaneously, without prior announcement or post-event documentation. As Bruce Conner commented: "Things just happened—sometimes they occurred only once; we did not feel compelled to name these events as 'happenings.' We did not document things the way they did on the East Coast; we were not self-conscious about inscribing ourselves into history."[3]

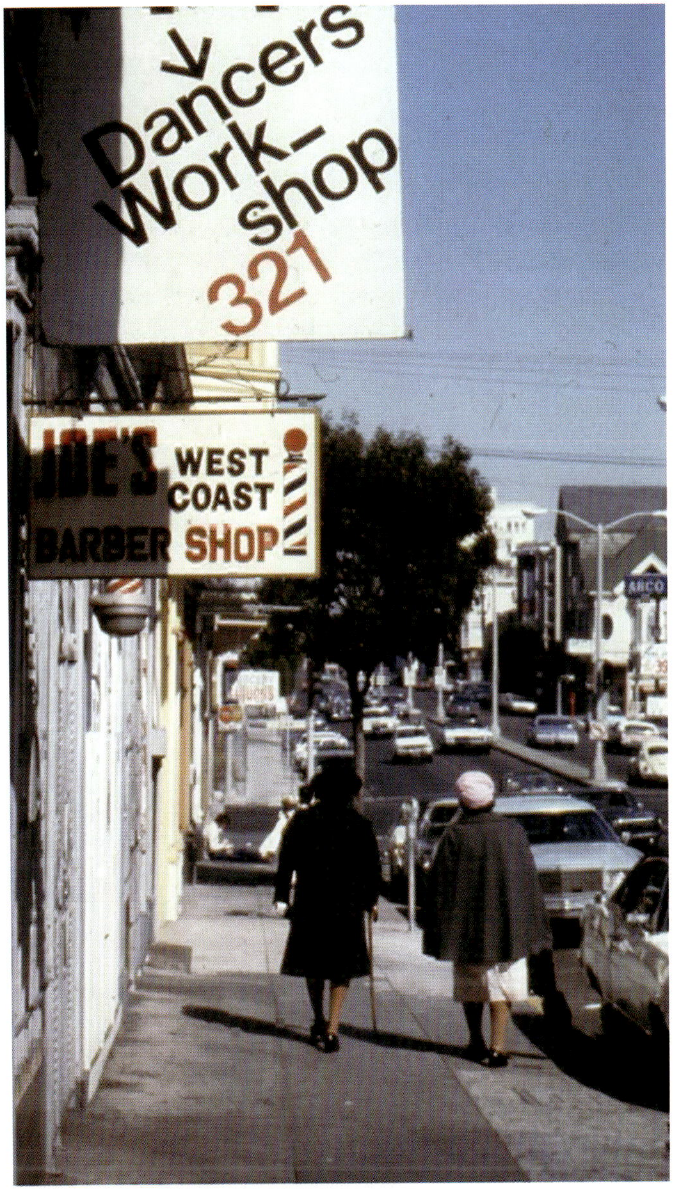

Fig. 2.2 San Francisco Dancers' Workshop storefront, 1955, San Francisco, California.
Photo: Courtesy of Anna Halprin.

Anna Halprin's San Francisco Dancers' Workshop, founded in a city storefront in 1955, became a laboratory for avant-garde practices combining visual arts, poetry, architecture, music, theater, and dance (fig. 2.2). Halprin formed the workshop to explore what she called "kinetic theater," which meant using everyday actions, tasks, and games to discover how the body would naturally and creatively react to new and demanding situations. As Richard Schechner has observed: "Halprin pioneered what was to be known as postmodern dance. Her work was a key that unlocked the door leading to all kinds of experimentation in theatre, music, happenings and performance art."[4] Early workshop performances occurred in nontraditional sites, such as Stern Grove in San Francisco, and later in other locales such as hotels and shopping malls.[5] Halprin became an important mentor, and several students in the troupe—Trisha Brown, Simone Forti, Steve Paxton, and Yvonne Rainer—relocated to New York and later became members of the Judson Church Dance Theater Group.

The task-oriented nature of Halprin's work and its empirical art-meets-life emphasis linked her early experiments to concurrent work by Merce Cunningham, who "shared an interest in reflecting in art the arbitrariness of modern life through radical juxtapositions of disparate activities, undercutting narrative logic and reacting against the emotional coloring of the modern dance establishment."[6] And, like John Cage, Halprin used ordinary materials, objects, and props, then combined these with music, found sounds, and spoken words. She also developed her own charting system to score dances where these disparate elements could transcend specific cause and effect. Halprin's written scores and use of a methodology resembling Cage's chance operations prefigure the rules and systems of both Conceptualism and pedestrian dance. In 1963, she also began

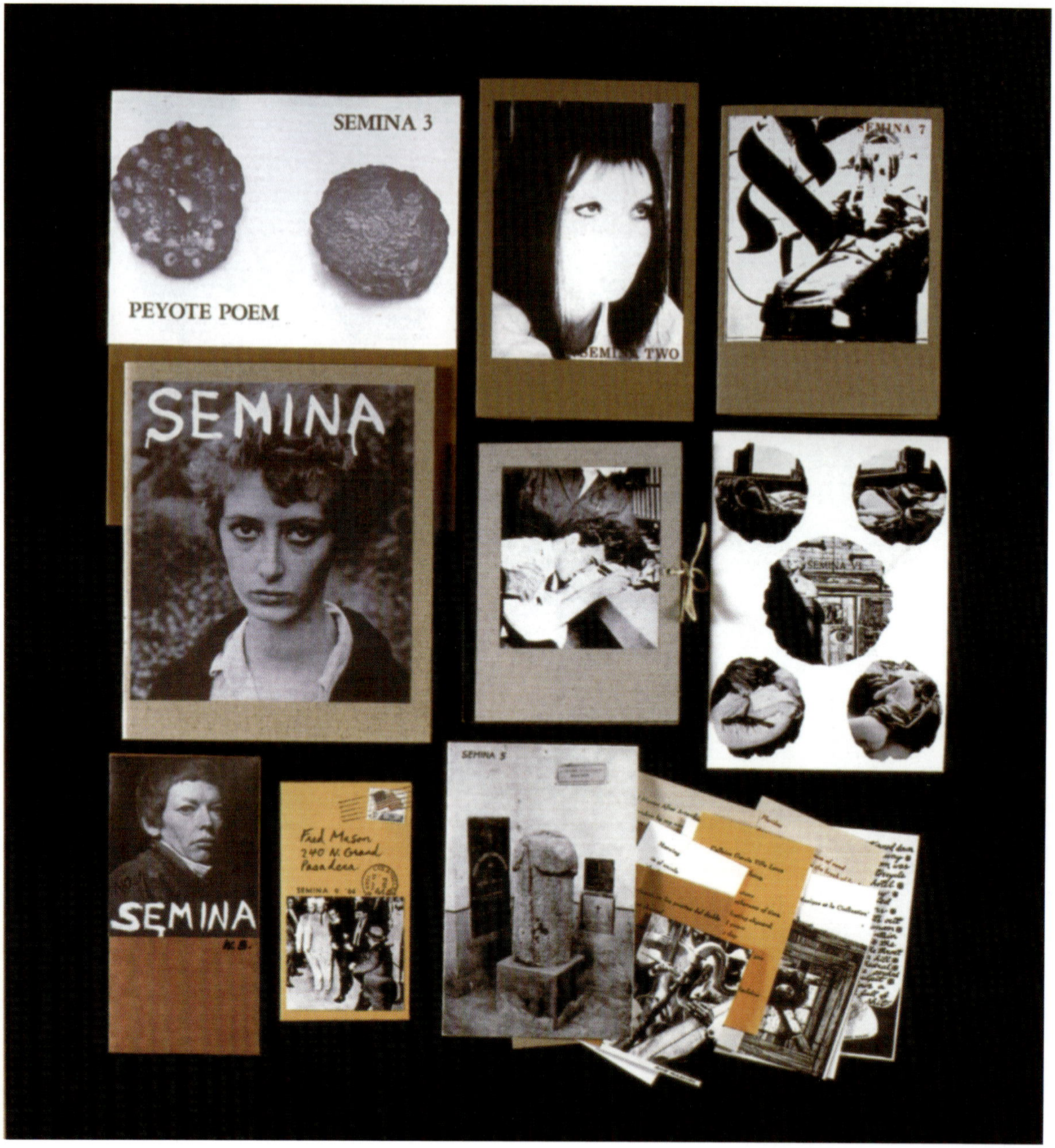

Fig. 2.3 Wallace Berman, *Semina,* vols. 1–9, 1955–64/1992. Publication series: offset lithography and letterpress printing on paper, in cardboard box. University of California, Berkeley Art Museum and Pacific Film Archive; Museum purchase: Bequest of Thérèse Bonney, Class of 1916, by exchange.

>>

Fig. 2.4 Wallace Berman, Semina Floating Gallery, 1961, Larkspur, California. Image: Courtesy Michael Kohn Gallery.

to incorporate audience participation into her work, writing event scores that called for nondancers to perform onstage with members of the workshop.[7]

By the late 1960s, the San Francisco Dancers' Workshop became steeped in the counterculture, melding pop music, dance, and film into intermedial spectacles. In a performance at the Fillmore Auditorium, where Ginsberg chanted his poetry and the Grateful Dead played music, workshop members danced and painted each other's bodies with fluorescent paint that became a screen for film projections.[8]
Halprin's dancers also participated in a Fluxfest concert in 1969 at Longshoremen's Hall with a Fluxus orchestra, the San Francisco Mime Troupe, and psychedelic rock bands Quicksilver Messenger Service and Wildflower. Most memorably, the workshop performed a version of Fluxus artist Benjamin Patterson's *Lick Piece,* in which the dancers licked fifty gallons of strawberry jam off of a brand-new sports car.[9]

In addition to these hybrid events combining high and popular cultures, during the 1960s Halprin collaborated with composers in the Bay Area's experimental music scene.[10] Terry Riley and La Monte Young, then students at University of California, Berkeley, composed Minimalist musical scores for Halprin's *Stillpoint* and *Vision* (1960) and joined visual artist Walter De Maria for collaborative events at UC Berkeley and the San Francisco Art Institute.[11] Riley and Young also collaborated on a concert presented at the Old Spaghetti Factory and Excelsior coffee shop on Green Street in San Francisco.[12] These events in art schools, universities, and North Beach restaurants were just the beginning; Bay Area artists, working across disciplines, would continue to seek nontraditional sites for their avant-garde activities throughout the decade.

Art Meets Life in Los Angeles

Visiting the galleries along La Cienega, one begins to picture Europe as the Renaissance, New York as the Avant Garde and L.A. as the orgiastic future that year by year becomes more actual and immediate, replete with an art that is more actual and immediate.

Barbara Rose, quoted in "Cultural Scenes," *The Sixties Revolution,* ed. Carey McWilliams (New Turk Grossman)

As Rose noted, art in Los Angeles in the early 1960s became even more actual and immediate as local artists as well as those from New York and Europe came to the city for exhibitions or to premiere live performance works. Like the Bay Area, the cultural milieu of Los Angeles in the late 1950s and early 1960s pivoted on a close network of artists, dealers, and curators. Here the network centered around the galleries on La Cienega Boulevard in West Hollywood.[13] The Ferus Gallery, initially founded by curator Walter Hopps and artist Edward Kienholz in 1957, then sold to Irving Blum the following year, mostly included such artists as Larry Bell, Billy Al Bengston, Robert Irwin, Kienholz, and Ed Moses, who were associated with Los Angeles's so-called Cool School of Pop and Minimalism. A notable exception in this stable of artists was the enigmatic and charismatic Wallace Berman, who favored a neo-Dada, proto-Conceptual use of image and text in his work.

Disseminating his ideas through various media, Berman produced not only assemblages and Verifax collages but also the artists' journal *Semina* (1955–64; fig. 2.3). Each *Semina* publication had a unique design and format constructed from multitextured, neutral-tone poster papers and cardboard, and was filled with packets of drawings, photographs, poems, and other texts. Referring to seeds, germination, and proliferation, *Semina* recalls the literary journals of the early European avant-garde and was influenced by the Dada assemblages of Man Ray, whom Berman reportedly met through photographer Edmund Teske in 1948. Defying codification and classification, like much of Berman's work, *Semina* evoked the spirit of Surrealism, as it synthesized the diverse ideas and materials of many artists into one intermedia publication.[14] Berman self-published the journal

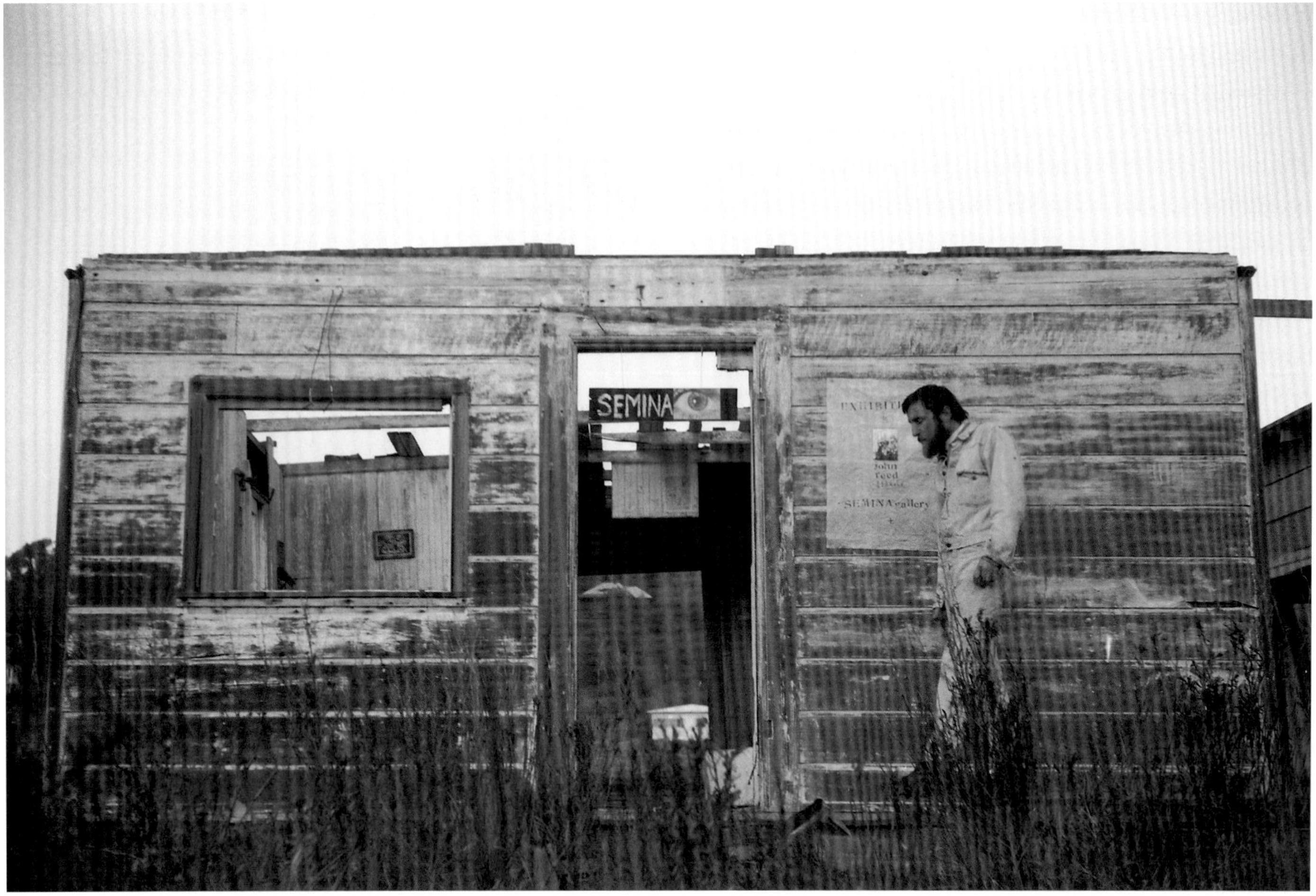

on a small printing press. He assembled images by his artist friends Bruce Conner, George Herms, and Llyn Foulkes, along with texts by deceased writers such as Hermann Hesse, Antonin Artaud, and Jean Cocteau, as well as contemporary poets whose work espoused revolutionary ideas, described drug-induced mental states, and referenced ancient myths. Printed with rubber stamps throughout *Semina,* Berman's own mantra—"Art is love is God"—expressed his belief that one could transcend the negative aspects of American society through art practices that connect with spirituality.

Produced in limited, handmade editions, *Semina* was described by contributor and poet Michael McClure as "a scrapbook of the spirit":

> Friends are drawn together into the assemblage of the magazine, but the magazine is also sent to acquaintances who are drawn into the circle of friends, so it expands and becomes a larger event. Friends are respondents, to Berman, and some of them become correspondents to the magazine . . . one is chosen . . . I see it on the lip exactly between love and generosity and selfish appetite: Wallace's appetite for art, friendship and spirituality.[15]

Bringing together Berman's art, life, and friends with a messianic fervor, *Semina* became both a social event and a collaborative intermedia production. Its do-it-yourself process created a sense of intimacy that was absent from mass-marketed journals, and, because Berman controlled the mailing list, it could not be sold or consumed anywhere else.

After Berman's first solo show at Ferus Gallery in June 1957, the Los Angeles vice squad asked him to remove a print of a copulating couple made by his artist friend Cameron; when Berman refused, the police closed the exhibition and arrested him.[16] At the end of the juryless trial, Berman told poet Robert Duncan and artist Jess, "I will continue to print *Semina* from locations other than this city of degenerate angels." He then relocated to the San Francisco Bay Area, where he became a key figure in the arts underground, in an attempt to further integrate his art and life by eschewing the repressive behaviors and conventions of the bourgeoisie and participating in the burgeoning counterculture.[17]

In Larkspur, in Marin County, Berman and Herms opened an alternative gallery on Berman's houseboat: the Semina Floating Gallery (fig. 2.4). There they showed their own work and that of others, such as Charles Brittin, whose photographs chronicle the San Francisco Beats. Occasionally, they exhibited in other sites, such as Berman's 1958 show of his photographs of artist Jay DeFeo in a one-day exhibition at his San Francisco apartment.

Berman continued to produce *Semina* while in the Bay Area and formed a crucial link between Northern and Southern California. At the time, his orientation toward the mystical and the spiritual probably contributed to his lack of reception by the New York art establishment, but today he is universally regarded as an important progenitor of an intermedial sensibility that prefigures Fluxus, artists' books, and mail art of the 1960s and 1970s, all of which will be discussed later in this essay.

In 1959, Virginia Dwan founded her Los Angeles gallery, where she exhibited both American Pop artists and French *nouveaux réalistes.* In May 1961, Dwan hosted the first Los Angeles exhibition of Yves Klein. The following year, *nouveau réaliste* artist Niki de Saint Phalle staged her first two "shooting" performances—protofeminist actions that clearly satirized Jackson Pollock's drip paintings—in the United States. That same year (1962), Saint Phalle's partner, Jean Tinguely, exhibited at the Ellin Gallery, showing his viewer-activated kinetic sculptures—smaller versions of *Homage to New York,* the machine that had destroyed itself in the Museum of Modern Art's sculpture garden in 1960.[18] The Ellin Gallery also sponsored avant-garde dance performances by Cunningham with music by Cage and sets by Robert Rauschenberg.

Claes Oldenburg came to Los Angeles in 1963 for an exhibition with Dwan and also staged the performance event *Autobodys.* Based on a score of five poems and presented in a large parking lot at the American Institute of Aeronautics and Astronautics on Beverly Boulevard, the work was, according to Michael Kirby:

> A Happening performed at night with numerous cars and a concrete truck. Its special features included the use of flashing headlights, the sound of revving engines, aggressive driving or maneuvering. . . . A motorcyclist in a white helmet was rolled along, lying on his back, in an immobile, rigid position. At the end he was placed back on his motorbike where he awoke once again to the bustle. The Happening was particularly aimed at the car-oriented city of Los Angeles and the violent elements were consciously connected with the murder of John F. Kennedy on November 22, 1963.[19]

Oldenburg's title, *Autobodys*, refers to his initial visits to Los Angeles, when he was struck by the sheer isolation that one feels from the city streets. He has said that he was thinking about how, in Los Angeles, people become "automatic bodies" as they move through the endless expanse of the city and seem to conflate their self-identities with their various wheeled vehicles.[20] The artist has also noted that he planned the Happening prior to the devastating November 22 assassination of President John F. Kennedy, but the ubiquitous televised image of the black Cadillac motorcade became etched in his mind.[21] He decided to add a black hearse to the vehicles in the performance to trigger the viewers' collective memory of the indelible scene that had been repeated incessantly on national television during the preceding two weeks. One of the first major performances by a New York artist to occur in Southern California, Oldenburg's event specifically referenced Los Angeles culture: the omnipresence of the automobile, the

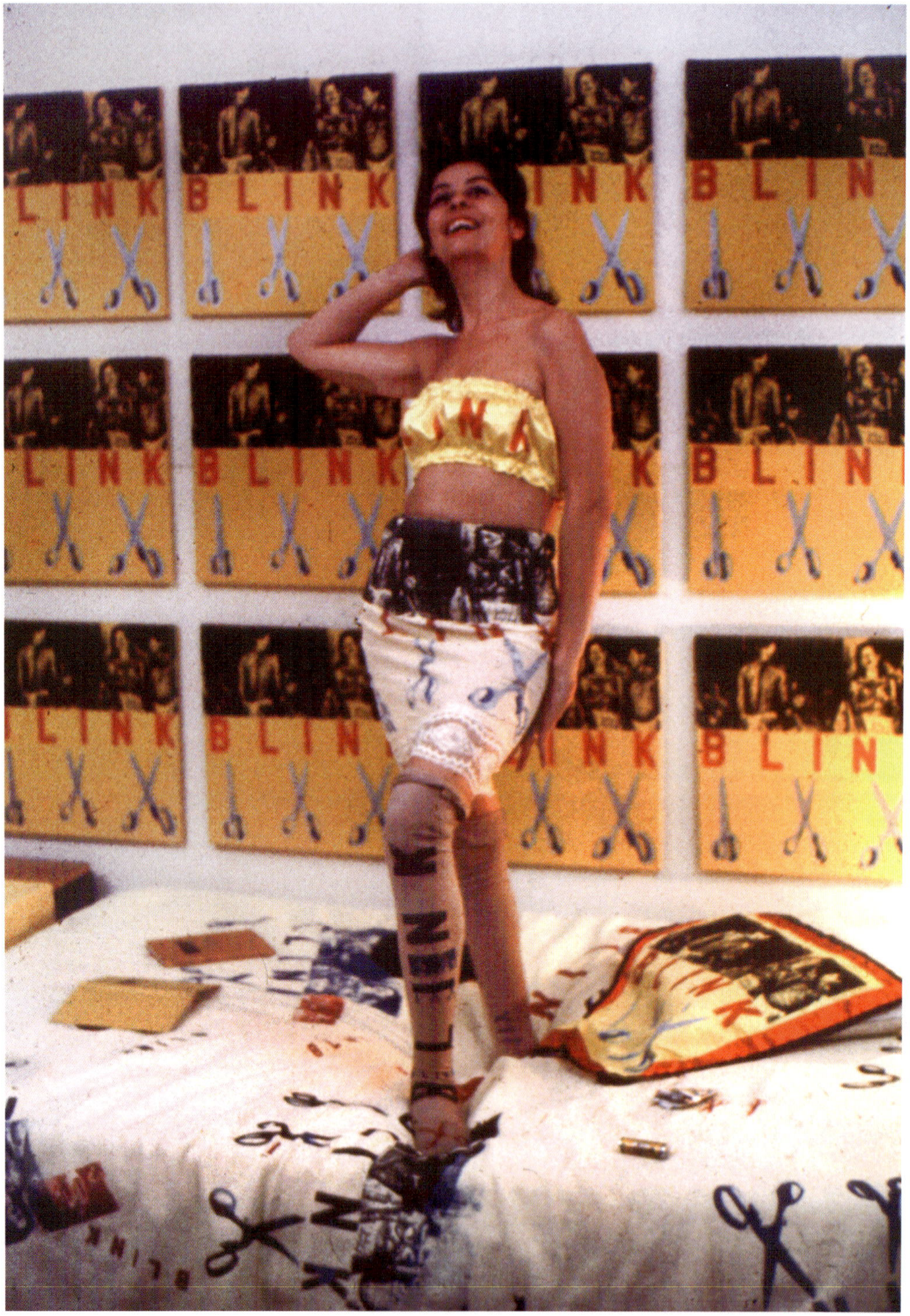

Fig. 2.5 The Sissor Brothers Warehouse (George Brecht, Alison Knowles, Robert Watts), BLINK, 1963. Installation and performance at Rolf Nelson Gallery, Los Angeles. Image: Courtesy Robert Watts Archive, New York. Photo: Robert Watts.

>>

Fig. 2.6 Anna Halprin Dancers, *Parades and Changes,* 1970. Performed prior to the opening of the Berkeley Art Museum (then University Art Museum), University of California, Berkeley. Photo: Courtesy of Anna Halprin. © Paul Fusco, Magnum Photos, NY.

sense of human isolation one feels in the seemingly endless urban sprawl, and the city as a site for the production of fictive, simulated film and television realities.

That same year, three Fluxus artists—George Brecht, Alison Knowles, and Robert Watts—did an exhibition at the Rolf Nelson Gallery, a small, artist-run space on La Cienega, under the randomly selected pseudonym "The Sissor Brothers Warehouse." Brecht and Watts met at Douglass College at Rutgers, where they "cooked up the idea of the Yam Festival (1963)," an ongoing series of Fluxus objects, performances, and events.[22] Shortly thereafter, Brecht and Watts planned the Sissor Brothers Warehouse event with their associate, Knowles, who had studied with Cage and had trained as a master printmaker.[23] Without consulting with one another, the three collaborating artists each made an image, which Knowles then silk-screened together onto one canvas in the most random manner possible. The resulting allover yellow canvas has three tattooed torsos at the top, the word "blink" in red letters across the middle, and three pairs of silver scissors across the bottom.

For their exhibition installation, the artists stamped the composite image with the words "Sissor Brothers Warehouse," plastered it all around the gallery, and printed it on various everyday objects including gloves, light bulbs, jewelry, tool chests, and floor mats. Artist Letty Lou Eishenhauer wore a "BLINK" dress and acted as the gallery docent, adding a live, performative element to the installation (fig. 2.5). By choosing the word "BLINK," Watts refers to the bodily reflex and to the process of looking, reiterating the viewer's voyeuristic gaze at the live female object/performer who intermittently lounged on a bed. The paintings sold for forty dollars each, and the gallery offered to custom stencil the word "BLINK" onto anything else for a small fee. To commemorate the occasion, Watts also made a series of "BLINK" stamps, which he used in later mail-art projects. This event satirized the dominance of Pop art at that time and reflected the core aesthetic and strategy of early Fluxus works: using everyday objects, actions, and language to merge art and life; refuting single authorship and uniqueness; and critiquing the commodity status of art.

When New York artists came to Los Angeles, they felt free to experiment in this new context and had a wider range of venues in which to present their work. Far from New York City's critical and commercial hegemony, traditions were not as ingrained in Los Angeles; however, because of a smaller artistic community in California, artists had to "turn to one another for both audience and space."[24] This accounts for the interactions among artists across disciplines and generations. For example, in addition to working with young dancers Forti, Paxton, and Rainer, and such composers as Riley and Young, Halprin was also involved with visual artists like Ant Farm's founders Chip Lord—who took her workshop—and Curtis Schreier—who was her photographer. Although Berman died tragically in a motorcycle accident at the early age of forty, he became a legend to many young artists in both Northern and Southern California. Though Oldenburg, Brecht, Knowles, and Watts eventually achieved greater recognition for their later work, they still consider these early performances—rediscovered by subsequent generations of artists—as critical to the development of their respective practices.[25]

The artists' use of unusual public spaces for their performances and their appropriation of popular culture and mass media also reveal the specific zeitgeist of the booming post-1960s California economy and its burgeoning counterculture. Without preexisting prototypes to draw from, California artists looked to the rock concerts, street theater, and political and social events of the 1960s as models, allying "[themselves] very closely with life . . . there was only a thin membrane separating the life of the performance from that of the artist and of his or her audience of close friends."[26] This art–life agenda influenced a younger generation of art students who went on to develop Conceptual practices and new genres in the later 1960s and 1970s.

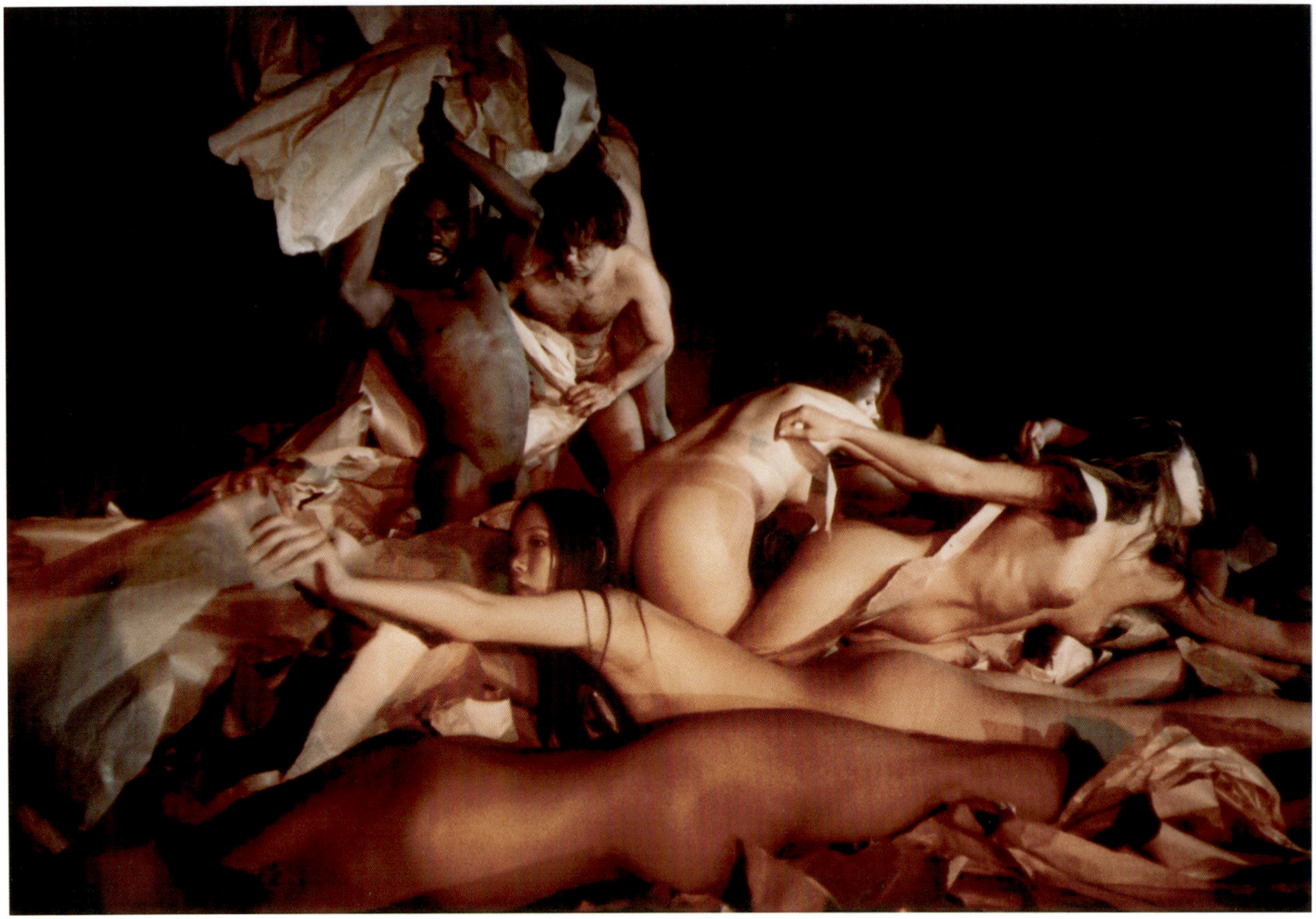

MUSEUMS: BREATHING LIFE INTO THE MAUSOLEUM

As artists in California continued to mine personal experiences and the context of everyday life, they moved away from static objects and traditional materials to more intermedial and performative sensibilities. And as their practices revolved around events and situations in specific sites and environments, their work became less and less conducive to the sterile white cube of the museum.

Opened in 1935, the San Francisco Museum of Art (SFMA) primarily organized exhibitions of modern artists even though it did not add the word "modern" to its title until 1975. Although it remained devoted to more traditional painting, sculpture, and printmaking, the museum created in 1967 the Society for the Encouragement of Contemporary Art (SECA), a collectors' group that awarded an exhibition to a contemporary artist every two years.[27] Initially established as part of the Los Angeles Museum of History, Science, and Art in Exposition Park in 1920, the Los Angeles County Museum of Art (LACMA) became a separate entity in 1961 and opened its new building in 1965. While the museum organized important contemporary exhibitions—such as *Seventeen Artists: Sculpture in the 1960s* (1966) and *Art + Technology* (1968)—that paired artists with corporations, many of the artists in these programs were not based in California, and LACMA's commitment to contemporary art was limited at that time.

Amid the relative conservatism of these larger museums in Los Angeles and San Francisco, a handful of cultural institutions in the late 1960s began to accommodate more challenging work. These venues—primarily small museums and university art galleries—became sites of experimentation for the rethinking of the practice, presentation, and reception of art that was integral to the advent of Conceptualism and other new genres. Additionally, with more artists interested in a critique of the various apparatuses of the art world, including the museum, there existed a tacit will to "de-institutionalize" even these smaller institutions.

Founded in 1963 with a donation of artwork and funds from the painter Hans Hofmann, the University Art Museum, Berkeley (UAM) was initially located in an old power plant on the campus. Known as the Power Plant Gallery (and the Barrows Lane Gallery), this site showcased both local and international contemporary artists such as Joan Brown, Robert Arneson, Jean Tinguely, and Pol Bury. *The Eighties*—curated by Brenda Richardson and Susan Rannells and on view between March 17 and April 12, 1970, at the Power Plant Gallery—featured younger, Conceptually oriented Bay Area artists.[28] With a prescient title referring to the next decade, the show was conceived by its curators to "encourage communications and the free flow of ideas about the future, the quality of life as it may exist in the eighties, and, equally important, ideas about the function of the museum in a radically changing world."[29] Presenting the gallery as studio or laboratory space, the exhibition included such installations as Jim Melchert's hanging Plexiglas wishing well and sound works such as a recording of William T. Wiley's voice murmuring "This is the eighties, this is the eighties" on repeat. On opening night, Terry Fox performed his infamous *Defoliation* (described in Constance Lewallen's essay in this catalogue), which both replicated and protested the horrific, pervasive napalm bombing in Vietnam (see fig. 1.25, p. 39).

During the course of the exhibition, artists came to the gallery to converse with the public, who was also invited to present its own ideas and to work within a special "free space" marked by a neon sign. As a result, artists had the opportunity to reveal more about their own processes, and audiences were able to more actively participate here than in the passive viewing conditions normally found in galleries and museums.[30]

In 1965, UAM held an architectural competition to design its new building, and the commission was awarded to San Francisco architect Mario Ciampi and associates.[31] In November 1970—during the apex of the antiwar student protests, less than six months after the tragic Kent State University shootings—the museum inaugurated its multi-ramped, concrete Brutalist building. The new director, Peter Selz, organized a series of opening events: Happenings by Wiley as well as Robert Hudson; poetry readings by Gary Snyder, Richard Brautigan, and Robert Duncan; a new music concert by Steve Reich; and a work, *Parades and Changes* (1970; fig. 2.6), by Anna Halprin's dancers.[32] The score instructed performers to embrace, dress and undress, then crumple and tear paper, and Halprin's intermittently nude dancers acted out these simple tasks while ascending and descending the concrete ramps of the building, "defining" its site. Paul Cotton did an unscheduled performance at the opening: Dressed as one of his characters, Astral-Naught Rabb-Eye, he engaged with a George Segal sculpture.[33]

After moving into the new building, Richardson organized other contemporary exhibitions and performances. A one-man show, *Terry Fox* (1973), featured a series of everyday actions and odd rituals with objects—basins, vials, candles, and mirrors. The work was performed behind a muslin curtain viewed "backstage," rendering the artist's ritualistic actions even more mysterious. That same year, Richardson presented *Stephen Laub: Bodies of Water*, a series of photographs and a book documenting the artist's task-oriented performance in which he attempts to hold water in crevices of his body, such as behind his knee.

Performance/Art/Artists/Performers (1975), a group of nineteen site-specific installations and performances

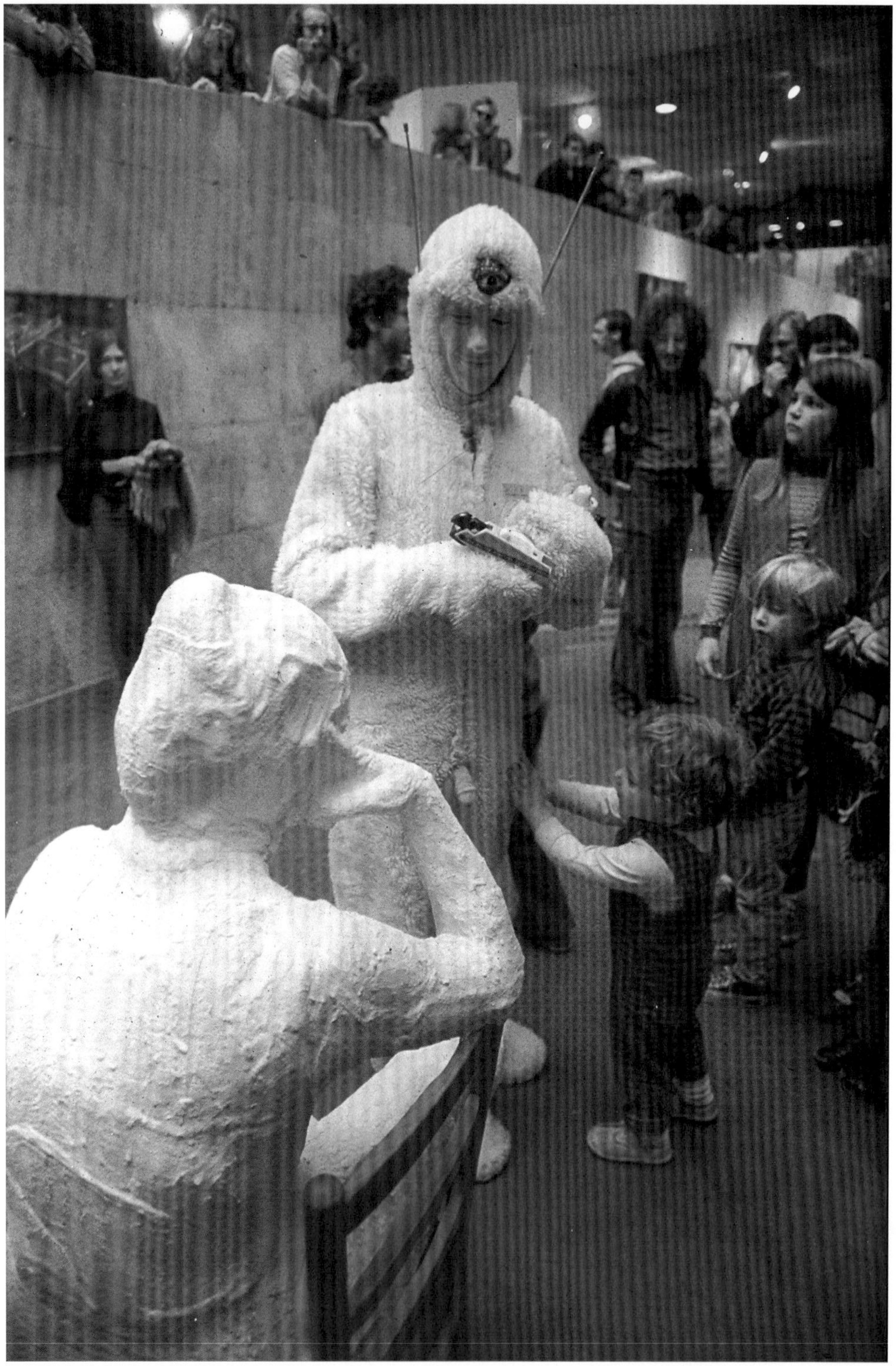

Fig. 2.7 Adam II (the late Paul Cotton), *Meditation on the Time Being,* November 8, 1970. "Creators' Proof of the living Astral-Naught's three-hour silent sculptural dialogue with George Segal's seated woman. This Act of Creation was captured photo-graphically by a museum visitor during William T. Wiley's 'Impossible Dream' at the opening of the University Art Museum." Arty-fact: Ben Blackwell, courtesy of Trans-Parent Teachers' Ink.

Fig. 2.8 Linda Mary Montano, *Lying: Dead Chicken, Live Angel (Chicken Bed),* 1972. Performance documentation.

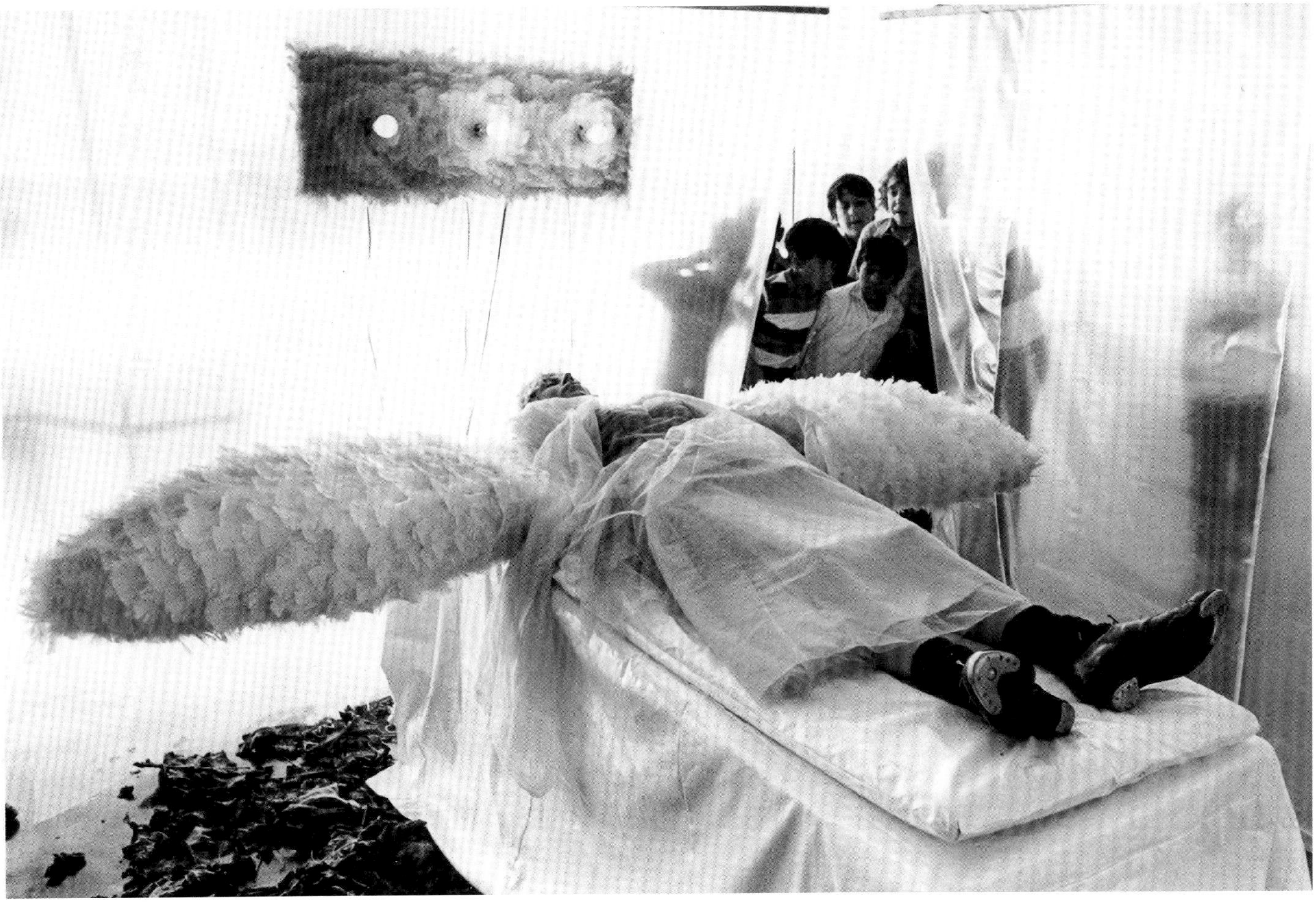

organized by guest curator Carlos Gutierrez-Solano, included two very different endurance performances. For *Splitting the Axis,* Darryl Sapien and Michael A. Hinton dressed as loggers and installed a thirty-four-foot-tall wooden utility pole in the lower atrium of the museum; they then climbed the pole with wooden mallets and wedges.[34] After reaching the top, they hammered wedges into the pole as they descended, splitting it lengthwise. Simultaneously, strategically placed video cameras and contact microphones captured fragmented images and audio from the performance, transmitting them around the periphery of the museum into the different galleries in real time.

For Linda Mary Montano's *Hypnosis, Dream, Sleep* (also called *Dreaming in Berkeley*), a hypnotist placed the artist in a trance and suggested that she could sleep, dream, and sing in her dreams.[35] Lying upon a bed with white linens, and with an amaryllis bouquet at her head and a chicken carcass in an old birdcage at her feet, Montano "slept" for three hours; she awoke several times and sang her dreams.[36] No stranger to endurance performance, Montano had done a similar installation—*Lying: Dead Chicken, Live Angel (Chicken Bed)* (fig. 2.8)—at UAM in 1972 and was famously handcuffed to artist Tom Marioni for a period of three days in 1973 (fig. 2.9). However, her gentle trance in the shrinelike setting of

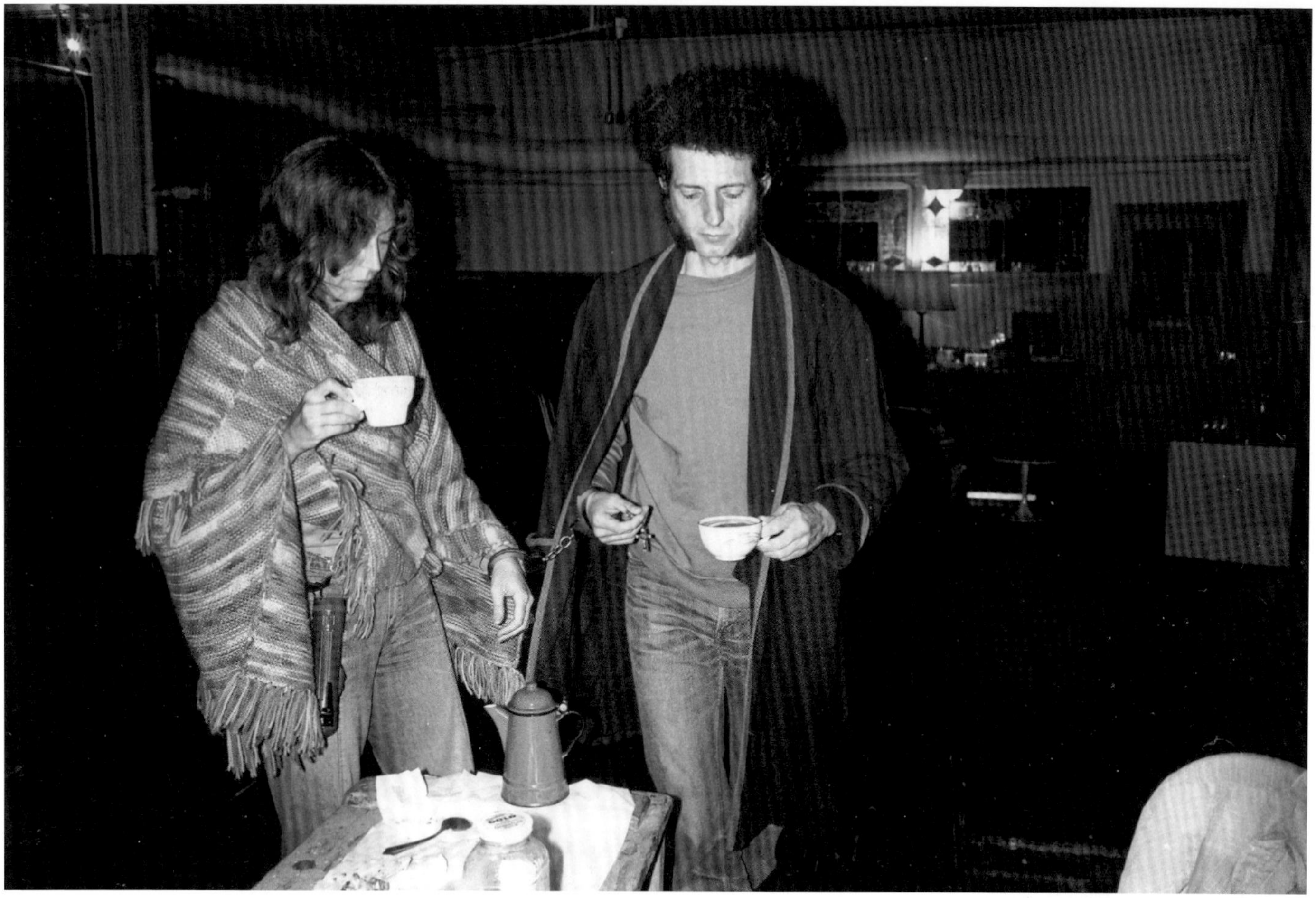

Hypnosis, Dream, Sleep contrasts to Hinton and Sapien's macho demonstration of a dangerous feat. Ultimately, both projects involve ritualistic actions that physically transform the site and expand the notion of what can take place within a museum. These adventurous exhibitions and pioneering live performance events put UAM on the map as an important venue for experimental practices of the period, not only in California but also nationally.[37]

Another Bay Area institution, the Oakland Museum, with a mission to be a "museum for the people," opened in 1969 in a multiterraced building in an urban park designed by Kevin Roche.[38] Focusing on the art, history, and science of California, the Oakland Museum presented mostly the work of younger, primarily Bay Area, artists such as Marioni, whose signature piece, *The Act of Drinking Beer with Friends Is the Highest Form of Art,* was inaugurated on the occasion of his 1970 exhibition:

> I invited sixteen friends to the museum on a Monday while it was normally closed. . . . I told the curator, George Neubert, to get the beer and to be there. Everybody showed up, and we drank and had a good time. The debris was left on exhibit as a record of the event. Basically, the show consisted of the evidence of the act. It was an important work for me, because it defined Action rather than Object as Art.[39]

While Marioni is still the author of the event, his convivial action was aided and abetted by friends who served as

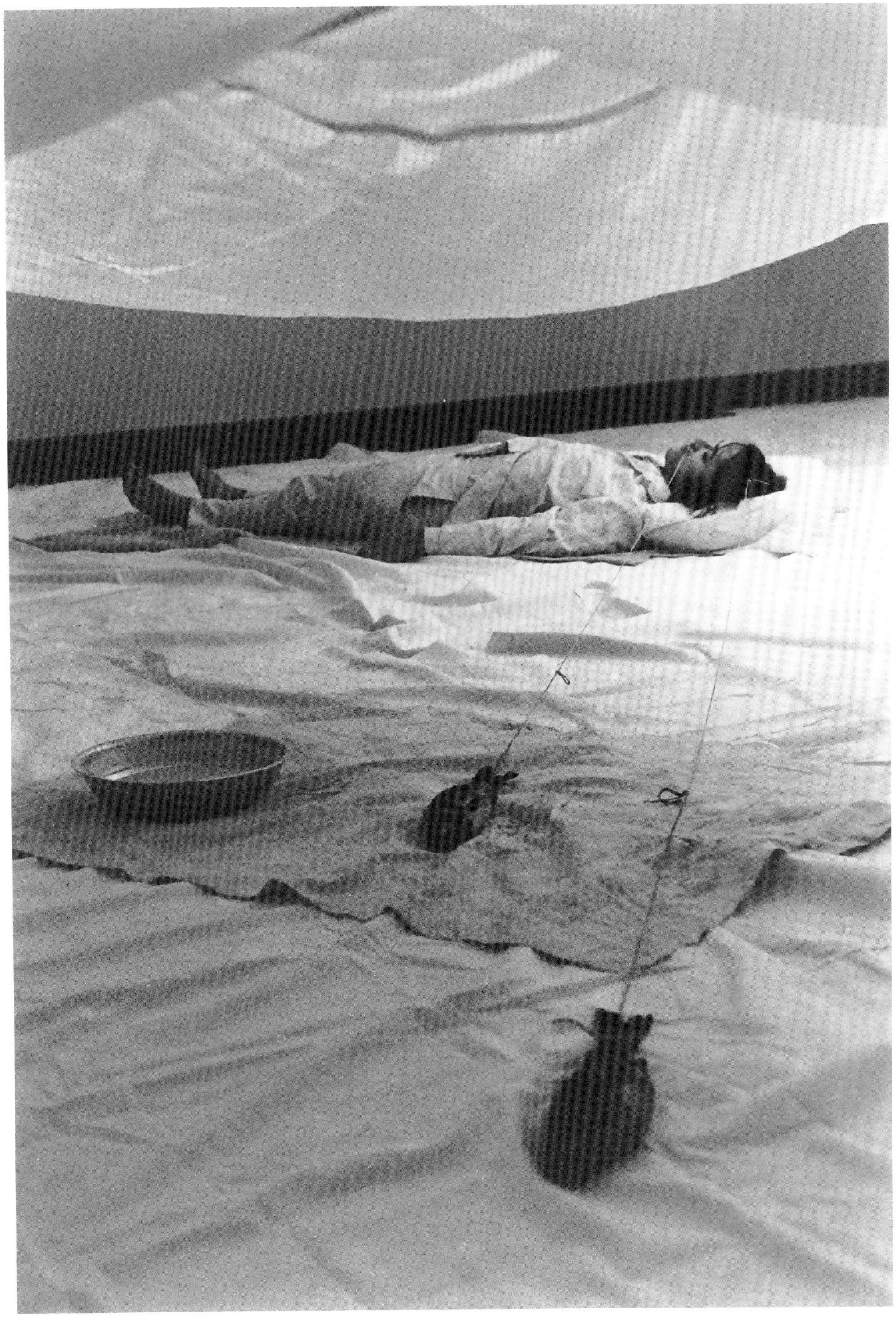

Fig. 2.9 Linda Mary Montano, *Linda Montano Will Be Handcuffed to Tom Marioni from 9 pm November 2 to 9 pm November 5, 1973,* 1973. Photographic documentation.

Fig. 2.10 Terry Fox, *Pisces,* February 2 and 3, 1971. Performance documentation *Fish, Fox, Kos,* Museum of Conceptual Art (MOCA), San Francisco, and de Saisset Art Gallery and Museum, Santa Clara. Photo: Joel Glassman, courtesy SFMOMA Research Library and Archives.

bartenders and beer drinkers; he constructs a social sculpture, disrupting the usual preordained or normative conditions of the institutional space through this collaborative and participatory process. However, when viewers came to the museum the next day (and for the duration of the exhibition), they saw only the detritus of the revelry and a refrigerator marked "FREE BEER," underscoring the ephemeral nature of the event. While Marioni temporarily shifted the conditions of display and introduced the possibility of sociability and humor into the galleries, the remains reminded visitors of what they had missed, exposing the limits of communality within the museum and the institutional critique.

Another small Bay Area museum, the de Saisset Art Gallery at Santa Clara University (SCU), directed by Lydia Modi-Vitale, exhibited several challenging performance and installation projects circa 1970. In *Fish, Fox, Kos* (1971), Marioni (working as Allan Fish) took his $500 honorarium to purchase a used Fiat 500 that he then drove through the front doors and parked in the gallery for the opening.[40] While he sat in the car, drinking champagne and conversing with visitors, a microphone and video camera recorded everything. Paul Kos showed an aerial photograph documenting his performance, *revolution,* in which he discharged 375 rounds from a Winchester rifle into a plywood target suspended from a scale. For his *Pisces* performance, Terry Fox tethered two fish to his teeth and hair, then slept on the floor as the audience watched from an adjacent room. Bright lights that hung from the ceiling and two flashlights pointed at a line of flour on the floor became progressively dim until they burned out: These functioned as correlatives of both the expired fish and the artist's somnolent body (see fig. 2.10; see also fig. 1.68, p. 81).[41] Fox's enigmatic evocation of life and death is intensely personal, since at that time he suffered from Hodgkin's disease. Finally, for the exhibition *Four,* Bonnie Sherk's environmental work—replete with trees and living animals—echoed her earlier *Portable Parks* projects, which are discussed later in this essay (see fig. 1.11, p. 25). All of these works pushed the usual boundaries of gallery content and exhibition practice.

In Southern California, too, it was the smaller, less established museums that exhibited the most challenging art. Initially founded in 1921, the Pasadena Art Institute reorganized as the Pasadena Art Museum (PAM) in 1954 to focus on acquiring and displaying modern and contemporary art created after 1945. The ambitious new director, Thomas Leavitt, arrived in 1957 and hired a young curator, Walter Hopps, to work with him on a Richard Diebenkorn exhibition in 1960.[42]

As a teenager, Hopps had visited the Walter and Louise Arensberg collection before it was acquired by the Philadelphia Museum of Art in 1954.[43] Maintaining his interest in Dada, Hopps organized a Kurt Schwitters retrospective (1962), followed by the first Duchamp retrospective (1963). These two historical exhibitions of Dadaists greatly influenced Los Angeles's younger generation of artists, including Ed Ruscha, who met Duchamp through Hopps.[44] That very same year (1963), Ruscha began to extend Duchamp's notion of the *objet trouvé* when he photographed "found" subjects in the urban landscape—buildings, apartments, gas stations, and palm trees—for his monothematic artists' books.

When Hopps was invited in 1965 to curate the São Paulo Biennial, John Coplans took on curatorial and publications responsibilities at PAM. Coplans curated *Allan Kaprow* (1967), a survey of the artist's work that traveled nationally and included *Fluids,* a Happening in which Kaprow and his collaborators built throughout the urban environment seven enormous structures using these simple instructions: "During three days, about twenty rectangular enclosures of ice blocks (measuring about 30 feet long, 10 wide and 8 high) are built throughout the city. Their walls are unbroken. They are left to melt."[45] Focusing on issues of labor, participation, and the ephemeral, Kaprow's project "[used] the fantasy of communal work as a means to dissolve the walls between individuals."[46]

Unfortunately, PAM was unable to sustain this adventurous programming due to an incompatibility between the avant-

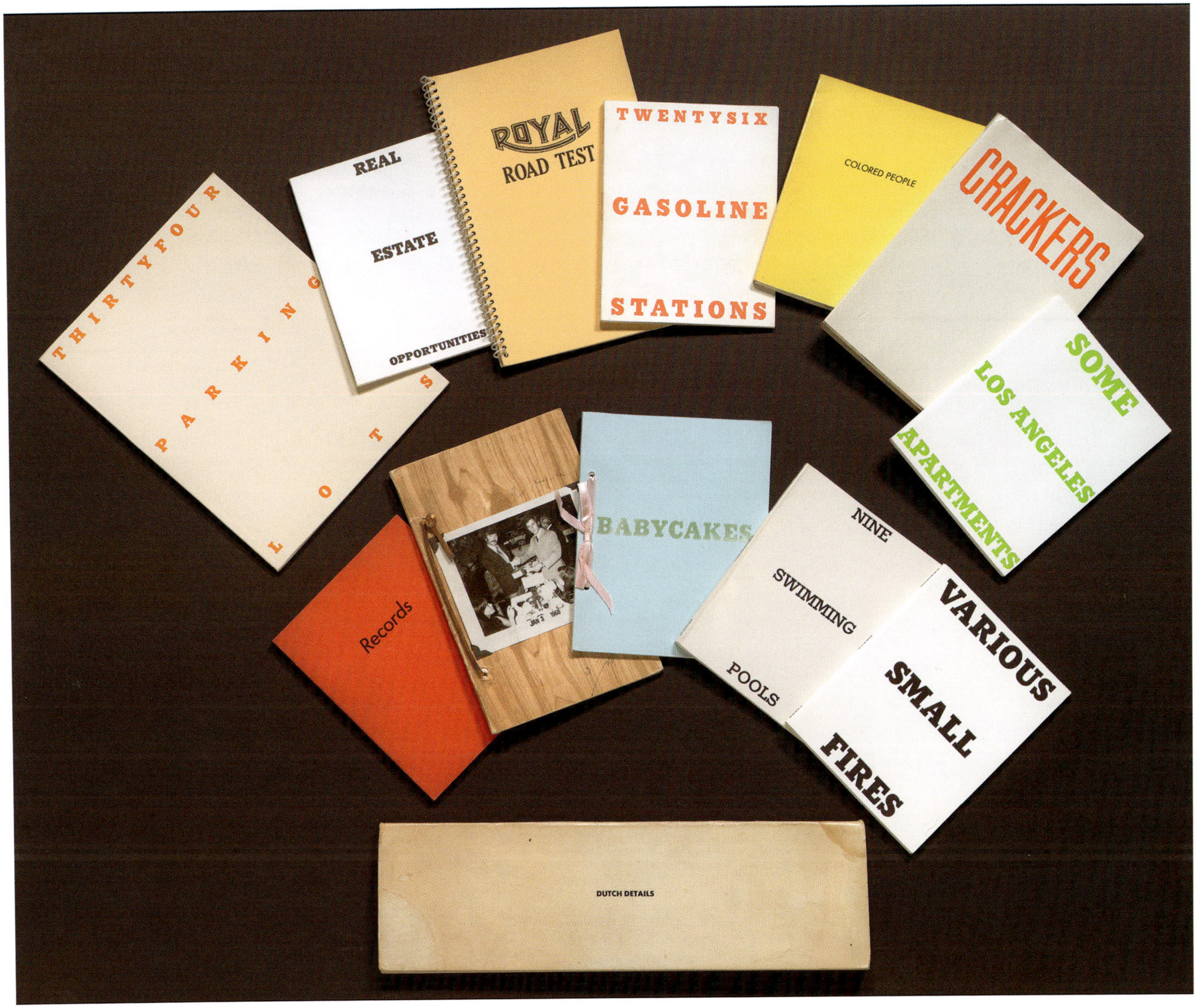

Fig. 2.11 Ed Ruscha, various artists' books, 1962–72. Dimensions variable.

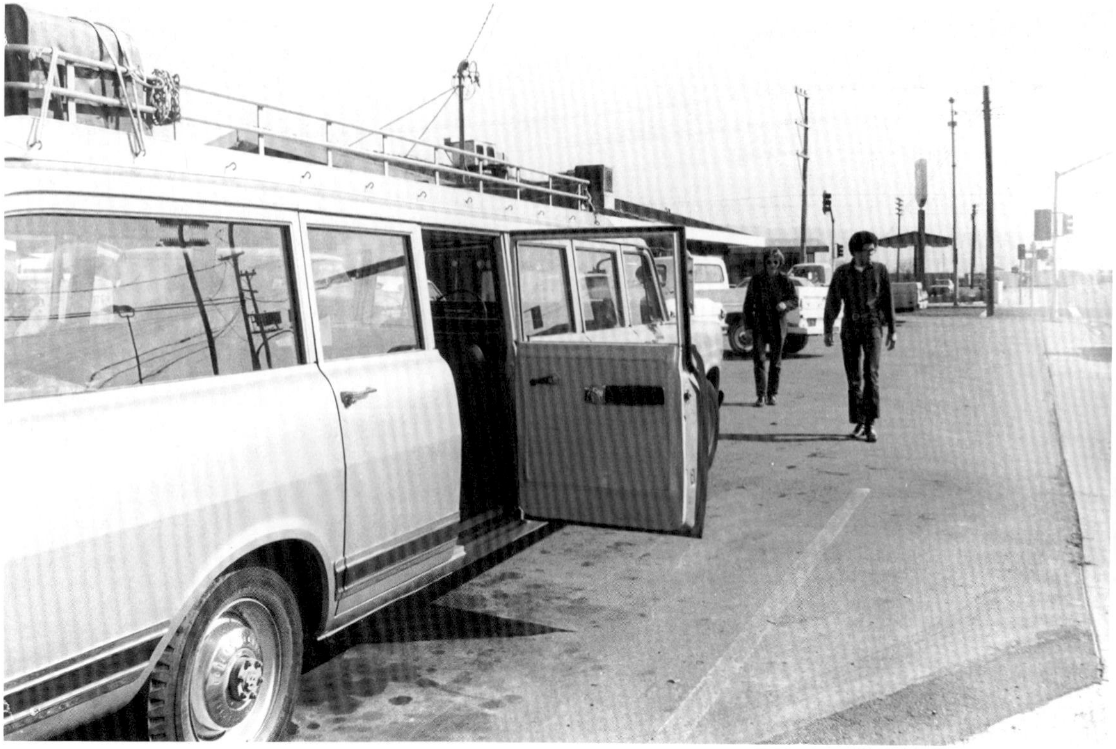

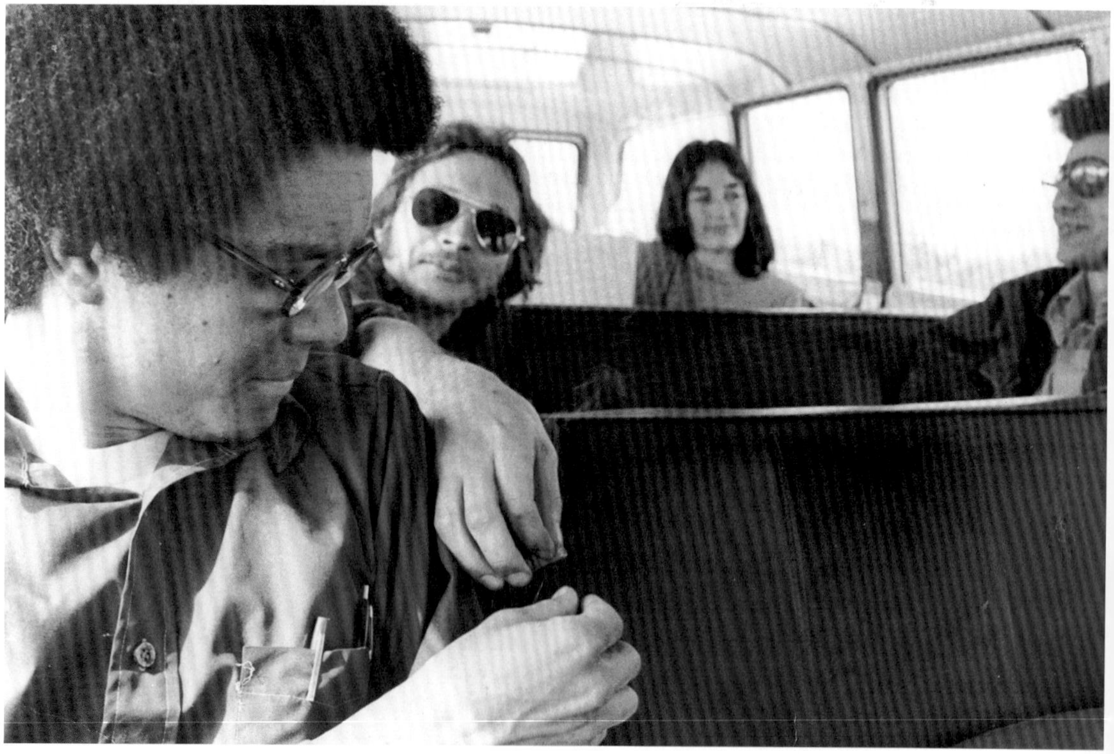

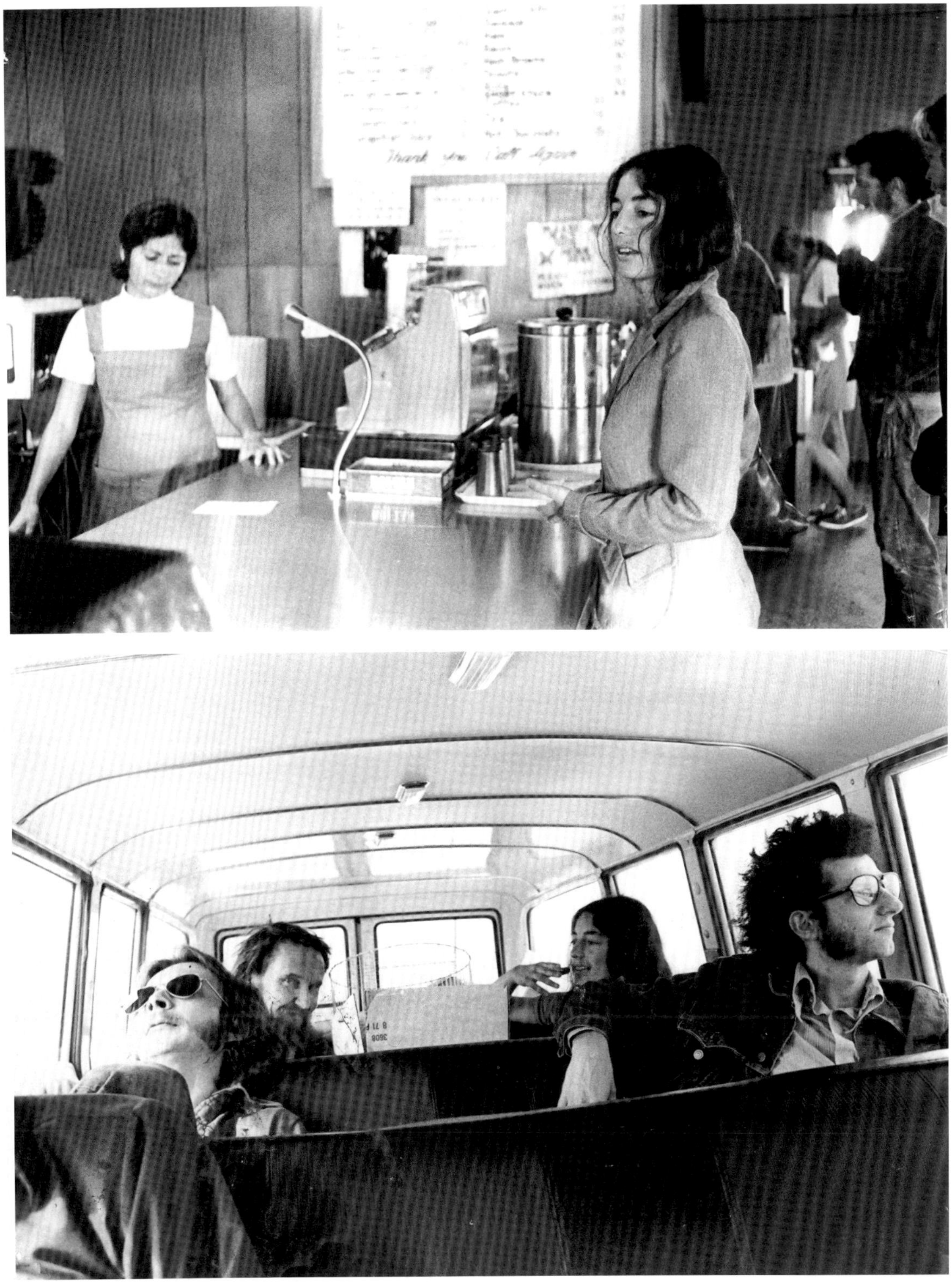

Fig. 2.12 Tom Marioni, *The Trip* (detail), 1972. Photographic documentation from *The San Francisco Performance,* March 12–April 16, 1972, Newport Harbor Art Museum, Newport Beach, California.

garde nature of the museum and the conservative politics of the community.[47] As a result, several key supporters and staff departed. Confronted by continuing economic difficulties, PAM became the Norton Simon Museum in 1975, when the Los Angeles industrialist after which it is named took charge and transformed it into a more historical museum.[48]

Another institution that made a strong commitment to emerging contemporary art was the Newport Harbor Art Museum, initially named the Balboa Pavilion Gallery. Constructed in 1906, the Balboa Pavilion became a seaside recreation center at the southern terminus of the Pacific Electric Red Car Line. In 1961, a group of thirteen ambitious women, known as the Balboa Pavilion Fine Arts Patrons, renovated the space's 8,000-square-foot second floor in exchange for permission to use it rent-free as an art museum. When it first opened, the Balboa Pavilion Gallery presented such exhibitions as *Morris Graves: Retrospective* (1963), *California Hard-Edge Painting* (1964), and a Richard Diebenkorn solo show (1965).[49] Rechristened the Newport Harbor Art Museum (NHAM) in 1965, the venue hired a professional director, Thomas Garver, and became an increasingly important space for contemporary art: Its first exhibition in 1968 featured now well-known Southern California artists like Ed Ruscha and Joe Goode.[50] NHAM also became one of the first museums on the West Coast to show emerging Conceptual art, performance, and video.

Appearing/Disappearing Image/Object (1969), organized by Garver at NHAM, included both artists who made tangible images or objects as well as those whose work was more Conceptual and dematerialized. Garver's curatorial statement relates:

> The artists whose work is seen here are of a disparate temperament and the work they produce is by no means uniform in philosophical intent and appearance. They are all involved, however, in a restructuring of the traditional means by which a work of art is conceived and executed by themselves and perceived by the viewer who might more accurately be called the participant, for these works demand more than a passivity of a spectator and involve more than a visual sense.[51]

Included in the exhibition, Michael Asher's no title (1966–67) consisted of a column of pressurized air that was perceived only when a viewer walked through it. Asher applies the same formal properties inherent in making a solid sculpture, yet here he creates the perception of planes, lines, and volumes through the carefully controlled air vent. Rather than seeing it with their eyes, viewers sense the air as it hits their bodies. Another work in the exhibition, Allen Ruppersberg's *Location Piece* (1969), had already been included in an exhibition at the new Eugenia Butler Gallery, though that is not where it was actually seen. When viewers arrived at the gallery, they found a sign on the door directing them to Ruppersberg's studio at 7507 Sunset Boulevard. Once inside, they encountered a small room constructed of stretched canvases within a lighted, museum-like display that included a cow's skull, rocks, and dried leaves—an ironic juxtaposition of nature and culture. Relocated in 1969 to NHAM's Balboa Pavilion, Ruppersberg's room-size work, with its stagelike environment and decaying objects, informed his subsequent performances/installations *Al's Café* (1969) and *Al's Grand Hotel* (1971), which are discussed in other essays in this book (see figs. 1.29–1.30, pp. 43–44; see also figs. 4.13–4.14, pp. 238–39).[52]

John Baldessari was represented in *Appearing/Disappearing Image/Object* by his early hand-lettered text paintings *Pure Beauty, A Painting That Is Its Own Documentation,* and *Voluble Luminist Painting for Max Kozloff* (all 1966–68; see fig. 1.89, p. 102). In this last work, Baldessari extracts a portion of Kozloff's 1968 *Artforum* article. By taking it completely out of context and reproducing the critic's high-falutin language, Baldessari reverses the typical dynamic between artist and critic: here the artist proposes a critique of the writer. In this exhibition, all three artists—Asher, Baldessari, and Ruppersberg—subvert or alter the normal viewing conditions in a museum as well as the expectations of its visitors.

Another early and important NHAM exhibition, *The San Francisco Performance* (1972), was guest curated by Marioni and highlighted Bay Area performance, video, and Conceptual art. In the newsprint catalogue, he discussed the transition from sculptural to time-based media:

> Today artists are using videotape to record unedited the stream-of-conscious flow of life. . . . The life span or performance of the piece is shorter and the methods for recording the artist's hand today are in keeping with the materials (technology) that are available to the artist. . . . The new sculpture demands the artist execute his work in the space it is to be shown in. That way the artist has control over all aspects of its environment.[53]

In keeping with his statement, Marioni, for his own project for the exhibition, documented a ride down the coast from San Francisco. He hired Larry Fox to take photographs and George Bolling to make a video of the trip. They smoked copious amounts of marijuana and took a jaunt to the Forestiere Underground Gardens in Fresno.

Mel Henderson's contribution to the NHAM show was a video documenting a performance that referenced the infamous 1971 riot at Attica Prison in New York. The night before the exhibition opened, he spelled out the word "Attica" in flashing Christmas-tree lights on a hillside owned by the Irvine Company. Henderson and his collaborator, Paul Kos, were arrested for trespassing. Kos spent the night in jail, and eventually the charges were dropped (see figs. 1.22–1.24, pp. 36–38). For his *Newport Wallpaper*, Howard Fried first made a pen-and-ink abstraction, holding the steno pad at the closest possible distance to his eye at which he could still see the image. He then reproduced the small drawing onto large sheets and installed them in a repetitous mirrored pattern across the gallery wall.

Fried tests the limits of his body and senses in the process of making the work, as he continued to do in performances like *Inside the Harlequin: Approach-Avoidance III and II* (1971; see figs. 2.13–2.14; see also figs. 1.58–1.59, pp. 74–75). Bonnie Sherk's installation *Traditional Performances: a piece, within a piece, within a piece, etc. (Demonstration of struggles)* (fig. 2.15) was a tentlike, mesh structure that housed a pregnant rat which gave birth to ten pups—a live "performance" of the tasks of motherhood and nest building for offspring. When one of the rats unexpectedly bit a visitor, the artist was asked to remove the animals and the museum closed temporarily. Sherk's interest in the interrelationships between humans and animals is also apparent in *Public Lunch.* In this piece, which is discussed in Lewallen's essay (see fig. 1.13, p. 27), Sherk dined in a cage at the San Francisco Zoo's lion house. Finally, Kos's untitled interactive/performative installation consisted of a pool table positioned in a corner of a room with animal traps hung on the walls. The work simultaneously beckoned visitors to play the game while creating a potentially hazardous situation for anyone who did so.

The radical new Conceptual and performance art at the UAM, PAM, and NHAM was atypical of what had been shown within the hallowed halls of a museum, and these works transformed the institutions into sites for living art. As the decade continued, other museums began to better integrate post-studio practices into their programs.[54] However, in spite of the efforts of these venues, some artists preferred to control production and presentation of their art by creating their own spaces or organizations where they were free from the constraints of more traditional institutions and commercial galleries.

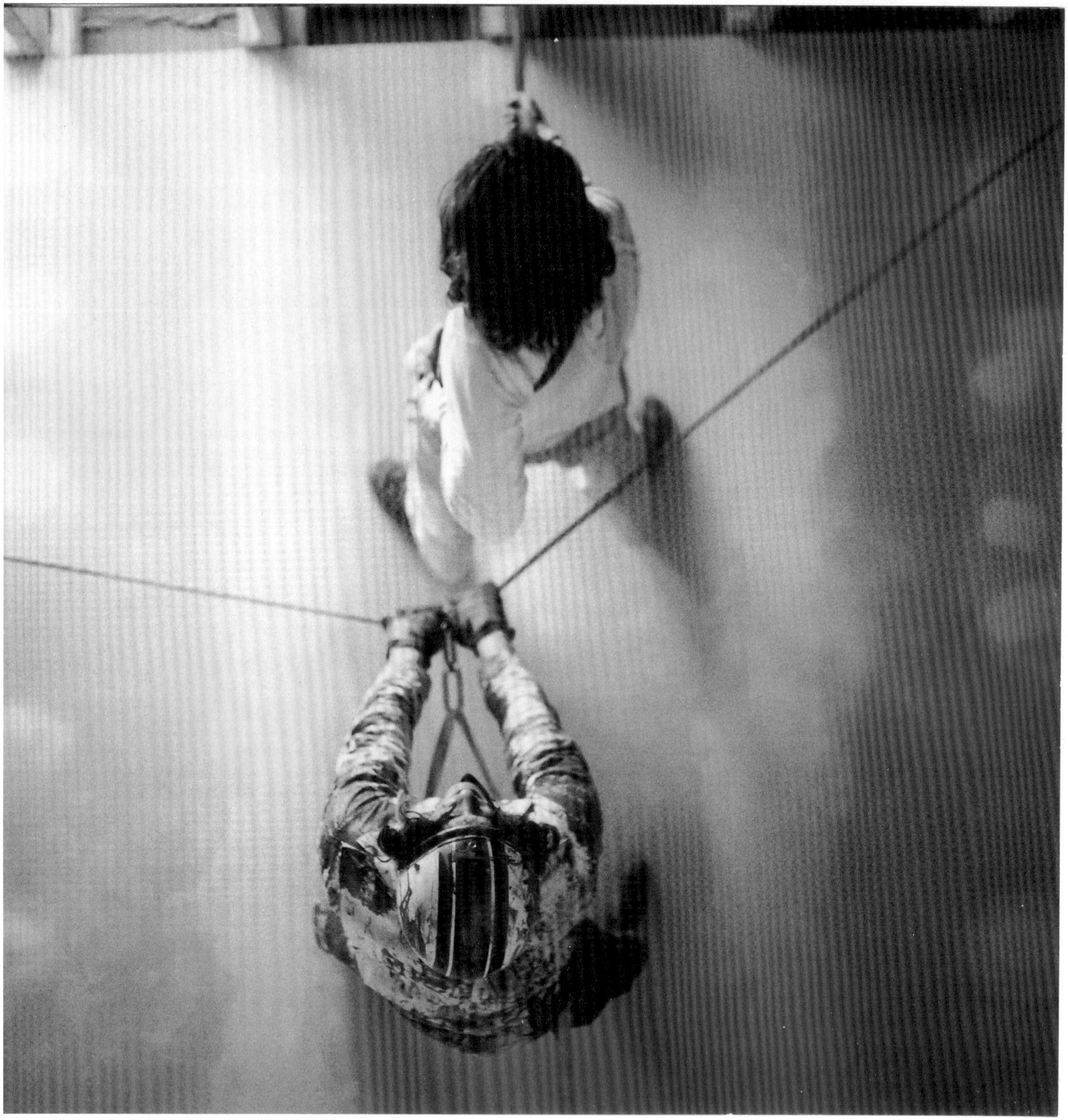

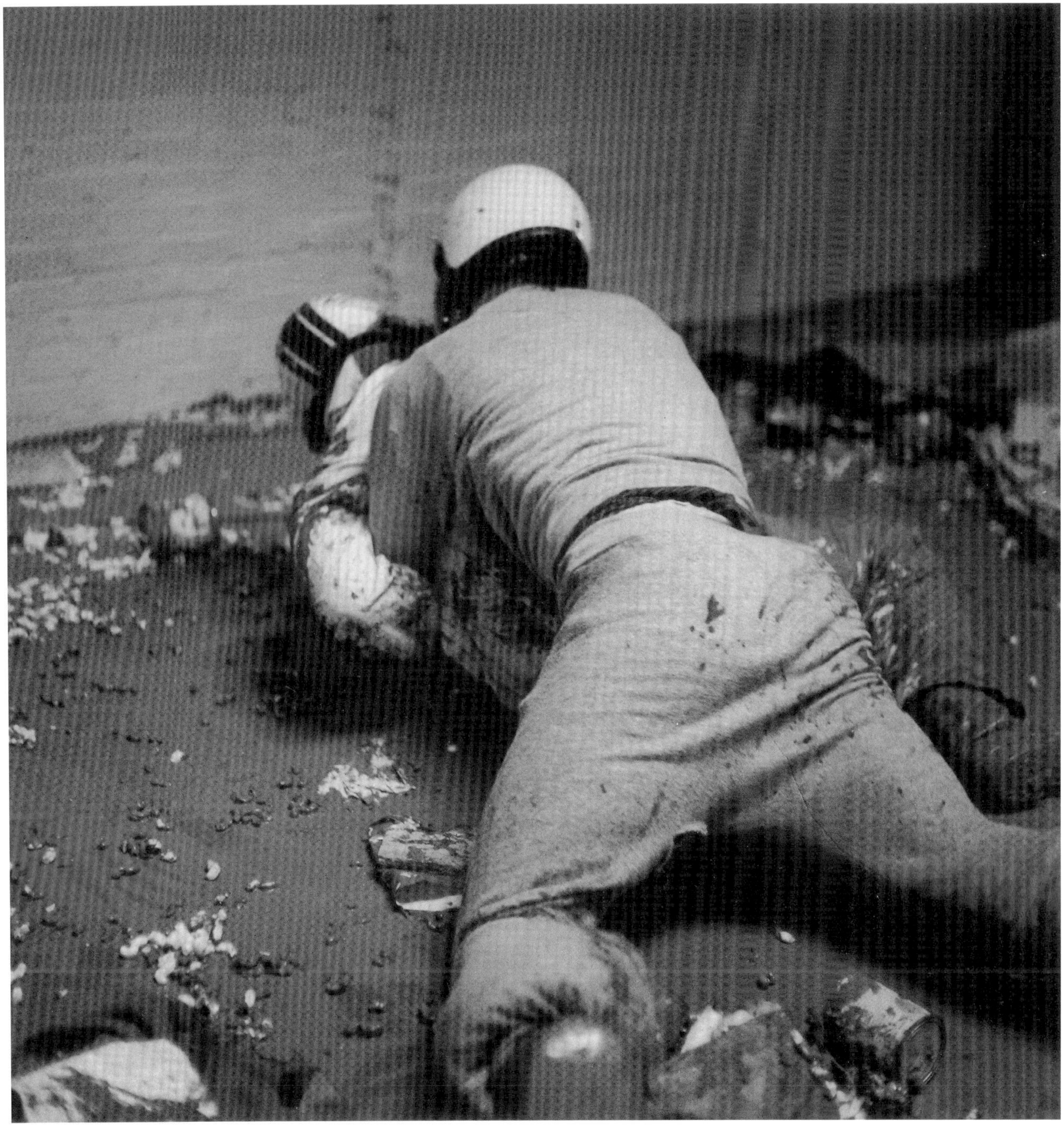

Figs. 2.13–2.14 Howard Fried, *Inside the Harlequin: Approach-Avoidance III and II,* 1971.
 Gravity decimation (*opposite*): James Pennuto, Howard Fried. Wrestling Possesions (*above*): Howard Fried, David Sherk. Production stills: Edmund Shea.

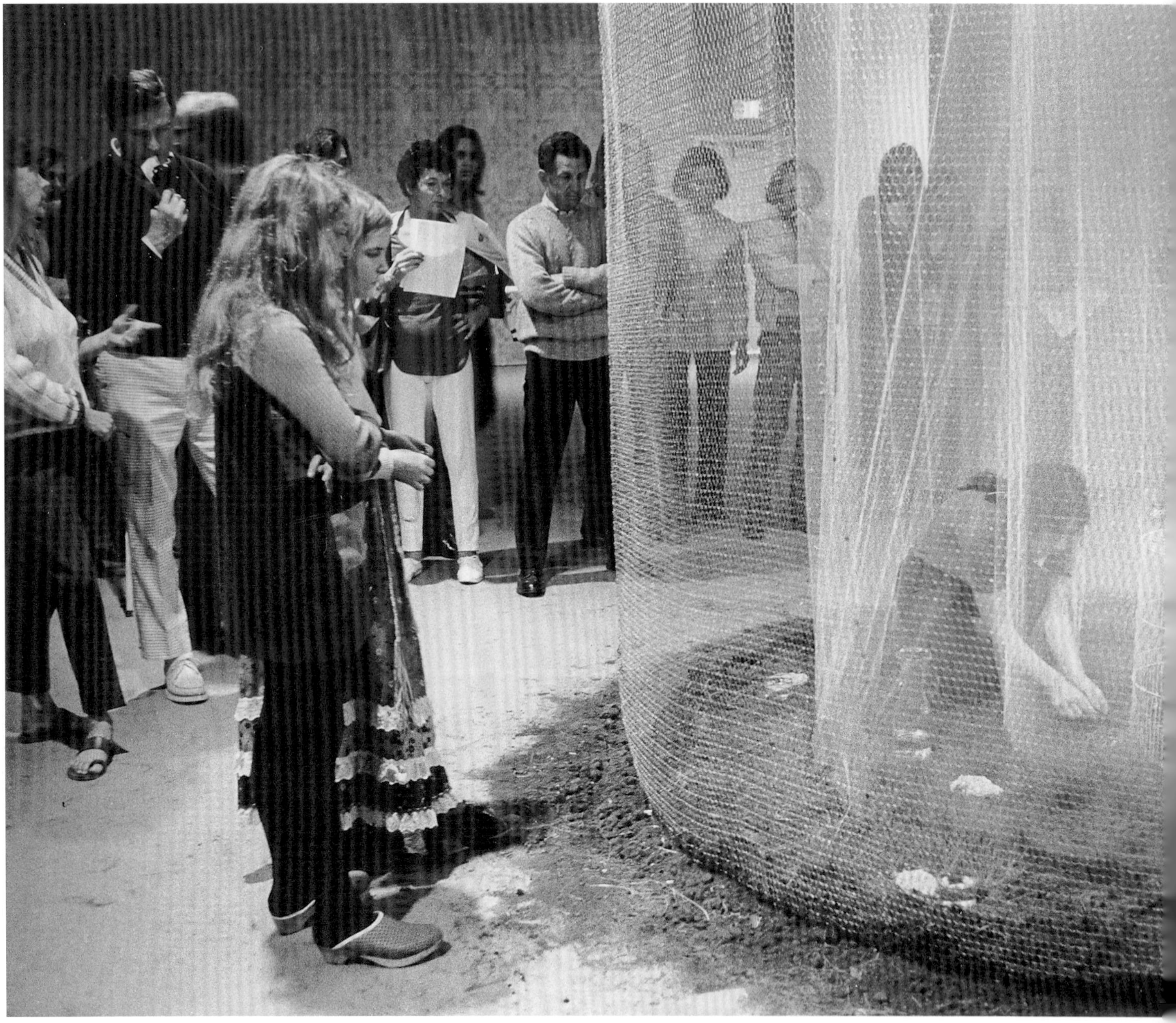

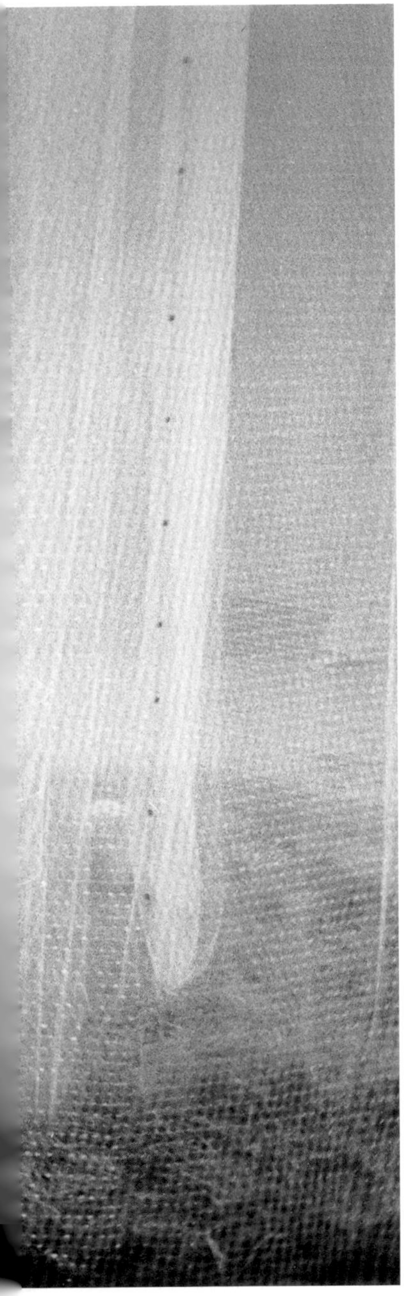

Fig. 2.15 Bonnie Sherk, *Traditional Performances: a piece, within a piece, within a piece, etc. (Demonstration of struggles),* March 12, 1972; from *The San Francisco Performance.* Photo: Larry Fox, courtesy SFMOMA Research Library and Archives.

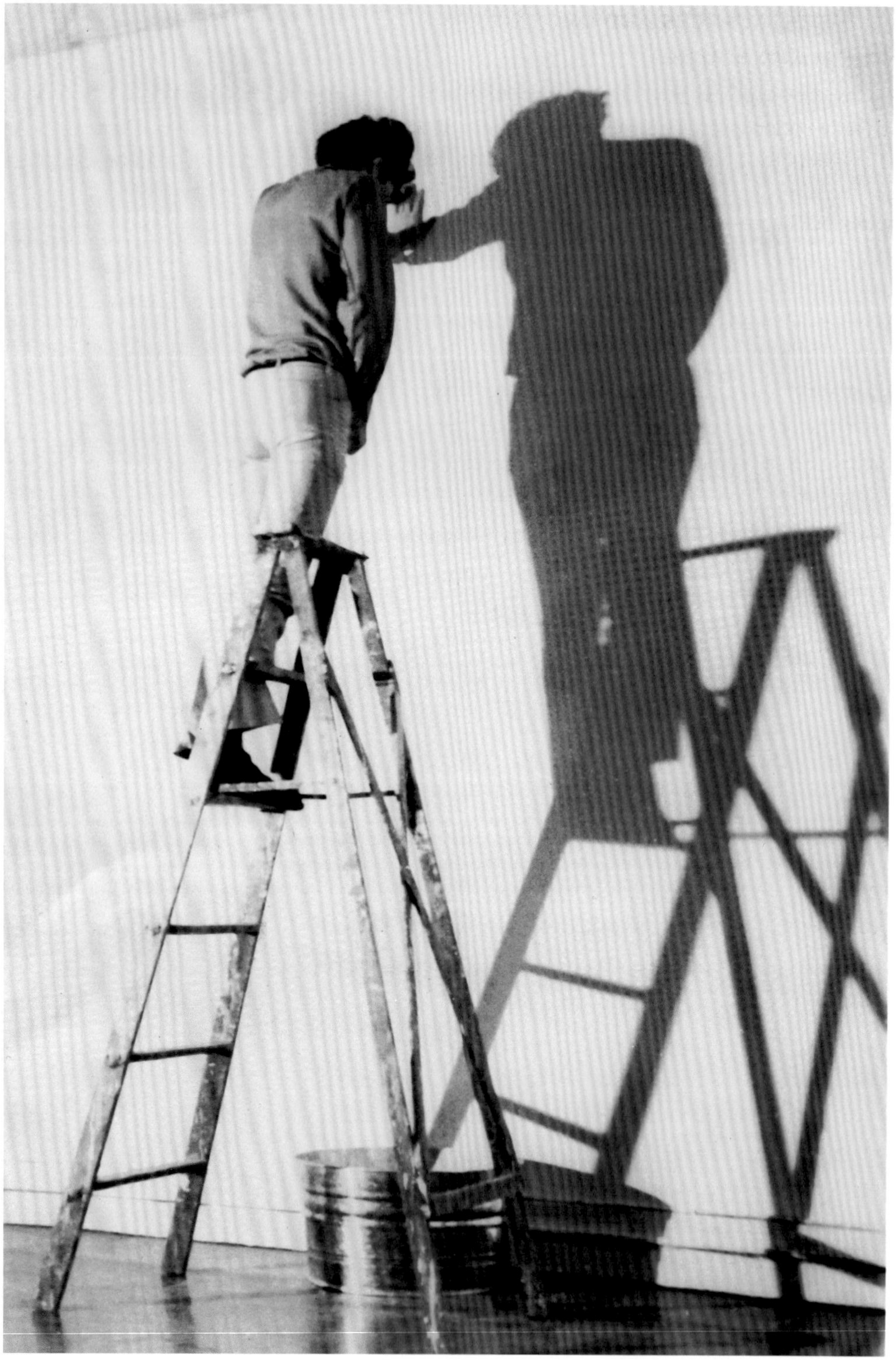

Fig. 2.16 Tom Marioni a.k.a. Allan Fish, *Piss Piece,* 1970; from *Sound Sculpture As,* April 30, 1970, Museum of Conceptual Art (MOCA). Performance documentation.

ARTIST-RUN SPACES AND ORGANIZATIONS, NORTH AND SOUTH

For artists of the seventies, the new alternative spaces offered virtually the only venues for the development of conceptually oriented, non-commercial forms such as video, installations and actions. . . . Non-traditional curatorial practices also characterized the new alternative spaces: Most relied on artists to curate shows, rather than professional curators. And, most radical of all, artists received fees for exhibiting.

Robert Atkins, "On Edge: Alternative Spaces Today," *Art in America* 86, no. 11 (November 1998): 57

As Atkins notes, artists who created Conceptual, noncommercial, and nontraditional art established their own alternative spaces to both curate and exhibit their works. In 1970, the National Endowment for the Arts instituted several new grants, including the workshops category for artists' organizations that had a strong commitment to new art forms and placed artists in key policy-making positions. Motivated by lobbying from the Congressional Black Caucus and other political activists, the NEA began to offer grants for community-based art activities in 1972. As Renny Pritikin has observed, the field of artist-run organizations employed the Students for a Democratic Society credo that "inspired rhetoric for self-determination, consensual decision-making and participatory democracy translated from the political struggles to the microcosm of the art world."[55] While some alternative spaces were established by artists working in a particular aesthetic or a specific medium, others began as cultural and service organizations by specific communities.[56]

A few artist-run organizations evolved specifically to accommodate Conceptual art and new genres, and provided larger, less formal, more flexible spaces that facilitated greater experimentation. These venues presented opportunities to work outside the confines of galleries, museums, and—perhaps most importantly—the contemporary art marketplace. In the Bay Area, Marioni became an influential figure as both artist and curator. Toward the end of his tenure as curator at the Richmond Art Center, where he was known for his "provocative and daring exhibitions," Marioni founded his own space, the Museum of Conceptual Art (MOCA), on Third Street in downtown San Francisco in 1970. It was a "large-scale social artwork and interactive installation" that became his "life's work for a decade."[57]

At the time, there was no other place like MOCA in San Francisco, and Marioni used this project to offer not only an exhibition venue but also a social space that could cultivate a community of Conceptual artists. Of MOCA's mission, which emphasized the production of work that combined visual art, performance, and sound, Marioni has said: "In '70 when I started MOCA as a specialized sculpture action museum, I made my own rules and defined Conceptual art as idea-oriented situations not directed at the production of static objects."[58] His notion that time-based, multidisciplinary production emanated from sculpture and actions elicited a series of exhibitions at MOCA, including *Sound Sculpture As, Body Works,* and *All Night Sculptures.*

For *Sound Sculpture As,* Marioni invited nine artists to participate in a one-night event on April 30, 1970; the only curatorial criterion was that the works utilize sound as their primary medium.[59] He announced that Allan Fish (his artistic alter ego) had sent instructions to perform a piece in his absence: he climbed to the top of a stepladder and urinated into a galvanized tub with his back to the audience as they applauded. Titled *Piss Piece,* this work recalls the short, body-oriented performances by Fluxus artists, specifically George Brecht's *Water Drip Piece* (1959), which has a score that reads: "For single or multiple performance. A source of dripping water and an empty vessel are arranged so that the water falls into the vessel."[60] Marioni humorously reinterprets Brecht's Fluxus score, which was intended to be performed by others as they wished. For *Sound Sculpture As,* Paul Kos collaborated with musician Richard Beggs to create *Sound of Ice Melting* (see fig. 1.77, p. 92). Here, boom microphones were trained on two twenty-five-pound blocks of ice, producing an absurdly humorous, Zen-like piece that evokes John Cage's *4'33"*—his "silent" composition that consists only of ambient sounds.

Body Works—a video exhibition conceived by the New York–based curator and *Avalanche* editor Willoughby Sharp and coordinated by Marioni—took place on October 18, 1970, at Breen's Café in San Francisco.[61] With artists from both the East and West Coasts—Vito Acconci, Terry Fox, Bruce Nauman, Dennis Oppenheim, Keith Sonnier, and William Wegman—the show featured videos in which the artists' bodies become the material, serving as both the object and subject. Acconci burns the hairs around his nipples; Nauman walks around his studio, and, in *Tonguings,* Fox manipulates his tongue (see fig. 1.66, p. 79).[62] The relaxed, informal setting afforded by Breen's was emblematic of the kind of social interaction Marioni encouraged in both his artwork and curatorial practice.

All Night Sculptures—presented from sunrise to sunset at MOCA on April 20–21, 1973—included a series of interactive installations and performances by nine artists.[63] In her iconic performance *Feed Me,* a nude Barbara T. Smith occupied a room in the gallery, and a recording of her voice repeated the phrase "Feed me" (see fig. 1.44, p. 58). Boldly beckoning a personal exchange, the work invited viewers to literally feed her or to "feed" her psychologically, or even sexually. Placed in a vulnerable situation with mostly male spectators, Smith, in this feminist performance, embodied the objectification of women and revealed power relations between genders.

MOCA also functioned as a social space for like-minded artists to gather together. As artist Jim Melchert said: "Often performances were done for one another . . . this communal activity among a certain group of artists was not just a matter of hanging out, but a way of working outside the studio."[64] Though MOCA had phased out by 1977, Marioni continues to host weekly salons based on his original 1970 presentation of *The Act of Drinking Beer with Friends Is the Highest Form of Art* at the Oakland Museum of California. To this day, his studio's bar remains well stocked with beer for this weekly ritual, which is central to his relationships within the San Francisco art community where he has been an integral player for the past forty-plus years.

Artists in the Bay Area continued to open their own alternative venues into the mid-1970s. In 1974, artist Jock Reynolds, with funding from the San Francisco Art Dealers Association, bought and renovated the ground floor of a warehouse at 80 Langton Street, turning it into an artist-run space for installations, video, and performance. In 1975, the space opened with Peter d'Agostino's *Walk Series* (1973–74, figs. 2.17–2.18), a sequence of neighborhood walks documented with a hand-held video camera. Three different monitors aired the uncut, real-time footage, and installation elements were also on display. That year, Lynn Hershman also started the Floating Museum, an itinerant space that commissioned and exhibited public, site-specific, and performative projects from 1974 to 1978. Carl Loeffler, who first published the art journal *La Mamelle* in 1974, opened the 8,000-square-foot La Mamelle arts space at 70 12th Street in downtown San Francisco to support live art and electronic media. La Mamelle remained active from 1975 to 1995, distributing, producing, and screening video and eventually developing one of the first archives and online networks for media art.[65] Intersection for the Arts, incorporated in 1965, was San Francisco's first community-based, multidisciplinary art space.

Galería de la Raza, was founded in a storefront in 1970 in the Mission District.[66] Initiated by a twelve-member Latino artists' collective led by Ralph Maradiaga and René Yañez, Galería de la Raza emerged from the Chicano movement to organize exhibitions, neighborhood art programs, and cultural activities. San Francisco Camerawork—devoted specifically to exhibitions of photography and the publication of *Camerawork: A Journal of Photographic Arts*—and Southern Exposure, a space south of Market Street for emerging artists, opened in 1975 and 1976, respectively, and both continue to operate today. All four of these spaces remain active.

In Los Angeles there were fewer artist-run organizations and spaces, but, as in San Francisco, they were often devoted to particular communities or practices. One of the earliest venues was the Brockman Gallery, a space opened by brothers

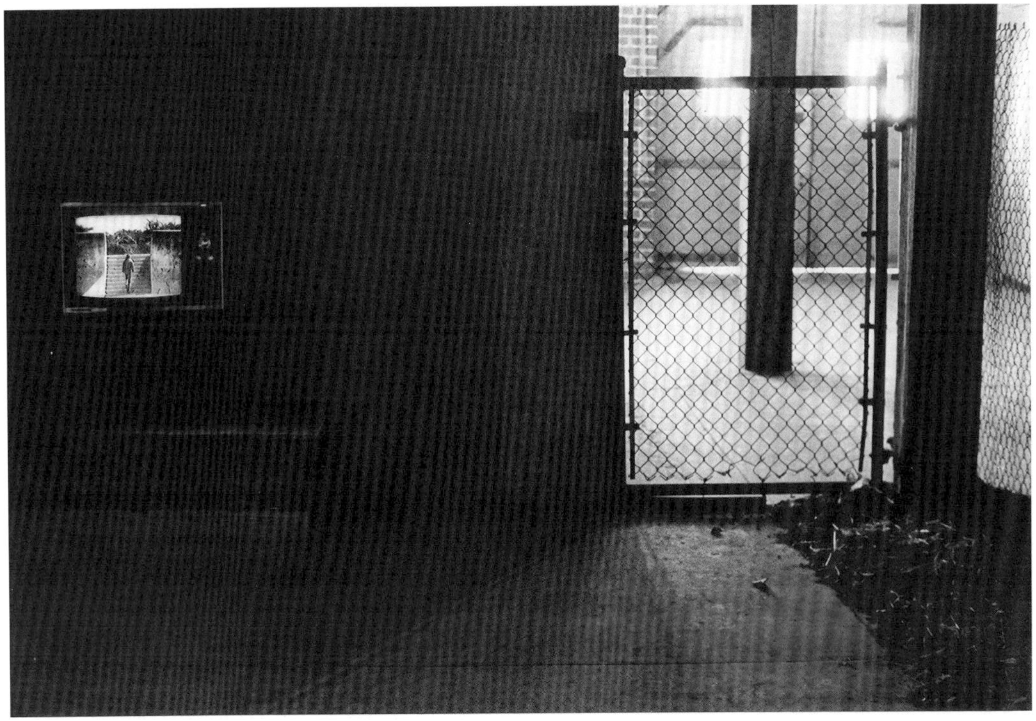

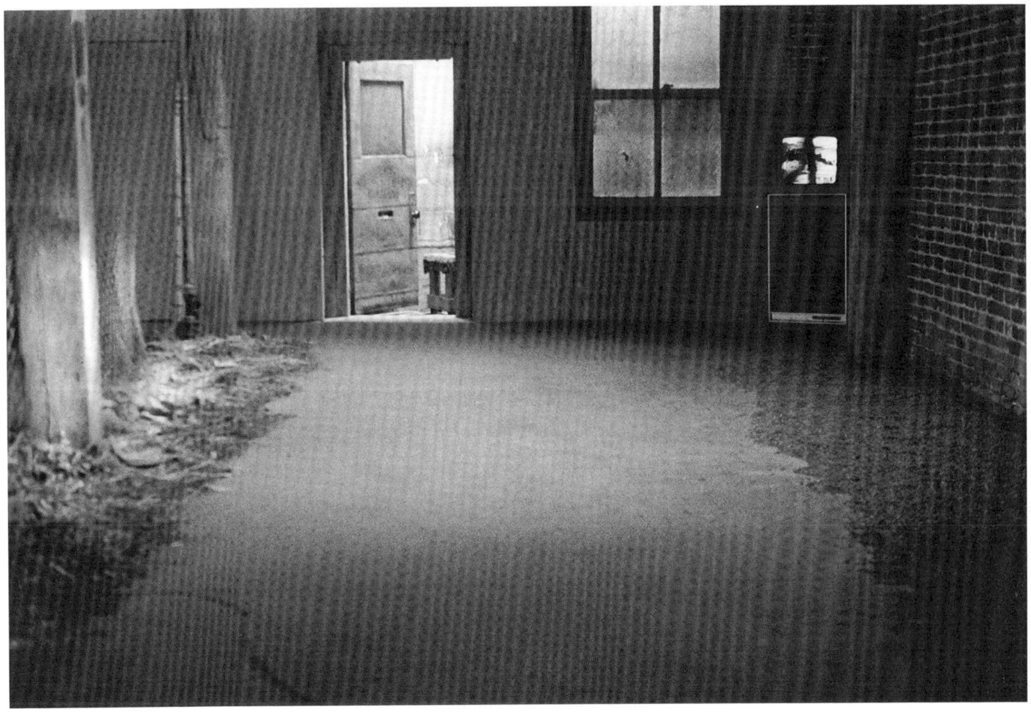

Fig. 2.17 Peter d'Agostino, *Walk Series*, 1973–74; installation view: 80 Langton Street, San Francisco, July 1975. Photo: courtesy of the artist.

>>

Fig. 2.18 Peter d'Agostino, *Walk Series: roof walk, fence walk, beach walk*, 1973–74. Video: black and white; 61:16 min.

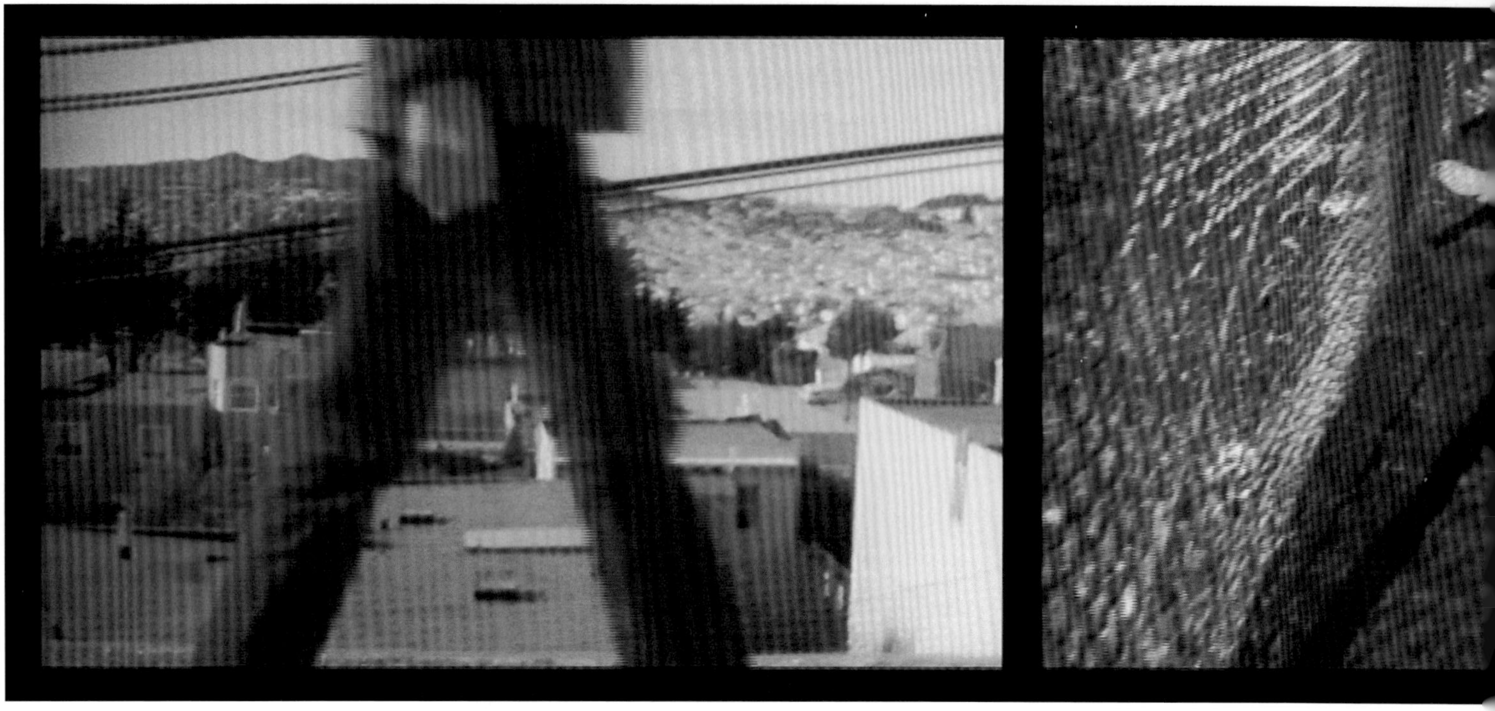

Dale and Alonzo Davis on Degnan Boulevard in South Los Angeles in 1967. Brockman nurtured emerging African American artists, including David Hammons and John Outterbridge, and exhibited established figures, such as Romare Bearden. Another early space, Beyond Baroque, was founded by George Drury Smith in 1968 in a storefront on West Washington Boulevard before relocating to the old Venice City Hall later in the decade. Primarily devoted to literary arts, Beyond Baroque became a meeting place for artists and writers, a space for performances, and a repository of the most extensive collections of "underground" or alternative publications.

In July 1969, the Los Angeles branch of the national artists' organization Experiments in Art and Technology (EAT) formed in Pasadena. Founded as an adjunct to Billy Klüver's original New York EAT, the Los Angeles group, like its East Coast counterpart, consisted of artists and scientists interested in experimental projects that occurred in nontraditional spaces. Most of EAT/LA's activities in the 1970s focused primarily on the intersection of art and technology. But one of the organization's most memorable events was the multimedia event *Moon Landing Celebration,* which included performances by artists Barbara T. Smith, composer Joe Byrd, and dancers Alex Hay and Steve Paxton, among others. The impact of the 1969 lunar landing on the public's and artists' collective imagination is apparent in other works, such as Richard Jackson's *Moon Piece* (1970; figs. 2.19), a systematic, minimal rendering of the subject in a series of eight sequential photographs, and Vija Celmins's *Moon Surface (Luna 9) #2* (1969, fig. 2.20), a meticulous multilayered drawing made from photographic maps taken in space.[67]

Other early artist-run spaces in Los Angeles included those initiated by feminists and other cultural activists who sought alternatives from dominant, often exclusive cultural institutions. In 1973, artist Judy Chicago, graphic designer

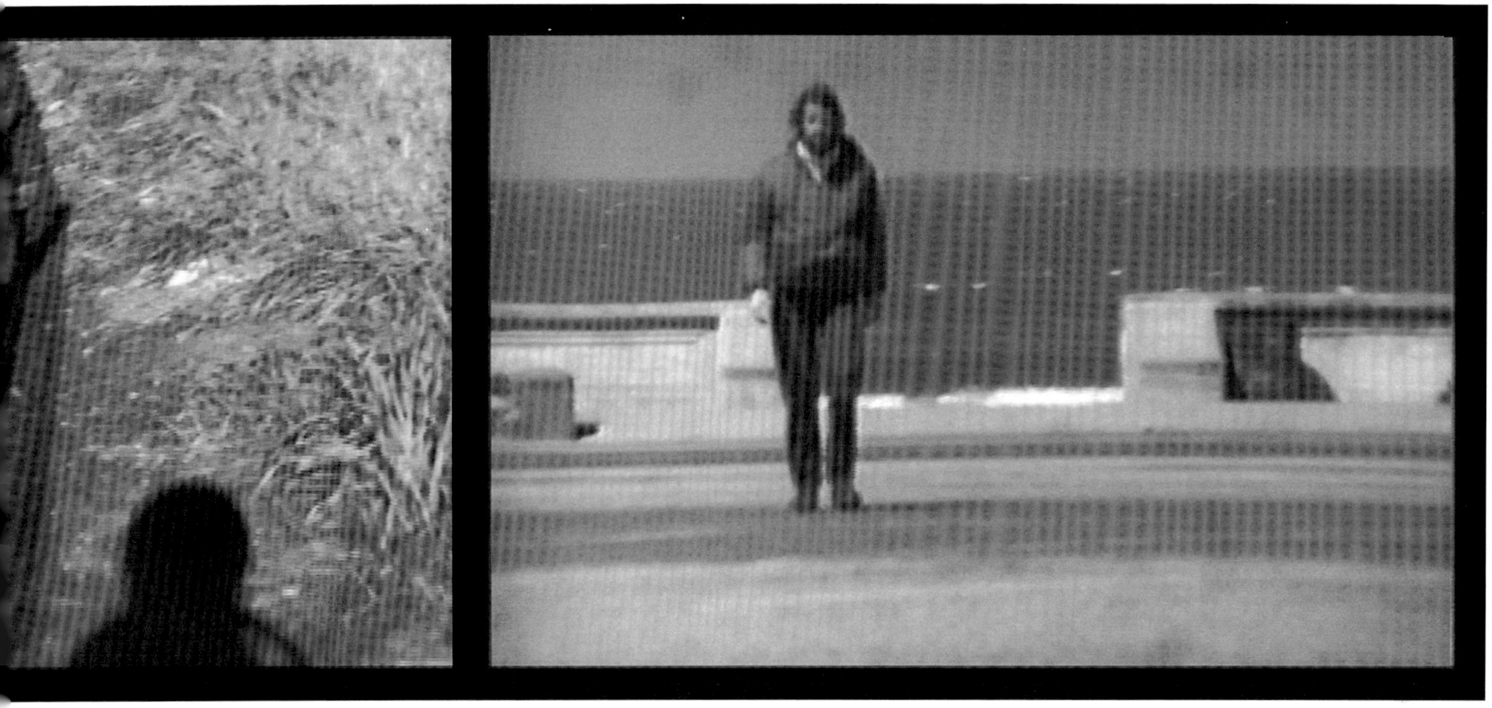

Sheila Levrant de Bretteville, and art historian Arlene Raven founded the Feminist Studio Workshop (FSW), an outgrowth of the feminist art programs at Fresno State University and California Institute of the Arts (CalArts). That year, FSW moved to the new Women's Building, which occupied the site of the old Chouinard Art Institute near MacArthur Park near downtown Los Angeles. Several other feminist galleries—Womanspace, Grandview, and 707—also opened in the vicinity. Self-Help Graphics & Art, a Chicano arts organization and workshop started by a small group of artists working out of a garage in East Los Angeles in the early 1970s, is still active today. Similarly, Centro Cultural de la Raza, founded in 1970, is a Chicano community cultural center and alternative space in the San Diego/Tijuana region that has been open for forty-plus years.

Los Angeles Institute of Contemporary Art (LAICA), an artist-run, artist-service organization established by Robert L. Smith in 1974, was a three-part institution that operated a gallery space in Century City, published the bimonthly *LAICA Journal* with critical writing about current arts activities, and created a slide registry open to all Southern California artists. LAICA's program alternated between exhibiting international avant-garde and local artists, and the organization also sponsored events such as *The New Artspace,* an important conference of alternative spaces in 1978. In 1987, with ongoing financial and administrative troubles, LAICA had to redefine its mission to focus only on its magazine, which was then edited by artist, critic, and art historian Howard Singerman, which became the organization's most enduring and erudite legacy.

Many other artist-run organizations in Los Angeles that opened between 1975 and 1978 also succumbed to financial or organizational woes. An exception was Los Angeles Contemporary Exhibitions (LACE),[68] which was started by members of a community-arts mural program funded through

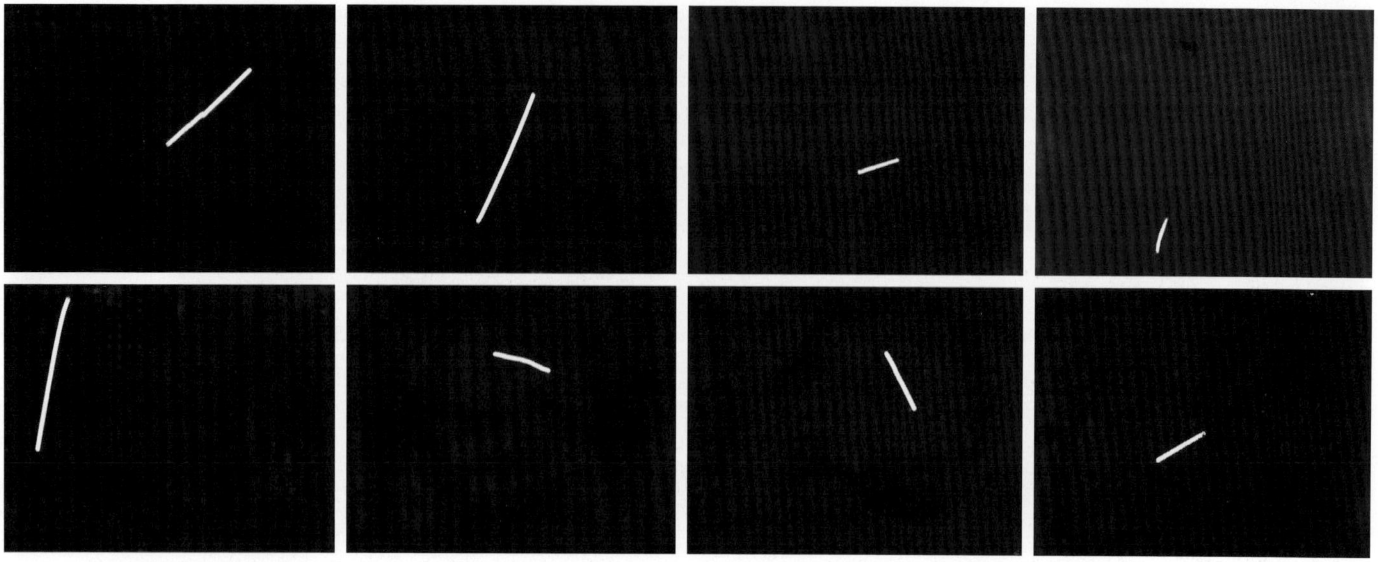

the Comprehensive Employment and Training Act (CETA). The acronym LACE was apropos given the organization's original location in the Victor Clothing Company building on Broadway, where muralist Kent Twitchell painted *The Bride and Groom* (1972). This artist-run venue for exhibitions, performances, new music, video, and workshops has had several incarnations, and it continues to thrive today in its Hollywood Boulevard location, where it serves a new generation of young artists, many of whom have emerged from California's diverse art schools and university art departments.

Fig. 2.19 Richard Jackson, *Moon Piece*, 1970. Eight black-and-white photographs; 8 × 10 in. each.

Fig. 2.20 Vija Celmins, *Moon Surface (Luna 9) #2,* 1969. Graphite on acrylic ground on paper; 14 × 18¾ in.

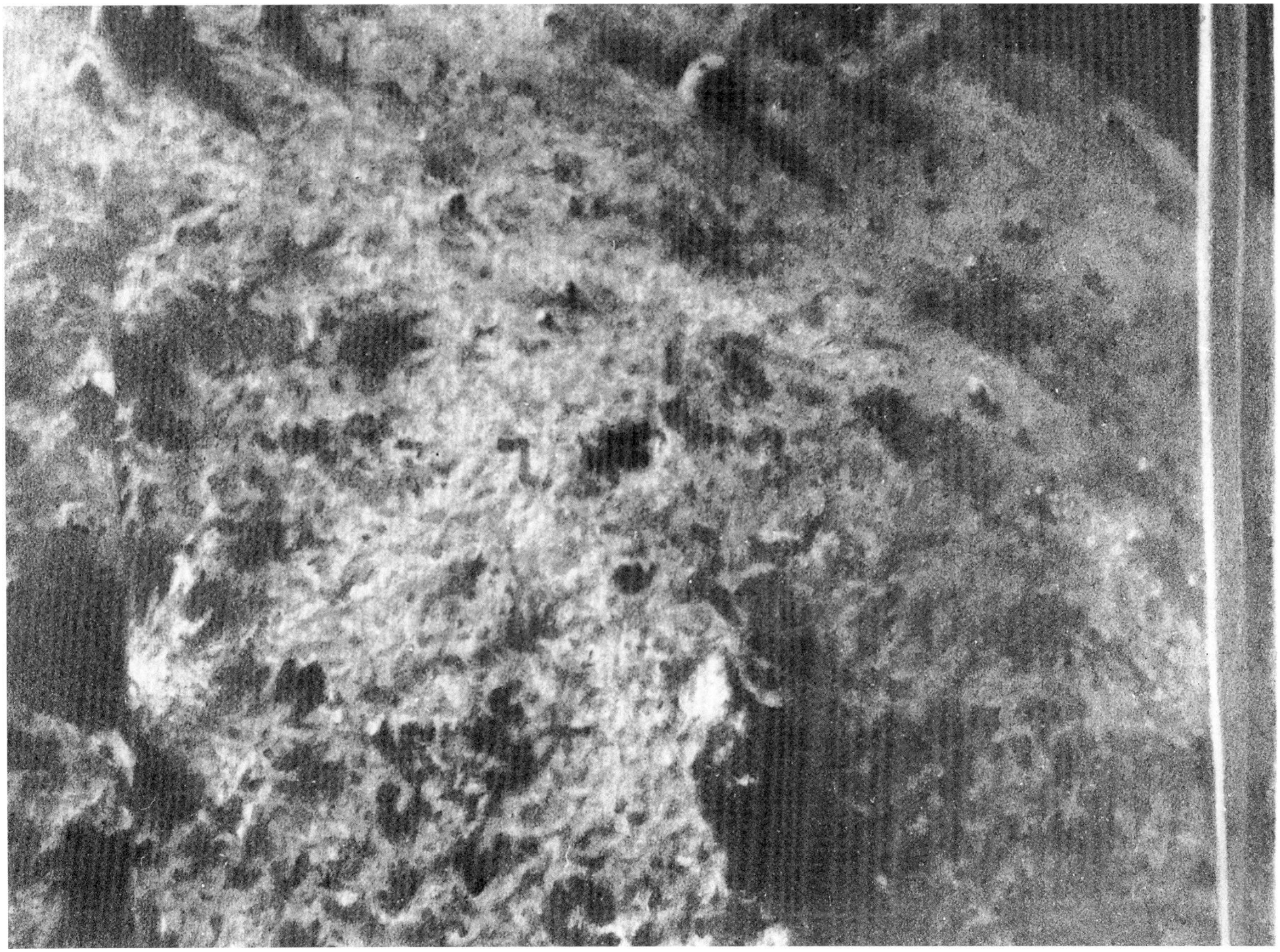

ALTERNATIVES IN THE ACADEMY: EXPERIMENTAL EDUCATION IN COLLEGES, UNIVERSITIES, AND ART SCHOOLS

Conceptual art of the 1960s—with its treatises and theses, its substitutions of publications over exhibitions and its redefinition of works of art to include esoteric criticism and speculations about art—appear to be a genre of academic art finely adapted to the pressures of the new university habitat.

Judith Adler, *Artists in Offices* (New Brunswick, NJ: Transaction Books, 1979), 17

In her sociological study on the California Institute of the Arts (CalArts), *Artists in Offices* (1979), Judith Adler discusses how the analysis of knowledge, production of meaning, and institutional critique and intervention inherent in Conceptualism complemented the ethos of experimental education in the 1960s and 1970s. Interdisciplinary teaching methodologies at both art schools and universities of the period mirrored new artistic practices that were no longer discipline-based or medium-specific. Special treatises and initiatives developed at schools offered "blueprints" for curriculum and, along with funding, brought these forays in experimental education to fruition.

The same activist impulses that instigated artists to form their own galleries and alternative spaces also precipitated experimental education in public universities and private art schools. In the early to mid-1960s, colleges and universities throughout California became epicenters for the antiwar movement. Faculty and students demanded educational reform and transformation of the university; they challenged the notion of campuses as isolated ivory towers. Established public educational systems and private art schools tried to adjust to myriad social and political changes. The University of California built three new campuses and hired prominent artists to start new art programs, while the state college system created experimental colleges and art departments.[69] Traditional academies like the Chouinard Art Institute and Los Angeles Conservatory of Music merged into the innovative new California Institute of the Arts (CalArts). Within both the state college system and long-established fine art academies, the formation of new, more experimental departments and programs aimed to break down the rigid barriers of these institutions. As a result, in California during the late 1960s and early 1970s, art schools and experimental colleges became the primary venues for artistic production.

The Experimental Ethos

Responding to the demands for educational reform, San Francisco State College established the Experimental College in 1965 to offer alternative courses, including those in the arts. Jeff Berner, a San Francisco–based artist and writer, taught "Astronaut of Inner Space: A Survey of the European Avant-Garde, 1880 to the Present," which addressed symbolism and Dada as well as the then-current work of Fluxus, Group Zero, and the *nouveaux réalistes.*[70] He also edited *Stolen Paper Review*, with criticism, poetry, and manifestos of the historical and contemporary avant-garde.[71] The class and journal served a rather limited group of artists and students until Berner was invited to use his moniker, "Astronaut of Inner Space," for his *San Francisco Chronicle* column of 1967–68, which significantly extended his audience and informed the general public about these avant-garde activities.

Ken Friedman, another instructor at the Experimental College, first became acquainted with Fluxus artists Dick Higgins and George Maciunas in New York in 1966. When Maciunas suggested Friedman open a Fluxus center when he returned to California, Friedman agreed and set up two "Fluxus West" locations, one in San Diego in the fall of 1966 and another in San Francisco at the end of that year.[72] From these two new centers, Friedman made his own art, disseminated information and works of other artists, and a taught an Experimental College course, "Intermedia," to engage Fluxus ideas and sensibilities with students.[73]

Throughout his career, artist Allan Kaprow worked in various educational capacities. In the early 1960s, he began to participate in conversations about pedagogy and the presence of artists within schools and museums. During 1968–69, Kaprow collaborated with educator Herbert Kohl on *Project*

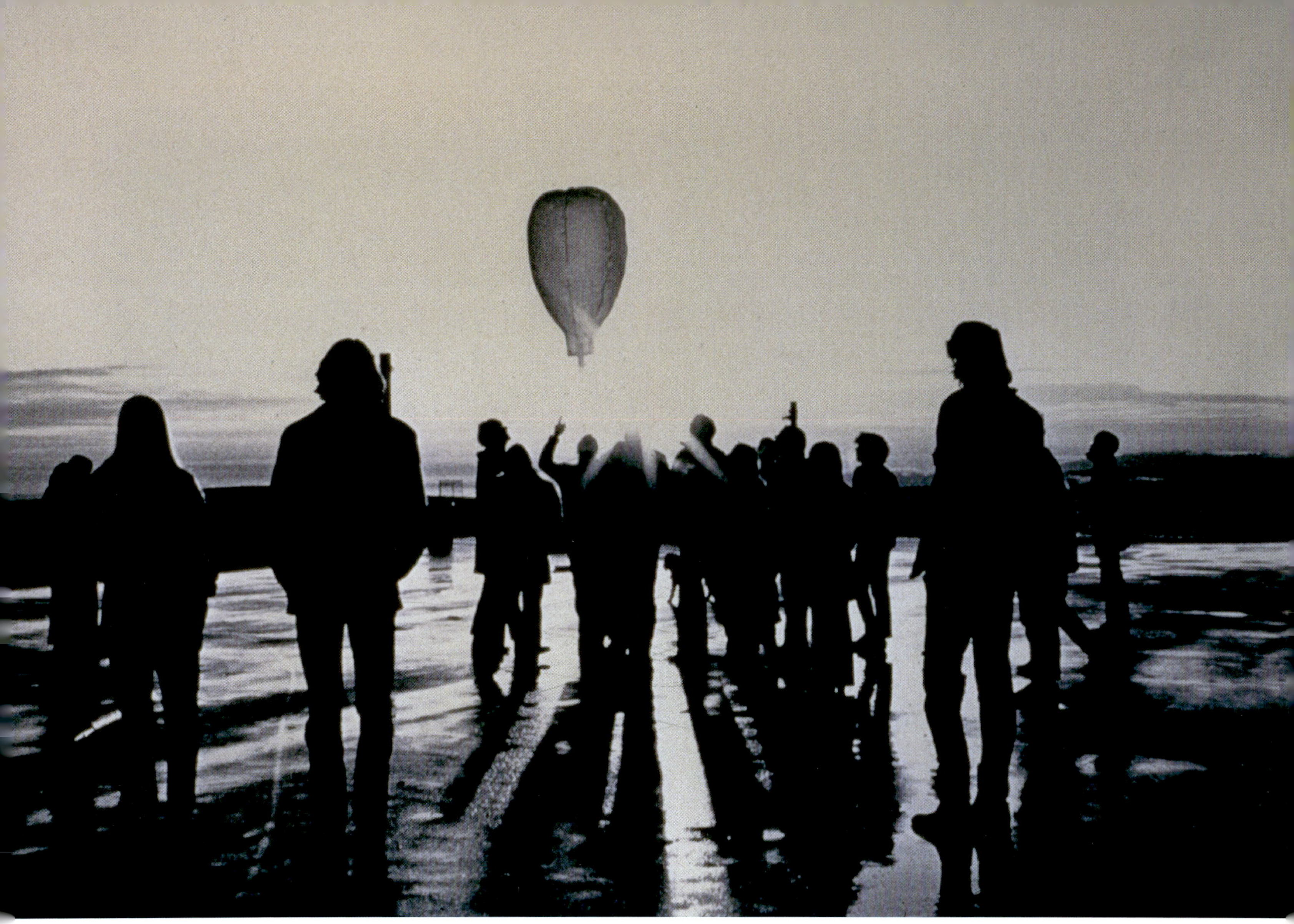

Fig. 2.21 Robert Watts, *Balloon Flight,* 1968, Experimental Workshop, University of California, Santa Cruz. Image: Courtesy Robert Watts Archive, New York.

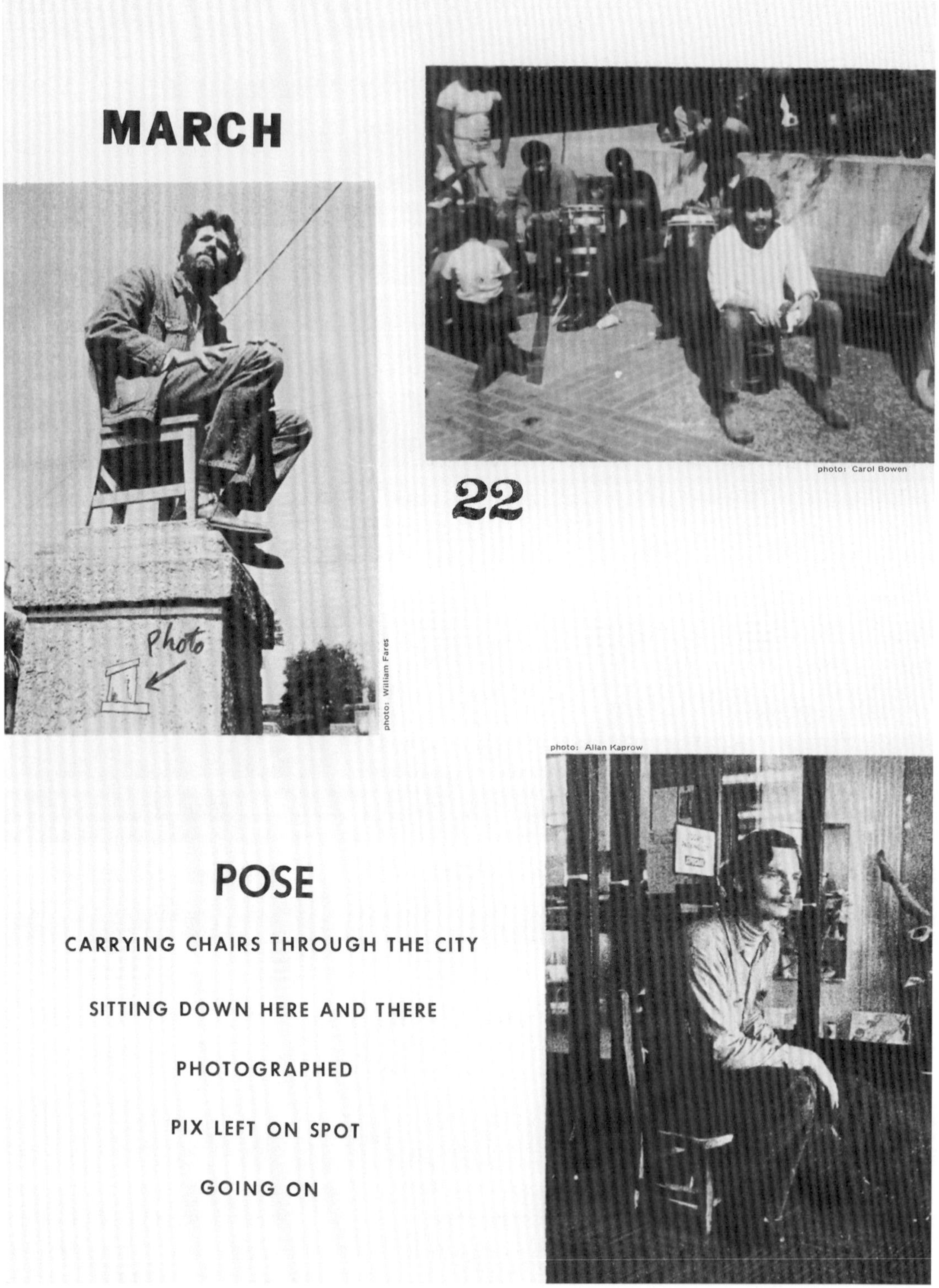

Fig. 2.22 Allan Kaprow, *Pose, March 22, 1969* (detail), 1970–; a record of an event to be continued infinitum. Offset lithography on card stock in envelope; seven cards: 10 ¾ × 7 ¾ in. each; envelope: 12 × 9 in.

Other Art Ways, a venture done in conjunction with the Berkeley Public Schools and sponsored by the Carnegie Foundation. Operating in a Berkeley storefront, Kaprow and Kohl wrote lessons that students would experience/learn outside of the classroom. In *Six Ordinary Happenings*, students received scores for simple actions that were to be performed on the streets. For example, *Pose (March 22, 1969)*(fig. 2.22) read: "Carrying chairs through the city, sitting down here and there, photographed pix left on spot, going on."[74] Pedagogically, these Happenings epitomized John Dewey's concept of "learning by doing" and coincided with Kaprow's own activity booklets—instructions for simple, playful tasks that can be performed by anyone. They also hark back to his influential articles, "The Education of the Un-Artists, Parts I and II," in which Kaprow calls for artists to remake themselves, first and fleetingly, as non-artists and then, more permanently, as un-artists who will use humor, play, and intermedia to reinvigorate themselves and society.[75]

A contemporaneous project in 1969–70, also funded by the Carnegie Foundation, occurred at the University of California, Santa Cruz (UCSC)—the "experimental" campus of the UC system. At this time, students and professors had criticized UC for becoming increasingly large and impersonal—a "multiversity" more interested in research than in teaching. UCSC was the antidote to this.[76] Formed under the aegis of visionary educator and political scientist Dean McHenry, UCSC consisted of eight small, semi-autonomous residential colleges where students lived and studied together in contemporary residences nestled in the redwoods.[77] When the university opened in 1965, the notion of this in-depth but laid-back countercultural education proved so popular that UCSC attracted the brightest of California's students.

In this highly experimental, nontraditional environment, McHenry hired Gurdon Woods, former director of the San Francisco Art Institute, as head of the UCSC art department. Woods and Fluxus artist Robert Watts co-conceived the Experimental Arts Workshop for the Carnegie Foundation. This new program brought avant-garde artists such as James Lee Byars, John Cage, Merce Cunningham, Dan Flavin, Allan Kaprow, George Maciunas, and George Segal to lecture and contribute to a report on experimental education.[78]

According to Jock Reynolds, who was a sculpture student at UCSC, Watts's teaching methodology centered on the Fluxus ideals of collectivity and collaboration: he was not particularly didactic, pedagogic, or theoretical, and he participated as an equal in the projects.[79] The tightly knit Experimental Arts Workshop initiated collaborations in which each person conceived an action that was scored as a performance. Their events included a journey down a country road in a bus that crashed into "brick" contact paper and set off an alarm; a giant balloon launch on the beach in Santa Cruz (fig. 2.21); and an event where everyone took a pill that changed the color of their urine. These actions reflect the Fluxus obsession with humor, surprise, physical movement, and bodily functions. Occasionally, the workshop participants would go to other campuses for collaborative activities, such as the March 1969 trip to participate in a Dada-like *Fur Family Parade* held at UC San Diego (UCSD).[80]

In its early years, the UCSD art department faculty was steeped in the avant-garde and included artists David and Eleanor Antin, John Baldessari, Paul Brach, Helen Mayer Harrison and Newton Harrison, and Allan Kaprow. As department chair Brach said in 1968: "The campus was an island of intellectuals in a sea of John Birchers."[81] In particular, scientist/poet Jacob Bronowski, political theorist Herbert Marcuse, and others who came to the Jonas Salk Institute became acquainted with the art faculty. From its inception, the department embraced Conceptualism and interdisciplinary practices, particularly performance.

Martha Rosler, a graduate student at UCSD, and Allan Sekula, an undergraduate, began to make significant work with political content while still attending the university. When Sekula started at UCSD in 1968, his first instructor was John Baldessari, who soon left to go to CalArts; photographer Fred

Lonidier convinced Sekula to stay at UCSD. Although Sekula considered himself to be a photographer, he recalls participating with Lonidier in *Body Bags* (1970), a protest of the Vietnam War. Surrogate body bags made from meat, bags, newspaper, and rocks were placed in UCSD's Revelle Plaza and then burned. The event lasted only one day, as the campus health department took the body bags to the cadaver locker where Lonidier later photographed them. The bags were incinerated, but because they were made with rocks, they ruined the equipment.

From 1970 to 1974, Rosler studied at UCSD, where she did several key performances. For her *Monumental Garage Sale* (1973), the artist set up an ordinary garage sale, with racks and tables displaying household goods, in the campus's Mandeville Art Gallery. Rosler assumed the persona of a struggling single mother and took cash in exchange for the items. As in her earlier video, *A Budding Gourmet* (1974), she used everyday experience and domesticity to make witty, ironic critiques about class, gender, and consumption.[82]

By the late 1960s, the UC Irvine (UCI) Studio Art Department, founded in 1965, had become an important educational institution known for faculty and students interested in Conceptual art, light and space, performance, and video. John Coplans, cofounder of *Artforum* magazine, directed the University Art Gallery—where he curated exhibitions of Andy Warhol, Roy Lichtenstein, and Robert Rauschenberg—and brought to the faculty such artists as Vija Celmins, Robert Irwin, and Bas Jan Ader.

With the advent of Conceptualism and performance in the late 1960s, academics and artists alike had a renewed interest in Marcel Duchamp. Recognizing this, art historians Moira Roth and Barbara Rose organized a UCI Duchamp festival in 1971. In addition to a month-long exhibition of work by Duchamp and his followers, the festival also hosted a two-day symposium featuring prominent art critics and historians Robert Hughes, Annette Michelson, Richard Hamilton, and Walter Hopps, among others. During this event, Alison Knowles and Allan Kaprow enacted Knowles's performance *The Identical Lunch,* where they ate the same lunch—a tuna fish sandwich with a cup of soup—each day throughout the exhibition. Extending a simple action into durational performance typifies the simple, Zen-like, quotidian nature of the Fluxus score and Kaprow's preference for non-art subjects in his own practice.

During this same time, students in UCI's MFA program organized and ran the F Space Gallery in an industrial building in nearby Santa Ana. The space is best known for the infamous Chris Burden performance *Shoot* (1971), when a marksman shot the artist in his left arm with a .22 rifle while the guests in the gallery watched the "crime" take place (see fig. 1.71, p. 84). Though Burden had intended for the bullet to only graze his arm, it penetrated his flesh. As Kristine Stiles has discussed, Burden had been thinking about what it would be like to be shot ever since the Kent State University shootings in 1970. *Shoot* foreshadows what would become Burden's ongoing interest in risk-oriented performances that explore the dynamics of power, issues of spectatorship, challenges to the physical body, and the redefinition of the parameters of the artist and artwork.[83]

In the summer of 1972, the Newport Harbor Art Museum, in collaboration with F Space, organized the exhibition *New Art in Orange County,* which included artists Gary Beydler, Nancy Buchanan, Burden, and Barbara T. Smith.[84] For Burden's *Jaizu* performance on June 10–11 (fig. 2.23), he wore dark glasses and sat at one end of a gallery. He faced the other end of the space, where there were two cushions and a small bowl of marijuana cigarettes. Visitors could chat with the artist and/or smoke, and they assumed he was watching them; however, his glasses were painted black on the inside, rendering him blind. This element of inviting the viewer to participate in an action with the artist, with a potentially unknown outcome, and the notion of spectatorship hark back to Burden's work at F Space, *Being Photographed: Looking Out, Looking In,* February 4–20, 1971 (see fig. 2.24; see also figs. 1.52–1.56, pp. 70–71).

Another work in the exhibition, Smith's *Artifacts: Trunk Piece* (1972), consisted of an installation of an old trunk on an oriental rug surrounded by crystal balls, magic wands, bottles,

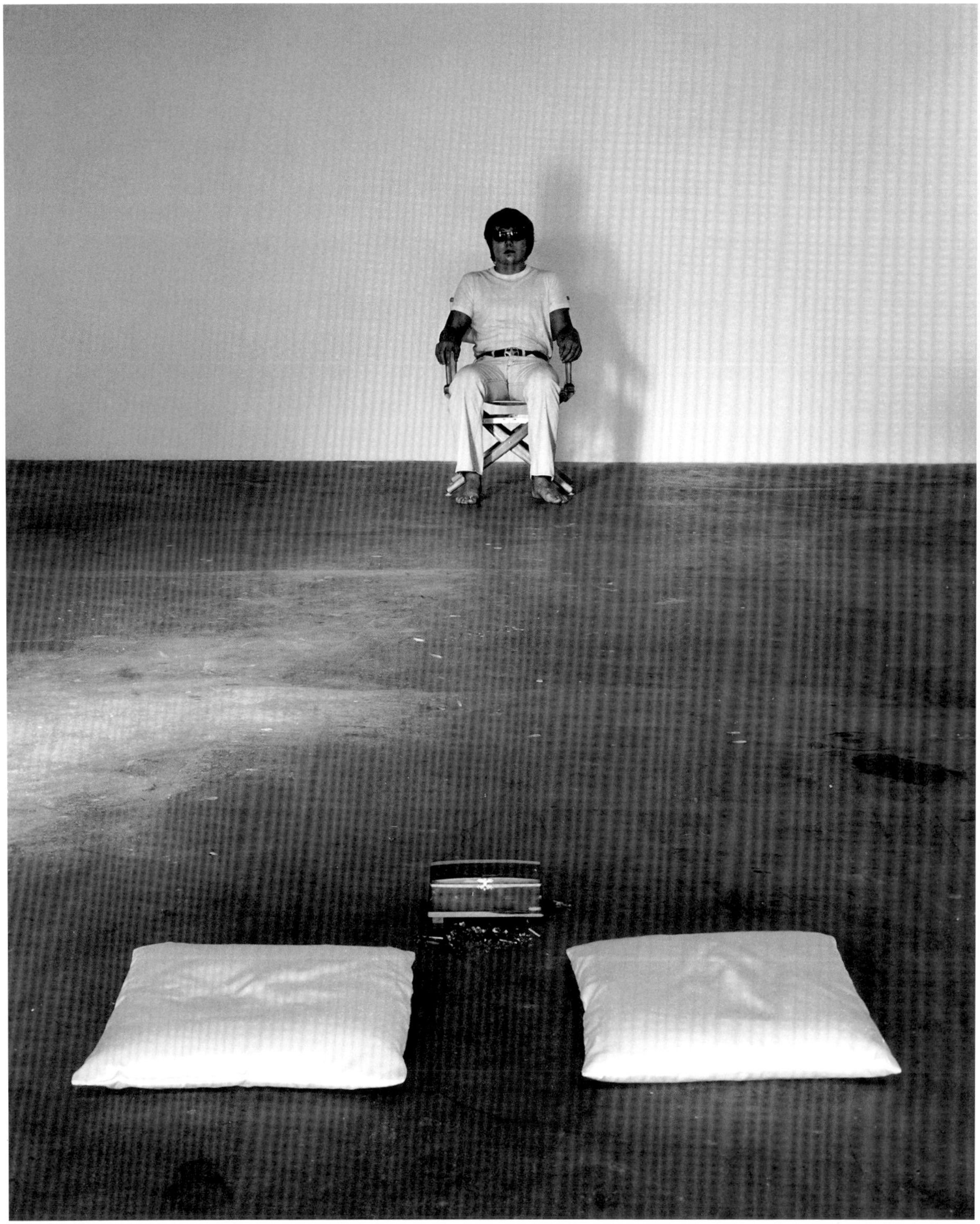

Fig. 2.23 Chris Burden, *Jaizu,* June 10–11, 1972. Performance at Newport Harbor Art Museum, Newport Beach, California. Photo: Courtesy of the artist, Topanga, California.

and other oddities. At that time, Smith was in the process of making a large-scale installation project out of resin; she used the leftovers to encase the found objects in globes that she later incorporated into performances. Smith's large-scale project *Field Piece* (1968–72) was an interactive installation of nine-foot-tall multicolored resin "blades" of grass that would light up when triggered by viewers' feet, thus illuminating the field (see fig. 2.1, pp. 118–19). When the work was originally presented, the artist asked the audience to remove their clothes, so most of the original spectators experienced *Field Piece* in the nude as an intimate, sensory, tactile environment.

Finally, for *Hair Transplant* (1972), Buchanan shaved moustache and body hair from fellow UCI student Robert Walker and pasted it onto her body; she then cut her own hair and pasted it onto him. This transplant, or overlay of one gender onto the other, is one of several works by Buchanan that addresses male-female stereotypes, roles, and power relations. Ultimately, these works in *New Art in Orange County* share different tropes of performance from this time: long durations and testing the limits of the body; masquerade and/or the appropriation of other personae; and gender role reversal and audience participation.

Art Schools

The San Francisco Art Institute—originally founded in 1871 by artists and writers as the San Francisco Art Association, and renamed California School of Fine Arts in 1916 and then San Francisco Art Institute (SFAI) in 1961—is one of the oldest art schools in the western United States. Throughout its history, SFAI has been a locus for new forms of art, from early fine art photography and Abstract Expressionist painting to the establishment of one of the first performance/video departments to accommodate new genres and hybridized forms of art.[85]

In 1969, Eugenia Butler organized at SFAI an exhibition entitled *18′6″ × 6′9″ × 11′2½″ × 47′ × 11 3/16″ × 29′8½″ × 31′9 3/16″* (the exact measurements of the gallery space; fig. 2.26). The show presented both California and East Coast Conceptualists.[86] Each artist submitted a proposal to use the entire gallery for a

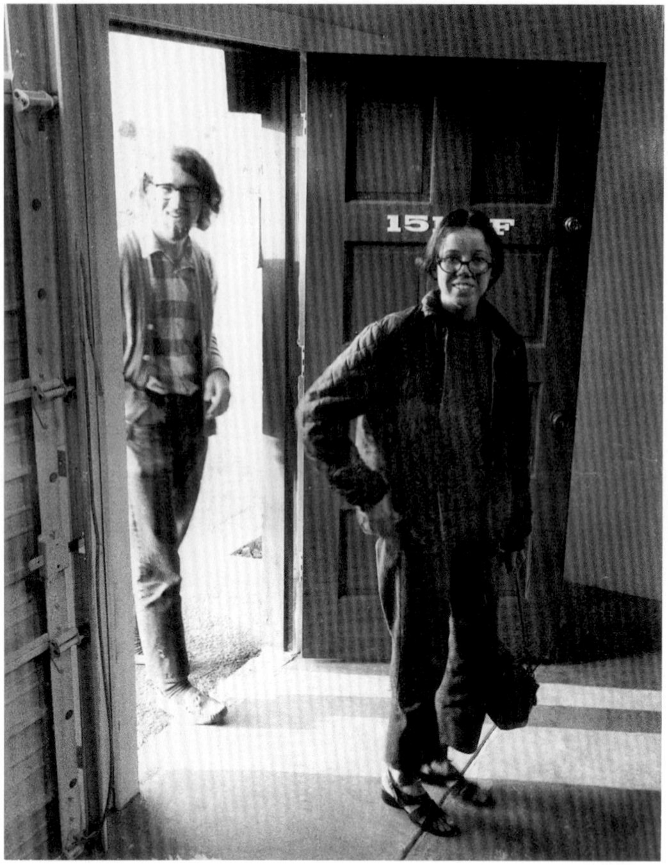

Fig. 2.24 Chris Burden, *Being Photographed: Looking Out, Looking In* (detail), 1971. 140 Polaroid photographs and one drawing; photographs: 25 × 133 in. overall; drawing: 25 × 33 in.

Fig. 2.25 Nancy Buchanan, *Hair Transplant*, 1972. Performance at F Space, Santa Ana, California, in conjunction with *New Art in Orange County*, an exhibition at the Newport Harbor Art Museum, Newport Beach, California.

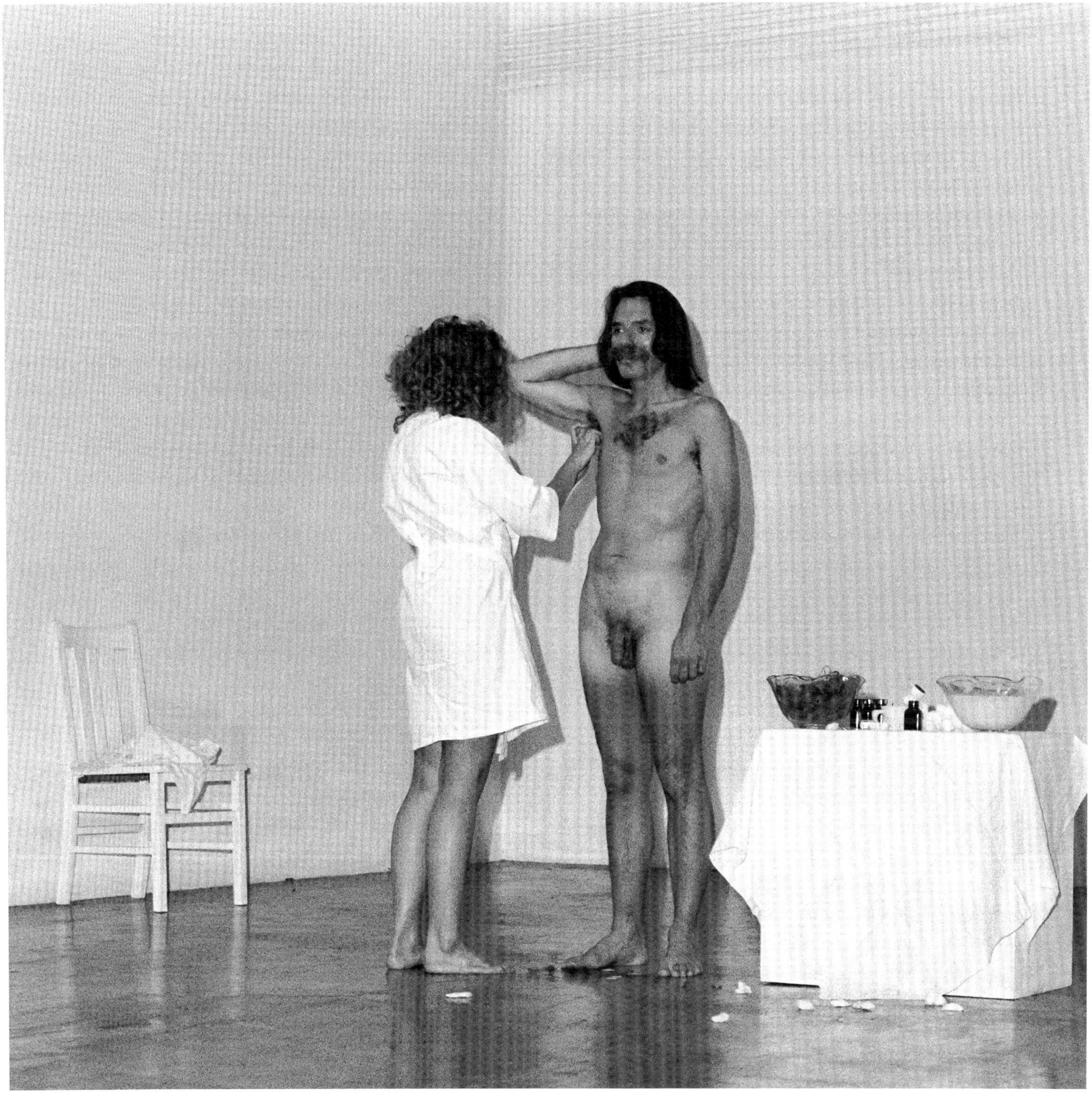

Blueprint for Counter Education

CURRICULUM • HANDBOOK

WALL DECORATION

SHOOTING SCRIPT

Maurice Stein and Larry Miller

Designed by Marshall Henrichs

Inside this box are three charts and a book, the tools for creating a new educational environment. This counter-university makes obsolete the traditional university process. Surrounded by charts, the participant will be confronted by ideas and issues that compel him to interact with everything going on around him—from movies, to riots, to political campaigns. There is no text book, no syllabus, no final exam; and the "faculty" includes Marcuse, McLuhan, Eldridge Cleaver, and Jean-Luc Godard.

THE REVOLUTION STARTS HERE.

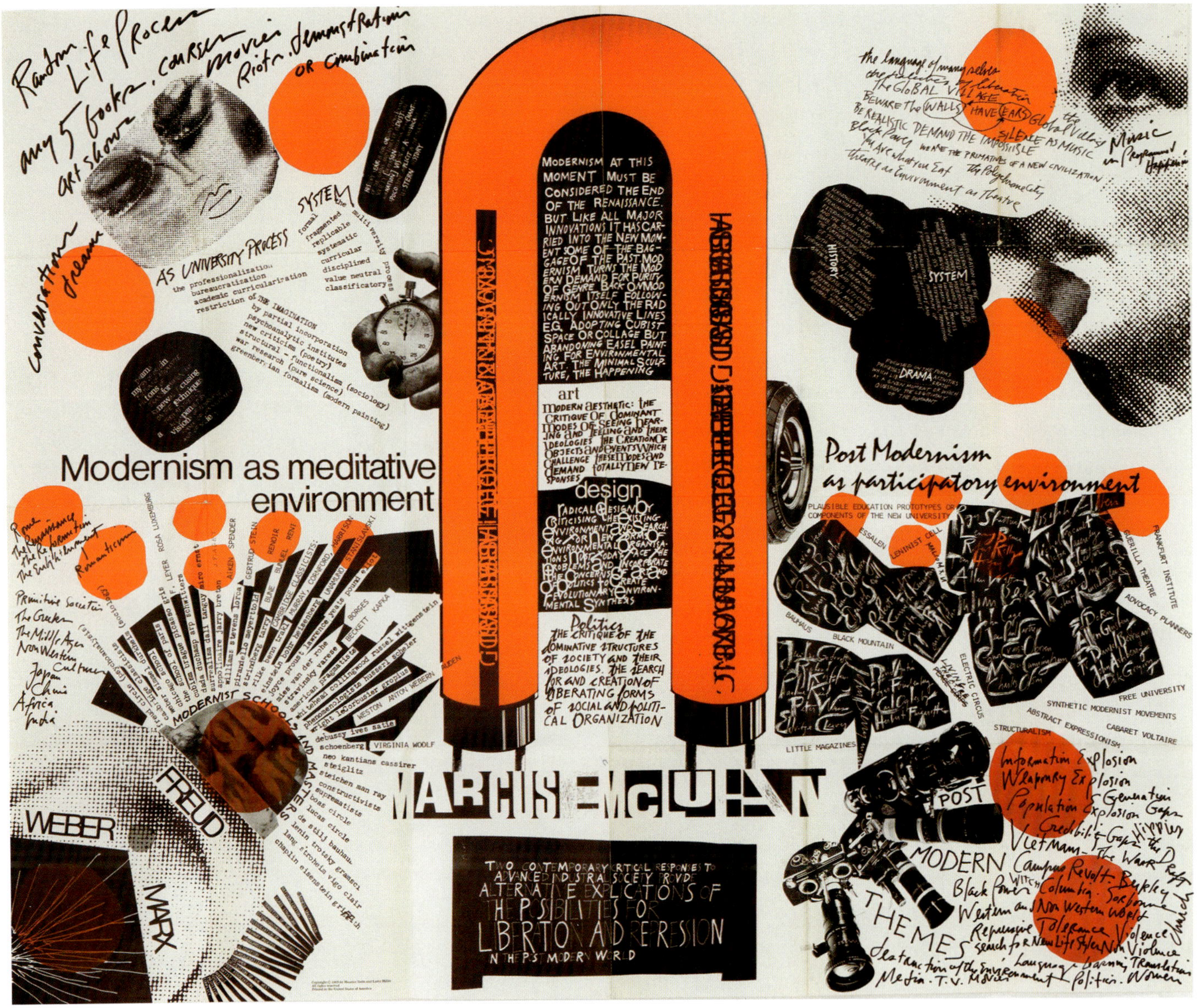

Figs. 2.27–2.28 Maurice Stein and Larry Miller, *Blueprint for Counter Education*, ca. 1968. *Left:* Box containing curriculum, handbook, wall decoration, and shooting script. *Right:* Poster designed by Marshall Henrichs. Photos: Scott Groller, courtesy California Institute of the Arts, Valencia.

Judy Chicago at Fresno State College originated the Feminist Art Program in 1970, and a year later she joined Miriam Schapiro at CalArts to co-organize a similar program there. Two of Chicago's students, Suzanne Lacy and Faith Wilding, came to CalArts from Fresno with her. In fall 1971, the members of the Feminist Art Program wanted to engage in a collaborative project and found on Mariposa Street in Hollywood an old house scheduled for demolition. They convinced the owner to donate it to them.[94] Using homemaking as their theme, they transformed the space into Womanhouse, a site of surreal installations that cumulatively made a biting feminist critique against domestic life and labor. According to Moira Roth, the works done at Womanhouse echoed the anger and despair of other women's performance work in Los Angeles and spawned a number of feminist spaces and organizations discussed later in this book.[95]

The importance of art departments and art schools in California circa 1970 cannot be underestimated. As Howard Singerman has asserted, the university played crucial roles as both patron and scene in the 1960s and 1970s because so much of the work necessitated the presence of the artist. Often works could not be simply bought and sold but instead had to be read or screened, installed, or performed and attended.[96] In art schools and universities, performance, video, and other Conceptual practices depended on the artists' actions and language; their presence and presentation as the preexisting audience often completed the work.

In 1997, Lars Nittve in *Sunshine Noir* noted that young artists in Los Angeles identified themselves by the art school or university where they received their degree or currently taught rather than by gallery representation, and this condition prevails even now.[97] As we have seen, since the late 1960s, art schools and university art departments have functioned as sites to meet mentors and visiting artists from multiple generations, and the phenomenon continues to this day.

Fig. 2.29 Alison Knowles with Robert Kaplan, *Computer Poem Drop* over *House of Dust*, 1971. California Institute of the Arts, Valencia. Photo: Courtesy of Alison Knowles.

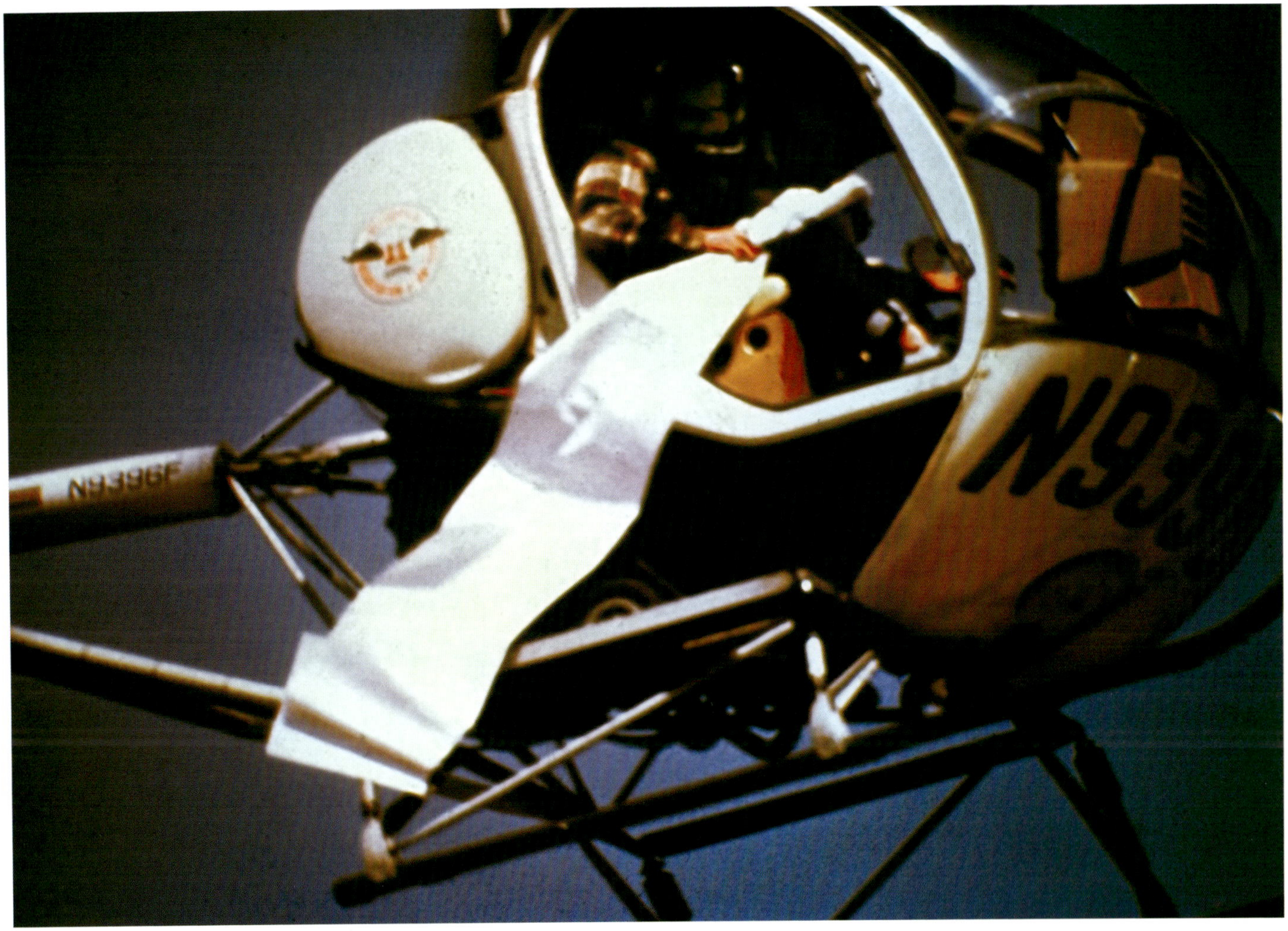
N9396F

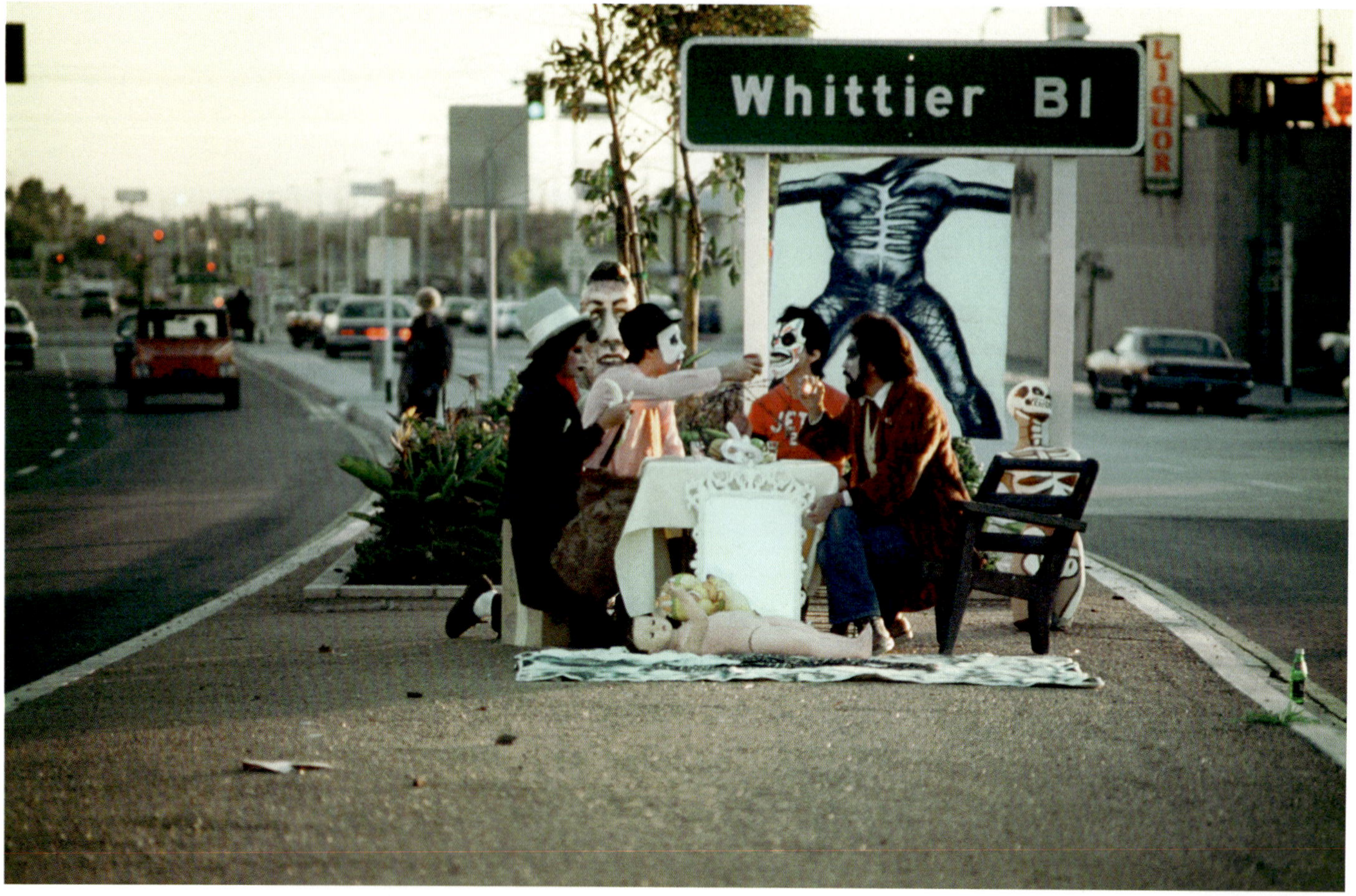

PUBLIC ADDRESS: INTERVENTIONS ON THE STREET, IN MEDIA, AND IN PUBLICATIONS

There is a tendency in San Francisco, as elsewhere, to "take to the streets" for various art activities now. Most of it (if not all) is oriented towards more or less political or environmental concerns. This direction seems significantly more relevant to more people (including many of the artists involved) than the traditional art channels of museums, galleries and collectors. . . . There seems to be an increasing wish to involve the various communications media in street events—particularly television, for both its creative and mass appeal potential.

Brenda Richardson in *Performance Anthology: Sourcebook for a Decade of California Performance Art,* ed. Carl E. Loeffler and Darlene Tong (San Francisco: Contemporary Arts Press, 1980), 10

As Richardson observed in 1970, what became more compelling to artists was not merely the representation of the urban environment but an intervention into the public sphere. Artists who "took to the streets" followed the Situationists' strategies of disruption and intervention within public space, staging events that responded to particular social issues. For instance, Paul Cotton appeared as *The People's Prick* (1969), wearing a full-body penis suit at the Berkeley People's Park demonstrations. He also made an impromptu visit to the Los Angeles County Museum of Art (LACMA), where he was ejected, and then appeared on the cover of the *Los Angeles Free Press* with a headline that declared "Art Museum Throws Art Out."[98]

Asco—an East Los Angeles Conceptual and performance collective that included writer Harry Gamboa Jr., painters

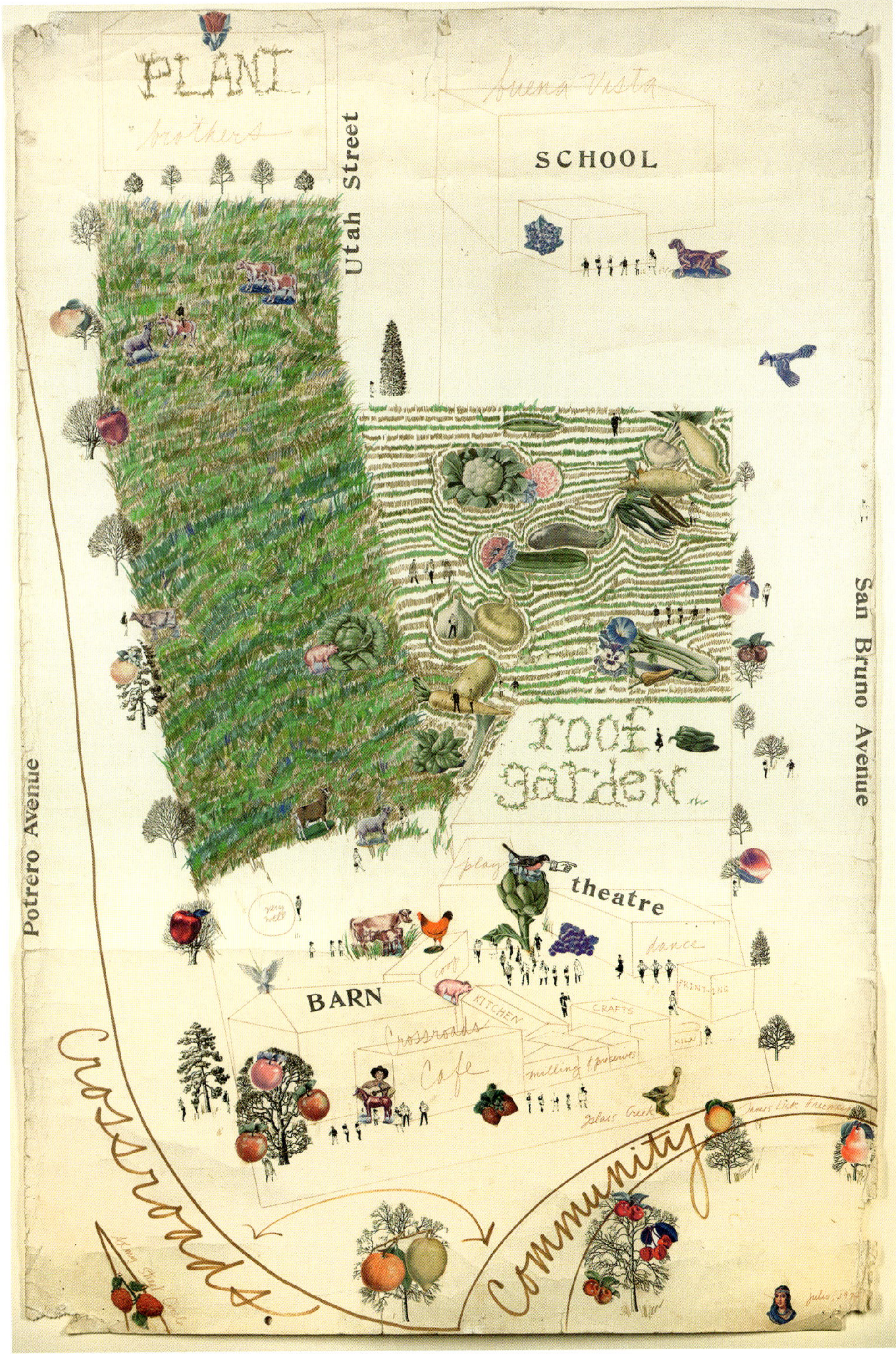

Fig. 2.30 Asco (Glugio "Gronk" Nicandro, Patssi Valdez, Willie Herrón III, and Harry Gamboa Jr.), *First Supper (After a Major Riot)*, 1974. Performance documentation (left to right: Valdez, Humberto Sandoval, Herrón, and Gronk).

Fig. 2.31 Bonnie Sherk, *Original Drawing for Crossroads Community (the farm)*, 1974. Pencil, ink, and collage on paper; 30 × 16 in. Courtesy of the artist, San Francisco.

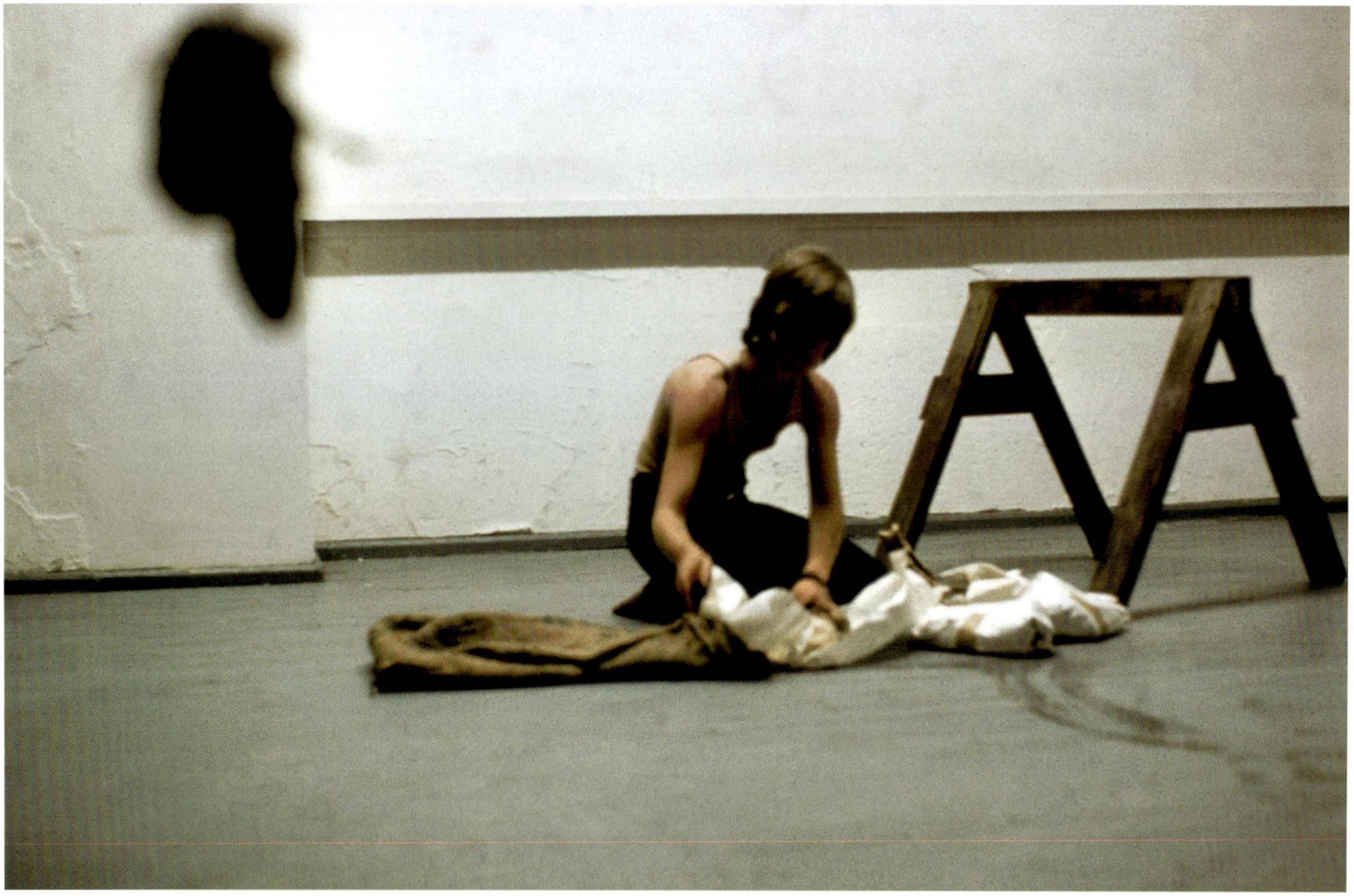

Patssi Valdez and Gronk, and muralist Willie Herrón III—made a more explicitly political intervention with their guerilla action *Spray Paint LACMA* (1972), in which three members tagged an exterior wall of the museum to protest its lack of works by Latino artists. For their *First Supper (After a Major Riot)* (1974), Asco staged a Christmas Eve meal on the traffic island on Whittier Boulevard. It was on this exact site, on January 31, 1971, that a police altercation had turned deadly. Asco donned absurd costumes and masks and placed a doll on a blanket to remind passersby of a tragic incident and to reclaim urban public space.

Artists in the Bay Area also made public interventions of a political and/or environmental nature. In *Dye,* Joe Hawley, Mel Henderson, and Alfred Young placed *a* yellow dye oil in the San Francisco Bay on June 12, 1969, to mark "the invisible line defining the limit of territorial fishing waters of the United States." The work questioned the notion of national borders, the depletion of ocean wildlife, and accidental fuel spills.[99] Another project, *Oil* (September 20, 1969; see the title page), more clearly referenced environmental disasters, while *Yellow Cabs* (November 19, 1969, p. xiv) was a proto–flash mob or swarm, in which Henderson hailed dozens of taxis to converge at the busy intersection of Castro and Market Streets in San Francisco.

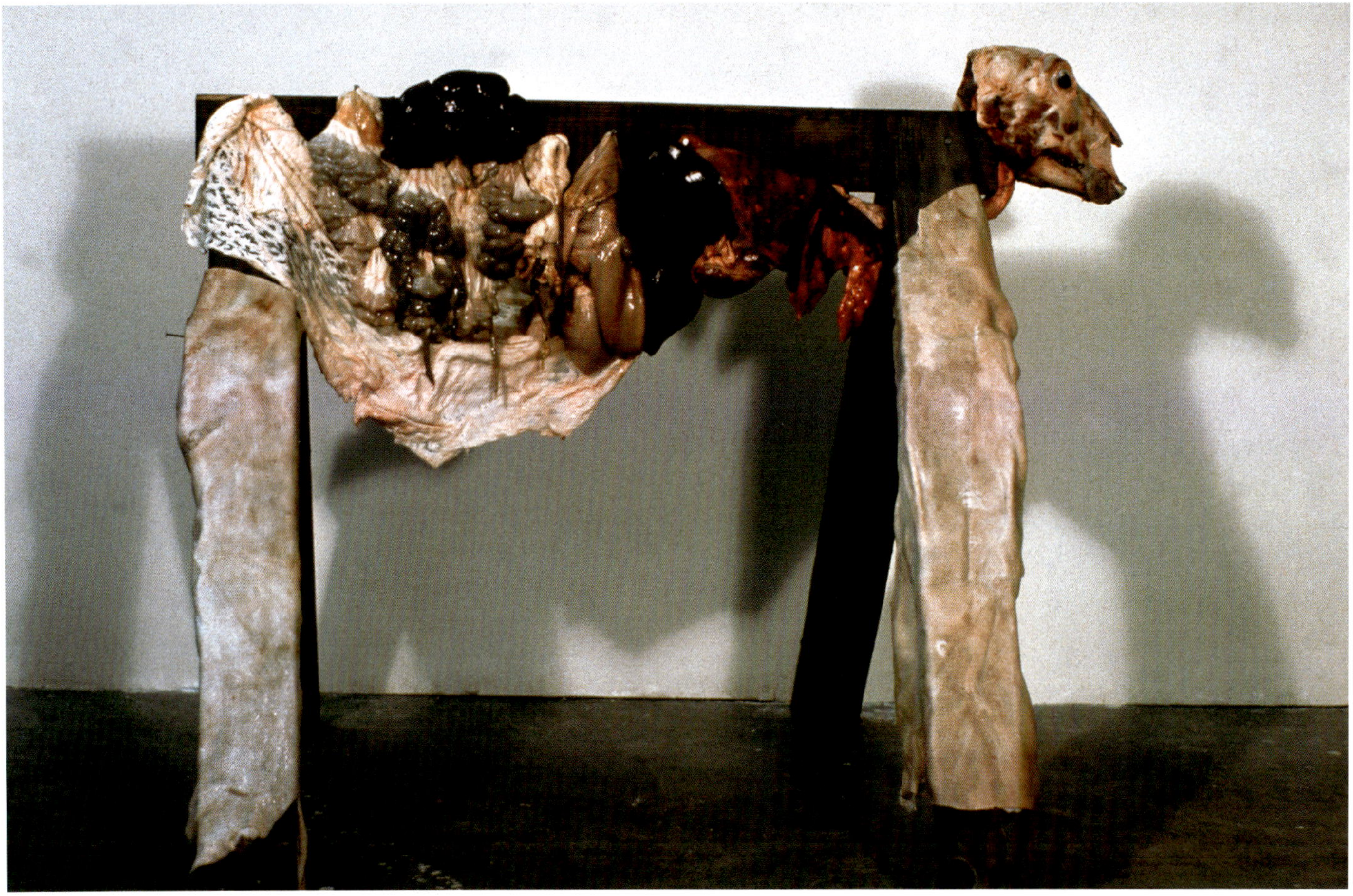

Bonnie Sherk, with Howard Levine, became well known for her environmental works, particularly her series of *Portable Parks*—temporary installations of green turf, palm trees, and animals in unlikely places in the urban environment, such as a freeway overpass, the intersection of Mission and Van Ness Streets, and Maiden Lane in downtown San Francisco (see fig. 1.11, p. 25). This led Sherk, in 1974, to establish *Crossroads Community (the farm)*, a seven-acre ecogarden/art space, replete with animals, built on the traffic meridians under a freeway overpass in San Francisco. The project, which lasted until 1980, also featured educational activities for children, internships, and performance-art events before it was transformed into a public park. Like other artists who make public interventions, Sherk was "no longer interested in the kind of object art that is shut up in museums, but in an environmental art that confronts people who do not necessarily go out in search of art."[100]

Figs. 2.32a–b Suzanne Lacy, *Lamb Constructions* (from the *Monster Series*), 1973. Performance documentation from Womanspace Gallery and the opening of the Los Angeles Women's Building, Los Angeles, California.

VIDEO AND PUBLIC MEDIA INTERVENTIONS

As artists in the late 1960s and early 1970s made performances and used their own bodies as both content and material, the introduction of the handheld video camera in 1967 became an important tool for documenting these live events. More easily handled and processed than film, video also enabled artists to record and distribute performance work to a broader audience, whether for sanctioned public broadcasting or for media intervention.

One of the earliest examples of artists' video made specifically for broadcast, *The Dilexi Series* aired on San Francisco public television station KQED in the spring and summer of 1969. Conceived and commissioned by James Newman, who ran the Dilexi Gallery from 1958 until 1970, the twelve-part weekly series included California-based artists and nationally known figures, and extended avant-garde contemporary art beyond the gallery and museum.[101] Filmmaker Robert Nelson and artist William T. Wiley used this opportunity to disseminate commentary on the broadcast media with an "in-studio" parody of the talk-show format. Terry Riley's *Music with Balls* combined his synthesized music and multilayered visualizations, while Philip Makanna's *The Empire of Things,* an experimental narrative original and found film, used electronic colorizing.

For other artists, *The Dilexi Series* allowed them to document performance work in a medium that would significantly extend their audience. Anna Halprin's *Right On* depicts two companies—her own San Francisco Dancers' Workshop and its collaborators, Studio Watts—as they prepare for a performance. *Dance Fractions for the West Coast* documents a rare solo dance and monologue by Yvonne Rainer at Mills College in Oakland. Land artist Walter De Maria's film *Hardcore* (1969) consists of slow shots of the subtle and sensuous play of light on a dry lake bed in the Black Rock Desert of northwestern Nevada—the same location used now for the annual Burning Man festival.[102] Andy Warhol contributed an excerpt from *The Paul Swan Film,* which follows Swan, an octogenarian and contemporary of Isadora Duncan, as he dances and recites poetry. Finally, Frank Zappa's *Burnt Weeny Sandwich,* filmed like a high-speed home movie, features the original Mothers of Invention along with Captain Beefheart. The work interjects eccentric pop music into an avant-garde series.

In the 1960s and 1970s, counterculture video collectives and guerilla television also utilized new video technologies. Michael Shamberg, who wrote *Guerilla Television* (1971), a do-it-yourself video production manual, was part of TVTV (short for Top Value Television), which he founded in 1972 along with Allen Rucker, Tom Weinberg, and Megan Williams. TVTV pioneered independent video using the new Sony Portapak to make socially activist work and political documentary; they covered the 1972 Republican and Democratic conventions as an examination of American consumerism in their 1974 film *Adland* (fig. 2.33). TVTV productions included artists Chip Lord, Doug Michels, Hudson Marquez, and Curtis Schreier, who also formed the Ant Farm collective.

Founded in 1968, Ant Farm consisted of radically inclined architects and artists who found alternatives to mainstream practices by using video, performance, and sculpture, often in public sites. Initially inspired by Buckminster Fuller and Paolo Soleri, the collective, during their early years, produced giant inflatable structures designed for a nomadic lifestyle that eventually evolved into *Truckstop Network* (1971), a cross-country tour of colleges and universities in a "Media Van." (fig. 2.35)[103] Equipped with a Portapak camera to facilitate constant documentation at each stop (and outfitted with an inflatable solar-heated shower), the Media Van was, quite literally, the vehicle for Ant Farm's itinerant video production. As Chip Lord has commented: "We brought an interest in high technology to the nomadic counterculture."[104]

Perhaps the most well-known instance of an artist using public media is Chris Burden's *TV Hijack* (figs. 2.36–2.39), a surprise assault on Phyllis Lutjeans, then curator of the Newport Harbor Art Museum, as she was interviewing him live on Channel 3 Cablevision in Irvine on February 9, 1972. Lutjeans asked Burden what pieces he had been thinking about, and he responded by demonstrating a TV hijack, holding a knife to

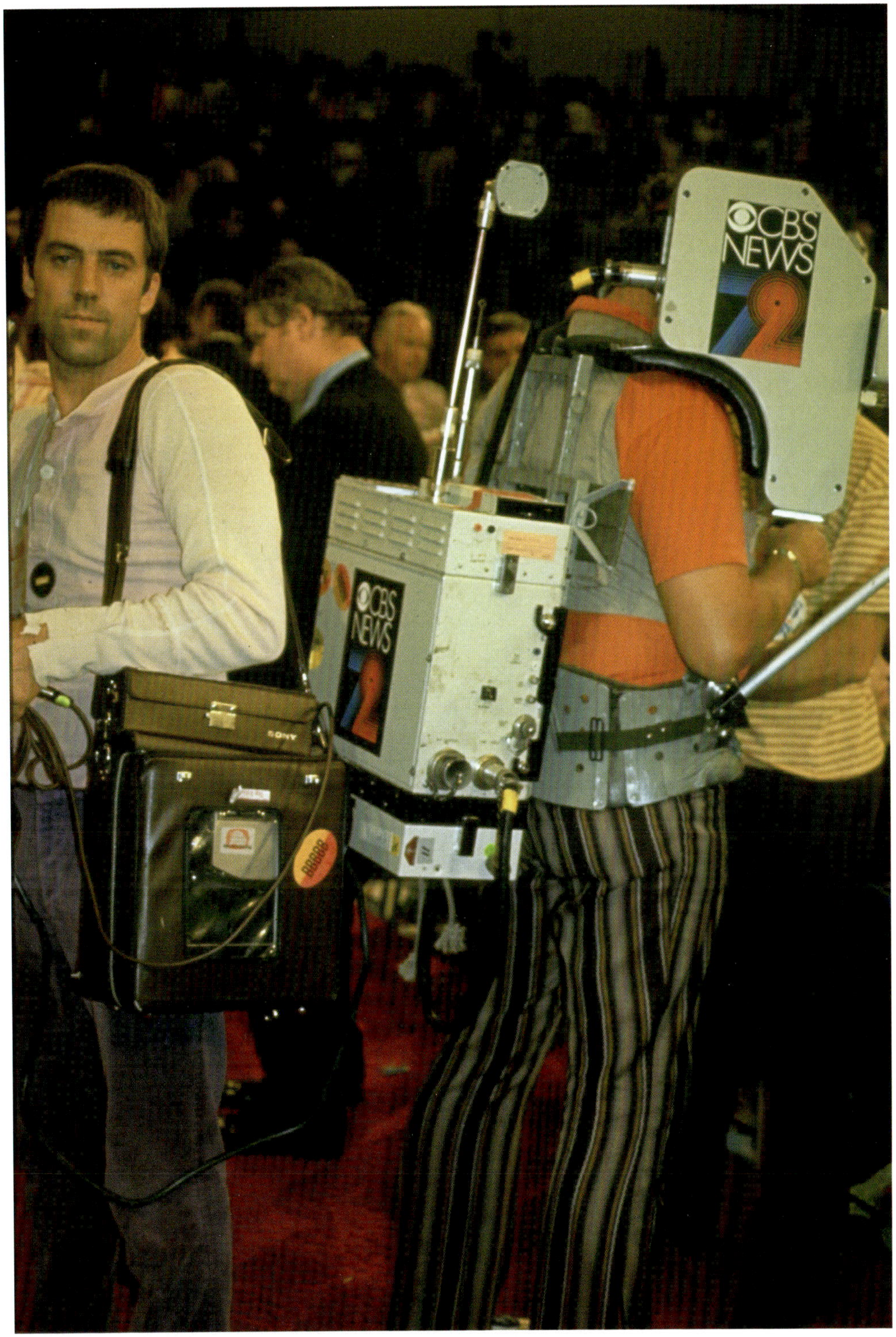

Fig. 2.33 Ant Farm: Doug Michels back-to-back with a CBS cameraman at the Republican National Convention, Miami Beach Florida, 1972. Photo: Chip Lord, courtesy of University of California, Berkeley Art Museum and Pacific Film Archive.

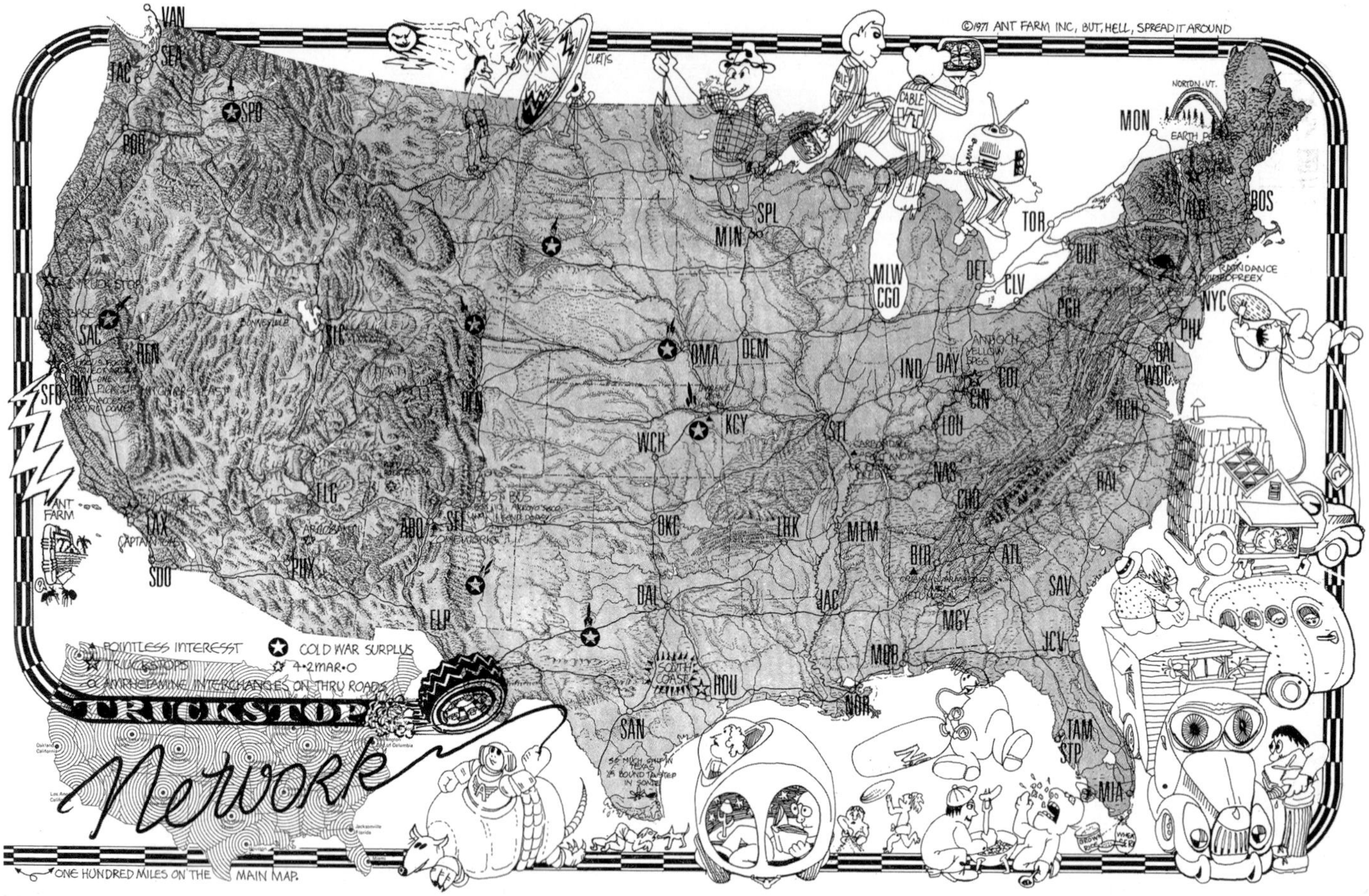

her throat and threatening her life if the station stopped the live transmission. When the recording stopped, Burden doused the tape in acetone to destroy it, infuriating the station manager. Lutjeans, completely unaware of Burden's plan, was terrified and truly felt threatened during this event.[105] *Relic from TV Hijack* (1972) is one of Burden's "relics"—artifacts left over from his performances that are placed on velvet in a Plexiglas case to represent the original event. In this case, the performance can never be seen again because of the destruction of the videotape. Burden's action implied a kind of mock yet ritualized violence, as it underscored the sensationalism of television coverage of such live, spectacular events as the airline hijackings so prevalent at that time.

A year later, in 1973, Burden purchased one month of airtime on KHJ–Channel 9 in Los Angeles to run a ten-second clip of a 16 mm film of his performance *Through the Night Softly,* in which he crawls through fifty feet of broken glass. Subsequently, in 1975 he did *Poem for LA,* a thirty-second spot on KHJ in which he is seen in a tight closeup uttering three phrases: "Science has failed," "Heat is life," and "Time kills." Played seventy-two times during a four-day period, the piece was another TV "hijack," as it disrupted viewers' customary commercial programming.[106]

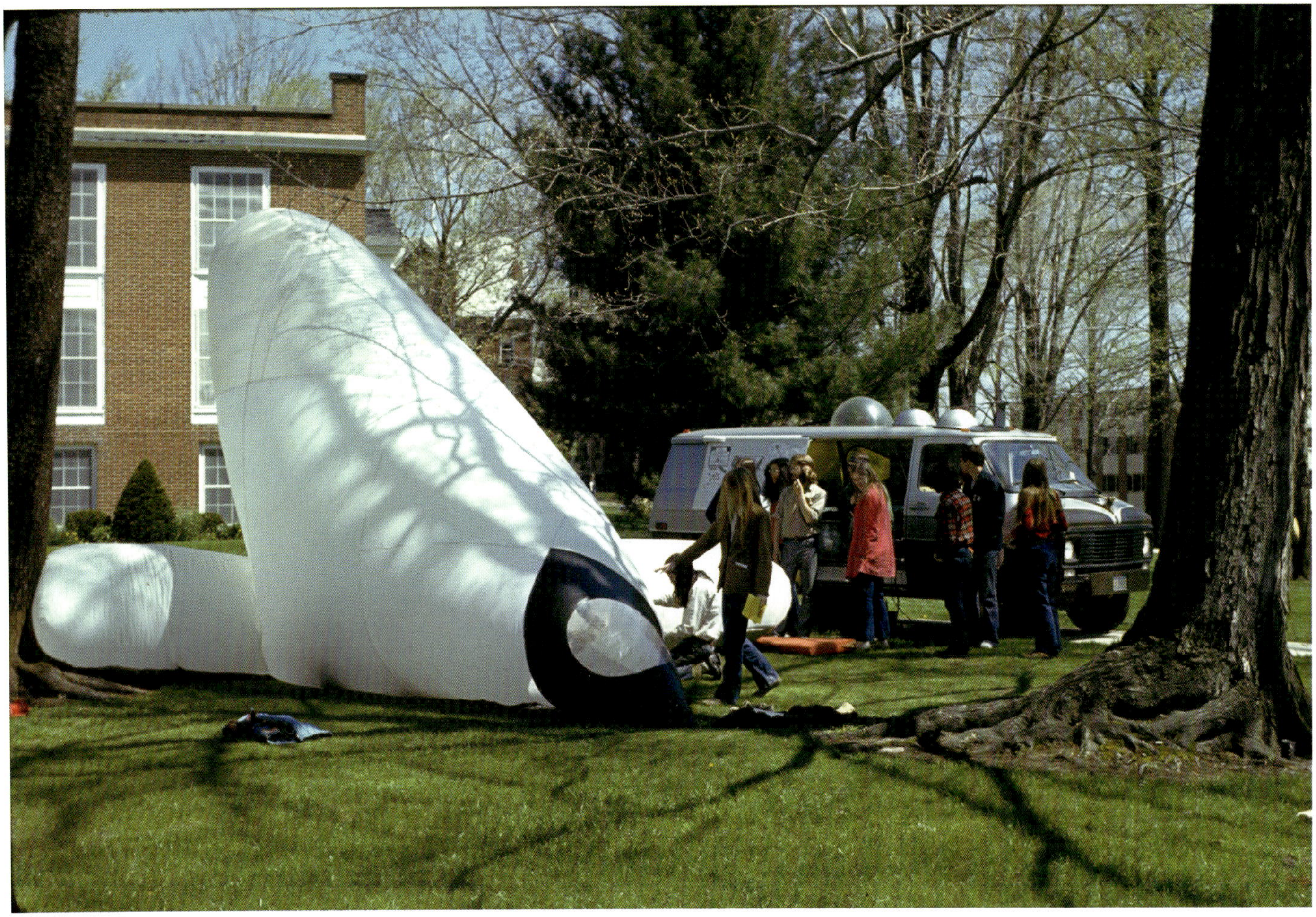

Fig. 2.34 Ant Farm, *Truckstop Network Placemat,* 1971. Offset lithography (two-sided); 11 × 17 in.

Fig. 2.35 Ant Farm, *Ice-9* and *Media Van*, 1971. Miami University, Oxford, Ohio. Photo: Doug Michels, courtesy University of California, Berkeley Art Museum and Pacific Film Archive.

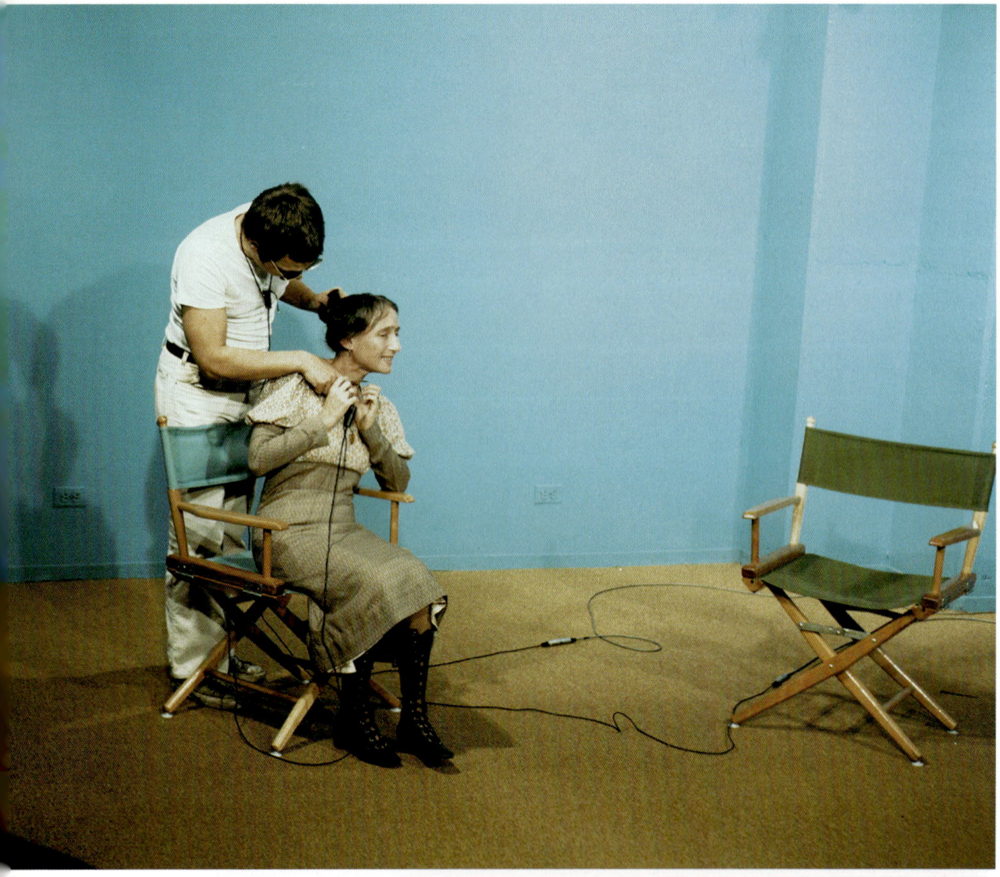

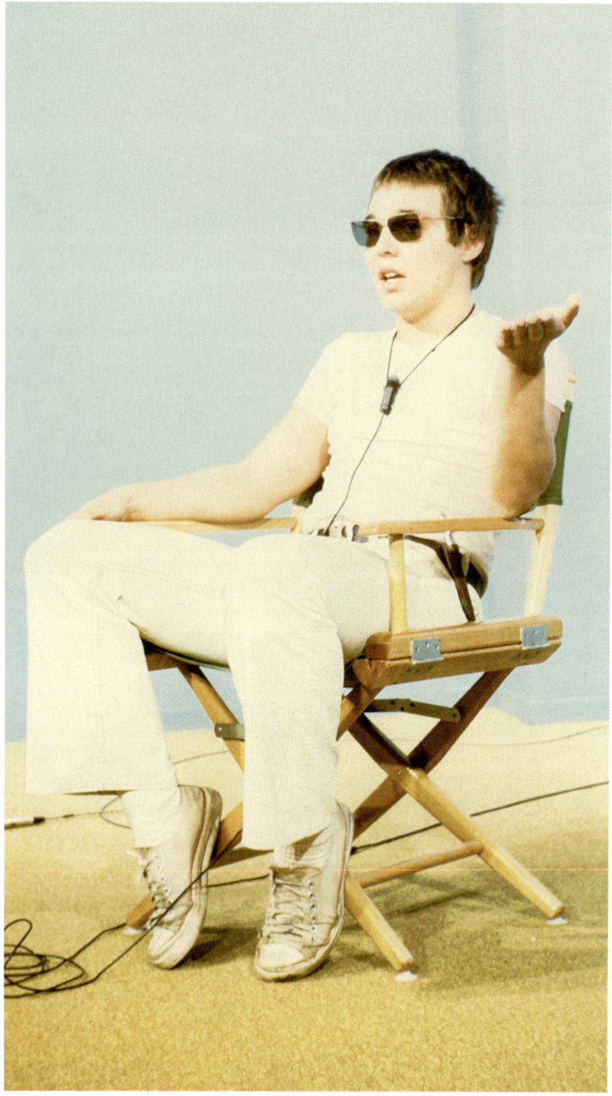

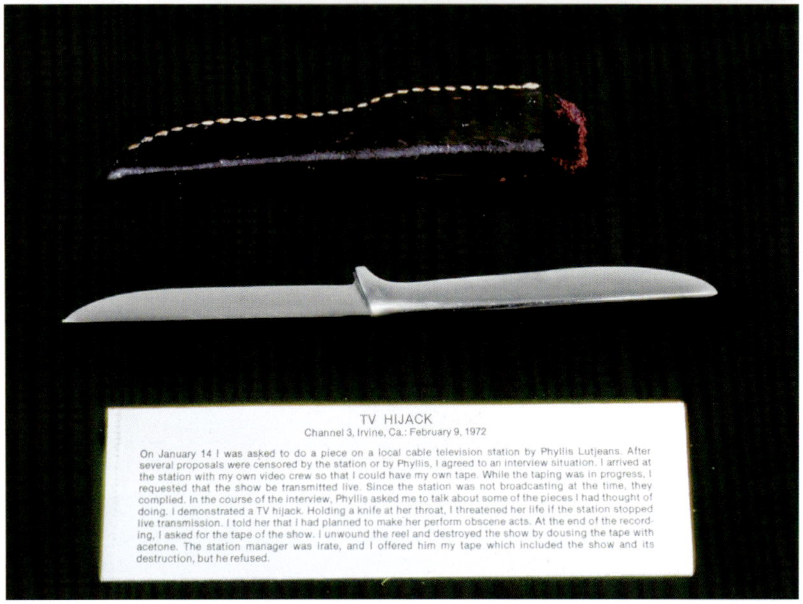

Figs. 2.36–2.39 Chris Burden, *TV Hijack,* 1972. Performance at Channel 3 Cablevision, Irvine, California. *Left: Relic from TV Hijack,* 1972. Knife, scabbard, case, and printed text; case: 5 ¾ × 10 ½ × 7 ⅞ in.

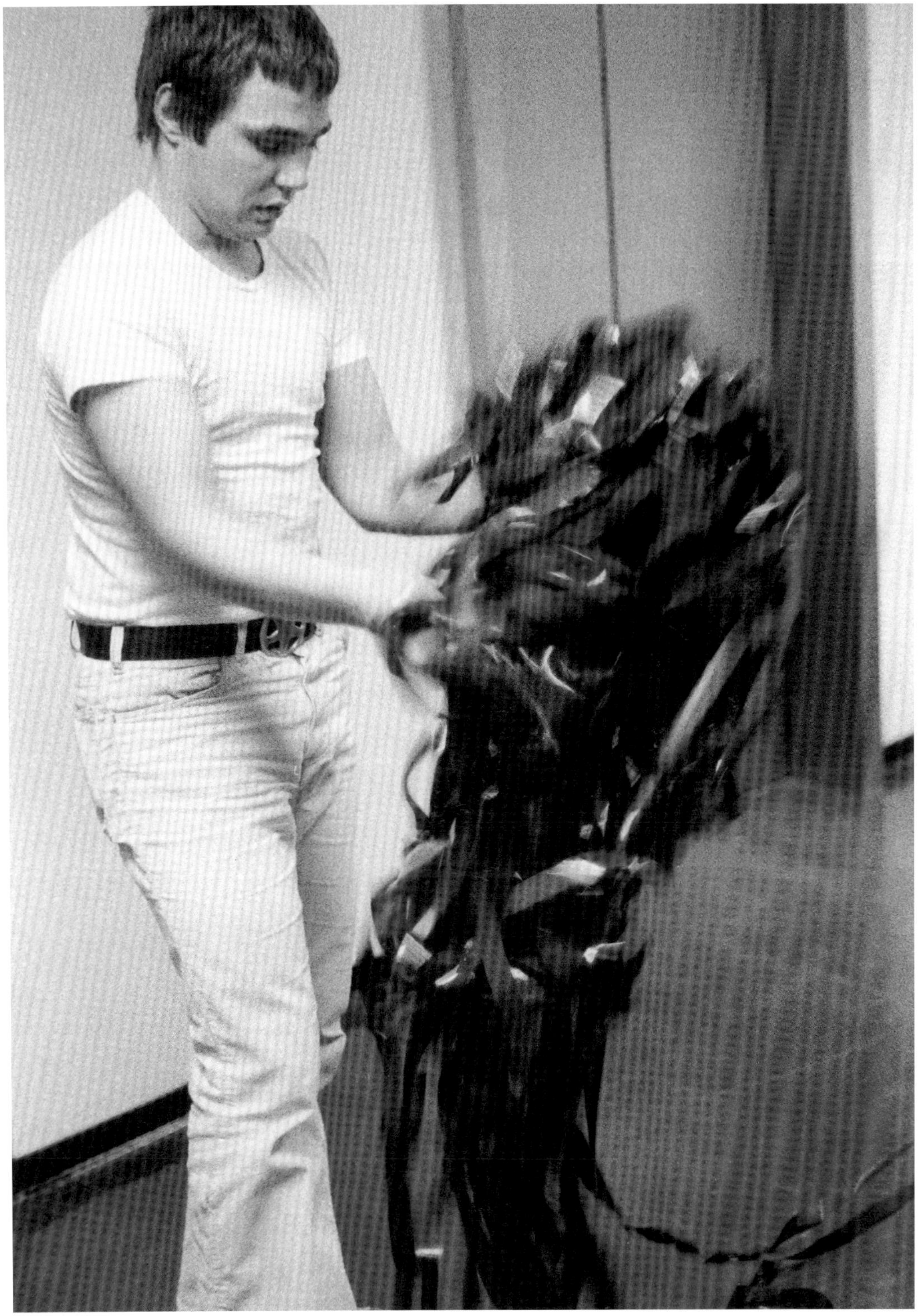

ARTISTS' PUBLICATIONS

Since the advent of the avant-garde, artists' publications have been an integral part of their production, often eliciting key aspects of their praxis. With the dominance of language in Conceptual art and the primacy of text in documenting ephemeral practices, the number of artists' publications expanded exponentially circa 1970. These works ranged from artists' books and journals to broadsides or posters, to post-cards and other forms of mail and correspondence art. Some pieces existed to document other ephemeral productions, serving as the only evidence of that action or event; others were produced as the primary art object. *Avalanche,* published from 1970 to 1976 by Willoughby Sharp and edited by Liza Bear, was the first major artist-produced periodical in the United States, and it disseminated documentation and information throughout the contemporary art community. Earlier artists' publications, such as Wallace Berman's *Semina* or George Maciunas's *Fluxus*—though generated for a particular network of artists or patrons—set an example for many others that emerged in the 1970s.

With an abundance of small, alternative presses and easily accessible printing facilities in art departments and art schools, California became a center of production for self-published, often handmade artists' books. Transcending the traditional bound-book format, these unique works of art take the form of scrolls, codices, foldouts, single sheets, or boxed materials. Although now artists' books may be mass produced, those of the late 1960s and early 1970s were typically one of a kind or issued in very small editions.

An early example of an artist's book, Ed Ruscha's fan-folded *Every Building on the Sunset Strip* (1966) documents his lived experience in the horizontal city of Los Angeles (see fig. 1.8, p. 22). Revealing Ruscha's penchant for everyday subjects and deadpan humor, this extra-long book replicates the endless repetition of apartments, gas stations, and other buildings that one experiences while driving. An equally banal sense of humor can be found in John Baldessari's *Throwing Three Balls in the Air to Get a Straight Line (Best of Thirty-six Attempts)* (1973; fig. 2.41). The artist performed this simple task thirty-six times—the standard number of shots on a roll of film—and eventually selected the "best" performance.

Always intrigued by images and texts appropriated from American popular culture, early in her career Alexis Smith made witty photographic collages such as *Charlie Chan Piece* (fig. 2.42), which are a corollary to her artist's books, often in eccentric formats.

Other larger-format artists' books follow specific sets of rules, sequences, or patterns, such as Guy de Cointet's *ACRCIT* (1971), a 17 × 22-inch newspaper filled with pages of completely encoded text in the form of letters, images, and symbols. Charles Gaines's *Regression Series* (1973–74, fig. 2.40), drawings of grids with numbered squares that rely on mathematical formulas, use counting as a system to map the spaces, and prefigure his subsequent conceptual paintings. He made four sets of seven drawings in 1973–74 and bound them into this larger-scale artist's book in 1978.

Fig. 2.40 Charles Gaines, from the *Regression Series,* 1973–74. Mechanical ink and pen on paper; 23 × 29 in.

REGRESSION: DRAWING #3 GROUP #2 WAS NOT DIVIDED

Fig. 2.41 John Baldessari, *Throwing Three Balls in the Air to Get a Straight Line (Best of Thirty-six Attempts)* (detail), 1973. Artist's book; 10 × 13 in.

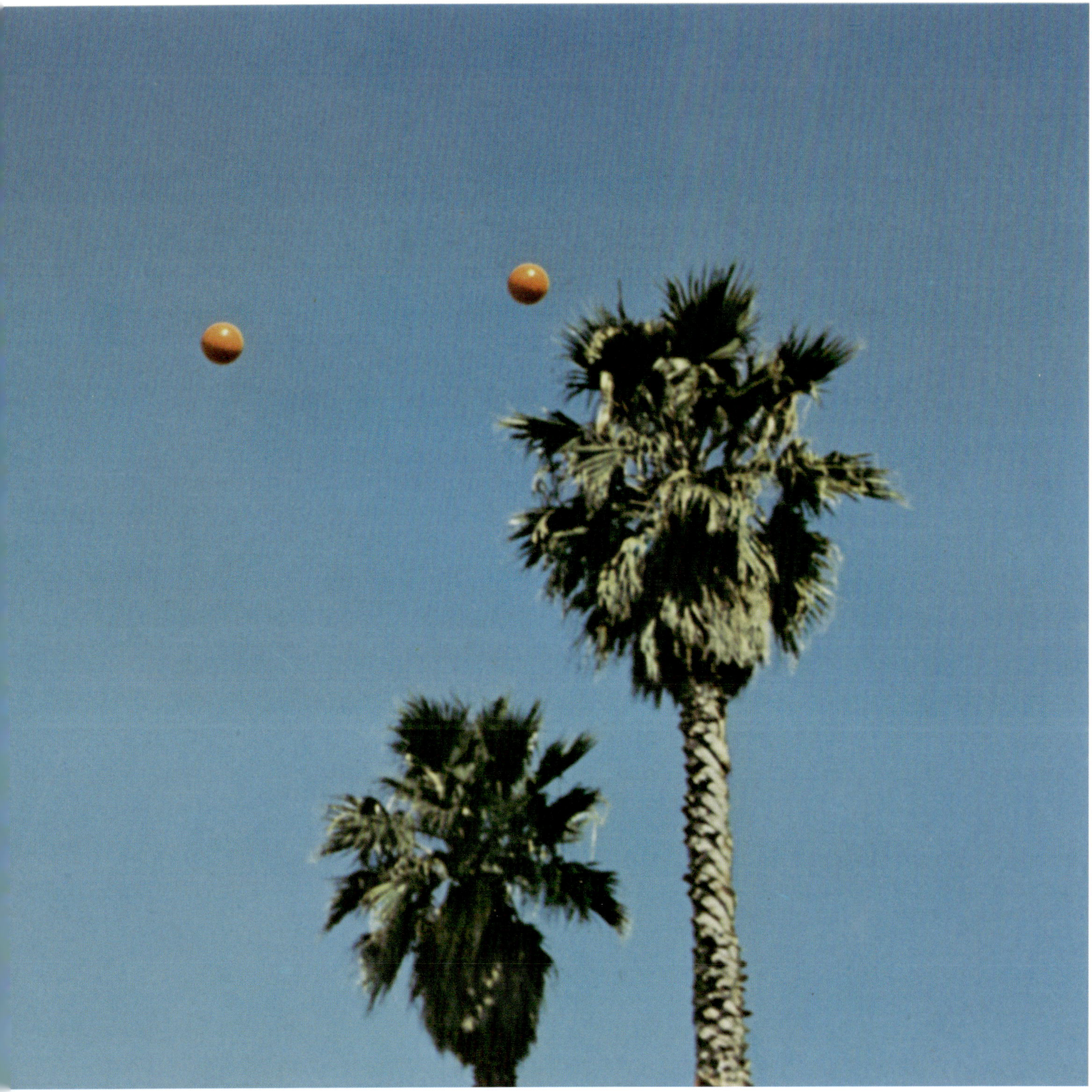

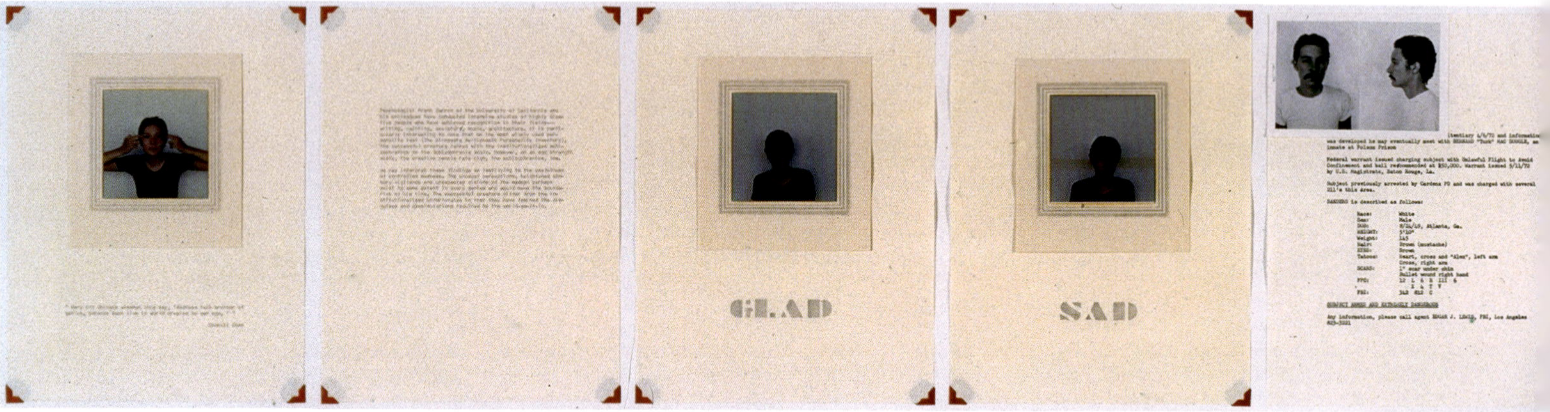

Fig. 2.42 Alexis Smith, *Charlie Chan Piece,* 1973.
Photographs and typed text; 12 × 45½ in.

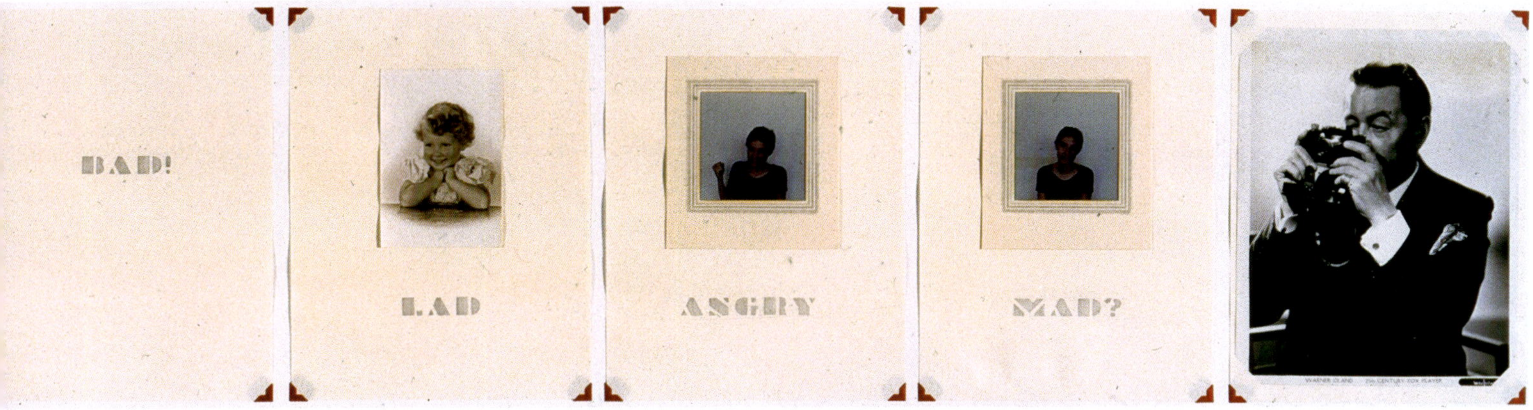
BAD!
LAD
ANGRY
MAD?
WARNER OLAND
20th CENTURY-FOX PLAYER

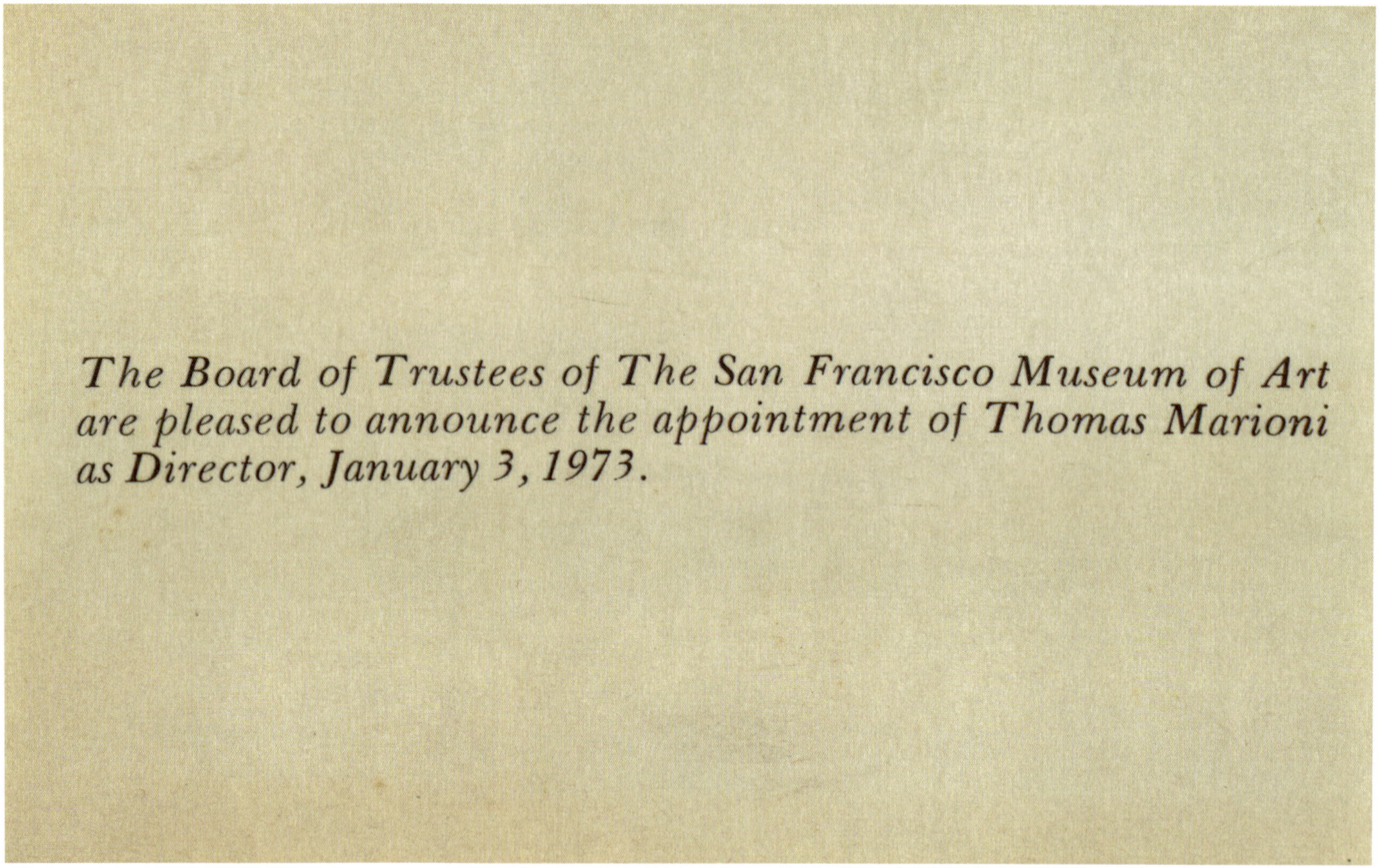
The Board of Trustees of The San Francisco Museum of Art are pleased to announce the appointment of Thomas Marioni as Director, January 3, 1973.

PUBLICATION INTERVENTIONS

Artists of this period also engaged in "publication interventions"—some infiltrated preexisting magazines and newspapers, while others took the form of correspondence or mail art. From November 1968 through November 1969, Stephen Kaltenbach inserted his artwork—with titles such as the double entendre "Art Works" (November 1968) and provocative phrases such as *Tell a Lie* (February 1969), *Perpetrate a Hoax* (April 1969), and *Build a Reputation* (May 1969)—as "ads" into eleven issues of *Artforum* (see fig. 1.39, pp. 52–53). Tom Marioni's postcard *The Board of Trustees of The San Francisco Museum of Art are pleased to announce the appointment of Thomas Marioni as Director, January 3, 1973* (1973; fig. 2:43) announced his fictitious new position, while *Museum News* (April 1973) featured a magazine ad stating the same.

As early as 1952, a group called Postfolks organized a network to distribute Conceptual artworks using the U.S. Postal Service, and mail art proliferated, particularly in California.[107] Some mail art functioned to extend site-specific installations and performances. For her *100 Boots* (1971–73; fig. 2.44), Eleanor Antin installed fifty pairs of boots in different public sites, photographed them, and then sent the black-and-

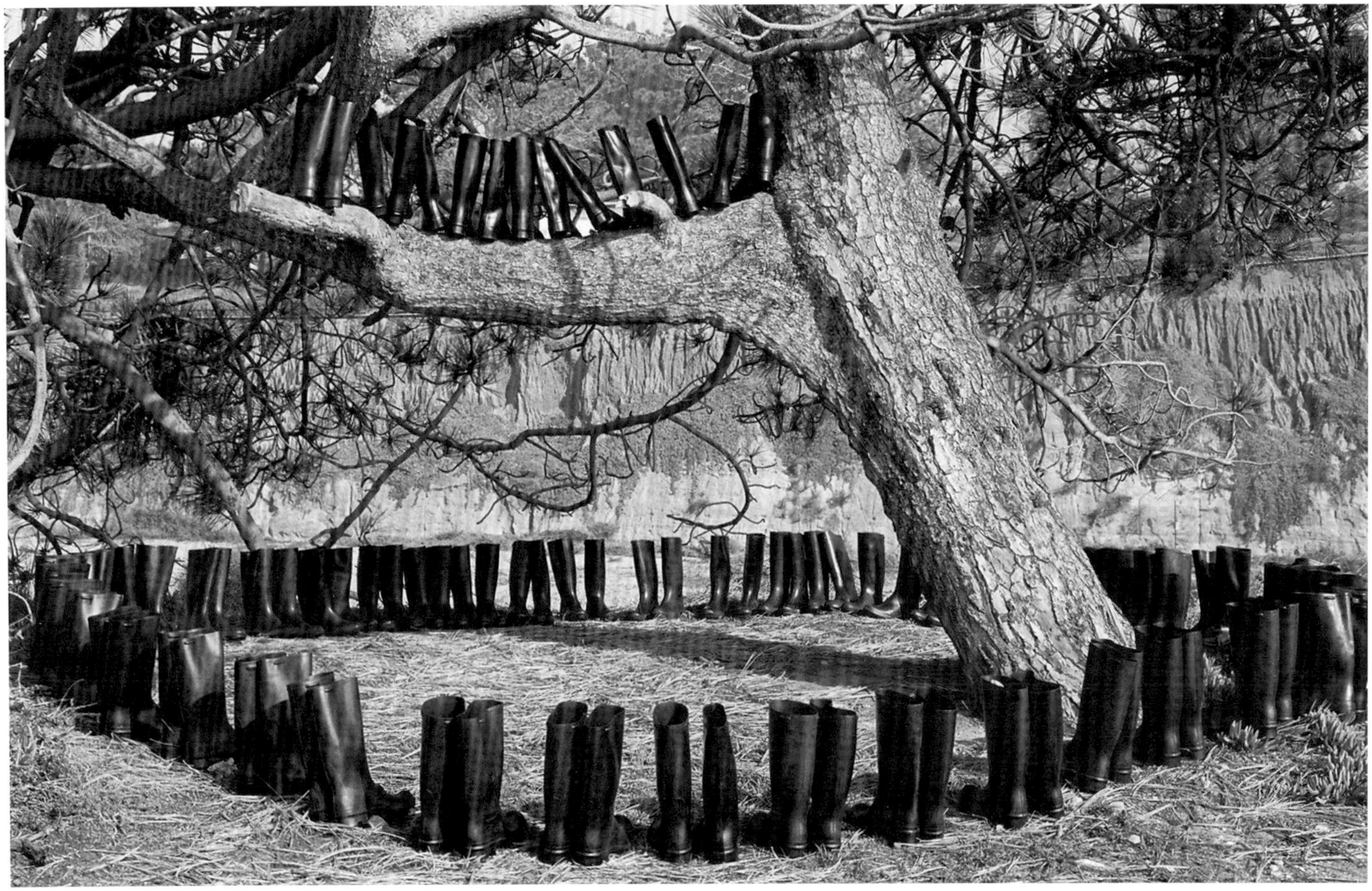

white photographs on postcards to people around the world. As the artist has commented: "Somehow it came to me in a dream. . . . Black boots! Big black boots. I got them at the Army-Navy Surplus then I printed them up on postcards. . . . Now it is a piece that I see as a kind of pictorial novel that was sent through the mail, came unannounced, unasked for. It came in the middle of people's lives." Antin's serial photographs of unoccupied boots may also pose a more somber reference to the legions of "absent bodies" of young men who perished during that time in the Vietnam War.

Fig. 2.43 Tom Marioni, *The Board of Trustees of The San Francisco Museum of Art are pleased to announce the appointment of Thomas Marioni as Director, January 3, 1973.* Offset lithography on card stock; 3¾ × 5¾ in.

Fig. 2.44 Eleanor Antin, *100 Boots in a Field,* Route 101, California, February 9, 1971, 3:30 p.m.; from *100 Boots,* 1971–73. Fifty-one black-and-white picture postcards; 4½ × 7 in. each.

>>

Fig. 2.45 Stephen Kaltenbach, *Artforum Ads* (detail: *Artforum,* April 1969 issue), November 1968–November 1969. Eleven issues of *Artforum* magazine with advertisements: offset lithography on paper; 10½ × 10⅜ in. each.

makes them. They're summing-up names, they tie a knot around the whole personality, and suggest the kind of bravura signature that underlines itself. Jeff Carter, Tess Millay, Mathew Garr, Guino Rinaldo, Buck Kennelley, Johnny Lovo, Molly Malloy, Cherry Valance, are dillies of names that indicate a Breughel type who creates a little world of his own, outfitted in every inch with picturesque hats, insensitive swagger, and good-natured snobberies.

Howard Hawks is a bravado specialist who always makes pictures about a Group. Fast dialogue, quirky costumes, the way a telephone is answered, everything is held together by his weird Mother Hen instinct. The whole population in *Scarface,* cavemen in quilted smoking jackets, are like the first animals struggling out of the slime and murk towards fresh air. *Only Angels,* a White Cargo melodrama that is often intricately silly, has a family unit living at the Dutchman's, a combination bar, restaurant, rooming house and airport run by a benevolent Santa Claus (some airline: the planes take off right next to the kitchen, and some kitchen: a plane crashes, the wreck is cleared and the pilot buried in the time it takes them to cook a steak; and the chief control is a crazy mascot who lives with a pet donkey and serves as a lookout atop a buzzard-and-blizzard infested mountain as sharp as a shark's tooth). The wonderfully dour reporters in *Friday,* the mawkish cowboys in *Red River,* are also strangely pinned in place by the idea of people being linked together in tight therapeutic groups, the creations of a man who is as divorced from modern *angst* as Fats Waller, whose whole movie-making system seems a secret preoccupation with linking, a connections business involving people, plots, and eight-inch hat brims.

The Mother Hubbard spirit gives the film a kind of romance that is somewhat Wasp-ish with a Gatsby elegance and cool. Both the girls in *Scarface,* like Zelda Fitzgerald, would fling themselves away over a Russ Columbo recording of "Poor Butterfly." Ann Dvorak, dancing with a big, bland-faced clod who is bewildered by all her passion and herky-jerky cat's meow stuff, is so close to *Tender Is the Night* in her aura of silly recklessness. The sophomoric pilots in Barranca, like Fitzgerald's expatriates in Paris, are ravished with each other's *soignée*: Bonnie playing psuedo-hot "Peanuts" with a whole saloon jammed around her piano cheering her on, is an embarrassing square version of super-square Chico Marx. The feeling of snobbery in any Hawks work is overpowering, whether it is a Great White Father (Grant) patronizing a devitalized native with a gift watch or the female Jimmy Breslin (Rosalind Russell) breezily typing a socko story. This romance which wraps the fliers-reporters-cowhands in a patina of period mannerism and attitude makes for a film that isn't dated so much as removed from reality, like the land of Tolkien's Hobbits.

It is interesting how many plots are interwoven into a scene. The whole last part of the *Front Page* remake is a fugue in fast humor, peculiar for the way each figure touches another in ricochets of wild absurdity. Molly Malloy, the killer's lady defender ("Ah come on fellahs, he didn't even touch me, I just gave him some tea, and he was shaking all over") jumps out the window and is forgotten; her boyfriend, who has been entombed forlornly inside a rolltop desk, is dragged to his cell, presumably to be hung the next morning; Hildy Johnson finally gets maneuvered back to the *Morning Star* by her arch heel editor; the mayor and the sheriff are politically destroyed for trying to bribe a fat Baby Huey, who turns up with a reprieve for the convicted killer. Then there's Louie, a terrific heist artist who steals a mother-in-law and gets mangled by a police car which was driving in the wrong lane. People who talk reams about great film comedy never mention this version of Hecht's play with its one twist, an elegantly played, pragmatic girl, sharp and immediately aware of everything in the ace reporter's role. It is a prime example of Hawks' uncelebrated female touch: the light flouncy foot, the anti-pomposity about newspaper problems, and the Mother Hen way of setting up family relationships. The ingenuity of its pragmatic engineering is that every gesture (she picks up the phone, it's funny) contributes to the plot, is laugh provoking, and adds up to a supply of intricately locked humor so large that there's hardly time to relish any one gag.

The films have a musical comedy hokishness joined to a freedom, a mellifluous motion which is summed up in the line "wherever they roam they'll be on my land," as a couple of cows — the start of a mighty herd: the man's bull and the boy's cow — wander off into a nice, sparse landscape. But the deep quality in any Hawks film is the uncannily poetic way an action is unfolded. Sometimes this portrayal of motion is thrilling (the cattle going into Abilene), funny (Abner Biberman's harmless hood: "everybody knows Louie"), gracefully dour (Karloff's enigmatic cockiness in a bowling alley, like a Muybridge photograph) or freakishly mannered (Karen Morley sizing up Scarface's new pad: "It's kinda gaudy, isn't it"), but it is always inventive, killingly expressive, and gets you in the gut. One blatantly colloquial effect is slammed against another. The last section of *Scarface* builds detail on detail into a forbidding whirlwind. As the incestuous duo shoots it out with the cops, slightly outnumbered eighty to one, the lighting is fabulous, Dvorak's clamoring reaches an unequaled frenzy ("I'm just like you, Tony, aren't I, I'm not afraid"), and there is an authentic sense of the primeval, life coming to smash the puny puffed up egos.

Not many moviemakers have gone so deeply into personality-revealing motion, the geography of gesture, the building and milking of a signature trait for all its worth. Hawks' abandon with his pet area, human gesture, is usually staggering, for better or worse. Why should Cary Grant get away with so much Kabuki-like exaggeration, popping his eyes, jutting out his elbows, roaring commands at breathtaking speed in a gymnasium of outrageous motion? Sometimes Hawks' human interest detailing falls on its face: the beginning of a cattle drive with Wayne a tiny speck moving down a channel of earth, the Knute Rockne of Cattledom, and then, those endless ghastly close-ups of every last cowboy, one after the other, giving his special version of a Yahoo.

Scarface, as vehement, vitriolic and passionate a work as has been made about Prohibition, is a deadly grim gangster movie far better than *White Heat* or *Bonnie and Clyde,* a damp black neighbor to the black art in Walker Evans' subway shots or the Highway 90 photographic shot at dawn by Robert Frank. Nowhere near the tough-lipped mentality or hallucinatory energy of Hawks' only serious film, *His Girl Friday* is still better than a clever, arch, extremely funny newspaper film. It's hard to believe that anything in Chaplin or W. C. Fields has so many hard, workable gags, each one bumping the other in an endless interplay of high-spirited cynicism. But rating these close camaraderie films, teeming with picturesque fliers-punks-pundits and a boy's book noble humanism, in the Pantheon division of Art and giving them cosmic conceptions is to needlessly overweight them.

A director who's made at least twenty box-office gold mines since 1926 is going to repeat himself, but the fact is that Howard Hawks' films are as different as they're similar. In each action film he's powerfully interested in the fraternal groups that he sets up, sticking to them with an undemonstrative camera that is always eye level and acute on intimate business, and using stories that have a straight-ahead motion and develop within a short time span. The point is that each picture has a widely different impact: from the sulphurous lighting and feverish style of *Scarface* to the ignorant blustering of John Wayne in a soft Western that doesn't have any pace at all. Within the devil-may-care silliness of his *Angels* picture, the difference in acting between Barthelmess (crafty and constipated), Thomas Mitchell (maudlin, weepy) and Jean Arthur (Good grief!) is so violent as to suggest the handling of three directors.

Hawks, a born movie manipulator who suggests a general moving around little flag pins on a battle map, is not very fussy about the pulp story figures nor the fableized scenery into which he jams them. The opening shots of his Andes airline movie are supposed to "vividly create Barranca, the South American town" in and around which the "completely achieved masterpiece" is set. This operetta seaport, with boas of smoke hanging in swirly serpentines and pairs of extras criss-crossing through the fake mist, might be good for a Douglas, Arizona high school production. In the next "vividly created" scene, Jean Arthur is be-

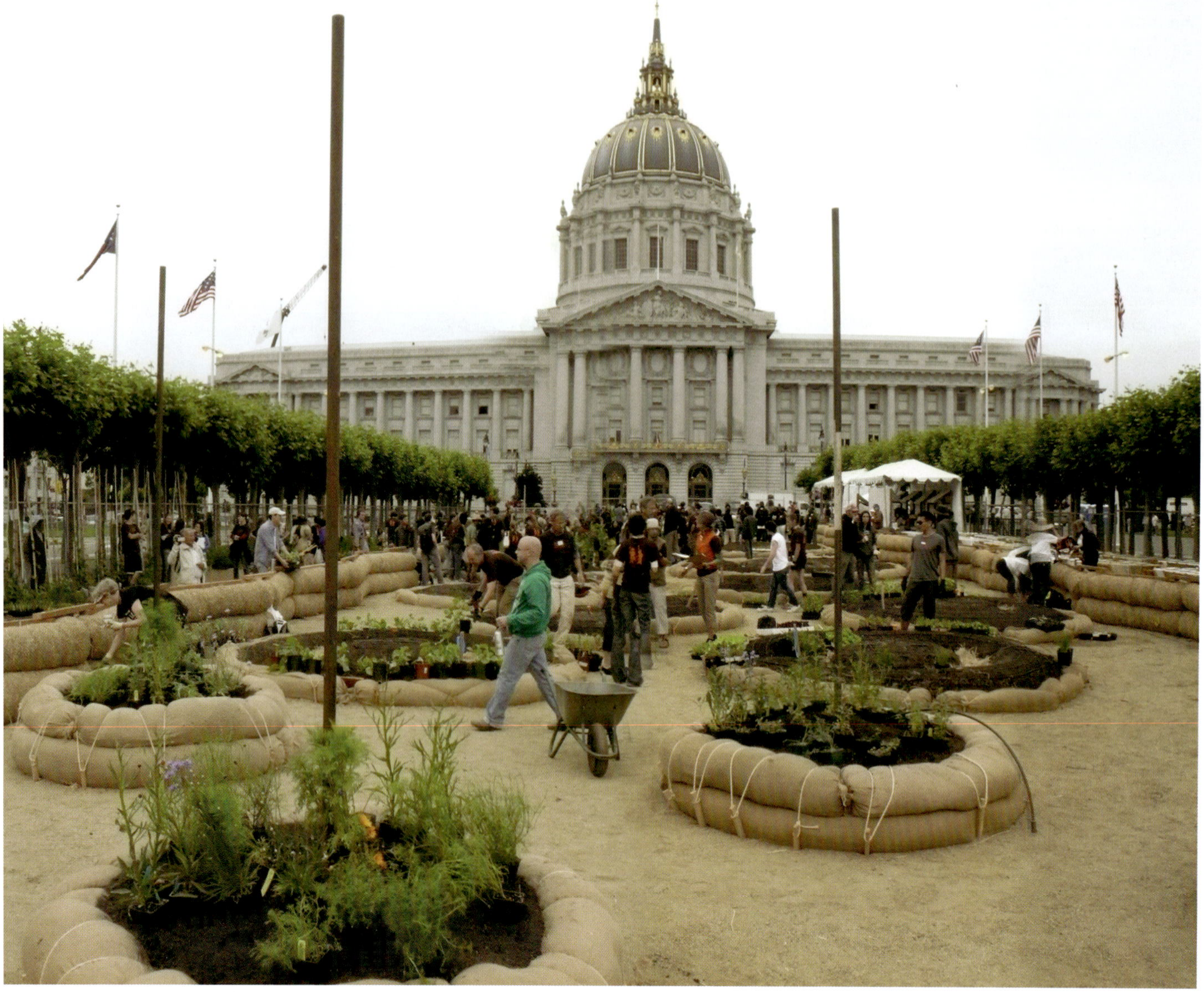

Fig. 2.46 Amy Franceschini (in collaboration with Slow Food Nation, CMG Architects, and Garden for the Environment), *Victory Gardens,* 2008; City Hall, San Francisco, California. Image: Courtesy Amy Franceschini / Futurefarmers.

CONCLUSION

The moment of conceptual art . . . is wide-ranging, covering a vast terrain in terms of its effect on traditional modes and categories of artistic production, exhibition and distribution. Indeed, one could argue that the influence of conceptualism can be found in almost all ambitious contemporary art—from the most direct lineage of "neo conceptualism" to the more obscure links of contemporary video, performance and public art. As an international movement that transcended national borders voicing common concerns about the role of the artist, the artwork, the public and the institutions involved, the questions and problematics posed by conceptual artists continue to be as important today as when they were initially raised in the 1960s and 1970s.

Alexander Alberro, *Conceptual Art: A Critical Anthology*, ed. Alexander Alberro and Blake Stimson (Cambridge, MA: MIT Press, 2000), xxx

As noted in the introduction to this essay, in today's globalized world it is increasingly problematic to speak about artistic practices from a specific geographic location. As Alberro observes, with its ongoing international influence, Conceptualism cannot be collapsed into a single moment or codified as a discrete movement: its genealogy encompasses not only the new genres that developed concurrently in the 1960s and 1970s but also new artistic practices that continue today. Conceptualism functions as its own genre or medium, particularly in California, where there are many highly visible artists working this way now.

However, as we have seen, this was not always the case. The cultural landscape in California circa 1970 was simultaneously absent and present: absent to the broader art historical discourse yet active, alive, and present in terms of the breadth and depth of the production of artists both in the north and in the south. And just as California had to be invented as a concept or "state of mind," so too did its cultural support system—more specifically, the sites for creating and displaying new work. A salient characteristic of artistic production in California was its hybridized, or intermedial, nature that combined actions and language; incorporated everyday experience; merged art and life; and produced work about the body or an embodied experience. This often demanded radically transforming existing institutions or inventing new alternatives. As artists' roles as cultural producers shifted and their authority ascended, they took greater control of the particular conditions of production and exhibition of their work. In determining specific sites, artists could respond to distinct contexts and incorporate spectators into the works—whether within an institution or a public space—as the reception of the viewer became paramount.

With their concerted effort to de-institutionalize institutions and/or to create work in the public sphere, often in eccentric locations, artists worked "outside the frame." As they eschewed the gallery system and the commodification of their art, many artists took an activist, antimaterialist, politically engaged position vis-à-vis critical cultural, social, and political issues. California was then, and continues to be now, a haven for counterculture, from Beats and hippies to punks and contemporary hipsters. Setting aside outmoded artistic hierarchies and hegemonies, artists freely appropriated attitudes and ideas from popular culture and made interventions into public media more than their East Coast counterparts did.

The impact of artists circa 1970 in California is most visible in the subsequent generation of Conceptual, video, and performance artists working in the state. Artists who came of age in the late 1970s and into the 1980s, a time associated with appropriation and other Neoconceptual practices, became influenced by mentors such as Michael Asher, John Baldessari, and Douglas Huebler at CalArts; Howard Fried, Doug Hall, and Paul Kos at the San Francisco Art Institute; and Chris Burden, Paul McCarthy, and Alexis Smith at UCLA.[108]

The legacy of the late 1960s and early 1970s is also apparent in the socially interactive, convivial relational art of the 1990s. In the introduction to his book *Relational Aesthetics* (1998), Nicolas Bourriaud compares the 1960s and 1970s with the art of the 1990s:

> The constitution of convivial relations has been an historical constant since the 1960s. The generation of the 1990s took up this set of issues, though it had been relieved of the matter of the definition of art, so pivotal in the 1960s and

> 1970s. The issue no longer resides in broadening the boundaries of art, but in experiencing art's capacities of resistance within the overall social arena. Based on one and the same family of activities, two radically different sets of problems emerge: yesterday, the stress laid on relations *inside* the art world, within a modernist culture attaching itself to the importance to the new and calling for linguistic subversion; today the emphasis is put on external relations as part of an eclectic culture where the artwork stands up to the mill of the Society of the Spectacle. Social utopias and revolutionary hopes have given way to everyday micro-utopias.[109]

Bourriaud is correct in stating that artists circa 1970—especially Conceptualists and those working in experimental genres—had to expand or, perhaps more accurately, eradicate the existing boundaries and a priori definitions of art. He implies that this effort operated primarily *inside* an art world that still fetishized Modernist "newness" and "social utopias" rather than focusing against the culture of spectacle; however, some artists did create external social relations and "micro-utopias."

Compare, for instance, the participatory, convivial, gallery-transforming works such as Marioni's *FREE BEER* with Rikrit Tiravanija's *Thai Curry* or Lee Mingwei's *Dinner Project.* Or note how feminist performance artists of the 1970s who assumed another profession—like Sherk's waitress, Montano's nurse, or Rosler's single mother—prefigure Andrea Fraser's impersonation of a docent in her *Museum Highlights* or Christine Hill's various roles as an apothecary, printer, and tour guide. Any number of artists—Burden, Fox, Montano, Barbara T. Smith, and others—occupied the gallery in new, quite radical ways, involving the spectator in their work. So do relational artists, such as Joseph Grigely and Ben Kinmont, who perform actions that require the audience, or Gabriel Orozco, Jorge Pardo, and Andrea Zittel, who alter the gallery by producing furniture or other objects and thereby shift the viewer's relationship to the space. While artists of the 1960s and 1970s focused on ideas about the environment, labor, feminism, gender, sexuality, and institutional politics—tackling tough *social issues*—their successors seemed initially more interested in themes of participation and *sociability*. Many of these young relational artists who began their careers in the recession of the 1990s abandoned their more ephemeral practices later in the decade—when the market grew stronger—and now often produce more commercial gallery-based work.

Today there is yet another generation of even younger artists—who are aware of or have studied with the artists who came of age in the 1990s—who have returned, once again, to more Conceptual, performative, and ephemeral practices. Some of them have created artist-run galleries or organizations and present exhibition programs such as Machine Project and the Outpost for Contemporary Art in Los Angeles, or 2nd Floor Projects and Queen's Nails Projects in San Francisco. Others have formed artist collectives—such as Finishing School and the Los Angeles Urban Rangers in Southern California or the Bureau of Urban Secrets in San Francisco. These groups use Conceptual, collaborative research methods to explore cultural, social, and urban issues. Some collectives have specific environmental agendas: Los Angeles–based Farmlab investigates land use, sustainability, livability, and health. Fallen Fruit, also in L.A., produces temporary events focused on urban space, neighborhoods, and new forms of community. Futurefarmers (whose motto is "raising consciousness since 1995") has made a series of *Victory Gardens (fig. 2.46)*, utilizing the model of the garden programs of World Wars I and II; the notion of wartime victory has been replaced by the desire to grow food in public sites, such as one near City Hall in San Francisco, and to educate people about urban sustainability.

It is this goal of educating the public that is shared by all of these artist collectives. In these socially engaged events, audiences are not only active participants but also co-learners in an investigative process that is informed by a sense of critical pedagogy.[110] Like their 1960s and 1970s forebears, these and other postmillennial artists continue to critique even more commodified art markets, spectacularized media, and insular institutions, with practices that engage with everyday life.

In the introduction to her 1997 edition of *Six Years: The Dematerialization of the Art Object from 1966 to 1972* (originally published in 1973), Lucy Lippard concludes:

> Conceptualists indicated that the most exciting "art" might still be buried in social energies not yet recognized as art. The process of discovering the boundaries didn't stop with Conceptual art. These energies are still out there, waiting for artists to plug into them potential fuel for the expansion of what art can mean. The escape was temporary. Art was recaptured and sent back to its white cell, but parole is always a possibility.[111]

Perhaps the zeitgeist of Conceptualism and related practices of the 1960s and 1970s has indeed found its place in the twenty-first century, as California artists continue to experiment with and innovate new methodologies, technologies, and sites for their work beyond the white cell.

NOTES

1 Alexander Alberro, *Conceptual Art: A Critical Anthology*, ed. Alexander Alberro and Blake Stimson (Cambridge, MA: MIT Press, 2000), xvii.

2 The Six Gallery was opened by poets Jack Spicer and John Ryan along with visual artists Hayward King, Deborah Remington, David Simpson, and Wally Hedrick.

3 Bruce Conner, panel discussion, "Beat Culture and New America" (remarks, Walker Art Center, Minneapolis, MN, June 2, 1996).

4 Richard Schechner, foreword to *Anna Halprin: Experience as Dance,* by Janice Ross (Berkeley: University of California Press, 2009), ix. Ross's volume is the most comprehensive book about Halprin's life and work to date.

5 These events include *Lunch* at the San Francisco Hilton Hotel (1968) and *Event in a Mall* at San Jose State University (1969). In 1965, Halprin moved her studio to Marin County, where her husband, the landscape architect Lawrence Halprin, designed an outdoor area to allow for new spatial and sonic relationships.

6 Anna Halprin, *Moving toward Life: Five Decades of Transformational Dance* (Middletown, CT: Wesleyan University Press, 1995), 3.

7 Halprin and the workshop later performed in other nontraditional sites: Halprin also participated in a Happening with Allan Kaprow, *Paper* (1964), an event in a multilevel parking garage at UC Berkeley that involved dancers, sweepers, and automobiles engaged in a frenetic series of interactions with newspaper.

8 Halprin, 102.

9 Jeff Berner, "Walker Talker," lecture presented at the Walker Art Center in a symposium in conjunction with the opening of *In The Spirit of Fluxus,* February 13, 1992. Venues such as Longshoremen's Hall and the Fillmore Auditorium hosted events combining rock, art, and politics, such as "The Rock for Peace" and the Week of Angry Arts Vietnam Mobilization, April 9, 1966.

10 Composers Charles Amirkhanian, Pauline Oliveros, Terry Riley, Morton Subotnick, David Tudor, and La Monte Young were among them.

11 James Lewes, chronology to *Fluxus Virus 1962–1992,* ed. Ken Friedman (Cologne, Germany: Galerie Schüppenhauer; Munich, Germany: Aktionsforum Praterinsel, 1992).

12 Lewes, chronology to *Fluxus Virus 1962–1992.* They performed *Simultaneous Performance of Four Compositions by La Monte Young, Terry Riley, Walter De Maria, and Dick Higgins.* Although Higgins was not there, this was the first time his work was presented on the West Coast and the beginning of his continued association with projects and people in California.

13 Susan Hapgood et al., *Neo-Dada: Redefining Art, 1958–1962* (New York: American Federation of the Arts, 1994), 53.

14 Sandra Starr, in *Lost and Found in California: Four Decades of Assemblage Art* (Santa Monica: James Corcoran Gallery, 1988), 64.

15 Eduardo Lipschutz-Villa, interview with Michael McClure, in *Wallace Berman: Support the Revolution* (Amsterdam: Institute of Contemporary Art, 1992), 60–61.

16 For detailed accounts of the Ferus censorship and court case, see Anne Bartlett Ayres, "Berman and Kienholz: Progenitors of Los Angeles Assemblage," in Maurice Tuchman, *Art in Los Angeles: Seventeen Artists in the Sixties,* ed. Jeanne D'Andrea et al. (Los Angeles: Los Angeles County Museum of Art, 1981), 12, 16; and Betty Turnbull, *The Last Time I Saw Ferus* (Newport Beach, CA: Newport Harbor Art Museum, 1976), unpaginated; and Starr, n.p.

17 Eduardo Lipschutz-Villa, interview with Michael McClure, 7.

18 Hapgood et al., 53.

19 Michael Kirby, *Happenings* (London: Sidewick and Jackson, 1965), 272–88.

20 Claes Oldenburg, interview with author, January 1993.

21 Oldenburg, interview with author, January 1993.

22 George Brecht, interview with Robin Page and Carla Liss, Tate Gallery Archives, 1981.

23 Art Seidenbaum, "Anti-Art Goes Out on a Limb," *Los Angeles Times,* October 3, 1963, part IV, 2. Seidenbaum's article is not a review but a curiosity piece in his "Spectator" column of the *L.A. Times.*

24 Moira Roth, "A Star Is Born: Performance Art in California," *Performing Arts Journal* 4, no. 3 (1980): 88.

25 Oldenburg, unpublished interview with author, January 1993; Alison Knowles and Larry Miller of the Robert Watts Studio Archive, interview with author, 1993.

26 Oldenburg, unpublished interview with author, January 1993; Alison Knowles and Larry Miller of the Robert Watts Studio Archive, interview with author, 1993.

27 This is ironic, as the museum did not add the word "modern" to its title until 1975. Mel Henderson was awarded the first SECA award in 1967.

28 The participating artists included Alvin Duskin, William Duval, John C. Fernie, Howard Fried, Tyrus Gerlach, Jay Hemingway, Mel Henderson, Kent Hodgetts, Henry Jacobs, Warner Jepson, Robert Kinmont, Paul Kos, Stephen Laub, James Melchert, Manuel Neri, William T. Wiley, and Alfred Young, plus other anonymous and group projects.

29 Susan Ranells and Brenda Richardson, in *Performance Anthology: Sourcebook for a Decade of California Performance Art,* ed. Carl E. Loeffler and Darlene Tong (San Francisco: Contemporary Arts Press, 1980), 6.

30 Constance Lewallen, "Commitment," Berkeley Art Museum/Pacific Film Archive, www.bampfa.berkeley.edu/about/aboutnotedetail.php?Nickname=TXT0011 (accessed August 3, 2010). As Lewallen has noted, the decision to blur the distinction between gallery and studio, spectator and artist (observer and participant), and art and life came out of several long and freewheeling conversations among the artists and curators, one of which was included in the exhibition's loose-leaf exhibition catalogue, *Free.*

31 Lucinda Barnes, "Collecting the Moment," Berkeley Art Museum/Pacific Film Archive, www.bampfa.berkeley.edu/about/aboutnotedetail.php?Nickname=TXT0009 (accessed August 3, 2010).

32 Peter Selz, as quoted by Jarrett Earnest, "Interview with Peter Selz and Lawrence Rinder on the Past and Future of the Berkeley Art Museum," *Talking Cure Quarterly* (August 2009): 69. Halprin's score is a more complex and extended version of the Fluxus *Paper* event; however, her dance works are more kinetic, expressionistic, and psychological than the simple Zen-like Fluxus performances.

33 Lewallen, "Commitment."

34 Darryl Sapien, "Performance Art Stills," Sapien Fine Arts, www.sapienfinearts.com/pages/performance_stills_index.html (accessed August 4, 2010).

35 Linda Mary Montano, "Resume," Linda M. Montano: 7 Years of Living Art, http://lindamontano.com/more/vita.html (accessed August 4, 2010).

36 William Kelb, "Art Performance San Francisco," *Performing Arts Journal* 1, no. 3 (Winter 1977): 47.

37 Throughout the remainder of the 1970s, the UAM presented performances by Tom Marioni, Lynn Hershman, and Paul Cotton, and also did a series, *Commissioned Video*

Works, by Eleanor Antin, David Askevold, John Baldessari, Robert Cumming, John C. Fernie, Paul McCarthy, Jim Melchert, and William Wegman. By the end of the decade, the new chief curator, David Ross, had established regular weekend video screenings at UAM, one of the first events of this kind in a museum.

38 Oakland Museum of California Board of Trustees, "Overview and History," Oakland Museum of California, http://museumca.org/overview-and-history (accessed August 6, 2010).

39 Tom Marioni, *Beer, Art and Philosophy* (San Francisco: Crown Point Press, 2003), 93.

40 Thomas Albright, *Art in the San Francisco Bay Area, 1945–1980* (Berkeley: University of California Press, 1985), 197.

41 Constance Lewallen, *Terry Fox: Articulations (Labyrinth/Text Works)* (Philadelphia: Moore College of Art and Design, 1992).

42 Hopps was initially named curator in 1962, acting director in 1963, and director from 1964–67.

43 The collection had first been offered to UCLA. Unfortunately, the donation fell through.

44 Art critic Peter Plagens noted how "no other show had the 'tectonic-plate-moving' effect of the Marcel Duchamp retrospective" upon Los Angeles artists in "Crown City Chronicle," *Radical Past: Contemporary Art and Music in Pasadena, 1960–1974* (Pasadena, CA: Armory Center for the Arts, 1999), 20.

45 The score originally included sites in Pasadena, South Pasadena, the San Fernando Valley, Los Angeles, and Watts, but in the end most were in Pasadena.

46 Annette Leddy, "Intimate: The Allan Kaprow Papers," in *Allan Kaprow—Art as Life,* ed. Eva Meyer-Hermann et al. (Los Angeles: Getty Research Institute, 2008), 45.

47 The Pasadena Art Museum in Los Angeles and California Institute of Technology co-presented the *Encounter* series of modern music from 1964 to 1973. The roster of national and international avant-garde composers included Luciano Berio, Pierre Boulez, John Cage, Elliott Carter, Charles Ives, Harry Partch, Terry Riley, Arnold Schoenberg, David Tudor, and La Monte Young. For a complete discussion, see Jeff von der Schmidt, "Musical from a Radical Past," in *Radical Past: Contemporary Art and Music in Pasadena, 1960–1974,* 23.

48 See Jay Beloli, "Lasting Achievements: The Pasadena Art Museum," in *Radical Past: Contemporary Art and Music in Pasadena, 1960–1974,* 16–18, for a complete discussion of the dissolution of the museum.

49 The Newport Harbor Art Museum eventually became the Orange County Museum of Art in 1997.

50 *The Audacious Years,* an exhibition catalogue with an introduction by Betty Winckler, gives an early account of the NHAM and was published by the museum in 1973.

51 Thomas Garver, curatorial statement in *The Appearing/Disappearing Image/Object,* exhibition brochure/poster (Newport Beach, CA: Newport Harbor Art Museum, 1969), unpaginated.

52 Allen Ruppersberg, artists' talk, Orange County Museum of Art, September 2007.

53 *The San Francisco Performance,* exhibition brochure (Newport Beach, CA: Newport Harbor Art Museum, 1972), unpaginated.

54 The La Jolla Museum of Contemporary Art presented numerous site-specific projects, including those by Robert Irwin, Bruce Nauman, Barry Le Va, Chris Burden, and Mowry Baden. The new Museum of Contemporary Art, Los Angeles, opened in 1979 with *Available Light,* a collaboration between composer John Adams, choreographer Lucinda Childs, and architect Frank Gehry. The event was organized by Julie Lazar, who later established MOCA's Media and Performing Arts Program. LACMA presented *The Museum as Site: Sixteen Projects* (1981), an exhibition of site-specific installations curated by Stephanie Barron, and initiated the New Talent Award in 1963.

55 Renny Pritikin, in *LACE 10 Years Documented,* ed. Karen Moss (Los Angeles: Los Angeles Contemporary Exhibitions, 1987), 14.

56 Vince Leo, *Timeline of Artist-Run Spaces and Organizations* (Minneapolis: National Association of Artist-run Organizations, 1990).

57 Marioni was dismissed from his position for presenting a performance in which a woman crawled along the gallery floor, spilling cow's blood from a milking machine strapped to her chest. Tom Marioni, *Crown Point Press Newsletter* (San Francisco: Crown Point Press, Winter 1993), unpaginated.

58 Marioni, *Crown Point Press Newsletter,* unpaginated.

59 Carl E. Loeffler and Darlene Tong, eds., *Performance Anthology: Sourcebook for a Decade of California Performance Art* (San Francisco: Contemporary Arts Press, 1980), 10.

60 Marioni's *Piss Piece* is most closely related to Brecht's *Drip Music, Fluxversion 1,* where the performer on a ladder pours water from a pitcher very slowly down into the bell of a French horn or tuba. See DADA and Radical Art, "Fluxus & Happening," George Brecht, Events and Performances, http://members.chello.nl/j.seegers1/flux_files/brecht_performances.html (accessed August 6, 2010).

61 Loeffler and Tong, 32.

62 Loeffler and Tong, 32.

63 They were Terry Fox, Joel Glassman, Mel Henderson, Paul Kos, Stephen Laub, Bonnie Sherk, Barbara T. Smith, John Woodall, and Frank Youmans.

64 Constance Lewallen and Jim Melchert, conversation with author, February 2010.

65 La Mamelle, "Art Spaces Archive Project," www.as-ap.org/content/lamemelle-incart-com (accessed August 6, 2011).

66 The original founders included Rupert García, Peter Rodriguez, Francisco X. Camplis, Gustavo Ramos Rivera, Carlos Loarca, Manuel Villamor, Robert Gonzalez, Luis Cervantes, Chuy Campusano, Rolando Castellón, Ralph Maradiaga, and René Yañez. This and all other information accessed from the Galería de la Raza Web site: www.galeriadelaraza.org/.

67 For an in-depth discussion, see Cécile Whiting, "It's Only a Paper Moon: The Cyborg Eye of Vija Celmins," *American Art 23* (Spring 2009): 36–55.

68 Carp (1975), founded by Barbara Burden and Marilyn Nix, organized single artists' projects such as an installation by Bruce Nauman, films by Vito Acconci, and a performance by Alexis Smith. Some Serious Business (1976), run by Nancy Drew, Elizabeth Freeman, and Susan Martin, presented more than seventy performances by Laurie Anderson, Philip Glass, Nam June Paik, Robert Wilson and others at video screenings and on cable television. Foundation for Art Resources (FAR), started by Claire Copley, Constance Lewallen, and Morgan Thomas, who had all run commercial galleries, featured works by John Baldessari and Douglas Huebler, among others, and in later years became committed to site-specific installations and a seminal lecture series, ArtTalkArt, for artists and critics.

69 The state of California's master plan for higher education, drafted in 1960, included a three-tiered college system: seventy-eight two-year community and vocational colleges, eighteen four-year California state colleges, and the six University of California campuses. Following the development of this master plan, the Regents of the University of California authorized the establishment of UC Irvine, UC San Diego, and UC Santa Cruz, and the student population in the state increased to nearly 600,000 full- and part-time students by 1968. This information is cited in Mel Wax, "The Knowledge Bonanza," in *The California Revolution,* ed. Carey McWilliams (New York: Grossman, 1968), 26.

70 Assignments for his class included writing a paper on "What Alfred Jarry Means to Me" or selecting a found object for a Duchampian valise.

71 *Stolen Paper Review* included essays by Beat veterans William Burroughs and Allen Ginsberg; Raoul Hausmann's "Dadaism and Today's Avant-Garde"; Otto Piene's "The Development of Group Zero"; and articles such as Marshall McLuhan's "Culture and Technology" and Fluxus artist Robert Watts's "In the Event."

72 In addition to Friedman, Maciunas also named heads of other Fluxus locations: Milan Knizak led Fluxus East in Prague; Ben Vautier headed Fluxus South in Nice; and Denmark's Per Kirkeby was named director of Fluxus North. Along with Maciunas, who "led" Fluxus in New York, these four men acted as a Fluxus "board of directors," but, in the true spirit of Fluxus, this quasi-bureaucratic structure did not meet regularly.

73 Friedman says that, to his knowledge, this was the first time the name "intermedia" was used for a course title at an American college or university.

74 Eva Meyer-Hermann et al., eds., *Allan Kaprow—Art as Life* (Los Angeles: Getty Research Institute, 2008), 207.

75 Allan Kaprow, "The Education of the Un-Artists—Part I," *Art News* 69, no. 10 (February 1971): 28–31; and "The Education of the Un-Artists—Part II," *Art News* 71, no. 3 (May 1972): 34–39. Both are reprinted in Allan Kaprow, *Essays on the Blurring of Art and Life,* ed. Jeff Kelley (Berkeley: University of California Press, 1993).

76 Clark Kerr's concept of "multiversity" of course goes back at least to his Godkin Lectures at Harvard University in 1963. Cited in Kevin Starr, *Golden Dreams: California in an Age of Abundance, 1950–1963* (Oxford: Oxford University Press, 2009), 236.

77 Prominent architects, among them Charles Moore, designed the colleges,

modeled after Swarthmore College and the English universities at Oxford and Cambridge, with the stipulation that buildings could not disturb the trees or obscure views of Monterey Bay.

78 *The Experimental Workshop Carnegie Foundation Report,* located in the Special Collections Department, McHenry Library, UC Santa Cruz, provided details about this program.

79 Thanks to Jock Reynolds for sharing his personal recollections of the Experimental Arts Workshop with me in an interview in August 1991. Reynolds studied with Watts and says this course provided the roots for his later collaborative installation and performance work.

80 When Watts returned to Rutgers in 1970, at least one UCSC student continued studying with him; others went to Southern California to work with Fluxus artists who had recently come to teach at the new California Institute of the Arts (CalArts).

81 Paul Brach, "CalArts: The Early Years," *Art Journal* 42, no. 1 (Spring 1982): 27.

82 Rosler has since presented this now iconic installation/performance for more than thirty years at international locations, including La Mamelle (1977).

83 Kristine Stiles, "Burden of Light," in *Chris Burden*, coordinated by Fred Hoffman and edited by John Bewley and Jonty Tarbuck (Newcastle-Upon-Tyne, United Kingdom: Locust + Publishing, 2007), 29.

84 The other artists in *New Art in Orange County* included John F. Becker, Jerry Byrd, Robert Cumming, Ned Evans, Stephen Harger, Don Henricks, Tom Holste, Don Karwelis, Brian Longe, Brian Miller, Stephen Moore, John Okulick, Roger Seeman, John Stanphill, Ludwig Stein, Jean St. Pierre, and Jim van Geem.

85 Founded in 1907, California College of Arts and Crafts (CCAC), now known as California College of the Arts, was the other major art school in the Bay Area. The college emphasized printmaking and painting, so its most prominent faculty were known for figurative art and photorealism rather than Conceptual practices.

86 The *18′6″ × 6′9″ × 11′2½″ × 47′ × 11³⁄₁₆″ × 29′8½″ × 31′9³⁄₁₆″* exhibition included artists Michael Asher, Eugenia Butler, Stephen Kaltenbach, Edward Kienholz, and Eric Orr, as well as New York Conceptualists Robert Barry, Joseph Kosuth, Barry Le Va, Dennis Oppenheim, Robert Watts, and Lawrence Weiner.

87 "Art Series Opens Soon at Art Institute," *San Francisco Chronicle,* April 10, 1969.

88 "Disney's Dream School," *Newsweek* (November 8, 1971): 67; and James Real, "It Was Disney's Dream," *Change* (January–February 1971): 23–25. The "dream school" also became a training ground for animation students who would often be recruited by the Disney Studios.

89 Real, 23.

90 Real, 24.

91 Real, 24. Stein produced the *Blueprint for Counter-Education,* fifty pages of text and charts alluding to an alternative education environment, designed to be read in a nonlinear fashion. Although I have not had the opportunity to see Stein's publication, it will be interesting to see if it has a Conceptual link to the utopianism of Henry Flynt's "Blueprint for Higher Living."

92 Dick Higgins, interview with author, July 7, 1992.

93 These titles are culled from course syllabi at the California Institute of the Arts (CalArts) Archive. Tenney, who has taught several generations of CalArts students, is the only artist from this original group who stayed for an extended period of time.

94 Judy Chicago and Miriam Schapiro, introduction to *Womanhouse* (Valencia, CA: Feminist Art Program, California Institute of the Arts, 1972), unpaginated. Three Los Angeles artists—Sherry Brody, Carol Mitchell, and Wanda Westcoast—also participated in *Womanhouse.*

95 Moira Roth, *The Amazing Decade: Women and Performance Art in America, 1970–1980* (Los Angeles: Astro Artz, 1983), 108–109, describes this project in detail. The space had a dining table filled with platters of food; a sensuous pink *Nuturant Kitchen,* with wall-to-ceiling breasts that became fried eggs; and a nude torso that appeared to be trapped in a linen closet. Live on-site performances featured women obsessively engaged in household activities—Sandy Orgel's *Ironing* and Chris Rush's *Scrubbing*—as well as an elaborately costumed enactment of the lives of *Three Women.*

96 Howard Singerman, *Art Subjects: Making Artists in the American University* (Berkeley and Los Angeles: University of California Press, 1999), 136.

97 Lars Nittve and Helle Crenzien, *Sunshine & Noir: Art in L.A., 1960–1997* (Humlebaek, Denmark: Louisiana Museum of Modern Art, 1997), 9.

98 Loeffler and Tong, 49.

99 Loeffler and Tong, 19.

100 Loeffler and Tong, 29.

101 This and all other information about *The Dilexi Series* derive from the Pacific Film Archive program notes, October 17 and 24, 1991.

102 This film was screened for the Museum of Modern Art exhibition *1969* and is cited in the *1969* Film Program Screening Notes, January 30–31, 2010, MOMA, www.moma.org/visit/calendar/events/8766 (accessed August 12, 2010).

103 Chip Lord, quoted by Scott Rappaport in "Film Professor's Revolutionary Past to Be Featured in Berkeley Art Museum Retrospective," *UC Santa Cruz Currents,* http://currents.ucsc.edu/03-04/01-19/ant_farm.html (accessed August 15, 2010).

104 Rappaport, "Film Professor's Revolutionary Past to Be Featured in Berkeley Art Museum Retrospective."

105 The description of this event derives from Burden and Lutjean's own accounts during a panel discussion for *Art since the 1960s,* Orange County Museum of Art, April 2007. It is also fully documented in Burden's handmade artist's book *Chris Burden 71–73* (1974).

106 In addition to these television spots, Burden staged a famous radio intervention when he went on the air on KPFK-FM with *Send Me Your Money* (1979). In this piece, he asked viewers to consider sending him money, thereby violating the noncommercial regulations of the station.

107 Michael Crane and Mary Stofflet, eds., Introduction to *Correspondence Art: Source Book for the Network of International Postal Art Activity* (San Francisco: Contemporary Art Press, 1984).

108 Barbara Bloom, Meg Cranston, Jack Goldstein, Mike Kelley, Stephen Prina, David Salle, James Welling, and Christopher Williams at CalArts; Karen Finley and Tony Labat at SFAI; and David Bunn, Martin Kersels, and Jason Rhoads at UCLA, to name a few.

109 Nicolas Bourriaud, *Relational Aesthetics* (Nice, France: Les Presse du Reel, 1998), 116.

110 Henry A. Giroux, *Border Crossings* (New York: Routledge, 2005), 148, cites how critical pedagogy within cultural practices is a method for a new language that opens up borders of knowledge and learning in new ways. See also Ken Ehrlich, ed., *Art, Architecture, Pedagogy: Experiments in Learning* (San Francisco: Blurb.com, 2010), for specific references on how contemporary artists working in collaborative, collective, public practices employ these ideas of critical pedagogy.

111 Lucy Lippard, *Six Years: The Dematerialization of the Art Object from 1966 to 1972* (Berkeley and Los Angeles: University of California Press, 1997), 38.

Fig. 3.1 Cockettes, *Hibiscus as Madame Butterfly at Sonoma State College,* 1970. Performance documentation. Rumi Missabu Collection. Photo: Kreemah Ritz.

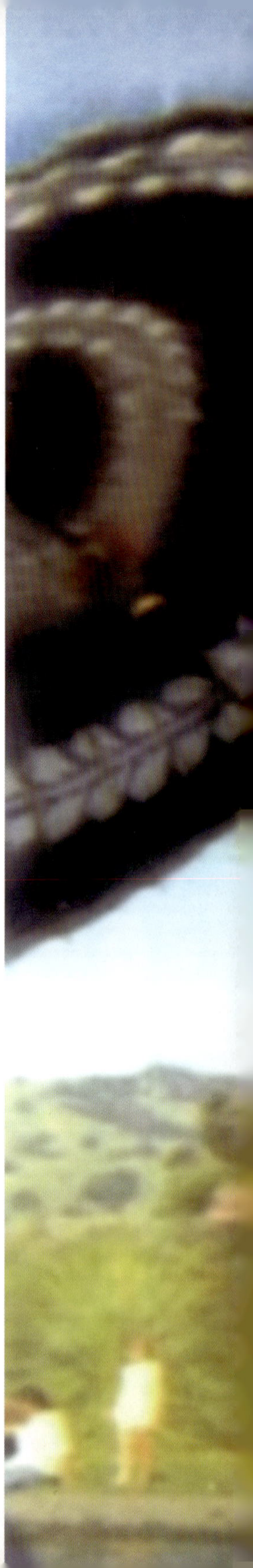

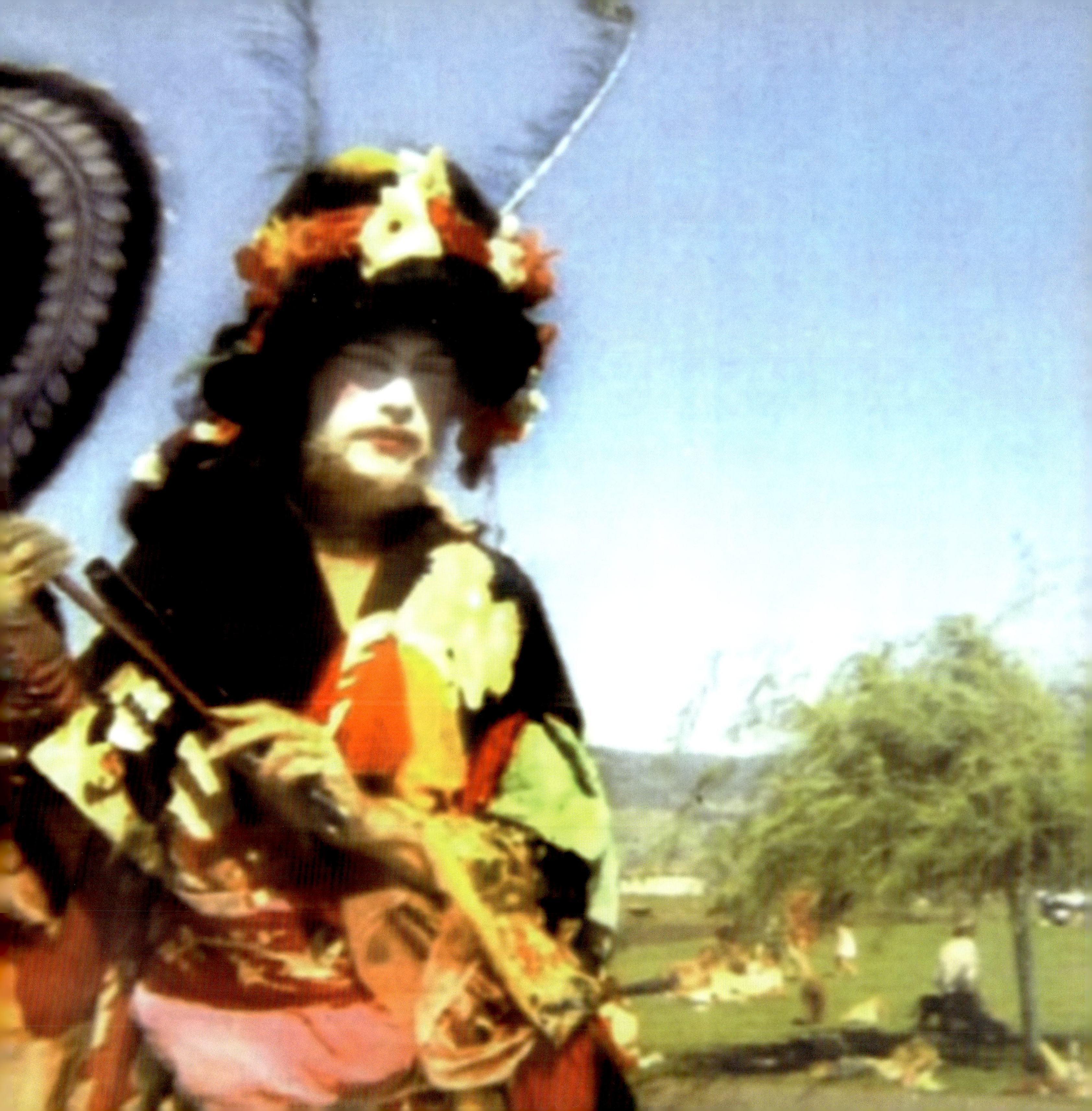

TO MOVE, TO DRESS, TO WORK, TO ACT

PLAYING GENDER AND RACE IN 1970S CALIFORNIA ART

Julia Bryan-Wilson

TO MOVE

To wander the streets in California in the early 1970s was to court some curious encounters. In San Francisco, Hibiscus, the charismatic central figure of the fabled drag troupe the Cockettes, might glide past with glitter in his beard, full makeup, and a theatrical outfit from another time and place (see fig. 3.1, overleaf, and fig. 3.4). Or artist Linda Mary Montano could traipse by in a blue prom dress, tap shoes, and an elaborate chicken-feather headdress. Meanwhile, in Los Angeles, the Chicano collective Asco could be spotted marching down Whittier Boulevard in their *Walking Mural* (fig. 3.2). Costumed as absurdly vivified icons, the group portrayed caricatures of typical mural imagery—including the Virgin of the Guadalupe and an inverted Christmas tree, which was actually the artist Gronk in tiered vintage chiffon skirts.

Man/woman, woman/bird, human/tree: What sorts of creatures are these? And should we consider these gestures performance art? Theater? Guerrilla protest? Or some altogether new combination? Each has been historicized in somewhat distinct realms: Hibiscus and the Cockettes are largely understood within the rubric of West Coast countercultural life, Montano is central to feminist art history, and Asco is heralded as a pioneering moment for Chicano art and Conceptualism. Seen together in the context of the exhibition *State of Mind*, however, these street interventions clearly also had significant commonalities—separate snapshots within a much larger photo album of costumed California practices. The three examples above employ cast-off, used, or found clothing (indicating thrift due to lack of resources as well as a keen-eyed scavenger aesthetic), and all three are engaged in an exaggerated or unraveled version of masculinity and femininity, from Hibiscus's queer Madame Butterfly to Montano's embodiment of woman-as-egg-bearer to Gronk's flouncing neck ruff. All three also deploy whitened faces—though to quite different effects—which raises questions about race and how formations of race, gender, and sexuality are complexly intertwined. Indeed, this essay asserts that California in the early 1970s fostered a unique flowering of diverse practices that used dress and play to upend or trouble conventional codes of race, gender, and sexuality. It is organized episodically, focusing on a series of action verbs—taking off on Richard Serra's famed *Verb List Compilation: Actions to Relate to Oneself* (1967–68)—in order to point

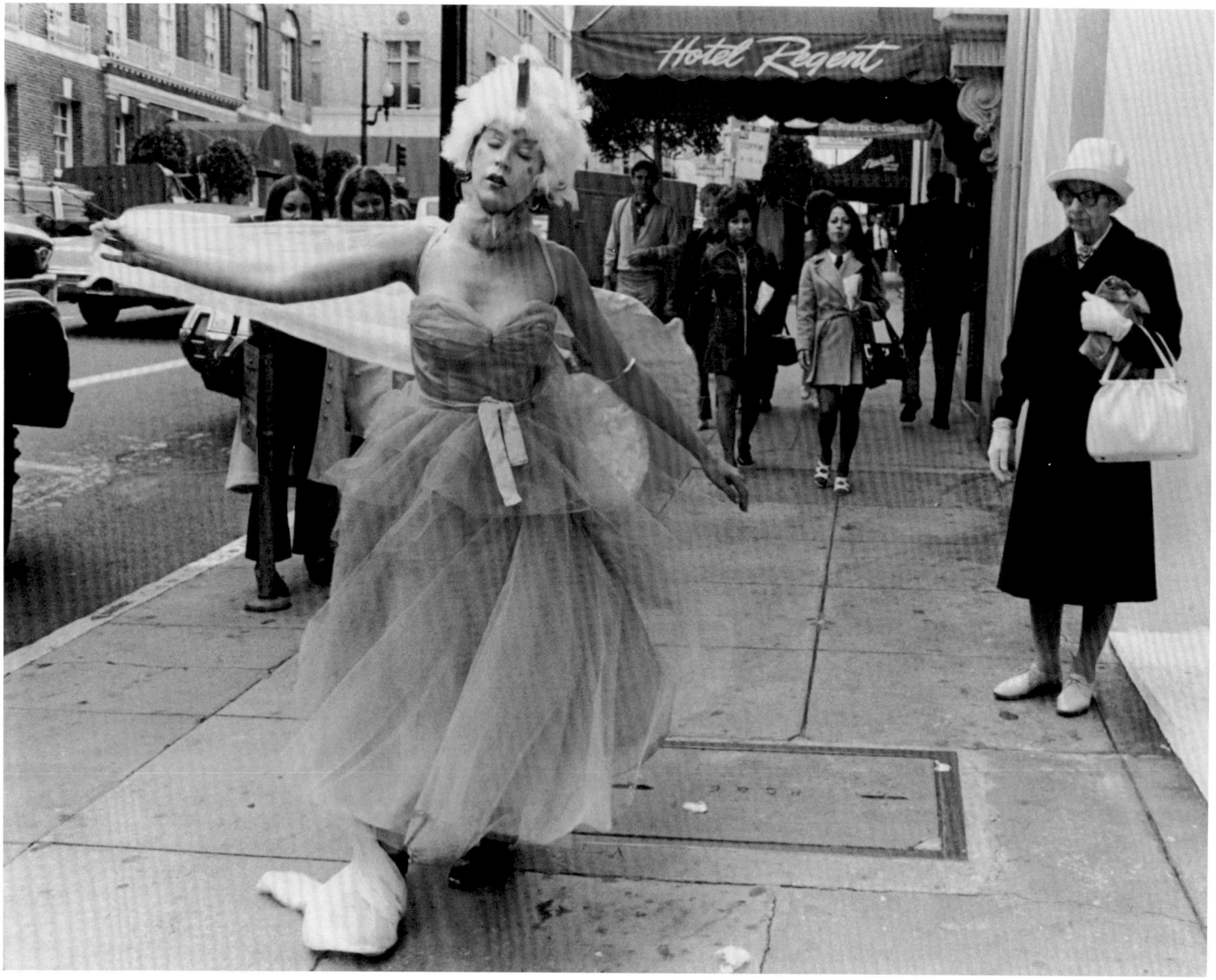
Hotel Regent

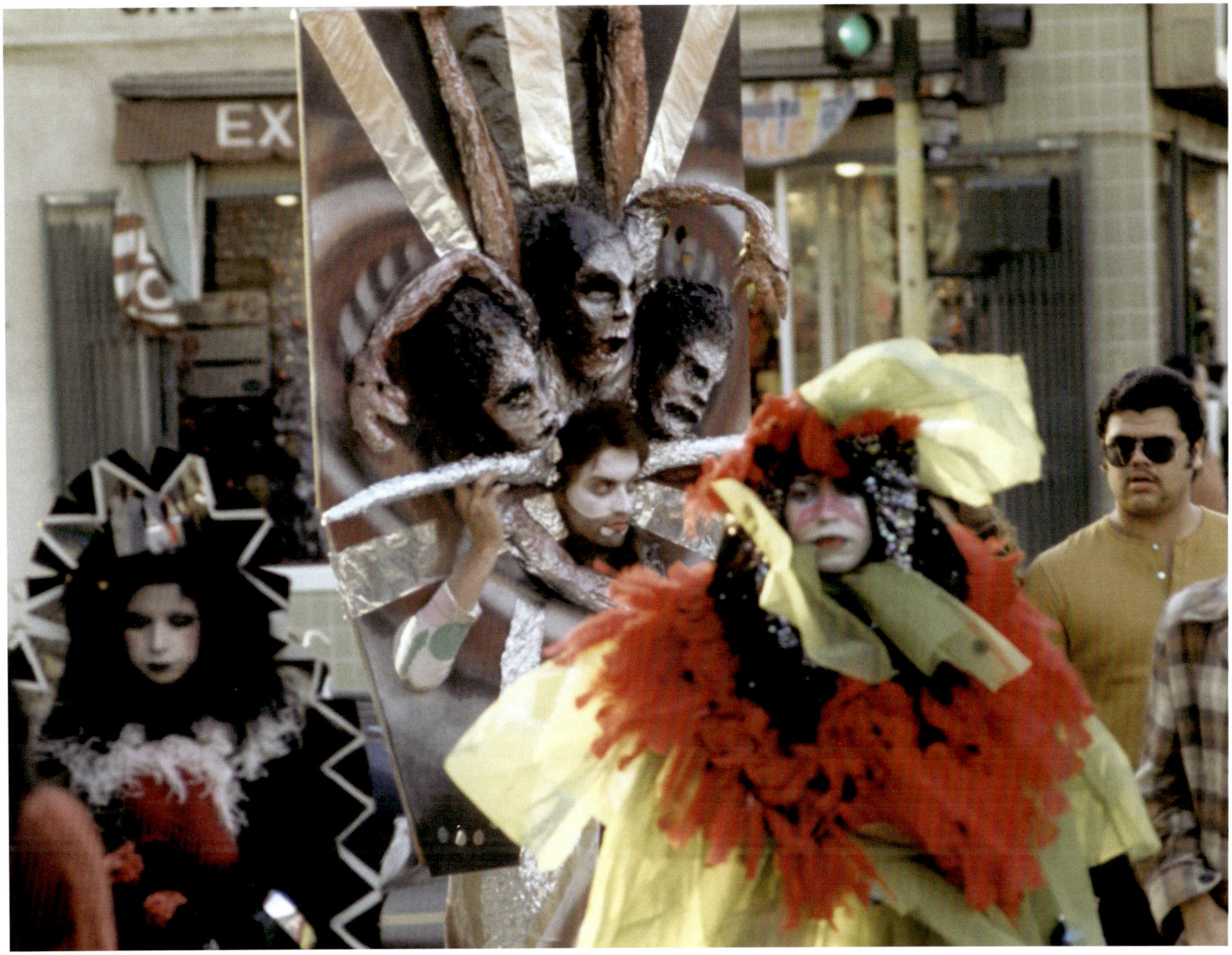

Fig. 3.2 Linda Mary Montano, *Chicken Dance: The Streets of San Francisco,* 1972. Performance documentation.

Fig. 3.3 Asco (Glugio "Gronk" Nicandro, Patssi Valdez, Willie Herrón III, and Harry Gamboa Jr.), *Walking Mural,* 1972. Performance documentation (left to right: Valdez, Herrón, and Gronk).

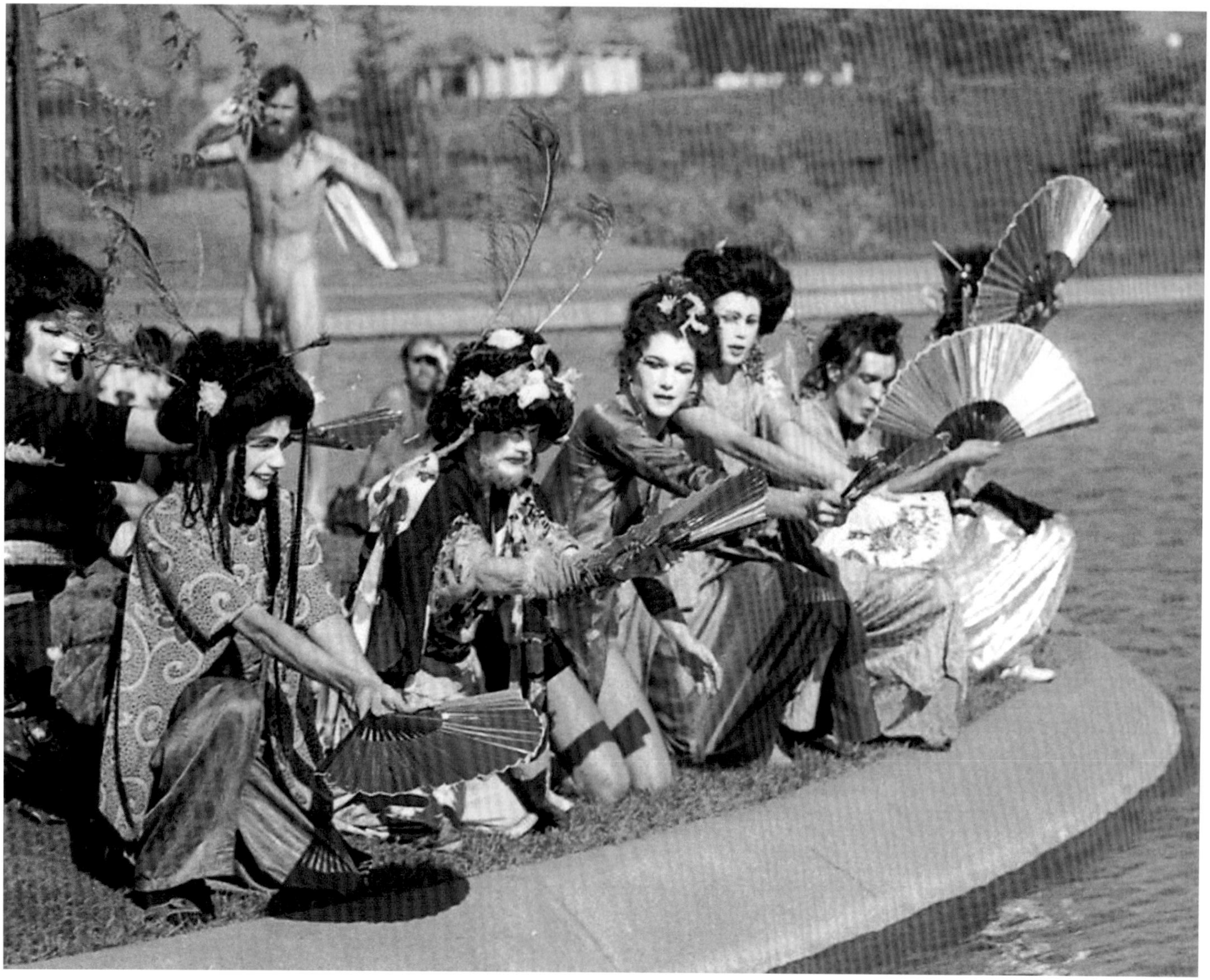

Fig. 3.4 Cockettes, *Madame Butterfly at Sonoma State College*, 1970. Performance documentation. Photo: Fayette Hauser.

toward the vitality and animating force of bodies in space. Whether gussying up or stripping down, dancing or walking, artists' gestures contested notions of cultural identity.

Such bodies in motion were intimately (if sometimes obliquely) connected to other kinds of movements—namely, social movements. In the early 1970s, many artists were swept up in the tide of transformative upheavals and revolutions within the United States as the civil rights movement, feminism, and gay liberation challenged how race, gender, and sexuality were defined and embodied. Peter Selz has argued that California art since 1945 was shaped by the particular regional formations and political agitations specific to the West Coast.[1] The conjunction of alternative cultures and experimentation in art led to a rare openness toward Conceptualism and performance, and the blossoming of feminism and queer lifestyles in California infused such work with a special awareness of bodily politics.

Hence the Cockettes were a defiant San Francisco phenomenon, an outgrowth of its famed gay and lesbian scene. And Montano has stated that the local artistic community nurtured her early actions, especially its permissive and accepting gender dynamics, declaring the early 1970s in the Bay Area "performance ecstasy time."[2] The late 1960s and early 1970s were also a time in which California took the lead as a key site of civil rights resistance, with the formation of the Black Panther Party in Oakland in 1966, the organization of farm workers in the Central Valley, the occupation of Alcatraz Island by activists in the American Indian Movement, and the flowering of the Brown Power movement in Southern California. Asco on the move down Whittier Boulevard had direct connections to East Los Angeles–based Chicano liberation strategies of creative protest. With its queer blendings—Gronk camping it up as a decorative Christmas symbol—*Walking Mural* further "suggested how nationalism occluded issues of gender and sexuality within the Chicano movement," as Chon A. Noriega writes.[3]

Why might this kind of gender play have been so prevalent within California art at this moment? And what does "playing gender" mean? It was a phrase in circulation in the era, as is evidenced by the following: "He is playing masculine because she is playing feminine. She is playing feminine because he is playing masculine. . . . She is stifling under the triviality of her femininity. The world is groaning beneath the terrors of his masculinity. . . . How do we call off the game?"[4] So begins the preface to *Masculine/Feminine*, a collection of texts related to the burgeoning women's liberation movement, published in 1969. Coedited by husband and wife Theodore and Betty Roszak, this foreword lays out some of the stakes of radical gender critique in this moment. Though thinkers such as philosopher Judith Butler would later refine and theorize the idea of gender as a systematized, repetitive series of gestures over time,[5] the Roszaks use the theatrical notion of "playing" to point out that the roles of male and female are not fixed and stable but rather a "game" of relational, ever-shifting identities implicated in power.

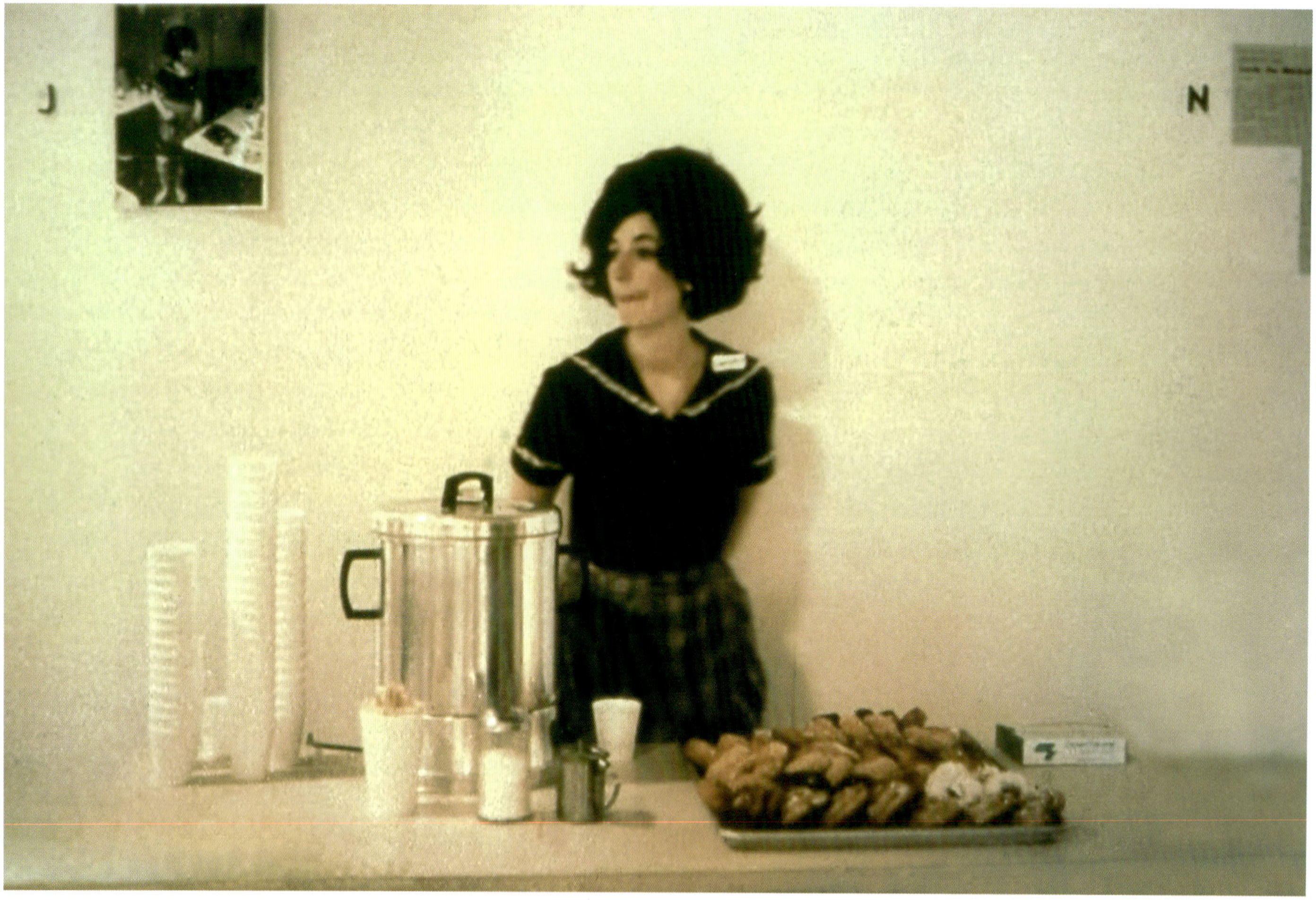

TO DRESS

Montano's *Chicken Dance: The Streets of San Francisco* was performed in 1972 in nine different public spaces in the city, including "museums, galleries, and the Golden Gate Bridge"—at this last location, Montano was picked up by the suicide prevention squad for holding up traffic.[6] In a photograph taken outside the Hotel Regent, she spreads her wings wide while a prim older woman, complete with gloves and handbag, pauses to take her in. The spectator's white hat formally echoes the flamboyant bird cap worn by the artist, and this parallel underscores how both the older woman's "normal" clothing and the artist's eccentric get-up are charged with carrying social norms about comportment and sartorial choice. Both outfits take the measure of gender identity—in the case of Montano, the proper ball gown is undone by both its unusual accessories and its spatial and temporal displacement. Instead of being worn inside a dance hall of long ago, the dress is twirled and swooped on the street alone in bright daylight.

Other feminist artists in California at this moment, including well-known artists Lynn Hershman and Eleanor Antin, used costumes, uniforms, and other forms of dress to comment on gender roles.[7] Lesser-known figures were similarly engaged in questioning the importance of dress as a form of social identification. Bonnie Sherk, for instance,

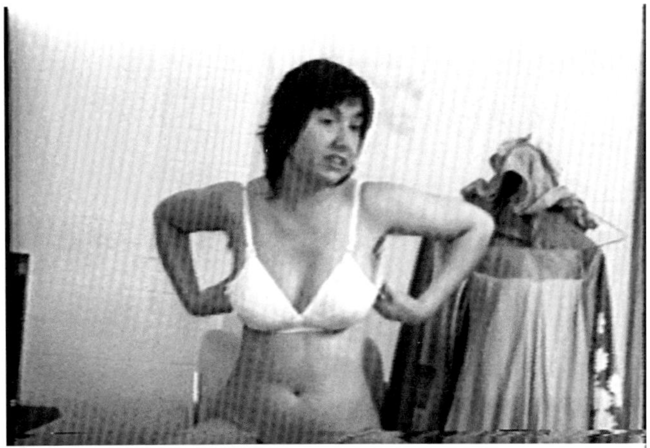

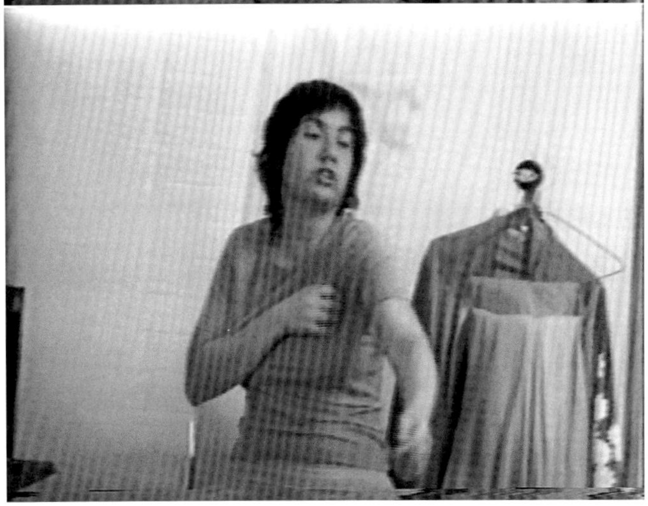

Fig. 3.5 Bonnie Sherk, *Waitress in Well Liked and Learned Lawyers Win Cases,* 1974. Performance documentation from Exhibit J2 Live, UC Davis Art Gallery, Davis, California. Image: Courtesy of the artist, San Francisco.

Fig. 3.6 Susan Mogul, *Dressing Up,* 1973. Video: black and white; sound; 7:06 min.

commenced a series in which she worked temporarily in a number of service jobs and decided to consciously reframe these roles as performance pieces. Uniforms are often required for such positions, and Sherk donned various outfits as she "played the part" of her employment. As a waitress she wore the requisite black-and-white nylon dress with a plaid apron; a bouffant wig completed her stereotypical look. Sherk's intervention here might be termed hushed or inverted drag, for though she passes, undetectable, as "normal," she in fact draws attention to the strangeness of so-called ordinary work clothes like those of waitresses and cooks. Sherk was especially interested in how our "cultural costumes" are implicated in the wider theatricalization of society, laden with custom and ritual.[8]

Susan Mogul's wry video *Dressing Up* (fig. 3.6) from 1973 likewise highlights that garments are always freighted as markers not only of gender and sexuality but also as signifiers of status, money, and class. In this short piece, the naked artist faces the camera and slowly gets dressed while discussing the purchase of each item that she puts on. Clothes tell stories; they register certain familial patterns and habits about spending and saving. "My mother brought me up on sales—never buy anything full price," she recounts as she matter-of-factly chomps CornNuts. *Dressing Up* was made under the auspices of the Feminist Art Program at the California Institute of the Arts (CalArts); as such, it emphasizes the West Coast as an especially fertile ground for feminist thought. Institutions such as CalArts (with faculty Judy Chicago and Miriam Schapiro) and UC San Diego (with artists such as Martha Rosler) alongside initiatives like Redstockings West, the Berkeley-based Women's History Research Project (started by Laura X in 1968 as the first feminist archive in the country), the Women's Building in Los Angeles (which opened in 1973), and the Los Angeles Women's Liberation Center (founded in 1970) created loose affiliations between feminist artists and activists. What is more, though the gender revolution was palpable across the country, much attention was focused on San Francisco as an historical hotbed of gay and lesbian community formation, which dovetailed with the alternative, fringe edges of the counterculture as exemplified by the wildly inventive Cockettes with their emphasis on glamorously excessive self-styling.

But the focus on clothes and appearance was not the exclusive realm of women or queer artists. Take, for instance, Chris Burden's piece *I Became a Secret Hippy* (1971; fig. 3.7). For this work, a friend hammered a biker's stud into Burden's chest and shaved his head; the artist then wore a dark suit (he referred to it as "FBI clothes") to cover up the hardware implanted in his sternum. Though he appears to be a regular man, he carries with him an undetectable element of rebellion, like an undercover agent whose long sleeves hide tattooed arms. Burden here is "playing masculine" as much as Sherk's waitress plays feminine. Unlike Sherk's inverted drag, Burden injects an element of physical pain and bodily injury to parody straight or "square" culture of male respectability, or what Andrew Perchuk and Helaine Posner have referred to as "masculine masquerade."[9] Given that the FBI is clichéd as a province of white men, it is crucial to recognize that Burden's work is also about race—that is, about the powers and privileges of white skin. Whiteness in such performances should not be naturalized, taken as invisible, or cast as insignificant, for such racial marking never is; Hibiscus's appropriative, orientalizing Kabuki makeup and Montano's self-described "whiteface" make that clear.

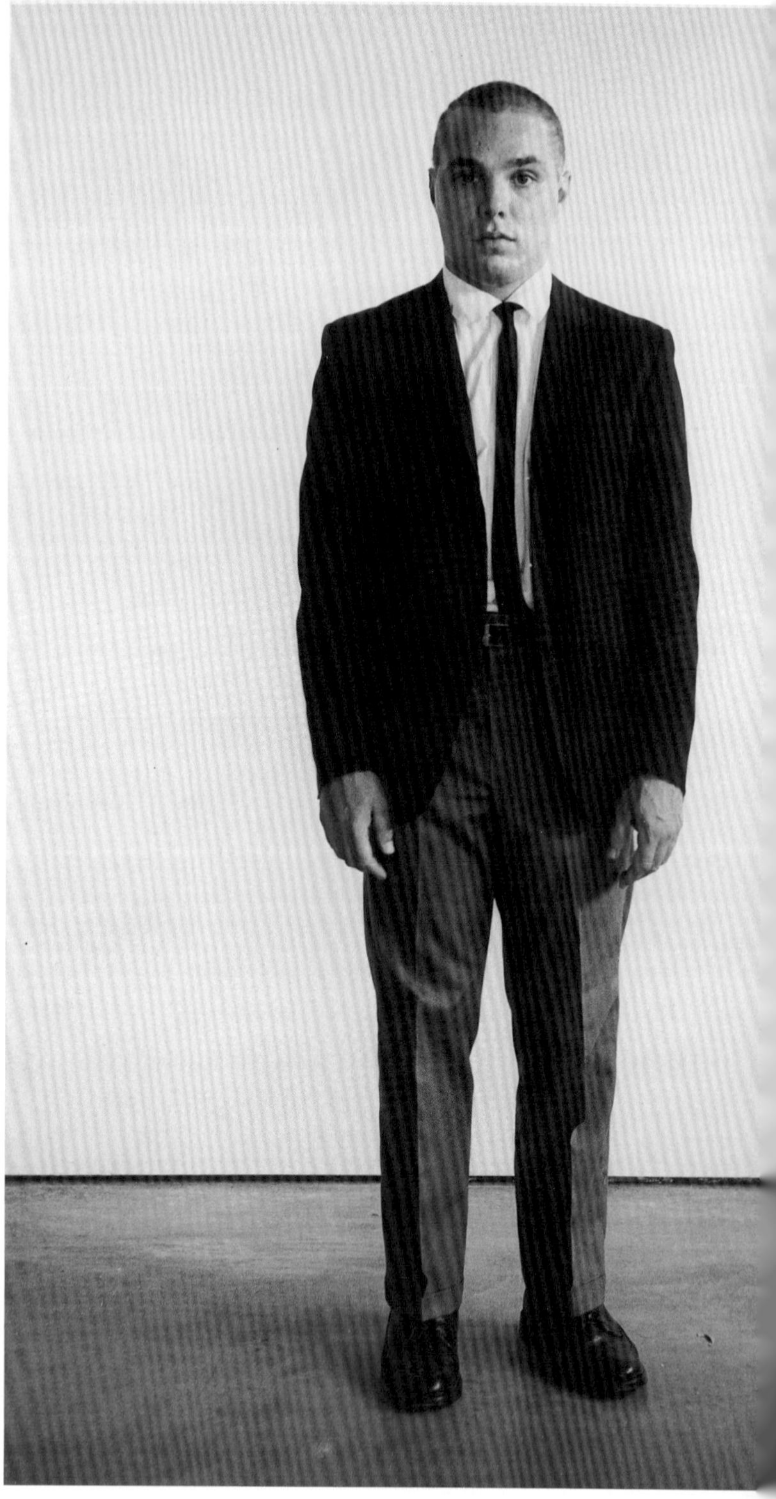

Fig. 3.7 Chris Burden, *I Became a Secret Hippy,* 1971. Performance at Museum of Conceptual Art (MOCA), San Francisco, California.

Fig. 3.8 Linda Mary Montano, *Home Nursing,* 1972. Performance documentation.

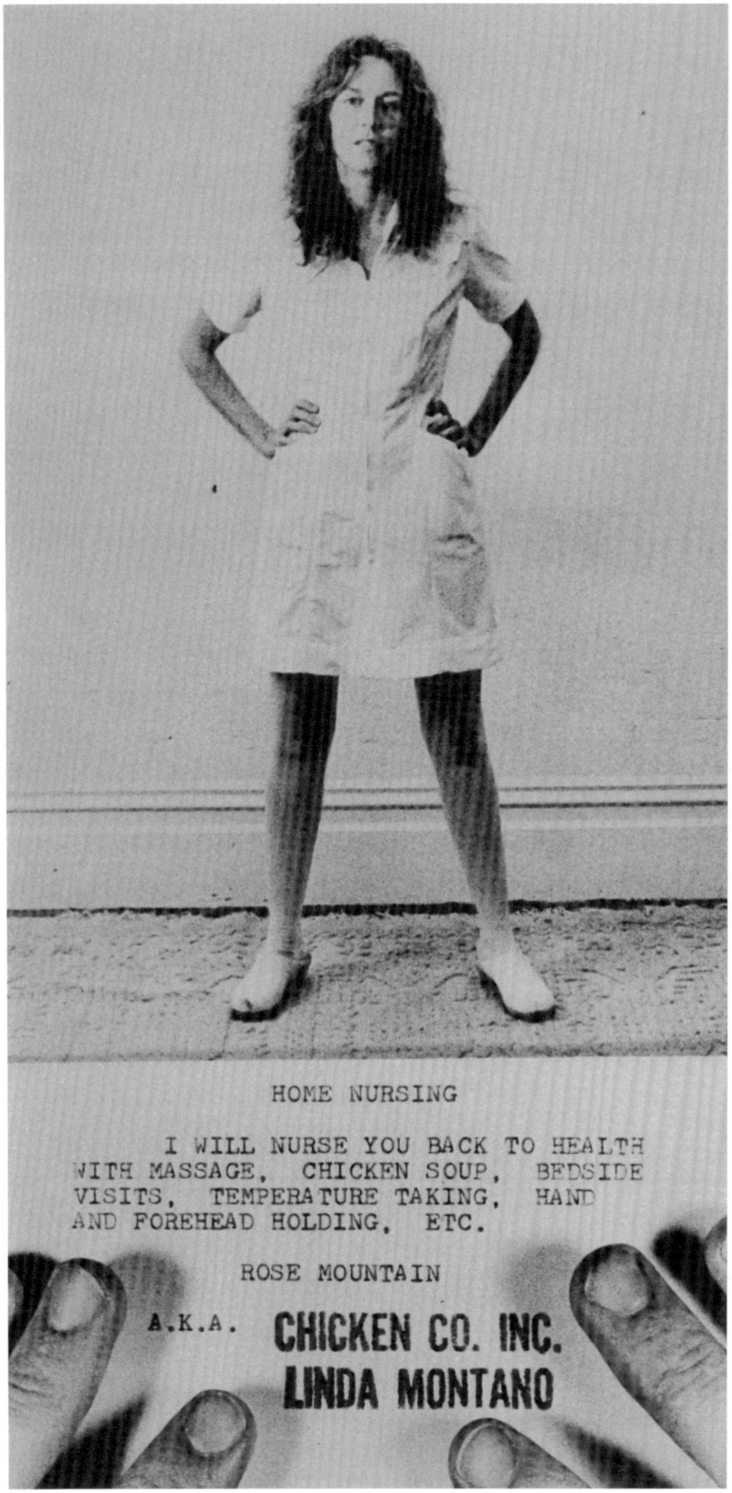
HOME NURSING
I WILL NURSE YOU BACK TO HEALTH WITH MASSAGE, CHICKEN SOUP, BEDSIDE VISITS, TEMPERATURE TAKING, HAND AND FOREHEAD HOLDING, ETC.
ROSE MOUNTAIN
A.K.A. CHICKEN CO. INC.
LINDA MONTANO

TO WORK

The adoption of alter egos of different professions was an important strategy in the Conceptual and performance practices of West Coast artists. For example, Sherk's decision to brand her workaday job as a waitress a piece of performance art was preceded by another such project, *Short Order Cook*. Over the course of nearly a year (June 1973–May 1974), Sherk worked the night shift every weekend at a donut shop in the Castro district of San Francisco. She wore jeans and a T-shirt that read "Florida," topped with an apron and a chef's hat. Though she garnered the typical cook's wage as she fried up eggs and buttered toast, she also labored under the rubric that such actions could be repositioned as art.

What kind of "work" is this, and how did it function as "art" if it was imperceptible to her bosses and customers alike? Conceptual art often thwarts expectations of artistic legibility, as ordinary objects or actions become art solely by virtue of nomination. In addition, in *Short Order Cook* and *Waitress*, Sherk questions the porous line between art making and other forms of work, drawing attention to how various forms of labor are differently valued and compensated, not least with respect to gender and class. If it is somehow less surprising to see her in a waitress outfit than executing duties typically associated with working-class men, it is no wonder—short-order cooks are one of the most male-dominated professions, and waitresses one of the most heavily feminized, in the gendered "occupational segregation" of the U.S. labor market.[10]

Montano, too, undertook wage labor as art. In her series *Odd Jobs* (1973), she printed up cards announcing her availability for "cleaning attics and cellars, interior painting, gardening, light hauling."[11] For Montano, this was an attempt to integrate making money with an artistic sense of awareness, and she noted that she "liked what [she] was doing when [she] called it art, probably because [she] was in a state of wakefulness which [she] associated with the art-making process."[12] Appropriate clothing became critical to Montano's ability to inhabit such roles; in her piece *Home Nursing* (1972; fig. 3.8), the artist bought a nurse's dress at a thrift store and told her friends she would make house calls when they were sick. Her attempt to achieve a more heightened existence through art-as-work, as well as her experiments with spiritual notions of fulfillment and purpose with regard to labor, were somewhat distinct to the West Coast.

While artists in California were performing gendered, classed work—literally inhabiting various occupations like housepainters and cooks—East Coast artists took up the issue of artistic labor quite differently. In 1969, artists in New York organized themselves into the Art Workers' Coalition, a short-lived but influential organization that came together to push for artists' rights. They began to identify themselves as "art workers," regardless of what kind of art they made (and many Conceptualists were in the ranks of the coalition). At the same time that they embraced the term "worker," they were ambivalent about their association with actual blue-collar laborers. Aside from Minimal artist Carl Andre, who consistently wore overalls, those in the Art Workers' Coalition did not generally use drag or utilize dress as a way to secure their somewhat fraught affiliation with the working class.[13]

Other approaches to representing work were taken up by California-based Conceptualist Allan Sekula, who employed documentary photography to depict the somewhat deadening managerial routines of labor. In *Untitled Slide Sequence* (figs. 3.9–3.12), from 1972, he photographed workers at an aerospace plant in San Diego as they left the factory at the end of the day shift. Taken during the Vietnam War, these images were snapped covertly over the space of about twenty minutes. Men in suits and ties jostle alongside those in more casual attire such as zippered sport coats, their security badges still pinned to their clothes. The sequence of images is poignant; the faces of some of the workers who stream toward the exit are weary from the efforts of the day, in an instance of what Sekula has described as the relentless disciplining of the working body.[14] Yet some appear to visibly relax as they approach the top of the staircase. One image captures two women with similar haircuts walking side by side, smiling with conspiratorial grins. Next to them, a man ascends the stairs, his jacket slung over his shoulders as an indication that the day is over. The demarcation between on and off the clock is often registered in these small adjustments in wardrobe, as personal comfort takes over from the regulatory force of workplace dress.

Just as defrocking signals the end of a shift, so too are outfits changed when certain forms of work begin. In Martha Rosler's video *Semiotics of the Kitchen* (1975), she recites the alphabet in a deadpan parody of a cooking show; she begins by donning an apron, which stands for the letter *A*. With the apron, she suits up for the feminist lesson that commences, and her alphabet of kitchen implements and gestures grows violent in order to resist the naturalization of domestic labor as the sphere of women. Indeed, the early 1970s were a time in which feminists around the globe organized to raise awareness about the invisible, uncompensated, and undervalued labor of housework, the vast majority of which was done by women. Utilizing Marxist critiques about the gendered division of labor, theorists and activists advocated for such housework as childrearing, cooking, and cleaning to be fairly paid and, in 1972, founded the International Wages for Housework Campaign.[15]

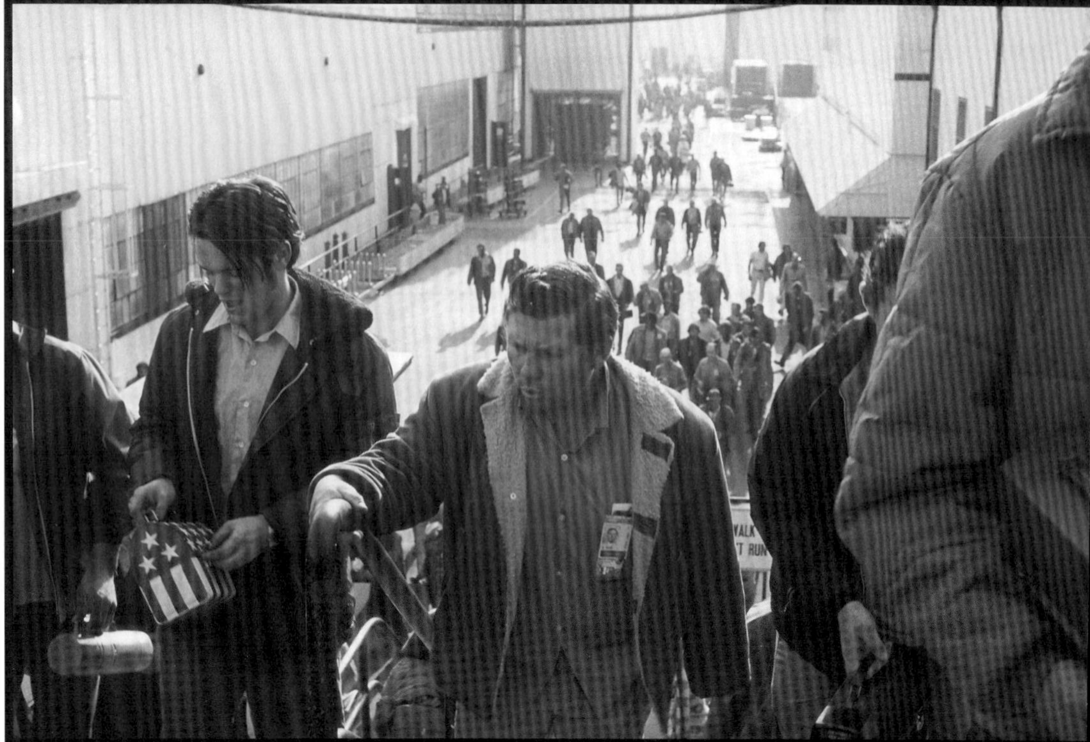

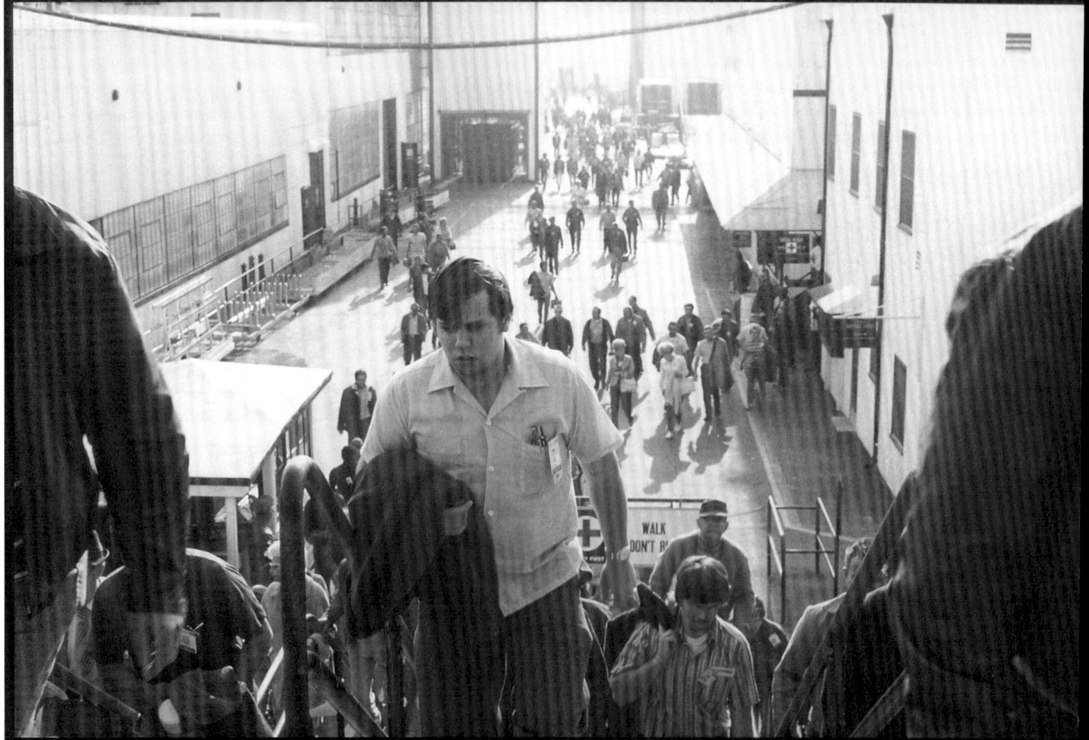

Figs. 3.9–3.12 Allan Sekula, *Untitled Slide Sequence* (detail), 1972. Twenty-five black-and-white slides in slide carousel; dimensions variable.

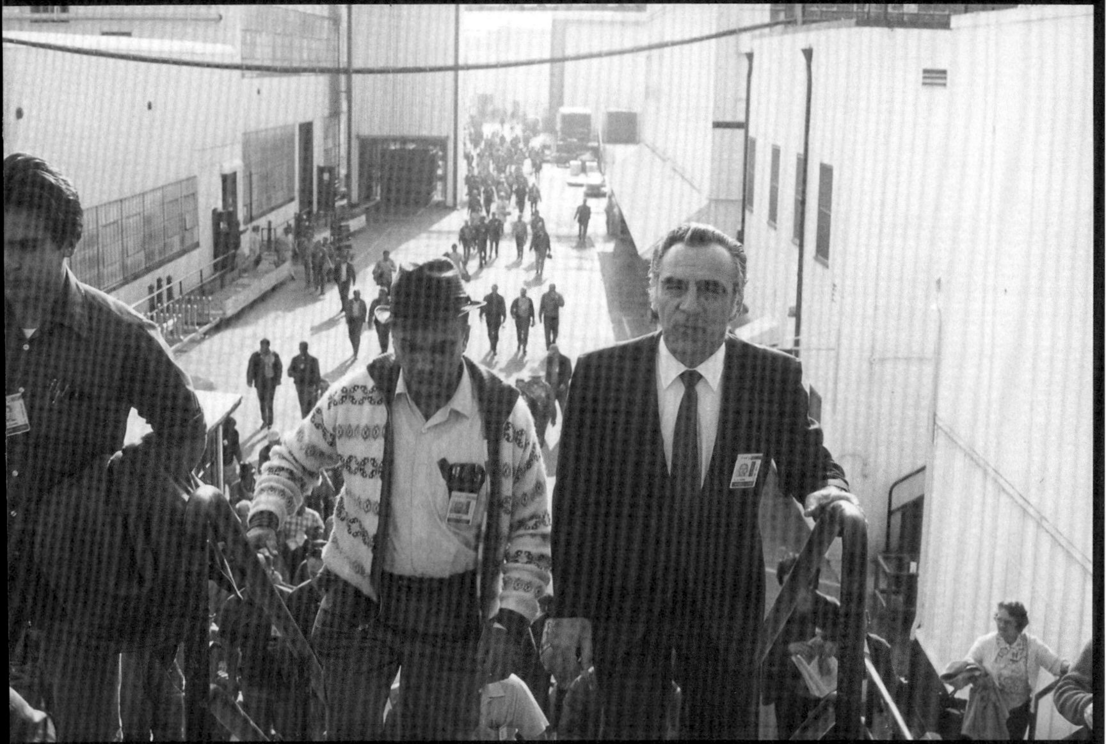

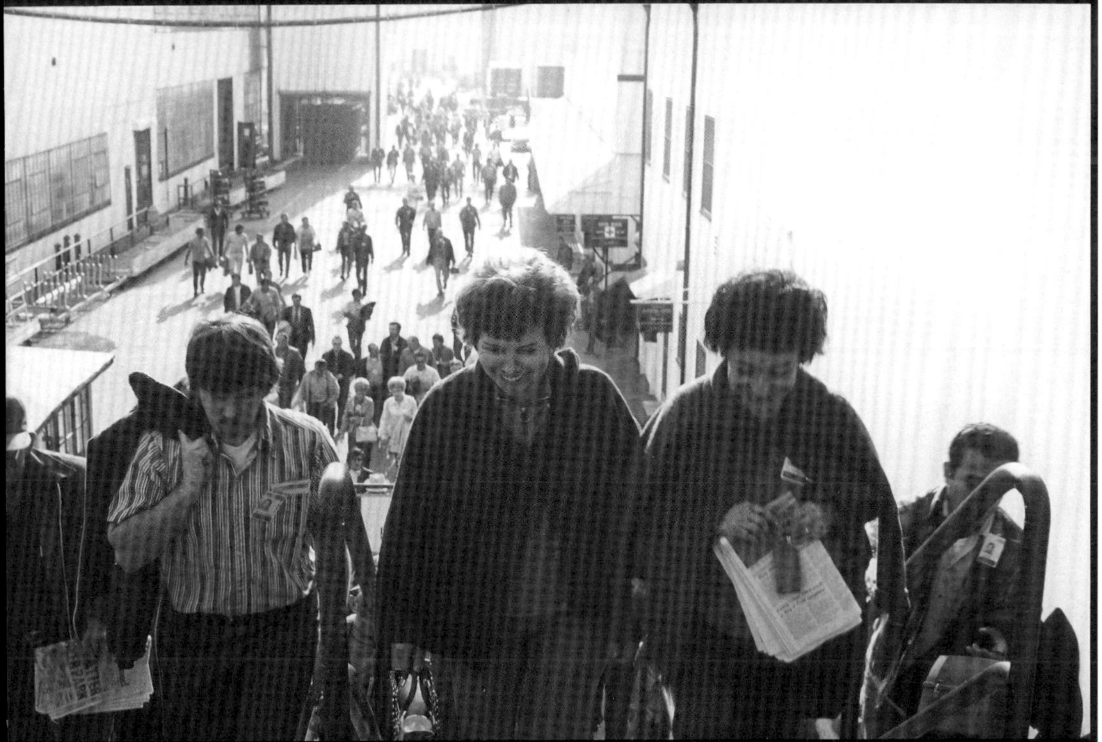

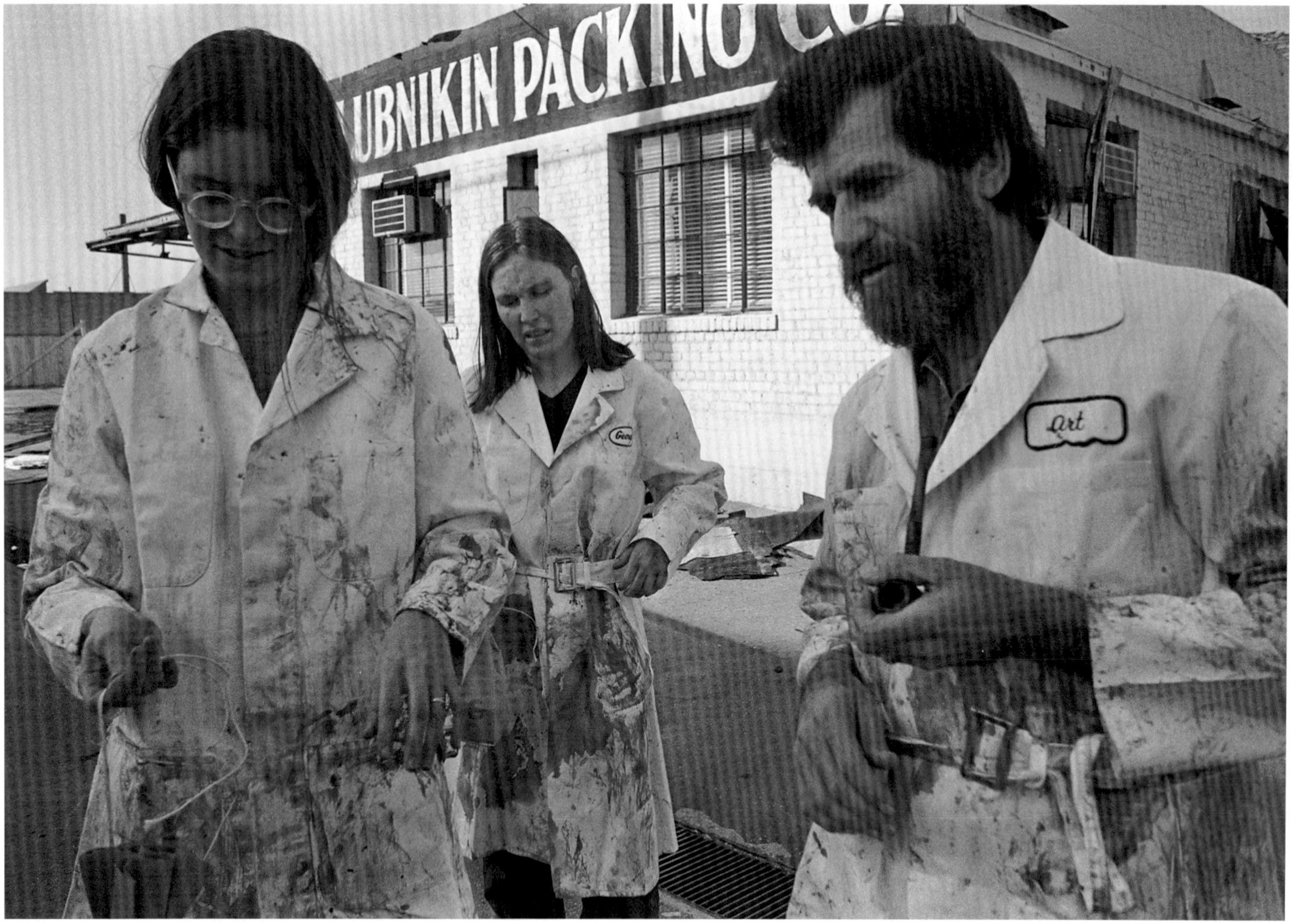

Fig. 3.13 Suzanne Lacy, *Maps,* 1973; a Happening with Allan Kaprow and California Institute of the Arts students that began in Valencia and ended in the Vernon meatpacking district in Los Angeles. Photo: Susan Mogul, courtesy of the artist.

TO ACT

As Angela Davis notes, "Although the history of this state is often told as a story of renewal, hope, and utopian possibility, a parallel story of disaster and catastrophe—of a dystopia shaped by fires, earthquakes, war, and prisons—also informs the California imaginary."[16] Many artists have confronted these darker edges of the Golden State: Fred Lonidier explored governmental repression and union activism, and Suzanne Lacy's feminist performances raised awareness about violence against women. Lacy in particular has been concerned about spectacles of violence; in the early seventies, she made her *Monster Series* that critically commented on various aspects of dehumanization and objectification. *Maps* (1973; fig. 3.13), which was produced for a class taught by Allan Kaprow at CalArts, involved an extended scavenger hunt for its participants in which they followed Lacy's maps to different destinations around Los Angeles, such as a hospital for the developmentally delayed and an abandoned slaughterhouse. For the final segment of the piece, the participants were given a meatpacker's gown to wear as they attempted to put lamb organs into a shape resembling a live animal. In this bloody work, it is not the artist's but the viewer's body that must costume itself and assume a potentially unfamiliar, even destabilizing or uncomfortable, role, as the gown interpolates its wearer into a butcher.

In his 1971 book *The Performing Self*, literary critic Richard Poirier argues that performance—which he defines as "any effort to find accommodation for human shapes or sounds"—is inevitably "an act that partakes of political meaning."[17] Lacy's *Maps* partakes in play-acting, but it is also acting as activism: California Conceptual and performance artists circa 1970 illuminate how such seemingly simplistic gestures as walking and getting dressed ramify into wider issues, from gender identity to violence against animals. To walk is not only to propel the body simply through space but also, depending on the context, to join a major march—think of the historic civil rights "walks" through Alabama. And demonstrations with bodies on the street were a crucial aspect of 1960s and 1970s protest politics. On both the East and the West Coasts there was a wealth of activity by groups like the San Francisco Diggers, Bread and Puppet Theater, the San Francisco Mime Troupe, and El Teatro Campesino that mixed theater with guerrilla street intervention. These groups catalyzed a wide variety of public interventions that were both improvisational and tightly scripted, from distributing free food to staging plays with elaborate sets and masks for political events, such as rallies for farm workers' rights or protests against racism and the Vietnam War. Though Bread and Puppet was founded in New York and then moved to Vermont, the troupe also traveled and performed in Northern California; they shared the bill with the mime troupe and Teatro Campesino at the 1968 Radical Theater Festival held at San Francisco State College.[18]

Many California artists were in an explicit dialogue with the wider context of theatrical antiwar activity; Terry Fox, for example, performed his controversial *Defoliation* at Berkeley's University Art Museum in 1970 (see fig. 1.25, p. 39). For this piece, Fox employed a flamethrower (similar to the type used in Vietnam) to methodically and systematically burn a section of flowers planted on campus. This aggressive act, in which Fox performs the part of a military man in order to register his dissent against such policies, could be seen as another iteration of drag. "The world is groaning beneath the terrors of his masculinity," write the Roszaks; the war is "playing masculine" at its most imperialist and horrifying.[19]

Feminist artists, too, were commenting on the gendered dynamic of war; in Rosler's *Bringing the War Home: House Beautiful* photomontages (1967–72; figs. 1.27, p. 41, and 3.14, p. 212), first published in an alternative newspaper, various well-coiffed women go about their household activities while the war rages outside their windows. Rosler's collages comment not only on female domestic labor—a woman vacuums drapes, oblivious to the soldiers behind her curtains—but also on the brutal racialization of the Vietnam War. Again insisting that gender and race are always mutually interpenetrating, it is significant that the models in the images are overwhelmingly

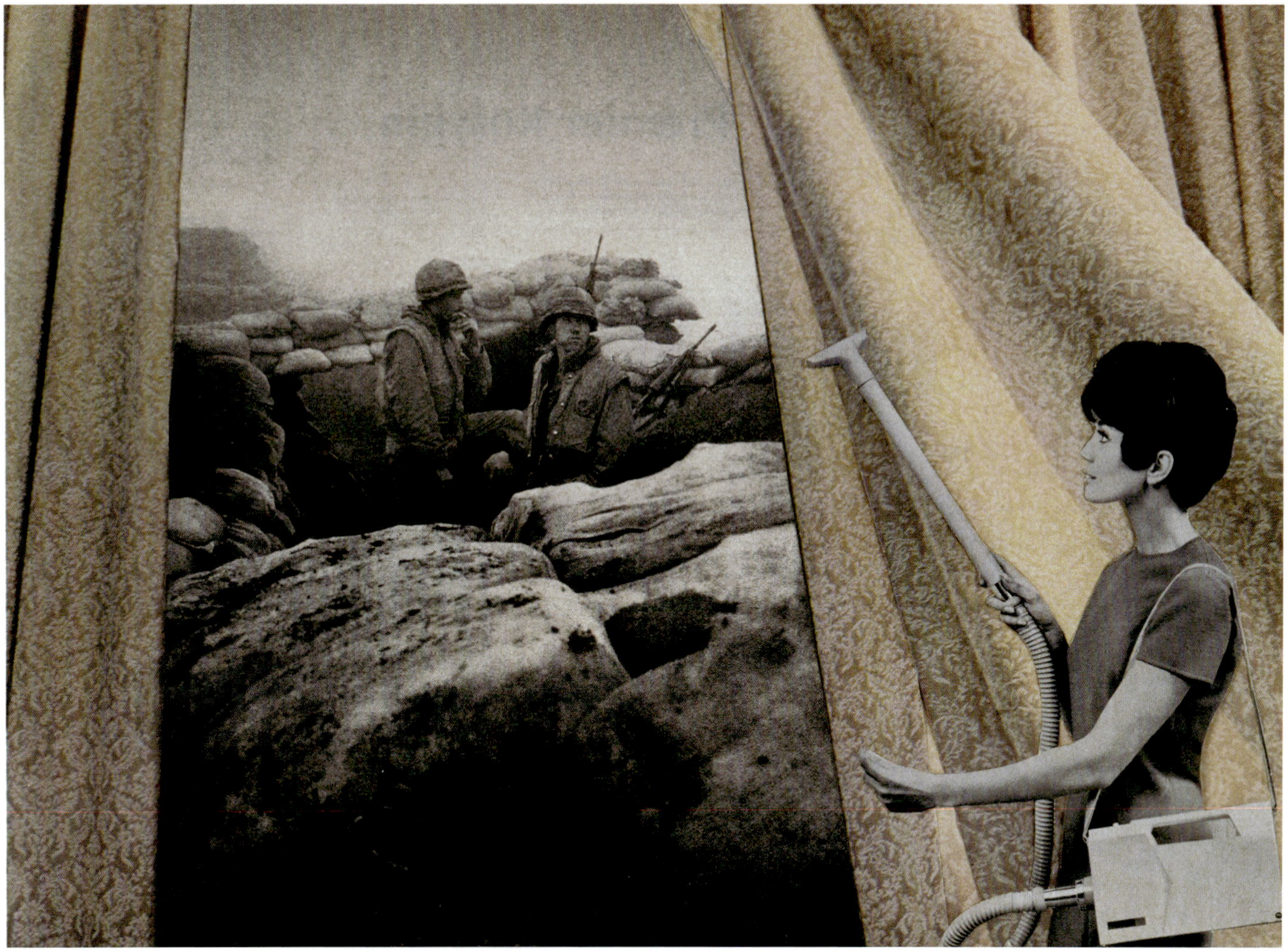

Fig. 3.14 Martha Rosler, *Cleaning the Drapes,* from the series *Bringing the War Home: House Beautiful,* 1967–72. Photomontage; 20 × 24 in.

Fig. 3.15 Bernie Boston, *Flower Power,* 1967. Gelatin silver print.

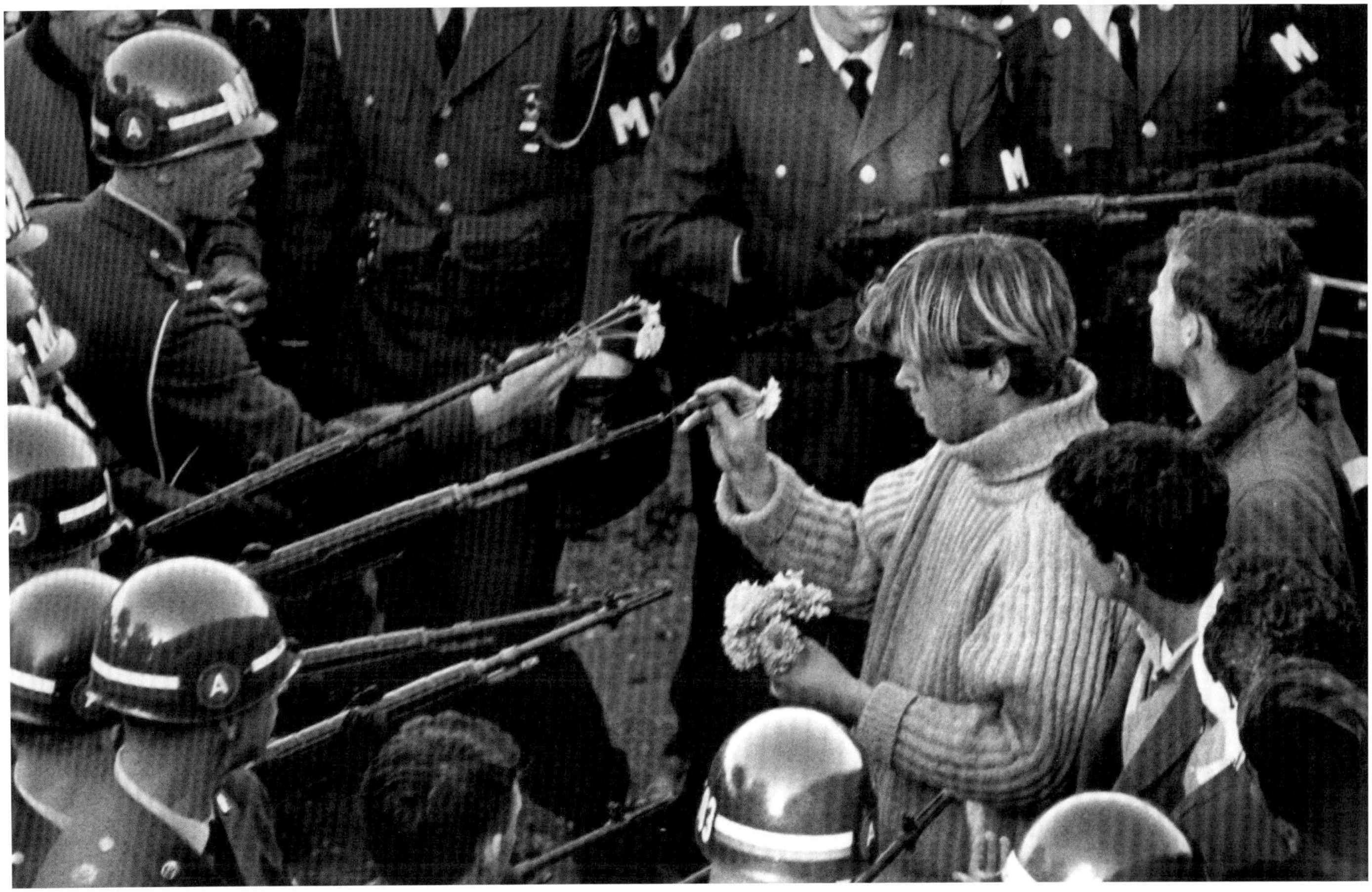

white; this collage, featuring a potentially nonwhite woman, is a striking exception. There are several interiors in which the majority of furnishings, walls, floors, and surfaces are white as well. In Rosler's works, whiteness is not a neutral background but a powerful organizing force and almost blinding visual field.

Such hard-hitting protests against the Vietnam War might seem disconnected from the somewhat more fanciful image of Hibiscus playing dress-up in full drag. Yet there are surprising continuities between antiwar organizing and the countercultural, queer, and feminist refusal to live by traditional gender roles: both modes of protest insist upon remaking a broken and damaging system by imagining a world of other possibilities, whether it be whimsical dances or deadly serious defoliations. One of the most iconic photographs of the Vietnam War era is of a young man tenderly inserting a flower into the barrel of a National Guardsman's gun at a demonstration at the Pentagon in 1967—that young man is Hibiscus (then George Harris, Jr.), a few years before the founding of the Cockettes. This action was organized by Michael Bowen, who brought two hundred pounds of daisies to the Pentagon in what could be called a mass performance-art protest event. (Bowen also organized the first "human be-in," in 1967.) The photograph depicts bodies: acting, moving, confronting each other, but also held back in tense confrontation. Harris's tousled wisps of blonde hair and the almost sculptural swooping lines of his cowl-necked pullover stand out against

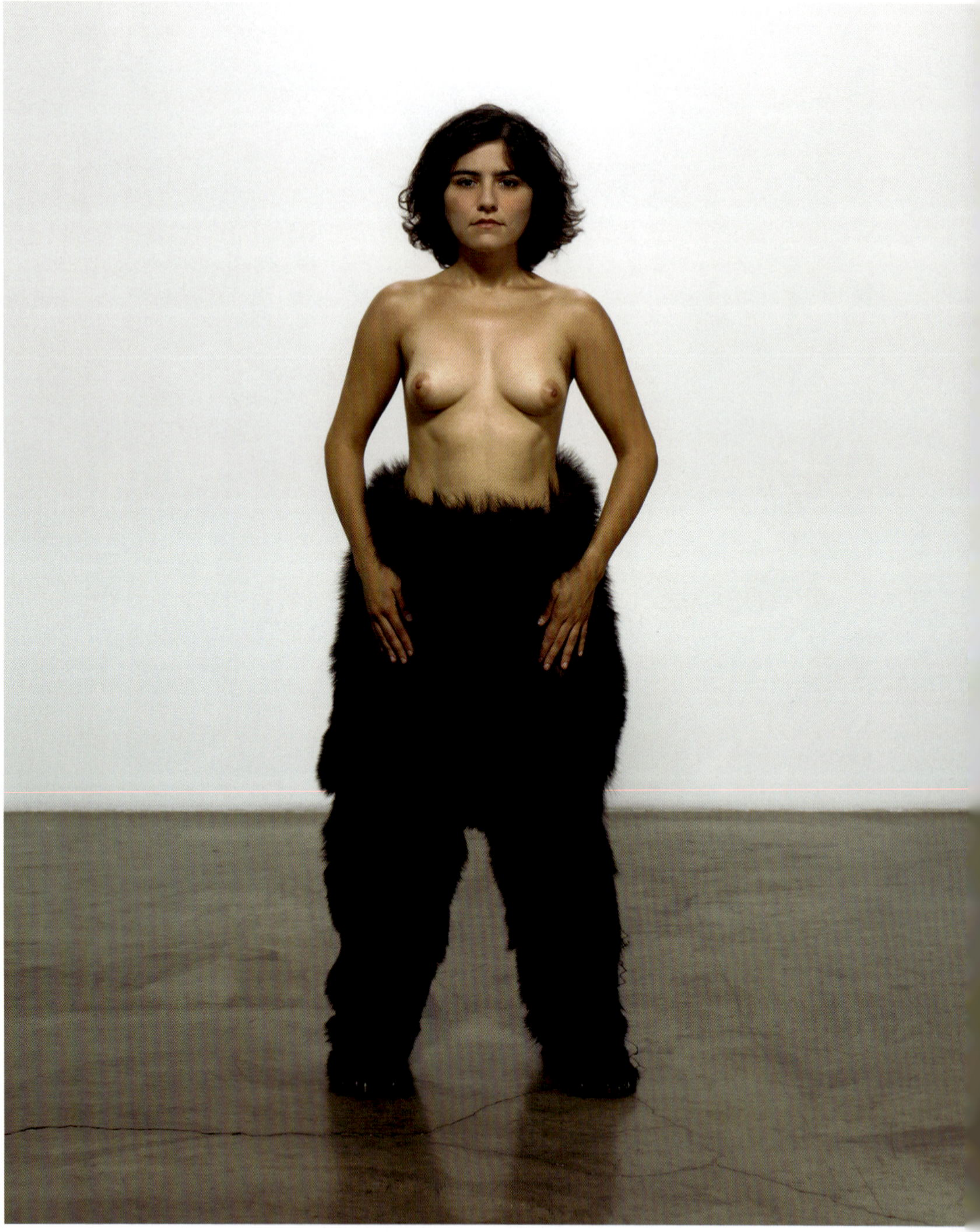

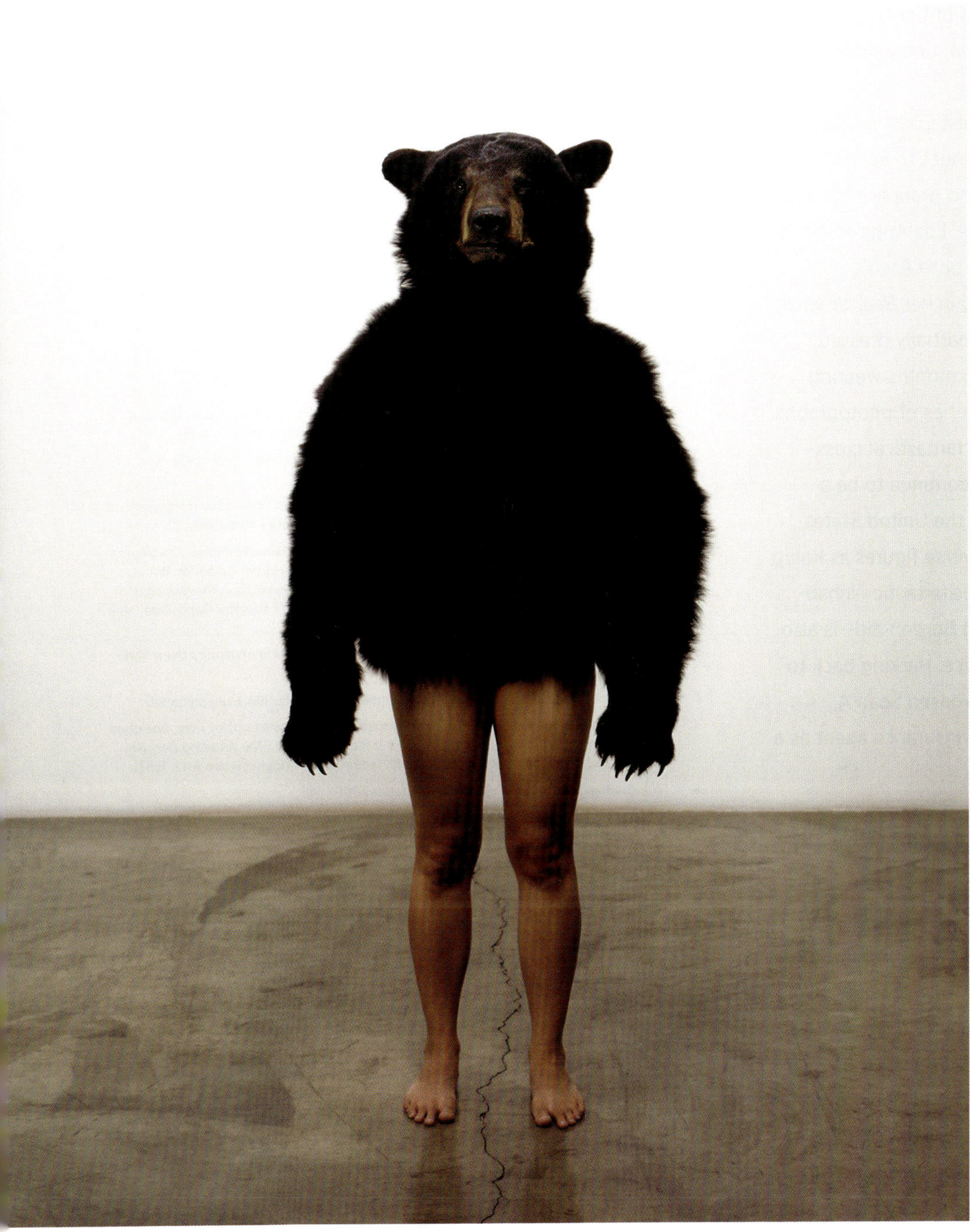

Fig. 3.16 Carlee Fernandez, *Bear Study Diptych,* 2004. C-print; 20 × 16 × 2 in. Courtesy of the artist and ACME., Los Angeles.

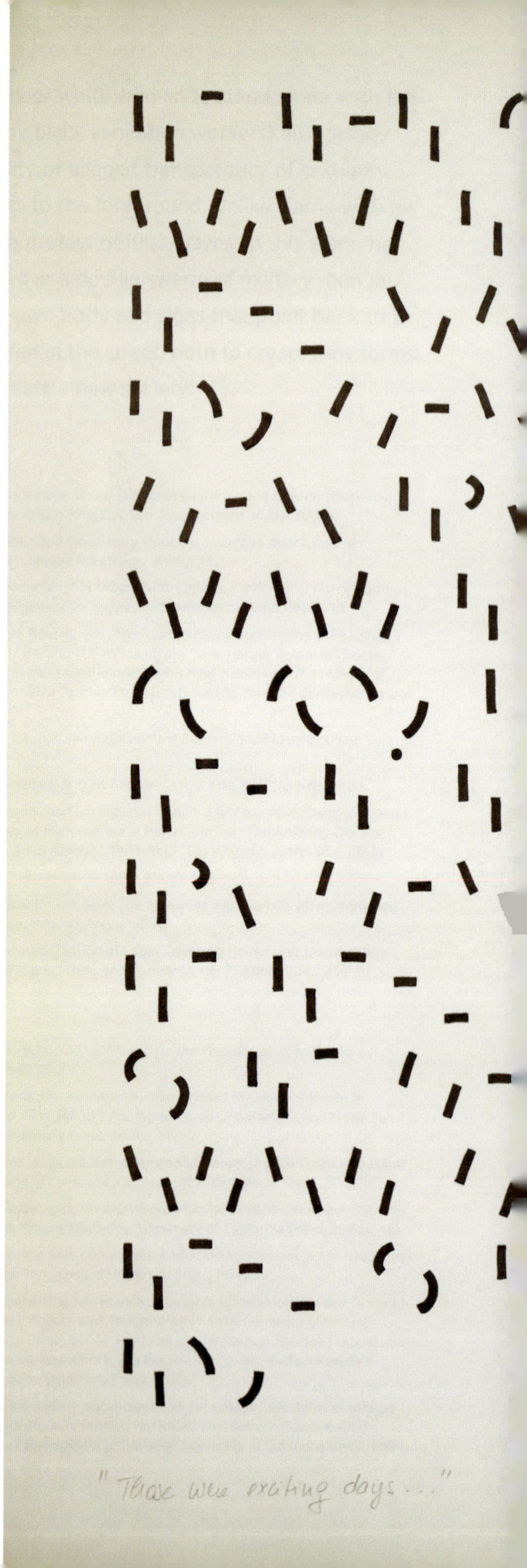

Fig. 4.1 Guy de Cointet, *These were exciting days . . .*, 1971. Ink on paper; 25½ × 30½ in.

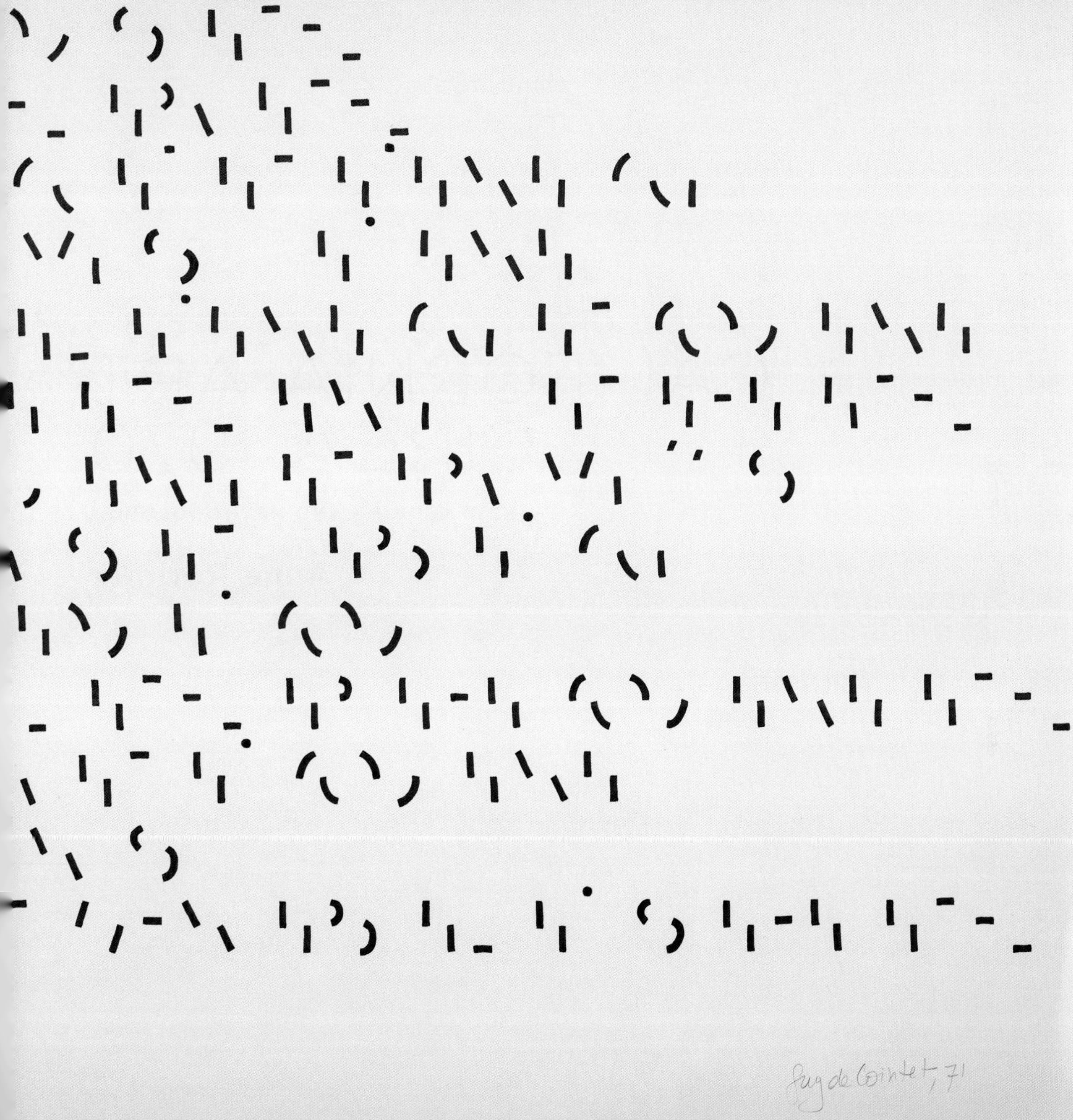
Guy de Cointet, 71

CALIFORNIA ART CIRCA 1970

NEW MEDIUMS AND METHODOLOGIES

Anne Rorimer

The groundswell of aesthetic activity on both sides of the Atlantic in the mid- to late 1960s irrevocably transformed the nature of art as previously defined in North America and Europe. *State of Mind: New California Art circa 1970* bears witness to this radical shift, which entailed the reassessment—and, for the most part, the rejection—of the age-old categories of painting and sculpture. Artists in this country and abroad succeeded in formulating new ideas about the object and objectives of art under the rubric of Conceptual art, as the use of new mediums and methodologies in the late 1960s and early 1970s has come to be termed. From West Coast to East Coast and in geographical centers abroad, many artists simultaneously sought to investigate ways to redefine art's traditional representational methods, modes, and meanings.

It is not possible to adequately synthesize the far-ranging, path-finding aesthetic practices that simultaneously began to develop internationally around 1970 with their wide variety of individual interests and intents. One can, however, state the prime importance of the fact that the medium specificity pertaining to painting and sculpture—so famously promulgated by renowned critic Clement Greenberg to be the linchpin of Modernism—was called into question by a substantial number of artists who, at the start, did not necessarily know of each other. California Conceptualists, therefore, belong together not solely by virtue of their geographical place of residence at the outset of their careers, but even more so by their shared pursuit of a wide range of aesthetic strategies devoted to reinvigorating worn-out practices of art making. The artists included in the current exhibition do not ultimately constitute a specific, California-based group; however, some of them, working or exhibiting together, have necessarily shared ideas and approaches in common (especially in the area of performance art, with its socially aware and critical "edge"). For this reason, the diverse production issuing from California included in this exhibition may best be considered under the extremely broad umbrella of Conceptual art.

Conceptual artists extended the preceding innovations of Minimal and Pop art in the process of turning away from the medium-specific disciplines of painting and sculpture. The replacement of traditional paint on canvas and of three-dimensional, sculptural materiality with alternative forms of

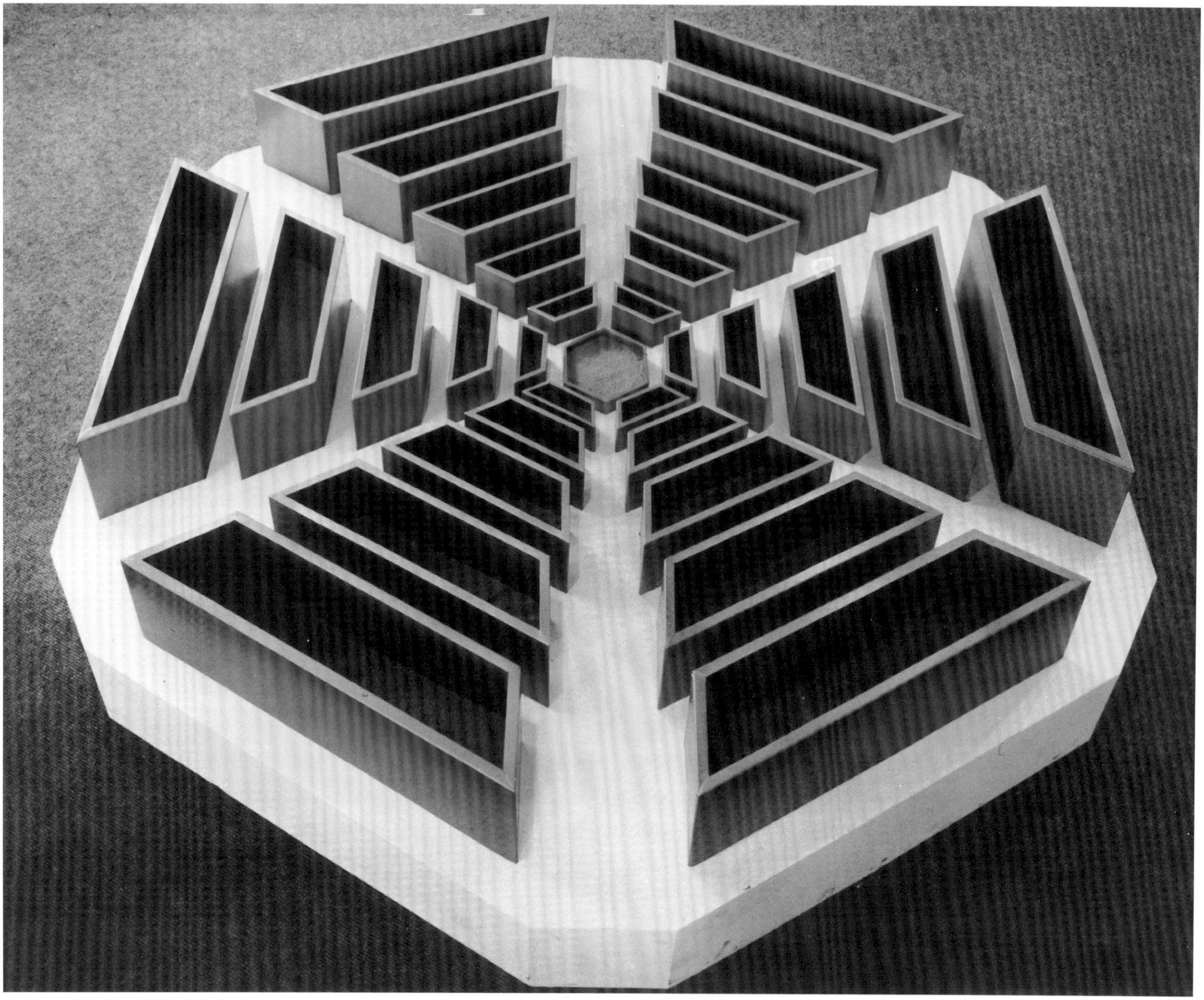

Fig. 4.2 Robert Smithson, *A Nonsite, Pine Barrens, New Jersey,* 1967–68. Wood, aluminum, and sand; 12 × 66 in. diameter. Private collection. © Estate of Robert Smithson / licensed by VAGA, New York. Image: Courtesy James Cohan Gallery, New York.

Fig. 4.3 Robert Smithson, *A Nonsite (Pine Barrens),* 1967. Cut Photostat and typewritten text on paper; 12 ½ × 10 ¼ in. © Estate of Robert Smithson / licensed by VAGA, New York. Image: Courtesy James Cohan Gallery, New York.

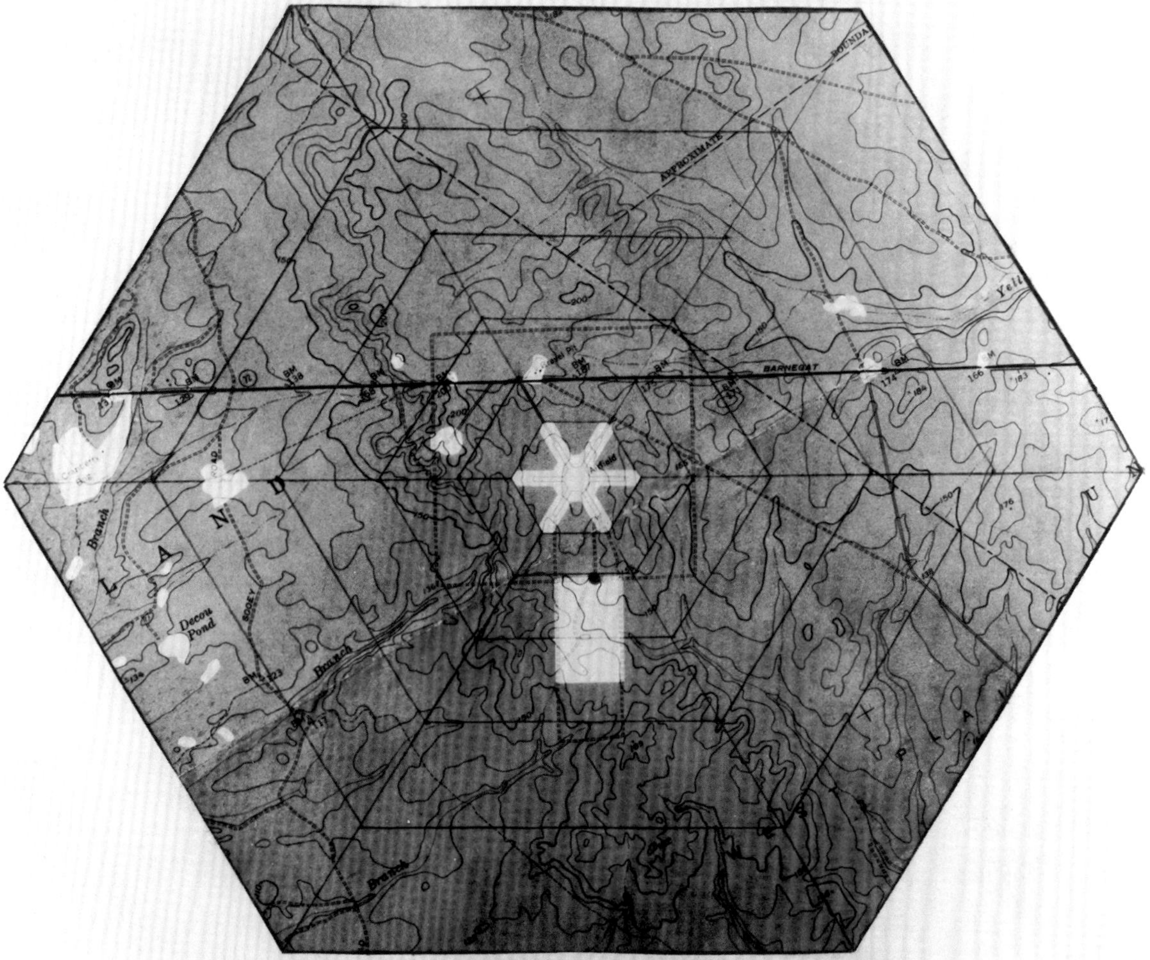

A NONSITE (an indoor earthwork)

31 sub-divisions based on a hexagonal "airfield" in the Woodmansie Quadrangle - New Jersey (Topographic) map. Each sub-dividion of the Nonsite contains sand from the site shown on the map. Tours between the Nonsite and the site are possible. The red dot on the map is the place where the sand was collected.

representation is what, speaking all inclusively, may be said to be the principal, underlying characteristic of Conceptual art as practiced on the West Coast.

The alternative representational mediums and modes fundamental to Conceptual art often overlap each other in a single work, and many artists moved freely between them. These various mediums and modes will nonetheless be separately considered in this essay for the sake of analysis: first, with regard to the use of photographic, linguistic, and/or cartographic means; second, with regard to the use of film; third, with regard to installation practices; and, last, with regard to video and performance.

The following discussion aims to foreground the desire on the part of Conceptual artists (both in and outside of California around 1970) to reconsider the ever-changing contract between art and reality. This reality may be thought of, for one, simply in relation to the material art object. As well, it may be thought of on a purely idealistic plane, where art empowers itself to be a lever for raising questions about issues of social justice.

Photography and language in Conceptual art may be utilized separately or in conjunction with each other, and frequently in association with numbers or maps. Photography, as an imprint on light-sensitive film of an actuality captured by a camera lens, and language, whose lexical components self-referentially convey semantic meaning, came to function independently from, and in lieu of, painting and sculpture with the advent of Conceptual art. Mechanical reproduction and/or text replaced the painted image or the carved, hewn, modeled, cast, etc., object. Considering the photographic and/or language-based work of East Coast artists—such as Robert Smithson (1938–73) and Robert Barry (b. 1936), and the British artist Richard Long (b. 1945), to mention only a very few—offers a comparative backdrop for looking at works by similarly minded artists of the same generation residing in California. The selection of artists discussed in this essay was chosen for the sake of comparison and represents only the smallest subset of internationally prominent figures.

The Nonsites by Robert Smithson (figs. 4.2–4.3) mark a transitional moment from Minimal to Conceptual means insofar as photography, text, and cartographic information are concerned. Similar to Minimal sculptures, the Nonsites accommodate three-dimensional, geometrically shaped, and serially arranged metal bins. They contain industrial or natural debris culled from a particular site, and accompanying descriptive photographs, texts, and maps designate the location from which this debris was taken. Non-art contexts on the fringes of civilization are thereby linked with the interior, art context of an exhibition space through the union of volumetric form with flat—and deliberately flatfooted—objective documentation. Notably, in works by San Diego artists Helen Mayer Harrison and Newton Harrison, such as those in *The Book of Lagoons,* photographic, textual, and cartographic representation in a Conceptual manner carry the full weight of aesthetic meaning (see fig. 1.5, p. 18). In geographically far-ranging works—from Sri Lanka to the Salton Sea, for example—which examine plant and marine systems, the Harrisons have long addressed "the ecological predicament" by treating the "surface of the world as their canvas."[1] In the early 1970s, they imported sizeable containers into gallery exhibitions. *Portable Farm: Survival Piece No. 6* (1972) presented plants and trees in containers—as opposed to in vitrines—as possible sources for food in the future. This work followed *Portable Fish Farm* (1971), in which catfish at each stage of their life cycle swam in water-filled steel tanks.[2] Subsequently, maps became the focal points for large-scale ecological proposals and replaced the need for the display of containers or tanks inside of exhibition spaces. These proposals present expansive schemes for calling attention to the threatened natural environment. The work of the Harrisons, although it possesses clear parallels with Smithson's Nonsites, is not concerned with connecting interior art and exterior non-art contexts. The artists have set their sights more specifically on saving the planet through works that, ideally, could be realized in the context of nature rather than solely in the context of art.

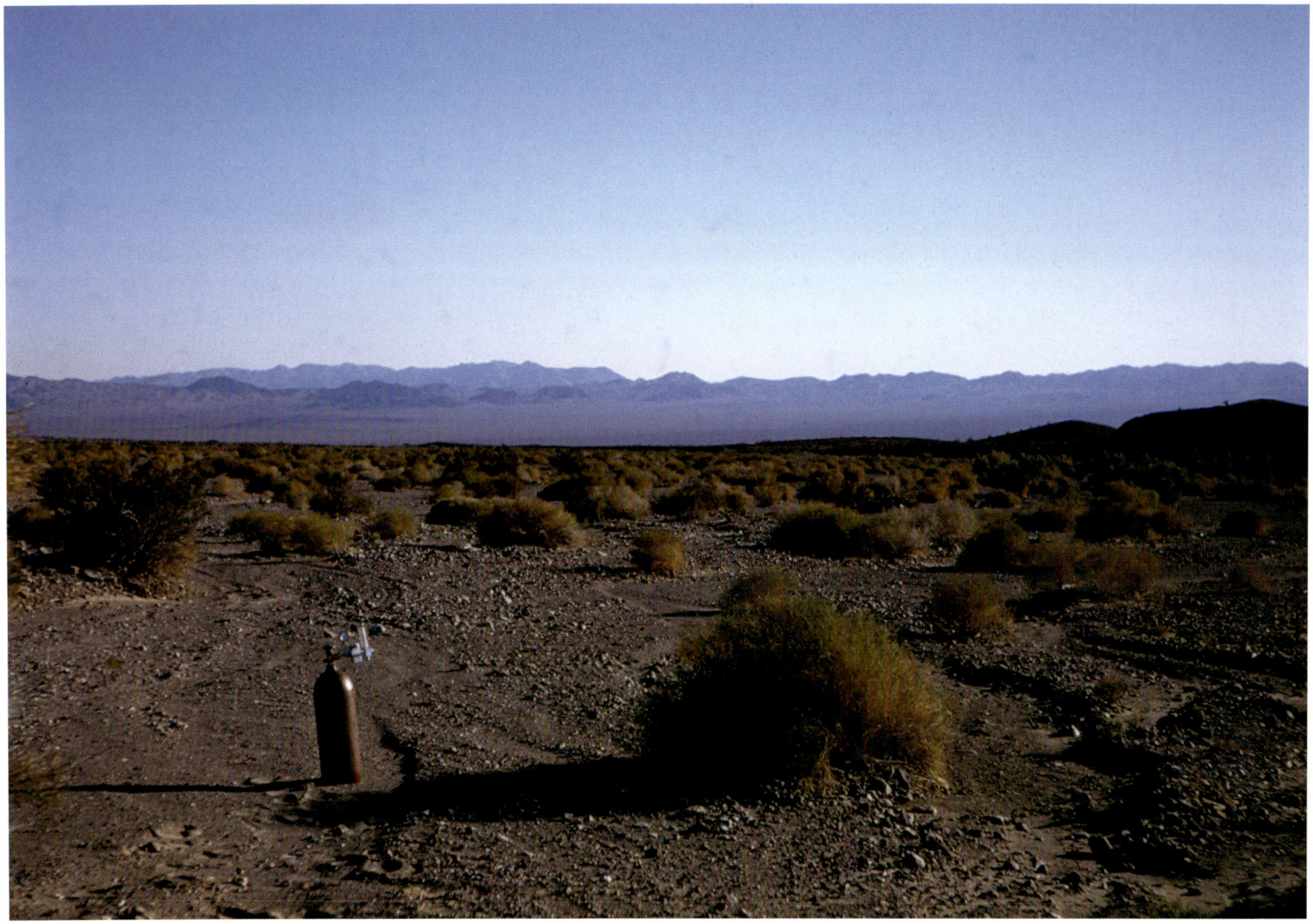

Text and photographic-image use in Robert Barry's *Inert Gas Series* (1969; fig. 4.4) and Richard Long's *A Hundred Mile Walk* (1971–72; fig. 4.5) make the otherwise invisible visible within the frame of representation. An *Inert Gas* piece by Barry evidences his release of a measured volume of gas—such as helium, krypton, or neon—into the atmosphere at a particular place on a particular date. Barry's work is about expanding the physical limits of a material substance—albeit an unperceivable one—to fill the vast, open-ended atmosphere rather than placing objects in a gallery space. For his part, using similar representational means, often with the inclusion of maps, Long gives form to the wide open spaces of the great outdoors by recording distances covered by his walks in the English countryside. Both artists inform the viewer photographically and textually of the measures they took to consider alternatives to the traditional material, static object.

Similarly, works in the exhibition by veteran Conceptualists like John Baldessari and Douglas Huebler further suggest the breadth of photography's reach, whether or not it is accompanied by language. Both of these artists turned to photography in the primary interest of, once again, repudiating the material singularity of a stationary object.

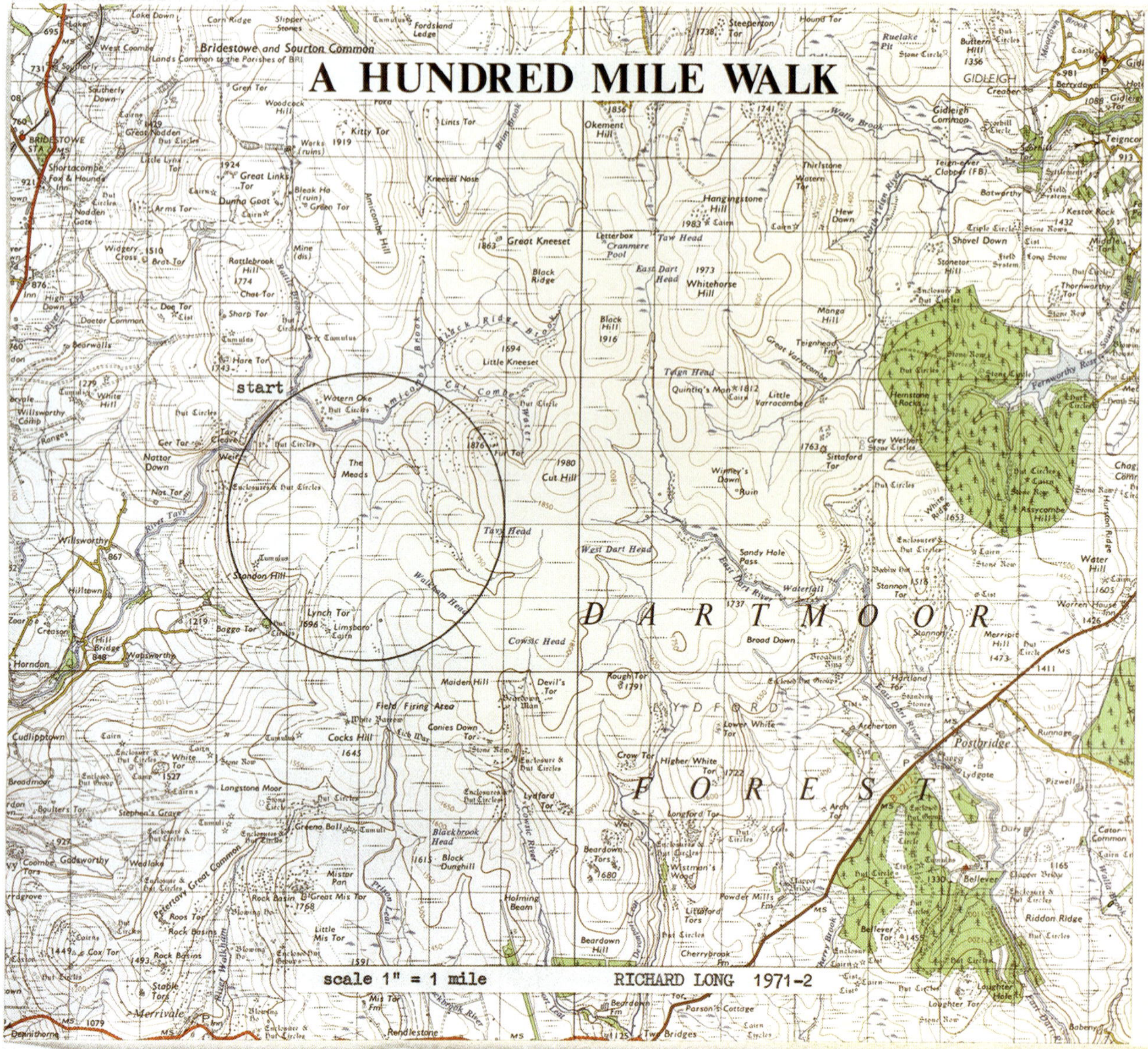

<<

Fig. 4.4 Robert Barry, *Inert Gas Series,* 1969. Helium; 2 cubic ft. © Robert Barry. Photo: Courtesy of the artist and Yvon Lambert Paris, New York / DACS, London.

Fig. 4.5 Richard Long, *A Hundred Mile Walk,* 1971–72. Pencil, map, printed text, photograph, and labels on paper, unique. © Tate, London; purchase 1973. © Richard Long, Artists Rights Society (ARS), New York.

Day 1 Winter skyline, a north wind

Day 2 The Earth turns effortlessly under my feet

Day 3 Suck icicles from the grass stems

Day 4 As though I had never been born

Day 5 In and out the sound of rivers over familiar stepping stones

Day 6 Corrina, Corrina

Day 7 Flop down on my back with tiredness
Stare up at the sky and watch it recede

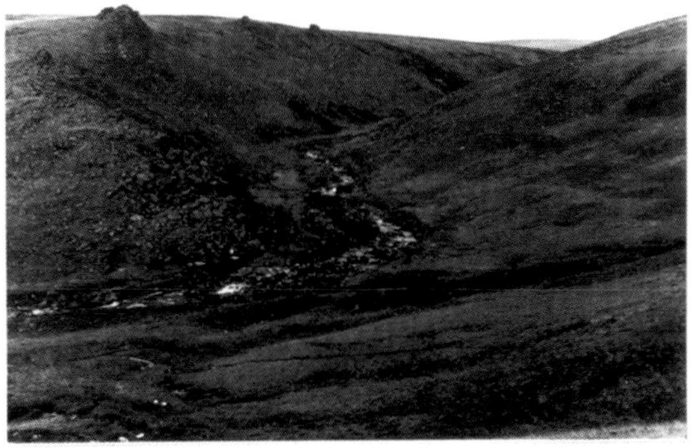

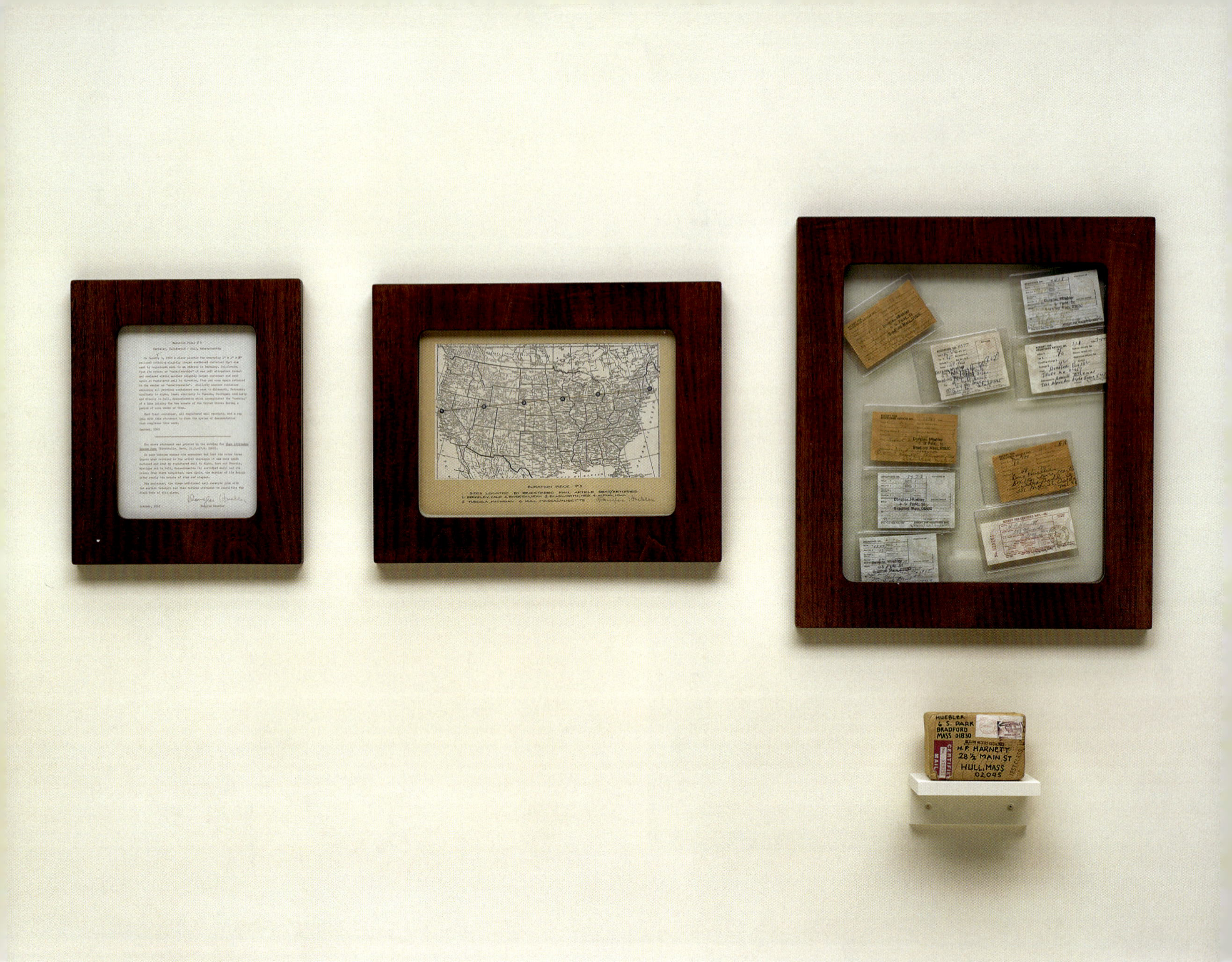

Fig. 4.6 Douglas Huebler, *Duration Piece #9, Berkeley, California—Hull, Massachusetts, January–October, 1969,* 1969. Statement, map, nine mail receipts, and box; statement: 11 × 8 ½ in.; map: 10 × 14 ½ in.; framed receipts: 22 ⅜ × 19 ¼ in.; box: 2 ⅞ × 5 ⅛ × 3 ½ in.

Baldessari has stated that "by late 1965 [he] was finished with painting . . . and began wondering if straight information would serve."[3] *California Map Project Part I: California* (1969; frontispiece) is the artist's first use of photographs independent from a canvas. The work, structured on the word "CALIFORNIA," consists of ten color photographs along with a map of the state and an explanatory text (see frontispiece). As per the text and notations on the map, Baldessari made and placed each of the ten letters in C-A-L-I-F-O-R-N-I-A in different locations, recording them in each instance with his camera. By means of photography, therefore, he was able to bring together geographically far-flung segments of reality.

For Huebler, too, as for Baldessari, the camera became an indispensable instrument for use in combination with language and, in some instances, with maps. In most of Huebler's early work, multiple shots taken in accordance with the stipulations of a text pinpoint facets of extant spatial reality or moments of an ongoing, otherwise unstoppable, sequence of movements. In much of Huebler's prolific oeuvre, photographs present multifaceted angles of situations that otherwise could not be perceived all at once. In *Duration Piece #9, Berkeley, California—Hull, Massachusetts, January–October, 1969* (1969; fig. 4.6), the assembled mail receipts replace the factual, documentary function of photographs.

Carving: A Traditional Sculpture (1972), by Eleanor Antin, a New Yorker by birth who moved to California in 1968, wittily synthesizes Conceptual methods—such as those employed by Baldessari and Huebler—that are founded on the premise of photographic neutrality (see fig. 1.42, p. 56–57). As indicated on an accompanying wall label, Antin documented her naked body from the back, front, and sides over a span of thirty-six days in a series of small black-and-white shots. Exhibited sequentially—one above the other in four long rows—the photographs show the progression of her weight loss. With reference to social standards of feminine beauty and the treatment of women as objects, Antin's work photographically follows the carving of her own curvilinear form day by day. In this way, the artist ingeniously comments on the Conceptual rejection of sculptural three-dimensionality, paradoxically, by means of shaping her own body.

Photography allows the artist to step back from any hands-on involvement in the process of aesthetic production to give the ideational impression that a work has taken its own logically self-propelling course in accordance with the directives set up for it. Thus suppressing overt signs of an authorial presence in a work's fabrication, Conceptual artists retained the Modernist notion, handed down from Abstract Expressionism via Minimal and Pop art, of art's self-referential nature. At the same time, they were able to reject pure solipsism along with materiality inasmuch as photographs make contact with recognizable aspects of reality.

The assumption of documentary truth attributed to mechanical reproduction, in large degree, is preserved in highly disparate bodies of work of the late 1960s and early 1970s. (At the end of the decade this, of course, would be overtly challenged by a slightly younger generation of artists known as the Pictures Generation.) The droll, playful work of Dutch artist Ger van Elk—who came to Los Angeles in the early 1960s to join his father, an animator at Hanna Barbera Studios, whose work included *The Flintstones*—for instance, marks a stark contrast with the socially probing work of Fred Lonidier.[4] Whereas van Elk employs photography to walk the line between reality and fiction, Lonidier enlists it to bring to light the darker side of the human condition.

Van Elk commented in an interview that his early decision to adopt photographic means was based on the fact that "you immediately get something resembling . . . reality."[5] His photographic works of the early 1970s record staged scenarios in which he, himself, often performs. In the three-part *The Co-founder of the Word O.K.—Hollywood* (1971; fig. 4.7), the artist acts out the two letters of the word "O.K." in three locations on Hollywood Boulevard in Los Angeles. The *O* hangs on a stick slung over his shoulder, while his arms and legs make the shape of the *K*. Because a camera can isolate and frame an

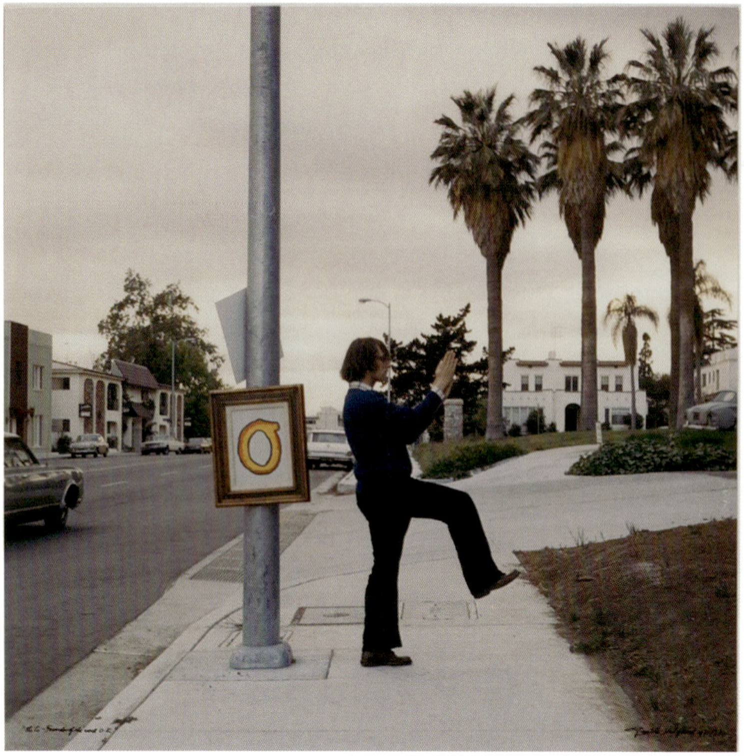

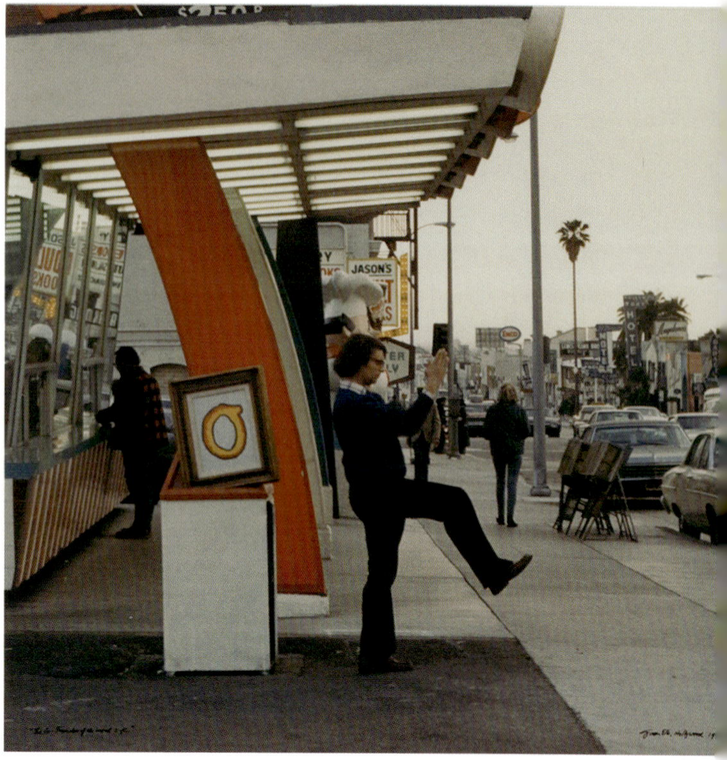

action, van Elk has been able to "figure" in works, wittily conceived, wherein his presence contributes to the reformulation of traditional representational form.

The camera serves, in van Elk's work, as a purely objective instrument for rendering verisimilitude and for binding together the real and the staged. In Lonidier's work, photography lends visual proof to scenes and situations that are not staged but are, actually, "for real." Lonidier is not involved with issues of aesthetic artifice in the manner of van Elk, but, quite the contrary, focuses on issues of social justice. *29 Arrests: Headquarters of the 11th Naval District, May 4, 1972, San Diego* (1972) details in twenty-nine shots the arrest of activists during a peaceful antiwar protest against the United States' bombing of Cambodia (see fig. 4.8, and figs. 1.1, pp. 6–7, and 1.28, p. 42). Lonidier stood directly behind a police officer as the man photographed the strong-armed tactics of his colleagues. The knowledge that the artist's photographs parallel non-art photographs—that here capture instances of brutality—reinforces the work's focus on images of physical and political force in the context of everyday life.

29 Arrests clearly manifests the straightforward, unquestioned, convincing, documentary capability of mechanical reproduction to come face-to-face with real-life situations. Lonidier's work is in line with that of the New York–based German American artist Hans Haacke (b. 1936), who for decades has similarly incorporated photographs into his investigatory, politically charged, socially conscious oeuvre. The 142 black-and-white photographs in *Shapolsky et al. Manhattan Real Estate Holdings, A Real-Time Social System, As of May 1, 1971* (1971; fig. 4.9) illustrate the facades or empty lots of properties in Manhattan that were owned by a single family. The photographs join exhaustive data from public records as well as

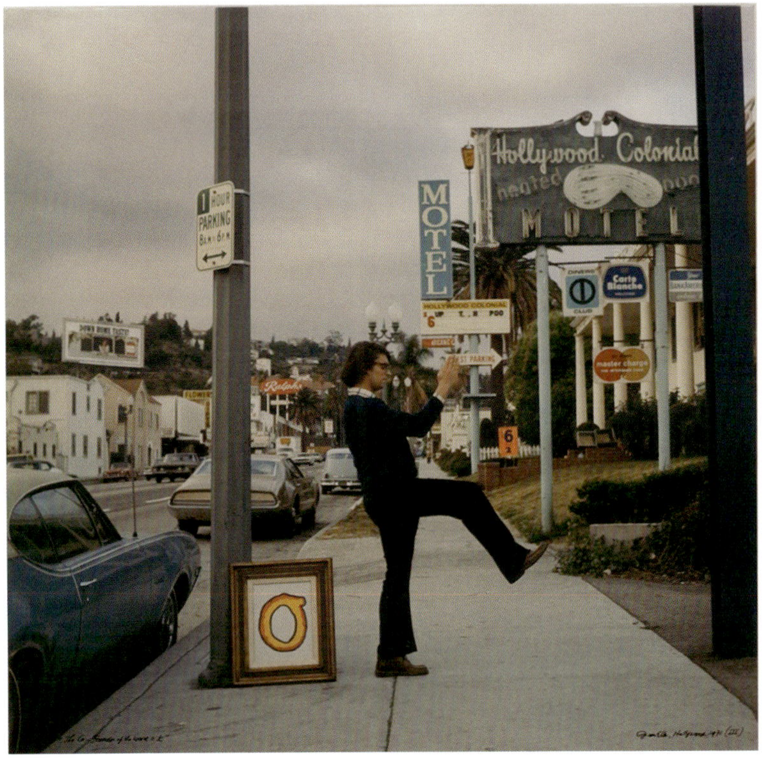

Fig. 4.7 Ger van Elk, *The Co-founder of the Word O.K.—Hollywood,* 1971. Three color photographs; 22 ¼ × 22 ¼ in. each.

charts of business transactions and maps plotting the geographical locations of the properties in low-income neighborhoods. *Shapolsky* opens the door to critical speculation about the hidden, underlying socioeconomic factors that privilege one family over those at lower echelons of the social scale. Photography, in *Shapolsky,* as in Conceptual art more generally, lends validity to the work by vouching for its visual veracity; this is especially relevant when works convey pointed political and social content, as much West Coast production often did.

Whereas language often acts in tandem with photography in numerous Conceptual works, in the art of New York–based artists Joseph Kosuth (b. 1945) and Lawrence Weiner (b. 1942)—as in the work of Guy de Cointet, who chose Los Angeles as his residence over his native France—words take over from pictorial and sculptural convention to supersede painted illusion and the substantive materiality of delimited objects. Enlarged photostats by Kosuth of definitions from dictionaries in *The First Investigation* (subtitled *Titled: Art as Idea as Idea [Water]*) (1966; fig. 4.10) are simply that which they describe. They are, that is, descriptions "through-and-through" inasmuch as flat, printed words provide lexical, formal, and semantic meaning all at once. Kosuth's dictionary definitions privilege written legibility over painted abstraction or figuration by substituting linguistic "forms" of definition, quite literally, for pictorial ones. In so doing, the definitions eliminate illusory depth of field at the same time that they possess visual, not literary, meaning.

Weiner reached the conclusion in 1968 that actual construction of his sculptures was not necessary and could remain optional. This has remained the case for hundreds of works, which, as single words, brief phrases, or lengthy statements, have taken—and continue to take—all manner of

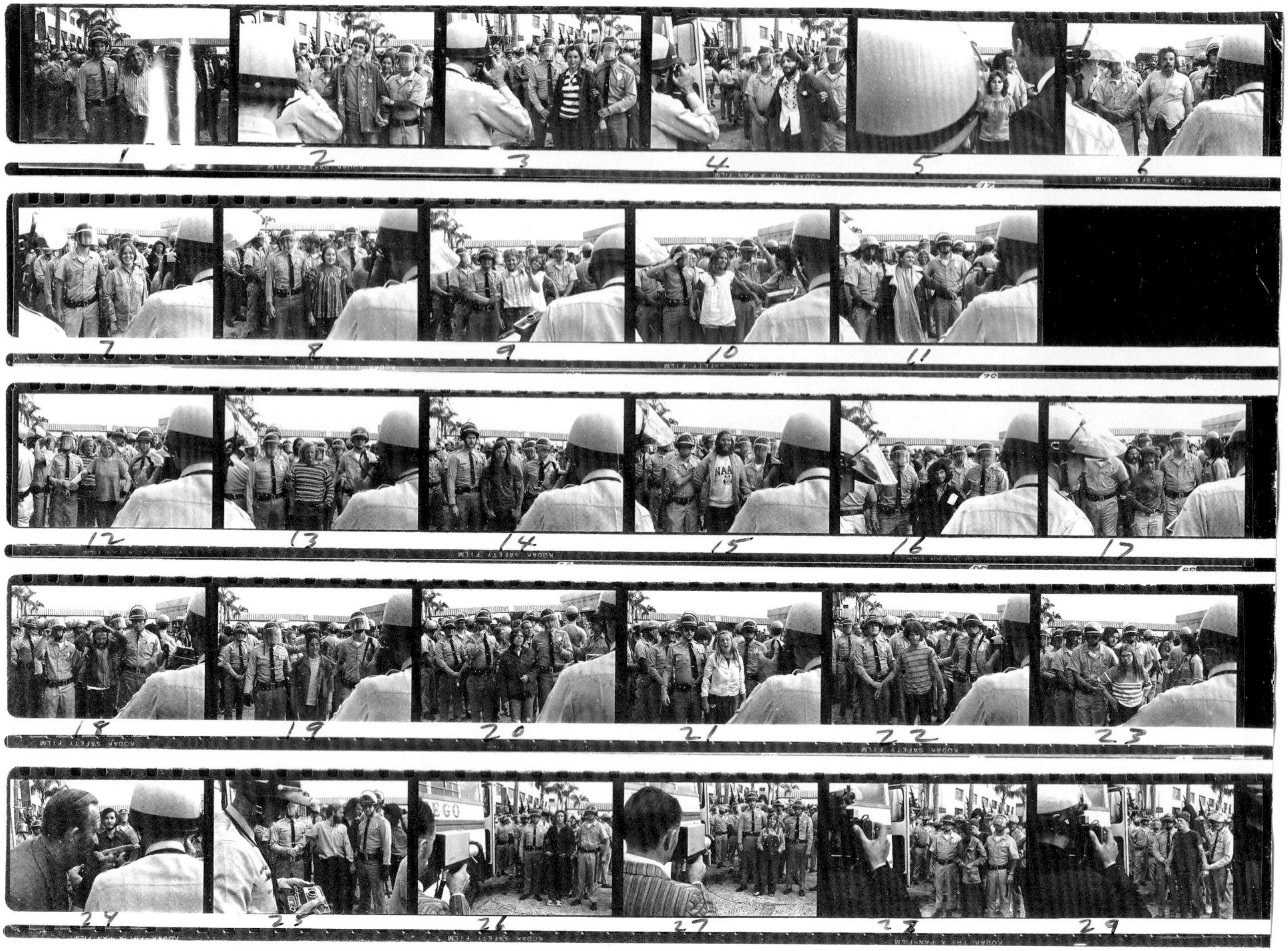

Fig. 4.8 Fred Lonidier, *29 Arrests: Headquarters of the 11th Naval District, May 4, 1972, San Diego* (contact sheet).

Fig. 4.9 Hans Haacke, *Shapolsky et al. Manhattan Real Estate Holdings, A Real-Time Social System, As of May 1, 1971*, 1971. Photo: Fred Scruton.

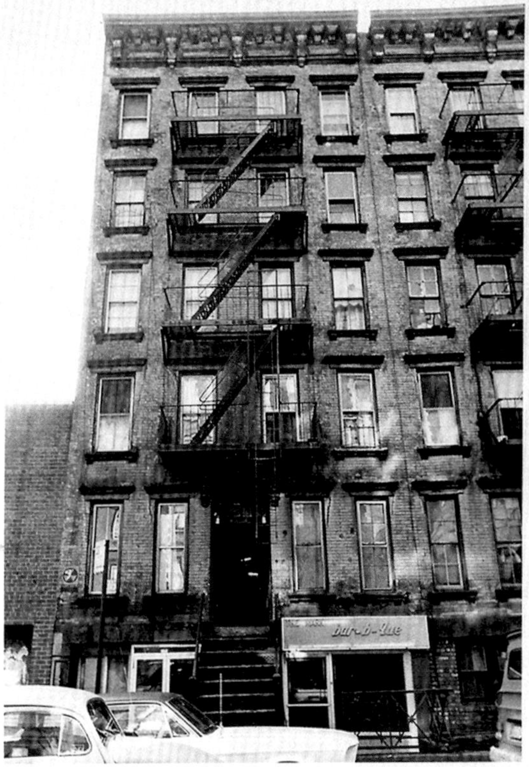

216 E 3 St.
Block 385 Lot 11
5 story walk-up old law tenement

Owned by Harpmel Realty Inc., 608 E 11 St., NYC
Contracts signed by Harry J. Shapolsky, President('63)
Martin Shapolsky, President('64)
Principal Harry J. Shapolsky(according to Real Estate Directory of Manhattan)

Acquired 8-21-1963 from John the Baptist Foundation, c/o The Bank of New York, 48 Wall St., NYC for $237 600.-(also 7 other bldgs.)

$150 000.- mortgage at 6% interest, 8-19-1963, due 8-19-1968, held by The Ministers and Missionaries Benefit Board of the American Baptist Convention, 475 Riverside Drive, NYC (also on 7 other bldgs.)

Assessed land value $25 000.-, total $75 000.- (including 212-14 E 3 St.) (1971)

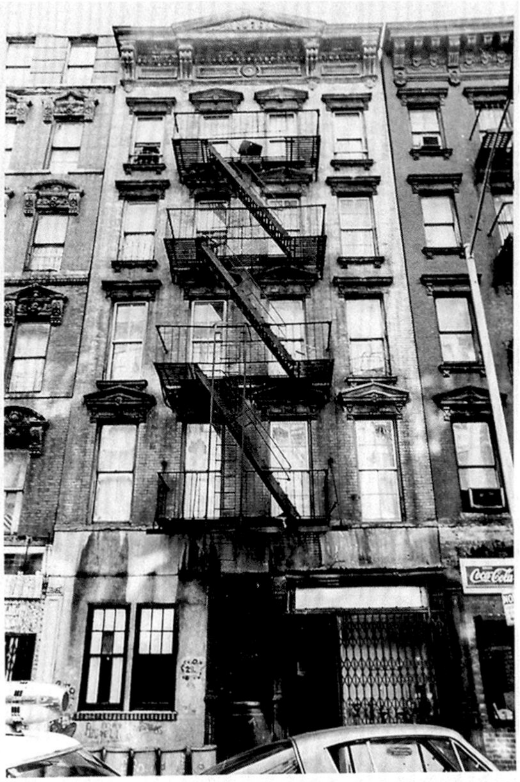

228 E 3 St.
Block 385 Lot 19
24 x 105' 5 story walk-up old law tenement

Owned by Harpmel Realty Inc. 608 E 11 St. NYC
Contracts signed by Harry J. Shapolsky, President('63)
Martin Shapolsky, President('64)

Acquired from John The Baptist Foundation
c/o The Bank of New York, 48 Wall St. NYC
for $237 000.- (also 5 other properties) , 8-21-1963

$150 000.- mortgage (also on 5 other properties) at 6%
interest as of 8-19-1963 due 8-19-1968
held by The Ministers and Missionaries Benefit Board of The American Baptist Convention, 475 Riverside Dr. NYC

Assessed land value $8 000.- total $28 000.-(1971)

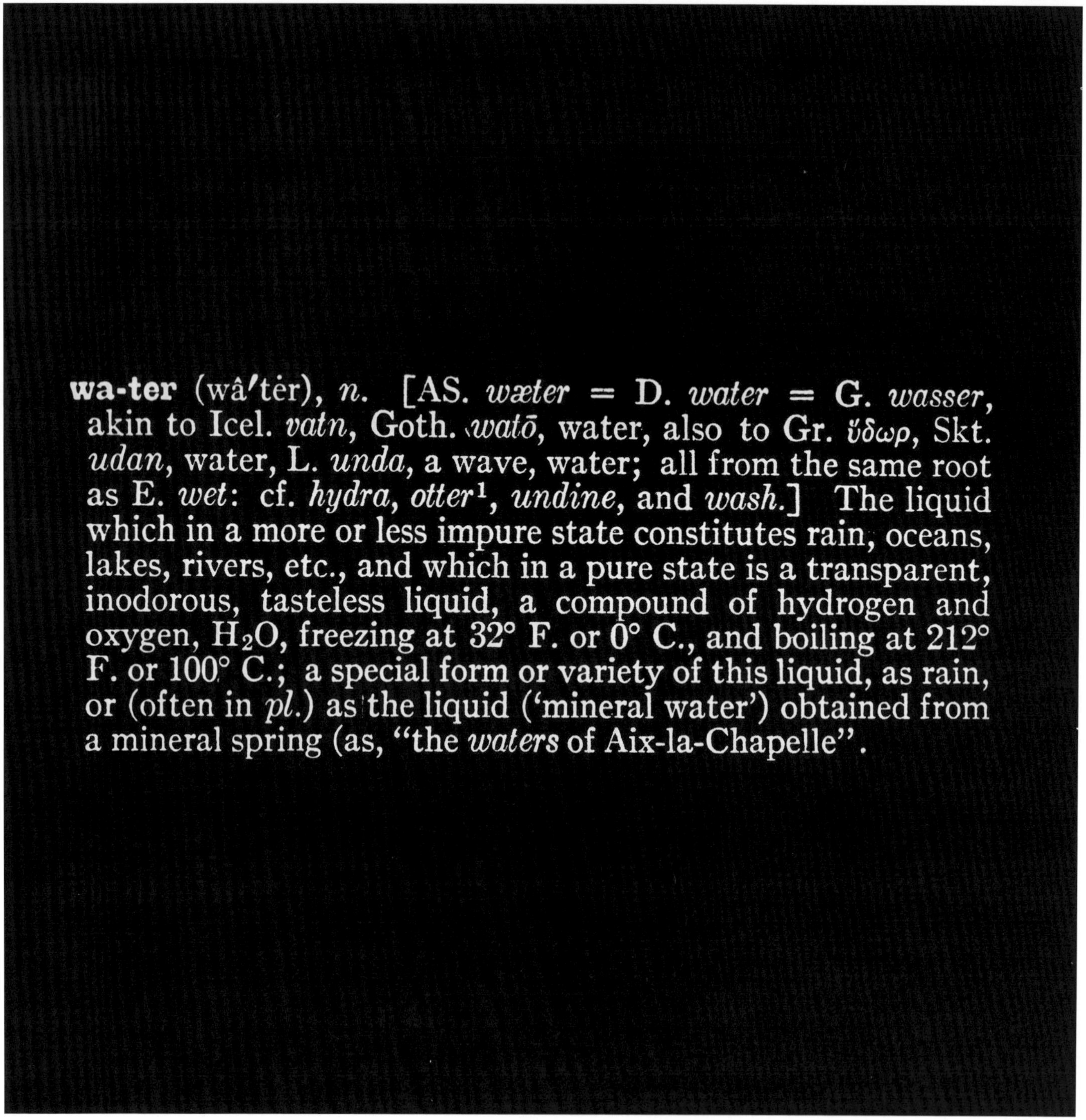

wa-ter (wâ′tėr), *n.* [AS. *wæter* = D. *water* = G. *wasser*, akin to Icel. *vatn*, Goth. *watō*, water, also to Gr. *ὕδωρ*, Skt. *udan*, water, L. *unda*, a wave, water; all from the same root as E. *wet*: cf. *hydra*, *otter*[1], *undine*, and *wash.*] The liquid which in a more or less impure state constitutes rain, oceans, lakes, rivers, etc., and which in a pure state is a transparent, inodorous, tasteless liquid, a compound of hydrogen and oxygen, H_2O, freezing at 32° F. or 0° C., and boiling at 212° F. or 100° C.; a special form or variety of this liquid, as rain, or (often in *pl.*) as the liquid ('mineral water') obtained from a mineral spring (as, "the *waters* of Aix-la-Chapelle".

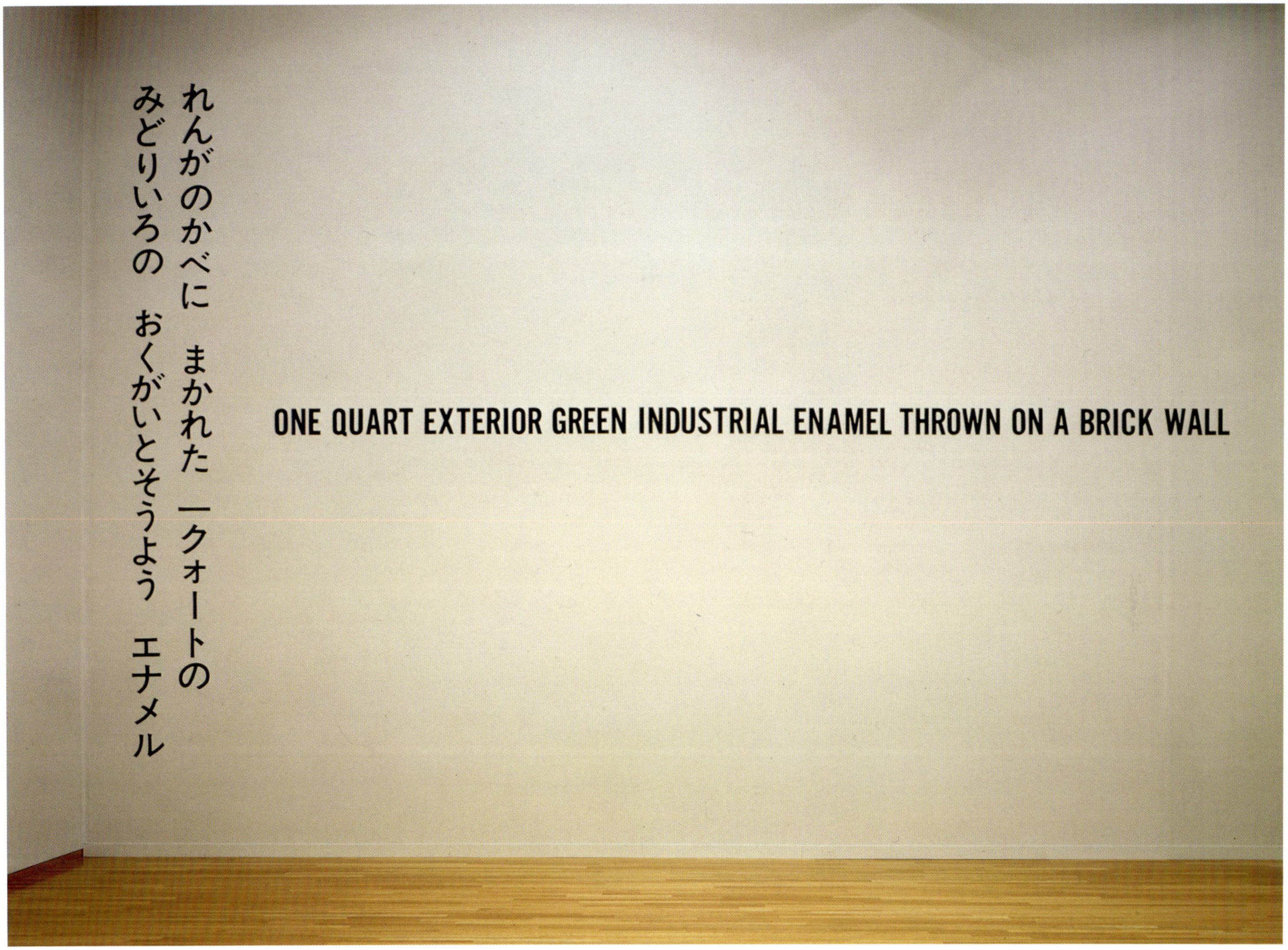

Fig. 4.10 Joseph Kosuth, *Titled (Art as Idea as Idea [Water])*, 1966. Photostat mounted on board; 48 × 48 in. Solomon R. Guggenheim Museum, New York, Gift, Leo Castelli, New York 73.2066. © 2010 Joseph Kosuth / Artists Rights Society (ARS), New York.

Fig. 4.11 Lawrence Weiner, *ONE QUART EXTERIOR GREEN INDUSTRIAL ENAMEL THROWN ON A BRICK WALL* (installation view), 1968. Museum of Contemporary Art, Tokyo; *Revolution in Contemporary Art: The Art of the Sixties,* 1995. Collection Alice Zimmermann Weiner (on extended loan to the Dia Art Foundation). Photo: Courtesy Moved Pictures Archive.

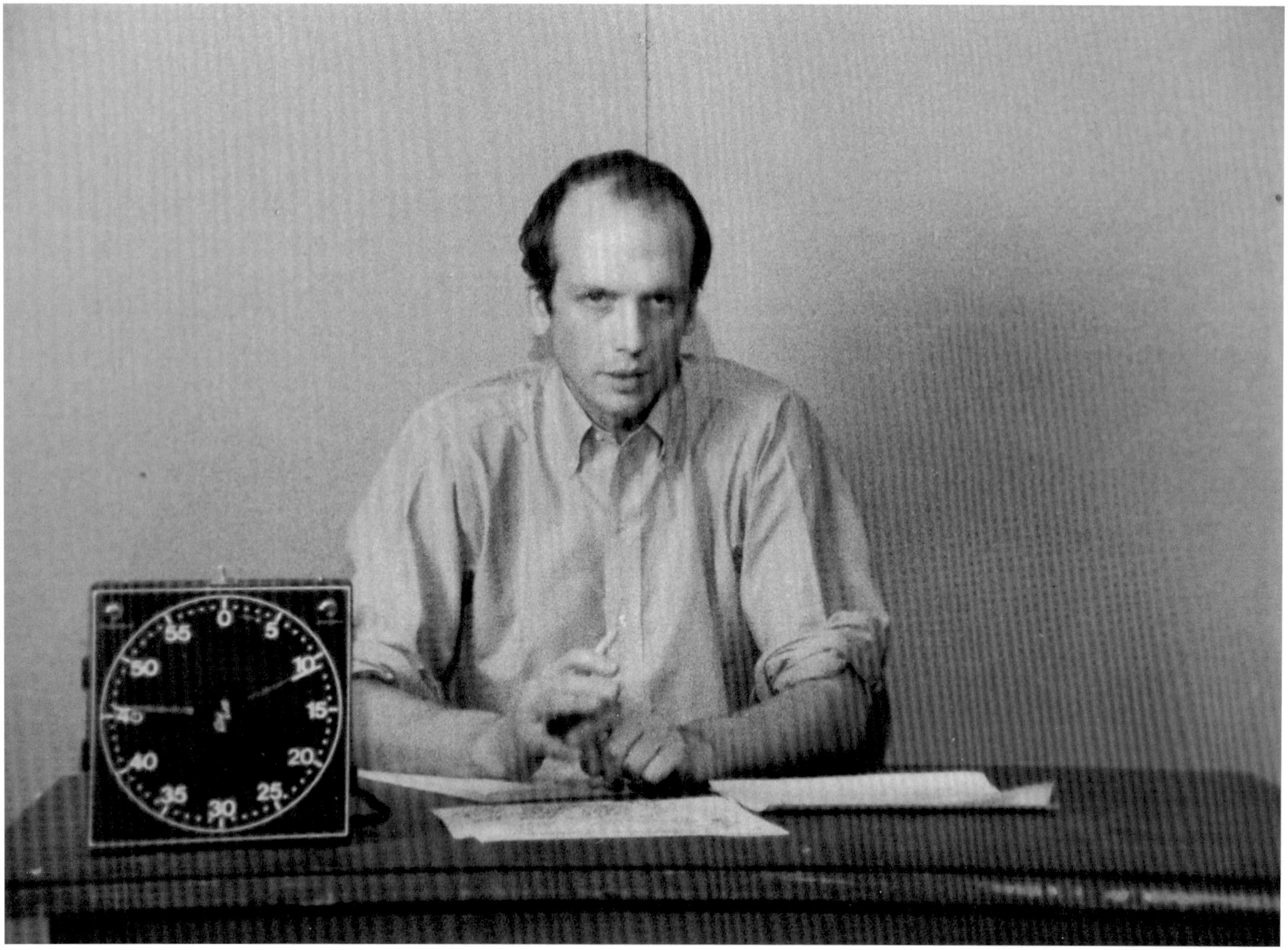

Fig. 4.12 Morgan Fisher, *Picture and Sound Rushes,* 1973. 16 mm film transferred to video; black and white; sound; 11 min.

written or verbal presentational forms. Never conclusively descriptive, the meaning of any work by Weiner is dependent on how it might be registered in the mind's eye of any one receiver. His work may be installed in public or private, in art or non-art contexts, contained in individual books or printed on a wide range of common objects, from stickers to pins to tableware, etc. Weiner's creations, synonymous with their titles, evade the tangible materiality of traditional sculpture while being capable of bonding ubiquitously with an endless number of surfaces and contexts (fig. 4.11) .

Language plays a predominant role in the two-dimensional work of Cointet as it did, quite literally, as a theatrical presence in his staged performances. Distinct from works by Kosuth and Weiner wherein information or images are contingent on comprehendible words and linguistic sequences, drawings by Cointet, such as *These were exciting days . . .* (1971), appear to be in code (see fig. 4.1). The rhetorical question as to how aesthetic meaning is determined is raised in works whose essential message pertains to the idea that art, a communicative system in its own right, can equally embody the verbal and the visual. Cointet's works disable determinable semantic function, often through the play of disconnected letters or numbers which are sometimes interspersed with coherently linked words. It thereby enables language to perform freely on—and as—its own terms; that is, his work points to the idea that language is able to supply endless possibilities for envisioning visual form. In obvious differentiation from a dictionary definition by Kosuth, Cointet's drawings are not clear-cut statements of fact but enigmatic cryptograms. As such, they bypass the strict Conceptual endeavor centered on bringing material reality directly into play.

The medium of film, a sequence of edited images projected on a screen, usually in combination with sound, unites photographic and aural or written linguistic representation with the passage of time. Numerous individual frames of a reel of developed celluloid progress seamlessly from sprocket to sprocket to present stationary viewers with a constructed, yet immaterial, reality moving in front of their eyes. With the Conceptual shift from traditional to new mediums, film, substituting a rectangular screen for canvas, was adopted subsequent to, but separately from, post–World War II experimental cinema. It provided a vantage point for mounting a critique of painting and sculpture in which these static mediums could not, in and of themselves, participate on account of being fixed in time and space as singular, two- or three-dimensional objects on a wall or on the ground.

Black-and-white films as different from each other as *I'm Too Sad to Tell You* (1971) by Dutch artist Bas Jan Ader, who moved to Southern California in 1963 for his studies, and *Picture and Sound Rushes* (1973; fig. 4.12), by Los Angeles filmmaker Morgan Fisher, use the artists themselves instead of professional, hired actors. Atypical of commercial cinema, neither artist performs in a character role or takes part in a narrative plot; both men sought to "entertain" previously inaccessible visual ideas. In his silent film, Ader faces the camera while he sheds tears for three-and-a-half minutes. In notes connected with the work, he wrote, "Descend, Rogier van der Weyden/Giovanni Bellini, tears exhaustion tears/ Picasso Guernica."[6] Ader's brief remarks stress that *I'm Too Sad to Tell You* is about siphoning off the tears of crying figures throughout the history of painting to achieve generalized and abstracted expression outside the framework of a particular story or set of circumstances. Paradoxically, the film drains all personal expression from the work by portraying an emotional state as a purely representational one—a distillation of sadness signaled only by facial contortions and falling tears.

Fisher, as a narrator of sorts, also looks directly at the camera in *Picture and Sound Rushes*, an eleven-minute black-and-white film with sound. The film's "plot" is the visualization of the process of the work's own construction, which is based on the permutations of the different combinations of picture and sound relationships that occur in film production. In the standard terminology of professional film production, "sync" refers to picture and sound taken together; "MOS" to picture

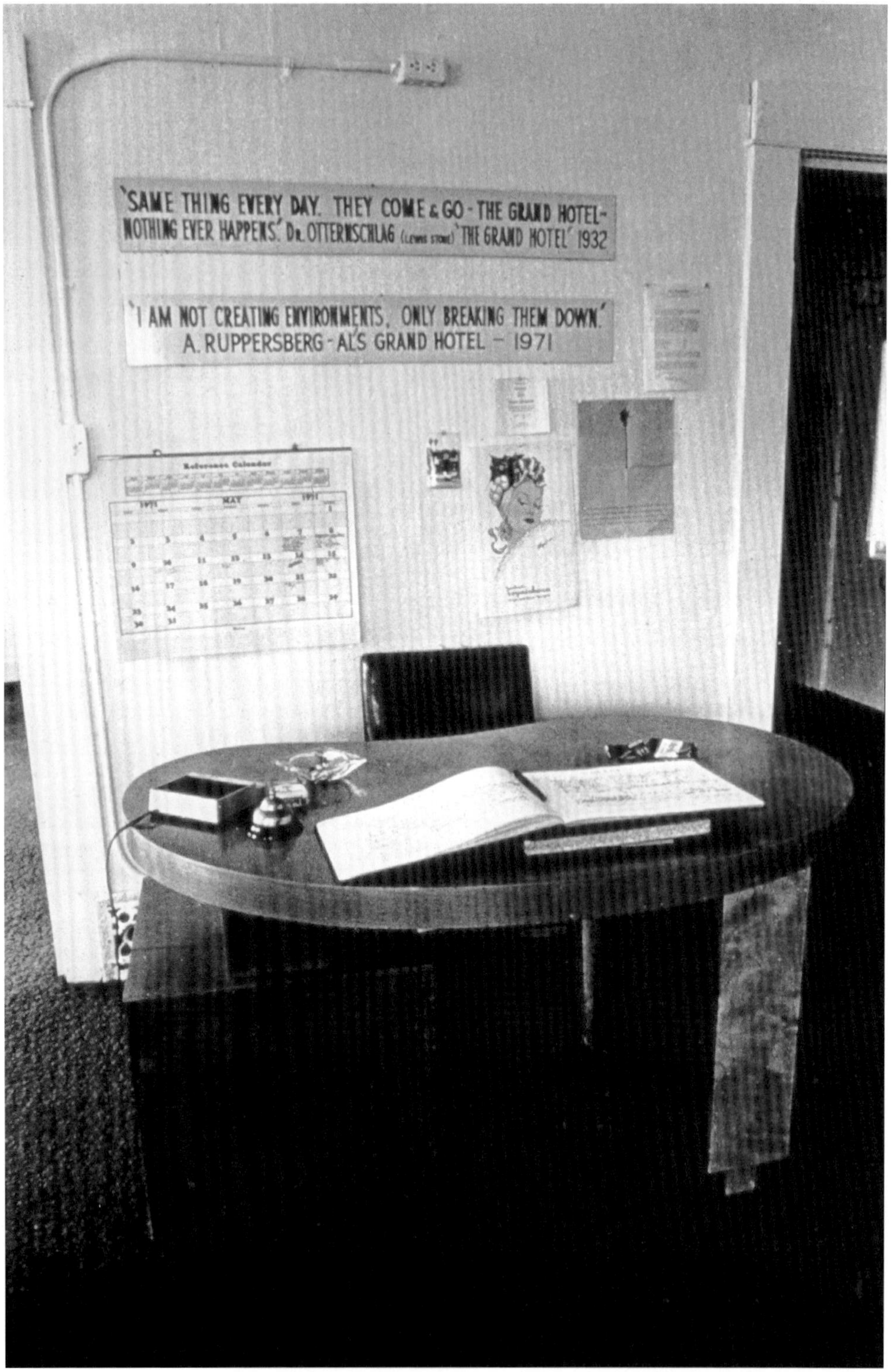

Fig. 4.13 Allen Ruppersberg, Reception desk, from *Al's Grand Hotel,* 1971. Installation at 7175 Sunset Boulevard, Hollywood, California. Photo: Courtesy of the artist.

Fig. 4.14 Allen Ruppersberg, Exterior of *Al's Grand Hotel,* 1971. Installation at 7175 Sunset Boulevard, Hollywood, California.

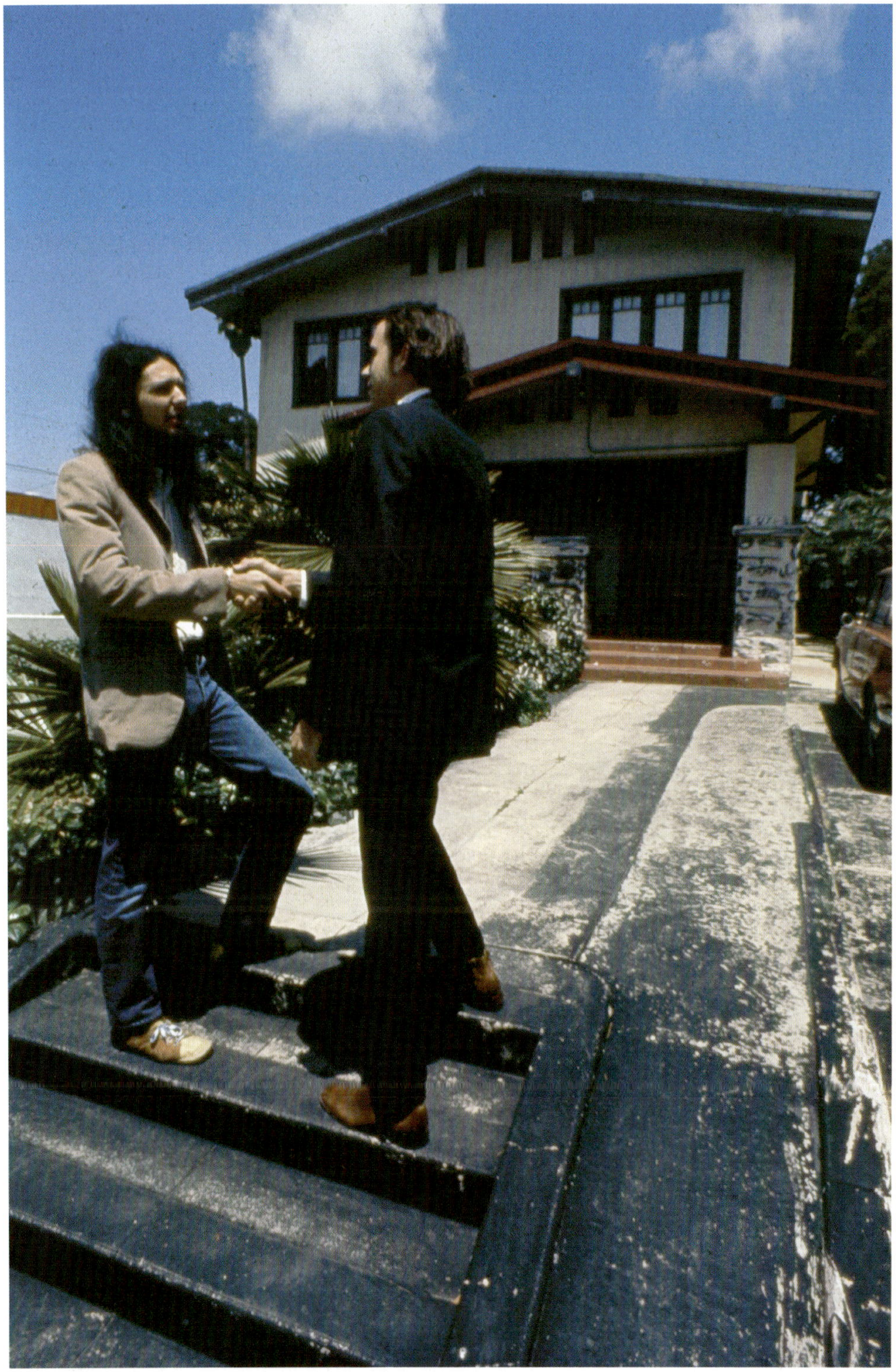

without sound; and "wild sound" to sound recorded without a picture.[7] For a fourth, and totally implausible, possibility of having neither sound nor picture, Fisher invented the term "null" to name the intervals of combined darkness and silence that the construction of *Picture and Sound Rushes* requires.

At the same time that the artist/speaker continuously delivers an improvised talk from notes about how the film has been organized, the cinematographer and the sound recordist, both offscreen, turn their equipment on and off in accordance with a preset score. This score determined the order of sync, MOS, wild sound, and "null" that are divided into a total of twenty-four segments—six segments for each of the four different sound/image combinations—during the temporal span of the film. The film opens with picture and sound taken together as Fisher is seen addressing the audience. When the film switches to MOS, he continues to speak, but we cannot hear him. Alternately, when the camera is turned off, Fisher disappears, although we continue to hear him. When the condition of "null" is in play, only a darkened screen is seen and silence reigns. This unprecedented rejection of sound and image is the ideational climax of a film whose self-referential, untraditional narrative structure gives "null" equal time with the three pictorial/auditory combinations associated with filmmaking. *Picture and Sound Rushes* presents a critique of cinematic illusion and fiction while employing the medium's own technical means.

In the late 1960s, artists seeking to take issue with illusion turned not only to photography, language, or film, but also to installation art, as exemplified by works in *State of Mind*—including *Yellow Room (Triangular)* (1973) by Bruce Nauman, *Al's Grand Hotel* (1971) by Allen Ruppersberg, and no title, a vertical column of accelerated air adapted from 1966–67 pressured-air projects by Michael Asher (see figs. 4.13–4.14; see also figs. 1.29–1.30, pp. 43–44, and fig. 1.51, p. 69). Installation works are frequently enterable. And, for the purposes of argument here, they may be defined as being experiential, environmental, expressions of their own contextual situation, or a combination of these generalized categories.

The diverse, multifaceted work of Nauman encompasses installations that fall into the category of the experiential. For *Yellow Room* to be operative, viewers need to step inside its triangular structure to become mentally and physically awash in the harsh yellow light emitted by fluorescent tubes. Nauman wrote to Konrad Fischer, who first exhibited the work in his Düsseldorf gallery, that "the room is very hard to stay inside of—I can't stay very long myself."[8]

Yellow Room inverts the traditional viewer–object relationship by removing the usual spatial divide between the two. Rather than being a discrete object located at a remove from a viewer in a shared, surrounding space, Nauman's room encapsulates viewers within its interior. Its discomforting lighting ensures that viewers do not become lulled or "wrapped in contemplation"; it stimulates a heightened perceptual attentiveness at the same time that it questions the nature of traditional sculpture.

Totally differentiated from *Yellow Room, Al's Grand Hotel*, an environmental work, was filled with, instead of emptied of, the objects contributing to its realization in Los Angeles. Of particular note, this work was not a lifelike room environment reminiscent of the well-known, influential social genre installations by Edward Kienholz (1927–94), but rather a fully functioning hotel. Offsite from a museum or gallery space in a house on Sunset Boulevard, *Al's Grand Hotel* "was like a real hotel where you could spend the night" on Fridays and Saturdays from May 7 to June 12, 1971, in one of several rooms.[9] This temporarily operative hotel/artwork brought socially based reality together with aesthetically based fiction.

The internationally influential production of Los Angeles–born Asher, one of the principal and most rigorous originators in the later 1960s of a site-specific modus operandi, is rooted in extant reality. For more than forty years, Asher has discovered ever-new ways by which to engage with facets of physical, architectural, and social reality without resorting to the creation of a previously nonexistent, material object. No title (1966–67) presages his ensuing analyses of the

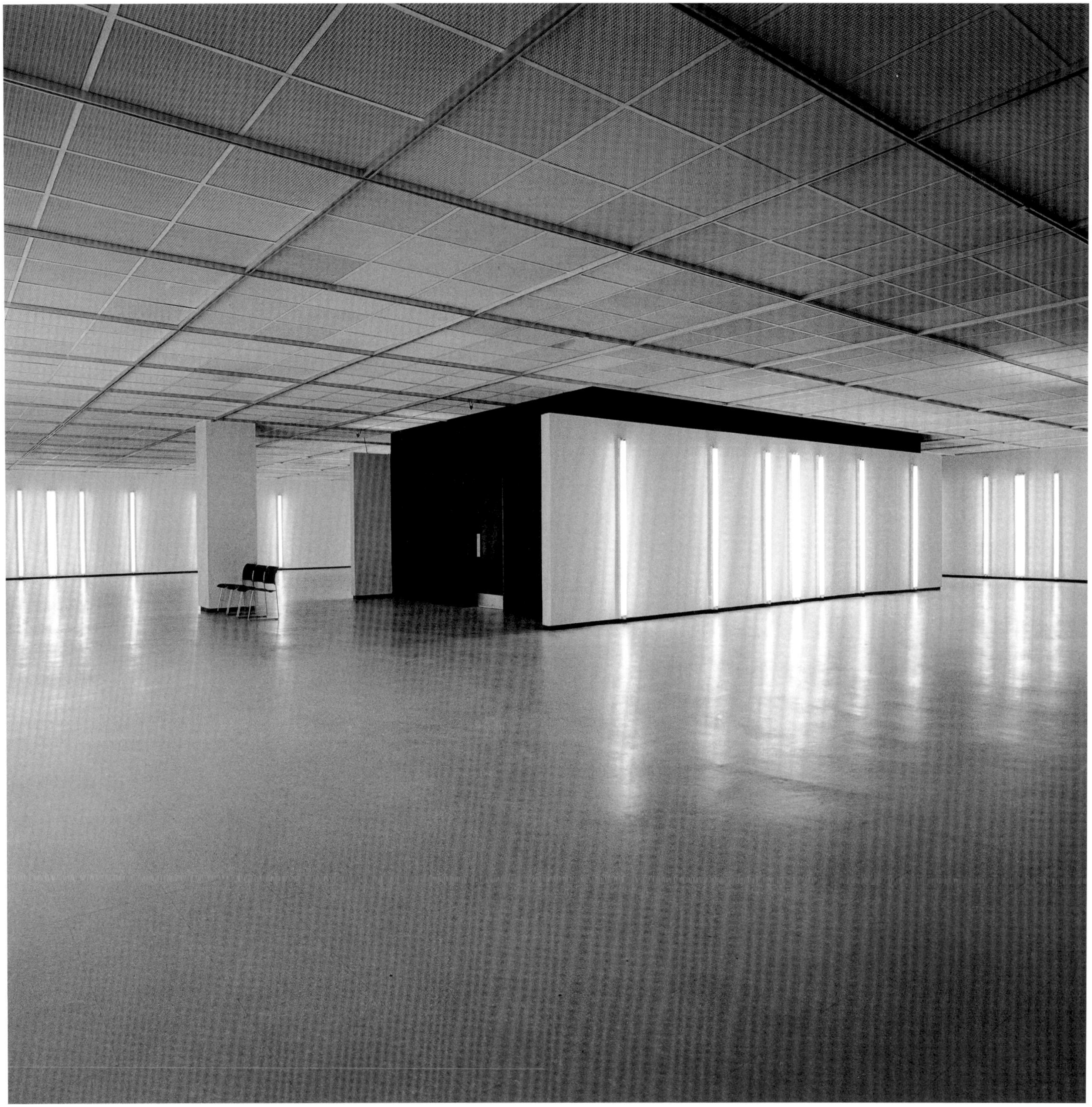

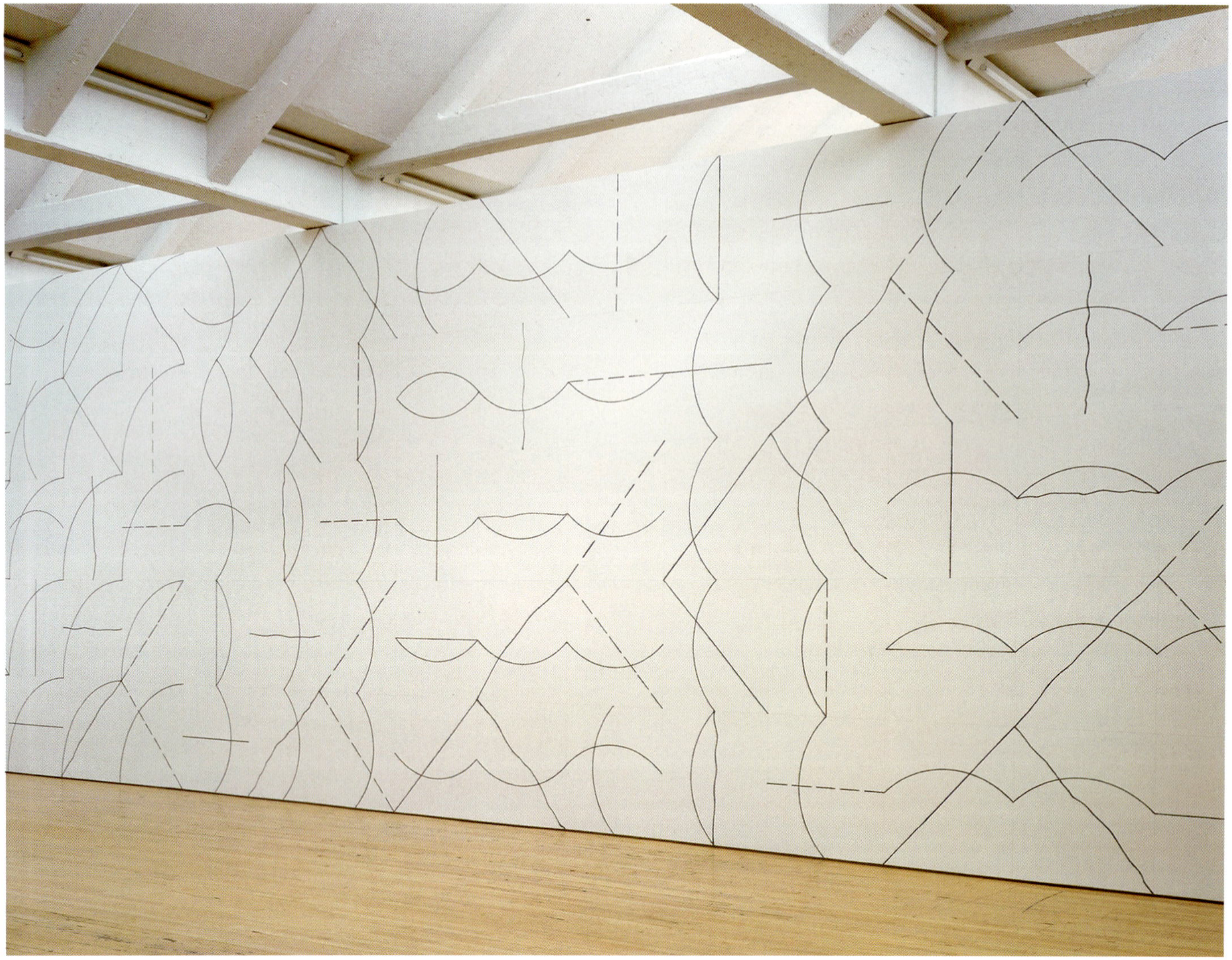

<<

Fig. 4.15 Dan Flavin, *alternating pink and "gold"* (installation view), Museum of Contemporary Art, Chicago, December 9, 1967–January 14, 1968. Photo: © Museum of Contemporary Art, Chicago. © 2010 Stephen Flavin / Artists Rights Society (ARS), New York.

Fig. 4.16 Sol LeWitt, *Wall Drawing #136: Arcs and Lines,* 1972. Two lines crossing; a 36-in. grid covering the wall; all possibilities of two lines crossing arcs from corners and sides, straight lines, not straight lines, and broken lines; two lines in each 36-in. square. Graphite and water-soluble crayon on wall; installation view at Dia Beacon. Photo: Bill Jacobson. © 2010 The LeWitt Estate / Artists Rights Society (ARS), New York.

contextual conditions underlying architectural and institutional sites. For his participation in the present exhibition, Asher has presented a column of accelerated air, a version of which was exhibited in the Whitney Museum of American Art's seminal exhibition of 1969, *Anti-Illusion: Procedures/Materials.* At the Whitney, an invisible current of air, just barely detectable to the touch, was ejected from a concealed air blower in the ceiling above a passageway between two exhibition areas. Made of the all-pervasive, yet imperceptible, substance required for breathing and existence, Asher's column of air neither visibly alters its surroundings nor impinges on the space of the viewer.

Installations of the Conceptual period challenged the material and thematic autonomy of the traditional object in its disconnection from physical and/or social reality by contending with the entirety of their exhibition container. A comparative look at relevant work in this regard by Dan Flavin (1933–96), Sol LeWitt (1928–2007), Daniel Buren (b. 1938), and Maria Nordman (b. 1943) illustrates various approaches to the conflation of a work's content and context. Installations by East Coast artists Flavin and LeWitt embody the mural confines of the spaces in which they are shown within the content of the work—the former by means of fluorescent light fixtures and the latter in *Wall Drawings.* For Flavin's first solo museum exhibition in December 1967 at the Museum of Contemporary Art, Chicago, he embraced the museum's main, ground-floor exhibition space within the totality of a multipart work, *alternating pink and "gold"* (1967; fig. 4.15), which consisted of fifty-four eight-foot fluorescent tubes. The artist divided the fixtures, mounted perpendicularly at baseboard level, between the museum's six available walls; he used a serial progression based on a two-foot interval measured outward from each wall's center, where the alternating pink and yellow lamps were paired. With his radical move of constructing a work from a commonly (until recently) and commercially available lighting system, Flavin was able to illuminate the outer boundaries of exhibition areas rather than allowing walls to stand merely as neutral backdrops. The pink and yellow rays of light in the Chicago work—in this particular case conceived specifically for a given architectural situation—permeated the interior of an otherwise vacant space to fill it with an almost palpable, luminescent ambiance.

Comparable with Flavin's light-filled spaces, LeWitt's pencil, crayon, or chalk *Wall Drawings* from the 1970s similarly "draw" their supporting walls into the work's overall content to present an all-encompassing environment (fig. 4.16). Generated by a predetermined system of lines, repeated, open, linear forms enmesh with the walls of their architectural surrounds.

Pushing the thematic investigation of art's support beyond the walls of the exhibition spaces, French artist Buren, based in Paris, has worked in situ, as he phrases it, since 1967. His site-specific works since that time have been governed by the placement of vertically striped material of alternating white and colored bands. They have often, moreover, been realized outside of conventional museum or gallery spaces. An exhibition at the Wide White Space Gallery, Antwerp, *Travail in situ* (1969; figs. 4.17–4.18), conjoined the traditional bifurcation of interior and exterior exhibition space by means of vertically striped paper, scaled to the invitational poster, which the artist glued both to the building's plinth outside and to one of the gallery's walls inside. The running length of the outdoor stripes, which extended from a hydrant some distance from the entryway door, determined the length of the indoor stripes. Like ensuing works by Buren, *Travail in situ* could not be physically disconnected or intellectually disassociated from its architectural and institutional site.

Nordman, working internationally as well as in California, has chosen to confront the observable world without resorting to representational forms such as photography or video. With the construction of moveable walls in the enclosed space of her former studio at 1014 Pico Boulevard, Los Angeles, for *Untitled 1969–* (1969–), Nordman defined illumination from the sun as a major component of her oeuvre. The rays from the sun serve as the artist's medium in conjunction with architecture and,

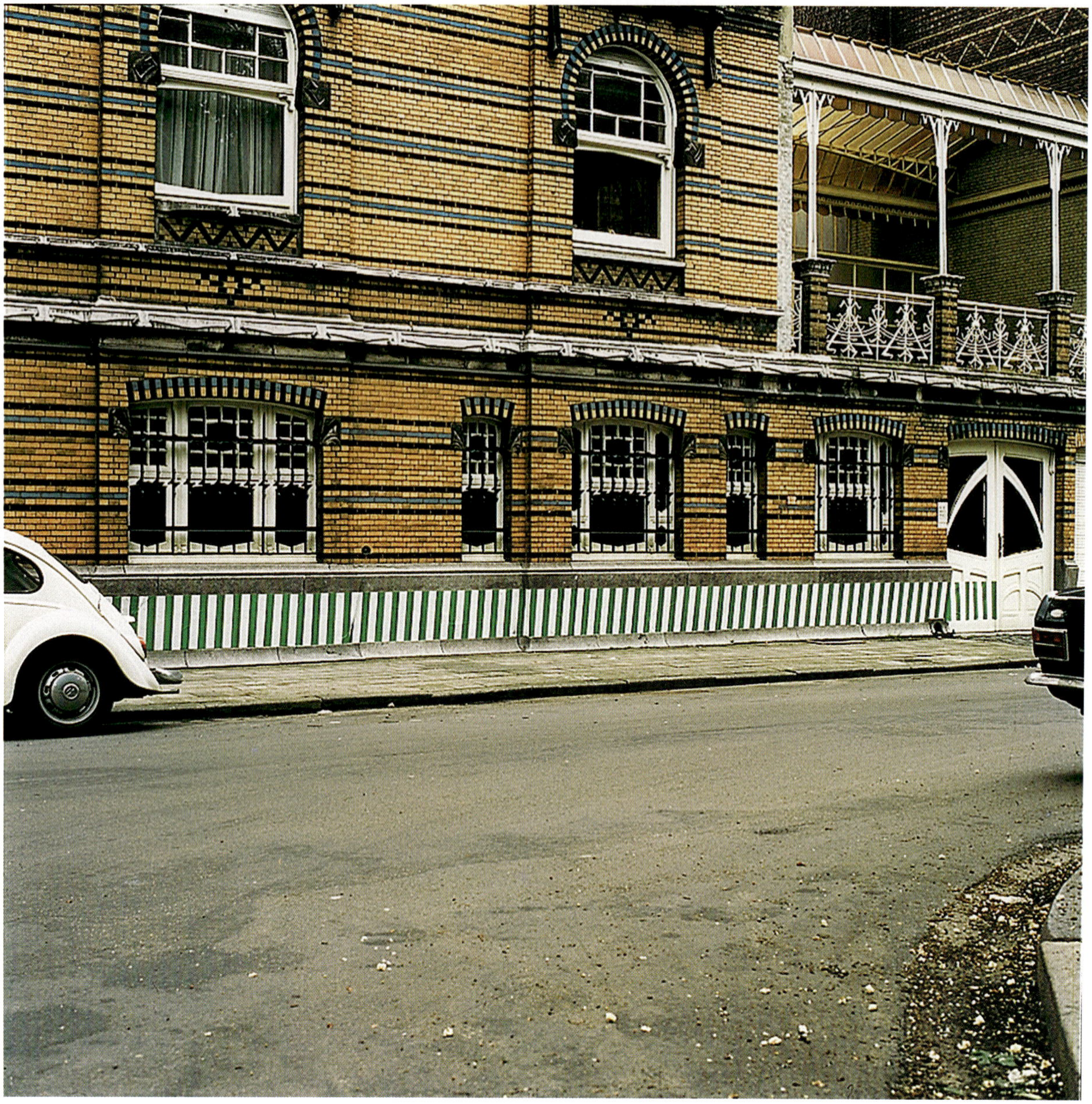

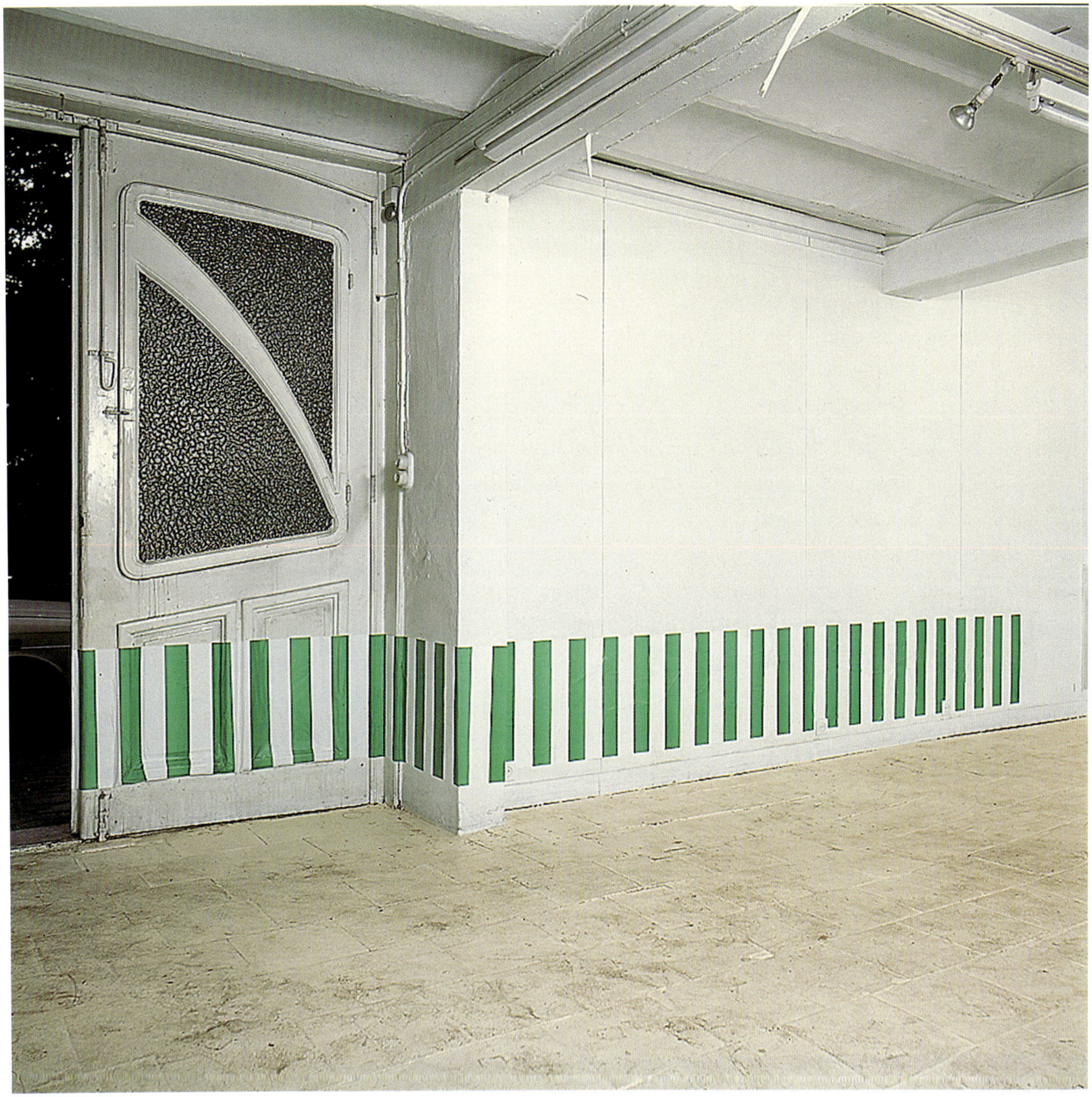

Figs. 4.17–4.18 Daniel Buren, *Photo-souvenir: Sans titre, travail in situ* (detail), 1969. Wide White Space Gallery, Antwerp, 1969. © D.B.-ADAGP, Paris / Artists Rights Society, New York / ADAGP, Paris.

>>
Fig. 4.19 Maria Nordman, *INTER-PRESENCING, MOVEABLE WALLS*, 1969–. Textual image. Courtesy of the artist.

significantly, with architecture in the context of urban life. Natural light as directed by the artist has allowed for unmediated perceptual and conceptual experience of the work.

When *Untitled 1969–* is set up, the sun entering through a slit in the door casts light into a room entirely painted black. In the course of the day, the light, changing in its intensity, moves around the walls and/or is absorbed by them. The walls sit on wheels and therefore may be repositioned from time to time. The continuously shifting relationship between light, shadows, and mural surfaces defines materiality in terms of luminosity, while the walls sometimes disappear into darkness. Subsequent works would similarly question the traditionally fixed image, which exists at a remove from firsthand interaction between perceiving subject and perceived object.

Considering art to be an activity involving cooperation and rejecting terminology such as "viewer," "spectator," or "observer," Nordman prefers the notion of the "the unknown person" or of "any person arriving by chance." She repudiates language that has long been associated with standing back from an art object and which presupposes an informed audience conditioned to looking at art in spaces exclusively reserved for such a purpose.

In marked contrast to the material and experiential components characterizing most installation-based works, *I Assumed* (1972, fig. 4.20) by California artist John Knight exists linguistically in the mind. Knight conceived this work in response to an invitation from a short-lived alternative space in Cambridge, Massachusetts. Since he was not able to visit the actual space, he imagined fifty features it might have. Statements printed individually on index cards represent conjectures such as "The space to appear new but be quite old" or "The space to be on the third floor." By using language to propose probable and particular attributes an exhibition facility could have, *I Assumed* constructs a space to be entered mentally. It also assumes viewer participation by highlighting, within its linguistically based structure, the imaginative processes required not only for art production but also for its reception.

Installation practices, with their concomitant attention to architecture and walls, on occasion, dovetail with works that fall into the category of performance art. This happens in *Changing Walls* (1971), a slide projection work by UC Berkeley professor Jim Melchert (see figs. 1.79–1.82, pp. 94–95). Slides filling a carousel, first, detail the total covering of a white, papered surface of a wall with red paint and, subsequently, the tearing off of the paper to lay bare the white wall underneath it. Painting becomes an enactment of its own process, while the work joins the self-referential, Conceptual critique of the purported white-wall neutrality of the gallery.

Performance art—with roots in Allan Kaprow's (1927–2006) Happenings and the international Fluxus events that began in the late 1950s—casts a wide net in terms of its subject matter, as the large percentage of works in *State of Mind* suggests. One-time works are documented by a series of photographs or time-based mediums, such as Super-8 film and video.

Integral to performance art in a variety of ways, video, a medium that first gained aesthetic currency in the late 1960s and early 1970s, serves above and beyond its capability to simply document a performed event. With an ability to trace movement in any and all directions, the video camera enables the production of works that, dealing with spatial effects, take place on a screen in actual time, as evinced, for example, in works by Peter d'Agostino. Very differently, video also makes possible sustained, indelible narration by the artist, appearing "in person," who, viewable on a monitor as witnessed in *A Budding Gourmet* (1974) by Martha Rosler, may be watched over and over again by anyone, anywhere, anytime (see fig. 1.40, p. 54).

D'Agostino's black-and-white, three-channel *Walk Series* (1973–74) demonstrates how the video camera can serve as an eye—independently from the actual eye of the artist—for tracking and registering movement in relation to whatever route the artist has chosen (see figs. 2.17–2.18, pp. 149–51). Sound in this work, having been recorded in tandem with the image (not separately from it, which occurs in making a film), conjoins with the representation of the camera's pictorial path. In *Walk Series,*

MARIA NORDMAN ***INTER- PRESENCING***

MOVEABLE WALLS 1968 - 9 - -

FOR ANY PERSON ARRIVING BY CHANCE OR BY CHOICE

from a street context during daytime

into a black room having black-painted walls on wheels:

drywall black latex metal wheels

IN A BLACK ROOM WITH TWO DOORS & AN ANTE-ROOM ON STREET LEVEL

WITH THE TIME & SITE AS PART OF THE CHOICE OF THE WORK

FOR ANY PERSON ARRIVING --

the panels are positioned & re-positioned from time to time

IN CONCERT WITH CHANGES IN THE ATMOSPHERIC PROJECTIONS

THE WALLS OF SHADOWS &

THE WALLS THEMSELVES EXCHANGE POSITIONS. \

UNPREDICTABLY WITH THE CONDITIONS

OF THE TIME OF DAY

a continuous work for a street-level siting --

first opened on Pico Santa Monica

this text & its layout constitutes part of the work

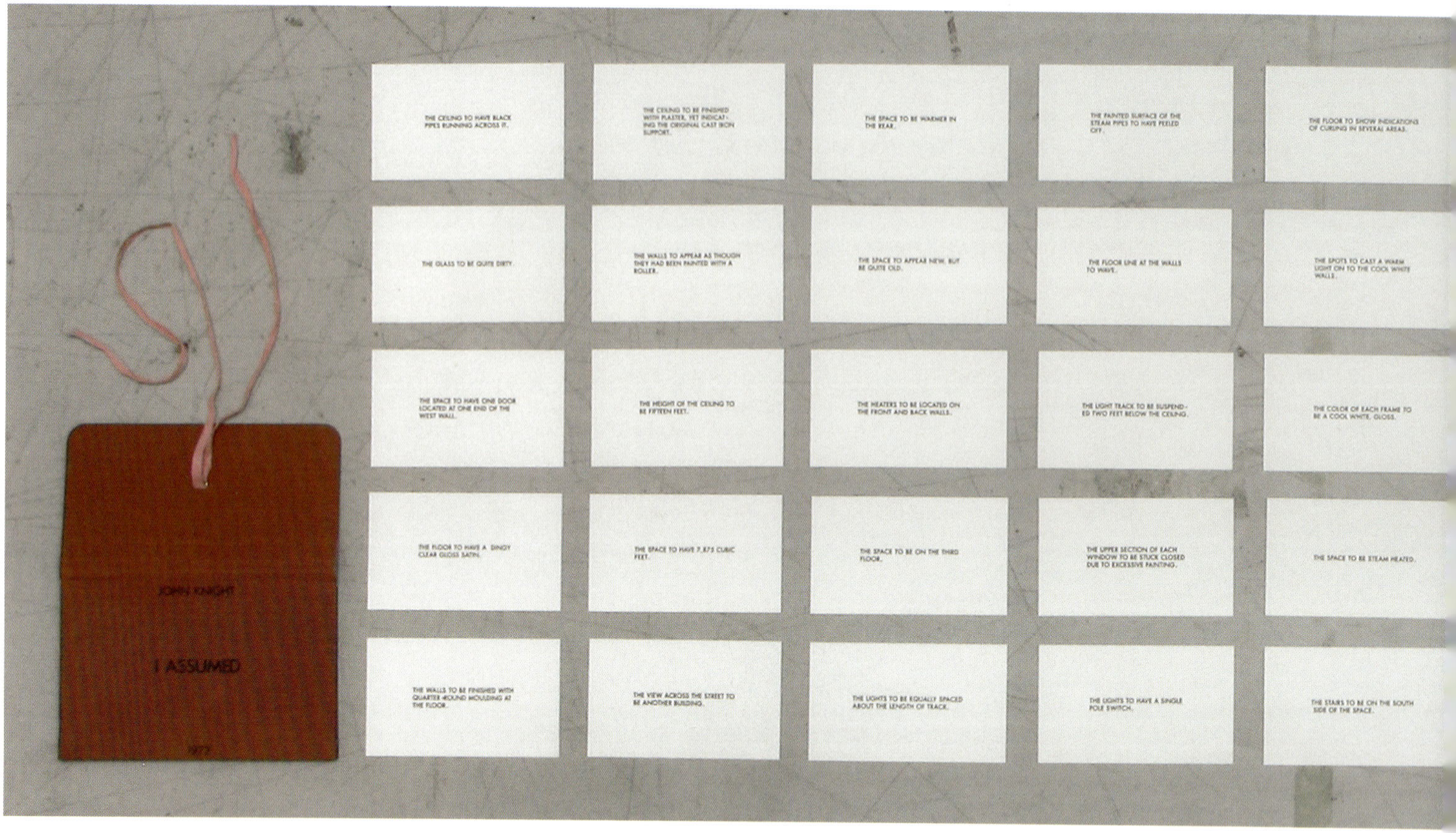
JOHN KNIGHT
I ASSUMED
THE CEILING TO HAVE BLACK PIPES RUNNING ACROSS IT.
THE CEILING TO BE FINISHED WITH PLASTER, YET INDICATING THE ORIGINAL CAST IRON SUPPORT.
THE SPACE TO BE WARMER IN THE REAR.
THE PAINTED SURFACE OF THE STEAM PIPES TO HAVE PEELED OFF.
THE FLOOR TO SHOW INDICATIONS OF CURLING IN SEVERAL AREAS.
THE GLASS TO BE QUITE DIRTY.
THE WALLS TO APPEAR AS THOUGH THEY HAD BEEN PAINTED WITH A ROLLER.
THE SPACE TO APPEAR NEW, BUT BE QUITE OLD.
THE FLOOR LINE AT THE WALLS TO WAVE.
THE SPOTS TO CAST A WARM LIGHT ON TO THE COOL WHITE WALLS.
THE SPACE TO HAVE ONE DOOR LOCATED AT ONE END OF THE WEST WALL.
THE HEIGHT OF THE CEILING TO BE FIFTEEN FEET.
THE HEATERS TO BE LOCATED ON THE FRONT AND BACK WALLS.
THE LIGHT TRACK TO BE SUSPENDED TWO FEET BELOW THE CEILING.
THE COLOR OF EACH FRAME TO BE A COOL WHITE, GLOSS.
THE FLOOR TO HAVE A DINGY CLEAR GLOSS SATIN.
THE SPACE TO HAVE 7,875 CUBIC FEET.
THE SPACE TO BE ON THE THIRD FLOOR.
THE UPPER SECTION OF EACH WINDOW TO BE STUCK CLOSED DUE TO EXCESSIVE PAINTING.
THE SPACE TO BE STEAM HEATED.
THE WALLS TO BE FINISHED WITH QUARTER-ROUND MOULDING AT THE FLOOR.
THE VIEW ACROSS THE STREET TO BE ANOTHER BUILDING.
THE LIGHTS TO BE EQUALLY SPACED ABOUT THE LENGTH OF TRACK.
THE LIGHTS TO HAVE A SINGLE POLE SWITCH.
THE STAIRS TO BE ON THE SOUTH SIDE OF THE SPACE.

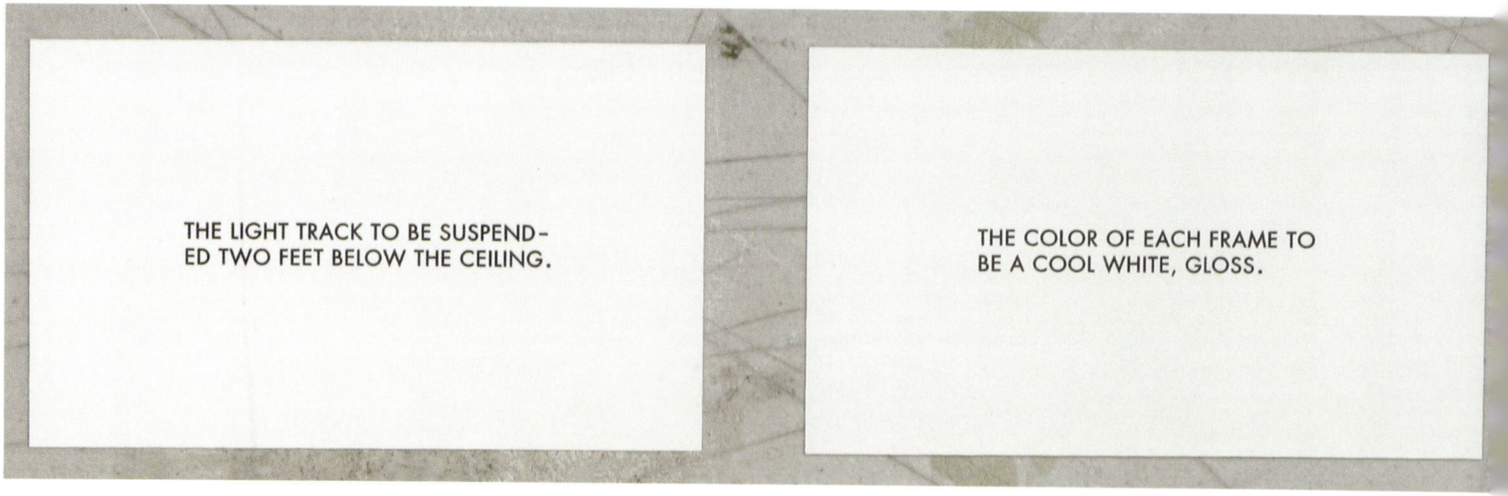
THE LIGHT TRACK TO BE SUSPEND-
ED TWO FEET BELOW THE CEILING.
THE COLOR OF EACH FRAME TO
BE A COOL WHITE, GLOSS.

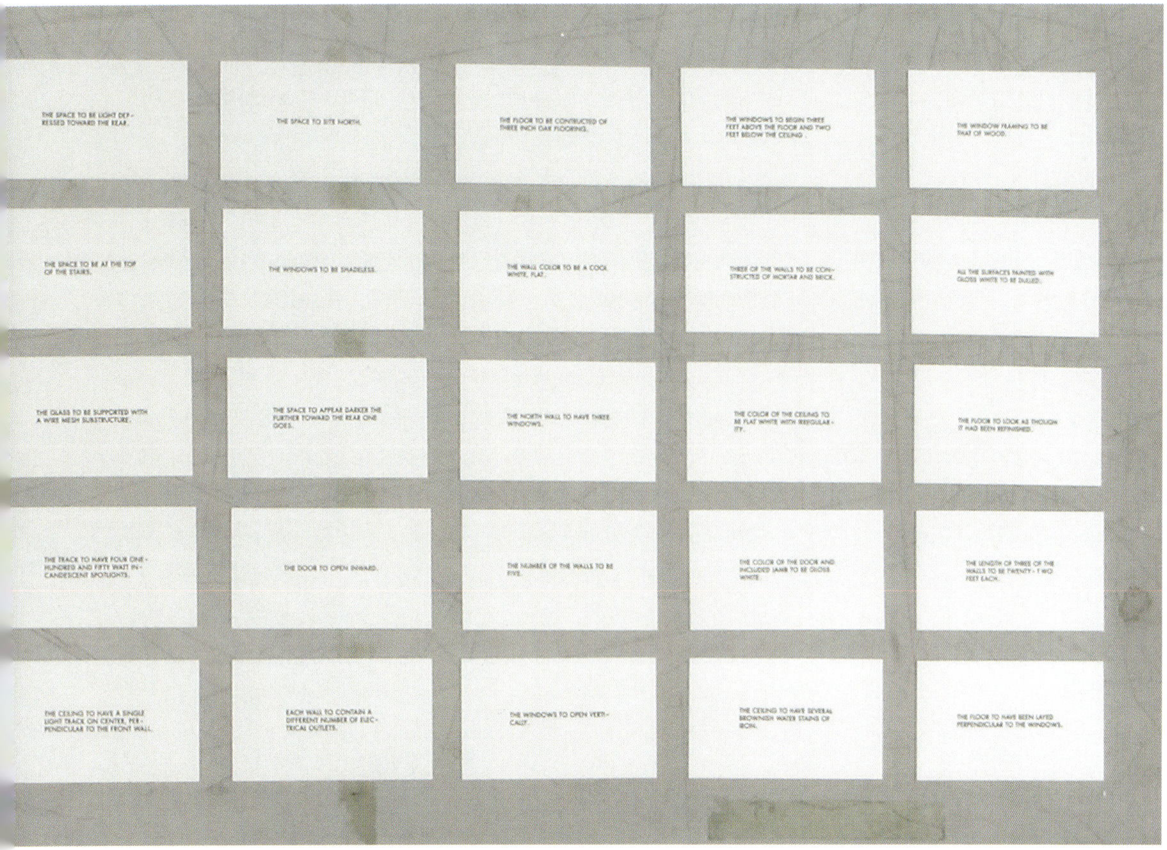

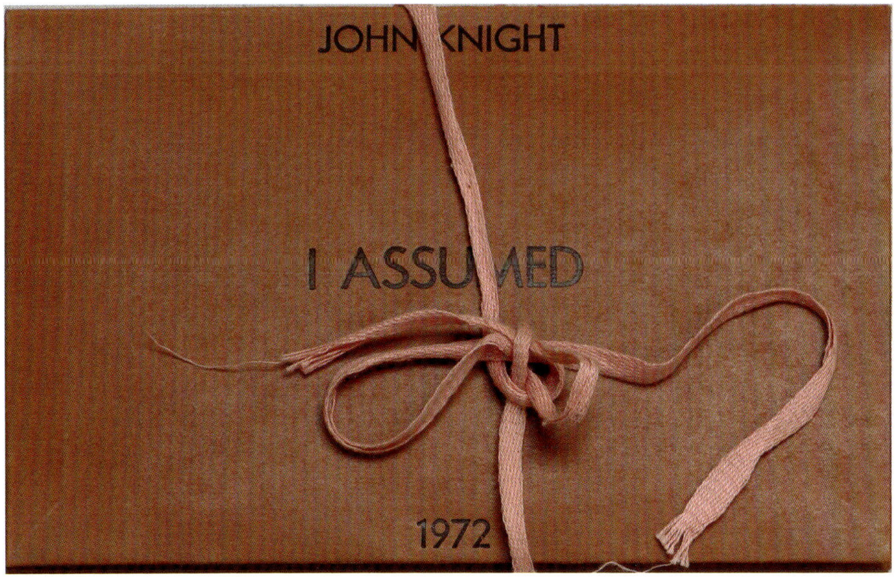

Fig. 4.20 John Knight, *I Assumed,* 1972. Fifty index cards and handmade envelope; cards: 3 × 5 in. each; envelope: 4 ½ × 7 in.

>>
Fig. 4.21 Adrian Piper, *Catalysis III* (detail), 1970. Performance documentation: three black-and- photographs on Baryta paper; 16 × 16 in. each. Collection of the Generali Foundation Collection, Vienna. © Generali Foundation and APRA Foundation. Photo: Rosemary Mayer.

d'Agostino succeeds in creating visual and audible effects that result from pursuing a course that first includes a walk at the edge of a flat, gravel-covered roof of a building; then along a cyclone fence in a city park; and, thereafter, in the direction of the freeway and Pacific Ocean. He thus creates a viewing/listening experience that is based in given reality but is beholden as well to the nature of the recording mechanism. The work, in short, expresses the peregrinations of artist-with-camera by means of visual blurring punctuated by clarity of focus as well as by the audible crunching of gravel beneath his feet or by the sound of cars or pounding waves.

Unlike d'Agostino's "narrative," which is contingent on video's ability to express movement by a camera through time and space in any and all directions, Rosler's *A Budding Gourmet,* made while she was a graduate student in art at UC San Diego, relies on video's capacity to focus, and remain trained, on whatever scenario is taking place in front of the camera lens. In this case, the camera follows Rosler as she gives a verbal presentation over a nearly eighteen-minute time span while other visual material, such as color photographs, are added. *A Budding Gourmet* (fig. 1.40, p. 54), initially in the form of a text written on a series of mailed postcards, was Rosler's first video, a medium the artist early on in her career discovered to be suitable for the purpose of expository performances laced with irony and tempered by humor. Rosler describes this black-and-white video piece as "a first-person fictional autobiography."[10] Commenting on culinary pretension—in relation to social discrepancies worldwide, whereby imperialism and consumerism feed upon each other—the work signals video's capacity for intertwining formal, feminist, and politically charged content.

In performance art, linked or not with video, the artist's body functions in large part as focus and locus. Of equal import as well, landscape or urban settings provide alternative contexts for spurring interactions that explore and attempt to mend the divide between a work of art and lived reality. Works performed by Howard Fried and Terry Fox illustrate aspects of the incorporation of an artist's corporeal presence, while works by Bonnie Sherk occurred outside of traditional exhibition spaces. The works of East Coast artists as different from each other as Vito Acconci (b. 1940) and Adrian Piper (b. 1948) share affinities of method and intent with their West Coast contemporaries.

Fried's *Inside the Harlequin: Approach-Avoidance III and II* (1971) is made up of two Super-8 films (transferred to video with sound, including that of the projector; see figs. 1.58–1.59, p. 75; see also figs. 2.13–2.14, p. 142–43). The artist interacts with the mural partitions of his studio in a work that fuses installation and performance modalities. His interaction includes hoisting himself up walls to dangle precariously while carrying unwieldy objects from room to room. The complicated narrative seemingly leads nowhere despite much arduous, back-and-forth activity, but the work metaphorically paints a picture of an artist wrestling with his workspace. He grapples with the work itself by confronting head-on the physical obstacles and psychological hurdles inherent in the creative process. Speaking about *Inside the Harlequin,* Fried maintained that he could ultimately "dissociate [himself] from those objects" and did "not have to be trapped in any one position."[11]

In Fox's *Levitation* (1970), the artist's body is also a central component of the work (see figs. 1.69–1.70, pp. 82–83). The principal element of resistance, in this case, is not that of external objects or spatial barriers but of gravity. Gravity plays a key, if invisible, role in *Levitation,* a work about endeavoring to give free reign to the human spirit by extricating it from corporeal limitation.

Levitation, on view at the Richmond Art Center before its closure by city officials, consisted of a large mound of earth with the imprint of the artist's body pressed into it. A poster on the door of the exhibition space described Fox's procedure for making the work and its parts: procuring of the earth; preliminary fasting; preparing the ring of the artist's blood and the four plastic tubes, respectively containing blood, water, urine, and milk, that radiated from the performance area; and sprinkling dust on top of the earth to suggest "that thou art dust and unto dust thou shall return."[12] The indentation of Fox's

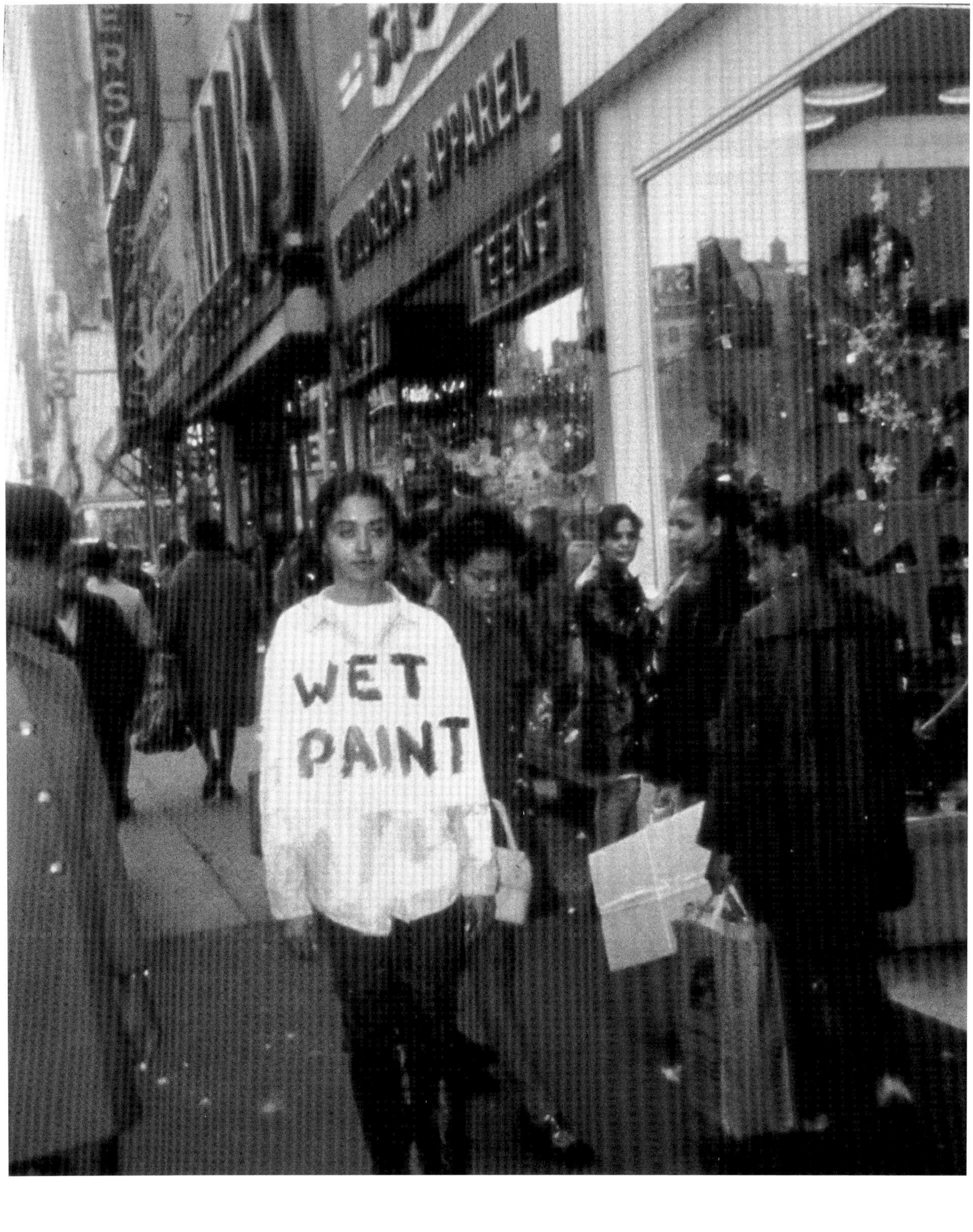
APPAREL
WET
PAINT

body resulted from a six-hour attempt "to levitate his body into the space he [had] created" and thereby to symbolically fill the exhibition space with his own mental powers and spirit while treating earthy and earthly matter as a ground.[13]

Where Fox used a space reserved for the display of art for the creation of *Levitation,* Sherk dramatically defied the conventions of presenting art by installing herself in unexpected locations in and around San Francisco. For the realization of *Public Lunch* (1971), she ate her lunch one Saturday afternoon in February not simply in the lion house of the San Francisco Zoo, but in the cage adjacent to where the large cats were being fed (see fig. 1.13, p. 27).[14] The aim was not to draw attention to herself alone but to foster a greater awareness of environments in the day-to-day surroundings in which animals and humans alike partake of the existing scenery. Situated alongside the beasts in their cages, Sherk included herself as an animal/object to be pondered. In this way, she staged a kind of one-person tableau vivant outside of the fictional framework of theater.

During the early 1970s, Piper was also carrying out actions in the public arena rather than in the context of art exhibition spaces. In her *Catalysis* series, "she was thinking more and more about [herself] as a three-dimensional object and . . . the difference between human objects, that is objects who have subjectivity, and other kinds of objects that do not, other kinds of nonsentient objects."[15] Photographs document Piper's works, which were performed anonymously in New York City. For *Catalysis I* (1970), she rode the subway at rush hour wearing clothes with a terrible stench. For *Catalysis III* (1970; fig. 4.21), she walked down a crowded Manhattan street and through a department store while wearing a "wet paint" sign across her chest. And for *Catalysis IV* (1970–71), she stuffed a hand towel into her mouth as she made her way through the streets. Not unlike Sherk, and during the same time period, Piper inserted herself into the non-art context of city spaces and streets as a socially incongruous object of display and, presumably, of dismay.

As opposed to performed works by Sherk and Piper, which severed all connection with museum or gallery enclosures, Acconci's *Room Piece (Room Situation: A Situation Using a Room)* (1970; fig. 4.22) reversed the traditional object and exhibition space relationship. Over the course of three weekends in January, the artist deposited items from his New York apartment on Christopher Street into the Gain Ground Gallery on West 80th Street. Whenever he needed something from the exhibition, he borrowed it temporarily and then returned it. By transferring household objects and personal effects into the setting of a gallery, and by acting as a go-between, Acconci breached the normally intransigent divide between art and non-art spheres of operation as well as the divide between public and domestic space, merging the one with the other.

Acconci's exhibition demonstrates yet one more initiative in Conceptualism's challenge to the autonomy of the singular, static object hanging on a wall or positioned discretely in an exhibition space. Whether by photographic, linguistic, installational, time-based, or performative means, the artists in *State of Mind,* along with their geographically widespread contemporaries, have broken new visual and intellectual ground in their reevaluation of the traditional painted or sculptural object. Replacing conventional materials and methods, works of Conceptual art—whether created by artists living in California, on the East Coast, or in Europe in the late 1960s and early 1970s—dramatically occasioned the reassessment of the traditional two- and three-dimensional art object in view of its former "detachment" from the real world, both materially and metaphorically. This reassessment has encompassed a broad range of subjects that, in one way or another, contend with, while seeking to counter, illusion on a multiplicity of fronts from the spatio-temporal to the sociopolitical. To this end, so-called Conceptual artists have taken the continuously evolving relationship between art and non-art reality to yet another level of investigation. They have thus succeeded in delivering new messages by mediums, means, and methodologies previously exempt from objects of art once defined, and circumscribed, by the traditional confines of painting and sculpture.

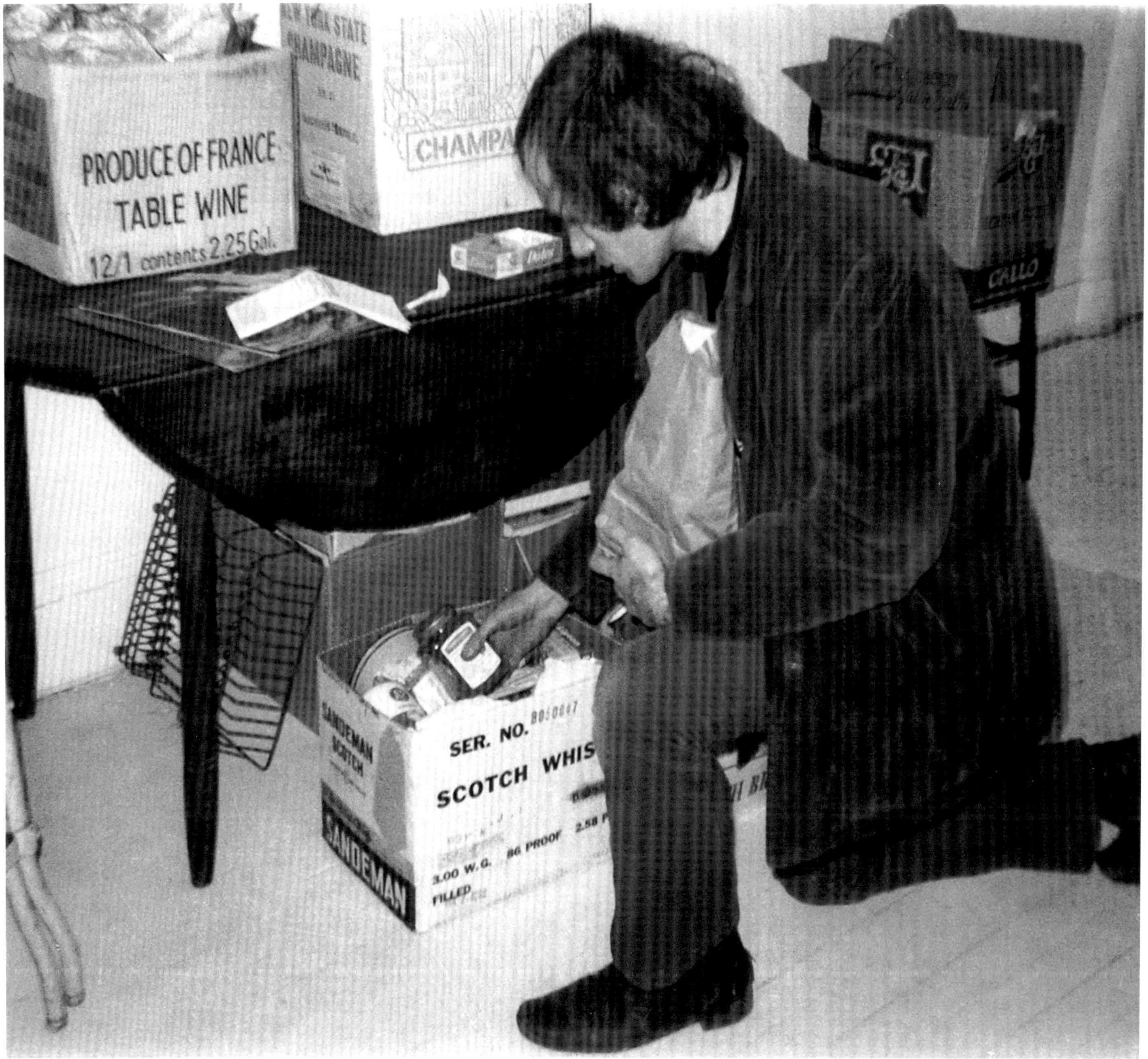

Fig. 4.22 Vito Acconci, *Room Piece (Room Situation: A Situation Using a Room)* (detail), January 1970. Activity/installation; three weekends, varying times each day; variable dimensions. © Vito Acconci. Image: Courtesy Acconci Studio, New York.

NOTES

With special thanks to Jesse Feiman.

1 Kim Levin, "Helen and Newton Harrison: New Grounds for Art," *Arts Magazine* 52, no. 6 (February 1978): 126.

2 See Carol Hall, "Environmental Artists: Sources and Directions," in *Art in the Land: A Critical Anthology of Environmental Art*, ed. Alan Sonfist (New York: E. P. Dutton, 1983), 24–25.

3 Baldessari quoted in *John Baldessari: Works 1966–1981,* ed. John Baldessari, R. H. Fuchs, Nelleke van Maaren, and Anna H. Berger (Eindhoven: Stedelijk Van Abbemuseum; Essen: Essen Museum Folkwang, 1981), 6.

4 Ger van Elk, interview with Christophe Cherix in *In & Out of Amsterdam: Travels in Conceptual Art, 1960–1976,* ed. Christophe Cherix (New York: Museum of Modern Art, 2009), 82.

5 Van Elk, interview with Gijs van Tuyl in *Reflection and Reality/Reflexion und Realitat* (Amsterdam: Visual Arts Office for Abroad of the Ministry for Cultural Affairs, Recreation and Social Welfare, 1976), 10.

6 Ann Goldstein, "Bas Jan Ader," in *Reconsidering the Object of Art: 1965–1975,* ed. Ann Goldstein and Anne Rorimer (Los Angeles: Museum of Contemporary Art; Cambridge, MA: MIT Press, 1995), 47.

7 In the early days of sound, a German émigré director working in Hollywood spoke English with an accent. When he wanted to shoot a silent scene, he would say, "We will shoot 'mit out sound,'" using the German word *mit* in place of the English *with.* The crew's notes on the slate thus developed into "MOS" and became a useful shorthand that is still used.

8 Nauman quoted in "Catalogue Raisonné #229," in *Bruce Nauman,* ed. Neal Benezra et al. (Minneapolis: Walker Art Center, 1994), 261.

9 Allen Ruppersberg, "Interview," in *Guest Informant: You and Me or The Art of Give and Take; Allen Ruppersberg,* ed. Constance M. Lewallen (Los Angeles: Santa Monica Museum of Art, 2009).

10 Glenn Phillips, ed., *California Video: Artists and Histories* (Los Angeles: Getty Research Institute and J. Paul Getty Museum, 2008), 199.

11 Brenda Richardson, "Howard Fried: The Paradox of Approach-Avoidance," *Arts Magazine* 45, no. 8 (Summer 1971): 31.

12 Suzanne Foley, "Artists: Terry Fox," in *Space/Time/Sound: Conceptual Art in the San Francisco Bay Area; The 1970s,* ed. Suzanne Foley and Constance M. Lewallen (San Francisco: San Francisco Museum of Modern Art, 1980), 61.

13 Foley, 61.

14 See Foley, "Artists: Bonnie Sherk," 81.

15 Adrian Piper, "Xenophobia and the Indexical Present II: Lecture," in *Selected Writings in Meta-Art 1966–1992,* vol. 1 of *Out of Order, Out of Sight* (Cambridge, MA: MIT Press, 1996), 262.

ARTIST BIOGRAPHIES

ADAM II (THE LATE PAUL COTTON)
Born 1939, Fitchburg, Massachusetts
BA, University of Rochester, New York, 1961
MA, University of Rochester, 1965
MA, University of California, Berkeley, 1967
Lives and works in Oakland, California

BAS JAN ADER
Born 1942, Winschoten, the Netherlands
BFA, Otis Art Institute, Los Angeles, 1965
MFA, Claremont University Center, California, 1967
Lived in Los Angeles, 1963–75
Died 1975, at sea

TERRY ALLEN
Born 1943, Wichita, Kansas
BFA, Chouinard Art Institute, Los Angeles, California, 1966
Lives and works in Santa Fe, New Mexico

ANT FARM

CHIP LORD
Born 1944, Cleveland, Ohio
BArch, Tulane University, New Orleans, Louisiana, 1968
Lives and works in San Francisco

HUDSON MARQUEZ
Born 1947, New Orleans, Louisiana
Attended Tulane University and Newcomb Art School, New Orleans, Louisiana
Lives and works in Los Angeles

DOUG MICHELS
Born 1943, Seattle, Washington
BArch, Yale University, New Haven, Connecticut, 1967
Lived and worked in Houston, Texas
Died 2003, Australia

CURTIS SCHREIER
Born 1944, Philadelphia, Pennsylvania
BArch, Rhode Island School of Design, Providence, 1967
Lives and works in San Francisco

ELEANOR ANTIN
Born 1935, New York City
BA, City College of New York, 1958
Lives and works in Solana Beach, California

ASCO

HARRY GAMBOA JR.
Born 1951, East Los Angeles
Attended California State College, Los Angeles, 1968–69
Lives and works in Los Angeles

GLUGIO "GRONK" NICANDRO
Born 1954, East Los Angeles
BFA, East Los Angeles College, 1975
MFA, California State College at Los Angeles, 1978
Lives and works in Los Angeles

WILLIE HERRÓN III
Born 1951, East Los Angeles
Attended Otis Art Institute, Los Angeles, 1971; East Los Angeles College, 1971–72
Attended Los Angeles Trade Technical College, 1972–73
Lives and works in Los Angeles

PATSSI VALDEZ
Born 1951, East Los Angeles
BFA, Otis Art Institute, Los Angeles, 1985
Attended Parsons School of Design, New York City
Lives and works in Los Angeles

MICHAEL ASHER
Born 1943, Los Angeles
BA, University of California, Irvine, 1966
Lives and works in Los Angeles

JOHN BALDESSARI
Born 1931, National City, California
BA, San Diego State College, California, 1953
Attended University of California, Berkeley, 1954–55
MA, San Diego State College, 1957
Attended Otis Art Institute, Los Angeles; Chouinard Art Institute, Los Angeles, 1957–59
Lives and works in Santa Monica, California

GARY BEYDLER
Born 1944, Los Angeles
MFA, University of California, Irvine, 1972
Lived and worked in Los Angeles
Died 2010, Los Angeles

NANCY BUCHANAN
Born 1946, Boston, Massachusetts
MFA, University of California, Irvine, 1971
Lives and works in Los Angeles

CHRIS BURDEN
Born 1946, Boston, Massachusetts
BFA, Pomona College, Claremont, California, 1969
MFA, University of California, Irvine, 1971
Lives and works in Topanga, California

VIJA CELMINS
Born 1938, Riga, Latvia
BFA, John Herron Institute, Indianapolis, Indiana, 1962
MFA, University of California, Los Angeles, 1965
Lives and works in New York City

PAUL COTTON
See Adam II (the late Paul Cotton)

ROBERT CUMMING
Born 1943, Worcester, Massachusetts
BFA, Massachusetts College of Art, Boston, 1965
MFA, University of Illinois at Urbana–Champaign, 1967
Lives and works in Whatley, Massachusetts

PETER D'AGOSTINO
Born 1945, New York City
BFA, School of Visual Arts, New York City, 1968
MA, San Francisco State University, California, 1975
Lives and works in Philadelphia, Pennsylvania

LOWELL DARLING
Born 1942, Jacksonville, Illinois
MFA, Southern Illinois University, Carbondale, 1970
Lived in Los Angeles, 1971–72
Lives and works in Rodeo, California

GUY DE COINTET
Born 1934, Paris, France
Moved to New York City, 1965, and to Los Angeles, 1968
Died 1983, Los Angeles

MORGAN FISHER
Born 1942, Washington, D.C.
BA, Harvard University, Cambridge, Massachusetts, 1964
Attended University of Southern California, Los Angeles, 1964–65
Attended University of California, Los Angeles, 1965–66
Lives and works in Santa Monica, California

TERRY FOX
Born 1943, Seattle, Washington
Attended Cornish School of Allied Arts, Seattle, 1961
Attended Accademia di Belle Arti, Rome, Italy, 1962
Lived in San Francisco, 1963–67; Paris, France, 1967–68; San Francisco, 1968–78
Lived and worked in Europe, 1978–2008
Died 2008, Cologne, Germany

HOWARD FRIED
Born 1946, Cleveland, Ohio
BFA, San Francisco Art Institute, California, 1968
MFA, University of California, Davis, 1970
Lives and works in Vallejo, California

CHARLES GAINES
Born 1944, Charleston, South Carolina
BA, Jersey City State College, New Jersey, 1966
MFA, Rochester Institute of Technology, School of Art and Design, New York, 1967
Lives and works in Los Angeles

DAVID HAMMONS
Born 1943, Springfield, Illinois
Attended Chouinard Art Institute, Los Angeles, 1966–68
Attended Otis Art Institute, Los Angeles, 1968–72
Lives and works in New York City

HELEN MAYER HARRISON AND NEWTON HARRISON

HELEN MAYER HARRISON
Born 1929, New York City
Attended Cornell University, Ithaca, New York, 1943–45
BA, Queens College, New York City, 1948
MA, New York University, New York City, 1952
Lives and works in Santa Cruz, California

NEWTON HARRISON
Born 1932, New York City
Attended Antioch College, Yellow Springs, Ohio, 1950–52
Attended Pennsylvania Academy of the Fine Arts, Philadelphia, 1955–57
BA, Yale University, New Haven, Connecticut, 1963
MFA, Yale University, 1965
Lives and works in Santa Cruz, California

JOE HAWLEY
Born 1938, Forsyth, Montana
BA, San Jose State University, San Jose, California, 1961
MA, San Jose State University, 1966
Lives and works in Cloverdale, California

MEL HENDERSON
Born 1922, Colfax, California
BFA, California College of Arts and Crafts, Oakland, 1961
Lives in Nevada City, California

LYNN HERSHMAN
Born 1941, Cleveland, Ohio
BS, Case Western Reserve University, Cleveland, 1963
MA, San Francisco State College, California, 1972
Lives and works in San Francisco

DOUGLAS HUEBLER
Born 1924, Ann Arbor, Michigan
BS, University of Michigan, 1952
MFA, University of Michigan, 1955
Lived in Newhall/Valencia, California, 1976–88
Died 1997, Truro, Massachusetts

RICHARD JACKSON
Born 1939, Sacramento, California
Attended Sacramento State College, 1959–61
Lives and works in Sierra Madre, California

STEPHEN KALTENBACH
Born 1940, Battle Creek, Michigan
BA, University of California, Davis, 1966
MA, University of California, Davis, 1967
Lives and works in Davis

ALLAN KAPROW
Born 1927, Atlantic City, New Jersey
BA, New York University, 1949
MA, Columbia University, New York, 1952
Died 2006, Encinitas, California

ROBERT KINMONT
Born 1937, Los Angeles
BFA, San Francisco Art Institute, California, 1970
MFA, University of California, Davis, 1971
Lives and works in Sonoma, California

JOHN KNIGHT
Born 1945, Hollywood, California
MFA, University of California, Irvine, 1973
Lives and works in Los Angeles

PAUL KOS
Born 1942, Rock Springs, Wyoming
Attended Georgetown University, Washington, D.C., 1961–62
BFA, San Francisco Art Institute, California, 1965
MFA, San Francisco Art Institute, 1967
Lives and works in San Francisco

SUZANNE LACY
Born 1945, Fresno, California
BA, University of California, Santa Barbara, 1965–68
Attended Fresno State College, 1969–71
MFA, California Institute of the Arts, Valencia, 1971–73
Lives and works in Marina del Ray, California

STEPHEN LAUB
Born 1945, Oakland, California
BA, University of California, Berkeley, 1968
MA, University of California, Berkeley, 1970
Lives and works in Water Mill, New York

WILLIAM LEAVITT
Born 1941, Washington, D.C.
BFA, University of Colorado, Boulder, 1963
MFA, Claremont Graduate School and University Center, California, 1967
Lives and works in Los Angeles

FRED LONIDIER
Born 1942, Lakeview, Oregon
Attended Yuba College, Marysville, California
BA, San Francisco State College, 1966
MFA, University of California, San Diego, 1972
Lives and works in La Jolla, California

MIKE MANDEL
Born 1950, Los Angeles
BA, California State College, Northridge, 1972
MFA, San Francisco Art Institute, California, 1974
Lives and works in Watertown, Massachusetts

TOM MARIONI
Born 1937, Cincinnati, Ohio
Attended Cincinnati Art Academy, 1955–59
Lives and works in San Francisco

PAUL MCCARTHY
Born 1945, Salt Lake City, Utah
Attended University of Utah, Salt Lake City, 1968–69
BFA, San Francisco Art Institute, California, 1969
MFA, University of Southern California, Los Angeles, 1972
Lives and works in Altadena, California

JIM MELCHERT
Born 1930, New Bremen, Ohio
BA, Princeton University, New Jersey, 1952
MFA, University of Chicago, Illinois, 1957
MA, University of California, Berkeley, 1961
Lives and works in Oakland, California

SUSAN MOGUL
Born 1949, New York City
BFA, Tufts University, Medford, Massachusetts, and Boston Museum of Fine Arts, 1972
Attended California Institute of the Arts, Valencia, 1973
Attended Feminist Studio Workshop, Los Angeles, 1973–75
MFA, University of California, San Diego, 1980
Lives and works in Los Angeles

LINDA MARY MONTANO
Born 1942, Saugerties, New York
MFA, University of Wisconsin, Madison, 1972
Lives and works in Saugerties

BRUCE NAUMAN
Born 1941, Fort Wayne, Indiana
BA, University of Wisconsin, Madison, 1964
MA, University of California, Davis, 1966
Lives and works in Galisteo, New Mexico

MARTHA ROSLER
Born 1943, Brooklyn, New York
BA, Brooklyn College, 1965
MFA, University of California, San Diego, 1974
Lives and works in Brooklyn

ALLEN RUPPERSBERG
Born 1944, Cleveland, Ohio
BFA, Chouinard Art Institute, Los Angeles, 1967
Lives and works in Santa Monica, California, and New York City

ED RUSCHA
Born 1937, Omaha, Nebraska
Attended Chouinard Art Institute, Los Angeles, 1956–60
Lives and works in Venice, California

SAM'S CAFÉ

MARC KEYSER
Born 1942, Salt Lake City, Utah
BA, University of Utah, Salt Lake City
BA, California State University, Hayward
Lives in Lompoc, California

TERRY KEYSER-COOPER
Born 1947, Los Angeles
BA, University of California, Berkeley
Attended MFA program, University of California, Berkeley
Lives in Reno, Nevada

DAVID SHIRE
Born 1947, Oakland, California
Attended University of California, Berkeley
BA, California State University, Hayward
Lives and works in Chico, California

DARRYL SAPIEN
Born 1950, Los Angeles
BFA, San Francisco Art Institute, California, 1972
MFA, San Francisco Art Institute, 1976
Lives and works in San Francisco

ILENE SEGALOVE
Born 1950, Los Angeles
Attended Loyola University
BFA, University of California, Santa Barbara, 1972
Lives and works in Santa Barbara

ALLAN SEKULA
Born 1951, Erie, Pennsylvania
Attended University of California, San Diego, 1968–72
Lives and works in Los Angeles

BONNIE SHERK
Born 1945, Bedford, Massachusetts
BA, Douglass College, Rutgers University, New Brunswick, New Jersey
MFA, San Francisco State College, California
Certificate in landscape architecture, San Francisco State University
Lives and works in San Francisco and New York City

ALEXIS SMITH
Born 1949, Los Angeles
BA, University of California, Irvine, 1970
Lives and works in Venice, California

BARBARA T. SMITH
Born 1931, Pasadena, California
BA, Pomona College, Claremont, California, 1953
MFA, University of California, Irvine, 1971
Lives and works in Venice, California

LARRY SULTAN
Born 1946, New York City
BA, University of California, Santa Barbara, 1968
MFA, San Francisco Art Institute, California, 1973
Lived and worked in Greenbrae, California
Died 2009, Greenbrae, California

T. R. UTHCO

DIANE ANDREWS HALL
Born 1945, Dallas, Texas
BFA, H. Sophie Newcomb College, New Orleans, Louisiana, 1967
MFA, Hoffberger School of Painting, Maryland Institute College of Art, Baltimore, 1969
Lives and works in San Francisco

DOUG HALL
Born 1944, San Francisco
BA, Harvard College, Cambridge, Massachusetts, 1966
MFA, Rinehart School of Sculpture, Maryland Institute College of Art, Baltimore, 1969
Lives and works in San Francisco

JODY PROCTER
Born 1943, Boston, Massachusetts
BA, Harvard College, Cambridge, Massachusetts, 1966
Lived and worked in San Francisco, 1969–80
Died 1998, Eugene, Oregon

GER VAN ELK
Born 1942, Amsterdam, the Netherlands
Attended Immaculate Heart College, Los Angeles, 1961–63
Lives and works in Amsterdam

WILLIAM WEGMAN
Born 1943, Holyoke, Massachusetts
BFA, Massachusetts College of Art, Boston, 1965
MFA, University of Illinois at Urbana-Champaign, 1967
Taught at California State College, Long Beach, 1970
Lives and works in New York City

JOHN WOODALL
Born 1940, Lakeland, Florida
BFA, San Francisco Art Institute, California, 1968
MFA, San Francisco Art Institute, 1969
Lives and works in Plant City, Florida

ALFRED YOUNG
Born 1936, London, England
Associate, Royal College of Art, London, 1962
Lived in California, 1968–75; New York City, 1975–88; and California, 1988–
Lives and works in Berkeley, California

WORKS IN THE EXHIBITION

Asterisks (*) indicate that the work or a related object is illustrated in the catalogue.

Adam II (the late Paul Cotton)

Rex-Erection of the Mystical Body
(1965–Eternal Present)
Keynote compilation of performance documentation; color; sound; 5:04 min.
Courtesy of the artist, Oakland, California

*Docu-Mentation of a Meating**
1969
Ditto print, with pencil notation
11 × 8¼ in.
University of California, Berkeley Art Museum and Pacific Film Archive; Museum purchase: Bequest of Thérèse Bonney, Class of 1916, by exchange, 1992.8.31
p. 111

WESTERN SUN-DAY II. BERKELEY'S LIVE OAK PARK. (The Age of Man)
April 2, 1972
Flyer: printed black on white paper, with purple rubber stamp
11 × 8½ in.
University of California, Berkeley Art Museum and Pacific Film Archive; Gift of the Naify Family, 1995.46.3.38

Bas Jan Ader

All works courtesy of Bas Jan Ader Estate & Patrick Painter Editions, Santa Monica, California, unless otherwise noted.

Fall
1970
Artist's book
7½ × 7½ in.
Collection of Steven Leiber, San Francisco, California

Four 16 mm films transferred to video; black and white; silent

*Fall I, Los Angeles**
1970
34 sec.
pp. 86–87

I'm Too Sad to Tell You
1971
3:34 min.

Night Fall
1971
4:16 min.

Untitled (Tea Party)
1972
16 mm film transferred to video; black and white; silent; 1:52 min.; edition of three

*In Search of the Miraculous (One Night in Los Angeles)**
1973
Eighteen black-and-white photographs with handwritten text in white ink
10¾ × 13½ in. each
Collection of Philip Aarons and Shelley Fox Aarons, New York
Photos: Courtesy of Bas Jan Ader Estate & Patrick Painter Editions, Santa Monica, California
p. 30

Bas Jan Ader and William Leavitt

Landslide, Brian Shitart
Feb. 13, 1969; twenty-fifth edition
Loose-leaf magazine, cover, and six sheets; heat-transfer printing process on card stock
11⅛ × 8¾ in.
Collection of Steven Leiber, San Francisco, California

Terry Allen

Terry Allen Live at Al's Grand Hotel, May 7, 1971
1971
Recording from three analog master tapes, 50 min.
Courtesy of the artist, Santa Fe, New Mexico

Ant Farm

Ant Farm Documentary Diptych (Route 66)
1970/2010
Two color photographs
11 × 14 in. each
Courtesy of Darrel and Marsha Anderson, Newport Beach, California

*Inflatocookbook**
1970
Loose-leaf book in plastic sleeve with rubber stamp title; first edition
11½ × 9¼ in.
University of California, Berkeley Art Museum and Pacific Film Archive; Purchase made possible through a bequest of Thérèse Bonney by exchange, a partial gift of Chip Lord and Curtis Schreier and gifts from an anonymous donor and Harrison Fraker, 2005.14.88, 92
p. 173

*Media Van (mobile vt studio)**
ca. 1971
Ink, collage, rubber stamp, and sticker on card stock
11 × 17 in.
University of California, Berkeley Art Museum and Pacific Film Archive; Purchase made possible through a bequest of Thérèse Bonney by exchange, a partial gift of Chip Lord and Curtis Schreier and gifts from an anonymous donor and Harrison Fraker, 2005.14.17
p. 175

*Truckstop Network: Phase One**
From the portfolio for *Truckstop Network* project
1971
Drawing with collaged elements: colored pencil, felt-tipped pen, stamped ink, India ink, embossing, stickers, and photograph
11 × 17 in.
University of California, Berkeley Art Museum and Pacific Film Archive; Gift of Chip Lord, 2006.57.7
Photo: Benjamin Blackwell
pp. 12–13

*Truckstop Network Placemat**
1971
Offset lithography (two-sided)
11 × 17 in.
University of California, Berkeley Art Museum and Pacific Film Archive; Purchase made possible through a bequest of Thérèse Bonney by exchange, a partial gift of Chip Lord and Curtis Schreier and gifts from an anonymous donor and Harrison Fraker, 2005.14.15
Photo: Benjamin Blackwell
p. 174

Truckstop Network & Truckstop Tour Video
1971/2008
Interactive video; color and black and white; 142 min.
Orange County Museum of Art; Gift of Chip Lord

Truckstop Scrapbook Page
Ca. 1971
Collage: offset lithography, Zip-a-tone, Whiteout, ink, marker, and colored pencil on paper
11 × 8½ in.
University of California, Berkeley Art Museum and Pacific Film Archive; Purchase made possible through a bequest of Thérèse Bonney by exchange, a partial gift of Chip Lord and Curtis Schreier and gifts from an anonymous donor and Harrison Fraker, 2005.14.250.6

Eleanor Antin

*100 Boots**
1971–73
Offset lithography: fifty-one black-and-white picture postcards
4½ × 7 in. each
University of California, Berkeley Art Museum and Pacific Film Archive; Museum purchase: Bequest of Phoebe Apperson Hearst, by exchange, 2010.37
Photo: Courtesy Ronald Feldman Fine Arts, New York
p. 185

*Carving: A Traditional Sculpture**
1972
144 black-and-white photographs and text panel
Photographs: 7 × 5 in. each
Collection of Gary and Tracy Mezzatesta, Burbank, California
Photo: Courtesy Ronald Feldman Fine Arts, New York
pp. 56–57

Representational Painting
1971
Eighteen black-and-white photographs
48 × 31¾ × 1½ in. framed
Courtesy of the artist and Ronald Feldman Fine Arts, New York

*Representational Painting**
1971
Video: black-and-white; silent; 38 min.
University of California, Berkeley Art Museum and Pacific Film Archive; Purchase made possible by the Norma H. Schlesinger, Andrew and Paul Spiegel Fund, 2010.43
Photo: Courtesy of the artist and Ronald Feldman Fine Arts, New York
p. 55

Asco (Glugio "Gronk" Nicandro, Patssi Valdez, Willie Herrón III, Harry Gamboa Jr.)

*First Supper (After a Major Riot)**
1974 (printed 2011)
Digital print of color photograph
26¾ × 40 in.
Courtesy of Harry Gamboa Jr.
Photo: © 1974 Harry Gamboa Jr.
p. 168

*Instant Mural**
1974 (printed 2011)
Digital print of color photograph
26¾ × 40 in.
Courtesy of Harry Gamboa Jr.
Photo: © 1974 Harry Gamboa Jr.
p. 40

*Walking Mural**
1972 (printed 2011)
Digital print of color photograph
26¾ × 40 in.
Courtesy of Harry Gamboa Jr.
Photo: © 1972 Harry Gamboa Jr.
p. 199

Michael Asher

no title
1966–67/2011
Pressured air
Dimensions variable
Courtesy of the artist, Los Angeles, California

no title*
1966
Heat-molded Plexiglas
34 × 40 in.
Collection of Carolina Bilbao and Richard Massey, Miami
Photo: Sid Hoeltzell
p. 66

John Baldessari

Baldessari Sings LeWitt
1972
Video: black and white; sound; 15 min.
Orange County Museum of Art; Museum purchase with funds provided through prior gift of Lois Outerbridge

*California Map Project Part I: California**
1969/2009
Twelve archival inkjet prints mounted on Dibond (exhibition copy, 2009)
Original work: color photographs and text
Photographs: 8¼ × 12¼ × 1¼ in. individually framed
Text: 8¼ × 10¼ × 1¼ in. framed
Courtesy of the artist, Santa Monica, California
Frontispiece

*I Am Making Art**
1971
Video: black-and-white; sound; 18:40 min.
University of California, Berkeley Art Museum and Pacific Film Archive; Purchase made possible by the Jan Boyce Fund for Contemporary Art, 2010.31
Photo: Courtesy Electronic Arts Intermix (EAI), New York
p. 103

I Will Not Make Any More Boring Art
1971
Video: black-and-white; sound; 31:17 min.
Orange County Museum of Art; Museum purchase with funds provided through prior gift of Lois Outerbridge

*Throwing Three Balls in the Air to Get a Straight Line (Best of Thirty-six Attempts)**
1973
Excerpt from artist's book
10 × 13 in.
University of California, Berkeley Art Museum and Pacific Film Archive; Gift of the Pitesky family in loving memory of Stuart F. Pitesky, Class of 1989
© John Baldessari
p. 181

*Voluble Luminist Painting for Max Kozloff**
1966–68
Acrylic on canvas
59 × 59 in.
Orange County Museum of Art; Gift of the Betty and Monte Factor Family Collection
p. 102

Gary Beydler

Stills from *Mirror*
1976
Seven color photographs mounted on mat board
11¾ × 50⅜ in.
University of California, Berkeley Art Museum and Pacific Film Archive; Anonymous gift, 1981.7.7

*Pasadena Freeway Stills**
1974
16mm film transferred to video; color; silent; 6 min.
Canyon Cinema, San Francisco, California
Photo: © Estate of Gary Beydler, courtesy of Academy Film Archive, Los Angeles, California
p. 98

*Venice Pier**
1976
16mm film transferred to video; color; sound; 16 min.
Canyon Cinema, San Francisco, California
Photos: © Estate of Gary Beydler, courtesy of Academy Film Archive, Los Angeles, California
pp. 100–101

George Bolling

Newport Beach Revisited
1972
Black-and-white film transferred to video; sound; 28:58 min.
San Francisco Museum of Modern Art Research Library and Archives

Nancy Buchanan

*Hair Transplant**
1972
Performance documentation
Black-and-white photograph (exhibition copy)
9½ × 14 in.
Courtesy of the artist, Los Angeles, California
p. 161

Chris Burden

*Being Photographed: Looking Out, Looking In**
Performance at F Space, Santa Ana, California
140 Polaroid photographs and one drawing
Photographs: 25 × 133 in. overall
Drawing: 25 × 33 in. with eleven date cards
Sender Collection, New York
Photos: Courtesy of the artist, Topanga, California
pp. 70–71; 160

Relic from *Being Photographed: Looking Out, Looking In*
1971
Copper
24 × 6 in.
Collection Barbara T. Smith, Venice, California

Chris Burden 71–73
1974
Artist's book: Fifty-three photographs (nine in color, forty-four in black and white, each signed on the back) and text in a loose-leaf binder with hand-painted cover
12 × 12 × 3 in.
Orange County Museum of Art; Gift of the artist

Documentation of Selected Works
1971–74
Video: black-and-white and color; sound; 34 min.
Orange County Museum of Art; Museum purchase with funds provided through prior gift of Lois Outerbridge

*I Became a Secret Hippy**
October 3, 1971
Performance at Museum of Conceptual Art (MOCA), San Francisco, California
Black-and-white photograph
10 × 8 in.
University of California, Berkeley Art Museum and Pacific Film Archive; Gift of the Naify Family, 1995.46.420.18
p. 204

*Shoot**
November 19, 1971
Performance at F Space, Santa Ana, California
Color photograph (exhibition copy)
20 × 13¼ in.
University of California, Berkeley Art Museum and Pacific Film Archive; Gift of the Naify Family, 1995.46.420.4
p. 84

*TV Hijack**
February 9, 1972
Performance at Channel 3 Cablevision, Irvine, California
Two panels: three black-and-white photographs and one photocopied text on mat board; three black-and-white photographs and one color photograph on mat board
Panel with text and photographs: 20 ¼ × 38 in.
Panel with photographs only: 20 ¼ × 45 ⅗ in.
Courtesy of the artist, Topanga, California
pp. 176–177

Relic from *TV Hijack**
February 9, 1972
Knife, scabbard, case, and printed text
Case: 5 ¾ × 10 ½ × 7 ⅞ in.
Orange County Museum of Art; Gift of the artist
p. 176

Through the Night Softly
September 12, 1973
Mixed media on cardboard
3 ½ × 5 ½ in.
University of California, Berkeley Art Museum and Pacific Film Archive; Gift of the Naify Family, 1995.46.420.5

Vija Celmins

*Moon Surface (Luna 9) #2**
1969
Graphite on acrylic ground on paper
14 × 18 ¾ in.
Orange County Museum of Art; Museum purchase with funds provided through prior gift of Ben C. Deane
Photo: Courtesy McKee Gallery, New York
p. 153

Robert Cumming

The Weight of Franchise Meat
1971
Artist's book
5 × 7 in.
University of California, Berkeley Art Museum and Pacific Film Archive; Gift of James and Mary Ann Melchert, 1995.43.11

*"A" Structure: Dana Atchley, Ken Friedman, Douglas Huebler, William T. Wiley**
1973
Black-and-white photograph
10 × 8 in.
San Francisco Museum of Modern Art; Gift of Arnold and Temmie Gilbert
© Robert H. Cumming Living Trust / Licensed by VAGA, New York
p. 113

*Ansel Adams Raisin Bread**
1973
Two black-and-white photographs
9 15⁄16 × 17 ⅜ in.; 24 × 30 in. framed
San Francisco Museum of Modern Art; Gift of Arnold and Temmie Gilbert
© Robert H. Cumming Living Trust / Licensed by VAGA, New York
pp. 106–107

Peter d'Agostino

*Walk Series**
1973–74
Three-channel video: black and white; sound: 61:16 min
University of California, Berkeley Art Museum and Pacific Film Archive; preserved from half-inch open reel master by Pacific Film Archive; PFA Collection
pp. 149–151

Lowell Darling

Fat City School of Finds Art
1972
Black-and-white photograph with ballpoint pen
8 × 10 in.
Courtesy of the artist, Rodeo, California

Fat City School of Finds Art
1974
Black-and-white photograph
14 × 11 in.
Collection of Max and Jane Reid, Oakland, California

Get Your MFA Friday
1972
Offset lithograph on paper
11 × 16 ⅞ in.
Courtesy of the artist, Rodeo, California

Lowell Darling with Fat City School of Friends of Art diploma at his alma mater, Southern Illinois University*
1972
Black-and-white photograph
11 × 8 ⅝ in.
Courtesy of the artist, Rodeo, California
Photo: Steve Sumner
p. 108

Guy de Cointet

*A Page from My Intimate Journal (Part 1)**
1974
Screen print
30 × 22 in.
University of California, Berkeley Art Museum and Pacific Film Archive; Anonymous gift, 1981.7.1
© Estate of Guy de Cointet, courtesy Air de Paris, Paris, and Greene Naftali, New York
Photo: Benjamin Blackwell
p. 112

ACRCIT
1971
Artist's book
17 × 22 in.
Courtesy of Cirrus Gallery, Los Angeles, California

*These were exciting days . . .**
1971
Ink on paper
25 ½ × 30 ½ in.
Nora Eccles Harrison Museum of Art, Utah State University, 2007.10. Gift of the Marie Eccles Caine Foundation, Logan, Utah. © Estate of Guy de Cointet, courtesy Air de Paris, Paris, and Greene Naftali, New York
pp. 218–219

Morgan Fisher

*Picture and Sound Rushes**
1973
16mm film transferred to video; black-and-white; sound; 11 min.
Courtesy of the artist and Galerie Daniel Buchholz, Cologne, Germany, and China Art Objects Gallery, Los Angeles, California
p. 236

Terry Fox

Blow through This Hole
December 1969
Offset lithography on card stock with a circular cutout
5 × 7 in.
University of California, Berkeley Art Museum and Pacific Film Archive; Gift of the Naify Family, 1995.46.426.12

Clutch
1971
Video: black-and-white; sound; 50 min.
Courtesy of de Saisset Museum, Santa Clara University permanent collection. 5.36

*Defoliation**
March 17, 1970
Performance at the opening night of the exhibition The Eighties, Power Plant Gallery, University Art Museum, University of California, Berkeley
Six black-and-white photographs (exhibition copies)
8 × 10 in. each
© Estate of Terry Fox. Courtesy Brenda Richardson, Baltimore, Maryland
Photo: Barry Klinger
p. 39

*Levitation**
September 17–21, 1970
Performance at Richmond Art Center
Black-and-white photograph (exhibition copy)
18 × 12 in.
© Estate of Terry Fox
Photo: Jerry Wainwright
pp. 82–83

Terry Fox, Richmond Art Center, Richmond, California, September 17–October 18, 1970
Poster: offset lithography on white paper
11 ¾ × 15 ½ in.
University of California, Berkeley Art Museum and Pacific Film Archive; Gift of the Naify Family, 1995.46.426.22

*Tonguings**
1970
Video: black-and-white; sound; 21 min.
University of California, Berkeley Art Museum and Pacific Film Archive; Purchase made possible by the Jan Boyce Fund for Contemporary Art, 2010.29
p. 79

*Untitled**
1970–71
Wood matchstick and glue on fiberboard
Four sheets: 14 × 11 in. each
Private collection, Berkeley
Photo: Benjamin Blackwell
p. 91

Howard Fried

Fuck You Purdue
1971
Video: black-and-white; sound, 31:39 min.
Courtesy of the artist, Vallejo, California

*Inside the Harlequin: Approach-Avoidance III and II**
1971
Two unsynchronized Super-8 film loops transferred to video with two unsynchronized audio loops
Projected images: 45½ × 120 in.; 120 × 126 in. overall
San Francisco Museum of Modern Art; Accessions Committee Fund purchase
Photo: © Howard Fried
pp. 74–75; 142–143

*Long John Servil vs. Long John Silver**
1972
Poster: offset lithography
17½ x 19¼ in.
University of California, Berkeley Art Museum and Pacific Film Archive, PFA Library Collection
p. 31

Charles Gaines

*Regression Series Drawings**
Drawings: 1973–74; book: 1978
Artist's book
12¼ × 16¾ × ¼ in.
Courtesy of the artist and Susanne Vielmetter Los Angeles Projects, Culver City, California
Photo: Robert Wedemeyer
p. 179

David Hammons

*Pray for America**
1974
Body print, silkscreen
60½ × 30 in.
Collection Hudgins Family, New York
Photo: Erma Estwick
p. 85

Helen Mayer Harrison and Newton Harrison

*The Book of Lagoons**
1974–84
Handmade book
28 × 21½ × 3 in.
Courtesy of the artists, Santa Cruz, California
p. 18

Joe Hawley, Mel Henderson, and Alfred Young

*Oil**
September 20, 1969
Performance event at Standard Oil docks, Richmond, California; nontoxic uranine marker dye on San Francisco Bay
Color photograph (exhibition copy)
21 × 30 in.
Courtesy of Mel Henderson and Susan Rannells, Nevada City, California
Photo: Robert Campbell / Chamois Moon
Title page

Video compilation featuring *Searchlights, Oil,* and *Yellow Cabs;* 7:28 min.
1969

Searchlights, June 3, 1969; performance event at Market Street from the Ferry Building to Twin Peaks, San Francisco, California

*Oil,** September 20, 1969; performance event on San Francisco Bay, Richmond, California

*Yellow Cabs,** November 19, 1969; performance event at Castro, 17th, and Market Streets, San Francisco
1969/1994
Film transferred to video; color; sound; 7:28 min.
Courtesy of Mel Henderson and Susan Rannells, Nevada City, California
p. xiv

Mel Henderson

*Attica**
March 11, 1972
From *The San Francisco Performance*, March 12–April 16, 1972, Newport Harbor Art Museum, Newport Beach, California
Black-and-white photographic documentation
8 × 10 in.
University of California, Berkeley Art Museum and Pacific Film Archive; Gift of the Naify Family, 1995.46.443.13
Photo: Larry Fox
p. 36

*Untitled (Attica, the Arrest)**
March 11, 1972
From *The San Francisco Performance*, March 12–April 16, 1972, Newport Harbor Art Museum, Newport Beach, California
Black-and-white photographic documentation
5 × 8 in.
University of California, Berkeley Art Museum and Pacific Film Archive, Gift of the Naify Family, 1995.46.443.10
Photo: Larry Fox
p. 37

Lynn Hershman

The Dante Hotel
1973–74
All works courtesy of the artist and Gallery Paule Anglim, San Francisco, California, unless otherwise noted

Dante Hotel Advertisement
Offset printing (exhibition copy)
10 × 7½ in.

Dante Hotel: Detail of Occupants of Room 47
7½ × 10 in.
Black-and-white photograph

*Dante Hotel—Dresser Graffiti by Trespassers to Room 47**
Black-and-white photograph
7½ × 10 in.
p. 273

*Dante Hotel Installation**
Black-and-white photograph
30 × 40 in.
University of California, Berkeley Art Museum and Pacific Film Archive; bequest of Thérèse Bonney, Class of 1916, by exchange
p. 45

Dante Hotel: Photograph of Lobby and Stairs, 1973
1973
Black-and-white photograph
7½ × 10 in.

Dante Hotel: Photograph Up the Stairs, 1973
Black-and-white photograph
10 × 7½ in.

Dante Hotel: Photograph of Stairs and Landing, 1973
Black-and-white photograph
10 × 7½ in.

Dante Hotel: Photograph of Hotel Room from Hallway Perspective
Black-and-white photograph
10 × 7½ in.

Dante Hotel: Photograph of Hotel Room with Sleeping Figures
Black-and-white photograph
10 × 8 in.

Dante Hotel Receipt
Paper receipt
6 × 4 in.

Four preliminary storyboards
Collage on paper
11 × 14 in. each

The Dante Hotel: November 30, 1973—August 31, 1974
Self-published catalogue
11 × 8½ in. overall dimensions
San Francisco, California

Douglas Huebler

*Duration Piece #9, Berkeley, California—Hull, Massachusetts, January–October, 1969**
January–October 1969
Typewritten statement, map with ink, nine mail receipts, and paper wrapped box
Statement: 11 × 8½ in.
Map: 10 × 14½ in.
Framed receipts: 22⅜ × 19¼ in. overall
Box: 2⅞ × 5⅛ × 3½ in.
Solomon R. Guggenheim Museum, New York; Panza Collection, Gift, 1992, 92.4129
© 2010 Douglas Huebler, courtesy Darcy Huebler / Artists Rights Society (ARS), New York
p. 228

*Location Piece #6, Los Angeles, March 1969**
March 1969
Typewritten statement and eight black-and-white photographs

Statement: 11 × 8 ½ in.
Photographs: 7 7/16 × 9 7/16 in. each
Solomon R. Guggenheim Museum, New York; Panza Collection, Gift, 1992, 92.4127
© 2010 Douglas Huebler, courtesy Darcy Huebler / Artists Rights Society (ARS), New York
pp. 16–17

Richard Jackson

*Moon Piece**
1970
Eight black-and-white photographs
8 × 10 in. each; 22 × 48 in. framed
Courtesy of the artist, Sierra Madre, California
p. 152

Stephen Kaltenbach

*Artforum Ads**
"Perpetrate a hoax,"* April 1969
"Build a Reputation," May 1969
"Become a Legend," Summer 1969
From series of eleven Artforum magazine advertisements
Offset lithography on paper
10 ½ x 10 3/8 in. each
Anonymous loan
pp. 53, 186–187

*ART WORKS**
1968/2005
From the *Sidewalk Plaques* series
Bronze
4 7/8 × 7 7/8 × 5/8 in.
University of California, Berkeley Art Museum and Pacific Film Archive; Museum purchase: Bequest of Thérèse Bonney, Class of 1916, by exchange, 2006.65.2
Photo: Benjamin Blackwell
p. 51

*Raised Floor**
1967/2011
Sheetrock and wood
168 × 168 in.
Courtesy of the artist, Davis, California
p. 68

Allan Kaprow

*Pose, March 22, 1969**
From *Artists & Photographs*, published by Multiples, Inc.
1970
A record of an event to be continued infinitum
Offset lithography on card stock in envelope
Seven cards: 10¾ × 7¾ in.
Envelope: 12 × 9 in.
University of California, Berkeley Art Museum and Pacific Film Archive; Gift of the Pitesky family in loving memory of Stuart F. Pitesky, Class of 1989
p. 156

Robert Kinmont

*8 Natural Handstands**
1969/2009
Nine black-and-white photographs
8 ½ × 8 ½ in. each
Courtesy of Alexander and Bonin, New York
Photo: Bill Orcutt
Cover, pp. 20–21

John Knight

*I Assumed**
1972
Fifty index cards and handmade envelope
Cards: 3 × 5 in. each
Envelope: 4 ½ × 7 in.
Courtesy of Cardwell Jimmerson Contemporary Art, Culver City, California
pp. 248–249

Paul Kos

*Sound of Ice Melting**
1970/2011
Two 25-lb. blocks of ice, eight boom microphone stands, mixer, amplifier, two large speakers, and cables
78 × 240 × 180 in.
Courtesy of the artist and Gallery Paule Anglim, San Francisco, California
p. 92

*Roping Boar's Tusk**
1971
Super-8 film transferred to video; one-minute loop
Courtesy of the artist and Gallery Paule Anglim, San Francisco, California
p. 93

*A Trophy/Atrophy**
1972
Video: black-and-white; sound; 3:08 min.
University of California, Berkeley Art Museum and Pacific Film Archive; preserved from half-inch open reel master by Pacific Film Archive; PFA Collection
Photo: Courtesy of the artist
p. 109

Suzanne Lacy

All works courtesy of the artist, Los Angeles, California, unless otherwise noted

A Gothic Love Story (From Three Love Stories)
1975–76
Six black-and-white photographs
11 × 14 in.

Anatomy Lessons #1—Chickens Coming Home to Roost (for Rose Mountain)
1975–76
Four cards with black-and-white photograph and text
4 × 6 in. each
Courtesy of Steven Leiber, San Francisco, California

Anatomy Lesson (After Mantegna) and Anatomy Lesson (Floating series 1)
1976
one 20 × 60 in.; two 11 × 17 in.
Three color photographs (exhibition copies)

Falling Apart
1976
Artist's book
Collage and typewritten text
8 × 10 in.

*Lamb Construction**
1973/2011
Sculpture (reconstruction from original performance artifact)
30 × 42 × 24 in.
Color photograph (exhibition copy)
16 × 24 in.
pp. 170–171

*Maps**
1973
p. 210

Frankenstein
1974
Video compilation of performances; color and black and white; 7 min.
p. 000

Monster Series: Construction of a Novel Frankenstein
1974
Two color photographs (exhibition copies)
20 × 30 in. and 16 × 24 in.

Skin
1974
Artist's book made from pigskin and collage
3 × 4 in.

Stephen Laub

Bodies of Water
1973
Artist's book
7 ½ × 6 ¾ × 1/8 in.
Courtesy of the artist, Water Mill, New York

*Relations (My father and a friend from school)**
1970–73
Color photograph (exhibition copy)
20 × 14 in.
Courtesy of the artist, Water Mill, New York
p. 89

William Leavitt

*Garden Sound**
1970
Artificial plants, plywood box, water, circulating pump, microphone, amplifier, and speaker
84 × 144 × 144 in.
Courtesy of the artist and Margo Leavin Gallery, Los Angeles, California
p. 72

Symbolic Images
1974/2008
Eight black-and-white photographs with acrylic ink; edition one of three
11 × 14 in. each
Orange County Museum of Art; Museum purchase with funds provided through prior gift of Lois Outerbridge

Fred Lonidier

*29 Arrests: Headquarters of the 11th Naval District, May 4, 1972, San Diego**
1972
Twenty-nine black-and-white photographs and one text panel
5½ × 8½ in. each; 48 × 60 in. framed
Courtesy of the artist, La Jolla, California
pp. 6–7; 42; 232

Mike Mandel

Myself: Timed Exposures
1971
Artist's book
5½ × 8½ in.
Courtesy of the artist, Watertown, Massachusetts

Mike Mandel and Larry Sultan

*How to Read Music in One Evening/A Clatworthy Catalog**
1974
Artists' book
8⅛ × 10¾ in.
Courtesy of Mike Mandel, Watertown, Massachusetts
Photo: Courtesy of Mike Mandel and the Estate of Larry Sultan
p. 50

Tom Marioni

Bay Area Roach Clip Show
San Geronimo Valley Art Center, October 21–22, 1972
1972
Flyer: offset lithography on yellow paper
8½ × 11 in.
University of California, Berkeley Art Museum and Pacific Film Archive; Gift of the Naify Family, 1995.46.441.23

Museum News
April 1973
Magazine
11 × 8½ in.
SFMOMA Research Library and Archives
Gift of John Bransten

Newport Drawing
1972
Performance documentation
Black-and-white photograph
10 × 16 in.
Private Collection, Long Beach, California

One Second Sculpture
1969
Black-and-white photograph
31 × 36 in.
Courtesy of the artist, San Francisco, California

*Process Print**
1969
Approximately thirty-four offset lithographs
24 × 30 in. each
Courtesy of the artist, San Francisco, California
p. 90

*The Board of Trustees of The San Francisco Museum of Art are pleased to announce the appointment of Thomas Marioni as Director, January 3, 1973**
January 3, 1973
Offset lithography on card stock
3¾ × 5¾ in.
University of California, Berkeley Art Museum and Pacific Film Archive; Gift of the Naify Family, 1995.46.263
Photo: Benjamin Blackwell
p. 184

The Return of Abstract Expressionism
September 25–November 2, 1969
Richmond Art Center, Richmond, California
Exhibition catalogue: offset lithography on paper
8½ × 11 in.
University of California, Berkeley Art Museum and Pacific Film Archive; Gift of the Naify Family, 1995.46.150.20

*The Trip**
From *The San Francisco Performance*, Newport Harbor Art Museum, Newport Beach, California, March 12–April 16, 1972
1972
Four black-and-white photographs (from box containing 139 black-and-white photographs, twenty contact sheets, and several negative strips)
4½ × 6⅝ in. each
University of California, Berkeley Art Museum and Pacific Film Archive; Gift of the Naify Family, 1995.46.443.15
Photos: Larry Fox
pp. 138–139

Tom Marioni a.k.a. Allan Fish

*Piss Piece**
1970
Black-and-white photograph
14 × 11 in.
Courtesy of the artist, San Francisco, California
p. 146

Paul McCarthy

*Black and White Tapes, Version 3**
1970–75
Video: black and white; sound; 32:50 min.
Courtesy of the artist, Altadena, California, and Hauser & Wirth
p. 80

Looking Out, Skull Card
1968
Cardboard and string
11 × 9 in.
Courtesy of the artist, Altadena, California

*May 1, 1971**
1971
Twenty-five projected slides
Courtesy of the artist, Altadena, California
Photo: Courtesy of the artist and Hauser & Wirth
p. 24

Jim Melchert

*Changing Walls**
October 1971
Eighty-one projected 35mm slides; 5:24 min.
84 × 56 in.
San Francisco Museum of Modern Art Purchase.
© Jim Melchert
pp. 94–95

Susan Mogul

*Dressing Up**
1973
Video: black and white; sound; 7:06 min.
Orange County Museum of Art; Museum purchase with funds provided through prior gift of Lois Outerbridge
Photo: Courtesy of the artist and Video Data Bank
p. 203

Linda Mary Montano

All works courtesy of the artist, Saugerties, New York

*Chicken Dance: The Streets of San Francisco**
1972
Performance documentation
Six black-and-white digital prints; one color digital print (exhibition copies)
9½ × 14 in. each
Courtesy of the artist, Saugerties, New York
Photo: Mitchell Payne
pp. 29; 198

*Lying: Dead Chicken, Live Angel (Chicken Bed)**
1972
Performance documentation
Black-and-white digital print (exhibition copy)
11¾ × 17 in.
Photo: Mitchell Payne
p. 133

*Home Nursing**
1972
Black-and-white photograph (exhibition copy)
17 × 9½ in.
Photo: Mitchell Payne
p. 205

Linda Montano Will Be Handcuffed to Tom Marioni from 9 pm November 2 to 9 pm November 5, 1973*
1973
Black-and-white photograph (exhibition copy)
13½ × 20 in.
Photo: Minnette Lehmann
p. 134

Bruce Nauman

Clea Rsky
1967–68
Artist's book
12 × 12 in.
University of California, Berkeley Art Museum and Pacific Film Archive; Gift of the Pitesky family in loving memory of Stuart F. Pitesky, Class of 1989

L A A I R
From *Artists & Photographs*, published by Multiples, Inc.
1970
Artist's book
12 × 12 in.
University of California, Berkeley Art Museum and Pacific Film Archive; Gift of the Pitesky family in loving memory of Stuart F. Pitesky, Class of 1989

*Studies for Holograms (Pinched Lips; Pulled Lower Lip; Pulled Neck; Pulled Cheeks; and Squeezed Lips)**
1970
Five screenprints
25 ¾ × 25 ¾ in. each
University of California, Berkeley Art Museum and Pacific Film Archive; Purchased with the aid of funds from the National Endowment for the Arts, 1970.97.1–5
Photo: © 2010 Bruce Nauman / Artists Rights Society (ARS), New York
p. 79

*Thighing**
1967
16 mm film transferred to video; color; sound; 4:36 min.
University of California, Berkeley Art Museum and Pacific Film Archive; Museum purchase: Bequest of Thérèse Bonney, Class of 1916, by exchange, and BAM/PFA Institutional Support, 2005.40.8
Photo: © 2010 Bruce Nauman / Artists Rights Society (ARS), New York
p. 78

*Walking in an Exaggerated Manner around the Perimeter of a Square**
1967–68
16mm film transferred to video; black-and-white; silent; 10 min.
University of California, Berkeley Art Museum and Pacific Film Archive; Museum purchase: Bequest of Thérèse Bonney, Class of 1916, by exchange, and BAM/PFA Institutional Support, 2005.40.12
Photo: © 2010 Bruce Nauman / Artists Rights Society (ARS), New York
p. 78

*Yellow Room (Triangular)**
1973
Painted wallboard, plywood, and fluorescent light fixtures with yellow lamps
Dimensions variable
Solomon R. Guggenheim Museum, New York, Panza Collection, 1991, 91.3835
Photo: © 2010 Bruce Nauman / Artists Rights Society (ARS), New York
p. 69

Newport Harbor Art Museum (now Orange County Museum of Art)

Poster from Appearing/Disappearing Image/Object, May 11–June 28, 1969
1969
Metallic ink on vellum
22 × 18 in.
Orange County Museum of Art Archives

Ephemera from The San Francisco Performance, Newport Harbor Art Museum
March 12–April 16, 1972

Tom Marioni

The San Francisco Performance
1972
Poster: offset lithography on white card stock
9 × 13¼ in.

The San Francisco Performance
1972
Exhibition catalogue: offset lithography on newsprint
17 × 12 in.
Orange County Museum of Art

Legal documents of arrest of Mel Henderson and Paul Kos during *The San Francisco Performance*
1972
Photocopies and carbon copies: printed black on white paper with handwritten additions, stapled
Dimensions variable
University of California, Berkeley Art Museum and Pacific Film Archive; Gift of the Naify Family, 1995.46.429.36

Martha Rosler

All works courtesy of the artist, Brooklyn, New York and Mitchell-Innes and Nash Gallery, New York, unless otherwise noted.

*A Budding Gourmet**
1974
Serial postcard novel in twelve parts
3 × 5 in. each
Collection of the artist, Brooklyn, New York
p. 54

A Budding Gourmet
1974
Video: black-and-white; sound; 17:45 min.
University of California, Berkeley Art Museum and Pacific Film Archive; Purchase made possible by the Jan Boyce Fund for Contemporary Art, 2010.30

*Bowl of Fruit, from the series Body Beautiful, or Beauty Knows No Pain**
1966–72
Photomontage
20 × 16 in.
Inside front cover

Brides Romance Language or Bianchi Bride, from the series Bringing the War Home: House Beautiful
1967–72
Photomontage
20 × 16 in.

*Cleaning the Drapes, from the series Bringing the War Home: House Beautiful**
1967–72
Photomontage
20 × 24 in.
p. 212

*First Lady (Pat Nixon) from the series Bringing the War Home: House Beautiful**
1972
Photomontage
20 × 24 in.
p. 41

Allen Ruppersberg

All works courtesy of the artist, Santa Monica, California and Margo Leavin Gallery, Los Angeles, California, unless otherwise noted.

Al's Grand Hotel
1971
Installation, 7175 Sunset Boulevard, Hollywood, California

Al's Grand Hotel
Brochure: Offset lithography
8½ × 11 in.

Al's Grand Hotel
Guest book
12⅛ × 9 × ⅝ in.
The Museum of Modern Art, New York, 300341.281.1

Untitled (standee)
Tinted photograph mounted on plywood
Approximately 72 in. tall

Untitled (standee)*
Tinted photograph mounted on plywood
Approximately 72 in. tall
Collection of Claire Copley and Alan Eisenberg, New York
Inside back cover

Al's Grand Hotel
Neon Sign
40 ¼ × 30 ½ × 6 ½ in.
Collection of Stanley and Elyse Grinstein, Los Angeles, California

Al's Grand Hotel
Rate Chart
8 ½ × 11 in.

Cafe Room
1971/2011
Duratrans light box
16 × 20 in.

*Exterior of Al's Grand Hotel**
1971/2011
Duratrans light box
16 × 20 in.
p. 239

Girl and Juke Box
1971/2011
Duratrans light box
16 × 20 in.

Girl in Print Dress in Lobby
1971/2011

Duratrans light box
16 × 20 in.

Terry Allen Performance at Al's Grand Hotel
Poster: color lithograph
23 × 29 in.

Untitled (Al with standees and their fabricator)•
Black-and-white photograph
34 ½ × 41 ¾ in.
p. 43

Television Documentation of Al's Grand Hotel from Le raid américain, La côte ouest ou le culte de la lumière, director: Jean-Marie Drot, Ina (Antenne 2)
August 16, 1976
Video; black and white; sound; 1:28 min.
Institut national de l'audiovisuel, Paris, France

Terry Allen Performance at Al's Grand Hotel
Poster: color lithograph
23 × 29 in. framed

*Untitled (Al with standees and their fabricator)**
Black-and-white photograph
34½ × 41¾ in. framed
p. 43

Television Documentation of Al's Grand Hotel from Le raid américain, La côte ouest ou le culte de la lumière, director: Jean-Marie Drot, Ina (Antenne 2)
August 16, 1976
Video; black and white; sound; 1:28 min.
Institut national de l'audiovisuel, Paris, France

Documentation of Al's Grand Hotel
Eighty 35 mm slide transparencies transferred to video

Untitled (City Limits)
1970
Five black-and-white photographs
11 × 14 in. each
Courtesy Artnow International: 101 Collection, San Francisco, California

Ed Ruscha

A Few Palm Trees
1971
Artist's book
7 × 5 ½ in.
Copy 1: University of California, Berkeley Art Museum and Pacific Film Archive; Gift of Eileen and Peter Michael, 1998.14.3
Copy 2: Collection Orange County Museum of Art, Newport Beach, California
© Ed Ruscha

*Baby Cakes**
From *Artists & Photographs*, published by Multiples, Inc.
1970
Artist's book
7 ½ × 6 in.
University of California, Berkeley Art Museum and Pacific Film Archive; Gift of the Pitesky family in loving memory of Stuart F. Pitesky, Class of 1989
© Ed Ruscha
p. 137

*Colored People**
1972
Artist's book
7 × 5 ½ in.
University of California, Berkeley Art Museum and Pacific Film Archive; Gift of the Pitesky family in loving memory of Stuart F. Pitesky, Class of 1989
© Ed Ruscha
p. 137

*Crackers**
1969
Artist's book
8 ¾ × 6 in.
Copy 1: University of California, Berkeley Art Museum and Pacific Film Archive; Gift of the Pitesky family in loving memory of Stuart F. Pitesky, Class of 1989
Copy 2: Collection Orange County Museum of Art, Newport Beach, California
© Ed Ruscha
p. 137

*Dutch Details**
1971
Artist's book
4 ½ × 15 in.
University of California, Berkeley Art Museum and Pacific Film Archive; Gift of Eileen and Peter Michael, 1998.14.2
© Ed Ruscha
p. 137

*Every Building on the Sunset Strip**
1966
Artist's book
7 ⅜ × 5 ⅞ in.
Copy 1: University of California, Berkeley Art Museum and Pacific Film Archive; Gift of the Pitesky family in loving memory of Stuart F. Pitesky, Class of 1989
Copy 2: Collection Orange County Museum of Art, Newport Beach, California; LAM/OCMA Art Collection Trust
© Ed Ruscha. Photo: Benjamin Blackwell
pp. 22–23

*Nine Swimming Pools**
1968/1978
Artist's book, second edition
7 ⅛ × 5 ½ in.
University of California, Berkeley Art Museum and Pacific Film Archive; Gift of the Pitesky family in loving memory of Stuart F. Pitesky, Class of 1989
© Ed Ruscha
p. 137

*Real Estate Opportunities**
1970
Artist's book
7 ¹⁄₁₆ × 5 ½ in.
Copy 1: University of California, Berkeley Art Museum and Pacific Film Archive; Gift of the Pitesky family in loving memory of Stuart F. Pitesky, Class of 1989
Copy 2: Collection Orange County Museum of Art, Newport Beach, California
© Ed Ruscha
p. 137

*Records**
1971
Artist's book
7 ¹⁄₁₆ × 5 ½ in.
Copy 1: University of California, Berkeley Art Museum and Pacific Film Archive; Gift of Eileen and Peter Michael, 1998.14.4
Copy 2: Collection Orange County Museum of Art, Newport Beach, California
© Ed Ruscha
p. 137

*Some Los Angeles Apartments**
1965/1970
Artist's book, second edition
7 ⅛ × 5 ⅝ in.
Copy 1: University of California, Berkeley Art Museum and Pacific Film Archive; Gift of the Pitesky family in loving memory of Stuart F. Pitesky, Class of 1989
Copy 2: Collection Orange County Museum of Art, Newport Beach, California
© Ed Ruscha
p. 137

*Thirtyfour Parking Lots**
1967
Artist's book
10 × 8 in.
University of California, Berkeley Art Museum and Pacific Film Archive; Gift of Eileen and Peter Michael, 1998.14.5
© Ed Ruscha
p. 137

*Twentysix Gasoline Stations**
1963
Artist's book
7 ¹⁄₁₆ × 5 ½ in.
Copy 1: University of California, Berkeley Art Museum and Pacific Film Archive; Gift of Eileen and Peter Michael, 1998.14.6
Copy 2: Collection Orange County Museum of Art, Newport Beach, California; LAM/OCMA Art Collection Trust
© Ed Ruscha
p. 137

Ed Ruscha and Billy Al Bengston

Business Cards
1968
Artists' book
8 ¾ × 5 ⅝ in.
University of California, Berkeley Art Museum and Pacific Film Archive; Gift of Eileen and Peter Michael, 1998.14.1

Ed Ruscha in collaboration with Mason Williams and Patrick Blackwell

*Royal Road Test**
1967/1980
Artists' book, fourth edition
9 ⁷⁄₁₆ × 6 ½ in.
University of California, Berkeley Art Museum and Pacific Film Archive; Gift of the Pitesky family in loving memory of Stuart F. Pitesky, Class of 1989
p. 137

Sam's Café (Terri Keyser, Marc Keyser, and David Shire)
All works courtesy of Terri Keyser-Cooper, Reno, Nevada, unless otherwise noted.

*Is America Disposable?**
1970
Poster: offset lithography on paper
30 × 20 in.
p. 47

Packaged Deal
1970
Offset lithography on seven sheets of paper
6 × 9 in. each
Collection of Steven Leiber, San Francisco, California

Sam's Collection Agency
1971

*Bill**
Offset lithography on paper
8 ½ × 6 ¼ in.
p. 48

Information Sheet
Paper
11 × 8 ½ in.

San Francisco Examiner, March 17, 1971 (You Owe $76.40)
Photographic reproduction
17 × 11 in.

San Francisco Chronicle, March 18, 1971 ($76.40 Hoax in SF)
Photographic reproduction
17 × 11 in.

San Francisco Chronicle, March 20, 1971 (Phony Bills Case)
Photographic reproduction
17 × 11 in.

San Francisco Chronicle, April 15, 1971 (Grand Jury Indicts 3 in $76.40 Hoax)
Photographic reproduction
17 × 11 in.

San Francisco Chronicle, October 13, 1971 (3 Sam's Café Artists Acquitted)
Photographic reproduction
17 × 11 in.

San Francisco Chronicle, October 13, 1971 (Judge Frees Sam's Café 3)
Photographic reproduction
17 × 11 in.

San Francisco Chronicle, October 17, 1971 (Conceptual Art—Just What Is It?)
Photographic reproduction
17 × 11 in.

San Francisco Chronicle, October 14, 1971 (An Artist's Responsibility)
Photographic reproduction
17 × 11 in.

Rotting Food Show
1969

*The Fine Art of Rotting Food: A Revolution in Decomposing**
Poster: offset lithography on glossy paper
17½ × 22½ in.
p. 48

Installation images of *Rotting Food Show*
Three black-and-white photographs
8 × 10 in. each

*Tenney Packet**
1970
Offset lithography on seven cards, one sheet of paper, and envelope
Cards: 5 × 7 in. each
Paper: 3 ½ × 6 in.
Envelope: 7 ½ × 5 ½ in.
Collection of Steven Leiber, San Francisco, California
p. 49

Darryl Sapien with Michael A. Hinton

*War Games**
July 16, 1973
Performance at Third and Howard Streets, San Francisco
Three color photographs and one offset lithograph on paper
Photographs: 11 × 17 in. each; lithograph: 6⅝ × 5 in.
Courtesy of Darryl Sapien, San Francisco, California
Photos: Phillip Galgiani, courtesy of Darryl Sapien
Courtesy of Darryl Sapien, San Francisco, California
Photos: Phillip Galgiani
p. 76

Ilene Segalove

*The Mom Tapes**
1974
Video: black-and-white and color; sound; 26:52 min.
Orange County Museum of Art; Museum purchase with funds provided through prior gift of Lois Outerbridge
Photo: © Ilene Segalove, courtesy of Video Data Bank
p. 58

Allan Sekula

*Untitled Slide Sequence**
1972
Twenty-five black-and-white slides in slide carousel; edition two of five
Dimensions variable
The Museum of Contemporary Art, Los Angeles; Purchased with funds provided by the Curatorial Discretionary Fund
Photos: Courtesy Christopher Grimes Gallery, Santa Monica, California
pp. 208–209

Bonnie Sherk
All works courtesy of the artist, San Francisco, California, unless otherwise noted.

Portable Parks I–III, Sitting Still,* Pacing, Public Lunch,* 1970*
Video: black and white; sound; 14:10 min.
pp. 25–27

Sitting Still Series
1971

Financial District: Bank of America Plaza, San Francisco
Two color photographs (exhibition copies)
11 × 11 in. each

*Financial District: Corner of Montgomery and California Streets, San Francisco**
Two color photographs (exhibition copies)
11 × 11 in. each

Mission and 20th Streets, San Francisco
Two color photographs (exhibition copies)
11 × 11 in. each

Sitting Still I, Facing Construction of 101 Freeway Interchange near Bayshore Boulevard and Army Street, San Francisco)
Two color photographs (exhibition copies)
13 × 20 in. each

Sitting Still II, Golden Gate Bridge, San Francisco*
Two color photographs (exhibition copies)
11 × 11 in. each
Photo: Robert Campbell / Chamois Moon, courtesy SFMOMA Research Library and Archives
p. 26

Public Lunch
Performance at Lion House, San Francisco Zoo*
1971
Black-and-white photograph (exhibition copy)
27 × 40 in.
Photo: Vincente Saval, courtesy SFMOMA Research Library and Archives
p. 27

Indoor and Outdoor Cages, San Francisco Zoo
1971
Performance documentation
Eight black-and-white photographs (exhibition copies)
11 × 11 in.

Alexis Smith

*Charlie Chan Piece**
1973
Photographs and typed text
12 × 45 ½ in.
The Museum of Contemporary Art, Los Angeles; Gift of Frank and Berta Gehry, 86.42A–B
pp. 182–183

Barbara T. Smith
All works courtesy of the artist, Venice, California, and The Box, Los Angeles, California

Field Piece
1968–72/2007
Sixteen fiberglass resin blades, Ethafoam, wood, light bulbs, and electronics
Installation: 48 × 96 × 120 in.

*Field Piece**
1968–72
Black-and-white photograph
48 × 72 in.
pp. 118–119

Light Watch
1971
DVD loop from time-lapse film; sound
Two vintage black-and-white photographs from part two of the performance
8 × 10 in. each
Original newspaper clipping of tide chart
Courtesy of the artist and The Box, Los Angeles

The Fisherman IS the Fish
1972
Four black-and-white photographs: 8 × 10 in. each
Two vintage black-and-white photographs: 16 × 20 in. each
One photocopy with dry fly lure: 8½ × 11 in.
One text written by the artist: 8½ × 11 in.

The Fisherman IS the Fish
1972
Video: black-and-white

Feed Me
1973
Audio recording and one 8½ × 11 in. text written by the artist

*Feed Me**
1973/2009
Two black-and-white photographs (exhibition copies)
48 × 36 in. each
p. 59

T. R. Uthco (Doug Hall, Jody Procter, and Diane Andrews Hall)

*8 Gestures**
1972/2011
Eight black-and-white photographs
16 × 12 in. each (largest); 14 × 11 in. each (smallest)
Courtesy of Doug Hall and Diane Andrews Hall, San Francisco, California
pp. 104–105

Ger van Elk

*The Co-founder of the Word O.K.—Hollywood**
1971
Three color photographs
22¼ × 22¼ in. each
Collection of Peter Morton, Los Angeles, California
Collection of Peter Morton, Los Angeles, California
Photo: courtesy of the artist and Margo Leavin Gallery, Los Angeles
pp. 230–231

William Wegman

*Selected Works 1970–1978**
Compiled 1981
Video: black and white and color; sound; 19:11 min.
Orange County Museum of Art; Museum purchase with funds provided through prior gift of Avco Financial Services
pp. 96–97

*Light On/Light Off**
1970
Two black-and-white photographs
11 × 11 in. each; 13 × 22¼ in. framed
Courtesy of the artist, New York, and Marc Selwyn Fine Art, Los Angeles
Photo: Robert Wedemeyer
pp. 62–63

*Artist**
1971
Black-and-white photograph
14 × 11 in.
Courtesy of the artist, New York, and Marc Selwyn Fine Art, Los Angeles
p. 97

*Selection of Unreleased Videos**
1971–72
Video: black-and-white; sound; 17:47 min.
University of California, Berkeley Art Museum and Pacific Film Archive; Preserved from unreleased half-inch open reel master tapes by Pacific Film Archive; PFA Collection
p. 60

*A Basic Guide to Lettering**
1972
Two black-and-white photographs
11 × 14 in. each
Courtesy of the artist, New York, and Marc Selwyn Fine Art, Los Angeles
pp. 64–65

Blondes/Brunettes
1972/1999
Thirty-two black-and-white photographs, diptych
10 × 8 in. each; 50 × 50 in. framed
Courtesy of the artist, New York, and Marc Selwyn Fine Art, Los Angeles

John Woodall

*Marking the Dilemma**
1973
Black-and-white photograph
8⅝ × 6 in.
Eyeglasses worn for the event
6 × 3 in.
Courtesy of the artist, Plant City, Florida
Photo: Sandra Woodall
p. 77

Alfred Young

*Coil**
1969
Inkjet print of original drawing on vellum (exhibition copy)
16½ × 25½ in.
Courtesy of the artist, Oakland, California
p. 32

SELECTED BIBLIOGRAPHY

Alberro, Alexander, and Patricia Norvell, eds. *Recording Conceptual Art: Early Interviews with Barry, Huebler, Kaltenbach, LeWitt, Morris, Oppenheim, Siegelaub, Smithson, and Weiner by Patricia Norvell.* Berkeley: University of California Press, 2001.

Alberro, Alexander, and Blake Stimson, eds. *Conceptual Art: A Critical Anthology.* Cambridge, MA: MIT Press, 2000.

Albright, Thomas. *Art in the San Francisco Bay Area, 1945–1980.* Berkeley: University of California Press, 1985.

Barron, Stephanie. *Made in California: Art, Image, and Identity, 1900–2000.* Los Angeles: Los Angeles County Museum of Art; Berkeley: University of California Press, 2000.

——. *Reading California: Art, Image, and Identity, 1900–2000.* Los Angeles: Los Angeles County Museum of Art; Berkeley: University of California Press, 2000.

Battcock, Gregory, ed. *Idea Art.* New York: E. P. Dutton, 1973.

——, ed. *New Artists Video.* New York: E. P. Dutton, 1978.

Bryan-Wilson, Julia. *Art Workers: Radical Practice in the Vietnam War Era.* Berkeley: University of California Press, 2009.

Camnitzer, Luis, et al. *Global Conceptualism: Points of Origin, 1950s–1980s.* New York: Queens Museum of Art, 1999.

Crow, Thomas. *The Rise of the Sixties: American and European Art in the Era of Dissent.* New York: Harry N. Abrams, 1996.

Fogle, Douglas. *The Last Picture Show: Artists Using Photography, 1960–1982.* Minneapolis, MN: Walker Art Center, 2003.

Foley, Suzanne, and Constance Lewallen. *Space/Time/Sound: Conceptual Art in the San Francisco Bay Area; The 1970s.* San Francisco: San Francisco Museum of Modern Art, 1980.

Frascina, Francis. *Art, Politics, and Dissent: Aspects of the Art Left in Sixties America.* Manchester, VT: Manchester University Press, 1999.

Goldstein, Ann. *A Minimal Future?: Art as Object 1958–1968.* Los Angeles: Museum of Contemporary Art; Cambridge, MA: MIT Press, 2004.

Goldstein, Ann, and Anne Rorimer. *Reconsidering the Object of Art: 1965–1975.* Los Angeles: Museum of Contemporary Art; Cambridge, MA: MIT Press, 1995.

Grenier, Catherine, ed. *Los Angeles, 1955–1985: Birth of an Art Capital.* Paris, France: Centre Pompidou, Musées Panama, 2006.

Hanhardt, John G., ed. *Video Culture: A Critical Investigation.* Layton, UT: G. M. Smith, P. Smith Books in association with Visual Studies Workshop Press, 1986.

Lippard, Lucy. *Six Years: The Dematerialization of the Art Object from 1966 to 1972.* New York: Praeger, 1973.

Loeffler, Carl E., and Darlene Tong, eds. *Performance Anthology: Sourcebook for a Decade of California Performance Art.* San Francisco: Contemporary Arts Press, 1980.

Marcus, Greil. *The Dustbin of History.* Cambridge, MA: Harvard University Press, 1995.

Mark, Lisa Gabrielle. *WACK!: Art and the Feminist Revolution.* Los Angeles: Museum of Contemporary Art; Cambridge, MA: MIT Press, 2007.

Meyer, Ursula, ed. *Conceptual Art.* New York: E. P. Dutton, 1972.

New Art in Orange County. Newport Beach, CA: Newport Harbor Art Museum; Santa Ana, CA: F Space Gallery, 1972.

Nittve, Lars, and Helle Crenzien. *Sunshine & Noir: Art in L.A., 1960–1997.* Humlebaek, Denmark: Louisiana Museum of Modern Art, 1997.

Phillips, Glenn, ed. *California Video: Artists and Histories.* Los Angeles: Getty Research Institute and J. Paul Getty Museum, 2008.

Rorimer, Anne. *New Art in the 60s and 70s: Redefining Reality.* London: Thames and Hudson, 2001.

Roth, Moira. "A History of Performance." *Art Journal* 56, no. 4 (Winter 1997): 73–83.

Schimmel, Paul. *Out of Actions: Between Performance and the Object, 1949–1979.* Los Angeles: Museum of Contemporary Art; London: Thames and Hudson, 1998.

Schneider, Ira, and Beryl Korot, eds. *Video Art: An Anthology.* New York: Harcourt Brace Jovanovich, 1976.

Selz, Peter. *The Art of Engagement: Visual Politics in California and Beyond.* Berkeley: University of California Press; San Jose, CA: San Jose Museum of Art, 2006.

Siegel, Jeanne, ed. *Artwords 2: Discourse on the Early 80s.* Ann Arbor: UMI Research Press, 1988.

Starr, Kevin. *California: A History.* New York: Modern Library, 2005.

Whiting, Cécile. *Pop L.A.: Art and the City in the 1960s.* Berkeley: University of California Press, 2006.

CONTRIBUTORS

Julia Bryan-Wilson is associate professor of contemporary art at the University of California, Berkeley, and the author of *Art Workers: Radical Practice in the Vietnam War Era* (Berkeley: University of California Press, 2009). She is also a frequent contributor to *Artforum* and has published widely on such topics as feminist art, art and politics, and Conceptual art in the Americas.

Constance M. Lewallen is adjunct curator at the University of California, Berkeley Art Museum and Pacific Film Archive, where she has organized many major exhibitions, including *Dream of the Audience: Theresa Hak Kyung Cha (1951–1982)* (2001); *Everything Matters: Paul Kos, a Retrospective* (2003); *Ant Farm (1968–1978)* (2004); and *A Rose Has No Teeth: Bruce Nauman in the 1960s* (2007), all of which toured and were accompanied by catalogues. Her most recent exhibition, for the Santa Monica Museum of Art, was *Allen Ruppersberg: You and Me or the Art of Give and Take* (2009).

Karen Moss is adjunct curator at Orange County Museum of Art, where she has organized numerous exhibitions, including the 2006 California Biennial; *Art since the 1960s: California Experiments* (2007-08); *The Paintings of Georgia O'Keeffe, Agnes Pelton, Agnes Martin, and Florence Pierce* (2009); and *15 Minutes of Fame: Photographs from Ansel Adams to Andy Warhol* (2010). Moss also teaches in the graduate programs at Otis College of Art and Design and USC Roski School of Fine Arts.

Anne Rorimer is an art historian and freelance curator. Formerly, she was a curator of twentieth-century art at the Art Institute of Chicago. She has published widely in art journals and was the co-curator of the exhibition *Reconsidering the Object of Art: 1965–1975,* organized by the Museum of Contemporary Art, Los Angeles, in 1995. She is the author of *New Art in the 60s and 70s: Redefining Reality* (London: Thames and Hudson, 2001).

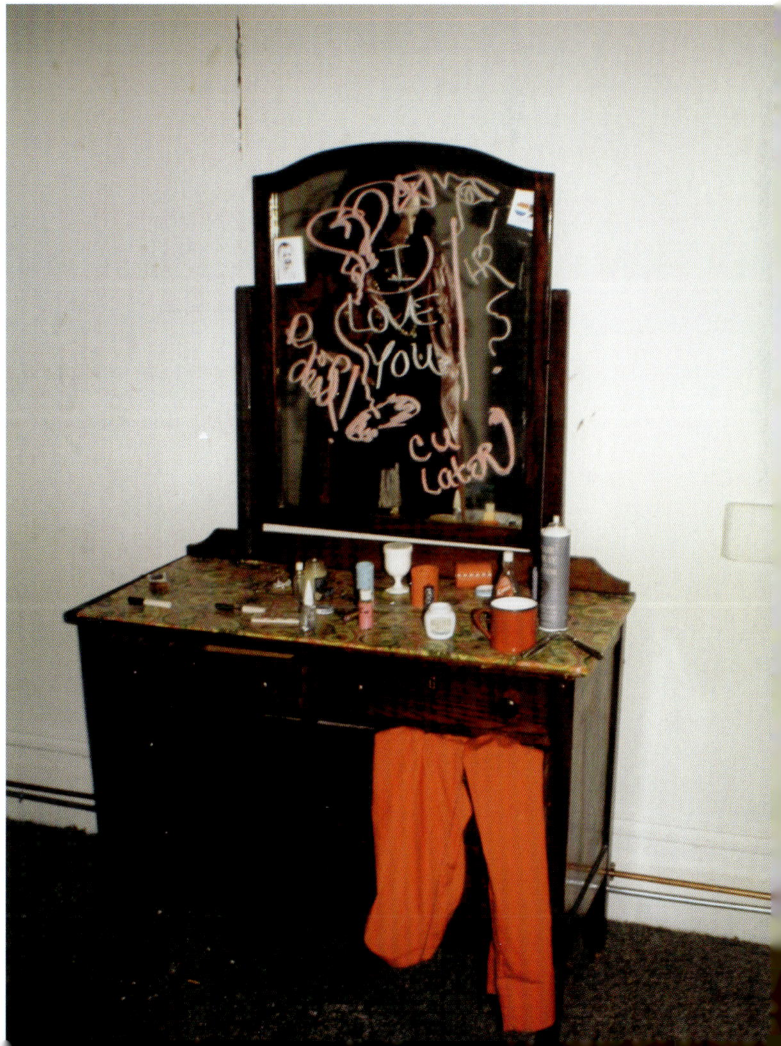

Lynn Hershman, *Dante Hotel — Dresser Graffiti by Trespassers to Room 47*, 1973–74.

INDEX

Page references given in italics indicate illustrations or material contained in their captions.

University of California Press, one of the most distinguished university presses in the United States, enriches lives around the world by advancing scholarship in the humanities, social sciences, and natural sciences. Its activities are supported by the UC Press Foundation and by philanthropic contributions from individuals and institutions. For more information, visit www.ucpress.edu.

Published in conjunction with the exhibition *State of Mind: New California Art circa 1970,* co-organized by the Orange County Museum of Art and the University of California, Berkeley Art Museum and Pacific Film Archive.

PACIFIC STANDARD TIME: ART IN L.A. 1945–1980

An initiative of the Getty with arts institutions across Southern California.

Presenting Sponsors The Getty Bank of America

EXHIBITION SCHEDULE

Orange County Museum of Art, Newport Beach, California
October 9, 2011–January 22, 2012

UC Berkeley Art Museum and Pacific Film Archive, Berkeley, California
February 29–June 17, 2012

State of Mind: New California Art circa 1970 is supported by a grant from the Getty Foundation as part of the *Pacific Standard Time: Art in L.A. 1945–1980. Pacific Standard Time* is an unprecedented collaboration of more than sixty cultural institutions across Southern California, coming together to tell the story of the birth of the L.A. art scene. Initiated through grants from the Getty Foundation, *Pacific Standard Time* will take place for six months beginning October 2011.

The Getty Foundation

National Endowment for the Arts

Additional support for *State of Mind* has been provided by the National Endowment for the Arts. Support from Ms. Robin Wright and Mr. Ian Reeves has made possible the presentation of the pressured air work of Michael Asher. Dr. Ameed Raoof and the Global Anatomy Project have provided support for Suzanne Lacy's *Lamb Construction*.

The catalog is supported in part by the Getty Foundation and by Furthermore: a program of the J.M. Kaplan Fund. *State of Mind* is co-organized by the University of California, Berkeley

Art Museum and Pacific Film Archive (BAM/PFA) and the Orange County Museum of Art (OCMA). The exhibition is co-curated by Constance M. Lewallen, adjunct curator at BAM/PFA, and Karen Moss, adjunct curator at OCMA.

Significant funding for the OCMA presentation of *State of Mind* is provided by Dr. James B. Pick and Dr. Rosalyn M. Laudati.

The presentation of *State of Mind* at BAM/PFA is made possible in part by the continued support of the BAM/PFA Trustees.

University of California Press
Berkeley and Los Angeles, California

University of California Press, Ltd.
London, England

ISBN 978-0-520-27061-9 (cloth : alk. paper)

Library of Congress Control Number: 2011935610

Manufactured in Canada

20 19 18 17 16 15 14 13 12 11
10 9 8 7 6 5 4 3 2 1

The paper used in this publication meets the minimum requirements of ANSI/NISO Z39.48-1992 (R 1997) *(Permanence of Paper).*

Sponsoring editors: Deborah Kirshman and Kari Dahlgren
Book designer: Mary Kate Murphy
Production coordinator: Pam Augspurger
Project editor: Laura Harger
Copy editor: Amanda Sparrow
Indexer: Kevin Millham
Text: Gotham Narrow
Display: Gotham
Typesetting: Grace Engels
Compositor: Berkeley Art Museum/Pacific Film Archive
Printer and Binder: Friesens

Frontispiece: John Baldessari: *California Map Project Part I: California*; 1969. Color photographs and text; photos: 11 at 8 × 10 in. each; text: 8½ × 11 in. Courtesy of John Baldessari

Inside front cover: Martha Rosler, *Bowl of Fruit*, 1966–72. Photomontage from *Body Beautiful, or Beauty Knows No Pain Series,* 1966–72 Courtesy of the artist, Brooklyn, New York, and Mitchell-Innes & Nash Gallery, New York.

Inside back cover: Allen Ru
ppersberg, Untitled, from *Al's Grand Hotel*, 1971. Installation, 7175 Sunset Boulevard, Hollywood, California. Tinted photograph mounted on plywood, 72 in. high (approx.). Collection of Claire Copley and Alan Ginsberg.